LOUISIANA BIRDS

RETucke

Louisiana Birds

By GEORGE H. LOWERY, JR.

Fellow, American Ornithologists' Union
Director of the Museum of Natural Science and
Boyd Professor of Zoology, Louisiana State University

Illustrated by Robert E. Tucker, John P. O'Neill, and H. Douglas Pratt

Published for the
LOUISIANA WILD LIFE AND FISHERIES COMMISSION
By **LOUISIANA STATE UNIVERSITY PRESS**

ISBN 0–8071–0087–0
Library of Congress Catalog Card Number 74–77662
Copyright © 1955, 1960, and 1974 by George H. Lowery, Jr.
Third Edition
All rights reserved
Manufactured in the United States of America

This book was designed by Dwight Agner. The type face is
Linotype Electra, designed by W. A. Dwiggins. Set by
Typoservice Corp., Indianapolis, Indiana, and printed and
bound by Kingsport Press, Kingsport, Tennessee. Color-
plates printed by R. R. Donnelley & Sons Company,
Chicago, Illinois.

TO JEAN
. . . anyone who knows her
will not wonder why

LOUISIANA WILD LIFE
AND FISHERIES COMMISSION

ACKNOWLEDGMENTS

THE WRITING of this book has been a pleasant task. As I have reviewed the birds of Louisiana, one by one, I have relived many memorable experiences. These reach back over the years to a never-to-be-forgotten July day nearly 27 years ago when Francis Marion Weston, the dean of Gulf Coast ornithologists, took the time to introduce a thirteen-year-old boy to the science of ornithology. I am sure that at least some of the field marks that I have employed for species in the following pages are the very ones Mr. Weston pointed out to me on my first field trip with him that day in 1927.

I have since been in the field with many of the leading ornithologists of the world, and from each I have learned something. Moreover, I have read scores upon scores of books about birds. How can one be sure which ideas are one's own instead of ideas gleaned from others? One thing is certain: no ornithologist can write on the identification of American birds without making use of information contained in Roger Tory Peterson's field guides to birds. Every serious student of birds now virtually memorizes these books as the first requisite to becoming proficient at species recognition. Peterson has attained such a high degree of perfection, both as an artist and as a field ornithologist, that it is doubtful if his books will ever be improved upon to any marked degree. I gratefully acknowledge the immense stimulation that his works and his personal communications have afforded me over the years.

Robert E. Tucker's copious illustrations for the book speak for themselves. But what the pictures do not tell is the boundless extent of Tucker's friendly cooperation and his painstaking efforts to satisfy my wishes. All this, coupled with the fact that he was once a student of mine and a companion on an expedition to southern Mexico, as well as on numerous field trips closer to home, has made our present joint undertaking a particularly pleasurable one to me. The numbered text figures, not initialed by Tucker, were done by Miss Joan Landry and myself, except where accredited to someone else.

The initial drawings for the book were instigated by Dr. Benjamin F. Mitchell and Mrs. May W. DeBlieux, of the Bureau of Educational Materials, Statistics, and Research, of the Department of Education at Louisiana State University. The original plan was to issue a much shorter book in the publication series of that bureau. Such a book could have contained only black-and-white illustrations and the barest textual material. During the execution of the drawings, but before the text was prepared, the planned scope of the book was enlarged, and the Wild Life and Fisheries Commission assumed sponsorship of the revised project. I wish, however, to express my sincere appreciation to Dr. Mitchell and Mrs. DeBlieux for providing the impetus that initiated the work and for relinquishing the earlier drawings that Mr. Tucker made at their request.

It is impossible for me to express adequately my gratitude to Mr. L. D. Young, Jr., Director of the Wild Life and Fisheries Commission, to the members of the Wild Life and Fisheries Commission itself, and to Mr. Ted O'Neil, Chief of the Commission's Division of Fur and Refuges. To these gentlemen goes the credit for endorsing the plan of the book here consummated and arranging for its publication. Mr. O'Neil particularly has devoted himself assiduously to helping me in every way possible.

President Troy H. Middleton, Dean Cecil G. Taylor, and Dr. Oscar W. Rosewall have given more than their mere administrative approval to my devoting a part of my university time to the work that has gone into the project. Each has followed its development with a very friendly interest. Since, however, museum and teaching duties regularly occupy most of my time, the actual writing of the text and the preparation of certain text figures and graphs was necessarily done for the most part in evenings, on weekends, and in periods that were ostensibly vacations. My family, through all this, has been indulgent.

Burgess Publishing Company and my good friends Drs. O. S. Pettingill, Jr., and W. J. Breckenridge have kindly granted permission to reproduce as Figure 13 portions of a chart that appeared in *A Laboratory and Field Manual of Ornithology*. Samuel A. Grimes, in addition to the personal attention that he has given to the engraving of the plates and other illustrations, has generously allowed the use of a number of his striking photographs, including the incomparable portrait of the dichromatic Common Screech Owls reproduced opposite page 64. Appreciation is also extended to Clair A. Brown, Allan D. Cruickshank, Claude H. Gresham, Jr., T. Kohara, Fred W. Lahrmann, James P. Morgan, Stephen M. Russell, Peter Scott, Fonville Winans, Davis Aerial Photographic Service, National Audubon Society, Saskatchewan Museum of Natural History, and the Standard Oil Company (N.J.) for permission to reproduce their photographs.

Every resident ornithologist in the state, without exception, has made all his notes available to me in order that the information might be used in the preparation of this book. In mentioning only a few of these people I am sure to omit the names of some who have been immensely helpful, but I would be guilty of reprehensible ingratitude if I failed to single out Jas. Hy. Bruns, Thomas D. Burleigh, Fred J. Buchmann, H. B. Chase, Jr., P. A. Daigre, J. L. Dorn, Miss Rose Feingold, John P. Gee, Thomas R. Howell, Horace H. Jeter, Dr. and Mrs. Robert W. Krebs, Mr. and Mrs. Robert B. Moore, Buford Myers, and Robert E. Tucker. But to say simply that my associate Robert J. Newman has been helpful would be a gross understatement. Not only has he offered many suggestions during the writing of the manuscript, applying his unexcelled abilities both as an ornithologist and as a scholar, but he has also been a daily source of assistance and intellectual stimulation.

Finally, it is more than proper that I express my appreciation to Mrs. Marguerite Ponder for her assistance and to Mrs. Lulu H. Patrick for her untiring labors in typing the manuscript and proofreading and for her many helpful suggestions.

For additional acknowledgments, see the chapter dealing with the history of Louisiana ornithology [and the preface to the third edition].

October 24, 1954

TABLE OF CONTENTS

ILLUSTRATIONS

PHOTOGRAPHS (Unnumbered)

ILLUSTRATIONS   xvii

FIGURES

PREFACE TO THE
FIRST EDITION

THIS IS NOT a state bird book in the traditional sense. Its one objective is to introduce the people of Louisiana to the absorbing subject of ornithology, mainly through the medium of that wealth of birdlife which is their heritage. Conventional state bird books usually combine such an end with a second one—that of assembling for convenient scientific reference the specific records and factual data upon which their generalizations concerning the various species are based. Though I am thoroughly in accord with the latter objective, I believe that in the present instance it is better to divorce that objective from the first one. The audience for whom this "introduction" to Louisiana birds has been prepared is composed mainly of people who have a potential interest in birds and a desire, perhaps, to learn more about them but who have not as yet been carried by that desire to a detailed study of ornithology. This audience would not, in my opinion, be greatly served by the precise documentation of each statement that is made; and, at the same time, such details would almost certainly decrease the readability of the text and greatly increase its length. In due course the basic factual data concerning the birds of the state amassed since the excellent summation by Harry C. Oberholser in 1938 will be made the subject of a more technical publication than the present one is intended to be.

In following the policy of nontechnical presentation, I have here further departed from the plan of most state bird books by omitting nearly all reference to subspecies, except for a brief discussion in one of the introductory chapters of the concept and some of its applications. Subspecies are the populations or combinations of populations within a species that differ suffi-

ciently from one another to be distinguishable and hence are given a name.
For various reasons, quite a number of species are represented by two or
more such subspecies in collections of specimens assembled from a single
state. Quite properly the names of these subspecies are included in the technical lists of the birds of that state. Although I am myself absorbed with
the study of subspecific variation and recognize its very special importance
to a better understanding of the problem of species formation and other
biological phenomena, I am nevertheless of the opinion that a detailed catalogue of subspecies recorded from a state is of no practical concern to the
vast majority of bird students. Only a few subspecies of birds in the whole
of North America can be recognized in the field with absolute certainty.
Generally speaking, only the museum worker, having access to comparative
material in the form of study skins, is in a position to decide to which subspecies a given specimen belongs. For this reason I am opposed to over-
emphasizing subspecies in books intended for the general public by devoting
two or more separate accounts to forms of the same species under distinct,
named headings. Indeed, I am opposed to giving subspecies distinctive common names at all, even when such names incorporate the name of the species
(such as Long-tailed Black-capped Chickadee, instead of Long-tailed Chickadee). The treatment of subspecies in technical ornithological publications
serves, of course, a valid scientific purpose, but their inclusion in this book
could only lead to confusion on the part of those for whom the work is
intended.

The space saved in omitting a catalogue of detailed records and in not
dealing with subspecies has enabled me to devote more attention to those
aspects of ornithology that I believe pertinent to the interest of the non-
specialist. The first step in the study of any group of objects or things,
whether they be minerals, plants, or animals, is to apply a correct name to
each entity. So it is with the study of birds. Consequently, in the pages that
follow, I have attempted to supply a means whereby the interested person
can correctly identify the birds he sees. To achieve this end I have given
concise diagnostic field characters of each species, that is, features that will
serve directly or otherwise to distinguish every species of bird in the state
from all other species that have been recorded within our borders. Obviously,
I don't need to tell how a Common Yellowthroat differs from a Brown Pelican. In the Yellowthroat's own family, on the other hand, there are many
small yellowish birds that are somewhat similar, but the male Common Yellowthroat may be distinguished from all of them by the single fact that it

wears a rectangular, solid black mask. The beginner needs further to be warned, however, that *rectangular, solid black mask* means exactly this— not the kind of disrupted black marking that partly surrounds the eye of the Kentucky Warbler.

No aid to identification is more effective than diagrams or paintings of birds grouped in such a way that similar species may be compared directly and their dissimilarities analyzed. In recognition of this fact, at least one illustration is included of each of the 377 species treated in the text. These bird portraits, which have been ably executed by Robert E. Tucker, are designed to facilitate species recognition and are not intended as mere decorations to the book. If Mr. Tucker's skill with pen and brush has produced pictures pleasing to the eye, that is so much the better.

In the species accounts I have given the status of each species with respect to its seasonal occurrence, employing standard ornithological terminology except with respect to the interpretation of the terms *casual* and *accidental*. Species that are represented regularly somewhere in the state in every month of the year are called *permanent residents*. Unless otherwise noted, this designation implies that the species in question breeds within our borders. The Spotted Sandpiper has often been recorded throughout the summer months, as well as at all other times of the year, but no nest, downy young, or other evidences of actual nesting have been found. Consequently, the species is classed as a permanent resident with attention being called to the hiatus in our knowledge concerning its breeding status. The term *summer resident* is employed for species that nest somewhere in the state but are not of regular annual occurrence here in winter. The term *summer visitor* is applied to species that ordinarily occur here only in summer but do not nest. An example is the Magnificent Frigatebird, which is seen in numbers along our coast in the warm months but does not breed anywhere in the United States. *Winter residents* are species that occur here in winter, usually arriving from more northern nesting grounds in late summer or in fall and remaining here until late winter or spring. Included in this category, for convenience, are a few birds that reach as far south as Louisiana only during periods of severe winter weather, drifting back northward as soon as conditions permit. *Casual visitors* are birds that wander to our state only at more or less infrequent intervals. Arbitrarily they may be defined as birds that have been recorded more than once but less than a dozen times all told. The term *accidental* applies to species for which there is but one record for the state. *Transients* are species whose regular occurrence in the state is limited to periods of migration, although an occasional individual may be seen at other seasons.

An attempt has been made to show major seasonal changes in the status of the various species where such changes occur. I have also tried to state in very general terms the usual times of arrival and departure of migrants. In Table 3, near the end of the book, much of this information is shown graphically, and the earliest and latest dates of occurrence are supplied. These extreme dates take into account all available authentic records from the time of Audubon to October 1, 1954. The preface to this table discusses some of the difficulties associated with trying to indicate the relative abundance of various species in terms of their population density or of the frequency with which they are seen. While the table employs only four degrees of abundance (*common, uncommon, rare*, and *very rare* or *irregular*), other shades of abundance are frequently indicated in the text itself, where use has been made of a graded series of modifiers, ranging from *extremely* through *very* and *moderately* to *fairly*. The device *not uncommon* is occasionally used to indicate a degree of abundance between fairly common and uncommon.

In the introductory chapters I have discussed briefly a variety of subjects relating to certain aspects of local ornithology, as well as to ornithology in general. I have included, for example, a discussion of the sequence of molt in birds because a knowledge of this subject is important in learning to identify birds in all their variations of plumages including those associated with age, sex, and season. Similarly, I think an understanding of the structure of a feather and the modifications of the avian skeleton is of interest to the layman and serves to enhance his appreciation of birds as living organisms. But the selection of topics is by no means an indication of the scope of the whole field of ornithology.

Not counted among the 377 species of birds here considered to compose the state list are three species included by Oberholser on the basis of evidence that I do not consider sufficient. Reference is made to these species in their proper sequence in the text, but the headings to the accounts are placed in brackets and the accounts themselves are set in a slightly different format. Accounts of four other species reported since the publication of Oberholser's book are handled in the same way because in each instance the evidence for the admission of the bird to the state list is again not wholly satisfactory. Three of these are pelagic species recorded only in our offshore waters.

The nomenclature, both scientific and vernacular, follows almost exactly the American Ornithologists' Union *Check-list of North American Birds* (4th ed., 1931, and its various supplements). Since a new edition of this highly important work is scheduled for early publication, I have tried to anticipate some of the changes it will include in order that the bird names used in this book will conform as closely as possible. Because of the influence of our French-speaking citizens, many colorful colloquial names exist for Louisiana birds. I have made no special attempt to list all of these French names, but I have included the ones I have most often heard in my travels in southern Louisiana.

GEORGE H. LOWERY, JR.

Museum of Natural Science
Louisiana State University
Baton Rouge, Louisiana
October 24, 1954

PREFACE
TO THE
THIRD EDITION

IN THE 19 years that have elapsed since the appearance of the first edition and the 14 years since the second edition of this work, many changes have taken place in the birdlife of our state. Some species are no longer present in their former numbers, and still others are now recorded with greater regularity than ever before. In 1955 the avifauna of the state comprised 377 species of known occurrence. Now the list is up to 411. The species that have been added and the revisions that have been required in statements regarding the relative abundance of numerous species have come about as a result of the mounting interest in our birdlife on the part of an ever-increasing number of people. Perhaps the various editions of *Louisiana Birds* have contributed in some measure to that end. As interest in our birds grows, so does our knowledge pertaining to them. In this completely revised edition I have attempted to synthesize all the information that is now available, and, in doing so, nearly every species account has been rewritten. To name all the people who have made significant contributions to Louisiana ornithology in the nearly two decades since the first edition of this book would require citing almost the entire present and past membership of the Louisiana Ornithological Society, a group of mainly nonprofessional students of the subject. But I would be remiss if I did not single out the continued good work of such stalwart "old-timers" as Marshall and Grace Eyster, Horace H. Jeter, Sidney A. Gauthreaux, John P. Gee, Mary Lewis, John T. Lynch, Buford Myers, Robert J. Newman, Ronald J. Stein, James R. Stewart, and the late Ava R. Tabor. To this list must now be added the names of Kenneth P. Able, Keith A. Arnold, Horace W. Belknap, Laurence C. Binford, W. H. Buskirk,

Matthew Courtman, Allan B. Ensminger, John Farrand, Jr., Richard Ferren, Leslie Glasgow, John W. Goertz, Robert B. Hamilton, James J. Hebrard, D. T. Kee, Joseph C. Kennedy, Burt L. Monroe, Jr., John J. Morony, Mac Myers, J. D. Newsom, Robert E. Noble, Larry P. O'Meallie, A. W. Palmisano, H. Douglas Pratt, R. D. Purrington, Stephen M. Russell, E. Ray Smith, Gayle T. Strickland, Jacob M. Valentine, Lovett E. Williams, Edwin O. Willis, and others.

I am especially indebted to John P. O'Neill for having executed a new colorplate and to H. Douglas Pratt for his numerous additional line drawings, in each case illustrating species that have been added to the state list since the book was first published with its portraits by Robert E. Tucker.

The new charts showing the seasonal occurrence of our birds include all species that have been recorded in the state and therefore they again provide a convenient checklist of the birds of Louisiana. The nomenclature in these charts and in the text itself has been altered to conform with the AOU *Check-list of North American Birds* (1957) and the recent (1973) supplement published by the AOU Committee on Classification and Nomenclature. The only departures that I have made are minor and have mainly to do with the sequence of species of shorebirds and wood-warblers.

Again I have followed the practice employed in earlier editions of treating species of hypothetical occurrence in the main sequence of the accounts but of placing the names forming the captioned headings in brackets to indicate the uncertain status of the species in question.

February 9, 1974   G. H. L.

LOUISIANA BIRDS

INTRODUCTION

NO ASPECT of natural history is more fascinating to a greater number of people than the study of birds. This fact is reflected in the large member-ships in bird clubs and ornithological societies, by the capacity audiences at public showings of wildlife films, and by the record sales of books pertaining to birds. No less indicative of the appeal that birds hold for the average man is the fact that seldom does one encounter a person who is not eager to dis-cuss them or to inquire about the proper identity of a bird he has seen. This interest manifests itself in a boy's elation when he finds his first mocking-bird nest. The sportsman, sitting in a duck blind on a cold winter morning, experiences a rare exhilaration when he beholds the beauty of a squadron of teal or a brace of pintails wheeling over the marsh in the morning mist. The farmer stops his tractor to watch a wedge of "honkers" pass over; the sailor follows the graceful forms of the gulls gliding over the wake of his ship; and the housewife puts crumbs on the ledge outside her kitchen window to attract the cardinals, whose bright red attire she admires. In the ranks of ornithologists there have been great statesmen, such as Thomas Jefferson, who published a list of the birds of his beloved Virginia, as well as men in many other walks of life. Indeed, I have found that often the simplest man, such as a peon tilling his *milpa* in a clearing in the depths of a remote Yuca-tan jungle, watches the birds around him and has names for most of them, including some of the smallest.

In the United States the study of birds is rapidly becoming a national pastime, as it has in England. The sale of nearly one and a half million copies of Roger T. Peterson's field guides to birds in the last four decades is in itself

1

ample proof of the mounting interest on the part of the general public. An activity that takes men and women of all ages, singly and in groups, out of doors in all kinds of weather and over all sorts of terrain—through mosquito-filled marshes, into tick-infested fields and thickets, and up boulder-strewn slopes of tall mountains—must indeed hold an appeal of magnitude, especially since these forays are repeated weekend after weekend with ever-mounting enthusiasm.

I think that everyone watches birds for much the same reason. As a hobby birds provide recreational opportunities unmatched by any other class of animals. As the highest of the vertebrates, next to mammals, they convey to us a feeling of kinship, based partly, perhaps, on the fact that they display personality, such as lower animals do not. And, unlike most of the mammals, which are difficult to observe in the wild, birds permit themselves to be seen and studied without exasperating effort. In doing so they provide a seasonally changing spectacle that is never quite the same for two months in a row, even from the vantage point of a single wood. Then, too, the great number of different kinds of birds and their color variations due to sex, age, and season provide an unending challenge to discovery and recognition, even under favorable conditions and with the aid of good binoculars. Birds are just elusive enough. They provide a quest, a lure, the end of which is attainable but never quite attained in any man's lifetime. If one should by chance find all of the birds that might conceivably visit one's garden, there remain others awaiting discovery in a nearby field or swamp, or still others in an adjacent state. Ultimately the quest for new birds may carry the real enthusiast to the Dry Tortugas, the Gaspé, or the Rockies, up the Alaskan or down the Pan-American Highway—all in the hope of seeing some bird he has not previously observed. This game of finding birds has an everlasting and enduring appeal, and it becomes more absorbing the deeper one delves into it.

But to many people the study of birds is more than a game or diversion. To the ornithologist it is the serious business of searching for new facts to fill the gaps in man's knowledge of the world of nature. The real student of birds is interested in a great deal more than adding new species to his list. He is absorbed in deciphering the intricacies of bird behavior or the perplexities of bird migration. He is interested in working out patterns of molt, the physiology of avian reproduction, the factors limiting avian distribution, or maybe the relationship of one group of birds to another on the basis of anatomy. He has participated since 1908 in the banding of over 30 million birds in the United States and Canada—20 million have been banded by nonprofessional ornithologists—whereby much has been learned from the 1.5 million recoveries concerning the movements of birds and their longevity, as well as their social organization. He has led expeditions that have visited the remote corners of the world, and he has been responsible for amassing great collections of study skins in our museums. In brief, the ornithologist is interested in one or more of scores of problems that are part of the biology of birds. Yet he is not necessarily an employee of a museum or a university laboratory. He is just as likely to be a lawyer or a chemist or a business executive who, by devoting his spare time to ornithological pursuits, is making contributions to science.

With this legion of enthusiasts ferreting out new facts, we have little cause to wonder why birds are now acknowledged by zoologists to be the most thoroughly worked and the best understood of all animal groups. This is not to suggest that our knowledge of birds is complete or even nearly so, for there are just as many unexplored horizons as ever. New discoveries merely open up new vistas; new facts suggest new avenues of inquiry. Some of the greatest gaps in our knowledge of birds are concerned with problems that the student can tackle in his own backyard. Indeed, the life history of no bird, even the commonest, is so well known as to preclude further careful study. All the beginner needs is a foundation of knowledge, and when this is gained, he soon begins to see for himself numerous problems that excite his curiosity and imagination.

LOUISIANA AS
A PLACE TO
SEE BIRDS

NO LESS THAN 411 species of birds have been recorded within the boundaries of Louisiana. This is more than half of all the birds known to occur regularly in North America, north of Mexico. Only six states (Texas, California, Arizona, Colorado, Florida, and New Mexico) have bird lists that include more species than does that of Louisiana. On the basis of the figures available to me, Louisiana, Massachusetts, New York, and Nebraska are tied for seventh place. A wholly accurate ranking would be difficult because I do not know the taxonomic treatment accorded certain forms on some of the state lists. For example, do all the lists treat the Bullock's type of the Baltimore Oriole as a subspecies of the Baltimore Oriole as I have done?

The presence here of a great array of species is not really surprising when one considers the several factors that make Louisiana such a splendid place to see birds. For one thing, our state's 48,523 square miles include no less than 3,346 square miles of water in the form of rivers, bayous, bays, lakes, and lagoons and 7,420 square miles of coastal marshes. Although the east-west breadth of the southern part of the state amounts to only 397 miles, the actual shoreline is 6,952 miles in length when one follows the numerous indentations formed by the many bays and sounds. The tremendous expanse of tidal beaches combines with the coastal waterways and marshes to provide an unexcelled habitat for gulls, terns, shorebirds, ducks, geese, herons, and other kinds of aquatic or semiaquatic birdlife. The remainder of the state possesses an assortment of hardwood alluvial swamplands, beech-oak-magnolia uplands, wide areas of pine forest, and even treeless grassy plains, habitats that are superbly attractive to land birds (see Fig. 1).

4

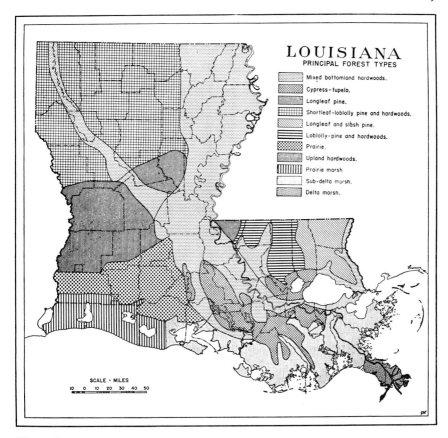

Figure 1

Possibly the greatest single factor, however, favoring Louisiana as a place to find many kinds of birds is its geographical position. It lies athwart the great Mississippi Valley migratory flyway, a route over which millions of birds wing their way twice a year in their annual migrations. This mass movement of a large segment of the avian population of the continent brings many northern nesting species to us in winter in incredible numbers. Others are with us simply as birds of passage, here only a few weeks in spring and again in fall as they pass to and from more southern winter homes. But in the period of their sojourn they add variety to our avifauna. Louisiana's geo-

Baldcypress Tree on Lake Verret

graphical position also gives it nearly all of the species that make up the distinctive breeding avifauna of the southeastern United States. Its southern location affords a mild climate, which encourages many northern birds to spend their winters here, along with the many southern birds that are resident throughout the year. But the state's important advantage over other southern states results from its strategic east-west location. It receives, at least in seasons of migration, nearly all of the species of the eastern United States and, at the same time, a strong representation of western forms. The latter are notably evident in fall when the southward migrations of western species, those of the Great Plains particularly and even those of the Rocky Mountains, are probably being swung southeastward by the general southeastward trajectory of much of the continental air flow at that time. Western

Baldcypress–Tupelogum–Waterelm Swamp Subject to Deep Flooding, Pearl River Area
CLAIR A. BROWN

migrants that are occasionally displaced eastward as far as Louisiana probably have a tendency to be concentrated along our Gulf Coast by the physical barrier imposed by the open waters of the Gulf itself. This tendency accounts in large measure for the fact that the great majority of records of western birds known from the state are from the southern tier of parishes, if not from the coastal ridges and islands themselves.

A breakdown of the 411 species of birds composing the state list is, for several reasons, illuminating in the present connection. For one thing, it shows the great potential of the state for receiving casual visitors or accidental strays. Moreover, the analysis demonstrates the seasonal variety of birds to be found in Louisiana. In assigning each species to one of the following categories, I have done so on the basis of the bird's primary seasonal status.

Shallow Water Baldcypress–Tupelogum Swamp at Weeks Island

STANDARD OIL CO. (N.J.)

Baldcypress Knees and Wind-blown Spanish Moss, Iberville Parish

The President of the Louisiana Live Oak Society, Near Hahnville, St. Charles Parish

For example, if a given species is here mainly during periods of migration, it is treated as a transient even though it may occur casually during the winter months. Likewise, if a species is here in large numbers in winter yet has been known on rare occasions to have remained to nest, it is still treated, for the purpose of this analysis, as a winter visitor and not as a permanent resident, which indeed it is on technical grounds.

Species recorded from the state but now extinct (Passenger Pigeon and Carolina Parakeet)	2
Species extirpated in Louisiana but still occurring elsewhere (Greater Prairie Chicken and Whooping Crane)	2
Species that formerly migrated to or through the state but for which there are no records in the past 50 years (Trumpeter Swan and Eskimo Curlew)	2
Species introduced and now well established as permanent residents (Black Francolin, Rock Pigeon, European Starling, and House Sparrow)	4
Accidental visitors (species recorded only once)	30
Casual visitors (species recorded less than 12 times but more than once)	37
Transient species, at least primarily so	59
Winter visitors primarily but often more numerous in periods of migration	120
Birds that are primarily summer residents that are known to breed in the state	49
Summer visitors, birds present regularly only in summer but not known to breed in the state (Wilson's Storm-Petrel, Masked Booby, Magnificent Frigatebird, and Wood Stork)	4
Native permanent residents that are known to breed or to have bred in the state	98
Species present the year around but not known to nest in the state (American White Pelican and American Avocet); not included here are, for example, many species of shorebirds for which casual nonbreeding individuals often remain throughout the summer	2
Total number of species known to have nested in the state, including those now extinct or extirpated (Carolina Parakeet, Greater Prairie Chicken, and Whooping Crane)	171

Another excellent illustration of the variety of the birdlife in Louisiana is provided by the results of what is known as the Christmas Bird Count, a project promulgated for 75 years by the National Audubon Society. Ornithologists throughout the United States and Canada spend a day afield counting the numbers and kinds of birds to be found in that one day in an area not exceeding 15 miles in diameter. The census period varies slightly

T. KOHARA

Loblolly Pine, Union Parish

from year to year, depending upon which day of the week Christmas falls, but the period usually extends from the Saturday before until the Sunday after Christmas. An unlimited number of people may operate within a prescribed circle, and, of course, the larger the personnel and the more extensive the coverage of the census area, the greater is the opportunity to obtain a long list of species. When the first censuses were made in 1899, only a few people at a few places participated. But in the three-quarters of a century that followed, more and more people became interested in birds, and the Christmas Bird Count soon developed into a nationwide ornithological endeavor. The census of 1972 involved 20,373 observers in 1,013 census areas in the United States, Canada, Mexico, Central America, and the West Indies. This horde of participants spent the amazing total of 57,918 party

Longleaf Pine, Rapides Parish

T. KOHARA

hours in the field and covered 70,824 miles (of which 30,898 were on foot). Forty-three censuses recorded 150 or more species each, and the grand total of all birds counted amounted to 71.2 million individuals.

With this explanation of the manner in which the censuses are conducted, let us now review some of the counts that have been tallied in Louisiana. In the St. Francisville–Port Hudson–False River area, 20 censuses have been made since 1945, and on 10 occasions the number of species recorded within the prescribed circle has exceeded 100, the highest one-day count being 114. The total number of birds observed on the counts has varied from 8,862 to as high as 190,910 individuals. Annual variations in the kinds and numbers of birds seen in a particular census area often reflect cyclic

Virgin Water Oak–Redgum Forest, Concordia Parish

T. KOHARA

Driskill Mountain, Highest Point in Louisiana (535 Feet), Bienville Parish

fluctuations in population densities, changes in roosting sites, effects of weather, and other natural phenomena.

The Sabine National Wildlife Refuge–Cameron count has now been made 18 times since 1950. On 10 occasions the high count of over 150 species has been reached, and on the 1959 census the number of species seen was an unprecedented 163, the largest list of birds ever observed in Louisiana during one day in winter. Up to the 1950s this number would have been the highest count in the nation. But since then counts have been organized at places in Florida, Texas, and California that have produced lists of 200 or more species. The all-time United States record is that of 226 species at

STEPHEN M. RUSSELL

Prairie North of Jennings, Jefferson Davis Parish

Freeport, Texas, in 1971. The Sabine Refuge–Cameron count could never be expected to even approach this mark because there the coastal marshes are so broad that nowhere could a circle 15 miles in diameter be drawn defining a census area that would incorporate Gulf beaches, heavily wooded upland forest, and pine savannas. Interestingly enough, though, the overall count of species on all Sabine Refuge–Cameron censuses comes to 233 species. But 26 of these have been seen on only one census, and all 26 are not likely to make a repeat appearance on any one day. Even species that are known to be present are sometimes missed on the day of the census.

Another census area of long-standing significance is that of Shreveport, where Horace H. Jeter and James R. Stewart have been responsible for annual counts for 24 consecutive years, beginning in 1950. Their censuses, combined with their other ornithological efforts in the Shreveport area, have contributed immeasurably to a better understanding of the status of the winter birdlife in northwestern Louisiana. The counts have varied from as few as 75 species to as many as 106, with the "century" figure having been reached or exceeded on seven occasions.

Also of special importance in recent years have been the Christmas counts conducted at New Orleans and Reserve and in the Venice–Buras area near the mouth of the Mississippi River. In these places, through the superb organizational efforts of Sidney A. Gauthreaux, Joseph C. Kennedy, Buford Myers, R. D. Purrington, Ronald J. Stein, and other members of the Crescent City Bird Club, highly noteworthy counts have been made during the past decade that have consistently included winter records of species that

Chenierelike Woods on Grand Isle, a Haven in Spring for Incoming Trans-Gulf Migrants
FONVILLE WINANS

Black Mangrove Marsh, Brush Island, St. Bernard Parish

CLAUDE H. GRESHAM, JR

Salt Marsh, St. Bernard Parish

The Mighty Mississippi Meets the Sea

do not normally occur anywhere else in the United States at that season except possibly in southern Texas or southern Florida.

The Christmas Bird Counts provide ample evidence of the general abundance of birds in Louisiana. This is particularly apparent when we consider the number of cases in which our count of individuals of a given species was higher than anywhere else in the nation. Between 1948 and 1972 this has happened 227 times, involving no less than 97 species (Table 1). In many other instances not listed, the counts in Louisiana were near the maximum for the country.

Table 1   Species for Which the Highest North American Christmas Bird Count Was Obtained in Louisiana (1948–1972)

Species	Year	Area	Number
Pied-billed Grebe	1950	St. Francisville	117
	1951	"	119
	1954	"	184
Brown Pelican	1955	Sabine Refuge	978
Olivaceous Cormorant	1950	Grand Isle	393
	1955	Sabine Refuge	19
	1958	"	70
	1959	"	252*
	1962	"	68
	1964	"	178
	1969	"	235
Little Blue Heron	1968	Venice	3,146
	1969	New Orleans	1,351
Cattle Egret	1955	Sabine Refuge	2
Louisiana Heron	1972	Reserve	600
Least Bittern	1953	Sabine Refuge	1*
American Bittern	1951	"	7
	1952	"	4*
	1955	"	16
	1961	"	14
White-faced Ibis	1950	"	131
	1951	"	68
	1953	"	1,259
	1954	"	2,036
	1955	"	881
	1956	"	250

* Tied with another census for high count.

Species	Year	Area	Number
White-faced Ibis (cont.)	1957	Sabine Refuge	279
	1958	”	358
	1959	”	5,627
	1961	”	2,103
	1962	”	263
	1964	”	2,736
	1969	”	654
	1971	”	5,400
	1972	”	2,692
Roseate Spoonbill	1957	”	250
	1969	”	800
Snow Goose (white morph)	1950	”	35,000
	1951	”	32,000
	1955	”	25,085
	1956	”	20,000
	1960	”	24,500
(blue morph)	1949	”	9,829
	1950	”	20,000
	1951	”	32,000
	1952	”	24,000
	1953	”	12,992
	1954	”	22,000
	1955	”	70,538
	1956	”	30,000
	1957	”	35,000
	1958	”	28,000
	1959	”	12,000
	1960	”	45,500
	1962	”	12,000
Mottled Duck	1951	”	50
Gadwall	1953	”	5,520
	1960	Venice	11,000
Green-winged Teal	1964	Sabine Refuge	16,011
Northern Shoveler	1964	”	4,105
Ruddy Duck	1950	St. Francisville	4,600
Swallow-tailed Kite	1968	Lafayette	1
Red-tailed Hawk (Harlan's type)	1959	Sabine Refuge	1*
Marsh Hawk	1951	”	134
	1962	”	82
Merlin	1959	”	4

* Tied with another census for high count.

Species	Year	Area	Number
King Rail	1951	Sabine Refuge	10
	1953	"	100
Clapper Rail	1949	Grand Isle	92
	1950	"	95
	1958	Sabine Refuge	60
Virginia Rail	1958	New Orleans	20
Sora	1949	Grand Isle	15
Black Rail	1955	Sabine Refuge	1
Common Gallinule	1960	"	398
Killdeer	1950	St. Francisville	362
Greater Yellowlegs	1949	Sabine Refuge	59
	1956	"	517
Lesser Yellowlegs	1957	"	78
	1959	"	64
	1960	"	244
Solitary Sandpiper	1949	St. Francisville	1
	1964	Venice	1
Wilson's Phalarope	1969	Lafayette	2
American Woodcock	1948	St. Francisville	3
	1959	Sabine Refuge	9
Common Snipe	1955	"	102
	1957	Shreveport	141
Long-billed Dowitcher	1964	Venice	235
Dowitcher (sp.)	1949	Sabine Refuge	450
Pectoral Sandpiper	1950	"	3
Laughing Gull	1955	"	2,581
Gull-billed Tern	1952	"	32
	1960	"	34
Forster's Tern	1949	Grand Isle	660
	1950	"	500
Common Tern	1958	Sabine Refuge	10
	1969	"	33
	1971	"	40
	1972	"	37
White-winged Dove	1956	New Orleans	1*
	1959	Sabine Refuge	3*
	1964	Venice	32
Yellow-billed Cuckoo	1969	Lafayette	1*

* Tied with another census for high count.

Species	Year	Area	Number
Groove-billed Ani	1959	Sabine Refuge	6
	1960	New Orleans	10
	1966	"	8
	1968	"	25
	1970	Sabine Refuge	19
	1971	"	31
Barn Owl	1953	"	14
	1960	"	11
Barred Owl	1948	St. Francisville	7
	1949	"	23
	1950	"	12
	1951	"	12
	1960	Shreveport	15
	1971	Reserve	43
	1972	"	36
Chuck-will's-widow	1950	Grand Isle	1*
Common Nighthawk	1960	New Orleans	1
Nighthawk (sp.)	1968	Lafayette	2*
Rufous Hummingbird	1955	New Orleans	2
	1956	"	3
	1957	"	1*
	1958	"	2
	1959	"	1
Red-bellied Woodpecker	1950	St. Francisville	105
Yellow-bellied Sapsucker	1948	"	41
	1950	"	38
	1951	"	18
	1954	"	39
	1960		44
Red-cockaded Woodpecker	1957	Shreveport	12
Wied's Crested Flycatcher	1965	Venice	1*
Eastern Wood Pewee	1971	Lafayette	2
Tree Swallow	1959	New Orleans	15,328
Rough-winged Swallow	1951	St. Francisville	50
	1953	"	112
	1955	New Orleans	110
	1956	"	200
	1969	Reserve	40
Barn Swallow	1962	New Orleans	200

* Tied with another census for high count.

Species	Year	Area	Number
Purple Martin	1956	New Orleans	2
Fish Crow	1957	St. Francisville	1,630
House Wren	1954	New Orleans	156
Winter Wren	1951	St. Francisville	29
Marsh Wren	1950	Sabine Refuge	40
	1952	,,	42
	1954	,,	98
Sedge Wren	1953	,,	57
	1958	,,	70
	1959	,,	90
	1964	,,	34
Northern Mockingbird	1954	New Orleans	2,000
Brown Thrasher	1948	St. Francisville	86
	1949	,,	73
	1950	,,	129
	1951	,,	80
	1953	,,	106
	1957	,,	109
	1960	Shreveport	110
Hermit Thrush	1948	St. Francisville	70
Eastern Bluebird	1956	Shreveport	284
Blue-gray Gnatcatcher	1950	Sabine Refuge	198
Ruby-crowned Kinglet	1948	St. Francisville	244
	1949	,,	177
	1950	,,	330
	1951	,,	260
	1953		273
	1954	New Orleans	501
Water Pipit	1957	St. Francisville	605
Sprague's Pipit	1954	Sabine Refuge	65
	1959	,,	9
	1960	,,	91
Loggerhead Shrike	1950	St. Francisville	209
	1951	Sabine Refuge	324
	1954	New Orleans	496
Solitary Vireo	1948	St. Francisville	7
	1958	,,	6
Orange-crowned Warbler	1948	,,	22
	1950	Grand Isle	57
	1951	St. Francisville	31

Species	Year	Area	Number
Orange-crowned Warbler	1953	St. Francisville	47
(cont.)	1954	Sabine Refuge	38
	1959	Venice	281
Lucy's Warbler	1959	"	1
Yellow Warbler	1953	Sabine Refuge	2
Pine Warbler	1958	Shreveport	98
Black-throated Gray Warbler	1952	Sabine Refuge	2
Black-throated Green Warbler	1960	New Orleans	1*
Blackburnian Warbler	1964	Venice	1
Magnolia Warbler	1969	"	1*
Myrtle Warbler (white-throated type)	1954	New Orleans	10,000
Bay-breasted Warbler	1967	"	2
Louisiana Waterthrush	1972	Venice	2
Worm-eating Warbler	1971	"	1
Common Yellowthroat	1954	New Orleans	487
Wilson's Warbler	1952	St. Francisville	5
	1953	Sabine Refuge	5
	1954	"	4
	1957	New Orleans	5
	1959	Venice	4
	1960	"	3
	1961	New Orleans	1
Yellow-breasted Chat	1958	Sabine Refuge	1*
Orchard Oriole	1964	Venice	1
	1966	New Orleans	3
	1972	Venice	1
Scott's Oriole	1958	Sabine Refuge	1
Baltimore Oriole (Bullock's type)	1955	"	1*
	1965	Venice	4*
	1968	"	6
	1969	"	2
	1971	"	4
	1972	"	8
Boat-tailed Grackle	1949	Grand Isle	2,375
	1951	Sabine Refuge	2,000
	1952	"	1,232
Scarlet Tanager	1965	Venice	1
Rose-breasted Grosbeak	1969	Lafayette	1*

* Tied with another census for high count.

Species	Year	Area	Number
Le Conte's Sparrow	1951	Sabine Refuge	16
	1955	Shreveport	56
	1962	"	27
	1963	"	25
	1968	"	15
Sharp-tailed Sparrow	1953	Sabine Refuge	25
	1955	"	28
Seaside Sparrow	1950	Grand Isle	640
	1951	Sabine Refuge	68
	1952	"	56
	1953	"	190
	1954	"	216
	1955	"	162
	1956	"	45
	1958	"	117
	1959	"	42
	1960	"	44
	1964	"	118
	1970	"	102
	1971	"	92
	1972	"	116
Vesper Sparrow	1949	St. Francisville	57
White-throated Sparrow	1958	"	2,138
Swamp Sparrow	1948	"	168
	1954	New Orleans	1,003
	1961	"	462

HISTORY OF
LOUISIANA
ORNITHOLOGY

ONE OF THE earliest naturalists of competence to visit Louisiana was Antoine Simon Le Page du Pratz, who came to New Orleans in 1718 and spent 16 years in various parts of the Louisiana province. In 1758, subsequent to his return to France, the first edition of his now famous work, *Histoire de la Louisiane,* was published, setting forth "a description of the countries that lie on both sides of the River Mississippi, with an account of the settlements, inhabitants, soil, climate, and products." M. Le Page du Pratz was a keen observer and, consequently, aside from giving us vivid accounts of life in this section of the country in a critical period of its development, he told of approximately 60 different kinds of birds that were known to him, including the then common Passenger Pigeon and Carolina Parakeet.

In the same year that M. Le Page du Pratz's narrative first appeared in print, the great Swedish biologist Carolus Linnaeus brought forth the tenth edition of his *Systema Naturae,* in which he laid the foundation of our present international system of zoological nomenclature. The twelfth edition of this classic, Volume I of which appeared in 1766, contained references to Louisiana birds, as well as the first acceptable technical descriptions of the Rose-breasted Grosbeak and Loggerhead Shrike, each of which was given the specific name *ludovicianus,* which means "of Louisiana." Linnaeus' descriptions of these two species were based only indirectly on Louisiana specimens since he himself did not visit Louisiana, nor indeed any part of America.

Between 1760 and 1790 other great ornithological works appeared that incorporated original descriptions, general accounts, or illustrations of Louisiana birds, including: Mathurin Jacques Brisson's *Ornithologia* in six volumes in 1760, Edme Louis D'Aubenton's drawings in his *Planches Enluminées d'Histoire Naturelle* in 1765, and John Latham's *Index Ornithologicus* in two volumes in 1790. The last-named work contained the first technical description of the Carolina Wren, which, despite the bird's vernacular name, was based on specimens from Louisiana, as its scientific name, *Thryothorus ludovicianus*, implies.

Although the famous artist-ornithologist, Alexander Wilson, made reference to Louisiana birds in various parts of his nine-volume classic, *American Ornithology* (1808–1814), he apparently spent only parts of May and June 1810 in the state. It was the illustrious John James Audubon who contributed the first real literature and extensive scientific knowledge concerning Louisiana birds. Endowed with magnificent artistic skill, an indomitable spirit, and a tenacity of purpose, Audubon set forth early in life to delineate faithfully the birds of America. His achievements toward this end rightfully earned him lasting fame and recognition as one of the greatest naturalists of all time.

Audubon never stayed long in one place, for he was continually searching for new birds on expeditions that led him north to Labrador and west to the Yellowstone country, as well as incessantly back and forth across the eastern and southern states. He was compelled to go many places, to England to find an engraver of the double-elephant folios of his drawings, *Birds of America* (1827–1838), and even to Scotland and France to peddle subscriptions to the work. Yet despite these journeys he spent several periods of his life in Louisiana, a place that he loved above all others. Particularly dear to him was the Feliciana country, with its deep beech-magnolia ravines, its river swamps, and the sand-lined shores of Bayou Sara. This he called his "Happyland."

Of the 435 plates that make up Audubon's original double-elephant folio, at least 167 are definitely known to have been done in Louisiana. No less than 66 of these were executed in West Feliciana Parish, at either Oakley or Beech Woods plantations. Here, too, was where he made many of his observations on the lives and habits of birds that later were incorporated in his *Ornithological Biography*. The first edition of this work appeared in five volumes, 1831–1839, as the letterpress supplementing the mammoth reproductions of his original drawings (untrimmed 29½ x 38½ inches). Later, essentially the same text was integrated with the reproduction of the *Birds of*

America in miniature, octavo size, the first edition of which appeared in five volumes between 1840 and 1844.

Audubon's last trip to Louisiana was in the spring of 1837, when he and his friend Edward Harris made a round trip by government cutter from New Orleans down to the mouth of the Mississippi and westward along the Gulf Coast to Galveston, stopping frequently en route to shoot birds on the coastal islands and in the expansive coastal marshes. On April 1, when the ship was anchored in Southwest Pass, Audubon saw a pair of Harlequin Ducks, the only ones ever recorded in Louisiana. On April 3 the expedition entered the Barataria Bay area, where in the following three days the ornithologists listed 104 different species of birds. On Isle Derniere Audubon saw 15 American Oystercatchers, bringing down two of them to establish the westernmost record of the species in this state. On Marsh Island, in the few days that they were there, the naturalists observed 97 species of birds. Many of the birds seen along the Louisiana shore were transient land birds that had just arrived from across the Gulf, as Audubon astutely noted in his journal. This seems to be the first clear reference in ornithological literature to the phenomenon of trans-Gulf migration.

Audubon lived until 1851, dying at the age of 66. His impact on the science of ornithology was immense. Although he himself was more of an artist-naturalist than a scientist, he gave the world, through his talents, his indefatigable labors, and his hardships and privations, a monumental work on the birdlife of this country that provoked further research and opened up an era of intensive ornithological inquiry and achievement. Soon to follow him in North America were Thomas Nuttall, Spencer Fullerton Baird, Thomas Brewer, Robert Ridgway, Elliott Coues, and J. A. Allen, whose scientific writings in the 50 years following Audubon's death filled in many of the details concerning North American birds left blank by the great "American Woodsman."

In the four decades following Audubon's farewell visit to his beloved Louisiana, naturalists devoted little attention to our avifauna. This is partially attributable to the War Between the States and to the hectic conditions that ensued. In 1881, however, Frank W. Langdon, writing in the *Journal of the Cincinnati Society of Natural History*, published an annotated list of 83 species of birds seen by him in West Baton Rouge Parish. One year later Charles Wickliffe Beckham wrote a similar article, appearing in the *Bulletin of the Nuttall Ornithological Club*, which described the occurrence of 86 species of birds recorded in the vicinity of Bayou Sara, Audubon's old stamping grounds. In 1887 Beckham supplemented this list, including notes on 27 additional species. By this time a resident of New Orleans, Joseph Gustave Kohn, had begun to assemble a collection of bird skins, most of which are now in the Tulane University Museum. Some of his specimens proved to be of species previously unknown in the state. As early as 1887 a series of short notes by Kohn and several other resident and nonresident ornithologists began to appear in *The Auk*, the official organ of the already well-established American Ornithologists' Union.

Just prior to 1900 four highly competent naturalists appeared on the Louisiana ornithological scene. They were H. H. Kopman, Andrew Allison, George E. Beyer, and Edward A. McIlhenny. Each contributed greatly to the knowledge concerning Louisiana birds. In 1900 Beyer published the first list of the birds of the state, which, on the basis of our present-day definition of a species, would include a total of 315 species. In a series of papers begun in 1906 and concluded in 1915, Beyer, Allison, and Kopman jointly compiled a list of Louisiana birds, this time including only 310 species, since several dubious entries of the previous list had been deleted. Prior to the completion of this résumé, Allison wrote a special paper on the birdlife of West Baton Rouge Parish, and Kopman was author of 13 papers, including one on the birds of Jefferson Parish and several highly important accounts of the migration of birds in the state. To McIlhenny we are especially indebted for his great work in the field of wildlife conservation and for his extensive bird-banding accomplishments. According to records on file in the U.S. Fish and Wildlife Service, McIlhenny is credited with having banded in his lifetime the amazing total of 189,289 birds, mainly ducks. Data obtained from returns on these bandings were eminently important in plotting migratory routes followed by North American birds.

The year 1918 saw the appearance of the first list of the birds of Louisiana to be published by the state—*The Birds of Louisiana* by Stanley Clisby Arthur. It was issued by the Department of Conservation, which then included what is now the Wild Life and Fisheries Commission. This brochure incorporated some species that are not now admitted to our state list because of insufficient evidence to support their occurrence here. Even with these deletions, the list totals 334 species. In 1931 Arthur prepared a full-length book on the birds of the state, and it, too, was published by the former Department of Conservation. This work is excellent for its interesting life history accounts, its explanations and derivations of colloquial names, and the fact that it constitutes the first attempt to summarize in book form available information on the seasonal occurrence of Louisiana birds. The demand for this publication was so great that the supply was quickly exhausted. Since Arthur was by that time submerged in numerous historical projects, including the preparation of his biography of Audubon (in my opinion by far the best one-volume account ever written on the life of the great naturalist), the Department of Conservation commissioned Harry C. Oberholser of the Bureau of Biological Survey, now the U.S. Fish and Wildlife Service, to undertake a complete revision of the 1931 book. This project culminated in the publication in 1938 of an 834-page treatise by Oberholser entitled *The Bird Life of Louisiana*. Again, because of a widespread interest in birds on the part of the people in Louisiana as well as those outside the state, the demand exceeded the supply, and this book also was soon unavailable for further distribution. Oberholser's work carefully summarizes the relative abundance of the birds of the state as it was known up to the beginning of 1938, giving an exhaustive listing of locality records, citations of specimens of Louisiana birds extant in the major museum collections of the country, some life history notes, and an excellent bibliography of nearly all papers relating in any way to the birds of the state published up to that time.

Unfortunately, the compilation of *The Bird Life of Louisiana* was completed when the most active period in the history of Louisiana ornithology was just getting under way. Though the Museum of Zoology at Louisiana State University was organized in 1936, its great collections had barely been started at the time of publication of Oberholser's book. So significant was the expansion of this institution and its programs in the years that followed that a separate chapter will be devoted to its activities. A later event of major importance in the history of Louisiana ornithology was the founding of the Louisiana Ornithological Society in 1947 (see p. 97) under the enthusiastic leadership of Earle R. Greene, with the support of a corps of ornithologically minded people from various parts of the state. The quickened tempo of fieldwork resulting from these two developments has since produced a wealth of new information adding to the distributional and other data given by Oberholser. Indeed, no less than 29 species of birds were added to the state list in the first 16 years following 1938, and, as a result of the great number of active ornithologists now resident in Louisiana, the number of species recorded in the state is continuing to grow.

Many people contributed to our knowledge of Louisiana birds in the 1940s and 1950s. Most notable were the members of a small but exceedingly energetic and capable group of students who attended Louisiana State

University and were instrumental in the development of its museum collections and the execution of its ornithological research. Likewise of great importance were the activities, collectively and individually, of the members of the Louisiana Ornithological Society. Field ornithologists who are especially deserving of commendation for the role they have played in the recent development of the ornithology of the state are: Earl L. Atwood, Samuel A. Arny, Horace W. Belknap, Mrs. Barbara M. Bodman, Donald M. Bradburn, Jas. Hy. Bruns, Fred J. Buchmann, Harvey R. Bullis, Austin W. Burdick, Thomas D. Burleigh, John Chapin, Henry B. Chase, Jr., P. A. Daigre, Father J. L. Dorn, Mr. and Mrs. H. A. J. Evans, Marshall B. Eyster, Miss Rose Feingold, Sidney A. Gauthreaux, Jr., John P. Gee, Leslie Glasgow, Earle R. Greene, G. Dale Hamilton, Thomas R. Howell, Mrs. Frances C. James, Horace H. Jeter, Mr. and Mrs. Robert W. Krebs, R. B. Lea, Miss Mary Lewis, John T. Lynch, Edward A. McIlhenny, Brooke Meanley, M. L. Miles, Oliver Miles, Mr. and Mrs. Robert B. Moore, Buford and Mac Myers, Robert J. Newman, Ted O'Neil, Sam Ray, Chandler S. Robbins, R. R. Rudolph, Charles R. Shaw, Edward McIlhenny Simmons, Alexander Sprunt IV, Ronald J. Stein, James R. Stewart, Miss Ava R. Tabor, James Tanner, Mrs. Ellen A. Taylor, Robert E. Tucker, Eugene Wallace, Eugene W. Wilhelm, Jr., and Richard K. Yancey.

Of special significance has been the work of Horace H. Jeter. His thorough field studies in the northwestern parishes have already done much to fill the gaps in what was previously one of the least-known areas of the state ornithologically. Still relatively unworked are the northern Florida Parishes and the parishes in the northeastern and central parts of the state. Actually, aside from the various state and federal wildlife refuges, the only areas that have had good year-around coverage by a resident ornithologist are the vicinities of New Orleans, Reserve, Avery Island, Lafayette, Baton Rouge, Monroe, Ruston, St. Francisville, Jonesboro, Natchitoches, and Shreveport. Although none of these border on the Gulf of Mexico, frequent field trips, amounting in the course of time to year-around coverage, have been made to Cameron and Grand Isle, the only two readily accessible localities on our coast.

THE LSU MUSEUM OF ZOOLOGY

THE ORGANIZATION in 1936 and the subsequent development of the Louisiana State University Museum of Zoology[1] inevitably led to advances in the more technical aspects of the ornithology of the state. In less than four decades the museum's bird collections have grown from a nucleus of six old unlabeled specimens of unknown origin to an array of over 78,000 skins. These collections include specimens of all the birds of Louisiana, examples of 97 percent of those of the United States and Canada, extensive and immensely important series of Middle and South American birds, and, finally, representatives of all the families of the birds of the world. Although a nearly complete series of native birds, mounted in the most lifelike poses that can be achieved by the art of taxidermy, is featured in the museum's exhibit halls, this assemblage, open to the general public, is but a fractional part of the entire collection. The ornithological material consists mostly of study skins, prepared in a very precise manner, each with an attached label giving the exact locality where the bird was obtained, the name of the collector, the date of collection, the sex, condition of the gonads, amount of fat, and often the weight and other pertinent data (Fig. 2). The skins are carefully classified, catalogued, and systematically arranged in steel cabinets,

[1] Under the university's expanded museum program, the Museum of Zoology is now set up as a research division within the Museum of Natural Science. Although the two museums are intimately tied together administratively and are both housed under the same roof, one of the primary functions of the Museum of Natural Science is related to exhibition and public education. The public displays, many of which are still in the planning stage while the museum awaits the acquisition of additional floor space, contain botanical and paleontological, as well as zoological, materials.

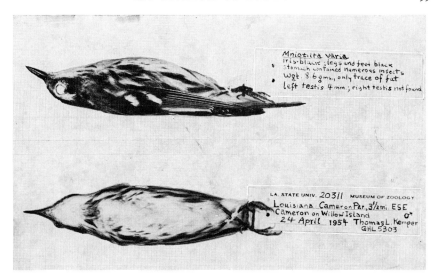

Figure 2   A typical museum study skin and its label.

where they are periodically fumigated and given every possible curatorial care to insure their safe preservation (Fig. 3). The oldest specimen in the museum is that of a Passenger Pigeon, taken near London, Ontario, in 1860, a gift by a Canadian ornithologist who was interested in the museum's welfare. This specimen is as well preserved as those collected in recent years.

Study collections are of immense scientific value. The preservation of specimens provides a means whereby the validity of a record can be checked and rechecked in the future. On January 2, 1954, for example, a Black-legged Kittiwake, the first ever known in the state, was seen and identified independently by two parties near the village of Cameron. In view of the competence of the observers who saw the bird, little or no uncertainty was attached to the correctness of the identification. Yet, in years to come, other ornithologists evaluating the sight record might well have questioned its validity, just as we now question whether Audubon was correct in his vague claim that he saw a kittiwake near the Florida Keys. Fortunately, there will be no occasion for doubting our kittiwake record, for the bird was collected and its skin preserved in the Louisiana State University Museum of Zoology. Even though ornithologists are not able to collect every bird they see (nor do they wish to do so), an attempt is made whenever possible to corroborate all

Figure 3 Photographs of portions of the interior of the Louisiana State University Museum of Zoology. *Upper:* A few of the 251 steel cabinets that presently house the museum's extensive research collections of birds. *Lower:* A close-up view of part of the contents of three specimen trays.

unusual or extralimital records of birds by a preserved specimen. Of course, in order to be able to collect nongame birds that are protected by law, ornithologists must procure special scientific collecting permits from both the state and federal governments.

Scientific study collections provide the material for important investigations relating to the classification of birds. Study skins can be assembled and conveniently handled in making detailed comparisons and measurements of structural parts. Despite the fact that such studies could not be undertaken in the absence of a large assemblage of specimens, the museum worker is often asked why it is necessary to collect more than one or two specimens of each kind of bird or why it is necessary sometimes to have whole trays of specimens of the same species. The answer is simple. The zoologist is interested in determining the range of variation in each species of animal. Variation expresses itself in several ways. Just as there are no two human beings in the world that are absolutely identical, neither are there any two birds of a given species that are identical. To find out the limits of this individual variation in a species, a large series of specimens must be studied critically. But there are still other kinds of variability. In some species age variation is pronounced. A Bald Eagle, for example, requires from four to five years to acquire its pure white head and white tail (see Pl. XIV). Individuals of intermediate age show various degrees of intermediacy in the amount of white on these parts. There is also the matter of sex differences, or what is called sexual dimorphism. The male Northern Cardinal is a brilliant red, but the young male and the female are drab in their attire (see Pl. XXXV). Seasonal changes account for additional variations, as we observe in the male Scarlet Tanager, which is a combination of scarlet and black in summer but a dull green and black in winter (see Pl. XXXIV). Variations in a species resulting from wear and fading and from dichromatism are discussed in the section on feathers and molt. The student of variation in birds must be aware of all these factors and be prepared to recognize them before he can pass on to the most important variations of all, those that we call geographic.

When a series of specimens of a certain species is collected throughout its range and careful comparisons are made of the various population samples represented, marked differences are often noted (Fig. 4). We designate these geographically variant populations within the species as subspecies or geographic races and accord them minor nomenclatural recognition. Sometimes the subspecific distinctions are minute, being nothing more than an average

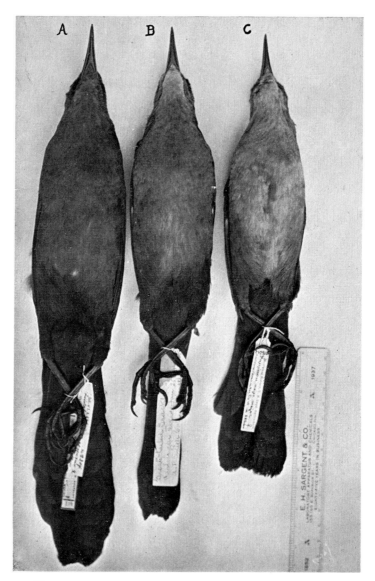

Figure 4 Photograph showing geographical variation in size and color in females from three populations of grackles. (A) *Cassidix mexicanus mexicanus*, of southern Mexico; (B) *C. m. prosopidicola*, of northern Mexico, southern Texas, and the western-northern Gulf Coast; (C) *C. major major*, of the central-northern Gulf Coast, Florida, and the southern Atlantic Coast. A and B are treated as subspecies since they interbreed freely in the areas where they come in contact. C is now regarded as a separate species because its range overlaps that of B without interbreeding taking place.

difference of a few millimeters in length of the wing, bill, or tail or a slight gradation in color from one locality to another. On the other hand, sub-specific variations may be of surprisingly great magnitude—so great some-times that they would suggest that two separate specific entities are involved, were it not for the fact that the observed differences are found to grade imperceptibly from one extreme to the other through a chain of interbreed-ing populations. But when two or more populations differ, if ever so slightly, yet nest in the same place without interbreeding, they are accorded full specific rank. Most vertebrate zoologists think that geographic variation pro-vides the means by which new species arise. The process is most likely to occur when the survival of the variation is favored by natural selection and when its spread throughout the entire species is prevented by physiographic barriers that produce isolation of populations.

Thus, the study of geographic variation in birds is of interest per se, as well as for the light it sheds on problems of avian taxonomy and on the ques-tion of species formation. In addition, a study of this type of variation in a single species enables the student of bird migration to trace the individuals of a certain geographical area from their breeding grounds along their migra-tion routes to their winter homes. For example, we know that the Palm Warblers that breed from Ontario, central Quebec, and Newfoundland south to southern Nova Scotia, New Brunswick, and Maine differ from the Palm Warblers that breed in central Canada and the north-central United States. The latter population of the species is decidedly paler than its eastern representative, the yellow of the underparts being confined mainly to the throat and to the lower belly and under tail coverts (see Pl. XXXI). The knowledge of this simple fact, arrived at by examining hundreds of speci-mens from known breeding localities, led to a still more interesting discovery when winter-taken specimens were examined. Ornithologists then found that the pale western population winters mainly from southeastern Louisiana to southern Florida and from the Bahamas to the Greater Antilles and Yucatan, while the brightly colored eastern population tends to migrate more southwesterly and to winter mainly along the central-northern Gulf Coast as far west as Texas. To a considerable extent the migratory paths of the two subspecies cross each other diagonally, and, although their winter ranges overlap in part, they are largely complementary, a fact that would have escaped detection had not studies of geographic variation in the breed-ing populations of the Palm Warbler been made.

In the winter of 1952–1953 there was a great invasion of western birds into the eastern United States. The effects were noticed in Louisiana possibly to a greater extent than anywhere else, which is not surprising in view of our geographical location. Attention was naturally focused on the large number of Great Plains and Rocky Mountain species that either appeared here for the first time on record or else in unprecedented numbers. The fact that the zoologist can often tell from where a bird comes by minor characteristics of its color and size greatly aided in the analysis of this invasion of western birds. Two notable cases may be cited by way of illustration. A Yellow-bellied Sapsucker collected near Baton Rouge on March 7, 1953, possessed a red nape, which marked the bird unquestionably as an example of the Rocky Mountain subspecies. It could have originated no farther east than the 104th meridian, which passes through eastern Colorado and New Mexico; east of that line the species lacks the red on the nape. Another interesting specimen taken in Louisiana in this eventful winter was a Hermit Thrush shot at Grand Isle. The bird was collected because it appeared to be unusually small and grayish above. On comparison of its preserved skin with a large series of Hermit Thrush skins in the museum from various parts of North America, the bird proved to be an example of the population that breeds in the high coniferous forests from southern British Columbia to southern California. The bird was far east of its known winter range when it appeared in Louisiana. These are but a few examples of the way studies in geographic variation of birds reveal facts pertaining to their migratory movements.

The extensive study collections in the Museum of Zoology are already a storehouse of facts relating to Louisiana birds, as well as the birdlife of the entire southern United States. But the activities of the museum are by no means confined to the acquisition of collections. Staff members and a small corps of graduate students are constantly engaged in other ornithological pursuits. Life history studies are being made of selected species. Thousands of birds have been banded by museum personnel to facilitate studies of the behavior of individual birds, as well as to learn about their molts, their longevity, their mating habits, their intraspecific relationships, and their movements. There is indeed no greater need in North American ornithology today than for better information on the life habits of our birds, for some of the commonest species are inadequately known.

Still another activity of the museum has been its investigations into the intricacies involved in the migration of birds. This endeavor has been concerned not only with local field studies of the phenomenon of migration in

Louisiana and in the general area of the Gulf of Mexico but also with problems of migration throughout North America. In 1945 museum personnel devised the lunar method of studying nocturnal migration on a continental basis. This technique employs a statistical analysis of the volume and direction of night migration, based on the counts of birds passing before the moon as seen through small telescopes. In brief, the method hinges on the principle that the sliver of open sky through which a bird must pass to be seen silhouetted against the moon is a measurable unit of space, the interceptive potential of which depends on the altitude of the moon at the time of the observation. The number of birds seen in this changing unit of space provides a statistical index to the total number of birds passing through a larger unit of space of standard dimensions. Moreover, the direction of flight of the birds seen passing before the moon can be determined with considerable accuracy even though what we actually see through the telescope is only a two-dimensional projection of the birds' flight paths against the lunar disc. By envisioning the moon as an upright clock and recording the pathway of a bird as clock coordinates and by applying simple trigonometric principles, we are enabled to ascertain the true direction of flight. When this is done for the scores, sometimes hundreds, of birds seen before the moon in one night at a given observation station, we are furnished with statistical insight into the probable average direction of flight for all the birds passing overhead that night in the vicinity of that station.

The cooperative study of night migration has resulted in thousands of hours of observation by over 2,400 collaborators at more than 300 stations operating throughout most of North America. At the end of each season of migration the leaders at the various stations send their lunar counts to the museum for processing and analysis. Several hours of complicated mathematical computations are required before the raw data obtained in one night at a given station are ready for comparison with results from other stations on the same or on different nights. Despite the difficulties involved in the analysis of lunar counts, the method has proved to be a successful means of deciphering some of the mysteries that have long surrounded the actual mechanics of night migration; otherwise the passage of birds through the night sky is veiled in darkness. Already many discoveries have been made, the most notable of which relate to the nightly temporal pattern of the flights (that is, the variation in the hour-to-hour volume of migration); to geographic variations in the volume of migration; to flight directions and their relationship to topographical features of the terrain; and to correlations between direction of flight and meteorological conditions. Any one of these basic facts so far learned in regard to the phenomenon of night migration more than justifies the tremendous effort that has gone into the work.

The Museum of Zoology has exerted still another influence in the development of the ornithology of the state through the instruction that its staff has given to a host of undergraduate and graduate students. These students are given every opportunity to make use of the collections, both to familiarize themselves with birds from many parts of the world and to carry out special research studies. An elementary course in ornithology, which is taught in the museum, is designed to acquaint the student with the basic principles of avian biology. The classes make regular weekly field trips, and by the end of the course the students are held responsible for the correct identification in the field or in the museum of approximately 175 species of birds. With this rather broad fundamental knowledge of the subject, the students are prepared to continue the pursuit of ornithology as an absorbing and pleasurable hobby for the remainder of their lives; in doing so, many of them make noteworthy contributions to the science itself.

HOW TO
IDENTIFY
BIRDS

THE FIRST STEP in the pursuit of ornithology is to learn to identify at least most of the common birds, particularly those in the vicinity of the home and the nearby countryside. The greatest progress in this direction is made after the beginner acquires some degree of familiarity with the general scheme of classification of birds into natural groups and is able to say that he knows at least one species in each of the main families. At that stage the illustrated bird book serves great usefulness, for in it the observer finds pictures and textual clues that lead him toward his goal. He knows that the species aggregated in any one family of birds are very similar in their general features, such as posture, body shape, proportions, and behavioral characteristics. Wrens, for instance, are elusive, small to tiny, drab brownish birds, with rather long and slightly decurved bills and usually rather short tails, which they often hold at a jaunty, upward tilt. When the beginner can say with confidence to himself that a certain bird in question is a wren, the job of identification is almost over, for there remains only the problem of deciding what kind of wren. This is done usually by looking for special markings that one particular species possesses and all others lack.

The beginner will find that identification becomes increasingly easy as each new bird is met and its identity solved. For example, after the Wood Thrush is recognized and carefully studied as to shape, size, and behavior, the student has some conception of thrushes in general, and his problem is simplified when he is confronted with other species of this family. He sees later what is obviously a thrush but one lacking the prominent black spots on the breast and the reddish brown head of the bird with which he has pre-

43

viously made acquaintance. He may experience difficulty at first in deciding if his new bird is a Veery or whether it is a Gray-cheeked, Swainson's, or Hermit Thrush, but at least he knows it is a thrush other than the Wood Thrush. The bird in question has an olive-colored back in contrast to its dull, reddish brown tail. The student soon learns that a Hermit Thrush has such markings, while the other species of thrushes have the tail and the back uniformly colored. And thus the beginner becomes aware of the diagnostic or key characters of each species, one after another, until he can recognize them all—even the most difficult species, such as the flycatchers, sandpipers, and sparrows.

When a new bird is encountered, the bird student should attempt to formulate a mental picture of it as quickly as possible, before it disappears from view. There are certain features in particular for which he should look. Are there any conspicuous markings? If so, exactly where are such markings located? Does the bird have a yellow rump patch, a white throat, a black crown patch, or a red malar stripe? Does it have an eye-ring or an eye stripe? If it does, what color is this marking? Are wing bars present, and how many are there? What is the shape of the tail—forked, emarginate, graduated, rounded, or square? Are the outer tail feathers white, only tipped with white, or simply like the others? Are there bars or some other distinctive pattern on the tail, such as a terminal band? Is the bill conical or thin and pointed, compressed or depressed, decurved or recurved? The diagrams in Figure 5 illustrate some of these and other features involved in the questions that a bird observer should immediately ask himself before consulting a book. After the bird is gone there will be ample time for a perusal of the book in search of a species that fits.

No less important in field identification are features of behavior and posture. Does the bird in question wag its tail like an Eastern Phoebe, flit its wings nervously like a kinglet, walk like a Water Pipit, or hop like a sparrow? If it is on the trunk or limb of a tree, does it climb head upward, holding its tail against the bark like a woodpecker or Brown Creeper, or does it run along upside down under limbs with its tail held away from the tree? If the bird is on the water, does its body float high like a duck's or mainly submerged as in the case of a cormorant? When taking to the air, does it spring up like a Mallard, or does it run along the surface for some distance like an American Coot?

Call notes and songs often provide clues to identification in instances when a bird cannot be clearly seen because it is hidden in a tree. Indeed, far

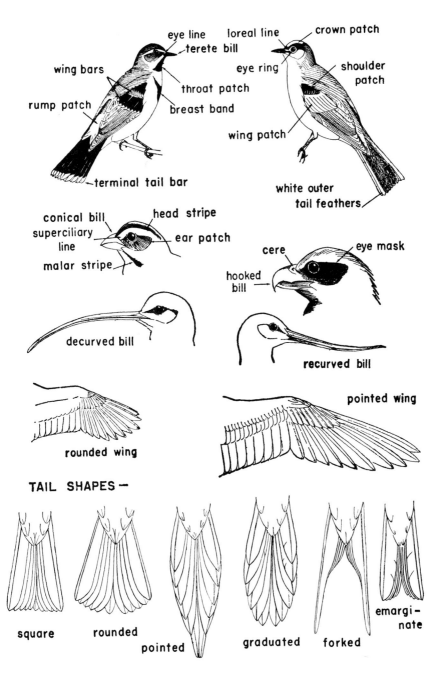

Figure 5 Some helpful field marks.

more small land birds are heard than are generally seen. Learning to recognize call notes and songs depends in some measure on the person and his ability, not only to hear sounds, but also to classify them. A common and highly useful practice among ornithologists is to translate bird calls into a simple phonetic expression. A Red-winged Blackbird seems to sing *ogurgleeee*; a Chestnut-sided Warbler, "I want to see Miss Beecher"; a Tufted Titmouse, "Peter, Peter, Peter." The names of some birds are conveniently derived from a phonetic rendering of their call notes, as in the case of a phoebe, pewee, chickadee, and others. Graphic representations of songs are also helpful, even when they may have meaning only to the one who devises them. To my ears the song of the Black-throated Green Warbler can be expressed, as was done by John Burroughs, by two straight lines, a "V," and another line: ——— ——— V ———. The use of descriptive words to characterize songs helps one to remember them. Among numerous words of this kind are: *ascending, buzzing, chattering, discordant, double-toned, flutelike, gurgling, liquid, metallic, nasal, plaintive, rattling, strident, slurring, twittering, throaty, weak,* and *warbling*.

In identifying a bird, one must also be aware of its known status in the area. If a beginner discovers, for example, what he believes is a Masked Duck, he should be immediately suspicious of his identification, for this tropical species has been recorded in Louisiana on only five occasions in well over one hundred years of observation by scores of ornithologists. Closer inspection is likely to disclose that the duck in question is a Ruddy Duck, a common winter resident and rare nester in the state. Similarly, if the beginner tentatively identifies in January what he believes to be a Gray-cheeked Thrush, he should scrutinize the bird further, for there are no unquestionable records of this species' being in Louisiana between October 29 and April 7. This is not to say that it is impossible for a Gray-cheeked Thrush to occur in Louisiana in January. However, despite the fact that unusual occurrences of birds are by no means infrequent, the probabilities are strongly against it. While the bird in question may be a Gray-cheeked Thrush, it is more likely the similar-appearing Hermit Thrush, which winters commonly in Louisiana, arriving in late September and remaining sometimes until as late as May 15. Consequently, a statement of the usual season of occurrence is given in each species account, and this information, together with the extreme dates of occurrence, is summarized graphically for the species of regular occurrence in the charts beginning on page 597.

Since this book is designed merely as an introduction to Louisiana birds and since there is a limitation on the amount of space that can be devoted to each species, many interesting facts must be omitted. The serious student is urged to supplement what he finds here with readings in other bird books. If he is desirous of pursuing his studies outside of the state, he is especially urged to obtain a copy of Peterson's A *Field Guide to the Birds* [of the eastern United States] or A *Field Guide to the Birds of Texas*. These are pocket-sized books, profusely illustrated by the author with colorplates and line drawings. Despite more than 45 years of almost daily experience in the field identification of birds, I constantly refer to Peterson's *Guides*, for they superbly and succinctly set forth, better than any other bird books ever written, the diagnostic field characters of birds in nearly all their variations. Still another excellent aid to the student of birds, published since the appearance of the earlier editions of this work, is *Birds of North America: A Guide to Field Identification*, by Chandler S. Robbins, Bertel Bruun, and Herbert S. Zim, illustrated by Arthur Singer.

Besides a field guide, there are two other valuable aids to the identification of birds. One is a good pair of field glasses. Ornithologists find that 6 x 30 or 7 x 35 prism binoculars are ideal. Anything less than six power is generally inadequate, and glasses with magnifications over eight power are either too heavy, too costly, or too poor in their light-transmitting qualities. The amount of light reaching the eye of the observer is determined by the diameter of the objective lens and the ratio of this diameter to the magnification. The relative brightness afforded by a binocular is computed by dividing the power into the diameter of the objective lens and squaring the quotient. The added advantage in magnification of an 8 x 30 over a 7 x 35 is more than offset, under adverse light conditions, by the fact that the latter provides a much brighter image. Factory coating of lenses, when it is done inside and out—that is, to all lens surfaces—greatly increases the brilliance of the image. Secondhand, but excellently reconditioned, binoculars are often obtainable at reasonable cost, but care should be taken to deal with a reputable concern. A good pair of binoculars will not only facilitate identification but will also make the observer's experiences in watching birds infinitely more enjoyable.

Almost as important as a field guide and binoculars is the ability of the observer to make a noise simulating a bird in distress. This is most effectively done by placing the fingers or the back of the hand against the lips and effecting a squeaking sound. Hawks, owls, some shorebirds, and nearly all small perching birds will fly toward the source of the sound, exhibiting great excitement and curiosity. When the observer is at least partially concealed, such birds as titmice, chickadees, and kinglets will sometimes alight on branches only a few feet away, scolding vociferously and thereby exciting and drawing up other species nearby in the forest or thicket. The technique operates most successfully in winter, when the largest number and greatest variety of birds are likely to respond. I have never understood why "squeaking" should not be more effective in the breeding season, but at that time the reaction is mainly confined to birds whose nests are very close by. At any rate, the stratagem always helps an observer obtain good views of many birds with retiring habits. The sound should be continued as long as any birds show interest; quite often the more wary species appear only after much inducement. A combination of squeaking and an imitation of the Common Screech Owl's call is more effective than squeaking alone, particularly with small woodland birds. The owl note is made by holding the head back and whistling through saliva held on the back of the tongue. If a Common Screech Owl is in the vicinity, it may answer the imitation of its call.

In order to make efficient use of the descriptive material in this and other bird books, the beginning student in ornithology needs to become familiar with the so-called topography of a bird. The various external components of the head, neck, trunk, wing, tail, bill, and foot all have special names that are used over and over again in descriptive ornithology. These names apply to precise features, definite areas, or certain particular feathers; consequently, they help immeasurably in accurately describing a bird in the fewest possible words. For example, to be able to simply say "lores" is better than having to say "the area between the anterior corner of the eye and a point just behind the nostril at the base of the bill" each time this part is mentioned. Figures 6 and 7 are designed to map and identify the principal external features referred to in ornithological works.

As one's knowledge of birds in the field increases, there is invariably a desire to read what is known about their habits, their distribution and migrations, and the various other aspects of their daily lives. Most libraries contain works that supply much of this information. Fortunately, Louisiana has had two books published on its birdlife, both issued by what is now known as the Wild Life and Fisheries Commission. Stanley Clisby Arthur's *Birds of Louisiana* appeared in 1931 and was followed in 1938 by Harry C. Oberholser's *Bird Life of Louisiana*. The student who can gain access to either of

Figure 6 External features of a bird.

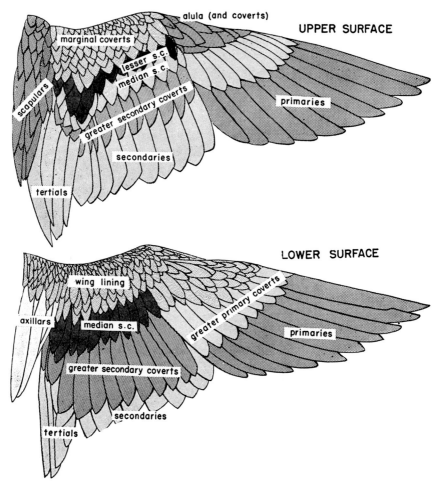

Figure 7 The classification of the feathers of the wing.

these publications will find much useful and interesting information concerning our state's avifauna. Unfortunately, both books are now out of print, but Oberholser's work was widely distributed in the state and thus can usually be located for reference purposes.

FEATHERS, PLUMAGE, AND MOLT

THE ONE unique external characteristic of birds is that they possess feathers. All their other features are distinctive only in combinations of two or more characters. For example, we cannot say that birds are the only animals with nucleated red blood cells, but we can say that they and camels are the only *warm-blooded* animals with nucleated red blood cells. Since feathers are peculiar to birds and are so marvelous in their structure and function, they should be thoroughly understood by the student of birds.

Birds appear to be covered by feathers, and in a literal sense they *are* covered; but by this we do not mean that feathers grow from all surface areas of the body. They are instead located in definite tracts, which are technically called *pterylae*, as opposed to the bare areas, called *apteria*. There are exceptions, such as in the case of penguins and ostriches and their allies, in which the body feathering is quite complete. The generalized distribution of the eight principal tracts is shown in Figure 8, but there are many minor deviations from this scheme that provide the basis for the important study known as pterylography. The pterylae in related groups of birds show certain peculiarities in shape and in relative size that distinguish them from the pterylae of other groups and, therefore, are useful in determining relationships.

Feathers can be classified into five major types: contour, down, semiplume, filoplume, and powder down. The first of these are the feathers that we see, which include, in addition to the body covering, the wing and tail feathers. A typical contour feather (Fig. 9) is one such as we might pluck from the breast of a crow. Close examination reveals that it consists

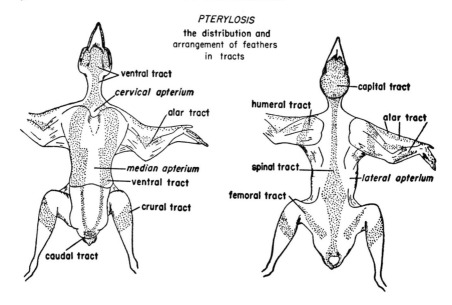

Figure 8

primarily of the *quill*, or *shaft*, and the *vane*. The former is divisible into two
clear-cut parts, the bare *calamus*, by which the feather is anchored to the
skin, and the *rhachis*, which bears a series of flat, platelike structures collectively called the web or vane. The base of the calamus is seen to have a
small opening, the *inferior umbilicus*, through which nutrient materials enter
the shaft in the period of the feather's growth and development. At the
point where the rhachis and the webbing begin, there is visible on the underside of most contour feathers a slight depression, the *superior umbilicus*, from
which a tuft of downy filaments protrudes. This tuft is called the *aftershaft*
or *hyporhachis*. In the feathers of many birds the aftershaft is poorly developed, but in others it is conspicuous—for example, in the Emu and the
Cassowary, in which it is as long or nearly as long as the main shaft (Fig. 10).
This "double feather" condition is believed to represent the type of feather
possessed by many ancient birds. Its retention in some modern forms, such
as in the grouse where the aftershaft is about half as long as the main shaft
(Fig. 10), perhaps serves a useful purpose by providing a heavier insulation
against the cold; feathers in general are a means whereby birds preserve their

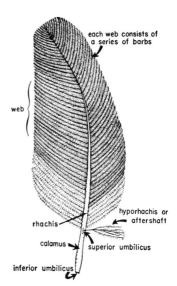

each web consists of
a series of barbs

web

hyporhachis or
aftershaft

rhachis

superior umbilicus

calamus

inferior umbilicus

Figure 9　A typical contour feather and its major components.

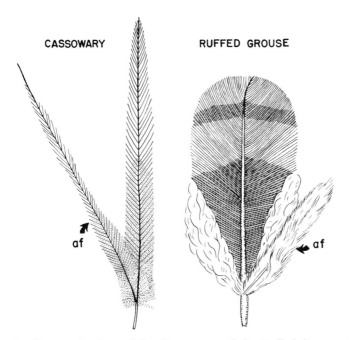

CASSOWARY

RUFFED GROUSE

af

af

Figure 10　Contour feathers of the Cassowary and the Ruffed Grouse, showing variations in the length of the aftershaft (af) or hyporhachis.

body warmth and exclude the cold. Feathers create a dead-air space, comparable to that in a thermos bottle; hence the colder the temperature, the more the feathers are fluffed in order to increase the depth of this insulating space.

Among the most remarkable features of a feather are the microscopic devices that interlock the plates composing the web. They are particularly essential in maintaining the rigidity of the flight feathers, which are subjected to great stresses as the bird beats its wings. If a single element of the web, called a *barb,* is pulled free from adjacent barbs and examined under a magnifying lens, it will be found to resemble a minute feather in that it consists of a shaft with webbing on each side. The subsidiary "barbs" making up the "web" on the true barb are called *barbules.* Those on the side toward the tip of the feather interlock with the barbules on the back side of the succeeding barb. Certain hooklike processes, *hamuli,* on the underside of one barbule fit into flanges on the top side of the barbules of the adjacent barb, thereby holding the entire web together (Fig. 11).

Contour feathers show many variations, of which color is the most notable. The almost infinite number of shades and tints displayed by the world's eight-thousand-odd species of birds is unsurpassed in any other group of animals, and only butterflies and flowering plants may be regarded as serious rivals. Modifications in the structure of contour feathers sometimes involve

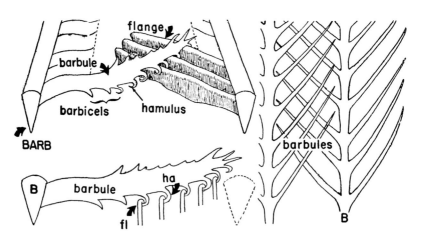

Figure 11 Diagrammatic drawings of the microscopic structural details of a typical contour feather. Note the devices (hamuli and flanges) that interlock the obliquely overlapping barbules.

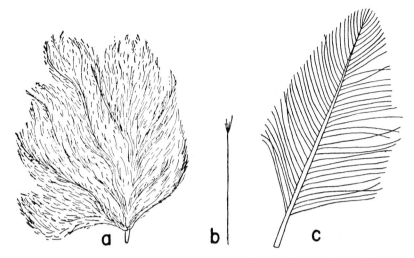

Figure 12   Typical down feather (a), filoplume (b), and semiplume (c).

an omission of the interlocking devices on the barbules, and this makes the feather filamentous or lacy. Such is the condition, for instance, in certain back feathers of the Snowy and Great Egrets, feathers that form the main *aigrettes* that these magnificent birds erect in their courtship. It is the modification of the normally small feathers covering the base of the tail, called the *upper tail coverts*, that supplies the well-known ornament of a peacock. An alteration of the tail feathers themselves creates the almost unbelievable adornment of the Lyrebird and some of the renowned vestures of the birds of paradise. Less spectacular are the variations in contour feathers that create crests, topknots, ruffs, "ear" tufts, forked or pointed tails, gorgets, and other outstanding features.

At the time of hatching many birds are covered, at least in part, with *down* (Fig. 12a). These short, usually dense, feathers possess a calamus but ordinarily no rhachis. The barbs arise from the top of the calamus in a tuft or from a soft rhachis, and, since they lack barbules and interlocking devices, they are fluffy. Down feathers are characteristic of ducks and the majority of water birds, even as adults. They occur in the natal stage of most other birds, although the higher types possess only a scant amount of them and some birds, such as woodpeckers and hummingbirds, lack them altogether. In any event, whether down is sparse or dense, there is an evolutionary tendency for birds to pass through the down stage as rapidly as possible. The Brush Turkey of Australia goes through the stage in the egg!

The *semiplumes* (Fig. 12c) are structurally somewhat intermediate between down and contour feathers. Unlike down, they have the entire shaft present and of firm texture, with the web on each side, but, like down, they lack hooks and flanges for holding the web together. Semiplumes are found chiefly on the underparts of the bird and are always covered by the main contour feathers.

The *filoplumes* (Fig. 12b) need no introduction other than to point out that they are the irksome hairlike structures that cause the discriminating cook inconvenience (along with pinfeathers, or feathers not yet mature and hence soft and mushy at their base). About the only way to remove the filoplumes is by singeing. Superficially they seem like hairs because of the exceedingly long, thin shaft, in which there is no marked separation into calamus and rhachis; on the end there is usually a tiny tuft of barbs.

The final category into which feathers are divided is *powder down*. These feathers arise as peculiar mats on the flanks, abdomen, or breast of all members of the heron tribe and even hawks and parrots. They are believed to be continuously growing down feathers, the tips of which are perpetually breaking up into a powdery substance. The feathers of herons in particular are quite powdery to the touch. Powder-down feathers are exceedingly oily at their base and perhaps serve to supply the birds that have them with supplementary lubrication and refurbishment for their plumage.

A bird's feathers are directly subjected to the adversities of the environment and consequently become gradually worn and abraded. Fortunately, nature has taken care of the situation to the extent that virtually no bird is required to retain one set of feathers for more than one year. This annual shedding of the feathers is called *ecdysis*, or *molt*, and when it happens but once a year, the event always follows the breeding season and hence is called *postnuptial* molt. This molt is complete; that is, every feather is shed and a new one is acquired in its place. In addition to the postnuptial molt, many birds undergo a *prenuptial* molt just before the breeding season. This molt is often partial, involving principally the feathers of the head. Birds with spectacular breeding plumage in contrast to a drab winter dress naturally must pass through a prenuptial molt.

Ecdysis takes place over a period of several weeks and usually by one or two tracts at a time; hence there is no period when the bird is nude of its covering. This is particularly important in the case of the wing and tail feathers, which are essential to the bird in maintaining its mobility. When we see a vulture soaring overhead with the fourth primary missing on the left wing, almost invariably the corresponding primary on the right wing is also missing. A classic exception to this manner of molting the flight feathers is provided by most ducks, which shed these feathers almost simultaneously and therefore become temporarily flightless during the period of the *eclipse plumage*. The characteristics of the *eclipse* molt in these birds are of special interest and will be mentioned in another connection.

The various plumage stages are clearly defined and fairly uniform in their sequence in all birds. Since many species assume radically different appearance in successive molts, the student of birds must familiarize himself with the names of the plumages, the molts by which they are lost, and the generalized scheme of their sequence. The plumages are definable as follows:

Natal Down—This plumage consists of down feathers, which are present on hatching or else acquired soon thereafter. As previously noted, it is a plumage stage that is passed through rapidly and in some birds, such as woodpeckers and hummingbirds, skipped altogether. In ducks and gallinaceous birds (for example, turkeys and chickens), the down covers the entire body, whereas in perching birds, such as sparrows, the down is limited mainly to the tracts on the upperparts. The plumage is lost by the postnatal molt, which is always complete.

Juvenal Plumage—Usually within a few days of hatching the young bird shows some evidence of acquiring the first set of contour feathers, which make up the juvenal plumage. In nearly all songbirds, the body covering is complete before the birds leave the nest, and the wing and tail feathers are full length, or almost so, within another week. The whole process from hatching to flying seldom requires much more than three or four weeks. At this point I should emphasize that in the majority of birds, the young, when they leave the nest, are just about as large as they will ever be. To be sure, there are numerous exceptions, as, for instance, the highly precocial young of ducks and grebes, which hit the water and swim with agility within an hour or so of hatching. Also, baby plovers run from the nest, a mere depression in the sand, as soon as the feathers are dry. On the other hand, young eaglets remain in the nest for three to four months, and when they finally leave they may even be heavier than their parents because of their rapid growth and lack of exercise. The juvenal plumage is often partially replaced or supplemented soon after departure from the nest, but sometimes the plumage remains intact until late summer or fall. The process by which the juvenal plumage is lost is called the postjuvenal molt. This molt may or may not be complete.

First Winter Plumage—This is the plumage that the young bird wears from late fall until the following spring. In some birds, such as chickadees, this plumage represents the pattern and coloration to be worn for life, but in other birds marked transformations occur before the first breeding season. In birds where the sexes are dissimilar, both the juvenal and the first winter plumages of males often resemble the hen more than they do the fully adult male. This is possibly always true where the adult markings are actually secondary sexual characters induced by sex hormones. The brilliant livery of the male Painted Bunting is brought on by secretions of the mature male gonads, which do not become activated until the spring following birth. Before this the male is attired like the female. Experimentally, in the laboratory, adult males can be made to assume the color of the female by the injection of female hormones. Conversely, the female can be made to take on the male attire by the injection of male hormones. On the other hand, the black throat and other male characters of the House Sparrow are unaffected by injections of even great quantities of female hormones, and, interestingly enough, the male characters are assumed in the postjuvenal molt, many months before the bird's initial sexual activity. In some birds the first winter plumage is retained as the first nuptial plumage, but in most cases it is at least partially replaced by the prenuptial molt. There are instances where a prenuptial molt occurs prior to the first nesting season but not thereafter.

First Nuptial Plumage—This is the first breeding plumage and, in many birds, it is less brilliant than the breeding dress acquired in subsequent years. In the Orchard Oriole, for example, the color and pattern of the male still closely resemble that of the female, the main difference being that a black throat is acquired by the first prenuptial molt. In other species, such as the Indigo Bunting and various warblers, the plumage of the male in the first breeding dress simply lacks the richness of color characteristic of older individuals. This plumage is always lost at the end of the nesting season by means of the first postnuptial molt, which is complete.

Second Winter Plumage—This term is applied to the plumage worn during the second winter, especially when it differs from the plumage worn the first winter. It is not usually distinguishable from the winter plumages that follow in successive years. It is lost by the second prenuptial molt, either wholly or in part, or it may be retained as the adult nuptial plumage. Birds with a breeding plumage distinct from the winter plumage naturally undergo at least a partial prenuptial molt.

Second Nuptial Plumage—This term has particular utility only when the second breeding plumage differs from the first. When the second breeding plumage or those of subsequent years do not differ, they are referred to simply as the *adult nuptial plumage*. The nuptial plumage is worn only during the breeding season and is lost by a complete postnuptial molt when nesting is over.

Third and Fourth Winter Plumages—These names are usually employed only in the case of the comparatively few birds (for example, the Bald Eagle and certain gulls) that have distinctive plumage characteristics in their third and fourth years. Otherwise the plumages are termed simply *adult winter*.

The following chart summarizes all the plumages and the molts by which each is lost. It should be memorized by the student, for there will be numerous occasions when the information will be needed. The plumages and the sequence of molt as it occurs in six selected species are shown in Figure 13.

Name of plumage	*Molt by which plumage is lost*
natal down	postnatal
juvenal	postjuvenal
first winter	first prenuptial
first nuptial	first postnuptial
second winter	second prenuptial
second nuptial	second postnuptial
third winter	third prenuptial
third nuptial	third postnuptial

Eclipse Plumage—A unique plumage sequence is observable in most male ducks. As soon as the female begins to incubate, the male rapidly loses all the wing and tail feathers, and its body feathers are partially replaced by a plumage that resembles that of the hen. For the next five to eight weeks the male is flightless, but then he undergoes another molt, whereby he regains his full regalia and is ready to migrate southward. The so-called eclipse plumage is equivalent to the winter plumage, and the molt by which it is acquired is actually the postnuptial molt of other birds; it is lost by a prenuptial molt that is moved forward some six months. In Figure 13 the so-called second winter plumage of the Mallard is actually the eclipse plumage. The second nuptial plumage is acquired by the eclipse molt and is worn

Figure 13 Sequence of plumages in the males of six species. (After Pettingill, 1946.)

FIRST NUPTIAL PLUMAGE   SECOND WINTER PLUMAGE   SECOND NUPTIAL PLUMAGE

the "eclipse" plumage

— in ducks only

Figure 13   (*concluded*)

through the winter and into the subsequent breeding season. Adult northern ducks that come down to Louisiana in late fall and early winter are consequently in their finest attire—in what amounts to their nuptial plumage, as well as their winter plumage.

Plumage changes occur by other means than molt. In a few birds this is accomplished by wear. The European Starling, for example, is profusely speckled in late fall and early winter following the postnuptial molt. By the time spring comes it is a highly iridescent black. This transformation is effected by the wearing off of the light tips to the black feathers, as shown by the drawings of the European Starling in Figure 128. The colors of other birds change through fading, as well as by abrasion. This is notably true of species in which there is no prenuptial molt and in which habitat preferences are for open, sunny situations or for coarse vegetation. The feathers of the little Carolina Wren, for instance, must last from one September to the next September. In this time the bird's attire becomes so badly faded and worn that it scarcely resembles the original richly colored, mahogany brown and buff plumage of early fall.

Color variations within a species are sometimes due to *dichromatism,* or the presence of two or more color phases. Some well-known examples are the red and gray phases in the Common Screech Owl (see photograph opposite p. 64), the whitish and yellowish phases in the Barn Owl, and the light and dark phases of the many kinds of hawks (Pls. XII and XIII). Some types of dichromatism are quite common within certain species, but others are rare. Abnormal blackness results from a phenomenon known as *melanism,* the preponderance of certain melanins, or dark brown or blackish brown pigments, in feathers. The complete absence of pigment produces *albinism.* Albino individuals are also pink eyed, since pigment is lacking from the iris of the eye, allowing light to be reflected from the underlying blood vessels in the vascularized portions of the retina. Technically there is no such thing as a "partial albino," for birds that are blotched with white may be so colored because of injury or because of a special genetic influence called the "spotting factor." All-white birds with black eyes are called "black-eyed whites" by the geneticist, who recognizes this variation as something entirely apart from pink-eyed whites, or true albinos. Two rarer variations are *erythrism* and *xanthochroism,* caused by excessive amounts of reddish brown and yellow pigments, respectively, deposited in the feathers.

THE BIRD
SKELETON

THE SERIOUS PURSUIT of ornithology, even as a hobby, should be implemented at the outset by at least a cursory study of the skeletal anatomy. This will serve to enhance the student's appreciation of the adaptations of the bird as a flying mechanism. The bird is, indeed, a bundle of marvelous evolutionary modifications, representing nature's greatest success in producing a large animal capable of sustaining itself aloft by its own power. By means of flight, birds escape enemies, secure food, and find mates. On outstretched pinions, they span the widest oceans and soar over the highest mountains. Thus they have been able to occupy all the continents of the world.

Flight in birds is accomplished primarily as a result of changes in the forelimb that have converted this structure from the conventional type of vertebrate organ of locomotion into a wing. In general, the primaries provide the propellers and the secondaries furnish the surface that creates the "lift" (Fig. 14). Together they make flight possible. The main functions of the bones are to furnish a firm anchorage for these feathers and to serve as a place of attachment for the muscles that move the limb. A consolidation of, and reduction in, the number of the elements in the limb (Fig. 15) would naturally increase its efficiency of operation by providing greater leverage and more rapid up-and-down motion. We are not surprised, therefore, to discover that this is precisely what happened when birds evolved from reptiles and the reptilian arm became a wing. The elements of the forearm (*radius* and *ulna*) and upper arm (*humerus*) remained essentially unchanged though the shoulder joint acquired a greater freedom of rotation.

63

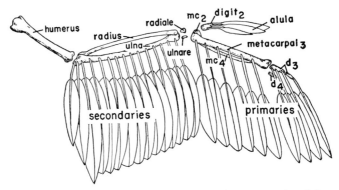

Figure 14   The bones of the wing and their relationships to the alula, primaries, and secondaries.

The most drastic alteration was the reduction of wrist bones (*carpals*) from the usual complement of eight to two, the *radiale* (articulating with the radius) and the *ulnare* (articulating with the ulna). This diminution in the number of wrist bones achieved greater simplicity and permitted the end of the limb to sweep more freely through its propellerlike motions, from which the bird gains propulsion. The hand (*manus*) has likewise undergone radical reduction in the number of elements. Five *metacarpals* were reduced to three. There is disagreement among authorities as to which two of the original five metacarpals are missing. Some comparative anatomists think the first, second, and third metacarpals are retained, that the fourth is missing, and that the fifth has become the so-called *ulnare*. Other anatomists believe simply that the first and fifth metacarpals are lost, with the second, third, and fourth remaining. Until more conclusive embryological studies have been made, I prefer to follow the latter interpretation. The second metacarpal is only knoblike and is fused to metacarpal number three, which is the largest, as well as the one to which the primaries attach. Metacarpal number four is a distinct bone, but it is fused at each end to metacarpal number three. Each of the three metacarpals continues to bear a digit, but the number of *phalanges* or joints in each is greatly diminished. Our own phalangeal formula is 2-3-3-3-3, whereas that of the bird is ordinarily 0-2-2-1-0.

Photograph on Opposite Page   Screech Owls at Their Nest   samuel a. grimes

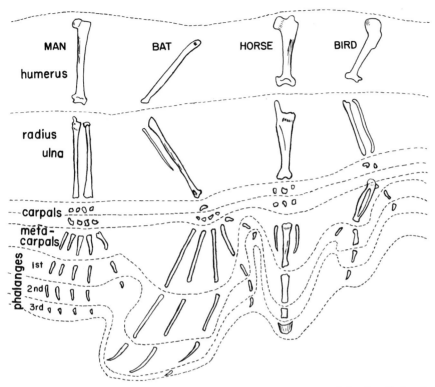

Figure 15 Diagram showing the homologies in the bones of the forelimb of a man, a bat, a horse, and a bird. (After Coues.)

By comparing the bones of the forelimb of a bat, horse, or man with those of a bird, we quickly see the extent of reduction that has occurred in the latter. Man has the humerus, the radius and ulna, eight carpals, five metacarpals, and five digits, the last comprising 14 phalanges—or a total of 30 elements. The typical bird has a total of only 13 bones in its forelimb. A diagrammatic comparison between the forelimbs of the bird, bat, horse, and man is shown in Figure 15.

There are many other skeletal modifications, aside from those that have taken place in the forelimb, that are superb adaptations for flight (Fig. 16). The forelimb requires firm anchorage, and we find it perched in a socket on a sort of tripod formed by the *scapula*, the *coracoid*, and one arm of the

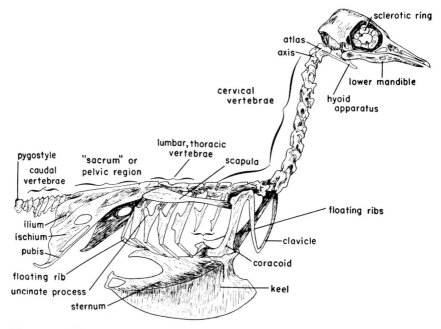

Figure 16 The axial skeleton and girdles of a bird. The bird represented is a Rock Pigeon.

furcula, or wishbone, which is nothing more than the two fused "collar bones." The muscles that operate the wing secure their main attachment across the broad breastbone and on its upright keel. Compactness and rigidity in the whole skeletal setup are provided by the extensive fusion of parts. This is particularly evident in the fusion of the pelvic bones with the vertebral column and from the special "struts," or braces, called *uncinate processes,* that connect one rib with the next. The hollow wing and leg bones reduce weight without loss of strength, and the lightness of the thin-boned skull helps to shift the bird's weight and center of gravity backward.

Few changes are more important than those manifest in the tail, where most of the vertebrae have been lost or else have moved forward to fuse into a single structure, the *pygostyle* (forming, along with other caudal vertebrae, the skeletal support to what is commonly called the "Pope's nose"). The pygostyle serves as an anchorage for the tail feathers. *Archaeopteryx,* the Lizard-tailed Bird that lived in Bavaria some 155 million years ago, retained a long series of tail vertebrae with feathers along each side (Fig. 17), but this must have been very unwieldy. Many modern birds can use their tails as effective rudders and elevators simply by moving the pygostyle, which in turn alters the position of the tail feathers.

The bird achieves buoyancy in the air and on the water not only by the lightness of its skeletal parts but also by its elaborate system of air sacs, which connect with the bronchial tubes and with the hollow spaces in the humeri and certain other bones. These sacs likewise increase the breathing efficiency of the bird by providing air spaces without using up vascularized portions of the lungs, which are the only places where an interchange of gases can take place with the red blood cells. In our own lungs a considerable part of the vascularized area is not used with full efficiency, since the air in the lower recesses of our respiratory organs is not always expelled at each exhalation. Because, as already noted, the air sacs connect with the hollow wing bones, we can readily understand why suffocating a bird with a broken humerus simply by closing its mouth and plugging its nostrils is virtually impossible. It breathes through the broken bone.

The hind limb, like its counterpart the forelimb, has undergone great alterations leading to a diminution of some elements and the fusion of others. Adaptive changes within certain groups of birds have converted the leg and foot into a paddle; in others, to a more efficient means of running. Above all, such changes have produced a structure that is eminently effective for grasping the limbs of trees, a modification that permitted the vast majority of birds to become arboreal, either wholly or in part.

There is a popular misconception concerning the identity of the bones of the hind limb (see Fig. 18). The knee of a bird bends forward as it should, but we generally do not see this part of a bird's leg. The thighbone, or *femur*, fits into a socket located far to the bird's rear, and since the bone is usually short, it and the knee are generally concealed by the feathers or may actually fail to reach the outside at all. The next section of the leg is the *crus*, or "drumstick," consisting of two bones—the larger, the *tibia*; the smaller, the *fibula*. With rare exceptions, as in some penguins, the fibula is merely a sliver of a bone. Technically this section of the leg is called the *tibiotarsus*, since it incorporates at its distal, or outward, end some fused tarsal elements. The junction of the tibiotarsus with the *tarsometatarsus* is the joint which is mistaken for the real knee. Actually it is the bird's heel. The succeeding section represents a consolidation of the remaining tarsal elements and the surviving metatarsal bones and is called the tarsometatarsus,

Figure 17 Impression in slate of the remains of the Lizard-tailed Bird (*Archaeopteryx lithographica*) found in Bavaria. (Photograph courtesy British Museum [Natural History], London.)

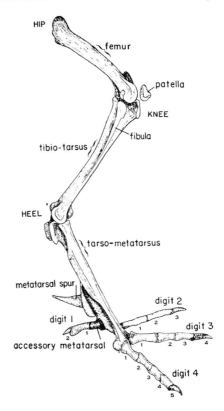

HIP
femur
patella
KNEE
fibula
tibio-tarsus
HEEL
tarso-metatarsus
metatarsal spur
digit 2
digit I
digit 3
accessory metatarsal
digit 4

Figure 18 The bones of the hind limb of a bird. The drawing is based on a chicken.

or often simply the "tarsus." There are no free tarsal bones remaining in the foot of the bird. The bird has become entirely *digitigrade*, that is, it stands on its toes, in contrast to man and several other animals that are *plantigrade* and stand on the entire foot. The bird's foot contains three or four digits, each with its complement of phalanges, or joints, the outermost ones always bearing a claw.

The student of birds should carefully study Figure 18 in order that he may know the proper names of the elements involved and, surely, under no circumstances confuse the heel with the knee. Examination of Figure 19 will disclose the true homologies of the bones of the bird's leg with those in man and the horse.

Some birds possess accessory structures on the wings and legs. The toes of reptiles possess *claws*; hence the fact that some birds also have small

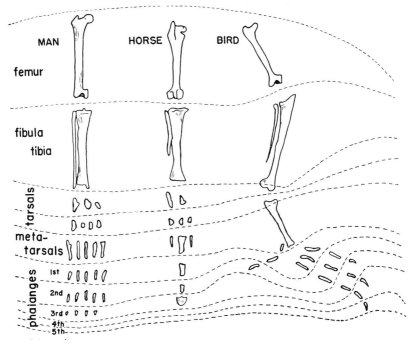

MAN HORSE BIRD

femur

fibula

tibia

tarsals

meta-
tarsals

phalanges 1st

2nd

3rd

4th

5th

Figure 19   Diagram showing the homologies in the bones of the leg of a man, a horse, and a bird. (After Coues.)

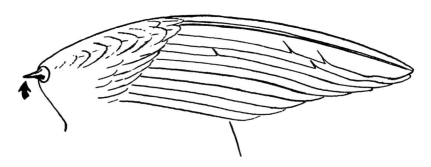

Figure 20   The metacarpal spur (indicated by arrow) on the wing of a Jacana.

claws on the digits of their forelimbs as well as on their toes is not surprising. Such rudimentary claws are to be found on the second finger of certain vultures and geese, as well as on some of the digits of other birds. In a South American bird, the Hoatzin, functional claws are found on the first and second fingers of the young, which use all four limbs to advantage in climbing and scrambling about on branches. Claws are, however, not to be confused with the *metacarpal spurs* on the wings of such birds as the Jacana (Fig. 20). These horny protuberances are comparable to the metatarsal spurs found on the tarsometatarsus of gallinaceous birds, such as the domestic fowl and the turkey. The latter appear only on the male, serving as offensive weapons, and are classified as secondary sexual characters, since they develop under the influence of male sex hormones.

For a more complete discussion of avian anatomy, the reader is referred to the classic account in Volume 1 of Elliott Coues' *Key to North American Birds* (6th ed., 1927). If this work is not available, I recommend a perusal of *Ornithology in Laboratory and Field* (rev. 4th ed., 1970) by O. S. Pettingill, Jr.

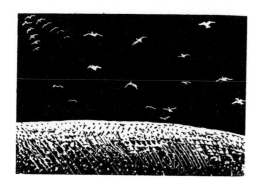

MIGRATION

TWICE EACH YEAR birds perform one of nature's most remarkable feats. Millions of them depart from their northern breeding grounds soon after the nesting chores are completed and fly hundreds, sometimes thousands, of miles to regions of warmer climate. After a sojourn in southern lands, sometimes even in faraway South America, the birds respond to some stimulus that sends them surging northward again. These incredible journeys are made not only by large, strong-winged birds of renowned prowess of flight but also by such small birds as swallows, wrens, warblers, tanagers, sparrows, and even the diminutive hummingbirds. The passage of small land birds is the more remarkable because it is accomplished in large part at night and because it carries many of them on long and perilous treks over great expanses of open water.

The identity of the stimulus that sets migration in motion has yet to be established with complete certainty, but day length is unquestionably of great importance. The internal physiological changes that occur prior to actual migration include an increase in the size of the sex organs and the deposition of excess amounts of fat, to be used later as a source of much-needed energy. But the exact nature of the psychological trigger that initiates the process of migration, even causing a bird to launch out into the night sky, is still a mystery; so is the nature of the orienting mechanism that sends the bird unerringly in the direction of its summer home. When we stand on a Gulf beach in spring and watch birds making a landfall after a trans-Gulf passage or even as we listen from our lawns on a cloudy night to the frequent flight calls coming down out of the darkness, is it any wonder that we marvel at what is taking place?

This semiannual event lends a real flavor to the study of birds and accounts for the interesting seasonal variations and for the general diversity of our birdlife on a local basis. If migrations ceased and all species remained the year around on their present nesting grounds, our state's avifauna would be reduced by approximately 62 percent. We could no longer, for instance, look forward in fall to the arrival of the hordes of ducks and geese, or the great array of sandpipers, plovers, swallows, and warblers, or the huge flocks of winter sparrows. The study of birds would be narrowed tremendously, and we would be denied one of our major enjoyments—the anticipation always of something new, such as a transient off its normal migratory route or a straggler from the distant North seeking to escape the cold and searching for food.

Space does not here permit a discussion of the many interesting facets of the study of migration. Whole books have been written on the subject without doing full justice to it. Features of migration, such as the punctuality with which many species arrive in certain localities year after year, the routes followed, the distances covered, the rate or speed of performance, and the possible explanations of the origin of the phenomenon itself, are among the topics admirably covered in such works as Frederick C. Lincoln's *Migration of Birds* (1939) or J. Van Tyne and Andrew Berger's *Fundamentals of Ornithology* (1959). Further remarks in this work will be confined to local aspects of the subject, to the visible manifestations of migration as they may be witnessed by the bird-student resident in Louisiana.

Since we are situated at the lower end of the great Mississippi Valley, a considerable portion of all southward migration in North America is funneled in our direction. Not only do we receive birds from the upper portions of the valley itself, but continental air currents apparently have a marked tendency to shift migrants from the Great Plains region in a southeasterly direction, often as far east as Louisiana. The general southward tapering of the continental landmass and the southwesterly slant of the Allegheny Mountains likewise appear to channel migrants from the eastern United States toward the central-northern Gulf Coast. These effects combine to make autumnal migration in Louisiana a steady daily procession of birds of many types.

The arrival of southbound birds in the state begins surprisingly early—

in mid-July in the case of many shorebirds, certain swallows, and a few warblers. The first 10 days of August find the tide of migration visible in force, but the peak is not reached until September. From late August until the middle of October our woods teem with transients. On some nights the sky seems to be filled with birds, judging by the call notes audible to the listener on the ground or by the number of birds actually seen passing before the moon (see p. 41). On the night of October 2–3, 1952, for example, over a thousand silhouettes of birds were counted through a single telescope at Baton Rouge. Considering the small size of the space through which a bird must pass to be visible against the background provided by the moon, one realizes that hundreds of thousands of birds must have passed over Baton Rouge on this night.

The spring concentrations of migrants in the state as seen in the day-time are more spectacular than those of autumn because the pageant is of shorter duration and the visible evidences of migration often come in bursts or waves that are associated with inclement weather. The Purple Martin sometimes returns to the state on the amazingly early date of January 23 and is regularly here in numbers by the middle of February. Its appearance is far in advance of that of other birds. The first wave of migrants generally reaches southern Louisiana in the first week of March, bringing in the Northern Parula, Black-and-white, and Yellow-throated Warblers and the Yellow-throated Vireo. Within two weeks these birds are joined by scores of Ruby-throated Hummingbirds, White-eyed Vireos, and Hooded Warblers. By the last week of the month the state is covered with summer resident birds, those scheduled to breed in our woods and swamps and about our homes and gardens. Among these are the Chimney Swift, Great Crested Fly-catcher, Wood Thrush, and Red-eyed Vireo, the Prothonotary, Worm-eating, and Kentucky Warblers, the American Redstart, Orchard Oriole, and Summer Tanager. Other common summer birds, such as the Blue Grosbeak, Painted and Indigo Buntings, Dickcissel, and Swainson's Warbler, normally do not appear in maximum numbers until after the middle of April, but, in any event, the vast majority of our breeding birds are on their nesting grounds and actually engaged in the selection and defense of territories, the choosing of mates, and even the building of nests when the transient migrants arrive in force.

The transient migrants comprise the host of species that winter to the south of us and breed to the north, merely passing through our state. Proceeding with them are transient individuals of some of the same species that breed in Louisiana, as well as at more northern latitudes. We observe, for instance, the passage of Purple Martins even in the last half of April, when the birds of our own local colonies have been here for two months or more and are already beginning to incubate eggs. These late arrivals are possibly individuals bound for the extreme northern limits of the range, where spring is only then appearing.

Although the spring return of the birds that are to occupy our summer woods and fields is to the ornithologist an exhilarating event, the real excitement of the season is provided by the appearance of transient migrants. Many of them are birds of exquisite colors and striking plumage patterns, and since their main passage through the state covers a period of only three to four weeks (or even less for individual species), we are never completely satisfied by our brief association with them. When we see transient migrants at all in southern Louisiana, we generally see them on the coast and in immense numbers, usually on a clear morning after a stormy night. Their appearance is associated with precise weather conditions, and the ornithologist in Louisiana is obliged to be familiar with the kind of weather that produces a precipitation of migrants if he is to assure himself of being in the field on the most advantageous occasions.

For a long time now ornithologists have known that many birds that migrate across the Gulf of Mexico in spring, en route from winter homes in Middle or South America, do not stop on reaching the northern shore but instead fly inland before alighting. The Louisiana Gulf Coast is not, as one might suppose, a strand where myriads of weary transients continually alight on the sight of land. That stretch of coast, which one might expect to be teeming day after day with multitudes of migrants that have just completed the overwater passage from Yucatan or Campeche, is actually, *during fine weather*, an "ornithological vacuum" as far as most small transients are concerned. *During inclement weather*, however, great numbers of trans-Gulf migrants are precipitated on the first available land, and this results in enormous concentrations on our wooded coastal islands and chenieres.

No written description can possibly convey a full appreciation of what the ornithologist experiences on one of these occasions. One who is fortunate enough to be on the coast following the advent of a norther is often bewildered by the number of birds present. Grand Isle, Cameron, Marsh Island, and other places on the Gulf shore are often refuges for such great hordes of incoming migrants that practically every bush contains birds. Small land birds may be counted by the hundreds as an observer stands in one place, and I have personally identified on such an occasion as many as seven species of warblers in one tree. When an event of this sort takes place at the height of the spring migratory movement, the bird student may see in one day most of the species of thrushes, warblers, vireos, tanagers, and grosbeaks that occur in the whole eastern United States. Two days later, however, the same place is likely not to produce a single transient!

The inclement weather that causes these immense concentrations of migrants on the coast is usually associated with cold-front storms. Masses of cold, dry air moving down from the north come in contact with warm, moist air approaching from the south. Advances of the cold air masses are usually called "northers" or "northwesters." Along the forward edge of the cold air (the polar front), the warm, moist air is forced to rise as a result of being underrun by the heavy wedge of cold air (Figs. 21 and 22). Under the decreased pressure at the higher levels, the warm air expands and cools.

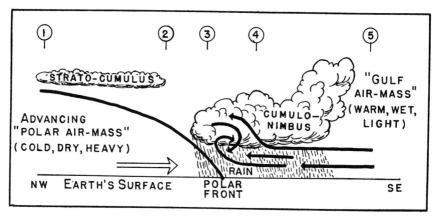

Figure 21   Idealized vertical section of an advancing cold front and its associated conditions. The above may be taken to represent a distance of 100 miles horizontally and 10 miles vertically, but the scale varies with individual fronts. The rate of advance may vary from 5 to 50 miles per hour. Point 1 lies in polar air; light to medium northerly or northwesterly winds and dry air are typical here. Point 5 lies in warm, humid Gulf air. Point 4 has dense cloud cover, heavy precipitation, and violent, gusty winds. Electrical storms are typical along this "squall line." Higher and thinner clouds, with less rain, characterize Points 2 and 3. At Point 2 there may be only a high cirrus haze. (Reprinted from Lowery, "Trans-Gulf Spring Migration of Birds and the Coastal Hiatus," *Wilson Bulletin*, 57, 1945:93.)

Condensation and precipitation result. The forced ascent of the warm, moist air is accompanied by squally winds and torrents of rain, sometimes by hail and violent twisters. As the polar front moves past a given point, the wind at that point shifts from the south into the north. A combination of adverse conditions associated with the meeting of the two air masses and with the northerly winds that follow is what apparently brings migrants down out of the sky. Never, though, are the concentrations that develop anywhere as great as those that appear on the Gulf islands and coastal ridges.

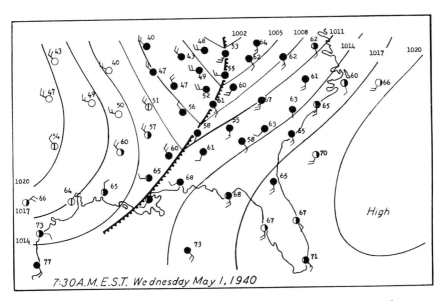

7:30 A.M. E.S.T. Wednesday May 1, 1940

Figure 22 Weather map showing position of cold front over the southeastern United States on May 1, 1940. The cold front is indicated by the barbed line; the warm front is not shown. The part of the country east of the cold front lies in warm, humid air; the part west of the cold front, in cold, dry air. This can be seen from the temperatures (in degrees F.) at each station. The direction toward which the wind is blowing is shown by the arrows pointing to the circles representing the stations. Wind velocity is indicated by the bars on the arrows, each full bar denoting approximately 10 miles per hour. The degree of cloudiness is indicated by the extent to which the station ring is filled with black. Figures on the solid lines show pressure in millibars. A record number of transient migrants was observed at Baton Rouge and on the coastal islands of Mississippi where ornithologists were afield on this date. (Reprinted from Lowery, "Trans-Gulf Spring Migration of Birds and the Coastal Hiatus," *Wilson Bulletin*, 57, 1945:94.)

There the amount of favorable habitat for land birds is limited because the wooded areas are surrounded by great expanses of marsh.

When the cold front passes the coastline, any birds still flying over the Gulf sooner or later encounter the adverse effects of the storms along the line of contact between the cold and the warm air masses, as well as the north winds behind the front. These forces impose a barrier of great magnitude to birds in northward flight, and, therefore, to find them dropping down on the first available land is not surprising.

The events of April 24, 1953, on the Gulf beach near the village of Cameron, in southwestern Louisiana, will serve to illustrate what the ornithologist may experience if he happens to be on the coast when conditions are favorable for the appearance of transients. Shortly after midday on this particular occasion the skies became heavily overcast and the southerly winds stronger and more variable. Both the temperature and the humidity were high. Since a norther was obviously in the offing, my companion and I immediately went to Willow Island—which is not really an island but a narrow ridge paralleling the Gulf, approximately four miles southeast of Cameron—and there made a search for transients. The only migrant that we found in a small woodland covering approximately 10 acres was a single Blackpoll Warbler. A few minutes later we walked out into a clearing not far from the Gulf beach and glanced up at the black clouds rushing overhead. Suddenly one of us noticed a succession of dark specks against the clouds, moving in the same direction as the clouds, from south toward north, hence from the direction of the open Gulf, and barely in the range of unaided vision. These specks, on close inspection with binoculars, proved to be hundreds of small birds.

Most of the birds observed passed out of sight to the north, but not infrequently we would see one suddenly pitch downward, almost as if it were flying headfirst toward the earth, to alight in the clump of trees along the ridge. Only two that we followed with our binoculars from the moment that they began their descent alighted near enough to be identified with certainty. One was an Indigo Bunting, the other a Chestnut-sided Warbler. A considerable number of the larger forms that we could make out against the clouds seemed to be thrushes, judging by their shapes and patterns of flight, but only a few of these were seen to descend. An interesting point is that, except for the main Cameron ridge, on which the highway between Cameron and Creole is located and which, like Willow Island, parallels the coast, no high ground lies to the north of this observation point until some

15 miles of deep marsh are crossed. Therefore, at this particular stage most of the incoming flight seemed to be passing over the coastal ridge and flying inland, the very thing that we believe nearly all transients do in fair weather.

After watching the spectacle from our clearing for 30 minutes or more, we could not resist investigating the changes that the descent of a portion of the overhead flight had effected in the 10-acre woodland, where a short while before we had been successful in finding only one lone transient. Walking back into the wood, we discovered that the trees were teeming with birds, some trees with as many as several dozen. Despite the windy and rainy weather conditions that prevailed for the remainder of this eventful afternoon, we identified 29 species of transients, including 14 kinds of warblers. The wind shifted temporarily into the north in midafternoon, but intermittent rain squalls continued until after dark, when the main cold front passed through the Cameron area, bringing cool air and clear skies by the following morning.

In situations such as this the observer cannot possibly inspect every bird carefully, even in a comparatively small area, because of the numbers involved and the nervousness of the birds under windy conditions. The morning following the passage of a cold front is the ideal time to study transients on the coastal islands and chenieres, provided the wind has abated. Small birds are then often very tame while they go about filling their empty stomachs and restoring their energies after their long Gulf flights. I have often stood among the oaks on Grand Isle in spring and in one spot watched dozens of warblers of several species not 30 feet away feeding on the ground and in trees, or drinking from small rain pools.

The birds precipitated on the coastal ridges resume their northward flights after a brief rest. The exodus for the bulk of them generally takes place the first or second night after their arrival, amply demonstrating the recuperative potential of small birds following a great expenditure of energy, as well as the force of the internal drive that sends them toward their summer homes.

An interesting feature of spring migration in the southern part of the state is the infrequency with which large concentrations of transient migrants are observed in the area lying just north of the coastal marshes. Although the problem requires much additional study, several obvious factors seem to contribute to making this area inferior. Trans-Gulf migrants that are not precipitated on the coastal ridges settle down in the extensive wooded swamps lying back of the marshes and are virtually lost in the vastness of these forests. Indeed, as already suggested, the spectacular character of the days when hordes of migrants are seen on the coastal ridges is in large measure the effect of concentrative forces. These forces bring large numbers of birds from the predominantly unfavorable habitat of the marsh or open water that lies in every direction into the narrow compass of a small but favorable wood. Moreover, when these concentrations resume their northward progress, their first night's flight carries them well over the southern parishes of the state.

At Baton Rouge, which seems to lie on the northern edge of the so-called coastal hiatus, the observation in spring of night migrants passing before the moon has often disclosed heavy flights involving thousands of birds per mile of migratory front. Since these birds began their journeys somewhere south of Baton Rouge and were destined to terminate them somewhere to the north of this place, not a single one of them could contribute to the migrant bird population on the ground in this intervening area, while areas farther north could anticipate an increase. Transient migrants are, in fact, observed in numbers and with regularity in northern Louisiana, although, as elsewhere, adverse weather conditions and the disposition of favorable habitat play an important role in producing outstanding concentrations.

In summary, the student of birds in Louisiana who is interested in observing spring migrants must also be something of a meteorologist. Being cognizant of the kind of weather that concentrates spring migrants enables one to plan field trips in such a way as to be out of doors at the most opportune times. Daily weather maps in newspapers and on television now make it particularly easy for the ornithologist to know well in advance when a norther is expected to reach his locality. Such weather maps and the expert forecasts that accompany them provide even the ornithologist living inland with the information he needs to reach the coast ahead of the critical weather and thereby be on the spot when transients begin to appear.

ECONOMIC
VALUE
OF BIRDS

DESPITE THE FACT that much has been written concerning the economic value of birds, many people still do not appreciate just how important birds are to man and what an essential role they play in preserving the balance of nature. Birds, by the things they eat, perform a service to man in four principal ways: they consume tremendous numbers of noxious insects, they are instrumental in controlling rats and mice, they destroy great quantities of weed seeds, and they help clean the countryside of carrion.

Let me emphasize at the outset that a great amount of study has been devoted to finding out what kind of food each species of bird eats and the proportion of each food in the total diet. This important work has been done mainly by biologists of the U.S. government, through its agency, the Fish and Wildlife Service of the Department of the Interior. Major food habits investigations were started as early as 1886, when the Fish and Wildlife Service was known as the Division of Economic Ornithology and Mammalogy. Thousands of bird stomachs have been examined, and untold numbers of observations have been made of living birds in the process of eating. Consequently, statements regarding the food of a given species of bird can now be made on the basis of much factual information.

The 1904 *Year Book of Agriculture* carries the statement that in that year the agricultural losses caused by insects in the United States amounted to $795 million. Moreover, we find elsewhere the assertion by the Department of Agriculture that insects cause a loss to our forestry and timber interests of approximately $100 million annually. Although we may find it difficult to comprehend the significance of these large figures in terms of our

81

own personal everyday welfare, they should make us realize the worth of any group of animals that feeds on insects and helps retard their increase.

Most birds have a predilection for a diet of animal matter, either wholly or in part. This is even true of the majority of small birds. A Yellow-billed Cuckoo was found to have eaten over 2,500 caterpillars, a chickadee had consumed 450 plant lice, and a Common Nighthawk had gorged itself on no less than 60 grasshoppers. The Common Flicker, unlike other woodpeckers, goes to the ground in fields and there has been seen to eat thousands of ants at one sitting, or, according to one observation, over 1,000 chinch bugs. A Scarlet Tanager on one occasion gulped down 630 gypsy moth caterpillars in 18 minutes, while a Common Yellowthroat ate 3,500 plant lice in 40 minutes, or at the rate of over 30,000 in the course of a single morning! We only need to watch the small birds of our yards and gardens to note that nearly all of them are continually in search of food, energetically peering under leaves and along the bark of trees, from which they pick off tiny insects one after another. Flocks of Chimney Swifts and birds such as swallows are seen winging overhead at all hours of the day, engulfing immense quantities of flying insects, such as mosquitoes and gnats.

On the basis of what we know of the volume of insects that birds eat each day, it would be conservative to state that, on the average, each insectivorous bird in Louisiana consumes as many as 100 insects a day. If we assume that there are at least five insectivorous birds per acre in Louisiana, we discover that no less than 22.5 million insects are ingested daily by birds in our state. Actually, the real figure is probably many times this number, since the assumption that each bird eats 100 insects per day is probably much too conservative. This simple computation serves to show us how important birds are in controlling the insect population.

Rats and mice also cause immense economic losses to man. They spread disease, eat grain and other field crops, and destroy seeds and seedlings of forest trees. One species, the Hispid Cotton Rat, is regarded by wildlife experts as the second worst enemy of our fine upland game bird, the Bobwhite. (Its worst enemy in many sections of the state is the fire ant that kills the young at pipping time.) Were it not, however, for the large birds of prey, the hawks and owls, small rodents would increase in numbers to the point where they would overrun the countryside. Ample proof of the value of our birds of prey is furnished by the following statistics selected from information gathered by biologists. Of 850 stomachs and crops of the Red-tailed Hawk examined, 754 held some kind of food remains; 654, or more than

86 percent of these, contained rats, mice, or other small mammals. Of 220 Red-shouldered Hawks examined, 142 held rodents and other small mammals. Broad-winged, Marsh, and Rough-legged Hawks, the American Kestrel, and the Barred, Common Screech, Short-eared, Long-eared, and Burrowing Owls subsist almost wholly on rodents, insects, and various kinds of reptiles and amphibians. Despite the unfortunate prejudice that most people hold against these fine birds because of the belief that they eat chickens and game, hawks and owls are actually worth millions of dollars.

Since we are everywhere plagued with weeds, the extent to which birds help us in effecting weed control is difficult to appreciate. One economic ornithologist has estimated that the American Tree Sparrow destroys no less than 875 *tons* of weed seeds each year in Iowa alone. The American Tree Sparrow is a rare bird in Louisiana, but we have many of its close relatives. Some of these are the resident Chipping and Field Sparrows and the hordes of White-throated and other species of sparrows visiting us in winter —all of which spend most of their wakeful moments picking up seeds that they husk in their tiny, conical bills.

Finally, there is the role of scavenger by means of which birds make our world a cleaner and more wholesome place in which to live. Vultures, or "buzzards" as we often call them, feed on virtually nothing but the flesh of dead animals. A carcass on the side of one of our highways that would quickly putrify in our generally warm, humid climate is reduced in a matter of hours by a flock of vultures to a heap of bones. And along our heavily populated bayous and rivers, such as Bayou Lafourche and the Mississippi River near the city of New Orleans, innumerable gulls are performing much the same function.

All these considerations are clearly defined, tangible ways in which birds are an economic asset. But there are still other indirect economic benefits. The state of Louisiana received $490,792 in fiscal 1972–1973 from the sale of hunting licenses, and the excise tax on guns and shells, most of which is used in wildlife restoration, amounts to hundreds of thousands of dollars annually. To this must be added the revenue derived by certain people of the state for guide services, for lodging to hunters, for sale of hunting gear, and for numerous other expenses incidental to the pursuit of game birds. No less important are the recreational benefits that birds afford the sportsman and the great many of us who pursue them with binoculars at all times of the year. In terms of human enjoyment and the benefits that accrue to one's health in being outdoors, birds are of inestimable value.

Every bird should be given man's unlimited protection unless it happens to be a species that can withstand hunting in proper season or unless it happens to be one of the very few species (and there are *only three or four*) whose habits are in some way seriously inimical to man's interest. With regard to the latter, even the much-indicted Great Horned Owl and the Cooper's and Sharp-shinned Hawks, which sometimes eat chickens and game, may indeed be essential in the preservation of healthy wild populations of the creatures on which they prey (see p. 217). We should, therefore, adopt the philosophy that every creature plays some vital part in the scheme of things. The more nearly we can preserve natural conditions, the less likely we are to upset the intricate relationships that exist between animals themselves and between animals and their environment. Each animal is part of the so-called web of life and may be likened to a cog in the wheels of a delicate machine. The unwise removal of a single cog may greatly impair or even stop the entire works. Consequently, we must make careful appraisal of all possible biological implications before we advocate the outlawing of any bird because of its alleged conflict with what we presume to be our best interests.

CONSERVATION
AND WILDLIFE
MANAGEMENT

LOUISIANA IS ENDOWED with an abundance of wildlife. Some of this wildlife demands rigid conservation if it is to be perpetuated for future generations of Louisiana citizens to enjoy. Fortunately, our state's Wild Life and Fisheries Commission, in conjunction with the U.S. Fish and Wildlife Service, is performing a highly efficient job in the administration of these valuable natural resources. This is being accomplished by the enforcement of our game laws, by creating more refuges and competently administering those already in existence, and by carrying on carefully planned research and management projects designed to increase our supply of "harvestable" game. Species that cannot withstand hunting pressure are given maximum protection, and those that can be hunted without danger of seriously reducing their effective breeding populations are assigned open seasons proportionate in length and bag limit to the amount of harvesting that each can tolerate.

Possibly the most important advances in bird protection in this country were the passage by the U.S. Congress in 1909 of the Lacey Act and the approval of the Migratory Bird Treaty Act of July 3, 1918. The Lacey Act stopped traffic in egret and other bird plumes, and the Migratory Bird Treaty Act supplied an agreement between the United States and Great Britain which enacted into law provisions for the protection of migratory birds. In 1936 the terms of the convention between these two nations were extended through a similar agreement between the United States and Mexico. The Migratory Bird Treaty Act provides that the taking of migratory birds is unlawful except as permitted by specific regulations and during

85

carefully prescribed open seasons, such as those indicated each year for certain waterfowl, rails, coots, gallinules, doves, and not infrequently the Common Snipe and American Woodcock. With two exceptions, the House Sparrow and the European Starling, *all* other birds are legally protected at *all* times. When any protected bird, such as the Red-winged Blackbird, is found to be doing temporary and local damage to crops and such alleged damage is duly reported to the director of the Fish and Wildlife Service, U.S. Department of the Interior, a careful investigation is immediately made by a competent biologist of that agency. If this inquiry into the facts of the case sustains the claim of damage, a special permit is issued to the landowner enabling him to take measures to stop the depredations.

Parents who buy their children air rifles and firearms should make the fact eminently clear that most cities have ordinances that prohibit the discharge of guns within their limits and that state laws forbid shooting from any state road or highway. Moreover, the responsibility of explaining that no nongame birds other than the House Sparrow and European Starling can be shot without violation of state and federal laws rests entirely on the parents. More fundamental still is the obligation of every parent to explain to the child the importance and need for wildlife conservation and why shooting nongame birds simply to test one's marksmanship is both unsportsmanlike and morally reprehensible. Our hope of maintaining for tomorrow an adequate supply of game and other wildlife depends in large measure on the training we give our young folks today.

On the other side of the picture, to undertake to interest and instruct young men and women in the art of hunting (and fishing) and the pleasures afforded by observing animals in the wild is a matter of real importance. These things provide clean, wholesome recreation. Furthermore, the enthusiastic sportsman is often the most ardent conservationist. He is aware that our natural resources are not a perpetual, inexhaustible legacy, to be enjoyed with no regard for the future.

Louisiana has a fair abundance of game—enough to supply the sportsman with hunting opportunities as long as the annual kill is proportionate to the productivity of the species in question. Quite often the natural crop of game can be greatly increased by improving the habitat conditions under which it lives through planting additional game foods and by supplying added cover. A corps of state and federal biologists is diligently engaged in the task of devising ways to increase the amount of "harvestable" game for the recreational benefit and pleasure of the masses. The determined efforts of these highly trained specialists are already paying tremendous dividends, and we may look with increased confidence to a future of continuing wildlife benefits.

One of the most vital instruments in a sound conservation program is a system of wildlife refuges. In some instances refuges are created to provide protection for a certain class of birds during the season of reproduction. This is the most critical time in the life of any animal, for it is then that the continuity of the species is at stake. Other refuges are set up either to provide a retreat or resting place during the winter hunting season or as way stations along a migratory flyway. We are amazed to watch ducks and geese in our southern marshes settle down on refuge property where the dividing line is simply a barbed wire fence, apparently knowing they are safe on one side of the fence and not on the other.

Refuges are as essential for sedentary birds as they are for migratory species, for in these protected spots maximal populations build up and overflow into surrounding areas. These state and federal refuges make up large blocks of land that are divorced from commercial interests, which are all too often adverse to the general welfare of wildlife. On privately owned lands monetary considerations lead to drainage, to the clearing of the forest, or to other exploitations that often make the land unsuitable for game and other wild creatures existing there. Indeed, an intensive nationwide drainage and land reclamation program in the 1930s, supplemented by a severe drought, nearly caused the extermination of several species of ducks and a drastic reduction in the population of others. Small potholes of marsh scattered through the central Great Plains region, where great hordes of ducks normally nested, became uninhabitable. When the birds failed to breed and raise new broods, only a few years elapsed before their population levels were below the critical threshold. Some species might have joined the ranks of the Labrador Duck and the Passenger Pigeon had not our nation awakened to the seriousness of the situation and plunged into the most vigorous conservation program ever undertaken anywhere. Large sections of submarginal land, forming a network from the Canadian boundary to the Gulf Coast and Mexican border, were acquired by the federal government and reconverted to duck marshes by the installation of dams and reservoirs to raise water levels and by the planting of duck foods. Bag limits were reduced and hunting seasons curtailed. Special schools were formed at a few leading universities to train wildlife specialists to carry on the expanding program of management and research. Biologists already well versed in the techniques of censusing wildlife journeyed north in summer to obtain a check on breeding success and traveled south in winter to appraise the winter

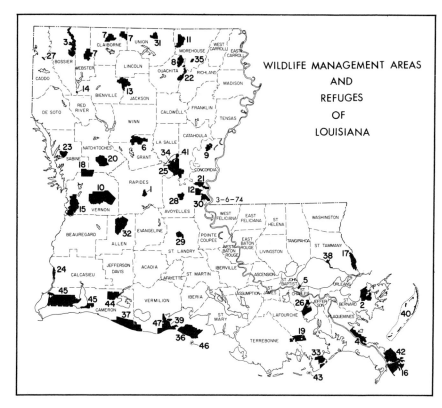

Figure 23

State Wildlife Management Areas

1	Alexander State Forest†	18	Peason Ridge†
2	Biloxi†	19	Pointe-au-Chien*
3	Bodcau†	20	Red Dirt†
4	Bohemia†	21	Red River*
5	Bonnet Carré†	22	Russell Sage*
6	Caney†	23	Sabine†
7	Catahoula†	24	Sabine Island†
8	Cities Service†	25	Saline*
9	Concordia†	26	Salvador*
10	Fort Polk†	27	Soda Lake†
11	Georgia-Pacific†	28	Spring Bayou*
12	Grassy Lake†	29	Thistlethwaite†
13	Jackson-Bienville†	30	Three Rivers*
14	Loggy Bayou*	31	Union†
15	Lutcher-Moore	32	West Bay†
16	Pass a Loutre*	33	Wisner†
17	Pearl River*		

State Wildlife Refuges

34 Catahoula Lake Migratory
 Bird*
35 Coulee†
36 Marsh Island*
37 Rockefeller*
38 St. Tammany†
39 State Wildlife*

National Wildlife Refuges

40 Breton Bird
41 Catahoula
42 Delta
43 East Timbalier
44 Lacassine
45 Sabine
46 Shell Keys

Other

47 Paul J. Rainey Wildlife
 Refuge and Game Preserve

* State owned; † state leased.

survival. Parasitologists and bacteriologists sought for the cause and possible treatment of botulism, a serious duck disease, and chemists explored ways of treating or coating the lead shot in shotgun shells to prevent the disastrous losses suffered by ducks from lead poisoning caused by swallowing spent shot. Wildlife technicians, aided by a host of amateur ornithologists, banded thousands of ducklings to find out where the breeding population of a given area spends the winter and the routes followed in getting there. Sportsmen in towns and cities everywhere organized local wildlife clubs, and these joined into state and national wildlife federations—all of which did a fine job of arousing public opinion in support of better wildlife legislation. The organization Ducks Unlimited came into existence and began an auspicious program of providing additional duck-breeding areas in the United States and Canada, greatly supplementing the works of the two governments. To all this effort was added the magnificent work of the National Audubon Society, which has long been devoted to a vigorous program of wildlife preservation.

The ever-increasing success of this enormous program is now common knowledge to every person interested in the conservation of wildlife. While much remains to be accomplished, we can at least look with pride on the fact that no longer is any species of waterfowl in the United States and Canada in danger of extinction. The Wood Duck, Redhead, and Bufflehead, which experts gloomily declared three decades ago to be doomed, are now back with us in numbers. Under the watchful eyes of the wildlife technicians, all major fluctuations in waterfowl populations are quickly detected and given careful appraisal. As long as the program remains operative, only a national disaster of the greatest magnitude can reduce wildlife conditions in this country to the low levels reached not so many years ago.

In Louisiana alone there are over 1,324,066 acres of state or federal wildlife refuges and wildlife management areas (Fig. 23.) Of this total approximately 1,088,215 acres are owned or leased by the state and administered by the Wild Life and Fisheries Commission, with federal aid, for upland game restoration, management, and protection and as waterfowl areas. Over 235,800 acres go to make up the federally owned Sabine, Catahoula, East Timbalier, Shell Keys, Lacassine, and Delta refuges, and the Breton Bird Refuge. The Paul J. Rainey Wildlife Refuge, in Vermilion Parish, consisting of 27,000 acres, is owned and operated by the National Audubon Society. Many of these coastal refuges, such as the Breton Refuge, are vitally important in the protection of our seabird nesting colonies.

ATTRACTING
BIRDS

A GREAT DEAL of everyday pleasure can be experienced by those who employ a few simple devices for attracting songbirds to their lawns and gardens. One of the easiest means is to set up feeding tables in view of living room, bedroom, or dining room windows where visitors to the trays will be in plain view. Feeding trays are best placed on an arm projecting from the side of a tree or else suspended from a limb. Table scraps that do not contain excessive amounts of salt make good bird food, but most people supplement them with cheap grades of cracked corn. An especially attractive food is pulverized pecan meat, which sometimes can be obtained cheaply as refuse from pecan-shelling plants. Pecan meat mixed with rendered suet is a more nutritious combination than either ingredient alone, and mixed with suet the pecan meat goes further. One user of pulverized pecan meat reports that no fewer than 42 species of birds have visited his feeding table.

Hummingbirds are often attracted in numbers to the garden if one hangs red-lacquered vials filled with sweetened water. I once knew a lady in Monroe who possessed the most remarkable aptitude for dispelling fear on the part of the feathered visitors to her gardens—a faculty so many of us lack, possibly because we do not possess enough patience. At any rate, I have seen this lady hold a vial of sweetened water between her lips and with her head tilted back have Ruby-throated Hummingbirds come and drink within inches of her face. What an experience it must be to look into the eye of a hummingbird, to be able literally to count the feathers of its flaming gorget!

Birdhouses are readily occupied by certain kinds of birds and sometimes

90

bring elusive species close to the home, where they can be enjoyed. The gregarious Purple Martin usually requires a special, multicompartmented box, but nest boxes for other species can be constructed along the simple general lines of the bottom diagrams in Figure 24, provided the relative dimensions are varied to suit the various species, with particular attention to the size of the entrance hole. Specifications for houses for birds of various sizes are given in Table 2. "Depth of Cavity" refers to the greatest inside depths of the box; "Height of Entrance," to the distance from the center of the hole to the floor. The front of the box can be made from a section of hardwood slabbing, with bark still intact, obtainable at a sawmill; this gives the box a rustic or natural appearance.

Few birds that can be attracted to the premises of our homes are as enjoyable as Purple Martins. They are highly sociable birds that seem to enjoy living near man. The male is resplendent in his blue-black coat, and his song and the answering notes of his mate are pleasant sounds indeed to hear outside our windows. Although the Purple Martin will nest in boxes of only a single compartment, it prefers nest boxes of many rooms.

My experience has been that the type of martin house illustrated in Figure 24 is superior to most others, particularly since all compartments face one side. This arrangement allows all the birds in the colony to be seen

Table 2   Recommended Specifications of Birdhouses for Certain Easily Attracted Species

Species	Floor of Cavity (Inches)	Depth of Cavity (Inches)	Height of Entrance (Inches)	Diameter of Entrance (Inches)	Height above Ground (Feet)
Wood Duck	10 x 18	22	16	4	10–20
Common Screech Owl	8 x 8	14	10	3	10–30
Downy Woodpecker	4 x 4	10	7	2	6–20
Red-bellied Woodpecker	6 x 6	14	10	2½	12–20
Great Crested Flycatcher	6 x 6	10	7	2	8–12
Purple Martin	7 x 7	7	2	2½	12–17
Carolina Chickadee	4 x 4	8	5	1¼	6–15
Tufted Titmouse	4 x 4	8	5	1½	6–15
Carolina Wren	4 x 4	9	6	1½	5–10
Eastern Bluebird	5 x 5	9	6	1½	5–10
Prothonotary Warbler	4 x 4	8	5	1½	4– 7

from a certain window or from a sitting porch, whereas in houses with compartments on all sides, only a portion of the colony can be observed from a single vantage point. This martin box has other desirable features: it can serve as a trap for those desiring to band the occupants, and it can be easily cleaned of the nests of House Sparrows. Access to the interior of each

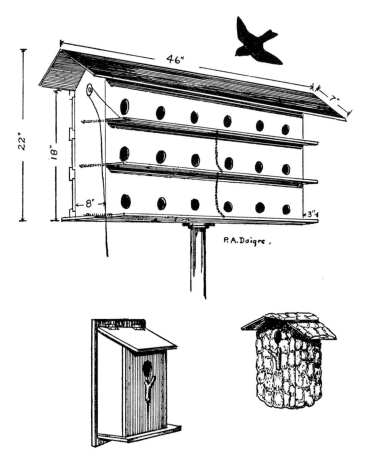

Figure 24 Birdhouses. *Upper:* A Purple Martin box, described in the text, that also serves as a banding trap. *Lower:* Two easily constructed boxes that can be made suitable for a variety of species simply by altering the proportions according to specifications given in Table 2.

compartment is readily gained simply by sliding one of the back panels to the right or left. Occupants are trapped for banding by pulling the cord that raises the hinged porches. A study of the drawing will show that there is a four-inch section of a screen door spring attached to the front edge of each porch and secured on the end wall of the house. The tension is straightaway, but as soon as a pull of the cord raises the front edge of the porch above the horizontal, the tension of the spring snaps the porch against the house, closing the entrance holes. The three porches operate in unison since they are connected by a small chain. The trap, of course, is sprung after dark when the occupants are at roost. Since there is ample ventilation, the martins can be left entrapped until the following morning, when banding can be done and the birds released in daylight.

Martin boxes are best placed on a pole in the open, or at least where the box itself towers above surrounding shrubbery. Fifteen feet above the ground is an ideal height, for the box can then be conveniently reached by climbing a 10-foot or 12-foot stepladder. A two-inch galvanized pipe set in a small amount of concrete makes the most satisfactory pole, especially when the weight of a 16- or 20-room house is involved. Since a standard length of pipe is 21 feet, one must either cut off several feet or else dig a very deep hole in the ground. One end of such a section of pipe comes already threaded; hence the box can be mounted on the pole by using a two-inch floor flange affixed to the bottom of the box with wood screws.

A martin box made of poor lumber and put together with nails will generally warp and come apart in one season, but a well-constructed box will last for many years. When built of cypress, put together with brass screws, covered with roofing material, and painted regularly every year or two, it will long withstand the elements. There is a box in my front yard that was constructed in January 1944, and it appears to be almost as good today as in the year it was built.

In building a martin house, care should be taken to put on plenty of porches, for the birds seem to prefer having these flat surfaces on which to alight and bask in the sun. Also, the bottom edge of the holes leading into the compartments should be close to the level of the porches to accommodate the martins, which, because of their short legs, would have difficulty in scrambling over a higher barrier. The main problem in trying to entice martins to boxes is the fact that House Sparrows sometimes take over before the intended occupants return from their winter quarters in South America. To combat the sparrows, I clean my boxes thoroughly in the last few days of

January, just before the martins return, and then repeat the job around the
end of February. Unless the sparrows are allowed to cram all the compartments with grass, the martins will claim their share of rooms and ward off
excessive numbers of uninvited guests. When there are only a few House
Sparrows, they may be either trapped or shot.

A birdbath is another effective means of attracting birds. Where there
is a hydrant at hand, an excellent birdbath can be made by building up a
pedestal of broken pieces of concrete and placing a pan on top in position
to catch the drip of water from the faucet. A low structure such as this,
however, may place the users at the mercy of cats. Anyone desiring to construct a more predator-proof birdbath at nominal expense can do so by
using a length of four-inch concrete pipe as the pedestal and two discarded
plow discs as part of the form for the construction of the bowl (see Fig. 25).
One well-greased disc is placed on a platform of wood with a six-inch length
of one-half-inch pipe standing upright through the square hole in the center
of the disc and set into a hole one-half inch in diameter drilled in the wooden
platform beneath. Two three-inch-wide strips of galvanized sheet metal are
wrapped around the perimeter of the disc and are fastened together on each
side with stove bolts, as shown in Figure 25. Reinforcing wires are placed
in proper position. Then concrete made with white cement is poured into
the form. The second greased plow disc is next pushed down into the concrete in the form and rotated on the upright pipe to smooth out air pockets.
The pipe in the center should be turned occasionally while the cement is
setting in order that it may be easily withdrawn later. The birdbath may be
supplied with water by passing a pipe up through the pedestal and out
through the center of the bowl. This is quite easy to do, since there is already
a one-half-inch hole in the center of the bowl. Otherwise, this hole must be
plugged with cement. The footing for the pedestal is made by building a
small boxlike form approximately 14 inches square and 4 inches in depth and
by standing the concrete pipe in its center, the flared end down, and finally,
by pouring cement into the box around the base of the pipe. The attachment
of the pedestal to the bowl is achieved by turning the bowl bottom side up,
standing the pedestal over the center, and pouring concrete into a special
metal collar about two inches wide and about eight inches in diameter. The
total cost of a homemade birdbath of this type is less than $3, only a fraction
of the price of those usually seen for sale.

Certain trees, shrubs, and herbaceous plants bear fruits that are attractive to birds. Such plants are in themselves ornamental, and they also serve to

Figure 25 An economically constructed homemade birdbath. The top figure shows the finished structure. The bottom figure shows the form into which concrete is poured to make the bowl. (See p. 94.)

draw birds away from cultivated fruits. As a rule birds like acrid or sour fruits that are generally unpalatable to man. When certain birds peck into cultivated fruits, they are often only after a· worm. A few red mulberry (*Morus rubra*) or wild cherry (*Prunus serotina*) trees on the premises will usually toll birds away from other fruits, for these two trees are prime favorites. Other attractive fruits are borne by privets (*Ligustrum*), the various hollies (*Ilex*), the hackberry (*Celtis laevigata*), the firebush (*Pyracantha coccinea*), the camphor tree (*Cinnamomum camphora*), the mayhaw and other haws (*Crataegus*), the pokeberry (*Phytolacca americana*), the spice bush (*Lindera benzoin*), the elderberry (*Sambucus canadensis*), the French mulberry (*Callicarpa americana*), Turk's-turban (*Siphonanthus indicus*), and numerous others. Red salvia (*Salvia splendens*), rosa-de-montana (*Antigonon leptopus*), and various kinds of *Hibiscus* are especially attractive to hummingbirds.

ORNITHOLOGICAL
SOCIETIES
AND BIRD
CLUBS

THE GREAT INCREASE in interest in birds on the part of the lay public in the last 40 years has led to a phenomenal expansion in membership in all the established ornithological organizations of this country and to the founding of many new ones, particularly groups of regional or local scope. The city and state bird clubs provide bird students of an area with the opportunity to become acquainted with persons of similar interest, to compare notes, and to enjoy field trips together. The national and some state organizations hold annual conventions and publish scientific journals, usually as quarterlies, that contain both short and long articles dealing with recent advances in ornithology, field observations, life histories, accounts of expeditions, and results of studies in the museum and laboratory.

Anyone in Louisiana who has a serious interest in birds should immediately affiliate with the Louisiana Ornithological Society. This organization was founded in 1947 and now has over 300 members. Membership is open to all persons regardless of their ages. Statewide meetings are held twice a year, once in the spring and again in the fall, usually in some place particularly favorable for birds, such as Grand Isle or Cameron. At one such weekend gathering of over 70 LOS members in Cameron, the group as a whole recorded 196 species of birds, and a good time was had by all.

The Crescent City Bird Club in New Orleans is quite active, as is also the Society for Nature Study in Shreveport. Monthly meetings and numerous field trips are scheduled, usually from September to May. The indoor gatherings feature short talks by members and guest speakers or the showing of movies. Anyone desiring to participate in the activities of the LOS or of any of the local organizations can do so simply by addressing an inquiry to the Museum of Zoology, Louisiana State University, Baton

Rouge 70803, and it will be forwarded to the secretary-treasurer of the LOS (currently Mrs. Grace Eyster, 226 Monteigne Drive, Lafayette 70501). Annual dues are $2. An interesting and attractive newsletter entitled the *LOS News* is issued to the membership at least four times a year.

The serious student of birds rapidly becomes engrossed in problems of avian distribution, the mechanics of migration, details of life histories and habits, or one or more of the other facets of ornithology. Therefore, he will want to affiliate with one of the national societies in order that he may attend its annual conventions and receive its journal, thereby keeping abreast of new discoveries in the science.

The largest and perhaps the most important ornithological society in the world is the American Ornithologists' Union, which was founded in 1883 and now has approximately three thousand members. Conventions held each year, usually in September or October, feature sessions for the reading of papers (some by the world's outstanding ornithologists), social gatherings, and field trips. The 1952 convention of the AOU was held in Baton Rouge with 288 persons attending, including representatives from five foreign countries. The official organ of the AOU is *The Auk*, which is now in its ninety-first volume. Each volume contains close to one thousand pages, and the articles cover every aspect of ornithology. The journal is free to all members, and membership in the organization is unlimited. Application blanks can be obtained from the LSU Museum of Zoology or by writing to any of the officers of the AOU, including the secretary, Dr. George E. Watson, National Museum of Natural History, Smithsonian Institution, Washington, D.C. 20560. Annual dues, $8.

Other important ornithological societies are:

Cooper Ornithological Society. Founded 1893. Organ, *The Condor*, published quarterly and free to members. Address: Jane R. Durham, Oakland Museum, 1000 Oak Street, Oakland, Calif. 90024. Annual dues, $12.

Wilson Ornithological Society. Founded 1888. Organ, *The Wilson Bulletin*, published quarterly and free to members. Address: Dr. Jerome A. Jackson, Department of Zoology, Mississippi State University, Mississippi State, Miss. 39762. Annual dues, $8.

National Audubon Society. Founded 1902. Publishes *Audubon Magazine* and *American Birds*, each six times a year, the latter including the Christmas Bird Count and seasonal summaries of the birdlife in the United States and Canada. Address: National Audubon Society, 950 Third Ave., New York, N.Y. Subscription for *Audubon Magazine*, $10 a year; for *American Birds*, $6 a year.

ACCOUNTS
OF THE
SPECIES

MAP OF

LOUISIANA

SHOWING PRINCIPAL LOCALITIES

MENTIONED IN TEXT

Figure 26

LOONS
Order *Gaviiformes*

The Loon Family
Gaviidae

COMMON LOON *Gavia immer* Figs. 27, 28

The expression "crazy as a loon," although often used, has little meaning to most people of this state, for the bird's mad, laughing call that has given rise to the phrase is uttered mainly on its breeding grounds in the North. I have heard this weird sound only once in Louisiana, and then it came from one of two birds, possibly a mated pair, that I watched late one spring afternoon as they flew up the Mississippi River—two birds that were possibly just beginning their long migratory flight to a wilderness lake, rimmed with spruce and fir, in some northern forest.

The first Common Loons come to us in the latter half of October, and a few nonbreeders sometimes remain far into summer; but the species is moderately common only from November through mid-April. Generally this species is a bird of large bodies of water, such as Lake Pontchartrain and the numerous bays and lagoons of our coastal belt, but it also occurs on our inland lakes. In our French-speaking sections it often goes by the name *grand plongeon*, the equivalent of "great northern diver," the official name by which it is known in Great Britain. For most of the time that this loon is with us the plumage is dark gray above and white below. In spring, though, the head and neck become black. The back also becomes black but is finely spotted with white. Its body bulk is about that of a goose. On the water it somewhat resembles the cormorants, or "nigger geese," but the latter have much smaller bodies and tilt their hooked bills decidedly upward. The bill of the Common Loon is held horizontally and is sharply pointed. The

American Anhinga, which also has a pointed bill, has a thin, snakelike neck, an exceedingly long tail, and the habit of swimming with its body submerged. Both the anhinga and the cormorants are quick to take flight when alarmed, and they perch in trees, while the loons seldom leave the water and never alight in trees.

Biologists regard the loons as "primitive" birds because in some of their structural characteristics, notably the bones of the skull, they are strongly reminiscent of reptiles, the group of animals that some 200 million years ago also gave rise to birds. But, despite the lowly position of loons in our system of bird classification, they are marvelously specialized in many ways, particularly in regard to their adaptations to a life on the water. The hind limbs are located just about as far back on the body as is possible, and they are shortened to provide greater leverage as swimming paddles; the toes are fully webbed. So well adapted is the loon for its aquatic habitat that it is helpless on land; it cannot take flight except from the surface of water. To escape its enemies it dives and swims great distances under water. But, as small and apparently as weak as the wings seem to be, they serve to carry the great bird hundreds of miles nonstop on its migratory flights to and from its nesting grounds.

Figure 27   Common Loon in winter plumage.

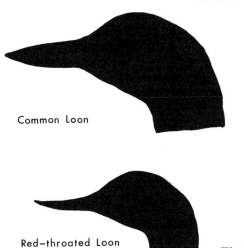

Common Loon

Red-throated Loon

Figure 28   Heads of loons in silhouette.

RED-THROATED LOON   *Gavia stellata*   Fig. 28

Only four Red-throated Loons have been recorded in the state: an individual observed by Robert J. Newman and me on several occasions from December 23 to 30, 1945, on False River, opposite New Roads, in Pointe Coupee Parish; one seen by Lovett E. Williams on December 17, 1962, in Calcasieu Pass; another identified by Joseph C. Kennedy on March 12, 1966, on Lake Pontchartrain; and a more recent bird studied in direct comparison with Common Loons by Robert B. Hamilton and others from December 4, 1971, through March 14, 1972, on Clear Lake, in Natchitoches Parish.

The Red-throated Loon resembles the Common Loon but is considerably smaller, being about the size of a Mallard. Moreover, the Common Loon is so dark a gray that it appears to be black at a distance, while the Red-throated Loon is ashy gray. Indeed, the gray of its head and hindneck is so pale that it merges into the white of the throat and foreneck without the sharp contrast characteristic of its larger relative. The bill of this species has a slightly upward curvature. It breeds far to the north, mainly in the Arctic Region. In the summer on its nesting grounds it takes on a much more ornate plumage, in which the throat is rufous red.

GREBES
Order *Podicipediformes*

The Grebe Family
Podicipedidae

THE GREBES are ducklike water birds of worldwide distribution and are closely related to the loons, but they differ structurally in many ways from both ducks and loons. The neck of most grebes is usually held more or less vertical, with the *pointed* bill at right angles; it is seldom hunched down on the shoulders as in the typical sitting posture of a diving duck. These features, together with their tailless appearance (indeed, the tail is a mere tuft of short straggly feathers), combine to distinguish them from ducks. The legs, like those of their relatives the loons, are located far back on the body as an adaptation for diving and swimming; but the toes, instead of being fully webbed, are provided with paddle-shaped edges and the toenails are broadly flattened to conform with the flat toes (see Fig. 36). The tarsi are likewise flattened laterally so that they knife through the water. The whole foot is, therefore, a combination of adaptations for swimming. A remarkable feature of the grebes is their ability to submerge instantaneously, hence the French name *sac-à-plomb*, or "sack of lead." One often hears it said that you cannot shoot a grebe as long as it is watching, for at the flash from the muzzle, the bird submerges and is gone before the pellets arrive. Still unexplained is the ability of grebes to sink straight downward, and to any desired depth. Sometimes only the head remains above the water. Most other birds that disappear below the surface usually lunge forward and then downward, bill first.

So bound are grebes to a life on water that they are rarely seen in flight. When danger approaches they simply submerge and swim away beneath the surface. To take flight, they must run for as much as 100 yards or more across

the surface of the water. I once kept under observation a Pied-billed Grebe
in a pond that was rapidly drying up, apparently without the grebe's being
aware of what was happening. When spring came the bird no longer had
sufficient space for takeoff; so it was obliged to forego its migration and
nesting. Despite reluctance of grebes to fly, most take to the air on their
short, stubby wings and travel great distances to nesting areas farther
north once the migratory urge manifests itself.

RED-NECKED GREBE   *Podiceps grisegena*   Pl. I; Fig. 29

The single Louisiana record of the Red-necked Grebe was obtained on
December 2, 1937, when a specimen was shot at Catahoula Lake. The
large size of the Red-necked Grebe as compared to that of most of the other
grebes found in Louisiana is shown in Plate I. This, together with its large
yellowish bill, distinguishes it readily in the field from all our grebes except
the Western, which has the front and sides of the neck pure white instead
of dark gray. The Red-necked Grebe might be mistaken for a Red-throated
Loon but differs in having the top of the head blackish and the neck dark
gray (instead of white in front and pale gray behind). Another distinctive
feature is the white, somewhat crescent-shaped mark on the head, extending
from the throat around the back of the cheek to the upper nape.

Figure 29   (1) Horned Grebe; (2) Red-necked Grebe; (3) Pied-billed Grebe.

HORNED GREBE *Podiceps auritus*   Pl. I; Fig. 29

The Horned Grebe is a fairly common winter visitor, seen from late October to the last week of March, on large lakes and bays, particularly in the southeastern part of the state. In the 1940s the species was especially numerous on False River, in Pointe Coupee Parish, where more than 50 individuals could sometimes be counted. Now its numbers there are reduced, possibly as a consequence of the greatly increased motorboat activity on this body of water. The north shore of Lake Pontchartrain is at present the place where one can be most certain of seeing the species. As many as 89 have been counted along a two-mile stretch of waterfront at Mandeville.

On the water at a distance, these grebes appear predominantly white in their winter dress, although the upperparts are actually gray and only the underparts are immaculate white. In these respects the Horned Grebe differs greatly from the common Pied-billed Grebe, which is brownish all over. For a comparison with the similar Eared Grebe, see the next account.

In southern Louisiana the Horned Grebe is called the *plongeur*, or "diver." Its molt into the breeding plumage, with its rufous neck, greenish black head, and large buffy "ear" patches (hence *Horned* Grebe), is sometimes completed just prior to the bird's departure in early spring.

EARED GREBE *Podiceps nigricollis*   Pl. I

Although the Eared Grebe, which is sometimes called the Black-necked Grebe, was not recorded in Louisiana until November 28, 1948, and only eight sightings were reported up to 1955, the species is now present in numbers each winter almost statewide and has a longer span of dates than that of the Horned Grebe. It occurs at least as far east as Mandeville, on Lake Pontchartrain, where, however, it is outnumbered by the Horned Grebe more than 20 to 1.

The Eared Grebe in winter plumage is similar to the Horned Grebe. It differs primarily in that its head, throat, and hindneck are much grayer (less whitish) than in the other species. A whitish spot just back of the ear stands out in contrast to the dingy color of the remainder of the head and upper neck, and this spot can be seen at a considerable distance. In breeding plumage this species and the Horned Grebe are striking in appearance and differently colored from each other, the Horned having a rufous neck, the Eared a black one. In the latter species, the bill is relatively longer and

Plate I   Heads and Silhouettes of Five Grebes in Winter Plumage

1. Red-necked Grebe (p. 105). 2. Pied-billed Grebe (p. 109). 3. Horned Grebe (p. 106).
4. Eared Grebe (p. 106). 5. Least Grebe (p. 107).

thinner, as well as slightly upturned. They both nest in the northern United States and Canada. But a June 13, 1970, observation by Robert J. Newman and Ronald J. Stein of a pair of Eared Grebes in breeding plumage near Holly Beach, in Cameron Parish, raises the possibility that this species may actually have nested in the state.

LEAST GREBE *Podiceps dominicus*   Pl. I

This grebe is known from Louisiana on the basis of a single record. One was detected on the lake behind our State Capitol in Baton Rouge on December 14, 1947. The individual was shot and later placed in the museum at Louisiana State University. Had the specimen not been secured, considerable doubt would have been attached to the validity of the identification, so closely does this species resemble the winter-plumaged Pied-billed Grebe. The size of the Least Grebe is approximately one-half that of the Pied-billed, but this difference becomes apparent only when the two are together for direct comparison. The bill is slimmer, relatively longer, less chickenlike in shape, and slightly upturned near the end. I suspect that the one Least Grebe record is that of an accidental wanderer, despite the fact that there is some evidence that the species may be slowly extending its normal range northward and eastward along the Gulf Coast from the lower Rio Grande Valley and Mexico.

The Least Grebe is one of some 18 species that seem to have moved in a northeasterly direction from southern Texas or Mexico to visit Louisiana, often at a seemingly inappropriate time, autumn or winter. The list includes, in addition to this species, the Black-bellied Tree-Duck, Masked Duck, White-tailed Hawk, Harris' Hawk, White-winged Dove, Inca Dove, Groove-billed Ani, Buff-bellied Hummingbird, Tropical Kingbird, Great Kiskadee, Sulphur-bellied Flycatcher, Wied's Crested Flycatcher, Vermilion Flycatcher, Curve-billed Thrasher, Painted Redstart, Scott's Oriole, and Bronzed Cowbird.

WESTERN GREBE *Aechmophorus occidentalis*   Fig. 30

On November 3, 1971, Mac Myers spotted what appeared to be a Western Grebe in the Mississippi River opposite downtown New Orleans. He returned the next day with binoculars and confirmed his suspicions. On November 5 he showed the bird to R. D. Purrington, who photographed it at

Figure 30   Western Grebe.

120 yards through a 400 mm lens. The resulting enlargement was easily recognizable as a Western Grebe and was reproduced in *Audubon Field Notes* (26, 1972:74). On November 6 Myers and several other observers studied the grebe from the Perry Street wharf in Gretna and verified the absence of a prominent white superciliary line, thereby excluding the possibility that the bird was a Great Crested Grebe from Europe. Thus was the Western Grebe added to the list of birds known to occur in Louisiana. Since then the species has been observed at two additional localities. One was found by James Stewart on Cross Lake on January 3, 1974, and two were seen there on several dates through January 16. Another was located on Mud Lake, south of the Sabine National Wildlife Refuge in Cameron Parish by Robert J. Newman and H. Douglas Pratt on February 2, 1974, and was subsequently seen by others as late as March 26.

    The species is easily distinguished from other grebes of North America by its large size, dark gray or blackish upperparts, and long slender neck, which is largely immaculate white with this color extending onto the cheeks. Both the top of the head and the back of the neck are black. The long neck that is held stiffly erect and the sharply contrasting black and white plumage are highly diagnostic. In flight the Western Grebe shows a single white wing patch that extends from the secondaries onto the primaries. The species breeds in the western parts of Canada and the United States and south over the Mexican plateau.

PIED-BILLED GREBE   *Podilymbus podiceps*   Pl. I; Fig. 29

Every Louisianian familiar in the least with the out-of-doors knows this common inhabitant of our lakes and ponds, although in most instances by the names "di-dipper" and "hell-diver." The species is widespread over the state in winter and by no means uncommon in summer, particularly in the coastal marshes. In 1963 Robert H. Chabreck found no fewer than 107 nests in a 200-acre impoundment containing brackish water on Rockefeller Refuge in Cameron Parish.

The floating nest is composed mainly of debris and is generally anchored to a few stalks of some aquatic plant. Almost as soon as the eggs hatch, the highly precocial downy young take to the water; within an hour they are swimming and diving like veterans. The name is based on the pied appearance created by the black ring that in spring and summer surrounds the bill near its end. In early spring the species undergoes a partial molt by which it acquires a black throat patch and a darker (less brownish) coloration throughout.

ALBATROSSES, SHEARWATERS, AND PETRELS
Order *Procellariiformes*

THE VAST watery expanse of the open oceans that make up approximately three-fourths of the earth's surface would seem to constitute a habitat probably devoid of birds, despite the great mobility that these creatures possess. To the contrary, the oceans are far from sterile of birdlife. The members of one whole order, the Procellariiformes, and to a lesser extent several others, are denizens of the sea and dependent on it for their existence. They come to land only to rear their young. Many of them nest in burrows in the ground or in crevices in rocks. The remainder of their lives is spent coursing over the waves of the high seas and presumably roosting at night on the water itself or on floating masses of seaweed or debris. In the hand a specimen of a procellariiform bird is seen to possess nostrils that open to the surface through tubular structures (Fig. 31) on the top of the bill instead of through mere slits—hence the name "Tubinares" that has been applied to the petrels and their close relatives. The classical albatross of the Ancient Mariner is the Wandering Albatross, a giant member of this same group with a wingspread of 11 feet.

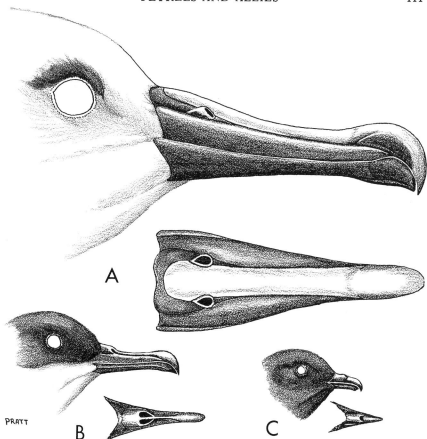

PRATT

Figure 31 Lateral and dorsal views of the bills of the Audubon's Shearwater (upper left), the Wilson's Storm-Petrel (upper right), and the Yellow-nosed Albatross (bottom). The nostrils in all three are tubular structures on the top of the bill. In the albatrosses the culmen separates the two tubes, but in the shearwaters and storm-petrels, the tubes lie juxtaposed on top of the culmen. In the shearwaters two distinct tubular openings are evident, but in the storm-petrels the dividing partition is not visible externally, and hence there appears to be only a single orifice.

The
Albatross
Family
Diomedeidae

YELLOW-NOSED ALBATROSS *Diomedea chlororhynchos*

Figs. 31, 32

The recording of a species of bird that occurs only accidentally in the state is often a consequence of fortuitous circumstances—that of an observer chancing to be at exactly the right place at exactly the right time. Such was the case on May 9, 1970, when Joseph C. Kennedy and James McDaniel were on the Gulf shore a few miles west of Holly Beach, in Cameron Parish, and observed an albatross flying eastward above the breakers. By making short dashes in their car, first passing the bird and then being passed by it, they were able to keep their find under observation for 15 minutes. Having in hand cameras equipped with telescopic lenses, both succeeded in obtaining several superb photographs of the bird before it reached Holly Beach, turned at a right angle, and flew out to sea, disappearing over the horizon. The photographs, one of which is reproduced as Figure 32, were studied by several competent ornithologists, including such experts on oceanic birds as George E. Watson and the late Robert Cushman Murphy. They all identified it as a Yellow-nosed Albatross, a species that breeds on Tristan da Cunha and Gough islands, in the South Atlantic Ocean, and on St. Paul Island, in the Indian Ocean, and ranges widely over the southern seas. Though the species has been recorded several times in waters off northeastern North America, the Holly Beach bird was the first albatross of any kind to be seen over the Gulf of Mexico. On May 14, 1972, approximately two years later, a Yellow-nosed Albatross was reported at the jetties of South Padre Island, Texas.

The huge bill, enormous wing span, and great size, which exceeds that of our pelicans, make albatrosses unmistakable. The Black-browed is the only species of albatross other than the Yellow-nosed that has been seen in the American or Canadian waters of the North Atlantic.

Figure 32 Yellow-nosed Albatross near Holly Beach in Cameron Parish on
May 9, 1970. (Photograph by James McDaniel.)

The
Shearwater
Family
Procellariidae

GREATER SHEARWATER *Puffinus gravis*   Fig. 33

I believe the Greater Shearwater is entitled to a place on the state list
despite the fact that no specimens or photographs are yet available as incontrovertible supporting evidence. Two shearwaters, one of which was

positively identified as this species, were seen on July 16, 1964, by Lovett E. Williams, Mac Myers, and R. W. Skinner 10 miles west of North Island in Chandeleur Sound. The stormy day with rough seas probably accounts for the presence of the birds in inshore waters. The observers felt that both were of the same species, though they did not note a white uppertail patch or all the other diagnostic features in one of the individuals.

The species certainly occurs in the state's offshore waters. Through the generosity of Harley Howcott, who is a bill-fishing expert and a true patron of science, my colleague Robert J. Newman often has been taken along as guest and ornithological observer on chartered boat trips to blue water offshore from the mouth of South Pass at the end of the Mississippi River delta. Newman thereby obtained the following sightings: two birds on September 4, 1970, and another on the following day, all 35 miles out; one on

Figure 33   Audubon's Shearwater (left) and Greater Shearwater (right).

August 11, 1971, at a similar distance; and one on May 3, 1972, about 20 miles out.

In their general appearance shearwaters suggest gulls but may be readily distinguished from gulls by the manner in which they rapidly, instead of slowly and gracefully, beat their wings in flurries and then sail for some distance on stiffly outstretched pinions over the surface of the waves. The diagnostic characters of the various species of shearwaters known from the Gulf of Mexico are treated at the end of the Audubon's Shearwater account.

AUDUBON'S SHEARWATER *Puffinus lherminieri*   Figs. 31, 33

Although all records of Audubon's Shearwater were once so far offshore that earlier editions of this book included it only as a species of extralimital occurrence, the bird is now entitled to an unequivocal place on the state list. Following Hurricane Carla 14 carcasses were picked up on September 15 and 16, 1961, on the beaches of Cameron Parish, and 13 of them were preserved as specimens in the LSU Museum of Zoology. On March 29, 1972, Rita Walther flushed an Audubon's Shearwater from the side of a shell road in Hackberry, in Cameron Parish, three-eighths of a mile from the Calcasieu ship channel. She was without binoculars, but she was within 20 yards of the bird, and her description is convincing. Hers is the first observation of a living Audubon's Shearwater within state boundaries. On May 4, 1972, Robert J. Newman added another along a rip dividing blue water from green, 8 miles from the mouth of the South Pass of the Mississippi River delta. The same observer has seen the species in numbers (15 on occasion) on other dates (May 4 to September 5) farther offshore from the mouth of South Pass and indeed collected a specimen on July 9, 1970, at 38 miles out.

The Audubon's Shearwater breeds in the West Indies, but, like other members of the order Procellariiformes, it seldom, if ever, visits land of its own accord outside the breeding season. Thus most of its life is spent wandering over the open seas.

The Audubon's Shearwater is sooty black above, including the top of the head and the hindneck, and is white below, except for the dusky brown undertail coverts and the dusky patches on each side of the breast. The rear edge of the tarsus and the outer edge of the outer toe are dusky, but the other parts of the tarsus and the toes are a vinaceous-pink. This species, which is less than 12 inches in length and has a wing expanse of less than 20 inches, is much the smallest of the shearwaters now known to occur in the Gulf of Mexico. The Sooty Shearwater, in addition to being larger, is dusky above and below. The Greater Shearwater is almost equal in size to the Ring-billed Gull, has the black cap distinct from the lighter-colored hindneck, and possesses a more or less crescent-shaped patch near the base of the tail on the upper surface. Cory's Shearwater is even larger than the Greater, from which it can be separated by its distinctly yellowish (not dusky) bill and by the absence of a black cap and white tail patch.

The Storm-Petrel Family
Hydrobatidae

LEACH'S STORM-PETREL *Oceanodroma leucorhoa*   Fig. 34

A specimen of this summer inhabitant of northern oceans was taken aboard the M/V *Oregon* at latitude 28°30'N, longitude 88°42'W, approximately 41 statute miles southeast of South Pass of the Mississippi River delta, by Harvey R. Bullis, on December 5, 1956, and is now in the LSU Museum of Zoology. The bird fell on the deck in a stunned condition at 2 A.M. but recovered and was kept on board a day or two before it finally expired. Other records for the species anywhere in the Gulf of Mexico are few, but on September 23, 1972, Phillip L. Bruner and James Rodgers found a Leach's Storm-Petrel on the beach at Grand Isle, in Jefferson Parish. It was sitting at the edge of the surf among a flock of shorebirds and flew when approached, showing the diagnostic field marks. It did not appear to be sick or injured. This species differs slightly from the Wilson's Storm-Petrel in having the tail forked and the webbing of the toes blackish instead of yellow.

Figure 34 Leach's Storm-Petrel (left) and Wilson's Storm-Petrel (right).

WILSON'S STORM-PETREL   *Oceanites oceanicus*   Figs. 31, 34

Louisiana is noted for the attraction that it affords to a great host of migratory birds. Our winter visitors and our spring and fall transients are nearly all species of birds that nest to the north of us. Their migration is, therefore, a movement from breeding grounds in the North to wintering grounds in the South and then back northward again the following spring. We have, however, one bird visitor, the Wilson's Storm-Petrel, that comes to us from the faraway Antarctic Zone and its environs. It nests there in December and January, the equivalent in the Southern Hemisphere of our summer, and then it moves northward across the equator to spend *its* winter, April to September, in the Gulf of Mexico and over the waters of the North Atlantic. Its habit of skipping over the water on its long legs is the basis for its name "Peter bird" or petrel, an allusion to the disciple Peter, who walked on water. In the anecdotes of the sea, all petrels are often called "Mother Carey's chickens." As the late Robert Cushman Murphy, who was a world authority on seabirds, pointed out: "The name of this vague demigoddess— no doubt the wife of Davy Jones, has been traced by some to prayers addressed by storm-tossed Mediterranean sailors to the Virgin, the *mater cara*, or 'dear mother'."

Sportsmen and commercial fishermen sometimes see small numbers of this species in the waters off the mouths of the Mississippi River and offshore from Grand Isle. Extreme recorded dates for Louisiana and adjacent waters are April 8 and September 9. The period when it is most likely to be seen is from June to early September, when as many as 15 have been seen on a single fishing trip.

The Wilson's Storm-Petrel is approximately the size of the Purple Martin, which it somewhat resembles because of its black color and its long, pointed wings. At the base of its tail, however, it has a conspicuous white patch. The toes are fully webbed, and the legs are so long that they reach beyond the tail when extended backward in flight—as the legs of Leach's do not.

PELICANS
AND ALLIES
Order *Pelecaniformes*

THE TROPICBIRDS, pelicans, boobies, cormorants, anhingas, and gannets are all members of this order of birds. One of the many structural characteristics that they have in common is the full, or totipalmate, webbing of the toes, which incorporates even the fourth or hind toe (Fig. 36). In other web-footed birds, the fourth toe is free of any connection with the three front toes and not infrequently articulates at a higher level on the foot than do the front toes. The members of this order are all aquatic, and the tropicbirds, boobies, and gannets are pelagic, usually coming to land only to nest.

The Tropicbird
Family
Phaethontidae

WHITE-TAILED TROPICBIRD *Phaethon lepturus* Fig. 35

This largely white bird, with striking black markings, a yellow bill, and a long streamer tail, is primarily a species of the open ocean. It breeds in the Bermudas and the West Indies and, prior to the 1960s, had been definitely recorded in the Gulf of Mexico on fewer than a dozen occasions. Vague reports by previous writers that at times it has been almost common in Louisiana in midsummer seem certainly unfounded. The only positive record of the species in the state is the identification of an individual in Sabine Pass, approximately a mile from the Gulf, on August 15, 1973. The bird was feeding in the ship channel and was carefully studied at a distance of 50 feet or less by O. W. Dillon, Jr., who was thoroughly familiar with the species in the West Indies. The sighting took place in the late morning following a day and night of severe thunderstorms that moved out of the Gulf and over land in the Sabine Pass area.

Figure 35   White-tailed Tropicbird.

The Pelican
Family
Pelecanidae

AMERICAN WHITE PELICAN *Pelecanus erythrorhynchos*

Figs. 36, 37, 61

This immense white bird, with its black-tipped wings and long, yellow, pouched bill, is one of our most conspicuous winter residents. Although American White Pelicans are not known to nest within our state, flocks numbering over one thousand individuals are sometimes present along our coast throughout the summer. In late October and early November large migratory flocks are not infrequently seen moving southward toward our coastal waterways, where the species is common in winter. Small flocks are also found on a few of the inland lakes in winter. Spring departure begins in April and continues through May. The principal breeding grounds for the American White Pelican are lakes in western Canada and in the northwestern United States, but since at least the late 1950s sizable colonies numbering sometimes over 500 pairs have nested on South Bird Island in Laguna Madre in southern Texas.

BROWN PELICAN *Pelecanus occidentalis*   Fig. 37; pp. 123, 126

In the 18 years following the first publication of *Louisiana Birds* in 1955, no bird in the state declined so dramatically and so frighteningly as the Brown Pelican. In the old days an observer could not visit any part of our coast at any time without seeing these birds in numbers splashing into the sea to catch fish or lumbering by in long, undulating lines. And breeding colonies that at different times were located at Raccoon Point at the western extremity of the Isles Dernieres, East Timbalier Island, the mud lumps at the mouths of the Mississippi River, Grand Gosier Island in the Chandeleur chain, North Island adjacent to the chain, and Isle au Pitre—all within our boun-

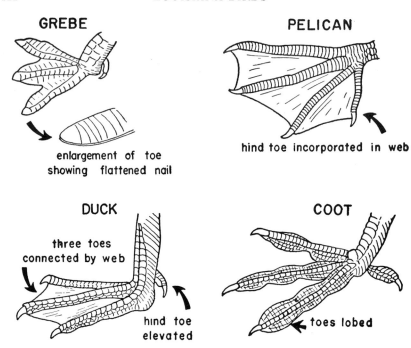

GREBE

enlargement of toe
showing flattened nail

PELICAN

hind toe incorporated in web

DUCK

three toes
connected by web

hind toe
elevated

COOT

toes lobed

Figure 36   Toes of some water birds.

daries—produced most of the Brown Pelicans seen along the entire northern Gulf Coast.

Although the species ranges widely through the Gulf and Caribbean areas and along the Atlantic and Pacific coasts from South Carolina and California to Brazil and Ecuador, Louisiana quite fittingly came to be known as the Pelican State. A family group of the birds had the honor of being emblazoned on our state seal and thus appears on all our official documents, along with the motto Union, Justice, and Confidence. Unfortunately, the legislation that named "the pelican" as our official state bird neglected to say what kind of pelican. The oversight led one year to the appearance of the American White Pelican on Louisiana automobile license plates. And by 1958, when the lawmakers finally got around to specifying the Brown Pelican as the choice really intended, almost no individuals of the species could be found anywhere on our mainland shores!

What had happened? The change came about so suddenly and so

swiftly that we do not really know. The first hint of trouble came in 1956, the year after the appearance of *Louisiana Birds*. From June 15 to 17, T. A. Imhof and party noted 20 to 25 dead adult Brown Pelicans around Dauphin and Petit Bois islands in Alabama and Mississippi, and on July 1, the H. A. J. Evanses counted 50 corpses on Isle au Pitre and found others on the Chandeleur Islands. Nonetheless, in the closing days of May in the following year, Robert J. Newman and P. A. Daigre reported the North Island colony continuing seemingly to thrive with well over one thousand nests. The fragmentary subsequent nesting data, all from North Island, follow: 1958—thousands of adults along with young of all ages on June 7 (W. H. Turcotte and others); 1959—no report; 1960—approximately 200 pairs nesting on April 20 (J. Valentine, J. Walther) and 300+ birds on September 9 (S. A. Gauthreaux); 1961—100 nests on May 21 (Valentine) increasing to 150 by June 6 (Walther, Valentine, R. Andrews); 1962—6 adults and no nests on June 6, 7, and 8 (L. E. Williams, S. G. Clawson).

Since 1962 no nesting of native stock is known to have occurred in the state. Thus the Chandeleur chain and associated islands, site of the first recorded "natural" colony in Louisiana in 1918, became 44 years later the site of the last.

"A Wonderful Bird Is the Pelican . . ."

ALLAN D. CRUICKSHANK

Figure 37   Brown Pelican (left) and American White Pelican (right).

Meanwhile on annual Christmas Bird Counts the Brown Pelican had undergone an even more rapid decrease. The totals were as follows: 1956—2 at New Orleans, 90 in the Cameron area; 1957—0 at New Orleans, 19 in the Cameron area; 1958—none on any count, though New Orleans, Reserve, and Cameron all turned in reports. The species has never since reappeared on a Louisiana Christmas count. A few birds were still occasionally sighted at odd times of the year in coastal parishes in the early 1960s, but by the middle of the decade even these reports had ceased.

The troubles of the species were by no means confined to Louisiana. Across the continent, in California, ornithologists were noting little or no production of young in the Brown Pelican colonies there. They discovered that the birds were laying eggs so fragile that the thin shells broke when the parents attempted incubation. Furthermore, they identified the causative agency as a chemical one, the chlorinated hydrocarbons widely used as pesticides. When rains fall, the runoff flushes the poisons from the soil and carries them to brooks and rivulets. Thence the substances move successively into larger streams, into rivers, and finally into the sea itself. All along the way, small fish are ingesting the chemicals along with normal food. Larger fish eat the smaller fish and are in turn devoured by still larger fish. At each transfer the concentration of poison in tissues intensifies. By the time a fish is swallowed by a large fish-eating bird high in the food chain, such as a cormorant, eagle, or pelican, the dosage can be dangerous indeed. Death seldom, if ever, ensues immediately; but the intruding hydrocarbons cumulate unnoticed in the fatty tissues. In times of stress, such as when storms impose unaccustomed physical exertion or when food is hard to procure for other reasons, pelicans can be forced to draw on energy reserves loaded with chlorinated hydrocarbons and then may be literally poisoned by their own fat. At such times they are likely to die. If they survive, they seem to do so as birds unable to reproduce effectively.

Sometime in the late 1950s, die-offs of fish began to become an annual event in Louisiana along the Mississippi and Atchafalaya rivers. In 1960 at least 30 large fish kills were reported to authorities, and in 1963 an estimated five million fish died. An investigation resulted that was eventually to identify the lethal agent as endrin and to pinpoint its source as a chemical plant in Memphis that manufactures this pesticide. Discharges of poisonous waste into the river by this plant were halted in 1965. During the years when Louisiana pelicans were disappearing, no chemical analyses of their eggs or tissues were ever conducted, but the similar timing of the fish kills and of the decline of the birds would appear to be more than mere coincidence.

I do not know how long a Brown Pelican normally lives, but I would guess that a bird reaching adulthood has a life expectancy of at least several years. Therefore one would expect the species to remain in evidence for a fairly long time after the production of young ceased. In Louisiana it did not do so. Brown Pelicans were still nesting in 1961, three and one-half years after the last individual was seen on a Christmas Bird Count; and the scarcity of the species on the Louisiana coast was noted before a drop-off in the numbers of breeding birds on North Island was noted. A possible explanation is that the North Island population may have consisted in large part of pelicans that lived for most of the year around the Chandeleurs, Mississippi Sound, and points east. These birds may not have been as immediately and as heavily subjected to doses of poison as were the birds farther west, nearer the mouths of the Mississippi River. At any rate, the disappearance of our Brown Pelicans seems not to have been a prolonged process brought about primarily by reduced fertility or weak-shelled eggs. The swiftness of the population collapse points to a direct die-off of adults.

Brown Pelican Rookery

In 1968, the history of the species in the state entered a new phase. That summer 50 young Brown Pelicans were imported from southern Florida by the Louisiana Wild Life and Fisheries Commission. Half were sent to Grand Terre, half to Rockefeller Refuge. In autumn of that year 30 of the birds were turned loose as free fliers—15 at Grand Terre in September and a like number at Rockefeller Refuge in October. By the time of their release, the latter birds had become so habituated to pen feeding that they made little attempt to fish on their own and continued to depend upon handouts for subsistence. To force them to support themselves, the Rockefeller biologists eventually denied the pelicans access to free meals. By this time, winter had come. A sudden cold snap was more than the birds could take. All died. At Grand Terre, meanwhile, the free fliers could be seen out over Barataria Bay plunging for fish. And they thrived through the winter.

In 1969, another 50 Brown Pelicans from Florida were split between Rockefeller Refuge and Grand Terre. This time the Rockefeller birds were allowed to fly free as soon as they were able. They responded by quickly disappearing, never to be seen again, dead or alive. At this point efforts to restore the species to western Louisiana came to an end. At Grand Terre the new releases remained in evidence and augmented the introduced Barataria Bay population. There the importation of more pelicans from Florida continued on an annual basis.

However commendable, this effort to reintroduce Brown Pelicans into Louisiana seemed to me to have a dim future. I could see no assurance that the causes that wiped out the species in the state, whatever they might have been, were not still in operation. But suddenly in the spring of 1971, only 31 months after the first release, the introduced pelicans began nesting. The small colony was on a perilously low and narrow shell reef conveniently close to the Wild Life and Fisheries Commission Grand Terre installation, separated from it by only a mile or so of open water. In the 13 nests there, 20 eggs were laid and 11 young hatched. Seven survived to grow to adult size.

The Brown Pelicans of Barataria Bay nested again in 1972 and 1973 but on a more suitable expanse of shell several miles farther east, on another island. The young surviving to the flying stage in these years numbered 17 and 24, respectively, but the totals represented an actual drop-off in production per number of eggs laid, since increasing numbers of adults were participating in the reproductive process.

Because chlorinated hydrocarbons are cumulative poison, building up in tissues progressively, one might anticipate that older adults would have a lesser capacity to reproduce than younger ones. So the initial breeding successes of transplants may be due to their youth. On the other hand, environmental conditions in Louisiana have improved to the point that there are fewer parts per million of chlorinated hydrocarbons in Barataria Bay than in the waters around the Florida rookeries whence our imports came. And eggshell thickness here, though somewhat subnormal, is appreciably better than in Florida and much better than in California.

At present, chemical contamination is probably doing less to impair reproduction than a combination of other factors. The introduced pelicans have brought with them the annual rhythm that governed their ancestors' activity in Florida. They begin to lay eggs in midwinter, a timing suitable in their native state but not in our climate. So the storms and low temperatures of late winter cause abnormal nesting mortality, aggravated by the fact that the birds are nesting on the ground, as I once found the pelicans doing on East Timbalier Island, rather than in low mangrove bushes, as they usually did on North Island. Be that as it may, limited nesting success and continued importation have increased the population in the Barataria Bay area to an estimated 400 birds. In the summer of 1973, Brown Pelicans were observed in Louisiana as far east as the Chandeleurs and as far west as East Timbalier Island.

The Brown Pelican lays from one to three eggs, which are either whitish or dirty brown in color. The young on hatching are naked, homely looking creatures but soon become covered with white down feathers. The adults feed their offspring by swallowing fish and then regurgitating partially digested portions back into the pouch. The baby pelican sticks its bill and head into its parent's pouch for its meal. The young grow slowly, and usually it is midsummer before they have completely lost their natal down, replaced it with contour feathers, and acquired their flight feathers. The full-fledged young are mostly gray in color and quite unlike their parents in their breeding dress. The front and back of the long neck of the adults are a rich mahogany brown and the top of the head and the sides of the neck are white. A few elongated feathers on the nape constitute some semblance of a nuptial crest.

Pelicans feed entirely on fish, almost wholly of noncommercial varieties. Turning in a half roll, they plunge bill first into the water and virtually disappear from sight in the resulting splash. The great pouch scoops up the prey and in doing so naturally scoops up several quarts of water. But the bird throws its bill upward, and this contracts the pouch, squeezing the water out through the corners of the mouth. The fish is then swallowed in an awkward gulp.

Pelicans are indeed queer birds. Despite their many marvelous structural adaptations, they have lost all vocal powers. The only sound ever heard from a pelican is the hissing, snakelike noise that the young make when intruders come near their nest. I never fail to marvel at the almost unbelievable differences between a pelican and, let us say, a hummingbird, as they appear in the field. It is difficult to believe that two creatures so superficially diverse could have stemmed from a common ancestor, although we know from their internal similarities they did just that millions of years ago.

The Booby
Family
Sulidae

MASKED BOOBY *Sula dactylatra*   Pl. II

Boobies are relatives of the pelicans to which externally they bear only a slight resemblance. In this species, which is sometimes called the Blue-faced Booby, the adult has a bluish black bare area around the bill. The plumage is pure white except for the black tail and black-tipped wing feathers. (In flight the entire rear edge of the wing is black, not just the tip.) The black tail serves to distinguish it from the adult Northern Gannet and the adult Red-footed Booby, both of which have white tails. The immature Masked Booby is dusky brown with a white breast and belly. In this respect it resembles the adult Brown or so-called White-bellied Booby; but the markings are much less sharply defined, the brown of the neck does not extend onto the chest, and the upper back has an indistinct whitish patch.

Although boobies and the Northern Gannet have been recorded comparatively few times in our state, they are doubtless present each year in our offshore waters. Commercial fishermen and sportsmen should be on the lookout for them. In late 1959 only two definite Louisiana records for the Masked Booby were available, but since that time at least seven birds have been obtained as specimens on land or in offshore waters. Still others have been seen 20 to 38 miles from the mouth of South Pass of the Mississippi River delta. Fourteen records span five consecutive months and are distributed as follows: May, 2; June, 3; July, 4; August, 3; September, 2. One of the specimens mentioned above was found on September 13, 1961, at Jackson, in East Feliciana Parish, during Hurricane Carla.

BROWN BOOBY   *Sula leucogaster*   Pl. II

The white belly sharply demarcated from the rest of the plumage, which is
solid dark brown, distinguishes adults of this species from other boobies
known to occur in Louisiana waters. The immatures are dark throughout
and therefore resemble the much larger immature Northern Gannet, but
they are blacker and more uniformly colored above (lacking white mottling)
and have yellow (instead of blackish) feet. The species is often referred to as
the White-bellied Booby. Two specimens were collected by George E. Beyer
in September 1884, approximately 50 miles below New Orleans; three were
seen at Red Pass, near the mouth of the Mississippi River, on January 15,
1901; a specimen was obtained in April 1929 at Grand Isle by E. S. Hopkins;
Harvey R. Bullis observed three individuals on September 8, 1951, in the
Gulf at 29°06′N latitude, 88°30′W longitude, which is approximately 30
miles east of Pass a Loutre; Lovett E. Williams saw one 31 miles south of
the Louisiana-Texas line on November 15, 1961; Williams, in company
with Mac Myers and R. W. Skinner, noted the species 10 miles west of
North Island, in Chandeleur Sound on July 16, 1964; and Robert J. Newman and Phillip L. Bruner observed an immature flying along the surf at
Elmers Island, in Lafourche Parish, on July 18, 1973.

RED-FOOTED BOOBY   *Sula sula*   Pl. II

A single immature specimen of this species taken at the mouth of Bayou
Scofield on November 1, 1940, and now preserved in the LSU Museum of
Zoology, is the only state record and, as a matter of fact, one of the few
unquestionable records in the United States. The immature is usually a light
brown throughout and cannot be readily distinguished in the field from the
immature Brown Booby. The adult Red-footed Booby has red feet and
is otherwise all-white except for the black-tipped wing feathers. The black
extends along almost the entire rear part of the wing, a character that it
shares with the Masked Booby, which differs in having a black-tipped tail.

Plate II   Gannets and Boobies

1. adult Northern Gannet (p. 131); 1a. immature. 2. adult Masked Booby (p. 129);
2a. immature from above; 2b. immature from below. 3. adult Red-footed Booby (p.
130); 3a. immature from above; 3b. immature from below. 4. adult Brown Booby (p.
130) from above; 4a. adult from below; 4b. immature from above; 4c. immature from
below.

In the Masked Booby the trailing edge of black is almost parallel-sided all the way to the juncture of the wing and body, while in the Red-footed Booby the black tapers almost to a point proximally. The adult Red-footed Booby is similar to the adult Northern Gannet in having the tail white, but differs in that the rear edge of the wing, not just the tip, is black. As the smallest of the boobies it is strikingly inferior in size to the Northern Gannet. The size ratio of the boobies to each other and to the Northern Gannet is indicated in Plate II.

NORTHERN GANNET *Morus bassanus* Pl. II

The Northern Gannet is the largest member of the Booby family; in fact, it is nearly the size of a Brown Pelican. It is also the most common member of its family in northern Gulf waters. Despite the fact that only one definite record for the state (a specimen taken in 1886) was available up to 1960, the species has now been recorded at least 15 times. For example, Jacob M. Valentine and John R. Walther counted 54 individuals between the north end of the Chandeleur Islands and Ship Island on March 15, 1960. Several additional specimens have been obtained, including an individual that was banded when too young to fly at Barachois, Canada, on September 7, 1968, and recovered on Grand Gosier Island in the Chandeleurs on April 26, 1970.

Boobies and gannets are highly pelagic and do not often come close to land except in their nesting season. The boobies are generally birds of tropical seas, but Northern Gannets breed at northern latitudes—for example, on the islands in the Gulf of St. Lawrence. In winter they move southward along the Atlantic Coast, and quite a few enter the Gulf of Mexico, arriving in northern Gulf waters as early as September and remaining as late as May 14. Whether they short-cut over the peninsula of Florida or come all the way around its tip in order to reach the Gulf is not known. When I crossed the Gulf in May 1945 and in April 1948, I saw gannets at various points between the mouth of the Mississippi River and Yucatan. Also, the species is observed regularly in winter at Pensacola Beach, where counts have run as high as 51 in a 45-minute period.

Their large size and the manner in which they wheel in circles over the ocean waves make gannets recognizable at once. They differ radically from gulls, even the large Herring Gull, in that the neck is much longer and the large bill is usually slanted downward toward the water. The tail is pointed, not fan-shaped. As Roger T. Peterson says, this gives them a "pointed-at-both-ends look." Like their relatives the pelicans, they hit the water with a great, spectacular splash; gulls rarely hit the water but instead pick food from the surface as they hover momentarily. Adult gannets are white with black wing tips (see also Masked Booby and Red-footed Booby); but immatures, which outnumber adults in the Gulf, are brownish gray, flecked with white. Subadults are mottled above with black and white, and, as in the adult Masked and Red-footed Boobies, the wing is black along the trailing edge even after the remainder of the plumage has become white.

The
Cormorant
Family
Phalacrocoracidae

DOUBLE-CRESTED CORMORANT   *Phalacrocorax auritus*

Figs. 38, 39

Often called "nigger goose" or "water-turkey," this is one of the common water birds of the state and, therefore, needs little introduction except by its proper name, Double-crested Cormorant. "Water-turkey" is a particularly unfortunate name, since it is often used for another species. Because of their fish-eating habits, cormorants enjoy no favor from sportsmen, and they are often shot in numbers. Killing them, however, is unjustified, for they eat very few game fish. If the truth be known, their fish-eating habits render them beneficial to sportsmen; actually they eliminate many predatory fish that would otherwise consume great quantities of small fry of perch and bass and other desirable species.

Double-crested Cormorants are most common in Louisiana in winter and early spring. Although a few were once known to breed in the state, such as in Devil's Swamp north of Baton Rouge and in Cameron Parish,

I find no evidence that they continue to do so. As a matter of fact, the species appears to be decidedly less numerous at all seasons in comparison with its status in the 1930s, 1940s, and 1950s. It used to be a winter fixture at City Park and University lakes in Baton Rouge, where it often perched on dead baldcypresses, but now its appearance on these lakes is unusual.

Most Double-crested Cormorants leave here in April to migrate far northward to nest, returning in early September. The nests, constructed of sticks and twigs, are in colonies and are generally placed on horizontal limbs over the water at various heights. The three eggs are laid in April or May and are very pale blue or bluish white, the color being more or less concealed by a chalky white covering.

The plumage of adults is entirely black with much iridescence at all seasons. Young birds less than a year old are light tan or brownish white below and on the neck. On the water, cormorants can be, and often are, mistaken for loons or for the American Anhinga (see account for that

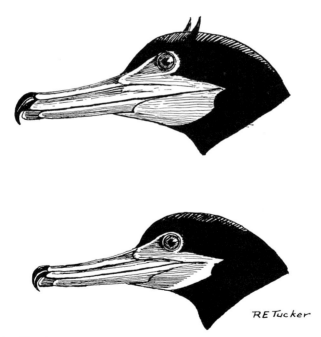

Figure 38 Heads of Double-crested Cormorant (top) and Olivaceous Cormorant (bottom).

Figure 39 Adult summer plumages of the American Anhinga and the cormorants: (1) male American Anhinga; (2) female American Anhinga; (3) Double-crested Cormorant; (4) Olivaceous Cormorant.

species). Loons, however, are white below and hold the neck hunched down on the shoulders, while our Louisiana cormorants are never pure white below and always hold the neck and head high. Moreover, the bill of the cormorant is tilted conspicuously upward, decidedly more so even than that of the Red-throated Loon. Cormorants dive and swim with agility, but, like grebes and loons, they often experience takeoff difficulties. In flight they resemble geese, both in size and in their manner of flying in long lines or V formations. These similarities and their black color are the basis for the name "nigger goose." Cormorants frequently perch in dead trees on our lakeshores and are often seen with their wings spread as they dry themselves.

OLIVACEOUS CORMORANT   *Phalacrocorax olivaceus*   Figs. 38, 39

This is a species whose range lies almost wholly to the south of us, extending all the way to the southern tip of South America, hence the name Neotropic Cormorant by which it is sometimes called. It barely enters the borders of our state. Our only positive records, except for a single individual seen near New Orleans on March 27 and April 4, 1959, by Sidney A. Gauthreaux and one observed at Baton Rouge on January 20, 1961, by Laurence C. Binford, are from southwestern Louisiana where it is a fairly common permanent resident, breeding in colonies in Cameron Parish. The four or five bluish white eggs are laid in late May on a stoutly constructed platform of sticks in trees and bushes growing in or near open water.

The body of this species is about half as large in bulk as that of a Double-crested Cormorant, and in the breeding season the throat pouch is bordered by a narrow edging of white feathers. In adult winter plumage, the Olivaceous Cormorant is more solid brownish black, especially on the neck, than is its larger relative. Immatures of the two species in the first winter plumage are indistinguishable from each other in the field except by size.

The Anhinga Family
Anhingidae

AMERICAN ANHINGA   *Anhinga anhinga*   Fig. 39

The American Anhinga, also known as the "water-turkey" or "snake-bird," is one of our most bizarre birds. It swims with the entire body submerged and only the long, black, snaky head and neck exposed—thus its name "snake-bird." Although somewhat similar to a cormorant, it differs in having a slimmer neck, a much longer tail (as long as the body rather than decidedly shorter than the body), and a pointed instead of a hooked bill. Adults have a great amount of white in the wings, the back is flecked and streaked with silvery white, and the tip of the tail is buffy white. Adult males are otherwise black, except for a few short brownish and white nuptial plumes that appear on the sides of the head and neck in the breeding season. Females have a brown throat, neck, and upper breast with a sharp line of demarcation at the junction with the otherwise blackish underparts. The young, less than a year old, show even more brown than the female. On the wing, the American Anhinga is one of the most arresting sights of our swamplands; it flies with the neck outstretched and the tail spread fanlike, sailing with rapid intermittent strokes of the wings or soaring on rising air currents, sometimes to considerable heights. It is rare in winter but very common in summer, being especially numerous as a nesting bird around the swamp lakes of northern Louisiana. The bulk of the population disappears by the end of October and reappears in March or early April. The nest is built of sticks, usually on the low limb of a cypress and usually over water. The three to five bluish white eggs are laid in the period from April through June. The young on hatching are naked and quite reptilelike in appearance.

The Frigatebird Family
Fregatidae

MAGNIFICENT FRIGATEBIRD *Fregata magnificens*   Fig. 40

These majestic birds of coastal waters and the environs of sea islands are rarely seen on the Louisiana mainland, and then usually only after storms. Following the hurricane of August 6, 1939, Magnificent Frigatebirds, or "man-o'-war-birds," as they are often called, appeared over the lakes in the city of Baton Rouge and at various places along the Mississippi River as far north as Natchez. Extreme dates of authenticated occurrence in the state are March 25 to December 31. These dates would suggest that the species breeds here, but it does not. In fact, it was not known to breed anywhere in the United States until 1970, when nests were found on the Marquesas Keys, west of Key West. Nesting otherwise takes place from the Bahamas, Campeche Bank, and the Caribbean area to as far south as northern South Amer-

Figure 40   Magnificent Frigatebird: (1) adult male; (2) immature; (3) adult female.

ica and the Galapagos Islands. The birds leave the breeding colonies in numbers as soon as the young can fly. In June and July thousands of these birds can be seen at one time around the North Islands, in the Chandeleur chain, and on June 11, 1941, a group of us estimated that as many as five to ten thousand were in the air at the same place. The majority of the individuals in these large aggregations are young of the year, as evidenced by their white heads and extensively white underparts.

Frigatebirds, adults and immatures alike, are readily identified by their eight-foot wingspread and their long tails, which are forked to a depth of 18 inches. Adult males are black with green iridescence, except for the featherless throat, which is red in the breeding season and expands balloon-like beneath the bill as part of the mating behavior. Adult females have white chests, but the black head and belly distinguish them from immatures.

Frigatebirds, despite their large size, are as agile on the wing as swallows and are expert fishermen. They dive from great heights to pluck their prey from the water with their hooked bills, without wetting a feather in the process. Often, however, they dine on stolen fish that they intimidate gulls into dropping or disgorging.

HERONS
AND ALLIES
Order *Ciconiiformes*

The Heron Family
Ardeidae

OFTEN IN LOUISIANA and in many other places, herons are incorrectly called cranes. They differ anatomically from cranes in many ways, and the two are confused only because both have long legs and a long neck. Herons fly with their necks pulled back on their shoulders in S-shaped fashion; cranes fly with their necks completely outstretched. Also, cranes are very rare in Louisiana; in the many years that I have searched for and studied birds in this state, I have yet to see here a single crane.

Included in the Heron family are the egrets, which were once virtually exterminated by plume hunters seeking feathers primarily for women's hats. Since the plumes are at their finest in the nesting season, the birds were killed mostly at that time. This persecution not only decimated the ranks of the adults but also left eggs unhatched and young to die in the nest. So completely was reproduction disrupted that the birds were soon on the brink of total extirpation. The passage in 1909 of the Lacey Act ended traffic in plumes in the United States and forbade their importation from countries south of our border. The aigrettes, as the nuptial plumes are called, are special lacelike feathers, situated mainly on the back, lower neck, and head. In the Snowy Egret those of the back are recurved, while in the Great Egret they are long and straight. All herons acquire nuptial plumes, but the egrets are adorned with the most filamentous, most lacy ones, which in courtship are raised in the most spectacular displays (see p. 150).

Most herons nest in colonies, which number from a few pairs to thousands of individuals. The nests are generally rather large platforms of sticks and twigs in bushes or in trees, often over water in some remote swamp. The pale bluish or greenish eggs are usually laid in April or May and require several weeks of incubation. Newly hatched herons are scantily covered with long natal down and are quite helpless. The parents nourish them by a curious method of regurgitative feeding, during which the young bird grasps the bill of the adult crosswise. Then by a rather comical pumping motion, the adult injects partially digested food into the throat of the offspring. Those who admire the quaint attractiveness of baby herons and aspire to raise one by hand should be fully apprised of this special feeding technique, which would be required of them as foster parents.

Adult herons are usually slow and deliberate in their movements. They stalk quietly along the shallows or stand motionless on the edge of a lake or marsh. But suddenly a long neck will dart out, and a bird will grab an unsuspecting minnow, frog, or crayfish in its heavy, pointed bill.

Much of Louisiana affords ideal habitat for herons, and consequently they have again become locally common and even sometimes abundant. The world-famous "Bird City" established by the renowned Louisiana conservationist, the late Edward A. McIlhenny of Avery Island, is now an immense colony of thousands of egrets and herons that nest on man-made platforms in an artificially created pond of several acres' extent. McIlhenny's efforts in behalf of the Snowy Egret were largely responsible for its survival.

One of the most interesting behavior patterns of herons is the extensive postbreeding wandering that carries individuals of some species north of their actual nesting range. The Snowy Egret, for example, has appeared in late summer in Ontario, and the Little Blue Heron has been observed in Nova Scotia—both places hundreds of miles north of the northernmost breeding colonies.

GREAT BLUE HERON *Ardea herodias*   Pl. III

This bird has the unchallenged distinction of being the largest member of the Heron family occurring in North America, since the Great White Heron is now considered merely a subspecies of the Great Blue Heron. It stands about four feet high when the head is raised. Size alone distinguishes it from other herons whose body color is not white. The call notes are a series of low, hoarse croaks that have been described as *frahnk, frahnk, frahnk*.

The species is statewide in distribution and a permanent resident that
is seen regularly in small numbers. In winter, nonmigratory populations in
the southern part of the state are supplemented by northern visitors.

GREEN HERON   *Butorides virescens*   Pl. III

This small, greenish-backed heron with its chestnut-colored neck and orange
legs and feet is well known to nearly every sportsman and schoolboy of this
state, although generally by one of its more colloquial names, such as "kop-
kop," "shipoke," or "fly-up-the-creek." In the air it somewhat resembles a
crow, but its wings have a more arched form in flight, and, of course, its body
shape is radically different. Its call is an explosive *kop-kop*, or a *sky-ow, sky-ow*.
     The Green Heron sometimes nests in small colonies, in a slough or over
a small pond, but frequently single pairs are found. It is rare in Louisiana
after mid-November, even in the coastal marshes, but by the third week of
March it can be found again throughout the state. It is one of the four members of the Heron family that migrate in significant numbers directly across
the Gulf of Mexico, instead of around it. The species is frequently seen in
spring over the open Gulf and in the act of arriving on our shores.

LITTLE BLUE HERON   *Florida caerulea*   Pl. III

The adult of this common species appears at a distance to be solid dark
blue. At close range, however, the neck is found to be dark vinaceous-purple.
The legs, feet, and tip of the bill are black. Immatures are all-white except
for the tips of the main flight feathers, which are dusky. Their greenish
yellow legs immediately distinguish them from the similarly white Snowy
Egret, which has black legs.
     Sometimes fair numbers of Little Blue Herons winter in the coastal
marshes and even at inland localities, but the vast majority leave for Central
America in October. In 1971, for example, Christmas Bird Counts recorded

---

Plate III   Herons and Their Allies

1. Great Blue Heron (p. 139). 2. immature Little Blue Heron (p. 140). 3. adult Little
Blue Heron (p. 140). 4. Great Egret (p. 144). 5. Reddish Egret (p. 143). 6. Snowy
Egret (p. 147). 7. Louisiana Heron (p. 147). 8. Green Heron (p. 140). 9. Black-crowned
Night Heron (p. 149), adult in front, immature behind. 10. American Bittern (p. 153).
11. Least Bittern (p. 151). 12. adult Yellow-crowned Night Heron (p. 151).

1

2

3

4

5

6

7

8

9

10

11

12

RET
'46

the species as follows: 38 at Natchitoches, 103 at Reserve, 29 at Sabine National Wildlife Refuge, and 55 at Venice. Migrants returning in spring move mainly up the coast of Mexico and Texas and by mid-March are again on their nesting grounds throughout the interior of Louisiana.

The heron often called "calico-bird" or "spotted crane" is the immature Little Blue Heron in the process of losing its white plumage and acquiring the blue. Hence it has a mixture of feathers of both colors. The first spring molt of immature birds takes place in the winter home, prior to migration, for by the time they return to the United States, nearly all have the adult plumage and cannot be distinguished from older adults.

CATTLE EGRET *Bubulcus ibis*   Pp. 141, 142

This small white heron, originally confined to Asia, Europe, and Africa, is a world rover without parallel. Within the lifetime of most of us, the Cattle Egret has crossed the oceans to become self-introduced on three continents. Its arrival in North America first became known in 1942 with the discovery of a flock in Florida, and within a decade and a half it had reached Louisiana. It was first noted here on October 17, 1955, when Claude Lard observed

The Cattle Egret Is Well Named

SAMUEL A. GRIMES

a flock of approximately 40 individuals a few miles south of Hayes, in Jefferson Davis Parish. Three days later, in the same general area, Lard and R. R. Rudolph counted no less than 113 individuals. Since its initial arrival the Cattle Egret has been observed regularly in numerous localities on numerous dates and just about in every parish. It has even established nesting rookeries in most parts of the state. The estimate of five thousand of these egrets nesting in 1971 on a small island in Clear Lake, near Natchitoches, shows that the species has invaded north Louisiana in force. In the same year the rookery on Lacassine National Wildlife Refuge, in Cameron Parish, contained approximately ten thousand individuals. The proliferation of the Cattle Egret has thus continued to be the great avian spectacular of this century.

The adult Cattle Egret (see photos on pp. 141, 142) resembles in size and color the Snowy Egret and the immature Little Blue Heron, although in some plumages the top of the head and back and a small patch of feathers on the lower neck are buffy, instead of immaculate white. The form is somewhat stockier, the posture is more erect, and the bill is stout, short, and yellow or yellow-orange. The legs are dark in winter, become greenish

Cattle Egrets at Nest in Florida

SAMUEL A. GRIMES

yellow in spring, and tend toward reddish at the height of the breeding season. The behavior of the bird, however, usually provides the first clue to its identity. As the name suggests, it is generally found in pastures in the company of cattle, feeding on insects that the cows stir up or that it pecks from the bodies of the animals themselves. The Cattle Egret sometimes alights on the backs of cattle, but Snowy Egrets also do this. So the presence of an egret in the vicinity of cattle should not be taken as absolute evidence that the bird is a Cattle Egret. Another reason why care must be exercised in making identifications is that white-plumaged immature Little Blue Herons likewise sometimes occur in such situations. Consequently, all such birds should be carefully scrutinized.

Even in the ancestrally unfamiliar Western Hemisphere, the Cattle Egret has remained largely a migratory bird. Observations made for the LSU Museum of Zoology by cooperators on offshore oil rigs have shown that at least some individuals migrate across the Gulf of Mexico in spring. Perhaps they do also in fall. Strange to say, the species has not been easy to find on Christmas Bird Counts in the Cameron area. Recent Christmas counts there recorded none in 1969, 1 in 1970, and 13 in 1971. Cameron Christmas Bird Counts, however, are not typical of the state at large. Even Natchitoches has done better—22 birds in 1971. But top honors go to New Orleans, which tallied 615 birds in 1969 and 106 in 1970. Lafayette had 107 in 1970.

REDDISH EGRET   *Dichromanassa rufescens*   Pl. III

This egret is a regular summer resident in coastal Louisiana, confined during the breeding season to small colonies in the Chandeleurs and associated islands and to Barataria Bay. It appears regularly in Cameron Parish in March and April, perhaps on the way to its nesting sites; so presumably it comes to us by way of Texas. It returns to Cameron Parish in midsummer and remains fairly easy to find there through early fall but is only rarely seen in the state in winter. The first definite breeding record for Louisiana is that of a nest, containing two young begging for food from two adults, found on North Island, in Chandeleur Sound, on June 7, 1958, by H. A. J. Evans and W. H. Turcotte. Presumptively breeding Reddish Egrets are seen on every trip nowadays to the Chandeleurs in summer, and nests have been found on numerous occasions. In one case photographs were taken. A survey of the Chandeleurs and related islands in 1971 produced a count of 44 individuals

—not many when compared with the entire breeding populations of Florida and Texas, but enough to create a sense of plentifulness when concentrated in a restricted area.

The fully adult Reddish Egret resembles the adult Little Blue Heron but is noticeably larger and bulkier and is lighter throughout in color, with the neck reddish tan instead of dark purplish. Also, in summer adults, the basal half of the bill is flesh colored, instead of black, a character that does not hold for immatures. The Reddish Egret is decidedly livelier in its movements than either the Little Blue Heron or the Snowy Egret. While feeding in shallow ponds or at the edge of the surf on the Gulf shore, it darts first one way and then another, grabbing the small fish that make up the bulk of its food.

Immatures are ashy gray, here and there suffused with rufous shades, fawn color, or various vinaceous tints, which may not always be visible in the field at a distance. The bill in these birds is uniformly dusky, and the legs and feet are dark greenish black. The full adult breeding plumage (in which the body is uniformly gray and the reddish feathers on the head and neck become long and scraggly) and the flesh-colored basal portion to the bill are not acquired until the prenuptial molt following the bird's second winter. An all-white color phase occurs regularly in Texas colonies and frequently in West Indian populations. It seems to be increasing in Louisiana. During the 1973 inventory of the birdlife of the Chandeleurs, 5 of the 41 Reddish Egrets found, or approximately 12 percent, were white, and the number equaled the total for all previous Louisiana sightings combined. In this phase the bird's larger size and dark, instead of yellow, toes serve, among other things, to distinguish it easily from the Snowy Egret. The bill, colored as in the dark phase, is sufficient to set it apart from the Great Egret, which always has a yellow bill.

GREAT EGRET *Casmerodius albus*   Pl. III; Fig. 61; pp. 145, 146

This large all-white heron is approximately half as large in bulk as the Great Blue Heron, but its long legs and neck give it nearly comparable stature. Its wholly black legs and feet, together with a bright yellow bill, form a combination it shares with none of the four other white herons known in Louisiana except at certain times the Cattle Egret, a bird so small and so stocky necked that it presents little real cause for confusion. The adult Snowy Egret has black legs and feet except for the *yellow toes*. (Re-

Great Egret Stalking Minnows

Great Egret—A Precision Landing

member that the first joint not in contact with the ground in a bird's hind limb is its heel; a bird stands on its toes only.) The bill of the Snowy Egret is black, and only the area called the lores is yellow. The immature Little Blue Heron has greenish yellow legs and toes, and the tips of the primary flight feathers are tinged with dusky. The Great Egret, which has in the past been called the Common or American Egret, is a permanent resident in southern Louisiana, moderately common in winter and abundant in summer. In mild winters fairly large numbers of individuals remain in the northern part of the state, but ordinarily at that season the bird is found principally in the coastal parishes. When the winter is severe, very few Great Egrets remain even there. Most of the known nesting colonies are scattered throughout the coastal parishes.

SNOWY EGRET *Egretta thula* Pl. III; pp. 148, 150

The Snowy Egret's immaculate white attire, with its adornment of delicate lacelike plumes, which it displays at the nest, harmonizes with its graceful form to make it one of the loveliest of all birds. It breeds commonly throughout the state, but the largest colonies, those comprising thousands of individuals, are in southern Louisiana. The number remaining in the coastal marshes in winter varies considerably, being large in some years and comparatively small in others. For example, on the Sabine Christmas Bird Count of 1956 only 18 were noted, but the following year 438 were tallied. In the interior of the state the species is rare or absent from November to mid-March.

The species is about one-half the size of the Great Egret and, like it, has black legs and tarsi. But the toes of the Snowy Egret are yellow instead of black. It also resembles the immature Little Blue Heron, which is all-white except for the dusky-tipped primaries; the legs and feet of the Little Blue are greenish yellow. It is also similar to the Cattle Egret; but in the latter the bill is never black, and the size is appreciably smaller.

LOUISIANA HERON *Hydranassa tricolor.* Frontispiece; Pl. III

This species and the Little Blue Heron occur together in winter and during migration in our coastal marshes, but when the breeding season comes they segregate ecologically. The Louisiana Heron remains primarily a bird of the marshes along the coast, where it is abundant and nests commonly in

Snowy Egret Going Places

mangrove thickets; the Little Blue Heron becomes almost entirely a bird of freshwater ponds and lakes and of riverbanks.

The abundance of the Louisiana Heron in winter varies from year to year. One-day counts in the last week of December and the first week of January in Cameron Parish, which provides some of the most favorable habitat for the species in the state, have ranged from as few as 3 to as many as 254, and a Christmas Bird Count in 1972 in the Bonnet Carré Spillway, near Reserve, tallied 600. By early March the marshes are again studded with Louisiana Herons and remain so until late November or early December.

In summer, when nesting is over, many Louisiana Herons desert the coastal, brackish-water marshes and wander northward over the state. In the environs of Baton Rouge they have occurred from late April to November, with the greatest frequency from June to September. As a consequence of the postnuptial wanderings, the species often appears at many other inland localities such as Natchitoches and Shreveport.

The dark-colored upperparts and contrasting white belly identify the present species at a glance. Birds of the year are, however, decidedly more rufescent than the adults, and the color of almost the entire neck is rufescent. Also, this species is somewhat larger than the Little Blue Heron.

BLACK-CROWNED NIGHT HERON   *Nycticorax nycticorax*   Pl. III

Night herons are distinguished from other herons by their much shorter legs and thick, heavy bills (hence the name *gros-bec* among Louisiana's French-speaking people). Adults of this and the following species are distinctively marked (see next account) and present no difficulty in identification when seen in good light; but unfortunately, as the name implies, night herons are sometimes not seen in good light. They usually leave their daytime roost just at sunset and hence are often observed as silhouettes. Even under these adverse conditions, however, two excellent field characteristics separate the Black-crown from the Yellow-crown: in flight only the toes of the Black-crown extend beyond the tail and the call is a coarse *quark*, while in the case of the Yellow-crown part of the tarsus also protrudes clear of the tail and the call is a less harsh *quak*. Immature night herons resemble the American Bittern but are a drab or grayish brown instead of a rich, yellowish brown. The Black-crowned Night Heron is fairly common throughout the state in suitable situations in summer, but in winter is almost entirely restricted to the southern parishes, where its numbers are greatly reduced in winter.

Snowy Egret in Nuptial Strut

YELLOW-CROWNED NIGHT HERON   *Nyctanassa violacea*
Pl. III; p. 152

The adult of this species is gray except for the black head with its white cheeks and creamy white crown. The adult Black-crowned Night Heron is black backed with the underparts white and with the neck and head gray except for the black crown, from which extend three long nuptial plumes. Immatures of the two species can best be distinguished by the degree to which the feet extend beyond the end of the tail as noted in the previous account. Experienced observers can recognize a young Yellow-crown by the grayer brown of its plumage, its somewhat scrawnier build, and the different facial profile produced by its heavier bill.

The Yellow-crowned Night Heron is a permanent resident, fairly common in summer but decidedly uncommon in winter, when it appears to be limited to the extreme southern part of the state and when it is much less numerous than the Black-crown. Participants in the annual Christmas Bird Count at Cameron have failed to find the species on half the occasions when the count has been taken. Migrants begin to leave early in September and to return by early March. As in the case of the Green Heron and the Cattle Egret, the routes of most seem to pass directly across the Gulf of Mexico.

LEAST BITTERN   *Ixobrychus exilis*   Pl. III

Bitterns, although members of the heron tribe, are greatly different from herons in many regards, particularly in their actions and behavior patterns. They are entirely marsh dwellers and are extremely secretive in their habits. Most often they are seen on the edges of mud flats in the marsh or on the edges of canal banks. At the slightest alarm they freeze and point the bill upward. The vertical streaks on the breast and throat align with the yellowish bill. The bird as a whole, even to the yellow eyes, becomes part of its mosaic background of marsh grasses, blending perfectly with it and becoming almost invisible. This habit of pointing the bill skyward earns for bitterns the name "sun-gazer" and provides one of the most striking examples of a behavior pattern associated with a device of protective coloration. That the bird instinctively knows that its upturned bill and vertically streaked breast blend with the grasses behind it is shown by the fact that, as the observer circles to one side or the other, the bittern slowly turns so as to keep its breast in sight.

Yellow-crowned Night Heron, Its Reflection, and Its Shadow

The diminutive Least Bittern, which is similar to a meadowlark in body bulk though not in shape, stands out from all other herons because of its very small size and buffy-colored wing patches, which contrast with its black back. Although resembling in general habits its larger relative the American Bittern, it differs in the main season of its stay with us. All but an occasional individual have left us by the closing days of October. A few early migrants reappear in our marshes in late February or early March, but most arrivals occur during the first part of April. Surprisingly, the paths followed make this seemingly weak flier the fourth in the quartet of trans-Gulf migrants among the herons. The species is a common summer resident in cattail marshes throughout Louisiana. The nest is suspended between stalks of marsh plants and is a woven mass of vegetation, sometimes containing twigs. The four or five eggs are bluish white.

AMERICAN BITTERN *Botaurus lentiginosus*   Pl. III

Compared with the preceding species, this bittern, our only other, is such a giant that an observer needs no additional means to tell them apart. In coloration, streaking, and size, the American Bittern most closely resembles immatures of our two night herons. But its plumage is a richer brown with a black mark usually visible on the side of the neck; and, as it takes flight on arched wings, the primaries and secondaries are seen to be blackish. It exposes itself somewhat more frequently than the Least Bittern. Sometimes, as we drive along the highways through the marshes of Cameron Parish, we spot an American Bittern standing completely unconcealed in the short grass on the shoulder of the road. If we alarm the bird by stopping the car, it comically seeks to escape detection by a trick that does not work in the open. It erects its neck and thrusts its bill skyward in an attempt to merge into a background of reeds, in a situation so far detached from reeds that the maneuver makes it only more conspicuous.

Technically, the American Bittern is a permanent resident in Louisiana. It has been recorded here in every month of the year, with most of the summer observations coming from noncoastal parishes. But we have had no clear-cut evidence of breeding since 1930. The furtiveness of the bird hardly suffices to account for the scarcity of records in summer, for at that season it advertises its presence with an arresting vocal performance that sounds like an old-fashioned water pump being primed or, at a greater distance, like a stake being driven into the mud by a wooden mallet. From October to May, however, as a result of the influx of migrants from the north, the species becomes quite numerous in the coastal marshes. The four or five buffy unmarked eggs are laid on a platform of rushes, cattails, and grasses built in a wet situation, usually at least a few inches above the ground.

The Stork Family
Ciconiidae

WOOD STORK *Mycteria americana* Pl. IV; Fig. 61; p. 155

Although formerly called the Wood Ibis, the present species is not an ibis at all but is instead a true stork. Its relatives in Europe often build their nests on rooftops of human dwellings and are, therefore, among the best known of all birds. The body of the Wood Stork is white, the flight feathers and tail are glossy black, the legs are long, and the black skin of the head is featherless. The last-named character is the basis for the vernacular name "gourdhead," by which the species is commonly known in this state.

The Wood Stork is said to have bred in the southern parishes as late as 1918, but now we have no known nesting rookeries even though it is fairly common to common throughout the state in summer. In Louisiana as a whole it has been recorded nearly every month of the year, but at Baton Rouge its occurrence has been limited to March and April and to late summer, when flocks are rather frequently observed in the vicinity of heavily wooded swamp areas of the state and in our coastal areas. Actual numbers vary appreciably from year to year, probably in accordance with fluctuations in water levels. In the summer of 1953, when swamps in Arkansas were largely dry because of drought, Wood Storks became unusually abundant in some sections of southern Louisiana, as, for example, in Cameron Parish.

"Gourdhead," or Wood Stork

There on July 10, John P. Gee estimated a single flock of Wood Storks at 350 to 400 individuals, and Robert J. Newman, as recently as July 29, 1973, reported an aggregation of 800 in Cameron Parish. Where these birds come from is a puzzle, because the breeding success of the Wood Stork in the United States in recent years has shown evidence of drastic decline. The species is now on the "Blue List" of *American Birds*, a publication of the National Audubon Society.

The Ibis
Family
Threskiornithidae

This family includes the ibises and spoonbills, all of which are long-legged, long-necked wading birds. In the former the bill is downcurved; in the latter, as the name implies, it is flattened and spoon shaped. They fly with their necks outstretched, not with their necks hunched back on the shoulders, S-shaped, in the manner of herons. Also, the flight of ibises is quite unlike that of herons. The former beat their wings much more rapidly and glide at frequent intervals, alternately flapping and sailing. Thus many characters serve to distinguish members of this family from herons and heronlike birds.

GLOSSY IBIS   *Plegadis falcinellus*   Pl. IV; p. 157

This species is an uncommon permanent resident in the state. It has been reliably recorded as breeding only in the Mississippi River delta and on islands in Barataria Bay but in rather sparse numbers. Because this species and the White-faced Ibis are extremely similar in appearance in their winter

---

Plate IV   Adult Ibises, the Greater Flamingo, the Roseate Spoonbill, and the Wood Stork

1. Glossy Ibis (p. 156) in breeding plumage. 2. White-faced Ibis (p. 157) in breeding plumage. 3. White Ibis (p. 158). 4. Roseate Spoonbill (p. 160). 5. Greater Flamingo (p. 163). 6. Wood Stork (p. 154). 7. Scarlet Ibis (p. 160).

1

2

3

7

5

4

6

RET
48

The Glossy Ibis Sometimes Appears to Have a White Face

plumage, differentiation between the two at that time is almost impossible, except under the most favorable circumstances. Consequently, we have no way of knowing the true relative abundance of the Glossy Ibis in winter. The two species can be distinguished when examined at close range with binoculars or a spotting scope, but most flocks do not permit such close inspection. The eye color is brown in the Glossy Ibis, red in the White-faced Ibis. And the bare skin of the face is dark grayish or blackish in the Glossy, reddish brown in the White-faced. Otherwise, in winter they each possess the same dull brown feathering on the head and neck that is flecked with white, and the color of the body, including the feathers of the wing, is the same dull iridescent green interspersed with some purplish feathers.

WHITE-FACED IBIS *Plegadis chihi* Pl. IV

In the rice fields and coastal marshes of southwestern Louisiana we commonly see flocks of these birds probing their long, curved bills into the water and mud for their food. At a distance they appear entirely black. At closer range the observer discovers that the coloration of adults in spring and early summer is mainly a rich maroon intermixed on the wings and back with highly iridescent purple and green and that a rim of white feathers borders the base of the bill, surrounds the bare facial area, and passes behind the blood red eye. From this white area the bird derives its name. The bare skin at the base of the bill is raspberry red but often appears blackish at a distance. In winter, White-faced Ibises, having lost the rich maroon coloration and white face in the annual postnuptial molt, are dark iridescent green above and brownish below, and the head and neck are brown, finely streaked with white. Only with great difficulty can this and the preceding species be distinguished at this season (see previous account).

In Louisiana the White-faced Ibis is so strictly a bird of the coastal marshes and rice fields that not even in southwestern Louisiana, where it is abundant, does it wander far from its preferred habitat. The species is quite common in the vicinity of Barataria Bay and in the delta region below New Orleans, where it is present the year around. The identity of dark ibises observed from time to time in the marshes at the west end of Lake Pontchartrain remains undetermined.

One of the largest rookeries of the White-faced Ibis in the state was for many years located at a place called "The Burn," in the deep marsh a few miles north of Little Cheniere in Cameron Parish. In some bygone year of great drought, marsh fires burned deep into the peat soil in this area, forming a depression that later became a pond surrounded by low bushes and a few willow trees. The area was the nesting site and winter roost for several thousands of these birds. I have not visited "The Burn" in recent years, but I have heard rumors to the effect that the site may now have been abandoned as an ibis rookery. The nest of sticks and rushes of the White-faced Ibis is placed in low bushes in the marsh and the three or four eggs are pale green in color.

WHITE IBIS *Eudocimus albus*   Pl. IV; Fig. 61; p. 159

The White Ibis is a permanent resident, almost entirely restricted in winter to the coastal marshes but nesting at least as far north as the swamps below Ponchatoula. It is most abundant from the middle of March to the end of September. In late summer, however, individuals wander northward over the state, even as far as Shreveport. White Ibises occur in freshwater swamps much more frequently than their relatives, but they also nest in mangrove communities in coastal bays. They build a nest of sticks and twigs and lay

White Ibis—A Study in Graceful Beauty

White Ibis Wading up to the Hilt

four greenish white eggs. An immense rookery of thousands of nesting pairs
of these birds is located in a wooded swamp lying near Pass Manchac between Lakes Pontchartrain and Maurepas. In 1941 another large rookery
was discovered in an almost inaccessible swamp a few miles from Thibodaux.
Individuals from these great rookeries fan out in all directions, sometimes for
considerable distances, in their daily search for food. In some years hundreds of White Ibises can be seen passing over the city of Baton Rouge each
afternoon in early summer, flying in the direction of the Pass Manchac
colony. In other years the afternoon flights pass south of the city, probably
because the most favorable feeding places are differently located. In any
event, many of the birds must travel daily well over 50 miles from their
homes.

The White Ibis is all-white except for its black-tipped wings and its reddish orange legs, bill, and facial mask. The immature starts out with the
neck streaked, the back and wings brownish, the tail blackish, and the uppertail coverts, rump, and belly white. As is true of all ibises, this species flies
with its neck outstretched, alternately flapping its wings rapidly and sailing.

[SCARLET IBIS   *Eudocimus ruber*]   Pl. IV

Although John James Audubon claimed to have seen three of these spectacular birds at Bayou Sara, near St. Francisville, on July 3, 1821, and I previously accepted the record, I now believe the species should be relegated
to the status of hypothetical occurrence in the state. The Scarlet Ibis occurs
only casually even in the West Indies and Central America, its center of distribution being in tropical South America. The bird is entirely scarlet except
for the black-tipped wing feathers, and some experts contend that it is only
a geographically restricted color phase of the White Ibis.

ROSEATE SPOONBILL   *Ajaia ajaja*   Pl. IV; p. 161

Roseate Spoonbills, which are also called "flame birds" or "pink curlews,"
are almost incredible birds. Their pink and white general color, highlighted
by areas of vivid blood red on the breast, wings, and lower belly, their long
legs, and their spoon-shaped bill, which is over six inches long, make a flock
of these birds the most spectacular sight in our marshes. As recently as the
1940s, the Roseate Spoonbill was considered rare in Louisiana, and any
day an ornithologist saw one here registered in memory as a special day indeed. Now the species has made such a strong comeback in Cameron and

Roseate Spoonbill, the "Flame Bird"

Vermilion parishes that it is probably as numerous there as it ever was in the past, even before plume hunting decimated the population. Two large concentrations found between Pecan Island and White Lake in March 1973 were estimated to total between 1,400 and 1,600 birds. The observer, John T. Lynch, thought the spoonbills were preparing to nest there; but our only present breeding sites known for certain are an island in Sabine Lake and the Lacassine National Wildlife Refuge, where the flame birds share a rookery with Olivaceous Cormorants, American Anhingas, and various species of herons. There, in well-built nests of sticks lined with dead leaves and bark, they lay their three dull white eggs streaked with brown.

Oddly, though the Louisiana colonies are the northernmost for the species and though spoonbills in Texas are to a large extent migratory, our populations do not vacate the southwestern parishes in winter. On the 1972 Christmas Bird Count, the Sabine National Wildlife Refuge total of 252 birds exceeded the figure of each of the several Texas areas reporting the species. The sedentary tendencies of Louisiana spoonbills are rather dangerous. During the ice storms of early 1973, at least 100 perished.

Records of the Roseate Spoonbill outside our two southwesternmost parishes are as yet few. Occurrence at Marsh Island, in Iberia Parish, and on the Isles Dernieres, in Terrebonne Parish, may be regular and, having been noted at the proper season, may even have involved nesting birds. But other records have a more vagrant quality. They have included since 1955 sightings in the following parishes: Calcasieu (near Lake Charles), St. Charles (Bonnet Carré Spillway), and East Baton Rouge (Walker). But the most unexpected observation of all, and the one farthest out of range, was made at Catahoula Lake on September 23, 1968, when Leslie Glasgow and Richard K. Yancey saw a flock of 20.

The
Flamingo
Family
Phoenicopteridae

Specialists are not in complete agreement on the taxonomic position of the flamingos. The birds possess a bizarre combination of characters—part heronlike and part swanlike. Indeed, they are so much like the latter that some experts would prefer to treat them as members of the Anseriformes, which includes the swans, geese, and ducks. Flamingos, like the swans and their allies, possess webbed feet, lamellate bills, and elevated hind toes. The newly hatched flamingo is heavily covered with down and is very cygnetlike in appearance. Adult flamingos are frequently seen to alight on deep open water and to swim swan-fashion with the neck in a graceful loop. In the vicinity of their nesting rookeries they utter low, conversational notes that are strongly reminiscent of the noises made by a flock of Snow Geese in the process of feeding or roosting at night on a prairie marsh. But, despite all these anserine features, the flamingos resemble the herons and ibises in certain anatomical respects and in the manner of their feather molt. Consequently, Dr. Alexander Wetmore, in drawing up his classification of the orders and families of the birds of the world—an arrangement almost universally followed by ornithologists—placed the flamingos in a separate suborder at the end of the Ciconiiformes and just before the Anseriformes.

GREATER FLAMINGO   *Phoenicopterus ruber*   Pl. IV

This large, grotesque, pink bird was formerly called the American Flamingo before taxonomists decided that one of the Old World members of the family belongs to the same species. It owes its inclusion on the Louisiana list to W. L. McAtee, the great authority on the food habits of North American birds, who saw a single individual on December 6, 1910, in Cameron Parish. The species has appeared on the coast of Texas on several occasions and for this reason might be expected to recur in Louisiana. A large colony of several thousand flamingos breeds in Yucatan, just across the Gulf of Mexico from Louisiana. An occasional stray individual could wander northward or be driven here by hurricanes that sweep up from that direction. Although the Greater Flamingo and Roseate Spoonbill are both pinkish in color, there is no reason for confusing them. As the accompanying illustrations show, the two are radically different in form. Only firsthand or carefully authenticated records, however, are acceptable, since the Roseate Spoonbill is sometimes erroneously called "flamingo," and since the possibility of birds escaped from captivity must be taken into consideration.

DUCKS
AND ALLIES
Order *Anseriformes*

The Swan, Goose, and
Duck Family
Anatidae

THIS FAMILY of birds in North America comprises, according to specialists, seven subfamilies—the swans, geese, tree-ducks, dabbling ducks, diving ducks, stiff-tailed ducks, and mergansers. Each has much in common with all the rest, as is evident from the fact that all belong to the same family, but each is likewise different in one or more notable structural characteristics. For instance, among other things, the tree-ducks are long legged; the mergansers have serrated, or sawlike, edges to the bill; and the diving ducks possess a prominent, fleshy lobe on the hind toe that the dabbling ducks lack. For the most part these are distinctions that can only be made when the bird is in the hand. Yet the experienced naturalist or the intelligent hunter is able to recognize at a glance not only the subfamilies but also various species in each group by characteristic differences, some subtle, some not—in general shape, posture on the water, outline in the air, or special markings—and often is able to do so nearly as far away as the duck can be seen (see Fig. 42).

Of all the birds that inhabit Louisiana, these are the ones for which our state is best known—for throughout the continent, the great Louisiana marshes are recognized as a duck and goose paradise. There the birds find hundreds of square miles of water, rushes, roseau cane, three-cornered grass, and other marsh vegetation that form superb habitat. When autumn comes, millions of ducks pour out of the northern lakes from Alaska and British Columbia to Labrador and funnel down into the Mississippi Valley, eventually settling for the winter in southern Louisiana. A good portion of the entire continental population of the Snow Goose winters in or near Cameron Parish. And from there to Mississippi, ducks of many varieties, along with the geese, abound in winter.

WHISTLING SWAN   *Olor columbianus*   Figs. 41, 61

The Whistling Swan is the only all-white bird presently occurring in Louisiana that habitually flies with its long neck outstretched. All the other long-necked largely white birds of similar flight posture found or likely to be found here—the Northern Gannet, White Ibis, Wood Stork, Snow Goose, and Whooping Crane—show conspicuous black markings, at least at the tips of the wings (Fig. 61). Swans are now extremely rare in this part of the United States. The present species has been positively identified less than two dozen times in Louisiana, although it is quite common on the Atlantic Coast in winter. The few records of it in our state are scattered from mid-November through mid-February.

The overwhelming probabilities are that any wild swan seen in Louisiana at present is a Whistling Swan. Another species, the Trumpeter Swan, presumably occurred here in the early years of this century, and the two are so difficult to distinguish from one another that we cannot place full confidence in identifications made in that bygone time. But the population of Trumpeters closest to Louisiana today (50 birds on the La Creek National Wildlife Refuge in South Dakota) is so small, so faraway, and so sedentary that the possibility of an individual straying to our state is now slim. Most

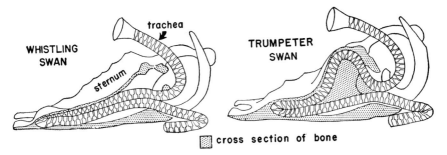

Figure 41   The arrangement of the trachea or windpipe in the breastbone of the Whistling Swan and Trumpeter Swan. In the former it merely loops on itself within the sternum, while in the latter a partition of bone separates a section of the tracheal fold within the sternum.

CHARACTERISTICS OF SUBFAMILIES OF DUCKS
AND THEIR ALLIES

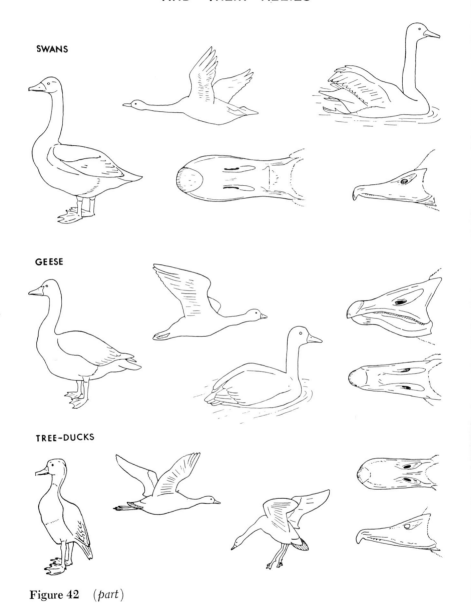

SWANS

GEESE

TREE-DUCKS

Figure 42   (*part*)

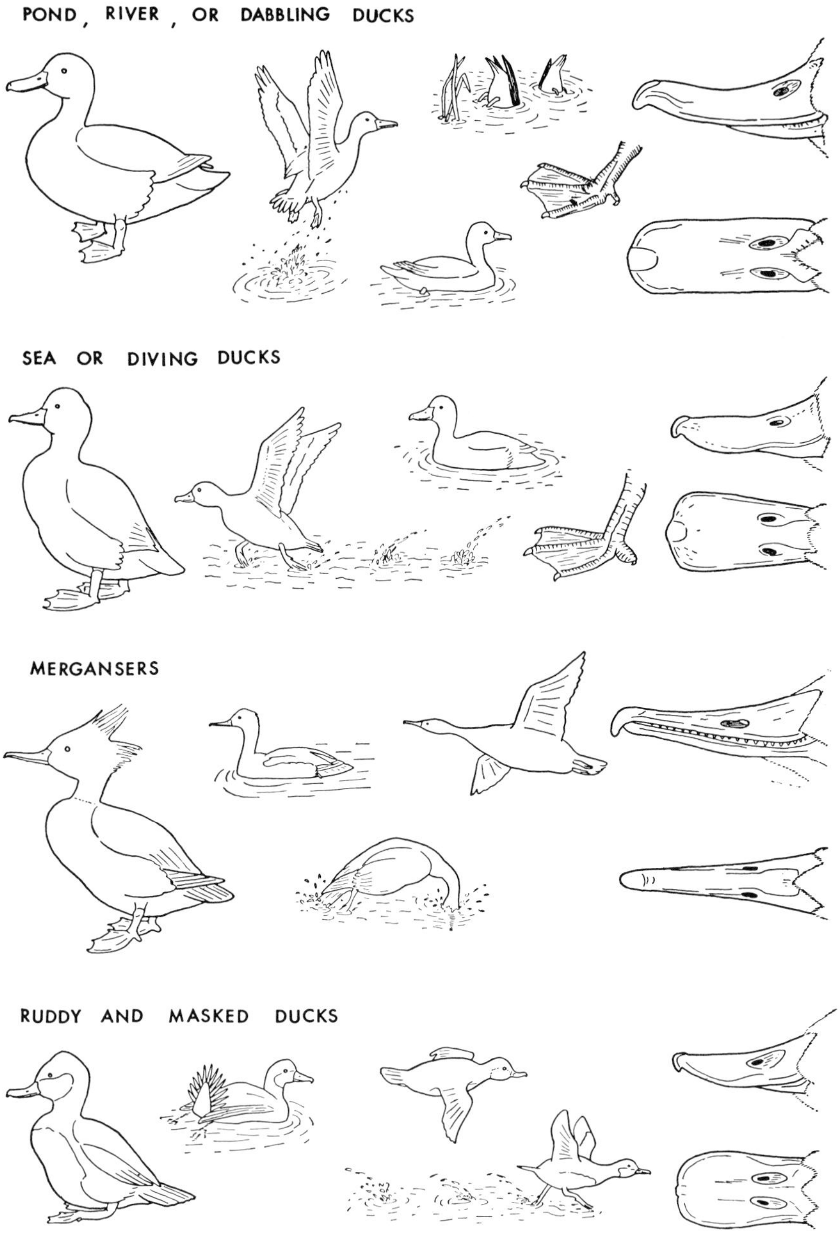

POND, RIVER, OR DABBLING DUCKS

SEA OR DIVING DUCKS

MERGANSERS

RUDDY AND MASKED DUCKS

Figure 42   (concluded)

adult Whistling Swans have an oval yellow spot at the base of the bill, a feature unique among swans, but some individuals lack this mark. So its absence does not establish that a swan is a Trumpeter. The distance of the nostril from the end of the beak, a character mentioned in some bird books, seems too variable to be dependable. Measurements and weights overlap; but, unless very thin, any full-grown native swan weighing less than 20 pounds is a Whistling Swan. By far the best criterion is in the relationship of the trachea, or windpipe, to the breastbone in the two species. In both, the windpipe loops through a cavity in the breastbone. In the Trumpeter, however, the windpipe has a loop over a bony hump in the breastbone. In the Whistling Swan the loop of the windpipe in the breastbone is at no point separated by a bony partition, and the windpipe simply folds on itself in passing in and out of the breastbone (Fig. 41).

The Mute Swan (*Cygnus olor*) is a European species that is now common in the feral state in the vicinity of Long Island and in other localities on the middle Atlantic seaboard. Wing-clipped individuals can be seen in some of the city parks in Louisiana. One of these birds might also go wild. Though none has yet been known to do so, the identification marks of the species should be kept in mind. In the adult Mute Swan there is a bulbous, black swelling at the base of the pinkish bill. In the immature, the bulbous knob is absent, but the dusky bill *is* suffused with pinkish. A distinction from the two preceding species diagnostic in birds of any age is that the trachea is simple, not entering the breastbone at all.

TRUMPETER SWAN *Olor buccinator*   Fig. 41

This magnificent swan, largest of all native North American waterfowl, was once believed to be on the brink of extinction. Now its name is no longer even on the list of rare and endangered species. The change came about partly through the painstaking efforts of conservationists to build up the populations on national wildlife refuges and in national parks and to maintain them under rigid protection. But a still bigger factor was the discovery in the 1960s that several thousand of the birds breed in Alaska. In 1973, the U.S. Fish and Wildlife Service estimated the number in Alaska as approximately five thousand—more than seven times the total residing in the lower 48 states. Originally Trumpeters nested as near to Louisiana as Indiana and Missouri. But the species requires almost complete solitude on its breeding grounds; hence, as more and more of the wilderness areas of the early American West were settled by man, the farther and farther back the bird retreated. In winter the Trumpeters abandoned much of their breeding season wariness and frequently exposed themselves to hunters. The resulting losses far exceeded reproductive gains, for the species is extremely unprolific. And so for a long time the known number of Trumpeter Swans sank lower and lower.

In the preceding account, I have explained that one cannot tell all Whistling Swans and Trumpeter Swans apart without internal examination. There I concentrated on points that enable ornithologists to identify some Whistling Swans. Here I shall call attention to external features that permit recognition of some Trumpeters. If a swan has a narrow salmon-colored streak on the mandibles or 24 instead of 20 tail feathers, it is a Trumpeter; but having fewer than 24 tail feathers would not prove it is something else. Any swan, other than a Mute Swan, more than 55 inches long, with bended wing of more than 23 inches and weighing more than 20 pounds is probably a Trumpeter.

To what extent earlier naturalists who reported Trumpeters in Louisiana were aware of the identification problems, no one can say for certain. And unfortunately no preserved specimen has come down to us to attest that the species ever occurred here. Indeed we have only one completely dated report, and it is surrounded by a measure of uncertainty. Oberholser's *Bird Life of Louisiana* says that Stanley C. Arthur photographed a Trumpeter Swan near Avery Island on January 7, 1915. In his own published account of the event, Arthur states that he first saw this bird in the winter of 1914–1915 but did not photograph it until its return in the *following* winter. Accordingly, if the picture *was* taken on January 7, the year must have been 1916. T. Gilbert Pearson has written that in November 1914 at Belle Isle Lake he saw a swan that was later shot by a fisherman and identified by Arthur as a Trumpeter. Arthur's own published works make no mention of this bird. Direct evidence that the Trumpeter Swan is entitled to a place on the state list is thus rather insubstantial. Circumstantial evidence, however, is strong because the general distribution of the species in the olden days practically guarantees its former presence here in winter.

CANADA GOOSE *Branta canadensis* Pl. V; Fig. 43

The "Canadian honker," as this now uncommon winter visitor is often called, needs little or no introduction, at least to the older generation. Up to the middle of the present century, when the first cool air from the north moved into Louisiana in early autumn, the first V-shaped formations of

Canada Geese would be seen winging their way southward over our state or settling on the sandbars along our large rivers. The majority of them would end up on the coastal prairies, particularly in southwestern Louisiana; however, the flats along the Mississippi River would also hold a few during the winter months. The main fall flights appeared by late September and the species remained with us in numbers until late March. Honkers were always much less numerous in Louisiana than the Snow Goose. But the establishment in the Mississippi Valley of many new waterfowl refuges, each of which is tending to retain more and more Canada Geese in winter, has wrought great changes in the status of the species in our state.

By the beginning of the 1960s, the number of Canada Geese reaching Louisiana had declined so drastically that the hunting of the big birds in our state was halted. At about the same time, biologists at Rockefeller Refuge began attempts to counteract short-stopping by establishing a nonmigratory population of Canadas in our marshes and prairies that included many birds of the subspecies *maxima*, the so-called Giant Canada Goose, which were imported from Minnesota. By 1973 the numbers of these resident geese had increased to an estimated two thousand, and the establishment of satellite

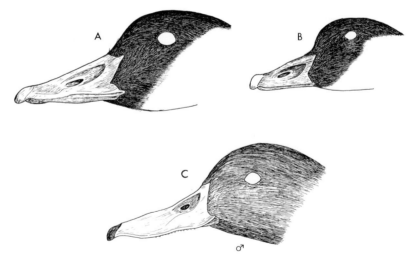

Figure 43   Head of one of the large forms of the Canada Goose (A) and that of its diminutive relative the "Richardson's" Goose (B) in comparison with the Mallard (C). Note particularly the size of the bill in each.

Plate V   Adult Geese

1. Canada Goose (p. 169). 2. White-fronted Goose (p. 173). 3. Blue morph of Snow Goose (p. 174). 4. White morph of Snow Goose (p. 174).

flocks away from Rockefeller Refuge was begun. The most distant of the releases was south of Gueydan, but, if plans work out, we may anticipate seeing Canada Geese at some future time almost anywhere in the coastal parishes on any day of the year.

Variation in color and size among the Canada Geese that have migrated into the state has been considerable. No hunter who has killed many of these birds has failed to note that some individuals are much darker breasted than others. And some are huge, long-billed, long-winged birds, while others are diminutive. Much of this variation is now known to be geographic in nature as a result of the work of specialists who have studied large series of specimens from various breeding populations. These studies have led to the description of several subspecies. Some ornithologists, however, believe that not all of the observed variation is subspecific. Instead, they contend that *two species* are involved, which, although very similar in color pattern, are actually discrete, noninterbreeding entities—or at least entities between which hybridization happens too infrequently to affect the overall complexion of the population. These specialists would recognize on the one hand, the Canada Goose (*Branta canadensis*), and on the other hand, the small Richardson's Goose (*Branta hutchinsii*). The latter, to be sure, is only a miniature edition of its larger relative, but the size differences are conspicuous. Indeed, the so-called Richardson's Goose is not much larger than a Mallard, and its bill is unusually small (Fig. 43). Also, there is evidence that this diminutive goose has numerous peculiarities in its behavior, such as its choice of nesting sites and the way in which it constructs its nest. Even on its wintering grounds it does not always associate with the larger birds, as was evident in the winter of 1952–1953 when a flock of 15 individuals of the *hutchinsii* type resided for two months on the Sabine National Wildlife Refuge in Cameron Parish. This little group was always seen apart from other geese, unquestionably avoiding their company.

Although the problem requires much additional study, based in part on the acquisition of breeding specimens from some of the more inaccessible parts of the Arctic, I, for one, would be inclined, on the basis of current evidence, to recognize the two species. But in order to conform here as nearly as possible to the AOU *Check-list of North American Birds*, I have treated them together under the name *Branta canadensis*. Most of the records of the diminutive form in Louisiana are from late November to late January and from the southwestern part of the state. But it never made up more than a tiny percentage of the Canada Geese wintering with us; and, now that the migration of the species into the state has been reduced to a trickle, it must be considered rarer than ever, even though one was seen at Gum Cove in a flock of larger geese as recently as 1973.

COMMON BRANT *Branta bernicla*   Fig. 44

Only two individuals of this species have been observed in the state. One was a bird that stayed from November 27 through November 30, 1960, in City Park, New Orleans, where it was observed by numerous ornithologists and photographed by Buford Myers. What was presumed to be the same individual was reported on the New Orleans lakefront in January 1961, and, interestingly enough, it was possibly, if not probably, the one seen in Mississippi Sound off Pass Christian, in the same month. Another Common Brant appeared on the Rockefeller Refuge on January 15, 1974, and was collected near the refuge headquarters in the late afternoon of January 17 by A. W. Palmisano. The specimen now reposes in the LSU Museum of Zoology.

The species resembles the Canada Goose but is smaller, and not only the head and neck are black but the chest as well. When the bird is afloat, the black of the chest extends to the waterline, whereas in the Canada Goose the black ends at the bottom of the neck, leaving much white showing above the waterline. The white throat and cheek patch of the Canada is replaced in the Common Brant by a flecking of white on the side of the neck (absent in immatures). In the latter species, the sides are whiter, and the rear is conspicuously white instead of largely black. The means of distinguishing the Common Brant from the Black Brant are discussed in the next account.

BLACK BRANT *Branta nigricans*   Fig. 44

On October 21, 1972, at the east jetty at the mouth of Calcasieu Pass, a Black Brant flew past three experienced ornithologists, Robert J. Newman, Ronald J. Stein, and Melvin Weber, giving them an excellent look at a range closer than 100 feet. The entire black belly and the slash of white on the neck were specifically noted by all three observers. The general form and the slash of white on the upper neck serve to distinguish this species as a brant, and the wholly black breast and belly separate it from the Common Brant. Although I would ordinarily hesitate to add a species to the

Figure 44 Common Brant (left) and Black Brant (right).

state list on the basis of a sight record alone, the competence of the observers in this instance seems to justify this action. But the matter may be
academic because in all probability the Black Brant is entitled to nothing
more than subspecific status as a race of *Branta bernicla*. It has been so
treated by such experts as Jean Delacour, James L. Peters, Peter Scott, and
Charles Vaurie. The last-named authority did, however, leave the matter
somewhat open to question. The AOU Committee on Classification and
Nomenclature still recognizes the Black Brant as a full species, and, for this
reason, I am likewise doing so.

WHITE-FRONTED GOOSE   *Anser albifrons*   Pl. V

This fine goose, which commonly goes by the name "specklebelly," is a
moderately common winter resident in Louisiana, sometimes abundant locally. Fall migrants begin to arrive in early October, and the last spring migrants are usually gone by April 15. Since the main North American contingent of the species winters in southern Texas and in Mexico, these geese
occasionally become somewhat less numerous here in midwinter. In the

Gum Cove area of Cameron Parish, White-fronted Geese congregate by the thousands and sometimes outnumber all other geese combined. The situation was the same over 60 years ago when W. L. McAtee wrote of the relative abundance of geese in Cameron Parish.

The adults are easily recognized by the irregular black blotches on the belly and by the white-feathered area that surrounds the base of the bill. The young, however, resemble the immature of the blue morph of the Snow Goose, from which they may be distinguished by their yellow instead of bluish feet and their light-colored bills. The flight note of the specklebelly is a clanging, high-pitched cackle that has been described as *kah-lah-a-luck*.

SNOW GOOSE   *Chen caerulescens*   Pl. V; Fig. 61; p. 175

In previous editions of this work and in virtually all other ornithological publications prior to 1973, the Snow Goose and the Blue Goose were treated as two separate species. Now, as a result of action by the AOU Committee on Classification and Nomenclature, these two geese are officially considered to be the white and blue morphs of a single species, the Snow Goose. The name alludes to the snow that is so characteristic of the bird's Arctic breeding grounds, not in any way to the largely snowy plumage of the white morph. The two forms are identical in nearly every feature except color, and they freely interbreed, producing individuals that exhibit an intermediate combination of the parental colors.

A common but unfortunate practice in Louisiana is the application of the name "brant" to this goose. The true brants, which have already been treated in previous accounts, are quite different. They are found in winter on the Atlantic and Pacific coasts, only rarely in the Mississippi Valley.

Each autumn tens of thousands of Snow Geese pass southward down the Mississippi Valley to winter in Louisiana's immense coastal marshes. Each spring they rise out of these same marshes to wing their way northward. For generations men have watched this seasonal procession and have never failed to be thrilled by it. But to those who studied birds and sought to learn about their lives and habits, the northward migration held, until 1929, a special challenge. Once the blue individuals in the flocks had passed over the forests and fields of southern Canada, they disappeared completely. No one knew where they went, where they laid their eggs, where they built their nests, the color of their eggs, or the appearance of their downy young. All these things then seemed momentous matters, for the blue morph was

Blue and White Morphs of the Snow Goose Fill the Sky

thought to be an unquestionably distinct species, and it was one of the very few common birds of the continent whose breeding grounds remained unknown to science.

The eventual finding of the nesting area was unique among similar accomplishments in the vast polar reaches of North America in that it was made as a "result of direct and intentional research, in contradistinction to fortuitous discovery." A concerted search, begun in 1923, lasted six years and covered an approximate distance of 30,300 miles. Then on June 26, 1929, J. Dewey Soper, acting for the Canadian Department of the Interior, discovered the species raising its young on the faraway tundra of western Baffin Island—"vast, sodden marsh-lands bounded by the reeking mud flats and the everlasting ice of Foxe Basin; . . . a gloomy land, haunted by leaden skies and harassed by chilling gales of rain and snow." After describing the setting in these terms in his classic report, *The Blue Goose*, Soper continues: "In such a land the Blue Goose is born and raised to take part in the long flight to the softer clime of his winter home on the coast of Louisiana." These words were written in a flush of high triumph over the discovery of nests of a "species" that ironically turned out not to be a species at all but only a Snow Goose in different dress! Yet Soper's finding was what began the train of events that led to the realization that Snow and Blue Geese constitute a single species.

In former years, the so-called Blue Geese had the reputation of taking off from staging areas on the shores of James Bay in Canada and flying for the most part nonstop to wintering grounds that lay mainly in Louisiana. The young birds of the year, with comparatively few hours of flying practice since pecking their way from the egg in midsummer, were the ones least consistently able to withstand the ordeal of the long journey and most likely to drop out of the flight to rest. And so in the lower Mississippi Valley, along the last leg of the long trek, one would not infrequently encounter "stopover blues," mostly immatures—in fields, along roadsides, or in small ponds and lakes.

Stopovers due to fatigue are a continuing feature of the fall migrations, but the situation is now complicated by a new factor. As previously noted with regard to the Canada Goose, the establishment of numerous refuges in the upper Mississippi Valley—where supplementary, artificial feeding and the maintenance of open water in winter are common practices—is causing increasingly large numbers of Snow Geese of both morphs to terminate their autumn flights long before reaching southern Louisiana. In 1971, for instance, a Christmas Bird Count at Shenandoah, Iowa, recorded 283,000 Snow Geese, a marked contrast to the 27,200 of these birds reported on the Sabine-Cameron count. The point may be raised that not all Snow Geese in Louisiana are within the Sabine-Cameron census area. But neither are all birds wintering outside Louisiana within the Shenandoah census area. Perhaps the resulting change in long-established habits accounts for the greater frequency with which small flocks of half a dozen or so Snow Geese are being found in winter in our northern parishes.

The adult blue morph of the Snow Goose, with its dark body and white head, is often called the "eagle-head goose." Seldom, however, is the head of either the blue or the white morphs immaculate white; it is instead highly

---

Plate VI Some Dabbling Ducks and the Fulvous Tree-Duck

1. Mallard (p. 181), male in front, female behind. 2. Black Duck (p. 182) in front; Mottled Duck (p. 183) behind. 3. Northern Pintail (p. 184), male in front, female behind. 4. Fulvous Tree-Duck (p. 180). 5. male Gadwall (p. 183). 6. Northern Shoveler (p. 187), male in front, female behind. 7. male European Wigeon (p. 188). 8. male American Wigeon (p. 189).

discolored with ferruginous stains acquired as a result of the bird's habit of "grubbing" in the marsh for its food of roots and tubers. A more startling color alteration is the dyeing being practiced by waterfowl biologists that results in the presence in our marshes of vivid yellow and bright red individuals.

The first Snow Geese arrive in the state in early September, but the main passage takes place after the first week of October, sometimes as late as the very end of that month. The bulk of the population departs in late April and early May, though a few nonbreeding individuals are sometimes found in the marshes in midsummer.

ROSS' GOOSE *Chen rossii*   Fig. 45

This goose, which is not much larger than a Mallard, is a miniature edition of the white morph of the Snow Goose. It differs further from its larger relative by lacking a "grinning" patch (broad black area between the closed mandibles) and by having on the base of the disproportionately small bill a series of warty protuberances, which, however, cannot be seen in the field at any great distance. The neck feathering commonly, but not always, shows a furrowing of the feathers. Size in direct comparison with Snow Geese and the abbreviated bill are the quickest clues to identity, but the observer should bear in mind that young Snow Geese of the year are only about two-thirds as large as adults and that Snow-Ross' Goose hybrids, intermediate in size between the parental species, are occasionally found in the state (see beyond). In the opinion of most of the state's waterfowl specialists, the Ross' Goose occurs in Louisiana each winter in small numbers. The scarcity of definite records may be attributed to several factors: the subtlety of the identification marks; the impossibility of seeing the smaller bird when it is on the ground in the midst of a flock of the larger Snow Geese; and the failure of waterfowl researchers to report observations of a bird too rare to be of great importance to sportsmen.

In addition to two old records of the species in southwestern Louisiana, recent observations include a flock of 11 seen near the Gibbstown ferry in Cameron Parish in the winter of 1967–1968. Three were shot and one of these was mounted and put on display in the Rockefeller Refuge headquarters on Grand Cheniere. It is an indubitable purebred Ross' Goose.

The species was long believed to nest only in the Perry River region on the Arctic Ocean and to winter almost entirely in California. Now, it is known to nest much farther east, on the edge of the breeding grounds of the

Figure 45   Head of the Ross' Goose, showing the warty protuberances at the base of the bill, which, along with the much smaller body size, serve to distinguish the species from the similar-appearing white morph of the Snow Goose.

Snow Goose, and there to produce hybrids with the white morph of the Snow Goose. Such intermediates between the two species have been captured, photographed in the hand, and banded by waterfowl experts on the Sabine National Wildlife Refuge, in Cameron Parish. The existence in the Mississippi Valley wintering population of geese of these hybrid crosses, which are intermediate in size between a purebred Ross' Goose and the small western race of the white morph of the Snow Goose, further compounds the difficulty of recognizing the Ross' Goose in the field.

BLACK-BELLIED TREE-DUCK   *Dendrocygna autumnalis*   P. 179

Since the last edition of this work, unimpeachable evidence has documented the right of the Black-bellied Tree-Duck to a place on the Louisiana list. The species is a strikingly handsome bird and one that sometimes seems to display a friendly affinity toward man. Indeed, the most attractive pets I have ever owned were four Black-bellied Tree-Ducks that I once kept free-winged in my yard. We called them our *qua-ne-quas*, a name derived from their call notes.

As a result of the bird's attractiveness, it has been procured for numerous live waterfowl collections in southern Louisiana, and at least some of the reports that have been received of the species in the wild are doubtless of escapees. On November 26, 1970, however, Scott Sealy and Mark Dickson, while passing a small pond on the Sealy farm, which is about five miles north of Bossier City, noticed an unfamiliar duck amid the decoys they had set there. Dickson shot the bird and later Scott called Horace H. Jeter, who went out to the farm to examine the specimen and found it to be a juvenal Black-bellied Tree-Duck, showing no evidence of having been in captivity. The specimen is now in the LSU Museum of Zoology. Still stronger proof of the natural occurrence of the species in the state is the shooting of one near Pecan Island on December 20, 1969, that had been banded on April 10, 1968, near Sinton, Texas.

Black-bellied Tree-Ducks have been purposely liberated at Rockefeller Refuge in Cameron Parish, and according to John T. Lynch they have nested there at considerable distances from penned enclosures. Under the circumstances, we can never again be sure that a Black-bellied Tree-Duck seen in Louisiana is a bird of wholly wild ancestry, unless, however, it again happens to wear a band showing that it was originally captured under natural conditions within the normal range of the species.

One glance at a tree-duck is enough to reveal, even to the uninitiated, why it is classified separately from other ducks. The legs and feet are exceptionally long and in flight extend well beyond the tail in a most unducklike manner. This species is easily recognized by the long, red legs and red bill, the black belly, the reddish brown upperparts and chest, the gray face and throat, and the predominantly white upper surfaces of the wings.

Black-bellied Tree-Duck

GEORGE H. LOWERY, JR.

FULVOUS TREE-DUCK *Dendrocygna bicolor*   Pls. VI, VII; Fig. 42

The Fulvous Tree-Duck is rather common in south-central and southwestern Louisiana, where it nests in rice fields. It can be found most consistently in the vicinity of Crowley, where most of the state's population of four to five thousand birds seems to be centered. The only record for northern Louisiana is the report of 12 seen by D. T. Kee and others on May 9, 1973, in a large flooded field seven miles southeast of Monroe; but during times of migration, in March and April and again in October, Fulvous Tree-Ducks can be observed along the coast, sometimes even on mud flats. By the first week of November, practically the entire population has moved southward to southern Texas or Mexico. Pen-reared birds set free at Rockefeller Refuge in small numbers have been inclined to winter, but, even before any known releases had occurred, observations had been made in the state in every month of the year.

One of the common names is "Mexican squealer," which is appropriate on two counts, because so much of the winter range is south of the border and because the call is a long, squealing whistle. The long, bluish legs and long neck, the tawny coloration, U-shaped white patch at the base of the tail, and the strong gooselike flight make the species easily identifiable. The wing-beat is slow, and the bird not infrequently glides. At a distance and in silhouette it somewhat suggests a White-faced Ibis. When coming in for a landing the body and neck assume an inverted V posture, much like that of a goose about to land, instead of feet first and head high like most ducks.

John T. Lynch, who has made a special study of the nesting of the Fulvous Tree-Duck in Louisiana rice fields, reports that nest building does not commence until the middle of July. He says that the nests are built on low rice field levees or on the dikes of the drainage canals and, not infrequently, are floating structures in the flooded rice stands themselves. These rafts are described as averaging 15 inches across and 10 inches deep, the immersed portion being 4 to 5 inches thick. Rice straw is the principal material used in the nest construction. Lynch further states that the clutch size varies from 10 to 15 eggs, 12 to 14 being the average.

Plate VII   Ducks in Adult Winter Plumage

(Males above when both sexes are shown) 1. American Wigeon (p. 189). 2. Blue-winged Teal (p. 186). 3. Northern Shoveler (p. 187). 4. Northern Pintail (p. 184). 5. Green-winged Teal (p. 185). 6. Wood Duck (p. 190). 7. Red-breasted Merganser (p. 209). 8. Hooded Merganser (p. 207). 9. Fulvous Tree-Duck (p. 180).

R.E.Tucker

Mallard Drake

MALLARD *Anas platyrhynchos* Pls. VI, X; Fig. 43; p. 181

This common winter resident is the best known of all North American ducks and requires no special introduction. It has been extensively domesticated and is thus often seen in barnyards and parks. Wild Mallards occur state-wide from mid-October to late April, and they remain in some localities throughout the year. The actual breeding of wild stock is known to take place occasionally in the coastal marshes, where, however, the few resident Mallards may tend to hybridize with Mottled Ducks. The male has an iridescent green head, a dark breast, a light upper surface, and a white ring around the neck. The speculum is iridescent bluish green, bordered by white lines. (The speculum is the rectangular patch of contrasting colors on the trailing edge of the secondaries that is found in most dabbling ducks.) Whereas the male can hardly be confused with other species, the female closely resembles both the Mottled and Black Ducks. From these she differs in being lighter colored and by having conspicuous, white outer tail feathers. The speculum is bordered by the two prominent white bars, whereas in the other species mentioned there is never more than one conspicuous white bar.

The Mallard is the first of the subfamily Anatinae, the dabbling ducks. The species in this group are also called pond ducks, since ordinarily they inhabit shallow lakes, ponds, and sloughs, where they can get their food by tipping up and dabbling, rather than by diving. Most of their food consists of material that they are able to reach with only the front half of the body submerged. Diving ducks (subfamily Aythyinae), on the other hand, go down to depths of 30 feet or more for their diet of fish and aquatic plants. The dabbling ducks usually swim with the tail high out of the water and spring straight upward into the air when taking flight. They generally have a pronounced speculum of iridescent colors in the wing and only a minute lobe on the hind toe. In contrast, the diving ducks typically hold their tails close to the water when swimming and have to run for some distance over the surface before becoming airborne. They also lack a speculum and have a well-developed lobe on the hind toe (see Figs. 36 and 42).

BLACK DUCK *Anas rubripes*   Pls. VI, X

This species winters annually in the state in small numbers, but its main wintering grounds are to the east of us. It arrives in early October and remains until the end of March. The best place in the state to look for the Black Duck is among the Mallards in the soybean fields of the northern half of the state. Catahoula Lake and the Saline Wildlife Management Area are especially convenient locations, but everywhere the Black Duck is outnumbered by the Mallard 100 to 1. Although the Mottled Duck sometimes wanders northward and may occasionally appear in northern Louisiana, any duck of the Black-Mottled type seen in the upper half of the state is likely to be the former species. In the coastal marshes the reverse tends to be true but with more exceptions.

Unlike the male and female Mallard, the sexes of the Black Duck are quite similar. The present species is a large blackish duck, with prominent white undersurfaces to the wings, which show in flight. The speculum is an iridescent purple. The Black Duck is most likely to be confused with the Mottled Duck, but the latter is paler with a less streaked head and neck, an immaculate throat, and a more greenish speculum, often bordered in back by a prominent white line. Even in fresh plumage the Black Duck has only a faint white line on the back of the speculum, and this is usually concealed in the folded wing. Field identifications that distinguish between the Black and Mottled Ducks should be made with great caution.

MOTTLED DUCK   *Anas fulvigula*   Pl. VI

This is the "summer duck," a bird well known to residents along our Gulf Coast, where the species nests commonly and often occurs in considerable numbers in winter. This is the only duck that breeds in large numbers throughout the great Louisiana marshes. Most ducks withdraw far to the north and west of us to hatch their young. This is not true of the Mottled Duck, however. A bona fide native, it would surely speak a special brand of Cajun, if ducks could talk, so typical is it of the French section of our state. By the end of March, Mottled Ducks are building their well-concealed nests of grasses, softly lined with contour feathers and down plucked from their breasts, and laying their 8 to 11 greenish white eggs. The nests are often but not always in a salt or brackish marsh, sometimes on the edge of a lake or pond, but not infrequently hidden away in a great expanse of reeds and rushes some distance from open water. The species also nests in marshes that are essentially freshwater and in the rice fields of the southwestern Louisiana prairies.

As already noted, the Mottled Duck resembles two of its close relatives that occur here. It is distinguished from the female Mallard by the absence of white outer tail feathers and by having only one white bar on the wing where the hen Mallard has two. It is considerably paler than the true Black Duck, has a greenish instead of purplish speculum, and has a white wing bar while the Black Duck has only a faint indication of one in fresh plumage, or none in worn plumage. The Mottled Duck is sometimes rather scarce in winter, when the bulk of the population possibly moves down along the Texas coast or even into Mexico. The species seldom ranges northward in the state above the coastal tier of parishes.

GADWALL   *Anas strepera*   Pls. VI, X

The Gadwall is generally known to sportsmen in Louisiana by the name "gray duck." The male is a drab, gray bird that on the water shows few distinctive markings; the female is even less well marked. The drake possesses a chestnut patch on the forepart of the wing and has a white, rectangular patch on the rear part of the wing, but when the bird is at rest the flank feathers sometimes cover these markings. The rump and the feathers under the tail are black, and the sharp contrast of these parts with the gray body provides the best feature for field identification. The female appears plain

Male Northern Pintail in Duplicate

brown at a distance and when at rest nearby can best be identified by the white patch in its wing and by its yellowish bill. It is browner (less grayish) than the female Northern Pintail, and the feet are yellow instead of gray.

From early October until April the Gadwall is one of the commonest ducks in the coastal regions of southern Louisiana, especially in Cameron Parish. It is less common in the interior, though in favorable locations it still ranks at least fourth among the dabbling ducks.

NORTHERN PINTAIL *Anas acuta* Pls. VI, VII; p. 184

Both sexes of this species may be easily distinguished by their long, pointed tails—particularly long in the males because of the great length of the central tail feathers. Furthermore, the adult male has a brown head with a white stripe on the side of the neck. The female is separable from other nondescript dabbling ducks by her greater slimness, proportionately longer and thinner neck, and bluish bill. The bill and feet of both male and female are bluish gray.

Pintails, or "sprigtails" as they are sometimes called, generally arrive in numbers from the North during the middle of September and are widespread and common over the state until April, sometimes lingering in coastal localities until May. Occasional birds remain to breed in the coastal marshes, for a female with a brood was seen in 1971 on the Delta National Wildlife Refuge, near the mouth of the Mississippi River. Pintails are highly esteemed by sportsmen as among the most delicious of all ducks.

GREEN-WINGED TEAL   *Anas crecca*   Pls. VII, VIII

In some years a special early season is arranged for the shooting of teal—and teal only. Its objective is to give hunters in the United States a chance to bag Blue-winged Teal, which pass in abundance in early fall but for the most part move on to the tropics before the main duck season begins. Federal regulations permit state game authorities to select for the early hunting of teal any nine-day period in September, and the Louisiana Wild Life and Fisheries Commission has usually set the dates as late as this formula allows. Yet, even though some Green-winged Teal have reached us by the closing days of August, the main flights of the species, which make it one of the commonest ducks in our coastal marshes, do not move in until after the early teal season has ended. In consequence only 20 to 25 percent of the teal killed in September in Louisiana have been Green-wings. For many years, when bag limits were on a strictly duck-for-duck basis, experienced hunters avoided shooting this species in the regular season, for one Mallard or an equally delectable Canvasback would outweigh a teal three to one. Under the point system, instituted in 1973, the Green-winged Teal finds its legal advantage diminished and its hazards increased.

Because of their small size and their distinctive markings, the three species of teal are not likely to be confused with other kinds of ducks. The male of the present species has a reddish head with a prominent green stripe through the eye and a conspicuous vertical white mark in front of the wing. At rest on the water the female can hardly be distinguished from the female Blue-winged and Cinnamon Teals except by her shorter bill and consequently different profile, unless she flutters her wings and reveals their color pattern. Green-wings, both male and female, have largely dark wings, whereas Blue-winged and Cinnamon Teals both have the whole forepart of the wing pale blue. The present species remains with us until the first of April, rarely later.

BLUE-WINGED TEAL   *Anas discors*   Pls. VII, VIII; p. 186

Some Blue-wings always remain in the Louisiana marshes during the summer to breed, laying 8 to 12 light, cream-colored, unmarked eggs in a down-lined nest of reeds and grasses on the margin of a pond or slough. Numbers have varied unaccountably from year to year from a barely perceptible presence to fairly impressive showings. A few individuals also occur here in midwinter, but the species is most abundant in the migratory seasons—in late summer and early autumn and again in spring. Blue-winged Teal winter abundantly in Mexico and even as far away as South America, and the passage of these intrepid travelers causes the seasonal fluctuations in local abundance. Migrant Blue-wings are by far the earliest ducks to appear in Louisiana as part of a southward migration; before the last week of August they are here in numbers, and by the time the other ducks pile into our marshes, the main body of Blue-wings has moved on to points farther south.

Identification of the adult male Blue-winged Teal is easy because of the combination of large blue wing patches and the crescent-shaped white marking on an otherwise dark head. Females and immatures, however, are difficult to distinguish when at rest from the females and juvenile males of the Green-winged Teal, in which the wings are dark with a small green speculum. No satisfactory means exists for separating the females and juve-

Male Blue-winged Teal and Its Mate

ALLAN D. CRUICKSHANK

nile males of Blue-winged and Cinnamon Teal, since all have a large patch
of blue on the forepart of the wing and are otherwise almost identical. The
latter species is rare in this state, and almost all nondescript ducks with blue
wing patches can be assumed to be the Blue-winged Teal. The similarly
colored female Northern Shoveler, of course, poses no problem because of
her distinctive profile.

CINNAMON TEAL *Anas cyanoptera*   Pl. VIII

This western species is not reported every year in the state, but it probably
occurs here with fair regularity in small numbers, despite the fact that less
than two dozen dated records are on file. The numbers by parishes are as
follows: nine from Cameron, three from Plaquemines, two each from Bossier, Caddo, Orleans, and St. Charles, and one each from St. Landry and
St. Bernard. Extreme dates are October 20 and April 21.

Hunters who happen to bag one should send the whole specimen packed
in dry ice to the LSU Museum of Zoology in order that the specimen can
be preserved. The highly attractive cinnamon red color of the head and
body of the male of this species and its lack of a white crescent-shaped mark
on the face make it easily identifiable. But in the case of all such birds of
rare occurrence, a preserved specimen is desirable. The young male, less than
a year old, and the female are indistinguishable in the field from Blue-
winged Teal of comparable age and sex. Specimens in these plumages can
be identified in the hand where a careful study is made of certain structures
such as the bill, but field identification should not be attempted except in
the case of adult males.

NORTHERN SHOVELER *Anas clypeata*   Pls. VI, VII

Sportsmen and men of the marsh country call this bird the "spoonbill"
because of the spoonlike shape of its long bill. Although much is rightfully
said of the beauty of the Wood Duck, the color pattern of the drake Northern Shoveler leaves little to be desired on this score. The head is green, the
back and tail black, the breast and shoulders white, the forepart of the wing
blue, and the sides nothing less than claret red. The female is rather drab
and inconspicuous. Like the male, she has a large patch of pale blue on the
forepart of the wing. In this respect she resembles the Blue-winged Teal, but
she is bigger and has a large spoon-shaped bill.

The Northern Shoveler usually arrives here in numbers in late September or early October and stays with us until late April and early May, sometimes through the summer, although none has yet been found nesting. It is one of our commonest ducks, being especially numerous in spring.

[EUROPEAN WIGEON   *Anas penelope*]   Pl. VI

Although all comprehensive works on the birds of Louisiana since 1918, including my own, have included this species without reservations, I now believe that the basis for doing so is insufficient. Accordingly, I am now placing it on the list of species of hypothetical occurrence. Three specimens, a male and two females, were allegedly killed in Cameron Parish in 1915 by W. B. Lea, at Cameron Farms, 14 miles south of Vinton, and a female that was identified as this species was collected by P. A. Daigre 3 miles north of Alexandria in about 1929. Unfortunately, in neither case was a specimen preserved or were any details supplied telling on what basis the identifications were made. Since the male of this species is strikingly different in coloration from all other ducks, one might suppose that the Cameron Parish record was surely valid, but we have no information concerning the competence of the collector, and we do not know what books were available to him at this early date that would have illustrated the species in color or given its diagnostic features. Both records were obtained before the advent of the first Peterson's *Field Guide* or of any of the other works stressing bird identification that have since become available. The Alexandria record, being that of a female, is highly suspect, despite the ornithological competence of the collector, because of the great similarity between females of this and the following species. If the specimen had been preserved, however, its identification could be verified at a glance by inspection of the dark color of the axillars beneath the wing.

The European Wigeon, which is also called the Eurasian Wigeon, is not known to breed in North America, except rarely in Greenland, but occurs rather regularly on both the Atlantic and Pacific coasts of the United States in fall and winter and inland in spring. It comes to us possibly from Iceland or Scandinavia, conceivably by some great circle route.

Plate VIII   Ducks in Adult Winter Plumage

(Males in foreground when both sexes are shown) 1. Blue-winged Teal (p. 186). 2. male Green-winged Teal (p. 185). 3. male Cinnamon Teal (p. 187). 4. Wood Duck (p. 190). 5. male Canvasback (p. 195). 6. male Redhead (p. 192). 7. Ring-necked Duck (p. 194). 8. male Common Goldeneye (p. 198). 9. Lesser Scaup (p. 197). 10. Old-squaw (p. 199). 11. Bufflehead (p. 199). 12. Ruddy Duck (p. 204).

In plumage pattern and outline the European Wigeon resembles the following species, but the male has a grayish (instead of brownish) back and sides and a reddish head with a cream-colored crown. In the American Wigeon, the head is grayish, finely streaked with dusky; there is a green band passing from the front of the eye to the nape and thence down the back of the neck; and the top of the head is usually white, although occasionally it is buffy. The female European Wigeon, when seen at close range, shows a slightly reddish tinge to the head, a color the female American Wigeon lacks. Hunters shooting female wigeons should inspect the axillars (see Fig. 7). If these feathers are *dusky* instead of pure white the bird is a European Wigeon and should be sent at once to the LSU Museum of Zoology. The species has been seen in winter in Texas on several occasions, and therefore observers in Louisiana should keep close watch for it.

AMERICAN WIGEON   *Anas americana*   Pls. VI, VII; p. 189

This is the species that was once officially known as Baldpate or simply "wigeon." The names "zin-zin," "whistling duck," and "whistling dick" are also applied to the species, all in reference to its call notes. The male utters

Male American Wigeon

ALLAN D. CRUICKSHANK

a rather musical *whew, whew, whew* that is repeated at frequent intervals. The notes of the female are *qua-awk, qua-awk.*

The American Wigeon is a common winter resident over the entire state; but like nearly all our ducks, it is much more abundant in the coastal areas. The main contingent of the species arrives in October and departs in late April or early May, although a few individuals sometimes reach here in September and others sometimes linger into the summer.

The male of this species is easily distinguished by the white (rarely buffy) top of its head and by the extensive area of *white* on the *forepart* of the wing. (The white in the wing of the Gadwall is on the speculum and hence toward the hind part of the spread wing.) In good light a green patch through the eye and black undertail feathers may be noted. Females and immatures resemble female American Pintails; but the body is browner in contrast to the gray head, the white patch is usually present on the forepart of the wing as in the male, and the elongated central tail feathers are lacking. The bill in both sexes is bluish with a black tip and is so short that its very size serves as a useful field character.

WOOD DUCK *Aix sponsa* Pls. VII, VIII

Most naturalists agree that the male Wood Duck is North America's most beautiful bird. Its color pattern is resplendent with rich chestnut, splashes of black and white, golden flanks, and even red eyelids arrayed amid iridescent greens, purples, and bronze. In addition to all this, the feathers of the head form a crest, as if a final touch of splendor were needed. The female has a rather nondescript grayish brown body and gray-crested head, with a prominent white ring around the eye. Even in flight at distances where none of its brilliant colors can be seen, the Wood Duck remains a distinctive bird. It holds its head above the level of the back with the bill pointed downward at a sharp angle. It also has a long, squarish tail and a short neck. The call note, which is often uttered in flight, is a squealing *hoo-eek, hoo-eek.*

This species and the Hooded Merganser are among the few North American ducks that normally nest in hollow trees. The nest of the Wood Duck is placed at heights varying from 4 to as much as 50 feet from the ground. The nest cavity itself may be quite shallow or as much as 6 feet deep. No materials are transported to the nest, but down feathers from the breast are used to cushion the normal complement of 10 to 15 dull white or creamy white eggs. Nesting boxes of the proper size, erected specifically for Wood Ducks, have met with great success.

The cutting of the forests, drainage of swamplands, excessive hunting pressure, and, probably above all, the commercial traffic in feathers for artificial trout flies nearly led to the Wood Duck's extinction. Timely action in 1918 forbade the killing of the species in both the United States and Canada, and the bird has now made a notable comeback. Since 1941 limited hunting has been permitted. In the point system currently in force, the Wood Duck is a 90-point bird. With the hunter being allowed 100 points, he can have in his bag two Wood Ducks, provided he has nothing else.

Some people object to the point system on the ground that learning to tell the species apart is too hard a task. But first-rate sportsmen already know how to recognize the various kinds of ducks both on the water and in the air, and beginners will find that mastering the art adds immeasurably to the fun of hunting.

A few brief words should be said about the classic debate among naturalists and sportsmen concerning the question of how young Wood Ducks get out of their nests high up in hollow trees. Some have said that the mother bird carries them in her bill down to the water. Others have claimed that the baby chicks ride on the mother's back or are carried between her feet. Still others have insisted that the ducklings climb from the floor of the

Ducks Rising Out of the Marsh

ALLAN D. CRUICKSHANK

nest to the entrance by using the sharp nails on their claws, jump spread-eagled into space, and hit the ground or water with their tiny feet outstretched. All three explanations have alleged eyewitness testimony to support them, though the last has been most frequently observed. Perhaps, as Audubon told us long ago, Wood Ducks vary their methods of getting the young to water according to circumstance.

Some years ago, I am told, an investigator trying to incubate and raise Wood Ducks in captivity for experiment met with great frustration. His hatchlings refused to eat and quickly died of starvation. Then one day he happened to drop one. Immediately, according to the story, it began to search for food. So he lifted aloft his other downy young Wood Ducks and let them fall. They began at once to look for something to eat. This tale led to the idea that a baby Wood Duck's life is a series of rigidly programed events, each of which is needed to trigger the next. Unfortunately for the theory, other breeders of Wood Ducks, notably Peter Scott, a British waterfowl specialist of worldwide fame, and our own John T. Lynch, have been raising these birds successfully without knowing that they needed to be dropped before commencing to eat.

The Wood Duck is a moderately common permanent resident throughout the heavily wooded swamps of the state. In the northern parishes it is possibly somewhat less numerous in winter than in summer, but in southern Louisiana its population appears to increase slightly in the cold months. Finding a Wood Duck in the coastal marshes is unusual, though a few instances are on record. But they seem out of place in a setting without trees. Possibly they go to the marshes only in the daytime to feed, returning at night to some wooded swamp on the northern edge of the marsh belt.

REDHEAD   *Aythya americana*   Pls. VIII, X; Fig. 46

This is the first of the species in the subfamily Aythyinae, the diving and sea ducks. Members of this group are generally found in deep waters. Unlike the preceding dabbling ducks, which simply tilt in the water, head down, tail and feet in air, feeding only as deep as the outstretched neck will reach, the diving ducks plunge under the surface and sometimes pursue fish to great depths or feed on plants growing on the bottom. The first step in the identification of a duck on the water is to decide to which of these subgroups it belongs (see Fig. 42). A diving duck usually sits with the tail close

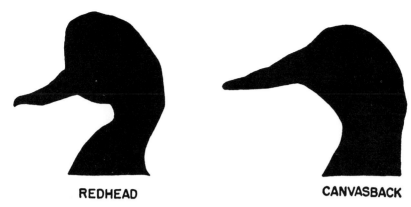

REDHEAD   **CANVASBACK**

Figure 46   Profiles in silhouette of two similarly colored ducks. In the Redhead the junction of the bill and the forehead forms almost a right angle, while in the Canvasback the angle is widely obtuse. The latter fact earns for the Canvasback its colloquial name "horse duck."

to water level rather than elevated, it runs across the water for some distance before taking wing instead of springing into the air, and it actually dives beneath the surface for food instead of dabbling.

As the name foretells, the male of this species has a red head, but so does the male Canvasback. The two may be distinguished by the color of the back, gray in the Redhead, all-white in the adult Canvasback; and in the present species the break between the *blue* bill and the forehead is marked by a sharp angle, whereas in the Canvasback a continuous and almost even slope connects the base of the *black* bill with the top of the head (Fig. 46). The female Redhead may be separated from the female Canvasback by its browner upperparts (less whitish) and by the angle between the forehead and bill, as described above. More confusion is likely to result between the female Redhead and the female Ring-necked Duck. The former has at best only a slight suffusion of whitish at the base of the bill instead of a well-defined white cheek patch, and it lacks the female Ring-neck's prominent white eye-ring.

Redheads are rather uncommon winter residents on our inland lakes, but sometimes they appear in great rafts of several thousands in our coastal waters, most consistently in Chandeleur Sound. They arrive in numbers during the first week of October and remain until the latter half of April.

Female Ring-necked Duck

RING-NECKED DUCK *Aythya collaris* Pls. VIII, X; p. 194

The name of this bird should have been ring-*billed* duck. Although it does possess a deep chestnut ring around an otherwise black neck, this feature is not nearly as conspicuous as the white ring around the bill. The Ring-necked Duck resembles the two kinds of scaups and often occurs with them, especially with the Lesser Scaup. If, however, one knows what to look for, the present species may be distinguished at great distances. The male Ring-neck, or "blackjack" as it is often called, has a black back and a prominent vertically elongate white patch before the wing. Drake scaups, on the other hand, have a salt-and-pepper-colored back that appears *very white* at a distance (suggesting the Canvasback at times), and they lack the slash of white in front of the wing. The bill of a scaup, instead of being ringed with white, is plain bluish with a black tip, hence the name "blue-bill." Females of the two are somewhat less distinct but still easily distinguished. Female Ring-necks have a white eye-ring and a light area around the bill that gradually blends in with the dark rear portion of the face and head, whereas female scaups have a prominent and sharply outlined creamy white patch at the base of the bill and no eye-ring.

Ring-necked Ducks are common to abundant in winter on the lakes inland in the southern half of the state, somewhat less numerous in our coastal areas and much less numerous in northern Louisiana. Like most of our ducks, they usually arrive in numbers in the middle of October and leave in April. The few individuals that rarely spend the summer here and there in the state are probably wounded birds that were unable to migrate when the time came for them to do so.

CANVASBACK *Aythya valisineria*   Pls. VIII, X; Fig. 46; p. 195

This duck is very popular among sportsmen, probably because of its large size and the fact that under most circumstances its flesh is delicious, particularly when the first migrants arrive. Later, in some situations a change of diet alters its flavor. Francis H. Kortright, in his book, *Ducks, Geese and Swans of North America*, gives the average weight of 102 specimens as three pounds.

The white body, rusty-colored head, and sloping profile (see Fig. 46 and

Female Canvasback, the "Horse Duck"

ALLAN D. CRUICKSHANK

discussion under Redhead) clearly distinguish the Canvasback in the field. Immature individuals are not nearly as white on the back as adult males, but the color of their heads and the slope of their profiles serve to identify them. The female is light grayish and brown but possesses the head profile characteristic of its mate. The French name, *canard cheval*, or "horse duck," is an allusion to the shape of the head.

The species is a late arriver in the fall, making its appearance ordinarily in late October. It is usually gone by the last half of April but sometimes remains until late May or even later. Records are available for every month of the year.

GREATER SCAUP   *Aythya marila*   Fig. 47

To distinguish between this and the following species on the water is a difficult feat. Its size is slightly larger, but this difference can be reliably ascertained only when the two are swimming in close proximity, thus affording direct comparison, or by measurements of a specimen in the hand. In the proper light, the head of the male shows a mostly greenish gloss, whereas in the Lesser Scaup the sheen is generally purplish, the colors varying somewhat with the incidence of light. In flight the Greater Scaup reveals a white stripe that extends, in both sexes, much farther toward the end of the primaries—well beyond the wrist instead of just to the wrist. Head shape is another alleged point of distinction but varies too much with the wetness of the feathers to be of much help. The comparative scarcity of records for this species in the state is attributable in part to the difficulty of distinguishing it from its smaller relative. One's tendency to call all scaups "lessers" probably leads to correct identification in the vast majority of instances, at least in freshwater situations. The conservative course in most instances, however, would be to record either species simply as "scaup." The salt-and-pepper color of the back, though it reflects in the sunlight as almost pure white, even at great distances, gives the scaups their common name of *dos-gris*. The other common name, "blue-bill," is self-explanatory (see discussion in connection with the Ring-necked Duck).

The Greater Scaup is said to frequent salt water more than the Lesser Scaup. Indeed, it is called *dos-gris de mer* in southern Louisiana. Nearly all records of its occurrence here range between November 2 and April 6. Specimens and good sight records are on file for the intervening months as well, and a specimen in heavy molt was taken five miles west of Cameron on July 24, 1971.

Figure 47 Wings of the Greater Scaup and Lesser Scaup. In the former species the white in the primaries is much more extensive.

LESSER SCAUP *Aythya affinis* Pls. VIII, X; Fig. 47; p. 198

This is one of our most abundant ducks and surely one of the best known. It goes mainly by two names, "blue-bill" or *dos-gris*. In size and color it resembles the Ring-necked Duck, but it has a blue bill, lacking the white ring around the tip. The back is speckled black and white and, in sunlight at a distance, reflects only slightly darker than the white sides, whereas the Ring-neck's back is black. Seen from the side the scaup lacks the prominent vertical white stripe, or slash, before the wing that is so characteristic of the male Ring-neck. In the female scaup the line of demarcation is very sharp between the creamy white area at the base of the bill and the dark face; in the Ring-neck this light area blends almost imperceptibly into the dark-colored area of the cheeks. The distinctions between the Lesser and Greater Scaups are discussed in the preceding account.

A few Lesser Scaup are almost always present on some of our larger lakes

Males of the Lesser Scaup, or *dos-gris*, in Formation

in summer, but there is no evidence that the species has ever nested in the state. Migration begins to bring in the wintering population around the first of October, although usually the species is not present in large numbers until the latter part of the month. Most of our scaups are gone by early April. Especially worthy of mention are the great rafts, often numbering into the thousands, that scaups form in winter along the rim of the Gulf.

COMMON GOLDENEYE *Bucephala clangula* Pls. VIII, X

The male of this species is a large black and white duck with a puffy dark green head (which appears black at a distance), a round white spot below and ahead of the eye, and white sides. The female has a gray body, a brown head, and a light collar around the neck. In flight large white wing patches, extending from the trailing edge of the wings almost to the dark leading edge, become visible on the upper side.

The Common Goldeneye is mainly a deepwater duck and therefore is seen most often on large lakes and on bays and lagoons along the coast.

Although never observed in large numbers in Louisiana, it occurs regularly. It arrives in November, and its early departure (late February in most cases) gives it one of the shortest stays of any of our ducks. Extreme dates of occurrence for the entire state are November 8 and April 22. Two of the best places to see this species in recent years have been the north shore of Lake Pontchartrain at Fontainebleau State Park and Mandeville and in the Calcasieu ship channel near Hackberry. It appears, however, from time to time on other large bodies of water.

BUFFLEHEAD *Bucephala albeola*   Pls. VIII, X

The Bufflehead, or "butterball," is a small duck (about the size of a teal) that because of its white underparts resembles a miniature Common Golden-eye. Instead, however, of a mere spot ahead of and below the eye, the male has a triangular white patch extending from below the eye over the back of the crown. The dark-headed, largely dark-sided female has an elongate white spot extending backward from *directly below* the eye.

Like the preceding species, the Bufflehead most often frequents deep water, and hence it usually stays far out in the middle of a lake or bay, where it can be studied to advantage only with powerful binoculars or a small telescope. And even when it is feeding near shore, it is likely to spend so much time beneath the surface that one glimpses it only intermittently. Although much easier to find than the Common Goldeneye, it seems never to occur in very great numbers even during its main period of residence with us, from early November to March (extreme dates are October 13 and April 23), yet such comparatively small inland lakes as False River, 20 miles northwest of Baton Rouge, have had 40 or 50 individuals wintering on them in years gone by. Now it is not easy to find them at False River because of the increased amount of motorboat activity on this body of water.

OLDSQUAW *Clangula hyemalis*   Pl. VIII

Seldom can the student of animal behavior lay down hard and fast rules to which exceptions do not sooner or later arise. Until the 1950s this account might well have read that the Oldsquaw was an extremely rare winter visitor to Louisiana and that it was most likely to be encountered near the coast if not actually in the waters of the Gulf itself. The species is, to be sure, decidedly maritime in its habitat preferences, but in the last two decades there have been more records at inland localities than at coastal ones. Moreover, there are now sufficient records to merit listing it as a rare to uncommon winter visitor from November 15 to sometimes as late as May 3. It is seen, however, much less often than the Common Goldeneye.

Neither the male nor the female is likely to escape detection, for each has its own unique pattern of black and white or brown and white, and the two central tail feathers are greatly elongated and pointed, particularly in the male. Unlike most other ducks, the drake Oldsquaw after leaving us assumes a distinctly different summer plumage. The head and neck change from predominantly white with a large dark facial patch to predominantly dark with a large white facial patch. The Oldsquaw is noted, especially in the Far North, for its vocal accomplishments. The continuous chatter uttered by migrants moving northward over Canada in spring is said to have given rise to the bird's common name. Further allusion to its vociferous tendencies is found in the scientific name; the word *Clangula* is the diminutive of the Latin *clangor*, meaning "noise."

HARLEQUIN DUCK   *Histrionicus histrionicus*   Fig. 48

For the only record of this northern duck within our state, we must go back to April 1, 1837, when John James Audubon "saw a pair in perfect plumage" in the Southwest Pass of the Mississippi River delta. This event occurred on the trip that he and Edward Harris made from New Orleans to Galveston in search of new birds along the Gulf Coast (see p. 30). The adult male is bedecked with such a lively pattern of chestnut and blues and such bizarrely shaped markings of black and white that, in the opinion of many, only one North American waterfowl, the Wood Duck, exceeds it in beauty.

WHITE-WINGED SCOTER   *Melanitta deglandi*   Pl. IX

The scoters are primarily ocean ducks. Since no concerted attempt has ever been made to study our offshore waters to ascertain what kinds of birds are found there, this and the following two species may be more common than the available records would indicate. Merely watching the open Gulf from the shore is not sufficient. The welling up of cool waters makes the area bordering the continental shelf extremely rich in plankton, which is one of the main links in the food chain of the sea. Seabirds find there an abundance of their preferred items of diet. The continental shelf, except

Figure 48   Harlequin Duck: male in foreground; female behind.

near the mouths of the Mississippi River, lies at a considerable distance from the Louisiana shore, in some places 150 miles out. Effective study of the offshore avifauna requires periodic excursions at different times of the year out to the edge of the continental shelf, and few such trips have ever been made by students of birds. Such a project would surely yield many valuable ornithological data.

The three scoters, the males of which are nearly all-black and the females almost entirely grayish brown, may be distinguished as follows: male and female White-winged Scoters have a *white patch* in the wing, which neither of the other two species possesses. The male also has the eye partially encircled by a small white patch, which is prominent in contrast to the black of the head. The females and juveniles sometimes show two white spots on their brownish faces (as in the Surf Scoter), but their *white wing patches* are diagnostic. The adult male Surf Scoter has a white forehead and nape; the adult female has two poorly defined light face patches (prominent in juveniles) and a dark crown. In the Black Scoter, the male is solid black except for the orange base of the bill; the female has a dark crown, like the Surf Scoter, but instead of two light areas on the face, the entire cheek is light in contrast to the dark crown.

From March 20, 1890, when the first recorded Louisiana specimen was shot near New Orleans, until the present time, the White-winged Scoter has been reported in the state on 21 different dates, in 17 different years. No less than 15 of the occurrences were in Cameron Parish, the most favored location being the surf between Holly Beach and Johnsons Bayou, where scoters of all three species now and again commingle with great rafts of scaups. Calcasieu, St. Mary, Jefferson, St. Bernard, St. Charles, and Pointe Coupee parishes round out the list with one record each. The Pointe Coupee Parish sighting, made by Robert B. Moore on January 13, 1962, at a borrow pit of the Mississippi River opposite St. Francisville, has the distinction of being the only Louisiana observation well inland from salt water. Most of the occurrences are of single birds. Although five White-winged Scoters were tallied on the Cameron–Sabine Refuge Christmas Bird Count of December 27, 1970, the total for all Louisiana records combined is only 27 birds.

By month, the distribution of reports is: one in October; three in November; eight in December; two in January; one in February; two in March; two in April; and one in May. One winter record did not specify the month. Extreme dates are October 17 to May 1, both occurrences near Holly Beach.

SURF SCOTER *Melanitta perspicillata*   Pl. IX

With the shooting of a specimen in the city of New Orleans on March 20, 1890, this scoter became the first to be accredited to the Louisiana list. But in the next 70 years the Surf Scoter fell into a distant second place behind the White-winged Scoter, which was recorded twice as many times. Then the Surf began to catch up: since 1960 it has been identified on more than 12 occasions, versus only 9 for the White-winged. Of course, birds seen on different occasions, even by different observers, at slightly different locations, may not actually be different birds. But the data indicate that the Surf Scoter has been the easier bird to find in the 1960s and 1970s. In terms of numbers of birds reported, the Surf is far ahead of the White-winged, with a score of 72 to 27.

As in the case of the White-winged Scoter, Cameron Parish has been the source of the most observations—13 of them. That parish has also provided our earliest date and our latest: November 8 (1964) and May 13 (1972). All the other records are for southeastern parishes: Plaquemines, one; Jefferson, one; Orleans, one; West Feliciana, one. The last-mentioned

---

Plate IX   Mergansers and Scoters

(Males above or in front; females below or behind) 1. Hooded Merganser (p. 207). 2. Common Merganser (p. 208). 3. Red-breasted Merganser (p. 209). 4. White-winged Scoter (p. 200). 5. Black Scoter (p. 203). 6. Surf Scoter (p. 202).

1

2

3

4

5

6

occurrence is particularly interesting. It involved 8 birds in company with 12 Black Scoters seen in the Mississippi River opposite the St. Francisville ferry. The date, November 24, 1963, together with the size of the flock, suggests that scoters may follow the great river as a migration route. But, if so, they seldom put down in its waters. The distribution of records by month is: five in November, five in December, one in January, one in March, four in April, and three in May. Characteristics useful in the field identification of the Surf Scoter are given in the preceding account.

BLACK SCOTER *Melanitta nigra*   Pl. IX

When the second edition of this book appeared in 1960, the Black, or Common, Scoter was the least frequently recorded of our trio of scoters, having been identified in the state only five times. One of the observations of this species, however, involved the largest group of scoters of any kind ever seen in Louisiana—a flock of 75 riding the waves of the Gulf, just off Holly Beach, in Cameron Parish, found by Eugene Wallace and myself on April 15, 1938. From 1962 on, as in the case of the preceding species, sightings increased in frequency. By 1973, the Black and Surf Scoters were tied with 19 records apiece. The year of greatest advance was 1972, when Black Scoters were noted on four different dates from April 8 to May 13, at various points between Holly Beach and Johnsons Bayou. Largely by virtue of the big count in 1938, the Black is our top-ranking scoter in terms of the number of birds reported, with a total of 120.

The species enjoys the highest rating in terms of points of record also. It has been found in nine parishes—10 times in Cameron Parish and once each in the parishes of St. John the Baptist, St. Charles, Orleans, Plaquemines, St. Bernard, St. Tammany, Natchitoches, and West Feliciana. A final record is from offshore in the Gulf, 25 miles from the mouth of South Pass. The sighting in Natchitoches Parish, made at Sibley Lake on May 25, 1970, by Robert B. Hamilton and Robert E. Noble, is the farthest inland in Louisiana for any scoter, as well as the latest ever in spring. The distribution of Black Scoter records by month is rather haphazard: two in October, four in November, one in January, one in March, six in April, four in May. The oldest record, which was represented by a specimen from Lake Catherine once preserved in the Gustave Kohn Collection (but now missing from the remainder of that collection at Tulane University), lacks a date, even for the year. Field marks for the Black Scoter are discussed in the White-winged Scoter account.

RUDDY DUCK   *Oxyura jamaicensis*   Pl. VIII; Fig. 49

The Ruddy and Masked Ducks are members of the subfamily Oxyurinae, which includes only eight species, often called stiff-tailed ducks. Most of them are found in the southern portions of the world. They differ from the diving ducks and the other subfamilies of Anatidae in a number of salient features (see Fig. 42). The tail feathers are stiff and spikelike and often held upright; the "nail" of the bill is strongly hooked downward at the tip and is sharply pointed; the legs are placed far to the rear of the body, even more so than in the mergansers, making it very difficult for them to walk on land; and their necks are thick and relatively short, drastically different in proportions from those of other ducks.

The Ruddy Duck is often seen in great rafts in some sections of the state in winter. False River, a lake formed by a meander cutoff of the Mississippi River above Baton Rouge, in some years has had a Ruddy Duck population estimated at ten thousand individuals, but now, because of the great motorboat activity there, such concentrations are no longer in evidence. The largest numbers seen on any of the recent Christmas Bird Counts in the state are those at Shreveport, where, for example, 2,500 were tallied on the 1972 census.

The species is easily distinguished from all our other ducks except the Masked Duck by its short, stiff tail feathers, which are generally held perpendicular to the body and furnish the basis for the name "stiff tail."

A regional name heard frequently is "God-damn," a blasphemy that is said, according to one explanation, to have originated in market-hunting days. Not infrequently in plucking the feathers of the back, which are deeply anchored, the market hunters would tear the skin before the feathers came out. This would expose the flesh, which, on contact with the air, turned black and rendered the bird less attractive for market display. This tearing of the skin frequently prompted the expletive noted above, and before long the words were in general use as a name for the bird itself. Another version of the interesting but profane colloquial name is given by Stanley Clisby Arthur: "In 1428 when Joan of Arc raised her white banner sprinkled with golden fleurs de lys against the English, the word *godons* (*God damus*) was used by the maid and her French soldiers to denote the English soldiers— this because the rough, fighting, red-uniformed English were continually using the expression. Therefore, in the early days anything that wore a red coat was a 'God damn' to the French and, when the early settlers found a

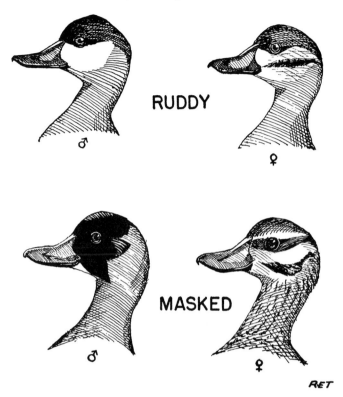

RUDDY

♂   ♀

MASKED

♂   ♀

RET

Figure 49 Heads of male and female Ruddy Duck and Masked Duck. The symbol ♂ denotes male, ♀ female.

little duck in Louisiana wearing a red coat, it was baptised by the profane name it is best known by today."

The Ruddy Duck and the Oldsquaw are the only two North American ducks with distinct winter and breeding plumages. When the first migrant Ruddies reach us in October they are brownish gray in color. The male has a dark cap and prominent white cheeks; in the female the cheeks are a dirty white and are crossed by a line beneath the eye. As spring approaches, the males begin to take on their breeding plumage, in which the back, breast, and neck become a rich ruddy red and the crown jet black. When the last of the migrant males leave us in late April or after the first of May, many are in full breeding plumage.

The species nests mainly in the central and western United States, northward to central British Columbia and northern Manitoba, but on June 5, 1969, John T. Lynch found six pairs of Ruddy Ducks in full breeding plumage in a marsh pond a mile or less west of Holly Beach, in Cameron Parish. One pair was accompanied by two one-third-grown young. On July 1 of the same year Lynch and Robert J. Newman returned to the pond and found 12 adults and 4 half-grown young. Thus was the Ruddy Duck first established as a breeding bird in the state. On June 8 and 30 and August 2, 1970, broods were noted by the same observers and others at the same pond, but no young have been seen there since, possibly because drought brought an end to breeding. The nest of the Ruddy Duck is generally located over water in dense stands of marsh vegetation, including bulrush. It lays 6 to 10 white eggs.

MASKED DUCK *Oxyura dominica*   Fig. 49

Although in 1960 I knew of only one record of the Masked Duck in Louisiana, at least five are now on file. A female was shot by a hunter a few miles south of Lake Charles on December 23, 1933. Then the species went unreported until April 3, 1967, when two out-of-state bird watchers, J. Miles and Barry Jones, observed five, including both males and females, on a pond along State Highway 27, some 10 miles south of Sulphur, in Calcasieu Parish. Even more exciting was the announcement by John T. Lynch that he had found a pair of Masked Ducks exhibiting courtship behavior in the spring of 1970 in the "Ruddy Duck pond" located less than a mile from Holly Beach (see preceding account). But several of us later visited the place repeatedly and were unable to find the birds. On January 7, 1971, a hunter, Jay Lafleur, shot a female Masked Duck immediately south of the southern boundary of the Sabine National Wildlife Refuge, along what state ornithologists refer to as the "Magnolia Road." This locality is less than two miles from the pond where Lynch observed the species in the spring of 1970. A fifth record of the Masked Duck is that of a female killed by a hunter, John Bernard, four miles southwest of Esther, in Vermilion Parish, on January 6, 1973, and initially identified by Marc J. Villien. This specimen and the other two already mentioned are now preserved in the LSU Museum of Zoology.

The secretive little duck, although until fairly recently believed to be of only casual occurrence anywhere in the United States, now appears regularly on refuges in southeastern Texas. On the basis of the Lynch observations, I believe it will sooner or later be found to nest in southwestern Louisiana.

The species is closely related to the Ruddy Duck and resembles it in appearance. As in that species, the tail feathers are stiff and are often held perpendicular to the body. The male has a black mask, a striking cinnamon coloration to the neck and body, and a prominent white patch in the wing. The female is light brown below and dark brown above, mottled with black, and has *two* black streaks on the cheeks while the female Ruddy Duck has only one. The female Masked Duck, like its mate, possesses two prominent white patches in the wing. The main range of the species is in the West Indies and Mexico and from there southward into South America. It builds its nest in situations similar to those used by the Ruddy Duck, rather than in trees as stated by one well-known field guide.

HOODED MERGANSER *Lophodytes cucullatus* Pls. VII, IX; p. 207

The mergansers are the so-called saw-billed ducks that make up the subfamily Merginae. The bill is long and very slender and the closing edges bear a row of "teeth" or serrations. From this fact stem many of their colloquial names—"saw-bill" and *bec-scie*, or "bexie." Because they feed largely on

Male Hooded Merganser

ALLAN D. CRUICKSHANK

fish, they are also called fish ducks and are seldom shot for food. They catch their prey by diving and pursuing it underwater, an art at which they are greatly adept. Mergansers float with a considerable part of their bodies submerged and do not seem to mind getting their tails wet, as do the dabbling ducks, which hold their tails high out of the water (see Fig. 42).

The Hooded Merganser is a moderately common winter resident and an uncommon breeder in Louisiana. Like the Wood Duck, it nests in tree cavities in the wooded swamplands and sometimes sets up housekeeping in nesting boxes. It lays 8 to 12 white eggs. The male of this smallest of our mergansers is readily distinguished by its black neck and brownish flanks and by the striking area of white that occupies most of its otherwise black head and extends over most of its large, rounded, fan-shaped crest. The male Bufflehead, our only other duck with a head patch of comparable prominence, has the white reaching all the way to the top and rear margin of the head; in the drake Hooded Merganser, the white of the head and crest is completely encircled by black. The female has an all-gray neck and a mostly dark head, which separate it from our other female mergansers, which have the front of the neck white and the head more extensively reddish.

COMMON MERGANSER *Mergus merganser* Pl. IX

The status of this large duck, common to three continents and called the Goosander in England, poses a special enigma. With its combination of a long and largely white body, a virtually uncrested green-glossed black head, and a merganser bill, the adult male does not closely resemble anything else that flies. The problem is that adult males almost never visit Louisiana. I have never seen one in the state myself, and I know of only one person who can claim that distinction—James R. Stewart, who chanced upon a flock of six drakes on Cross Lake, near Shreveport, on December 23, 1961.

Although sex is sometimes not specified, the probabilities are that 36 of the 37 definite reports available at present relate to birds in "hen" plumage—females or immature males. In this dress the Common and Red-

---

Plate X Ducks in Adult Winter Plumage
(Males above or in foreground when both sexes are shown) 1. Canvasback (p. 195). 2. Redhead (p. 192). 3. Common Goldeneye (p. 198). 4. Lesser Scaup (p. 197). 5. Ring-necked Duck (p. 194). 6. Bufflehead (p. 199). 7. Mallard (p. 181). 8. Black Duck (p. 182). 9. Gadwall (p. 183).

R.E.Tucker

breasted Mergansers are only subtly different. One must study them closely to identify them with certainty, and mistakes are a constant hazard, particularly since field guide illustrations make the distinctions seem more clear-cut than they actually are on some individuals. The female Common Merganser has a dark reddish head and neck that is usually sharply demarcated from her white throat.

The dark reddish color often, though not always, completely encircles her neck. The smaller female Red-breasted Merganser has a paler reddish head and neck, typically much paler, that blends gradually into her whitish throat patch. Her back is browner, less grayish; and sometimes at close range she reveals that she has a double, instead of a single, crest.

Even if all the available records are accepted as valid, we still must rate the Common Merganser as an uncommon winter visitor. Observations are on file for all the months from October through April, and there is a report of one bird, apparently a flightless cripple, on June 3. The single records for October, April, and June all date back to the 1930s or beyond. The distribution in other months is as follows: 2 in November, 16 in December, 6 in January, 7 in February, and 2 in March. Rather remarkably, reports have been filed from all the parishes bordering on the Gulf of Mexico, even though Cameron Parish with seven sightings and Jefferson Parish with two are the only strictly coastal parishes for which I can find more than one record. In northern and eastern parts of the range, the Common Merganser is considered more of an inland freshwater bird than is the Red-breasted. In Louisiana, conformably, 17 of 37 reports have come from noncoastal situations; the largest aggregation ever observed within our boundaries was 21 on University Lake in Baton Rouge on November 20, 1955; and the only specimen for the state is a female (LSUMZ 20459) taken on Lake Fletchers in Concordia Parish on December 4, 1955. Specific bodies of water where the species has been reported more than once include Cross Lake in Caddo Parish, False River in Pointe Coupee Parish, University Lake in East Baton Rouge Parish, Lake Pontchartrain in Orleans and St. Tammany parishes, and the Calcasieu Lake ship channel in Cameron Parish.

RED-BREASTED MERGANSER   *Mergus serrator*   Pls. VII, IX

This particular *bec-scie*, as all mergansers are called in southern Louisiana, is mainly a bird of the coastal waterways, moderately common from the last part of October until the end of April, with a few remaining until as late as June 22. It is especially numerous in Cameron Parish, in Barataria and Vermilion bays, in Lake Borgne, and in Chandeleur Sound. It has probably always been much less common on inland freshwater lakes, but this seems to have been particularly true since 1935. I counted over 100 individuals of this species on False River on December 13, 1934, but in more recent years I have seen it there only occasionally and in very small numbers. In terms of absolute frequency of reports from the interior, it runs a close second to the Common Merganser, and it too has been found as far north in the state as Caddo Lake; but a much smaller *proportionate* number of its sightings have been in noncoastal settings.

The male Red-breasted Merganser has a conspicuously crested, green-glossed blackish head that is separated from the dull reddish breast by a white collar. This combination of characters, together with its brownish sides, readily distinguishes it from the male Common Merganser, which is green headed but immaculate white or pale pinkish white on the entire breast and along the sides. The females of the two species are, however, much more difficult to separate. In each the head is reddish, but the two differ in the prominence of the white on the throat and at the base of the neck. In the Common Merganser the white throat stands out in sharp contrast to the reddish areas of the head and neck. In the present species the reddish part of the head and neck blend with the white of the throat and foreneck.

HAWKS AND ALLIES
Order *Falconiformes*

THIS ORDER of birds in Louisiana contains four families: Cathartidae, the American vultures; Accipitridae, the kites, hawks, and their allies; Pandionidae, the Osprey or "fish hawk"; and Falconidae, the caracaras and falcons. Twenty-four species are represented on the state list.

Although now treated as two separate orders, the hawklike birds and the owls were long regarded as members of a monophyletic order—the Raptores, or the so-called birds of prey. There are indeed certain striking similarities that suggest close kinship between them. Both, for example, have powerful, grasping toes with well-developed talons. But, as a matter of fact, hawks and owls are really much more closely related to various other kinds of birds than they are related to each other. Consequently, we now place them in separate orders rather far apart. The current treatment is based on careful anatomical studies of all the body organs and the entire musculature and skeletal structure, which disclose many dissimilarities and point to an independent origin of the two groups. The likenesses between them are merely expressions of the principle that zoologists refer to as evolutionary convergence, or the development of like structures in two unrelated groups as adaptations to similar ways of life.

Convergence can be, and often has been, the cause of erroneous interpretations of relationship. Thomas Jefferson, who was quite a well-informed paleontologist for his day, described a fossil claw as probably belonging to a giant, extinct carnivore, only to have the French zoologist, Cuvier, correctly point out that the claw was from an extinct ground sloth. Similar mistakes would be made more frequently if we always relied, as did Jefferson, on single characters. Woodpeckers and creepers both have stiffened tail feathers, which they hold against the tree trunk as a support; but despite this similarity in structure, these two groups of birds are quite distantly related, as we see from their other characteristics. A tern and a kingfisher have similar bills that are long and pointed and also flattened laterally, and each gets its food of fish by plunging into the water, but these similarities in bill structure and habits are again examples of convergence.

Conclusions regarding the relationship of one group of animals with another must always be made with caution and, wherever possible, on numerous lines of evidence, to avoid the pitfalls into which we may be led by adaptive convergence. Ornithologists studying probable relationships of two or more groups of birds now explore all avenues of evidence, to the extent of comparing nesting habits, song patterns, behaviorisms, and even ectoparasites, in addition to anatomical and physiological characteristics. Such methods usually reveal an aggregate of characters that reflect true relationships and show us, as in the case of the hawks and owls, errors in old concepts.

The American Vulture Family
Cathartidae

Vultures are commonly called "buzzards," which is an unfortunate colloquial name. The word *buzzard*, at least on the basis of first usage, applies properly to the large broad-winged hawks of Europe. Early British settlers gave American birds the names of birds back home that our birds seemed to resemble. The robin was so named simply because early New England settlers thought the American bird was related to their well-known Robin Redbreast. And so it was with the vultures; they must have suggested the familiar birds of prey that Europeans called "buzzards." Actually, Europe has no representative at all of the New World Vulture family, which is limited exclusively to the Western Hemisphere.

Vultures are important to us as sanitary agents. They are quick to clean up the remains of dead animals along our highways. In Charleston, South Carolina, they used to come down into the city streets, as they do in Mexico today, to perform a real service in increasing the cleanliness of the community. I can hardly imagine what Mexican villages and towns would be like without these birds, for these places are not usually equipped with any sort of street-cleaning department. More recently, vultures were thought to be the principal agent in the spread of anthrax and hog cholera. This idea was disproved by careful experiments made by William H. Dalrymple, Louisiana State University's eminent and beloved scientist, who made many contributions of economic importance to our state up to the time of his death in 1925.

The early French naturalist, M. Le Page du Pratz, who spent 16 years in Louisiana and who in 1758 published an account of his experiences and observations in this country, called attention to the economic value of vultures as agents of sanitation when he wrote: "The Spaniards forbid the killing of . . . [vultures] under pain of corporal punishment; for they do not use the whole carcass of the buffaloes which they kill, those birds eat what they leave, which otherwise, by rotting on the ground, would according to them, infect the air."

Some debate still centers on the question of how vultures find their food, some arguing that it is by their sense of smell, others by sight alone. The general belief now is that they find it mainly by their eyes, but that the olfactory sense is employed to some extent, especially by the Turkey Vulture.

Vultures build no nests but simply lay their one to three large, blotched eggs in stumps, in hollow trees, or under logs. At birth the young are covered with white or buffy down. Aside from a hissing and grunting sound made when excited, as when the "nest" is threatened, the young and the adults alike are voiceless.

TURKEY VULTURE *Cathartes aura*   Fig. 50; p. 215

Probably the majority of people in Louisiana do not realize that we have two kinds of vultures, the Turkey and the Black, which they commonly call "buzzards." These birds were once, within the lifetimes of most of us, almost daily in view to anyone outdoors, even when walking the streets of a city like Baton Rouge. Indeed, from shortly after sunrise to near sunset one or more of these graceful creatures could be seen gliding on outstretched wings. Unfortunately, in the last decade, a diminution in the vulture popu-

Figure 50 Two vultures in flight: Turkey Vulture on left; Black Vulture on right. The distant silhouettes call attention to the dihedral in the wings of the former and its absence in the latter.

lation has appeared to take place, and neither species is as numerous as it once was.

The two species can be distinguished at a glance, almost as far away as they can be seen. Try making a game of it! Here are the features to look for in the Turkey Vulture: (1) the long, pointed wings are gracefully arched and are bordered all across the rear undersurface by silvery gray; (2) in flight the wings are held above the horizontal, forming a dihedral (the wings of the Bald Eagle, which resembles a vulture in the air, form no dihedral); (3) the tail is relatively long, protruding from the body in flight at least twice as far as the neck and head; (4) the wings are seldom flapped except on the takeoff—the bird will sometimes soar for hours without beating a wing; and (5) the head, like that of the "Thanksgiving turkey," is featherless and red in color. In contrast, in the Black Vulture (1) the shorter, straight-edged wings have white patches toward the squarish tips; (2) the wings are held

Turkey Vulture

more on the horizontal; (3) the tail is short, hardly protruding beyond the feet, and no longer than the head and neck (in other words, the Black Vulture sticks out in front as much as behind); (4) the bird flaps regularly, seldom soaring more than a minute or so without beating its wings; and (5) the skin of the naked head is black.

The Turkey Vulture is a fairly common permanent resident throughout much of the state, and nesting records are on file for as early as March 28. The eggs are usually two in number and are chalky white, heavily blotched and spotted with reddish brown and dark chocolate brown. The eggs of the Black Vulture differ from those of the Turkey Vulture in having a slightly greenish tinge to the ground color and in being much less profusely marked with brownish spots.

BLACK VULTURE   *Coragyps atratus*   Fig. 50

The Black Vulture, sometimes called the "carrion-crow" but more often simply "black buzzard," is fairly common in Louisiana the year around, except in the coastal marshes, where it is often absent. In the southern part of the state it formerly seemed to be more numerous than the Turkey Vulture, although in the last decade it appears to have lost more ground than has the Turkey Vulture. The Black Vulture is more gregarious and therefore is seen in larger groups. The distinguishing differences between the two species are discussed in detail under the Turkey Vulture.

The Hawk
Family
Accipitridae

Representatives of this family in Louisiana fall into three fairly distinct categories: the kites and the accipiters, or short-winged hawks; the eagles and the buteos, or broad-winged hawks; and, finally, the harriers (one species, the

Marsh Hawk). The kites are long-tailed, long-winged birds that superficially
resemble the falcons (p. 242). The accipiters have long tails but short, round
wings. The buteos are characterized by broad, round wings and broad, round
tails. A mental image of three composite silhouettes, each representing one
of these categories, is a highly useful aid in accurate field identification (see
Pls. XI and XIV and Fig. 51). The kites of regular occurrence in Louisiana
and the accipiters are mainly woodland species. The latter, especially, are
swift fliers that dart in and out among the trees. The buteos are most often
seen soaring on outstretched wings with their broad, rounded tails widely
spread or else perched quietly in isolated trees in roadside pastures and fields.
Our one species of harrier, in contrast, flies low just over the top of the grass
or sedge of fields and marshes.

Intelligent people should make a real effort to learn how to identify the
different hawks. The vast majority of hawks have been proven over and over
again by scientific investigation to be extremely beneficial to man. But, unfortunately, most people subscribe to the principle that "a hawk is a hawk"
and that *all* hawks are murderers of game and poultry. This uninformed
prejudice is often voiced by sportsmen and by farmers, despite the fact that
hawks feed on rodents, which eat the eggs and young of game birds, destroy
crops, and spread diseases inimical to man. Facts and figures seem to do little
good in correcting false impressions regarding our birds of prey. I know a
farmer, though, who told me of shooting a "chicken hawk" as it flew away
from his barnyard with what he was certain was a young chicken. When he
walked over to examine the dead body of the supposed culprit, he found in
its talons a large rat! Henceforth this particular farmer was a hawk conservationist.

For the benefit of sportsmen, especially those in the South, only one reference need be cited to prove the value of hawks—namely, the results of the
famous Cooperative Quail Investigation sponsored jointly by a group of
sportsmen and the U.S. Fish and Wildlife Service. The final report of the
study, which lasted several years, listed the enemies of the Bobwhite in the
order of their importance. First was the fire ant, which gets into the eggs at
pipping time and kills the young about to hatch. Second on the list was the
Hispid Cotton Rat, our commonest native small mammal of fields and
thickets. Far down the list was casual mention that a few kinds of hawks
sometimes catch Bobwhites. The report demonstrated, however, the important role that hawks perform in keeping small rodents, like the Hispid Cotton Rat, in check. These animals reproduce prodigiously, and were it not for

Figure 51 Flight silhouettes of three categories of hawks: accipiter or "blue darter" (top); buteo or "broad-winged" hawk (middle); falcon (bottom).

the fact that their numbers are continually being decimated by the birds of prey, they would literally overrun the countryside, destroy our crops, and possibly eliminate our ground-nesting birds such as the Bobwhite.

WHITE-TAILED KITE *Elanus leucurus* Pl. XII

There is only one positive record in Louisiana of this kite, an individual shot by George E. Beyer on the bank of the Mississippi River opposite Kenner on October 11, 1890. The specimen now reposes in the Tulane University collections. A second record, about which there is justly some doubt, is that of an individual reportedly seen by me near Monroe on November 2, 1930. Although I was positive of the identification at the time, I now believe this record should be disregarded.

No additional records of this kite in Louisiana have been forthcoming since the old one by Beyer, but we can look forward with some confidence to a recurrence of the species in the state. It is increasing in many parts of its range, including Texas. Of 55 Christmas Bird Counts in 1972 in Texas, 5 reported the species, with a total of 52 individuals. A logical Louisiana locality at which to expect the White-tailed Kite is Smiths Island, in Cameron Parish, the closest place to Texas with good habitat.

The species has been known to breed in three widely separated areas— in California, in Texas and Oklahoma, and in Florida. Adults may be easily recognized by the white underparts, the pale gray upperparts, the blackish patches on the forepart of the wings, and the white tail from which the species derives its name. The food of this beautiful kite consists mainly of insects and small rodents.

SWALLOW-TAILED KITE *Elanoides forficatus* Pl. XI

Few birds possess the graceful beauty of the Swallow-tailed Kite. Unfortunately, it occurs only as a migrant and uncommon summer resident (extreme dates: February 15 and October 24) within the borders of our state and thus is not likely to be encountered except by one who goes in search of it. The most likely areas in which to find it are the Pearl River swamp in southeastern Louisiana, the Tensas swamp country of the northeastern part of the state, and the Atchafalaya Basin, although it occasionally appears elsewhere. A few still nest in the Atchafalaya swamp near Krotz Springs, where R. K. Dix saw an adult carrying nesting material on April 25, 1959, and where it has been seen on fairly numerous occasions in recent years along the basin levees leading south to Butte La Rose and north from Henderson. In migration it can turn up almost anywhere.

The Swallow-tail is a medium-sized hawk with respect to the size of its body bulk, but its long wings and tail give it the appearance of being quite large when seen in flight. It is black backed with a white head. The underparts are white except for the black tips and rear edges of the wings, which are especially noticeable in ventral aspect as the bird flies overhead. The tail is deeply forked, the outer tail feathers being about eight inches longer than the central ones. In flight it has an ease and agility almost unparalleled among birds of its size. Its food consists almost entirely of snakes, frogs, snails, and insects. The nest of sticks and twigs interspersed with moss and leaves is placed near the top of a tall tree in swamps or along a forest river. It has only a slight depression to hold the two white eggs, which are blotched with brown.

MISSISSIPPI KITE   *Ictinia misisippiensis*   Pl. XI

There is hardly anything more lamentable than the killing of one of these beautiful hawks simply because it happens to belong to a group of birds among which a few are destructive. As a matter of fact, no bird could be less obnoxious and more beneficial than the Mississippi Kite. Its diet is made up almost entirely of insects, mainly grasshoppers, cicadas, and dragonflies. The adult is readily identified by the sharp contrast of its slate-colored upperparts, black-tipped wings, black tail, and pearl gray head and breast. In shape this kite resembles the American Kestrel, a falcon, but is fully half again as large in both wing span and total length; and no falcon has a black tail. When soaring it will often wheel around and reveal another good field characteristic, a whitish streak along the back side of the wings. The brownish immatures are heavily streaked below and have a few indistinct, light bands across the dark tail. The beginner would do well not to record immature Mississippi Kites except when they are seen in the company of adults.

Plate XI   Adult Hawks Viewed from Below
1. male Peregrine Falcon (p. 243). 2. female Merlin (p. 245). 3. male American Kestrel (p. 245). 4. Swallow-tailed Kite (p. 219). 5. Mississippi Kite (p. 220). 6. female Cooper's Hawk (p. 224). 7. male Sharp-shinned Hawk (p. 223).

AFTER R.T. PETERSON

The species is a fairly common summer resident in the deciduous forests of Louisiana, being especially numerous in the batture areas adjacent to the Mississippi River, from below New Orleans all the way to the Arkansas border, as well as along other large streams that are bordered by cottonwoods. There it builds its platform nest of sticks and grasses, usually at a considerable height. The normal clutch consists of one or two plain white eggs.

Some typical high counts of Mississippi Kites are 53 along a 10-mile section of levee in the Atchafalaya Basin on August 11, 1956; 100+ in the Bonnet Carré Spillway on July 29, 1962; 150 near New Orleans on May 14, 1969; 50 to 60 along U.S. Highway 190 a few miles west of Port Allen on May 2, 1971; 75 individuals over 18 miles of Louisiana Highway 75, beginning at Bayou Pigeon, on July 18, 1973.

The Mississippi Kite ordinarily arrives in late April (rarely as early as February) and usually departs by the middle of September, although sometimes a few are seen in southeastern Louisiana in the fall months.

GOSHAWK   *Accipiter gentilis*   Fig. 52

On November 30, 1972, Cecil Koepp observed two hawks on his farm near Amite, in Tangipahoa Parish. They were perched near the pens where he keeps his special breeds of chickens. Although all hawks are now protected by federal and state laws, special provisions of the regulations permit a person to protect his property. Consequently, having fetched his gun, Mr. Koepp was prepared when one of the hawks swooped down and attempted to seize one of the chickens. When it did so, he shot it. On picking up the hawk, he was surprised to find that it bore a numbered U.S. Fish and Wildlife Service leg band. Later investigation showed that the bird had been banded exactly three months earlier at Duluth, Minnesota, by David Evans, operating under the permit of Charles Sindelar. Mr. Koepp mounted the hawk and later generously donated it to the LSU Museum of Zoology, where it was relaxed and made into a study skin. Such was the way the Goshawk, a far northern raptor, unexpectedly won a place on the list of birds known to have occurred in Louisiana.

I have since learned that the winter of 1972–1973 was the occasion for a great southward invasion of the eastern United States by Goshawks, which I understand is the subject of a detailed analysis now in preparation.

The Goshawk is a large accipitrine bird of prey; the male measures up to 22 inches in length, and the female ranges up to 24 inches. The species is bluish slate color above, except that the top of the head and a mask on the side of the head are blackish. A white line passes over and behind the eye. The underparts are evenly marked with irregular, wavy bars of gray and white, and the feathers of the throat and breast have dark shaft streaks. The grayish tail is tipped with white and crossed by four blackish bands.

Figure 52 Goshawk.

Immatures are brownish above, with the feathers margined with rufous, and white or buffy below, with large, guttate, black streaks along the shafts of the feathers.

The species breeds in the Boreal Region from northwestern Alaska across Canada south to the extreme northern United States. In winter only rarely does it wander in the eastern United States farther south than Tennessee and Virginia.

SHARP-SHINNED HAWK   *Accipiter striatus*   Pl. XI

The habits of this and the following species, which are both commonly called "blue darters," constitute virtually the entire basis for the bad reputation of hawks in general. Male Sharp-shinned Hawks feed almost exclusively on small birds; the females, which, as in all hawks, are larger than the males, sometimes catch Bobwhites and even small chickens. But more and more people are coming to realize that predators such as these perform an invaluable role in the natural scheme of things, that they help to keep the populations of their prey healthy and well conditioned by weeding out individuals that are sick or otherwise substandard. Unfortunately, the Sharp-shinned Hawks occurring in Louisiana today are such a pitiful remnant of their former numbers that they no longer can carry out this predatory function effectively. On the nine Christmas Bird Counts in the state in 1972, the total count was a single individual; and my colleague Robert J. Newman made more than 100 successive field trips in 1972 and 1973 without finding any. In recognition both of their increasing rarity and of the service they render, state and federal laws now forbid the killing of Sharp-shins, along with hawks of all other kinds.

Sharp-shinned and Cooper's Hawks, our two regularly occurring accipiters, are not at all difficult to identify. They are long-tailed hawks with short, rounded wings. The typical flight is several short, quick wing beats and a glide. As is implied by their colloquial name "blue darter," adults of both species have a great deal of bluish in their plumage and fly in a very swift, dashing manner that sends them in and out among the forest trees where they generally hunt. They are not often seen soaring in the open except in migration. The male Sharp-shinned Hawk is about 11 inches in length, while the female averages close to 14 inches. Adults are bluish gray above, except for the top of the head, which is black; the throat is white with fine black streaks; and the breast and belly are white, heavily *barred* with pale rufous. The sharp-cornered tail is ashy gray with blackish crossbars and a white tip. Immatures are brownish above and heavily *streaked* longitudinally with ochraceous-buff below. Comparative field marks are discussed in the following account of the Cooper's Hawk.

Small birds freeze in panic at the sight of one of these hawks, for it seems that nature has taught the birds that headlong flight is the surest way to get caught. I have often stood in a wood watching an active band of warblers, kinglets, and other small birds in a treetop and suddenly, on the appearance of a blue darter, lost sight of every one of these lively little creatures. Then, by close scrutiny with binoculars, I would be able to find birds sitting absolutely motionless here and there in a cluster of leaves or close to a limb or tree trunk. After a few minutes, however, the little birds would resume their activities as if nothing had happened to bring them perilously close to death.

The Sharp-shinned Hawk breeds, or has bred, sparingly in the state; actually the few records of its nest having been found here all date back many years. In early fall, however, migrants appear from the North, and the species is present in small numbers from then until the following April, rarely later. Louisiana ornithologists should be on the alert for accipiter migrations, particularly along the coast in the latter half of September, for few observations of seasonal movements are on record for the state.

The nest, which is generally placed high in a tree crotch, is made of sticks and rootlets and lined with grasses, leaves, and other fine materials. The usual complement of four eggs is sometimes laid as early as the first week of March. The nearly round eggs are bluish white, blotched with numerous shades of brown that render them among the most attractive of all bird eggs.

COOPER'S HAWK   *Accipiter cooperii*   Pl. XI

This hawk, which, like the preceding species, is known to many people as a blue darter, was once a moderately common permanent resident, but now it is infrequently seen. In the last decade or more its numbers have undergone drastic diminution, and its plight is serious. The species is at the top of a food chain, as much so as the Peregrine Falcon, and for this reason a ready explanation for its apparent decline is obvious. All hawks are now rigidly protected by both federal and state laws, but in the case of the Cooper's Hawk this help may have come too late.

Sex for sex, the Cooper's Hawk is larger (males 15½ inches in total length; females, 19 inches) than the Sharp-shinned Hawk, but since female hawks are larger than males, a female Sharp-shinned may sometimes approximate a male Cooper's Hawk in size. By the same token, a female Cooper's Hawk is several times as large in body bulk and seven or eight inches longer than a male Sharp-shinned; hence these two are easily distinguished by size alone. But when an accipiter circles overhead or otherwise shows the shape of its tail, it then most clearly reveals its specific identity —a Sharp-shinned has the end of the tail square; a Cooper's Hawk has it rounded or graduated.

Immatures of both species are brownish with a streaked breast. They can be distinguished from other hawks by their accipitrine shape and manner of flight and from each other by the shape of the tail.

The Cooper's Hawk, less rare as a breeding bird in Louisiana than the Sharp-shinned, usually builds its nest of sticks in the crotch of a tree, 25 or 30 feet up. The three to six eggs are pale bluish white when laid but soon fade to dirty white and are often considerably nest stained by the time they hatch.

RED-TAILED HAWK   *Buteo jamaicensis*   Pl. XIII; Figs. 53, 56

The Red-tailed Hawk is the first of the buteos, the hawks with particularly broad wings and broad tails. All the buteos are highly adept at soaring and therefore are frequently observed on outstretched wings high in the sky. This species is a permanent resident, rare in summer but abundant from early October until late March. It is the hawk most often seen along highways perched in trees, on fences, or on telephone poles. Since it has little wariness about it, countless numbers are shot each winter by gunners who do not seem to realize that they are eliminating a highly beneficial bird protected by federal and state law, often in addition to violating another statute by shooting a gun from a public highway. The large buteos, such as the present species, feed almost exclusively on small rodents—cotton rats, rice rats, harvest mice, and field-inhabiting House Mice. Sixty-five stomachs of Redtails that were examined one winter at Baton Rouge either held the remains of one or more of these rodents or else were empty. What better proof could be offered that Red-tails deserve protection?

The Red-tailed Hawk is the largest of our common buteos. Adults of most populations of the species have a highly diagnostic red uppertail surface, visible when the bird wheels about in one of its soaring spirals. Imma-

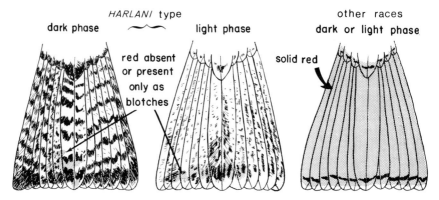

Figure 53 Tail patterns in Red-tailed Hawks: *harlani* type, left and center; red-tailed type, right.

tures have a banded tail and a usually prominent black belly band, also present in adults, formed by a concentration of streaks on the lower underparts. The bird's call is a drawn-out squealing whistle that sounds somewhat like escaping steam. The species is uncommon as a breeder in Louisiana except possibly in the extreme northern tier of parishes, where breeding birds are found in somewhat greater numbers than elsewhere. The nest is composed of sticks and twigs that form a platform in the fork of a tree, usually 25 to 30 feet above the ground. The two to four dull whitish eggs are sometimes irregularly marked with cinnamon-brown.

Until recently the so-called Harlan's Hawk was regarded as a species distinct from the Red-tail, but it is now considered a subspecies of the Red-tail. It is like other Red-tails except that it is somewhat larger and the tail is never solid red above. The bases of the tail feathers are usually extensively white, giving the appearance of a white "rump," and such red as it often has in the tail is in small blotches, patches, or streaks, along with a mottling of black, brown, and white. The melanistic or virtually all-black phase is not uncommon in the race *harlani*, but the same is also true of other races of the Red-tailed Hawk. Melanistic individuals of one of the other subspecies of the Red-tail, however, have red tails while a melanistic *harlani* has the tail colored as described above and illustrated in Figure 53.

Buteo jamaicensis harlani is of special interest to ornithologists of Louisiana, for St. Francisville was the locality where John James Audubon shot the first known specimen of this hawk, on which he bestowed the name of his good friend Dr. R. Harlan. The specimen in question was only a migrant, since the subspecies is now known to breed in Alaska and British Columbia. It winters extensively, however, in the central and lower Mississippi Valley and in Texas, arriving in Louisiana in early November and staying rarely until late March.

RED-SHOULDERED HAWK *Buteo lineatus* Pl. XIII; Fig. 54

This and the Red-tailed Hawk are the two birds of prey most often saddled with the name "chicken hawk," despite the fact that both are very beneficial. As proof of the value of the present species, I need only mention that of 220 stomachs examined by the U.S. Fish and Wildlife Service, only *three* contained poultry and only *twelve* some kind of wild bird. Of the same 220 stomachs, no less than 142 contained mice or other small mammals; 59 had snakes, lizards, or frogs; 92, insects; 7, crayfish; 2, offal; and 14 were empty. Despite figures such as these, many farmers and so-called sportsmen continue to shoot these useful birds on sight.

The Red-shouldered Hawk is mainly a woodland species, although it sometimes soars over open fields in the main province of the Red-tail. The call is a loud, piercing *kee-you*, a note often imitated by the Blue Jay. Adult Red-shouldered Hawks have a reddish breast and underparts that are often transversely barred with pale buff, particularly on the abdomen. The fore edge of the wing from the elbow to the wrist is reddish (hence "red-shouldered"). The *four* to *six* broad black tail bands are separated by white bands no more than one-third as wide. The mature Broad-winged Hawk, which sometimes is reddish brown below, has white spots on the ground color. Its tail has typically *three*, though occasionally four, broad black bands sep-

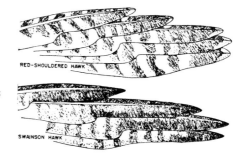

Figure 54 Diagrams showing the four notched primaries in the Red-shouldered Hawk and the three in the Swainson's Hawk. Of the buteos that occur in Louisiana, the Swainson's and Broad-winged Hawks alone have only three notched primaries.

arated by white bands that are always considerably more than one-third as wide. A difficulty is that in all species of hawks the tail coverts can hide the basal part of the tail and thereby prevent an accurate count of such bars as may be present. Most immature Red-shouldered Hawks have heavy streaking all over the underparts, whereas in the immature Broad-wing the streaking is much sparser, and in the Red-tail it is confined to the belly. Red-shouldered Hawks are distinctively larger than most Broad-wings but close enough in size to the still larger Red-tailed and Swainson's Hawks not to be reliably separable from them in the field on this basis. In flight all Red-shouldered Hawks reveal a diagnostic translucent light spot, often called a "window," near the insertion of the primaries, a feature shared with no other member of the genus in Louisiana except the almost entirely black and much larger dark phase of the Rough-legged Hawk. Infrequently one encounters immature Red-tailed Hawks in motley plumage that have light patches toward the end of the wing, but these areas are not at the base of the primaries and are not translucent.

The species is a common permanent resident throughout the state wherever persecution has not greatly reduced its numbers. The nest is built in a wooded area, usually 25 to 50 feet from the ground, in a tree crotch. The two to four dull white eggs are more or less splotched and sprinkled with various shades of brown.

BROAD-WINGED HAWK   *Buteo platypterus*   Pl. XIII

The Broad-winged Hawk is a locally common to uncommon summer resident in the heavily forested portions of Louisiana. It arrives in March and is generally gone by late October. Although once believed to be absent in winter, the species has now been recorded in that season on numerous occasions by many competent observers. Generally these sightings are of single birds, but on December 30, 1971, five were tallied in the course of the day at Venice, and six were seen there on January 8, 1972. Other localities where the Broad-wing has been noted in December and January are Diamond, Grand Isle, Grand Cheniere (specimen taken on December 2, 1962), and Cameron.

The time when Broad-wings are most numerous is during September and October, when migratory flights are passing through the state. At that time large aggregations sometimes seem to fill the sky. For example, on October 1, 1960, Richard K. Yancey observed four flocks 10 miles south of

Vidalia that he estimated to contain three thousand birds. In a smaller, but
still spectacular, flight on September 26, 1965, at Lafayette, the Eysters
counted 327 individuals, and 360 were seen in two groups in Cameron on
October 18, 1970, by Robert J. Newman and Larry P. O'Meallie.

Most Broad-winged Hawks are distinctly smaller than most Red-shouldered Hawks. Adults have the chunky, short-tailed proportions of the much
larger Red-tailed Hawk. Their three, or sometimes four, black tail bands are
distinct and wide and are separated by somewhat narrower white bands (see
discussion in preceding account). Their underparts are heavily mottled and
barred, usually with dull brown instead of the reddish coloration found in
the Red-shouldered. The immature is buffy or white below with large, tear-
shaped, blackish spots that string into sparse and scraggly, but prominent,
streaks. The underside of the immature Red-shouldered is more densely, but
usually not as sharply, streaked. Immatures of both species have numerous
alternating dull white and dusky bars. In the Red-shouldered the dusky bars
usually number more than eight and are broader than the white ones. In
the Broad-winged they are usually less than eight in number and are narrower than the white ones. Young Broad-wings are often much longer tailed
than adults and hence not so similar to a Red-tail in proportions. A specimen
can be identified with complete certainty by examining the primaries or the
main flight feathers. In the Broad-winged and Swainson's Hawks only the
outer three feathers are notched; in other buteos that are known to occur in
Louisiana, four or more primaries are notched (Fig. 54). The diagnostic
features of the Swainson's Hawk are given in the account of that species.

A further complication in the field identification of the Broad-winged
Hawk is the occurrence in that species of a melanistic phase, which closely
resembles the dark phase of the Short-tailed Hawk of Florida and Central
and South America. The latter species has been recorded on the northern
Gulf Coast at Panama City and at Dauphin Island and might conceivably
someday appear in Louisiana. Perhaps the only way to distinguish the dark
phase of the Broad-winged from a dark phase Short-tailed in the field is the
fact that in the latter the tail possesses six or seven distinct black bars,
whereas in the Broad-wing only two or three indistinct bands are present.
Light-phase adults of the two species are, however, easily separated by the
fact that the Short-tailed is almost black above, has virtually unstreaked
underparts, and possesses a tail with six or more narrow black bands alternating with white.

The Broad-winged, like the Red-shouldered Hawk, is a woodland species that only rarely catches small birds, for it feeds on rats, mice, reptiles, frogs, and, above all, insects. The nest is usually placed in the main crotch of a deciduous tree or on a horizontal branch next to the trunk when located in a pine tree. It is a poorly constructed assemblage of sticks, leaves, and bark. The Broad-winged usually lays only two eggs, fewer than the average for the Red-shouldered. Except in size the eggs of the two species are quite similar.

SWAINSON'S HAWK *Buteo swainsoni* Pl. XII; Fig. 54

At the time of the second revision of this work, in late 1959, only three reports of the occurrence of the Swainson's Hawk in Louisiana were available. The most important of the several records obtained since then is the only Louisiana specimen, one taken by Laurence C. Binford on December 6, 1963, two miles southeast of Fenton, in Jefferson Davis Parish. The localities at which the species·has now been seen, in addition to Fenton, are: between De Quincy and Kinder, December 29, 1952 (Newman); eight miles north of Shreveport, August 8, 1953 (Jeter); Cameron, December 28, 1958 (Tabor); Peveto Beach, Cameron Parish, November 28, 1959 (Lowery *et al.*); Robson, Caddo Parish, April 16, 1960 (Stewart); three miles northeast of Vinton, Calcasieu Parish, April 7, 1966 (Binford and O'Neill); Reserve, St. John the Baptist Parish, January 5, 1969 (Stein); Cameron, August 9, 1970 (Hamilton and Newman); Golden Meadow, Lafourche Parish, September 7, 1970 (Newman and Stein); and Cameron, a group of 10 on September 26, 1970 (Newman and Stein).

The fact that so few Swainson's Hawks have been seen over the years in Louisiana is surprising, since they appear regularly in eastern Texas and have been observed in numbers in southern Florida in winter. Possibly many have simply gone undetected among the host of buteos that invade our state each autumn.

In size the Swainson's Hawk is close to the Red-tail, which it resembles somewhat. The adult Swainson's in the light phase has a white throat and

---

Plate XII Adult Hawks Viewed from Below

1. White-tailed Kite (p. 219). 2. White-tailed Hawk (p. 231). 3. Ferruginous Hawk (p. 232). 4. Harris' Hawk (p. 233). 5. Audubon's Caracara (p. 242). 6. light-phase Swainson's Hawk (p. 230). 7. dark-phase Swainson's Hawk (p. 230).

1

2

3

4

5

6

7

AFTER R.T. PETERSON

R.E.Tucker

usually a wide *brown* or *reddish brown chest band.* The light-phase Red-tail almost always has a whitish chest and a band of dense, black spots *across the abdomen,* and in both phases the tail of the adult is reddish on its upper surface. Another good field mark of the light-phase Swainson's Hawk is the color of the underwing surfaces. The flight feathers (primaries and secondaries) are dark gray, while the wing linings are virtually all-white. In the light-phase Red-tail and our other large light-phase buteos, except the rare White-tailed Hawk, the flight feathers are white or at least appear to be lighter in color than the wing linings. Dark-phase Swainson's Hawks may have the wing linings slightly darker than the flight feathers, but the latter are always clouded, never white or whitish as in the melanistic Red-tail or Rough-leg. Immature Swainson's Hawks are dark brown above, buffy below, with fairly numerous streaks and spots. Both immatures and adults often glide with the wings held above the horizontal in much the same manner as does a Marsh Hawk. In the hand the species is easily distinguished, regardless of age and plumage variations, by observing that it has only *three* primaries notched. Other buteos of Louisiana, except the much smaller and differently colored Broad-winged Hawk, all have four primaries notched (Fig. 54).

WHITE-TAILED HAWK *Buteo albicaudatus*   Pl. XII

This beautiful hawk from Texas has been definitely recorded from Louisiana only twice. An immature was taken on November 18, 1888, in southwestern Calcasieu Parish, not far from the Texas state line, and an adult was seen by D. T. Kee and B. Wells 13 miles northeast of Bastrop, in Morehouse Parish, on January 19, 1972, as it circled overhead at a height of approximately 100 feet. In addition, I believe that a large buteo that I saw on December 7, 1972, approximately seven miles south of Pierre Part, in Assumption Parish, was an adult of this species. It was white below with a white tail and a distinct patch of reddish brown on the back. Unfortunately, I was unable to study the bird to my complete satisfaction before it circled out of range.

The pure white underparts, except for the throat, which is sometimes gray, the white tail with a black band near the tip, and the grayish dorsum with reddish brown scapulars and marginal coverts combine to make the adults of this species distinct from all other hawks of the United States. Juveniles are blackish, usually mottled and splotched below with white, and the tail is neutral gray with indistinct narrow bars of somewhat darker gray. Because of the apparent great rarity of the species in Louisiana and because there are other somewhat similarly colored dark hawks, a sight identification of one of these dark-plumaged White-tailed Hawks could hardly be accepted as a record.

ROUGH-LEGGED HAWK   *Buteo lagopus*   Pl. XIII

The Rough-legged Hawk is a rare winter visitor to our state. In some years it appears to be slightly more numerous than in others, but as many as five years may go by with none being seen. The highest count by one observer is that of E. Ray Smith, who reported 10 in central Louisiana in the winter of 1970–1971, five of them being on one day, the largest number ever recorded in the state in this span of time. The species seldom reaches as far south as Louisiana until December, and its sojourn with us is rather brief, for it has been recorded only once in October, twice in November, once in February, three times in March, and once in April. In December and January, on the other hand, it has been noted on 20 occasions. Extreme dates are October 30 and April 12. The species breeds in the northern part of the continent from the Aleutian Islands, Alaska, and British Columbia across Canada to Newfoundland but never within the United States.

The species has a light and a dark phase. In the light phase, the bases of the tail feathers are white, the belly is crossed by a broad black band, and the spread wings show prominent black "wrist" patches on the underside. In the dark phase the body is black, but the tail is light with a terminal bar, and the flight feathers are decidedly whitish at their bases. An excellent character that is discernible in the Rough-leg that happens to be perched within good binocular or telescope range is the feathering of the tarsus that extends all the way to the toes. Rough-legs have the habit of hovering in midair much oftener than the other large hawks. Indeed, any time a large, broad-winged hawk is seen poised on spread wings, it should be closely scrutinized to determine if it is a Rough-leg. One, though, should bear in mind that on windy days Red-tails are sometimes seen to hover into the wind.

FERRUGINOUS HAWK   *Buteo regalis*   Pl. XII

The Ferruginous Hawk is another bird of prey for which there are few records in Louisiana. An adult individual in the light phase was observed at very close range, perched on a telephone pole, near McCall, on January

14, 1938. This was in the winter of a great hawk invasion of our state; only one time since then, in the winter of 1952–1953, have hawks appeared in nearly comparable numbers. In each of these winters there was a lamentable slaughter of hawks, leaving alive tens of thousands of rats and mice that would have otherwise died.

Between November 1, 1957, and February 2, 1958, an adult individual was repeatedly observed by John P. Gee, Sidney A. Gauthreaux, Brian Donlan, Mary Lewis, Buford Myers, and others in the area beginning just east of New Orleans and extending to a point eight miles south of Slidell. On December 21 of the same year another adult Ferruginous Hawk, which exhibited all the typical field marks, was seen by Alfred Delahoussaye at Breaux Bridge. Other records of the species include one identified at Shreveport on March 8, 1959, by James R. Stewart; one seen at Johnsons Bayou, in Cameron Parish, on December 3, 1960, by John P. Gee and others; one observed at the Rigolets, in Orleans Parish, on February 23, 1970, by Joseph C. Kennedy; and one noted near Bunkie, in St. Landry Parish, on December 16, 1972, by Robert J. Newman.

The adult of the present species is a large, heavy-bodied buteo, which, in the light phase, is reddish intermixed with varying proportions of brown above and white below with a whitish tail that has no terminal band. The dark phase resembles the dark phase of the preceding species, but the combination of the white undersurface of the wings and the white, unbanded tail are adequate field marks. Immatures resemble young Red-tails but differ in having the legs feathered to the toes and in lacking prominent bands on the tail. No field guide to my knowledge warns the observer that the Ferruginous Hawk sometimes shows considerable red on the *upper surface* of the tail. The matter is important, because when a large hawk wheels and displays a reddish uppertail surface many observers would lower their binoculars and lose further interest in the bird, writing it off as a Red-tail.

HARRIS' HAWK   *Parabuteo unicinctus*   Pl. XII

The Harris' Hawk was named by Audubon from a specimen taken between Bayou Sara and Natchez, Mississippi. It has not been observed since in that area, although there is one other old published Louisiana record— that of a bird killed on an unspecified date in October in St. Mary Parish. It is a large blackish hawk with conspicuous white near the base of the tail and with a white band at the end of the tail. The female and immature

Marsh Hawks are brownish in color and have a white rump, but, unlike the present species, they show the white only on the upper surface (the white does not circle the tail). While the flight of the Harris' Hawk is labored and straightaway, that of the Marsh Hawk is graceful and bounding. At perch the adult Harris' Hawk shows chestnut patches on the wings and body, features that would immediately eliminate any of the black phases of foregoing species.

GOLDEN EAGLE *Aquila chrysaetos*   Pl. XIV; Fig. 55

This great raptor, whose main range is in the Far West, is not a familiar sight in Louisiana. Sometimes many years have gone by with no report of its presence. Nevertheless, the accumulated records extend from October 8 to March 12 and represent 13 parishes: Union, Ouachita, Morehouse, West Carroll, Madison, Beauregard, East Feliciana, East Baton Rouge, Iberville, Washington, Vermilion, Calcasieu, and Cameron. And I suspect that in past decades the Golden Eagle may often have been overlooked because of its similarity to the immature Bald Eagle.

Like almost all large predators, this species has been having difficulty in adjusting to the environmental conditions of the contemporary world. And its survival has been made doubly precarious by determined persecution in parts of the West, even in the face of protective federal regulations. Readers may recall accounts in the news media in the early 1970s that told of the pursuit of these proud birds by plane and helicopter in their mountain fastnesses and of their slaughter by the hundreds.

In view of this background, one might suppose that the Golden Eagle, rare in the state even when at its height of abundance in other places, would by now be just about impossible to find here. But for some reason—perhaps increased attention to the species—as many reports as ever have been received in the 1970s. Particularly enlightening is information furnished by John W. Goertz, who on February 10, 1973, followed up rumors that this seldom-recorded species could be seen on the Spring Bayou Plantation 12 miles south and 1 mile west of Tallulah. On that day he positively identified three immature Golden Eagles and learned from L. A. Hamilton, part owner of the plantation, that the species has been visiting this location regularly every winter for several years. A more or less constant supply of deer carcasses seems to be the reason why eagles gather in the area. There the animals roam wild in two hunting preserves covering hundreds of acres but enclosed by

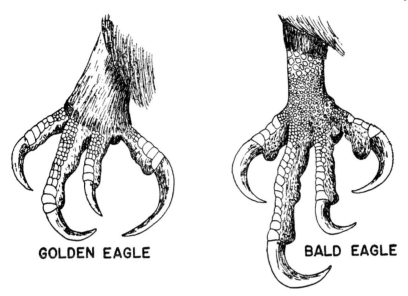

GOLDEN EAGLE   **BALD EAGLE**

Figure 55 Feet of the Golden Eagle and the Bald Eagle. In the Golden Eagle the feathering extends to the toes, while in the Bald Eagle the lower end of the tarsometatarsus is bare of feathers. This difference is particularly useful in separating immature Bald Eagles, which lack the white head and tail of the adult, from Golden Eagles.

high fences. Local residents say that dogs and coyotes frequently chase the deer until they run panic stricken into the fences and kill themselves, providing an abundant food supply for the eagles.

In the field the adult Golden Eagle appears uniformly black with white at the base of the tail feathers. Immatures show more white at the base of the tail, some white in the wings, and a sprinkling of white on the body where the white basal portions of the contour feathers occasionally show through. Both young and old Golden Eagles are easily confused with the immature Bald Eagle, which lacks the white head and wholly white tail characteristic of adults of its species. Inexperienced observers should be very careful in attempting to distinguish between the two species. A specimen in the hand or a mounted bird can be told at a glance, since the Golden Eagle has the tarsi feathered all the way to the toes, and in the Bald Eagle the tarsi are bare (see Fig. 55). Unfortunately, since we can seldom approach a living eagle close enough to see the feathers on its feet, this character is not always a useful one in the field.

Young Bald Eagles sometimes have a considerable amount of white in the wings and over the body and are hence less solid blackish brown. The bill of the Bald Eagle is nearly twice as long as in the Golden Eagle and is correspondingly more massive. The best distinguishing mark between immatures of the two species is the color pattern of the area between the dark terminal tail band and the insertion of the tail feathers. When Bald Eagles have terminal bands, these are usually irregular and ill defined, the white area adjoining is usually blotched with brownish, and the dark outer webs of the outermost rectrices frame the whitish area laterally. In immature Golden Eagles the intervening area is, if not immaculate, only lightly flecked with a darker color, and the white extends laterally to the outermost margins of the tail.

BALD EAGLE *Haliaeetus leucocephalus* Pl. XIV; Fig. 55

The Bald Eagle, the symbol of American freedom, is a bird that requires no introduction. Ever since its adoption by the founders of our country as the national emblem, its figure has adorned much of our money and all kinds of displays and posters of a patriotic nature. The Bald Eagle is a powerful and stately bird that fulfills most of the symbolic attributes assigned to it. Benjamin Franklin, however, in his usual great wisdom on all matters, was aware from the outset of one defect. He knew that the Bald Eagle is not averse to eating carrion, and because of this he argued for the adoption of that most magnificent of all North American game birds, the Wild Turkey, as the national bird. Despite the soundness of Franklin's opinions on nearly all matters, it is difficult to envision the portrait of a turkey on a quarter or five-dollar bill, much less on a national defense poster or a Marine Corps emblem.

The Bald Eagle's lack of disdain for carrion has been the main cause of its ill repute among livestock owners in some sections of the country and

---

Plate XIII Adult Hawks Viewed from Below

1. light-phase Red-tailed Hawk (p. 225). 2. dark-phase Red-tailed Hawk (p. 225). 3. dark-phase Rough-legged Hawk (p. 232). 4. light-phase Rough-legged Hawk (p. 232). 5. Red-shouldered Hawk (p. 227). 6. Broad-winged Hawk (p. 228). 7. female Marsh Hawk (p. 238).

1

2

3

4

5

6

7

AFTER R.T.PETERSON

even here in our own state. Wolves or wild dogs, or often natural causes, bring about the death of a lamb or newborn calf. Later a Bald Eagle is seen feeding on the carcass and is blamed for the actual kill. As a matter of fact, the chief food of the Bald Eagle is fish, which it either catches itself or steals from the Osprey. Many times I have observed a Bald Eagle perched quietly on a dead snag on the side of a bay or lagoon, while an Osprey circled out over the water in search of a fish. Suddenly the Osprey would plunge downward, hit the water with a terrific splash, and then reappear amid the spray with a fish in its talons. As the Osprey would begin to wing its way toward its favorite perch or its nest, the Bald Eagle would be seen to leave its lookout and to fall in behind the Osprey. Almost invariably when the eagle drew near, the Osprey would drop its fish, although I have never known an eagle actually to touch its victim. Generally the eagle follows the fish to the ground, but sometimes it may be seen to swoop down and pick the fish out of the air. When an eagle catches its own fish, it comes down in a terrific power dive but never strikes the water as does an Osprey. The descent ends just above the surface, and only the talons dip into the water to extract the prey.

Because fish are their favorite food, Bald Eagles are seldom found far from water, and their nests, which are massive structures of sticks that are added to from year to year, are usually built in trees along a shore. Mating takes place in late fall, and in our state the two dull white or pale bluish white unmarked eggs are usually laid before Christmas. The young eaglets spend three months in the nest before they make their first flight. The full adult plumage, characterized by an all-white head and tail, is not acquired until after four or five years. In this interim period, the immature is not easily distinguished from the Golden Eagle (see preceding account).

Bald Eagles are fully protected by state and federal laws, and not even museums are allowed to collect specimens for exhibition purposes. The killing of one of them is punishable by a severe fine, by imprisonment, or by both. The Bald Eagle deserves all the protection it can get, for it is now apparently much less numerous than it was in former years. Its current status in Louisiana is that of a decidedly uncommon resident. As one of the species whose ability to reproduce successfully has been diminished by the effect of pesticides, it is now on the U.S. Fish and Wildlife Service's "Red List"— species considered in imminent danger of extinction unless every possible preventive measure is taken. Ray Aycock, a biologist with the U.S. Fish and Wildlife Service, has been keeping a close tabulation of all verifiable reports of Bald Eagles in the state. In 1972 he came up with a truly astounding total of 48 individuals, although he could not eliminate the possibility that some duplication was involved. He also had reports of six or seven active nests, some of which he was personally able to confirm.

The Bald Eagle is infrequently seen in Louisiana in June, July, and August. Even in Florida, where the species is still present in some numbers as a breeding bird, records in summer are few except in Everglades National Park in the extreme southern part of the state. The remarkable eagle-banding efforts of Charles L. Broley in that state finally solved the mystery of the bird's diminution in summer. As a result of banding 814 Bald Eagles in Florida between 1939 and 1946, he received reports of recoveries of 48 individuals, 10 in Florida and the remainder at some point *north* of Florida. More than a third of the birds were recovered at least a thousand miles away. From this evidence one can conclude that part of the Bald Eagle population of Florida migrates *north* in late spring and summer. The scarcity of the bird in Louisiana at that time is possibly explainable on the same basis.

MARSH HAWK *Circus cyaneus*   Pl. XIII

The Marsh Hawk, or "marsh harrier," is a member of a distinct group of hawks that have slim bodies, long legs, and unusually long tails. The only representative of the group in North America north of Mexico is this species; and it is one of the easiest of all hawks to identify when seen cruising in a slow, bounding flight low over a grassy field, conspicuously showing its white rump patch. The females and young males are brownish in color, and the adult males are pale gray.

Since the Marsh Hawk frequents fields, the general impression of hunters unfortunately is that it preys on the Bobwhite. In fact, the diet of the Marsh Hawk is made up of rats, mice, and sometimes rabbits. The species breeds principally in the northern states and in Canada and does not regularly reach Louisiana until the first week of September, although it has been recorded at least four times in the latter half of August and once at the end of July. After this time it is fairly common, especially in southern Louisiana in the vicinity of cane fields and marshes. It sometimes remains, however, until late in May, much later than other winter-resident hawks. The individuals seen in late spring may be migrants that have gone as far as South America and hence are taking more time to get back toward their breeding grounds in the North. An adult female seen a few miles north of Jennings on July 28, 1954, was more than likely a straggler.

The Osprey Family
Pandionidae

The vast majority of birds possess characters or combinations of characters that leave little or no doubt as to their closest generic and family relationships. This is not true of the Osprey. Although comprising only a single species of nearly cosmopolitan distribution in the temperate and tropical regions of the world, the Osprey, because of its peculiarities, has at various times been treated as constituting a distinct suborder, family, or subfamily. Current opinion is still varied, but the consensus among specialists seems to be that the Osprey merits separation as a family. In its pterylosis it resembles the vultures, but in some of its other features it is more similar to the accipitrine hawks. From the latter, however, the Osprey differs in being wholly piscivorous and in having an entirely different foot structure that is unquestionably an adaptation for grasping slippery fish. The thighs and basal portions of the tarsi are covered with short, densely matted feathers, and the bare portions of the tarsi are extensively reticulate, that is, broken up into a multitude of polygonal plates. The fourth or outer toe is opposable, moving to the front or to the back, and the inner surfaces of all the toes are profusely covered with sharp spicules. The claws are massive and long and equal in length instead of graduated in size from the hallux, the largest, to the outer toe, the smallest. In cross section the claws are rounded instead of convex above and concave below. This feature, along with the uniform size of the claws, is unique among hawks and hawklike birds if not the entire class Aves (see Fig. 56).

OSPREY *Pandion haliaetus* Pl. XIV; Fig. 56; p. 240

Ospreys, also called "fish hawks," are surprisingly uncommon and scantily distributed permanent residents, must less numerous now than they were in

Osprey in Flight

ALLAN D. CRUICKSHANK

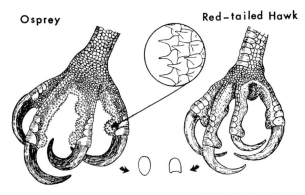

Figure 56 Feet of the Osprey and the Red-tailed Hawk. Inset drawings show an enlargement of the spicules on the pads of the Osprey and the unique shape of its claws as seen in cross section.

former years. A few individuals doubtless breed along the coast and on the borders of some of our inland lakes, but to my knowledge only one nest of an Osprey has ever been observed in the state. It was discovered by Mac Myers near Venice on March 30, 1974, just as this book went to press. The species has been recorded in the state in every month of the year. Surprisingly enough, although the greatest number of monthly records fall in April, the months of September through December are almost equally well represented.

The Osprey has been severely persecuted by fishermen, simply because of its fish-eating habits. It never seems to occur to fishermen to inquire about the kind of fish eaten by such a bird before passing judgment on it. Is the bird's diet mainly game fish, is it made up of game and nongame species, or does it consist of nongame varieties only? Investigations show that, although all classes of fish are eaten by the Osprey, its frequent selection of predatory fish more than compensates for the game fish it consumes. Of course, an Osprey in the vicinity of a fish hatchery is an entirely different matter. To illegal shooting a far worse hazard has now been added. Like the Brown Pelican and the Bald Eagle, the Osprey is suffering severely from the effect of pesticide residues ingested with the fish they eat. The poisons impede the production of eggshell and cause many birds to lay eggs that are too fragile to be hatched.

Superficially the Osprey resembles the Bald Eagle but is smaller; the underparts are white, instead of black as in the eagle; the white head has a prominent black line through the eye; and in flight the wings have a decided kink or swept-back appearance and conspicuous black "wrist" marks when viewed from below.

The nest of the Osprey is a bulky collection of sticks and sod that is often added to annually until the resulting enormous structure is heavy enough to break down the tree in which it is built. Almost invariably three eggs, occasionally two and more rarely four, are laid. Many oologists regard them as the most attractive of all bird eggs, at least among the birds of prey. The ground color may be white, pinkish white, light pinkish cinnamon, or many other variable shades, heavily blotched and spotted with dark rich browns and bright reddish browns.

The Falcon Family
Falconidae

Falcons are rather easily distinguished from other birds of prey. In flight they beat their long, pointed wings rapidly with powerful strokes. Their very long tails serve to separate them from buteos but not from accipiters. The family is represented in Louisiana by the Audubon's Caracara, American Kestrel, Merlin, and Peregrine Falcon. All except the first have a notch in the cutting edge of the bill near the tip. As a result the bill is double hooked.

AUDUBON'S CARACARA   *Caracara cheriway*   Pls. XII, XIV

The Audubon's Caracara, which is also called the Crested Caracara, is a member of the Falcon family but is aberrant in that it spends much time on the ground, where its small feet enable it to run with agility. It is also unlike its relatives in that it feeds extensively on carrion, along with the vultures. The latter, however, stand back at a respectful distance until the pugnacious caracaras have gained their fill.

The species is a decidedly rare permanent resident in Louisiana, recorded in every month of the year. It is most consistently seen on the Moore-Odom Ranch at Gum Cove, Cameron Parish, where it is definitely known to have nested successfully and where it perhaps continues to do so. The population there seems to be limited to a single pair of adults, or perhaps at times two pairs, plus one or two young, and this number seems to have undergone little variation over a span of many years. The owners of the ranch give the caracaras complete protection, and I would have thought that under the circumstances the numbers of birds would have increased. Unless one knows the exact whereabouts of the nest, which is usually built in the top of one of the clumps of Cherokee rose that dot the prairie, the birds are not easy to find, even at Gum Cove, for they spend much of their time on the ground and have the habit of retreating behind a mass of vegetation or one of the many pimple mounds in the area when an observer approaches.

Sightings of caracaras outside Cameron Parish are few. Robert W. Krebs reported finding one on December 10, 1949, at Crowley, the farthest point of record inland; and in his book on the birds of the state Harry C. Oberholser told of seeing a pair near Kenner in 1932 and an individual in St. James Parish in 1938. An Audubon's Caracara in the Jefferson Parish part of greater New Orleans achieved notoriety, swift execution, and a spot on TV in midautumn 1973 by unaccountably attacking a child and battling a neighbor's dog. At first it was thought to have been an escapee from the Audubon Park Zoo that had been attracting attention along the Lake Pontchartrain waterfront earlier in the year. But subsequent observation proved that the fugitive from the zoo was still alive and well in December.

On the ground the black-capped head, white throat and upper breast, black lower breast and belly, and white basal portion of the tail of the caracara are diagnostic. In flight, the bird reveals prominent white patches at the end of the wings. The pattern of the outstretched neck, unusually long for a hawk, in combination with the tail and the wings, which are often held flat on the horizontal, gives it a cross-shaped appearance in the air.

PEREGRINE FALCON *Falco peregrinus*   Pl. XI

Always a rather scarce bird, the Peregrine Falcon, or "duck hawk" as it is often called, has now become so decidedly uncommon in the United States that it is on the "Red List" as an endangered species. The main cause of its decline, as in the case of several fish-eating birds, is reputed to be poisoning through accumulation of the chlorinated hydrocarbons widely used as pesticides. The records of the past extend throughout most of Louisiana and are distributed from early September to mid-May. A pair with a nest in the top of a dead snag, observed near Tallulah on May 11, 1942, by Roger T. Peterson, furnishes the southernmost breeding record for the eastern United States and the only breeding record for Louisiana.

Nowadays, the species is likely to be found in the state only near our Gulf shores, where it finds an unlimited supply of food amid the clouds of gulls and terns, the myriads of sandpipers and plovers, and the hordes of ducks. The admission that it kills ducks will doubtless further prejudice hunters against this species, as well as against all hawks. A sportsman once told me, however, that he has experienced no greater outdoor thrill than that of watching from his duck blind the spectacle of a Peregrine Falcon in pursuit of a brace of teal. It is precisely this sort of drama in the wild that makes the study of nature so immensely intriguing. The ducks killed by Peregrines are, I am certain, few in comparison with the number that die from eating lead shot on the bottom of ponds or from being wounded by inexperienced hunters who fire when ducks are well out of effective range.

The Peregrine is a powerful bird that can climb almost vertically in the air in order to get above its quarry. Once this feat is accomplished there is little the hapless creature being pursued can do to escape. The Peregrine dives and strikes its prey with such force that death is usually instantaneous under the impact of the massive feet (Audubon called the species the Great-footed Hawk). It seizes the dead bird in midair or, failing in this, follows the body to the ground to devour it.

The crow size of the Peregrine, the long, pointed wings, and the dark "mustache" patches on the sides of the face serve immediately to identify this fine bird of prey. Adults are dark bluish slate above and whitish below, heavily streaked with black. Immature birds are brownish above.

Although nesting sites in the tops of dead trees, such as the one near Tallulah, were once not rare in that part of the bird's range where the terrain

---

Plate XIV Hawks Viewed from Below

1. adult Bald Eagle (p. 236). 2. immature Bald Eagle (p. 236). 3. adult Golden Eagle (p. 234). 4. immature Golden Eagle (p. 234). 5. Osprey (p. 239). 6. Audubon's Caracara (p. 242).

AFTER R.T. PETERSON

is flat, rocky ledges are preferred when available. The three or four hand-somely colored eggs are creamy white to pale pink, with numerous spots and fine dots of brilliant rich brown or reds, sometimes concentrated on one end.

MERLIN *Falco columbarius* Pl. XI

This small falcon, formerly known as the Pigeon Hawk, is now only a rare migrant and winter resident that occurs here from the middle of September to the last of April, or more infrequently into May and even June. Although it is seen nowhere in Louisiana in numbers, the species is observed most regularly in our coastal areas where, when not on the hunt, it takes up station on perches concealed in the dense foliage of live oak trees. Among the individuals encountered, females and immatures, which are brown backed and heavily streaked below, greatly outnumber adult males, most of which go farther south. The males are bluish on the back with a heavy streaking of dusky below. In color and pattern the species resembles the Sharp-shinned Hawk but has pointed, instead of rounded, wings and dis-plays a typical falcon, instead of accipitrine, wingbeat. The females and im-matures resemble the American Kestrel also, but they lack the dark cheek stripes and the rufous coloration on the upperparts and tail. The tail of adults of both sexes, as well as of immatures, possesses broad dark bars sep-arated by narrow white bars. The food of the Merlin is made up mainly of small birds and insects.

A strong—and, in my opinion, ill-advised—movement by some ornithol-ogists has resulted in the change of the familiar American names Pigeon Hawk and Sparrow Hawk to Merlin and American Kestrel, respectively, to make our names conform with the long-established designations for their European relatives.

AMERICAN KESTREL *Falco sparverius* Pl. XI

This little falcon, whose official American name used to be Sparrow Hawk, occurs fairly abundantly in Louisiana from mid-September until late April, and a small population remains to breed, especially in the piney woods sec-tions. American Kestrels may frequently be seen perched on telephone poles or telephone wires. The jerking motion of the tail when the bird is at rest is characteristic, as are also the male's bluish wings and reddish back and tail (which has a black terminal band). The female and immature birds have both the back and wings reddish brown, and the tail is crossed by numerous dark narrow bars instead of a single black terminal bar. The *reddish* brown color alone will separate them from the Merlin and the Sharp-shinned Hawk. The call is a *killy-killy-killy*, from which the local name "killy-hawk" is derived.

The diet of the American Kestrel consists almost wholly of insects, although it occasionally takes small sparrow-sized birds and mice. It has a habit of hovering in midair, an aerial feat that few birds have mastered, although one in which the Rough-legged Hawk, the terns, the Belted Kingfisher, and the hummingbirds are at least equally adept.

The American Kestrel builds its nest in a natural cavity of a dead tree or in a hole excavated by a flicker or some other bird of comparable size. It lays from three to five white, creamy white, or even pinkish white eggs that are rather evenly covered with fine dots and small spots of various shades of brown, often concentrated in a ring around the large end.

FOWL-LIKE
BIRDS
Order *Galliformes*

THIS IS A large and important group, not only because it includes the Jungle Fowl, from which our domestic chicken was derived, but also because it contains some of the world's finest game birds. The Wild Turkey and the celebrated Bobwhite are certainly among the most notable. These last-named species are the only native wild representatives of the order now present in our state, but several attempts have been made to introduce Asiatic species such as the Ring-necked Pheasant, Chukar, Jungle Fowl, and Black Francolin into the state. These efforts have been successful only in the case of the francolin. Other sections of the United States have a wider variety of gallinaceous birds—quail, grouse, ptarmigan, and prairie chickens.

The Grouse Family
Tetraonidae

GREATER PRAIRIE CHICKEN   *Tympanuchus cupido*   Fig. 57

The Greater Prairie Chicken is a member of the Grouse family, a group of large chickenlike birds that are mainly inhabitants of northern forests, tundra, sagebrush, and midwestern grassy plains. The prairies of southwestern Louisiana, however, were once occupied by a race of this species that is known as *Tympanuchus cupido attwateri*. Although this race is still fairly numerous locally on the coastal plains of the central Gulf Coast of Texas, where it enjoys protection from hunters, Greater Prairie Chickens were long ago extirpated in Louisiana. The last definite record in this state came from a secluded prairie 14 miles south of Vinton on February 26, 1919.

This splendid bird is famous for its unique courtship antics, which involve the coming together of all the birds of a rather large area in a spectacular communal dance, punctuated by terrific fights and a medley of loud,

Figure 57   Greater Prairie Chicken.

248

booming sounds and strange cries. How unfortunate that a few were not left on one of our refuges to multiply or at least to maintain a token representation for observation by the present and future generations of Louisianians! Had the few hunters who shot the last hundred or even the last dozen birds foregone the brief, transitory pleasure of killing a prairie chicken, the species might well have survived as an interesting member of our state's avifauna.

The Quail Family
Phasianidae

BOBWHITE *Colinus virginianus* Fig. 58

This is the South's upland game bird par excellence, a species familiar to all by the name of either Bobwhite, "quail," or "partridge." Its well-known call is a loud, ringing *bob-white* or *poor-bob-white*, in which the last syllable is very clear and emphatic.

The man who probably knew more about the Bobwhite than any other naturalist, the late Herbert L. Stoddard of Thomasville, Georgia, found in his years of intensive study that, contrary to popular belief, the males heard calling in the summer are unmated cocks and not indicators of second nestings. Only one brood a year is produced, but the average of 14 eggs produced by each mating gives the species a high breeding potential. If all the eggs from a mated pair hatched and all the birds survived, there would be 16 individuals at the start of the following season. Assuming that half of these were males and half females, the eight pairs would each produce an average of 14 eggs, and, again assuming all survived, 128 Bobwhites would be on hand to start the third season. If we carry this analysis further, we find that the theoretical Bobwhite population increase at the end of the third breeding season would comprise no fewer than 1,022 individuals—all from a single pair. Obviously, no such numbers result in nature, for the many decimating factors in operation bring the *potential* population down to a

Figure 58   Bobwhite (male).

much lower *actual* population. Some of the factors involved are those that kill directly, such as adverse weather, lack of food, hunting pressure, and predation. Other factors, such as improper cover, insufficient water, lack of various minerals in the diet, or insufficient grit, operate indirectly but effectively in taking their toll of the population. Indeed, no matter how perfect the environment or how inconsequential the killing by hunters or by predators, the maximum population density of the species is rarely more than one Bobwhite per acre.

A primary objective of upland game management, as it is now being carried on by a legion of biologists, is to provide the maximum number of Bobwhites per acre. This can be accomplished only by improving the environmental conditions of an area—that is, by providing better cover and more food. Experts agree that on farms that are improved for game according to recommended procedures, 50 percent of the Bobwhite population can be removed annually by hunting and the area will still maintain the year-to-year maximum population density that would be present *if not a single bird were shot!* To provide a contrast with the breeding potential of the Bob-white, let us examine that of another game animal, the deer. One mated pair will usually produce one fawn, which as a yearling will not breed. Thus, counting the original pair of adults and the three annual fawns and assuming that the fawn of the first year's mating found a mate when it became two years old, all we would have at the end of the third breeding season would be *six* deer! When we compare this to our figure of 1,024 for the Bobwhite, we discover that a tremendous disparity may exist between two species of animals in their breeding potentials. Fortunately, the Bobwhite's is high.

Sound management practices by landowners and the cooperation of sportsmen in limiting their kill in areas where the population is low will insure this fine game bird's survival. The enormous cost of rearing Bobwhites artificially in hatcheries cannot be justified on any basis, except possibly in areas where the species has been completely eliminated and a new "working stock" must be introduced, just as we would plant seedlings where all trees had been cut. The Louisiana Wild Life and Fisheries Commission has abandoned the practice.

The Bobwhite occurs throughout the state in habitats that include brushy coastal islands, chenieres, meadowland, and pine savannas.

BLACK FRANCOLIN *Francolinus francolinus*   Fig. 59

In the spring of 1961 and again in 1962, the Louisiana Wild Life and Fisheries Commission, in collaboration with the U.S. Fish and Wildlife Service, obtained a large consignment of Black Francolins from Pakistan for trial liberations in the state. Two sites were chosen that represented two extremely diverse types of terrain with respect to land use. One was the Moore-Odom Ranch at Gum Cove, in Cameron Parish, and the other was the Earl Barham Plantation at Oak Ridge, in Morehouse Parish. On the Moore-Odom Ranch, 110 birds were released in April 1961 and 201 in February 1962. On the Barham Plantation, 152 birds were released in April 1961 and 190 in May 1962. Although the experiment in Morehouse Parish is now regarded as unsuccessful, the species seems to be flourishing at the release site in Cameron Parish. Indeed, numerous nests and successful broods have been observed involving unbanded birds and hence not part of the original release, and the species is now a conspicuous part of the avifauna of the area. And there is good evidence that this import has expanded its range, for it has

Figure 59   Black Francolin (female and male).

been observed north of the Intracoastal Canal in Calcasieu Parish and near the Lake Charles airport south of that city. I have no hesitation in adding the species to the state list as a successfully introduced exotic.

In one respect, the introduction of the Black Francolin has, in my opinion, been a failure. It is likely to prove to be a poor game bird, for it is a skulker, one that can disappear behind mere wisps of grass. It tends to run rather than freeze and therefore cannot be effectively pointed by a dog. On the other hand, it is much larger than a Bobwhite.

In the breeding season, male Black Francolins lose all caution. They become blatant, unwary, and conspicuous. They mount to exposed positions —to the tops of fence posts, to bare spaces on low-hanging boughs near roads, and even to such places as the tops of chimneys rising above deserted shacks. There they utter their distinctive call that sounds rather like a giant cicada.

The male is about the size of a bantam rooster. The head and breast are black except for a reddish necklace and white ear patches; the flanks are black with large white spots and bars; the upper back is black, spotted and streaked with white and buff; the lower back, rump, and uppertail coverts are black with numerous narrow white bars; the lower belly and undertail coverts are chestnut; and the wings are a mixture of black and tan in the form of streaks and bars. The female is a rather nondescript brownish buff, heavily streaked and barred with black except for the throat, which is immaculate, and for the rump and tail, which are black, finely barred with white.

The Turkey Family

Meleagrididae

WILD TURKEY *Meleagris gallopavo*   Fig. 60; p. 254

Wild Turkeys entirely of Louisiana ancestry are now almost exclusively confined to the Florida Parishes and to a few areas in the northeastern part of the state. The Wild Turkey was at one time widely and commonly distributed, but with the inroads of civilization its numbers steadily decreased, and it became quite uncommon in most of the areas where it once occurred. Since 1963, however, widespread introductions of stock from Mississippi and Florida have been made in the wooded uplands of 38 parishes.

The original domestication of the Wild Turkey was accomplished by the Aztecs and by other natives of southern Mexico long before the arrival of the Spanish conquistadores in 1519. It was from the natives that the Spanish obtained the stock that was introduced into Europe and which became established there as early as 1540. About 100 years later the New England settlers brought the domestic turkey back to the Western Hemi-

Wild Turkey Gobbler with Full Beard

Figure 60   Wild Turkey (male).

sphere, only to find here an abundant native wild population. Blackish
body color and a white terminal band on the tail are both characteristic of
the Mexican turkey population, and even today much of our ordinary domestic stock retains these distinctive features. The native Wild Turkey of
the eastern United States has a beautiful bronze iridescence to the body,
and the terminal band on the tail is brown instead of white.

The nest of the Wild Turkey is a well-concealed, scooped-out depression containing a few dried leaves, located by the side of a log, in a dense
thicket, or in a fallen top of a tree. The eggs, which are creamy white with
numerous small red dots, vary in number from 8 to 15, rarely to 20. The
smaller sets are laid by young birds. Audubon makes this interesting observation: "When depositing her eggs, the female always approaches the nest
with extreme caution, scarcely ever taking the same course twice; and when
about to leave them, covers them carefully with leaves, so that it is very
difficult for a person who may have seen the bird to discover the nest. Indeed, few Turkeys' nests are found."

CRANES AND ALLIES
Order *Gruiformes*

The Crane Family
Gruidae

THE CRANES are long-legged, long-necked birds that superficially resemble members of the Heron family. They fly, however, with their necks outstretched, not doubled back in a loop as do the herons (see Fig. 61). Moreover, the face is almost bare of feathers, and the young emerge from the egg with a dense covering of down instead of being virtually naked. The call is a loud, buglelike note, which is totally unlike the simple croaks of the herons. Cranes are exceedingly rare in Louisiana; indeed, in all of my searches for birds in this case, covering over four decades, I have yet to see a living wild crane here.

WHOOPING CRANE   *Grus americana*   Fig. 61; p. 259

Standing over five feet in height, the Whooping Crane is the tallest bird in North America. It is all-white except for part of the head, the black legs, and the black-tipped wing feathers. The head is red on top, on the lores, and on the sides of the throat, and with a sprinkling of black hairlike feathers on these otherwise bare areas. This crane is one of the rarest of all North American birds, a species whose survival or extinction hangs delicately in balance. By actual count, fewer than 60 wild Whooping Cranes are left anywhere, and, although an intensive search for the breeding grounds of these few remaining individuals was made over a period of many years, these efforts met with no success until the early 1950s. Regardless of the amount

Figure 61 Large white birds in flight: (1) American White Pelican; (2) Whooping Crane; (3) Great Egret; (4) Whistling Swan; (5) Wood Stork; (6) White Ibis; (7) Snow Goose. Note the variously shaped black markings in five species.

of protection afforded the birds in winter, when the majority, if not all, of them are on the Aransas Refuge in Texas, they must receive attentive care in their summer retreat in far northwestern Canada and along their migration route if the species is to remain a living part of our American avifauna.

The Whooping Crane has a very low breeding potential. On the basis of the number of brown-colored juveniles that come down from Canada each fall, it is apparent that many of the adults either go unmated or are unsuccessful parents. In spite of all that has been done in recent years, it is discouraging to learn that in 1950, 1951, and 1952, in the period from May to October, when the birds were either in migration or on their breeding grounds, a total loss of 20 individuals was incurred, and only 12 young were produced! If the total population numbered a thousand birds instead of a pitifully small flock, even this low breeding productivity might be sufficient to maintain a comfortable stability. As it is, we cannot afford to lose a single adult bird by any cause, most certainly not by unnatural ones, without serious consequences. The protection of the few surviving birds even in winter is by no means easy, but the main hazard comes while they are making their long fall and spring migration flights between Canada and Texas. This is especially the case when they are passing through areas where people are not aware of the birds' identity and their great rarity.

Both the prairies and the marshes of southwestern Louisiana were once the wintering grounds for fairly large numbers of Whooping Cranes. Indeed, prior to the introduction of rice farming and the extensive settlement that followed, this area may have constituted the optimum winter habitat of the species and hence the center of its greatest abundance in the nonbreeding season. Even as late as 1899, the well-known naturalist, Vernon Bailey, wrote that "whoopers" were "common" in the prairie near Iowa Station, in Calcasieu Parish. Apparently the birds were here in numbers only in late fall, winter, and early spring, but at least a small portion remained each year to nest in the panicum, or *paille fine*, marsh north of White Lake, in Vermilion Parish. By 1919 both the Louisiana wintering and the breeding populations were drastically reduced in numbers, a result that is hardly surprising when we learn that in 1918 a certain rice farmer near Sweet Lake, in Calcasieu Parish, shot 12 of these magnificent birds because they were feeding on the rice that had fallen from the separator door of a thresher. According to Robert P. Allen, whose excellent studies of the history and habits of the whooper were published as Research Report No. 3 of the National Audubon Society, the year 1918 marked the virtual disappearance of the bird from the prairie habitat of Louisiana, although a small wintering group of less than two dozen individuals and an even smaller breeding population continued to inhabit the panicum marsh area until as late as 1939. In that year John T. Lynch, of the U.S. Fish and Wildlife Service, saw a pair of adults with two unfledged young near White Lake. In the winter of 1940, however, following a severe storm and a subsequent flooding of the marshes in this area, 7 cranes out of 13 known to have been present were presumably lost. This catastrophe, combined with the tragedy of additional mortality from birds being shot or caught in muskrat traps, rang the death knell to the existence of the Whooping Crane in Louisiana. The last whooper definitely identified within the state was a single individual found by Lynch near White Lake on December 2, 1949. It was seen on several dates thereafter until March 11, 1950, when it was captured with the aid of a helicopter and taken to the Aransas Refuge in Texas in the hope that it could be used to breed additional individuals. Unfortunately, this bird, called by the name Mac, was

Whooping Cranes over Saskatchewan, November 5, 1953

destroyed by a predator, presumably a coyote, before it could be used in a breeding experiment.

In 1973, there were 22 captive Whooping Cranes in the world, 18 at the U.S. Fish and Wildlife Service Patuxent Refuge near Washington, D.C., one named Crip in the San Antonio Zoo, and three in the New Orleans Audubon Park Zoo. One of the parents of the birds in the New Orleans Zoo was a female called Josephine or Jo that was shot and wounded in 1940 south of Eunice and may have been one of the seven birds that disappeared from the White Lake area following the flood referred to previously. In October 1948, she was taken to the Aransas Refuge and was mated there with Pete, a semicaptive individual that had been obtained several years before in Nebraska. In the first year, the pairing resulted in the laying of two infertile eggs, which, after 23 days of futile incubation, were broken up by the birds themselves. Then, in July 1949, Pete died, presumably of natural causes. The following year Jo was placed with a slightly crippled male, named Crip, that had been captured on the Aransas Refuge with the aid of

Whooping Cranes on Aransas Refuge in Winter

horses. In a special enclosure in a remote part of the refuge, the two birds built a nest, and on the night of May 24, 1950, the first Whooping Crane ever hatched in captivity broke its way from the egg. But despite a dawn-to-dusk vigil maintained by refuge personnel from a 20-foot tower more than 1,200 feet away, the little chick, dubbed Rusty, suddenly disappeared in the tall grass. At the time the parent birds were wandering at a distance of some 200 yards, but on their return to the spot where they had left the little chick, they seemed unable to find it. The observers were at a loss to explain just what happened, for the little crane was only six inches in height and was often concealed by the tall grass. Whether it was killed and eaten by a Turkey Vulture that was seen to alight a few minutes before near the last brooding site or fell prey to some wandering predator, such as a raccoon, is not known. Both Crip and Jo were subsequently returned to Audubon Park, where they were given every possible care and where they raised three young before Jo was killed by flying into a fence when a helicopter flew over the zoo during Hurricane Betsy in 1965.

SANDHILL CRANE *Grus canadensis* Fig. 62

The plight of the Sandhill Crane is fortunately not nearly so acute as that of the Whooping Crane. The Sandhill has a wide breeding distribution, which, although by no means continuous, extends roughly from Alaska and Hudson Bay southward through parts of the Great Plains of Canada and the northern part of the United States and includes parts of southern Mississippi, southern Georgia, and the Florida peninsula. In much of the southern part of this area it is now extremely rare. Like the Whooping Crane it has often been shot simply because of its great size and the fact that it offers a tempting target to the irresponsible gunner.

Figure 62   Sandhill Crane.

The species once nested in Louisiana, in the southwestern prairie section, and doubtless in the Florida Parishes, but I do not know of any reports of its having done so in either place since 1919. Indeed, I am aware of only four subsequent records of any sort: I found one dead, entangled in the wires of a fence, four miles east of Covington on February 10, 1945; two individuals remained on the Sabine National Wildlife Refuge for several years and were last reported there in the winter of 1950–1951; a bird was seen one mile west of the White Kitchen Cafe, near the mouth of the Pearl River, on October 19, 1957, by Sidney A. Gauthreaux and Rose Feingold; and one appeared in a field six miles south of Alto, in Richland Parish, in February 1971, and remained until April 21, when plowing procedures drove it out. The Alto bird was found by the landowner, John Landers, first identified by D. T. Kee, and later seen by several others.

A few breed each year in the flatlands of southern Mississippi, where, as is typical of the species, the bulky, elevated nest of sticks, grass, and other vegetation is placed on the ground in an open pine wood or savanna. Only two eggs are laid, and their color ranges from pale greenish to brownish buff, blotched and spotted with brown.

The Sandhill, like all cranes, flies with its neck extended. Adults are gray in color except for the almost bald, red-skinned forehead (immatures have the head feathered) and a varying admixture of buffy ochraceous, which in some individuals is extensive. This buffiness is said to be a discoloration, which the crane itself brings about by applying muddy water to its feathers.

[The Limpkin
Family
Aramidae]

[LIMPKIN   *Aramus guarauna*]

In the spring of 1935 Mr. Fred Weber told me of a bird that he had shot at Moss Lake, 10 miles north of Lake Charles. The specimen was not preserved, but Mr. Weber believed it to be an example of the Limpkin, and he described it in a rather convincing manner. I mentioned this incident to Dr. Oberholser, and through a misunderstanding the record was included in his book with my apparent concurrence. However, since the range of the Limpkin is supposed to be limited to areas where a certain large freshwater snail of the genus *Ampullaria* occurs and since this snail is unknown in Louisiana, I have never considered the evidence sufficiently strong to merit including the species on the state list.

The Rail
Family
Rallidae

Rails are usually birds of the marsh and are heard more often than seen. A rail may call from a distance of only a few feet, and when you dash to the spot from which the sound came, the bird calls again a few feet back of you. The expression "thin as a rail" is based on the fact that rails are capable of greatly compressing their bodies laterally and hence are able to slip between stalks of grass seemingly too close together to allow the birds to pass. They stick their bills out in front to deflect blades of grass one way or the other and scoot on their long toes through the vegetation almost as fast as if it were not there at all. The downy young of all our rails are glossy black, regardless of the color of their parents, and after they emerge from the egg and rest for a few minutes while the down dries, they begin to run around like baby chicks. Three species in Louisiana are permanent residents, but the others are winter residents and migrants only, particularly in evidence in our great coastal marshlands. Despite the reluctance of rails to fly more than a few feet at a time once they reach their winter haunts, the migrant species of the group take wing when spring comes, and some fly hundreds of miles to a northern nesting site, where they again become sedentary until the time for them to return southward with their young. The migration of any bird is a remarkable feat, but in hardly any instance is it more remarkable than in the case of the rails, simply because they are such poor fliers. One member of the family, the Laysan Rail, after unquestionably using its powers of flight to reach its mid-ocean retreat, proceeded then to lose the use of its wings altogether and to become flightless.

KING RAIL   *Rallus elegans*   Pl. XV

This and the following species are the largest rails in Louisiana, for they approach in size a half-grown chicken. The King and Clapper Rails are quite similar in appearance and are, for the most part, simply ecological representatives of each other. The former generally inhabits freshwater marshes and is widespread in the interior of the United States; the latter is confined to brackish or saltwater marshes on or near the seacoast. The King Rail is decidedly reddish in general coloration, both above and below, while the Clapper Rail is mainly olivaceous above and buffy below. Both have the throat white, the upperparts strongly suffused with black, and the flanks barred with dusky and white. There are brackish marshes in which both breed side by side without intermingling; but even though the King Rail does nest sometimes within a few hundred yards of the surf (as, for example, along the road between Cameron and Holly Beach), I have never encountered a Clapper Rail in a strictly freshwater situation.

Peterson describes the notes of the King Rail as *bup-bup, bup, bup,* or *chuck-chuck-chuck,* and the note of the Clapper Rail as a clattering *kek-kek-kek-kek,* or *cha-cha-cha-cha.* This seems to me to be a reasonably informative rendition of the slight difference in the call notes of these obviously closely related species.

The King Rail nests in suitable situations throughout the state, sometimes in a small cattail marsh and sometimes simply in a dense stand of grass in a roadside ditch. The 7 to 12 buffy white eggs, finely speckled with rufous brown, are placed in a nest of grasses on or near the ground.

The species is much more numerous in winter than in summer, since its

---

Plate XV   Rails

1. King Rail (p. 264). 2. Clapper Rail (p. 265). 3. Virginia Rail (p. 265). 4. Sora (p. 266). 5. Yellow Rail (p. 267). 6. Black Rail (p. 268).

1

2

3

4

5

6

50

numbers are augmented in fall by the arrival of northern visitors. At this season King Rails are a not uncommon sight in roadside ditches, in cane fields, and in grassy places where the ground is damp. Although the secretive habits of rails make assessment of their true abundance difficult, this species certainly vies with the Sora as the one most frequently encountered in marshy places in the interior parts of the state, and it occurs even on the coast in numbers comparable to those of the Clapper Rail.

CLAPPER RAIL *Rallus longirostris* Pl. XV

The field characters of the Clapper Rail, which is a common permanent resident in our salt and brackish marshes, are discussed in the preceding account along with those of its close counterpart, the King Rail. Here, however, I might add a word of caution. While the King Rail exhibits next to no geographic variation, the Clapper Rail is broken up into numerous subspecies. Our form, which was once called the Louisiana Clapper Rail, is much more similar in coloration to the King Rail than is the form inhabiting the coasts of the northeastern United States, the form most commonly depicted in standard bird guides. Beginners in Louisiana should study long and carefully the large rails they find in freshwater situations on the one hand and saltwater situations on the other before attempting to discriminate between the two species in the brackish habitats where both are likely to occur.

This rail builds its nest of grass near the ground in a marshy place usually in a clump of vegetation. Eight to 12 buffy eggs, blotched with reddish brown, are laid in April. It shares with our other marsh birds and the muskrat the danger of extirpation if the drainage and exploitation of our marshes continue. The only salvation of these species may lie in the acquisition and setting aside of large areas of marshland as natural sanctuaries on which controlled hunting and trapping may be allowed, but on which rigid guard is kept to prevent commercial exploitation without regard for the perpetuation of our living natural resources.

VIRGINIA RAIL *Rallus limicola* Pl. XV

The Virginia Rail is about one-half the size of a King Rail, that is, about as large as a Bobwhite but not nearly so plump. The sides of the face are entirely slaty gray, whereas in the King Rail the lower cheeks and neck, except the throat, are reddish. The Black and Yellow Rails and the Sora, which are also small in size, have short, chickenlike bills, entirely different from the long, slightly downcurved bill of the Virginia Rail.

The present species is a fairly common migrant and winter resident that is especially numerous in the coastal marshes. Migrants arrive in September and remain until late April, rarely into May. To Joseph C. Kennedy goes the credit of establishing that Virginia Rails sometimes remain to breed, although they had long been suspected of doing so. Kennedy found an adult with a brood of five young and photographed one of the chicks along the highway to Grand Isle, one mile south of Leeville, in Lafourche Parish, on May 25, 1969.

All rails are exceedingly shy and retiring, and unless one can recognize their call notes, they can be quite common in a marshy spot and remain undetected. One of the best ways to see the species is to ride through the coastal marshes in a marsh buggy, flushing the rails ahead of the machine. On the Cameron Christmas Bird Count of December 30, 1972, no fewer than 27 were tallied by this method in a small section of the marsh just south of the Sabine National Wildlife Refuge. The calls of the Virginia Rail consist of a variety of grunting sounds and a *kid-ick, kidick,* or *cut, cutta-cutta-cutta.*

SORA *Porzana carolina* Pl. XV

The Sora is a small rail about the size of an Eastern Meadowlark. It has a chubby, chickenlike bill instead of the long, slender bill characteristic of the King, Clapper, and Virginia Rails. The Black and Yellow Rails have similarly shaped bills but are distinguished by their diminutive size, which hardly exceeds that of a House Sparrow or one of the small plovers. The bill of the Sora is yellow, and adults have the throat and area around the base of the bill black, the upperparts olive, and the underparts gray. The immature lacks the black on the throat, and the general coloration is more brownish (less olive).

The species is a fairly common transient and winter resident in Louisiana, occurring mainly from early September until early May. It is found in all kinds of marshy situations, both fresh and saline, and it occurs also in grassy fields. The call of the Sora is frequently described as a whinny. It starts out on a high note and descends rapidly. Another note frequently heard given by the Sora here in winter is a *keek-keek* that is very suggestive of the calls of the chorus frogs (*Pseudacris*), especially the Ornate Chorus Frog (*P. ornatus*).

YELLOW RAIL *Coturnicops noveboracensis* Pl. XV

The story of the belated discovery of the Yellow Rail at Baton Rouge, where much ornithological work has been done, illustrates how easily rails may escape detection, even where they are actually common. Not until 1943, when I picked up a wing, with feathers intact, in a freshly mowed hayfield five miles below LSU, did I have any intimation of the presence of the Yellow Rail in the Baton Rouge area. The wing was unmistakably that of the Yellow Rail, since it had the characteristic squarish white patch in the secondaries, a mark so striking that it serves as an excellent field character to distinguish this small bird, which is otherwise a nondescript yellowish brown mottled with black. Later developments revealed that there were numerous Yellow Rails in these fields every fall, and that they could be seen simply by following the mowing machines. As the tractor with its cutting blade moved forward, the little rails would flush ahead of the machine a short distance. If they went into the cut section of the field, they ducked under the grass and froze. By running quickly to the spot and clamping the cupped hands or a hat over the mat of grass, one could often catch the rail alive. By this method we once captured seven Yellow Rails in a single week. Those that were injured were retained as museum specimens, and the remainder were released. If the flushed bird flew to the uncut side of the field, tragedy was apt to follow; for, instead of flushing again ahead of the cutting blade, the bird seemed to attempt to step over it. Consequently, its feet were often severed or the bird was otherwise maimed, sometimes fatally. Several specimens that we have captured have shown evidence of this sort of injury, and the wing that led to our unexpected discovery was doubtless that of a bird killed outright by the hay-cutting machine.

The mowing equipment involved in these early experiences of ours consisted of small tractors fitted with a scissor-type blade that projected to the side. One could easily keep up with such rigs on foot and be in position to move in for a capture the moment the rail alighted. A few of these old-fashioned contraptions are still in limited operation, but they have largely been replaced by apparatus with rotary blades attached *behind* huge high-speed tractors. The introduction of these newer machines has greatly altered "yellow-railing." For one thing, they and their accessory equipment get the hay cut and baled so fast that the job is often finished before the rails return in fall. In 1972 and again in 1973, mowing produced no records of Yellow Rails at all. For another thing, a man on foot can no longer keep pace with the tractor, so one must resort to riding on the rig itself or following it in a car. Neither alternative is really satisfactory for actually capturing the rails; but a rotary mower holds the record for the number of flushes—18 in three hours on October 23, 1969, at Longwood a few miles south of the LSU Baton Rouge campus. The new rigs probably cripple fewer birds than the old, since the tractor itself startles them into flight or other evasive action well before the cutting blades reach them. But any luckless enough to freeze would certainly be sliced to bits. The men who run mowing machines are quite familiar with the birds and call them "little prairie chickens." Another vernacular name for the species is "yellow crake." The note, which I have never heard, is said to be *tic-tic, tic-tic, tic, tic.*

Attempts to flush Yellow Rails in these fields by having two people drag a rope between them as they walk through the uncut grass have been unsuccessful. The rope, even with weights attached, rides too high on the grass, and the little rails evidently duck under it. Nevertheless, the several records from outside the vicinity of Baton Rouge, all from the coastal marshes except a specimen shot at De Ridder and single sightings at Reserve and near Lafayette, have been of birds that happened to fly up before people who were walking. Extreme dates for the state are October 6 and May 1.

BLACK RAIL   *Laterallus jamaicensis*   Pl. XV

When I recall my experiences with the Yellow Rail, as related in the previous account, I hesitate to proclaim that any kind of rail is rare in Louisiana. There are, however, only 14 dated records for the Black Rail in the state, all from the coastal marshes except two presumed migrants caught in the Baton Rouge area. The dates extend from November 9 to April 13.

This tiny rail, which is sometimes called the "little black crake," is about the size of a House Sparrow with a bobbed tail. Its color is black and grayish, with white speckling on the back and a brown patch on the back of the neck. The young chicks of all rails are black, but in this early stage the body is covered with down and the overall juvenile appearance is so pronounced that they can hardly be confused with the adult Black Rail, except possibly at a distance.

Personnel on the Rockefeller Refuge in Cameron Parish inform me that Black Rails are occasionally flushed in winter ahead of marsh buggies. It seems likely, therefore, that the elusive little bird has frequently escaped notice by ornithologists of the state and is actually much more numerous in our marshes than the eight dated specimens and six additional dated sight records would indicate. But, if so, one matter remains perplexing. The little rail has a highly distinctive call, aptly described as *kicky-dur* or *kicky-doo*. Field investigators have spent considerable time in Cameron Parish playing tapes of this vocalization without yet eliciting a response or even finding a marshman who could remember ever having heard it.

PURPLE GALLINULE *Porphyrula martinica* Pl. XVI

The chickenlike Purple Gallinule, or "blue peter" as it is often called, is without question one of the most beautiful birds in the United States. So striking is its gaudy coloration that the bird appears to be unreal and the product of one's imagination. It is brilliantly colored on the head and the underparts with rich, purplish blue; the back and wings are olive-green; the forehead is bare of feathers, forming a shield that is light blue in color; the feathers under the tail are white, in sharp contrast to the rest of the plumage; the bill is a deep red, tipped with yellow; and the legs are yellow. The juvenile is completely different from the adult, being yellowish below and greenish brown above, with the bill and legs yellowish brown. The species is one of our more common native birds, residing in summer almost throughout the state along marshy lakeshores, rice fields, reed-bordered ponds, and bayous choked with water hyacinths. Records in the southern part of the state are available for every month of the year, but the species is rare anywhere in Louisiana in winter. Migrants begin to arrive by the end of March and by early April Purple Gallinules are common. They remain so until late September, when their numbers begin to diminish. By the end of October most have departed.

The feet of gallinules are equipped with long, slender toes highly adapted for walking on lily pads and other floating vegetation, where the birds go in search of their food of snails, mollusks, and aquatic insects. They move with stealth, but the tail is jerked forward over the back with each step, thereby flashing the white undertail feathers. They have a laborious flight, since the wings are very short and rounded. Consequently, when approached, they seem to prefer hiding in the tall marsh grass to flying. Poor fliers though Purple Gallinules are, they still leave Louisiana when fall comes and make an extended migration to tropical America, presumably flying across the waters of the Gulf of Mexico (as they definitely do in spring). The nest is built on floating islands of vegetation in dense marsh grass or in rice fields. It is made of stems and leaves of various water plants, and often the surrounding plants are brought together over the nest to form a sort of roof as added protection and concealment. The eggs are buff colored with numerous fine drab or brownish dots and are six to eight in number. The downy young are jet black and, on hatching, immediately leave the nest in search of food. They are accompanied, of course, by the mother.

In Louisiana, Purple Gallinules occur most commonly in the southwestern section of the state, where they nest in rice fields. Here they are said to do some damage by eating the rice and by building nests of woven rice plants that clog the harvesting machines at cutting time.

COMMON GALLINULE *Gallinula chloropus* Pl. XVI

The Common or so-called Florida Gallinule is decidedly more cootlike in its general appearance and actions than is the Purple Gallinule. It spends a great deal more time in the water, instead of walking on floating vegetation. Any blackish ducklike or cootlike bird with a red bill and a red frontal shield certainly belongs to this species. The coot has a white bill, while that of the Purple Gallinule is red, tipped with yellow and bordered behind by a pale blue frontal shield. The Moorhen of Europe, about which much has been written in English literature, belongs to the same species as our Common Gallinule, being identical with it except for very minor geographical variations.

The Common Gallinule is with us the year around, common in summer, moderately common in winter when, however, it is mostly restricted to the southern parishes. Even in summer it is much more numerous in the coastal sections than elsewhere. The only winter observations in the northern half of the state were made by Robert B. Hamilton at the Natchitoches Fish Hatchery in 1971, when three birds remained until December 13 and one

---

Plate XVI Gallinules and the American Coot

Purple Gallinule (p. 269) standing in water. Common Gallinule (p. 270) on edge of marsh. American Coot (p. 271) swimming in center foreground and running and swimming on the water in background.

of them did not disappear until the vegetation in which it was residing was cleared out a week later.

The calls consist of a variety of chickenlike sounds and explosive, croaking noises that lend immeasurable charm to our marshlands. The nest is placed in thick marshy vegetation, either a few inches above the water or sometimes floating on it. As many as 12 buffy eggs finely speckled with brown are laid on dates ranging from late April to July.

AMERICAN COOT *Fulica americana* Pl. XVI; Fig. 36

This well-known slate-gray bird is the size of a small duck. It can be distinguished from a duck by its chickenlike, white bill. It resembles the Common Gallinule, which, however, has a red bill. The *poule d'eau*, as the coot is called in southern Louisiana, can be found on freshwater lakes and brackish ponds throughout the state in large numbers in fall, winter, and early spring. Sometimes we see coots making their way through the water like dark little ducks, nodding their heads forward and backward as they swim along. But they do not have webbed feet as do ducks. Their toes are equipped instead with flaps or lobes, which act as paddles (see Fig. 36). Usually coots stay closer to the shore than ducks; for, though they can be eaten, they are not as frequently hunted here during the gunning season and are not as shy. Often they come right out on the shore and walk around like chickens with feet two sizes too big. If we frighten one, however, or chase it in a boat, it spreads its wings and skitters away over the surface of the lake, splashing water in every direction before it finally manages to rise into the air.

Formerly in the winter as many as ten thousand coots could be counted on False River, in Pointe Coupee Parish, but now they are no longer seen there in such large concentrations, probably because of the growing popularity of outboard motorboating on this body of water. In spring, nearly all of our coots migrate northward. A few remain in the state, mating and laying 8 to 14 speckled buff eggs on a platform woven of reeds or sedge back in the marsh vegetation. Such a nest was found on the Lacassine National Wildlife Refuge on April 15, 1956, by Leslie Glasgow; Edward McIlhenny Simmons found a brood of young at Avery Island in the spring of 1960; and Robert B. Hamilton and Robert E. Noble discovered two nests at the Natchitoches Fish Hatchery in June and July 1970 and photographed one clutch.

SHOREBIRDS
AND ALLIES
Order *Charadriiformes*

THIS ORDER is large and diverse and its range is worldwide. It contains many subgroups, which, on first scrutiny, seem to be quite dissimilar—sandpipers, plovers, gulls, and terns, and even the Great Auk—but all these birds have much in common in their structure and in their habits. I never cease to marvel at the similarity in the silhouettes of a tiny plover and a great gull, as the two stand side by side on a sandbar on a beach in late afternoon.

Representation of the order in Louisiana is large, amounting to no less than 67 recorded species. They are nearly all inhabitants of the shores, either of our lakes and bays or of the Gulf itself. Louisiana has a fair number of species of nesting terns, but otherwise comparatively few of the birds in this order breed within our borders. In summer they are mainly denizens of the Far North, with the vast Arctic tundra abounding in both species and individuals. Many of them seem to dash northward, rear their young, and then dash southward again. The last of the transient shorebirds to go up in the spring must surely meet the first individuals of one species or another to start back, since there is never a time when these little waders are entirely absent from the state. In the group are some of our truly long-distance migrants. Some Sanderlings, for instance, cover approximately 22,000 miles in the round trip between the extreme limits of their summer and winter homes, for they breed within the Arctic Circle and winter in faraway Patagonia. A considerable part of the Sanderling population, however, goes no farther south than the Gulf shores to find food and climate to suit its winter tastes.

Louisiana's long and much-indented coastline and its great expanses of inland waters provide an ideal habitat for shorebirds and their allies; hence in some months they are with us by the hundreds of thousands. They are truly a fascinating group. Although the order Charadriiformes contains many species of similar appearance, not easily differentiated in the field, this difficulty provides a challenge to the serious student. Much enjoyment can be derived from studying their field characteristics and attempting to identify the various species.

The Oystercatcher Family
Haematopodidae

AMERICAN OYSTERCATCHER   *Haematopus palliatus*   Fig. 63

Black and white with a large red bill and standing at least a foot in height, the first shorebird of our list is a spectacular one, yet one that unfortunately is rare in Louisiana. It is primarily a bird of the Atlantic Coast, but even there it is seldom seen, since it prefers the most remote and uninhabited beaches. In Louisiana it seems now to be confined almost entirely to the secluded sandy and muddy strands of the Chandeleur chain and nearby islands. In June 1941, I found two on Isle au Pitre and four on North Island, where they were presumably nesting, but in none of my countless visits to other parts of our coast in the last 40 years have I had the slightest glimpse of it. The highest number that has been counted in Louisiana is the 21 seen on the Chandeleur and adjacent islands on June 11 and 12, 1971. This tally did not include birds on Isle au Pitre, which is adjacent to the mainland on the west side of Chandeleur Sound. The observation of a pair of these birds on Timbalier Island by Leslie Glasgow and Robert H. Chabreck on June 22, 1973, is the first record of the species west of the Mississippi delta since Audubon observed it on the Isles Dernieres in 1837.

Figure 63   American Oystercatcher.

The American Oystercatcher is presumably a permanent resident at the latitude of the northern Gulf Coast, but actual records for it in Louisiana are lacking for October and for the period from November 6 to March 26.

The Stilt Family
Recurvirostridae

The family in Louisiana includes two species, the American Avocet and the Black-necked Stilt. Each is extremely long legged and long necked for a shorebird. As the name Recurvirostridae suggests, many members of this family have the bill upturned toward the end. This is true of the avocets, but not the stilts, which have straight bills.

BLACK-NECKED STILT *Himantopus mexicanus* Pl. XVII; p. 275

The stilt is a well-named bird, for although its body is not much, if any, longer than that of a Killdeer, its legs are more than 12 inches in length—it literally stands on stilts. In many respects it is one of our most attractive shorebirds. The wings, top of the head, and hindneck are black; the rump, tail, and underparts are immaculate white; and the legs are brilliant red! The long needlelike bill is black and straight, not turned up as it is in most members of the family Recurvirostridae. Close inspection of a pair of stilts reveals sexual dimorphism in the color of the dorsum, which is jet black in the male, brown in the female.

Although stilts are generally confined to the coastal areas, where they are regular summer residents, they have been occasionally seen in New Orleans and even at Baton Rouge. One was observed on the edge of the LSU campus on May 7, 1961, by Robert F. Andrle, and eight were seen at the same place on September 10, 1965. The last incident is easily explainable, for it took place during Hurricane Betsy, the eye of which passed almost directly over the university.

Stilts are especially numerous in southwestern Louisiana. Some indi-

Black-necked Stilt at Nest

ALLAN D. CRUICKSHANK

viduals remain there all winter, but the population is drastically reduced at that time. The species builds its nest of a few sticks and twigs in the marsh or near the edge of a muddy flat, laying three to seven buffy or dull yellow eggs that are beautifully spotted with dark brown or black. It is a noisy bird at all seasons, the call being a loud yipping note. In the vicinity of the nest the species is especially vociferous as it displays itself conspicuously in an attempt to lead intruders away from its territory.

AMERICAN AVOCET   *Recurvirostra americana*   Pl. XVII

These graceful and handsome shorebirds went entirely unreported in Louisiana in the half century between 1889 and 1940. Since then spectacular increases have made their presence in numbers commonplace. On January 26, 1954, for example, a flock estimated at 1,100 was noted on the state-supervised Rockefeller Refuge in Cameron Parish, and the observation in recent years of 300 or more individuals in a single day in that part of the state has been by no means unusual.

The contrasting black and white pattern, bluish legs, and upturned bill make the American Avocet a bird that can be confused with nothing else on our shores. In spring and summer the head and neck become a pinkish tan. Breeding takes place, for the most part, in the Great Plains region of the western part of North America, but it is known to nest sparingly on the coast of Texas and hence may one day be discovered doing so in this state. Already records are available for every month of the year, and on May 25–27, 1971, Robert B. Hamilton, a practiced investigator of the behavior of recurvirostrids, observed what appeared to be mated pairs at Grand Cheniere engaged in what he interpreted to be postcopulatory display.

As the Rockefeller Refuge observation mentioned above clearly indicates, the American Avocet is now common in southwestern Louisiana in winter; and there are recent records of the occurrence of single individuals and of small flocks all along the coast. Inland records are still rather scattered and generally pertain to single individuals, but a sizable flock of 75 was seen on a sandbar two miles below Shreveport on October 23, 1949, and 30 were counted at the Natchitoches Fish Hatchery on September 24, 1970. These noncoastal records, all of which are in summer and fall, suggest that migrants pass through the interior of the state from early July to the second week of November.

The Plover
Family
Charadriidae

In their shape, plovers suggest miniature gulls. They are wading birds with thick, stubby bills (especially in comparison with their relatives the sandpipers), large eyes, and usually prominent body patterns involving solid areas of white, gray, black, or brown. The best-known representative of the family in Louisiana is the Killdeer, which occurs all over the state the year around. In certain seasons, however, our sandbars and Gulf beaches are sometimes studded with as many as six other kinds of plovers.

SEMIPALMATED PLOVER *Charadrius semipalmatus* Fig. 64

The main North American population of this species has long been known by the name Semipalmated Plover, *Charadrius semipalmatus*, because it is believed to be specifically distinct from the Ringed Plover, *Charadrius hiaticula*, of the eastern American Arctic, Greenland, and the Old World. Each summer the little "semipalms," as we sometimes call them for short, raise their young near the bleak shores of the Arctic Ocean. When their family chores are completed, they head southward, some of them going almost to the opposite end of the earth, to Patagonia.

In making this trek, the species passes through Louisiana and is rather commonly seen on our inland lakeshores and mud flats and even more frequently along our coastal beaches. It is, indeed, the commonest of our four small plovers, except in June and early July. It is especially numerous from early March to late May and again from mid-July to late November and is regularly present in small numbers along the Gulf shores even in the middle of winter. In fact, records are available for every month of the year. Although often seen on clean sandy shores and on the edges of beach pools, it prefers muddy situations, such as the shores east of the mouth of the Calcasieu River and the great flats on the bay side of some of our coastal islands.

The Semipalmated Plover suggests a miniature Killdeer, but it has only

Wilson's Plover Chick Finds a Shady Spot

one black chest band, while the Killdeer has *two*. It is most like the Wilson's Plover in plumage, but it has a stubby bill that is dull orange at the base instead of all black, and the legs are dull orange instead of flesh colored. The Piping Plover also is similar in pattern to the Semipalmated Plover, but the latter is *much* darker above.

WILSON'S PLOVER   *Charadrius wilsonia*   Fig. 64; p. 278

The Wilson's, or Thick-billed Plover as it has sometimes been called, is a permanent resident in Louisiana, common in summer, extremely scarce in winter. In this state it is almost entirely a bird of the seabeaches although it has occasionally been known to appear a short distance inland along tidal estuaries or along the spoil banks of waterways. We usually find it feeding on the front beaches in the intertidal zone or around ponds formed by high tides washing over the natural levee of the shore's edge. The nest, which is only a depression in the sand with maybe a few broken shells in it, is placed from several yards to as much as 100 feet or so back from the water, but always well above normal high tides.

The uninterrupted band across the chest of the Wilson's Plover is jet black in the male, dusky in the female. In these respects it resembles the Semipalmated Plover, but it may be distinguished from the latter by its flesh-colored legs and longer and much heavier bill that is solid black; the Semipalmated Plover has a small bill that is orange at the base and black only on the tip.

KILLDEER   *Charadrius vociferus*   Fig. 64

The Killdeer, or "killdee" as the species is often called, is almost too well known to require description. From early September until late May it is conspicuously abundant in fields and meadows, on golf courses, and in other open situations. Even in summer, when most plovers migrate far to the north

Figure 64   Heads of five plovers: (1) Semipalmated Plover; (2) Piping Plover; (3) Snowy Plover; (4) Wilson's Plover; (5) Killdeer.

to nest, the Killdeer remains at least moderately common throughout most of Louisiana. Its two solid black bands across the chest, its rufous tail with a terminal black band, and its loud, persistent call, *kill-deah, kill-deah,* repeated many times at the slightest alarm, are characters familiar to all.

The species is much less of a "shorebird" than its close relatives, for it oftentimes nests far from water, in cultivated fields, near gravel pits, or in the rough of golf courses. The nest, like that of other plovers, is hardly more than a concavity in the ground, although occasionally there may be a few strands of grass or several pebbles beneath the four buffy eggs, which are heavily splotched with chocolate brown. The young on hatching have a pattern almost identical with that of the parents. As soon as the chicks are out of the egg and have rested for a minute or two while the feathers dry, they begin to run about on the ground. Should an observer approach the vicinity of the nest or the young, the adults go through a most elaborate "broken-wing act." Amid loud vocal outbursts and fluttering, with one or both wings hanging limp on the ground or pitifully twisted over the back, the parent bird apparently strives to draw attention to itself and to lead the intruder away from the nest or the young. Whatever may be the true psychological basis of the behavior, its survival value cannot be denied.

PIPING PLOVER   *Charadrius melodus*   Fig. 64

This species is one of our five so-called ringed plovers—plovers that have one or two bands that either partially or completely encircle the birds' necks and chests. The well-known Killdeer, which is in this group, has two bands across the chest that join on the sides. The other four species—the Piping, Snowy, Semipalmated, and Wilson's Plovers—have but one band, and even it may sometimes be broken on the chest. In the adult Semipalmated and Wilson's Plovers it is always complete; in the Snowy it is always broken; but in the Piping, depending on season, age, and sex, the ring may be either complete across the chest or more or less interrupted. The Snowy and Piping Plovers are the two species most easily confused, since both are pale above in color and since the Piping sometimes lacks the complete black band on the chest. In the latter, however, the base of the bill is usually orange, the tip is black, and the legs and feet are also orange. In the Snowy the bill is blackish and the legs and feet are either black or slaty gray. When the two species are together the bill of the Snowy is noticeably longer and more attenuated. The immatures and winter-plumaged adults lack the black frontal patch on the crown that is characteristic of the breeding plumage. But when this mark is present it furnishes an additional means of separating our two light-plumaged plovers, for it extends to the eye in the Piping, but not all the way to the eye in the Snowy.

The Piping Plover breeds mainly in the Great Plains region of the northern United States and Canada and on the Atlantic Coast as far south as North Carolina. It is fairly common in coastal Louisiana in migration (early August to late October and early March to late April) but scarce in midwinter. At Baton Rouge, which is a fairly typical inland locality, it has been recorded only between August 8 and September 12. The lack of observations inland in spring is probably due to the general absence of mud flats at that season, when the Mississippi and other rivers are at or above flood stage and the water levels of ponds and lakes are high following the winter rains.

SNOWY PLOVER *Charadrius alexandrinus*   Fig. 64

This smallest of our plovers—smallest by a narrow margin—is a sprite of our beaches that seems to be rapidly passing from the Louisiana scene and, for that matter, from all the coasts of the southeastern United States. There it has become a top candidate for admission to the U.S. Fish and Wildlife Service's List of Endangered Species. Once fairly common in the state, particularly in autumn and spring, with records from mid-July to late April, it now sometimes goes unreported all year long.

The Snowy Plover nests on all the major continents and is one of the few shorebirds that does not retire to the seclusion of the Arctic tundra for the purpose. It is known to breed a short distance to the east of us, in northwest Florida, and a short distance to the west of us, on the Texas coast; but evidence is still lacking that it has ever done so in Louisiana. The increasing number of people that throng the Gulf beaches during the nesting season seems to be the chief reason for the decline of the species in recent years. One might suppose that, as other breeding grounds become less and less habitable, these little plovers might take up summer residence on some of our seldom-visited barrier islands. Perhaps they have, but the infrequency with which they are being seen on the more accessible parts of our coast makes the hope appear rather dim.

For the diagnostic characters of this species see the account of the Piping Plover.

AMERICAN GOLDEN PLOVER   *Pluvialis dominica*   Figs. 65, 67

Much has been written about the phenomenal migratory performances of this species. Our American Golden Plovers breed in the Arctic tundra, and in fall most of them move eastward to the coast of Labrador, where they take off southward over two thousand miles of open water of the Atlantic in the direction of Brazil. From the coast of Brazil they move still farther southward to the pampas of Argentina, where they spend the winter. In spring, however, the northward flight is overland across South America to the shores of Venezuela and the Guianas. From there they fly across the Caribbean and the Gulf of Mexico to alight in the central Gulf Coast region before continuing on up the Mississippi Valley to their summer home in northern Canada.

Because of this elliptical flight path, we should expect to find the species in Louisiana only in spring, and, to be sure, this is the season when they are most numerous. During or after the first week of March and thence to mid-May, rarely to the last week of the month, flocks of American Golden Plovers may be seen in freshly plowed fields and clearings, on golf courses and the runways of airports, and in other similar situations throughout the state. Generally these birds, during the first part of their period of passage, are still in their winter dress, that is, without black underparts; but, as the

Figure 65 American Golden Plovers: adult breeding plumage on left; winter plumage on right.

season progresses, particularly by April and May, a number of individuals are likely to be in full nuptial plumage. Contrary to former belief, not all members of the population that breeds in eastern Alaska and Canada move eastward in the fall to Labrador, for we find the species occasionally in Louisiana in fall and early winter. Golden Plovers seen at this time are apparently birds that have deserted the main contingent of the species and have moved directly southward down the Mississippi Valley.

The American Golden Plover, in each of its plumages, has a close counterpart in one of the seasonal or age variations found in the Black-bellied Plover. A summary of the diagnostic differences between the two species is given in the next account.

BLACK-BELLIED PLOVER   *Pluvialis squatarola*   Figs. 66, 67

This and the preceding species are difficult to distinguish in the field unless one knows just what characters to look for. The axillars, a group of long narrow feathers located in the armpit and hence obscured by the wing except in flight, are black in this species and pale gray in the American Golden Plover. Moreover, the Black-bellied Plover has a white rump patch that is

Figure 66   Black-bellied Plovers: winter plumage on left; adult breeding plumage on right.

Figure 67 Two plovers in fall flight: Black-bellied Plover above; American Golden Plover below. Note the black axillars in the Black-bellied Plover.

diagnostic. In the breeding plumage, when both have black bellies, the American Golden Plover may be distinguished by its black (instead of white) lower belly and undertail coverts, by the absence of a white rump, and by the speckling of yellow instead of white on the back.

Black-bellies are very numerous all along our coast but are seldom seen inland, even in migration. Nonbreeding individuals, which for some reason have failed to migrate northward, may be seen irregularly throughout the summer at Grand Isle, on the Cameron beaches, and elsewhere. The bird is common to abundant from early September to early May.

The
Sandpiper
Family
Scolopacidae

The Sandpiper family, which claims the godwits, curlew, yellowlegs, Dunlin, phalaropes, woodcock, and snipe among its well-known representatives, is nearly cosmopolitan in distribution. Wherever in the world there are wet meadows, muddy beaches, or wave-washed shores, we are more than likely to find at least a few of its members at all seasons, methodically probing their long bills into the ground in constant search for food. The great majority of them nest in the subarctic and cold districts of Europe, Asia, and North America. Consequently, their virtually worldwide occurrence is a result mainly of their intrepid migratory movements outside of the breeding season. Of the 32 species of the family on the Louisiana list, only 2, the American Woodcock and Willet, are definitely known to breed in the state. The remainder are transients, winter residents, or nonbreeding summer residents.

The family consists for the most part of birds of small to medium size, although a few, such as some of the curlew, are rather large. All have relatively long legs and long bills, the first being an adaptation to wading, the latter, an adaptation to probing in the ground. In the woodcock the tip of the bill is provided with tactile nerve endings to aid in the detection of subsurface organisms that cannot be seen, and muscles control the flexible tip that enables the bird to seize these organisms and withdraw them from the mud.

HUDSONIAN GODWIT *Limosa haemastica* Pl. XVII

Godwits are large shorebirds with long, upturned bills that are flesh colored basally. The Hudsonian Godwit is an uncommon spring and even less common fall migrant that was once, not long ago, considered extremely rare at any season. But enough records have now accumulated to make me feel confident that the species can be located every spring by careful search in the rice fields of southwestern Louisiana and perhaps suitable situations in other parts of the state. Recorded dates for northward migration extend from April 17 to June 5. Apparently the greatest number seen by one observer in one day was the 58 tallied by John P. Gee in a rice field near Gum Cove on May 9, 1956. I know of only five fall records: specimens taken at New Orleans on September 6, 1875, and on September 27, 1895; one seen by Brooke Meanley at Mamou, in Evangeline Parish, on August 6, 1955; one observed by Ava R. Tabor near Cameron on October 30, 1965; and a flock of nine noted by Robert J. Newman and H. Douglas Pratt at Cameron on October 27, 1973.

In spring the Hudsonian Godwit is extremely dark above and the breast is a dull reddish with numerous horizontal black bars, especially on the sides and flanks. In fall, however, it is a drab gray above and whitish below. Except for the slightly upturned bill, the broad black band on the terminal half of the tail, and the absence of the bold black and white flight pattern in the wing, it is a close counterpart of a winter-plumaged Willet. I believe that the Hudsonian Godwit may have more than once escaped detection in fall because of this striking resemblance to one of our commonest species. There are just too many Willets on our shores for each one seen in the course of a day to be scrutinized closely.

Plate XVII Six Long-legged Shorebirds

1. Whimbrel (p. 289). 2. Long-billed Curlew (p. 290). 3. Marbled Godwit (p. 287). 4. Hudsonian Godwit (p. 286) in winter plumage. 5. American Avocet (p. 276) in breeding plumage. 6. adult male Black-necked Stilt (p. 275).

1   2   3   4

5   6

RET
'47

MARBLED GODWIT *Limosa fedoa*   Pl. XVII

The Marbled Godwit is rather uniformly light brown to pinkish buff on the underparts, sometimes with faint transverse barring on the sides. The color above is brown, heavily mottled and barred with pale buff and vinaceous-buff. The secondary wing coverts, most of the flight feathers, and the wing linings are vinaceous or cinnamon colored, flecked with dusky. The tail feathers and uppertail coverts are dusky, distinctly and regularly barred with cinnamon-buff or vinaceous-buff. The legs and feet are bluish gray. This dress is maintained essentially unaltered in both summer and winter. The distinctly upturned bill is pinkish on the basal half. The similarly colored Long-billed Curlew has an all-dusky downcurved bill.

The species was doubtless in the 1800s a common migrant and winter visitor, but, like many other shorebirds, it was diminished in numbers toward the end of that century almost to the point of extinction by market hunting. When Oberholser wrote his *Bird Life of Louisiana,* he could find but two definite state records for the species, one in 1885, the other in 1888. Since 1938, when Oberholser's work appeared, Marbled Godwits have been seen on numerous occasions on the coast in every month of the year. I have found them in moderate numbers on East Timbalier Island in August and common there in November. The bird has likewise been noted frequently in the last decade in Cameron Parish and in other coastal areas.

Most spring migrants arrive in early April and are gone by the end of May. Fall migration covers the period from mid-August to the end of November. I know of only two individuals found inland in the state, a bird seen on the LSU campus in Baton Rouge on September 10, 1965, by Laurence C. Binford and Sidney A. Gauthreaux, following Hurricane Betsy, and one seen at the same place on April 13, 1969, by Robert J. Newman and others. But there is no reason why the species should not fairly often visit suitable situations away from the coast in migration. Since it breeds in the Great Plains region of the northern United States and Canada, it must necessarily pass over the interior of Louisiana, en route to and from its nesting and wintering grounds.

ESKIMO CURLEW *Numenius borealis*   Fig. 68

Eskimo Curlew once migrated through the southern parts of our state in vast numbers, and, as was the case elsewhere along their path, they were slaughtered unmercifully and without heed for the possibility of their ultimate extinction. Each spring they came to our prairies by the thousands, and each spring their bodies were hauled away by the wagonload for shipment to the markets. By 1875, however, their numbers were so depleted that market hunting was no longer profitable. The last Eskimo Curlew in the state identified with certainty was one killed in March at Rayne in Acadia

Figure 68   Eskimo Curlew.

Parish in 1889. Fortunately, this specimen was preserved and now is in the LSU Museum of Zoology. Eskimo Curlews are still occasionally reported, especially on the coast of Texas, at either Rockport or Galveston Island. I was privileged to see the species on Galveston Island in both 1961 and 1964, when Nancy Strickling led me to the pastures where she had previously spotted the birds. In 1964 two individuals were definitely present.

Some books have stated erroneously that this species can hardly be distinguished in the field from the Whimbrel, especially from a short-billed individual of the latter. Really, however, there should be no confusion at all. The Eskimo Curlew has less than half the body bulk of the Whimbrel; its bill averages half as long and is much thinner; the underside of the wings is cinnamon-buff instead of gray; its belly is a warm buff color instead of grayish brown; and the legs and feet are dark greenish instead of bluish gray as they are in the Long-billed Curlew and Whimbrel.

WHIMBREL   *Numenius phaeopus*   Pl. XVII; p. 289

The Whimbrel, which was once called the Hudsonian Curlew, has about half the body bulk of the Long-billed Curlew and a bill that is only two and

Whimbrel

ALLAN D. CRUICKSHANK

three-fourths to four inches in length. Both the buffy line over the eye and the buffy stripe down the center of the otherwise unstreaked crown set this species apart from the larger bird; and the underside of the wing is gray instead of cinnamon-buff.

Whimbrels are sometimes seen on the Gulf beaches or around tidal pools near the shore, but most often they are birds of the coastal prairies and wet meadows lying a few hundred yards to a few miles inland. The species has been observed in Louisiana in every month of the year, but is common only in spring. The main flights arrive from the south of us during the first half of April and continue to pass through until the end of May. In late April I have seen flocks of several hundred on the coastal prairie near the town of Cameron in southwestern Louisiana. The only record of the species in the state outside the coastal parishes is that of three seen by Ronald J. Stein on a beach at the west end of Lake Pontchartrain on April 30, 1959. But the Whimbrel must surely pass over the interior of Louisiana during its migrations in spring and fall, for it breeds only in the high Arctic.

LONG-BILLED CURLEW   *Numenius americanus*   Pl. XVII

Long-billed Curlews are not just ordinary birds. There is something indefinably exciting and special about them. Perhaps the feature that gives them character is their grotesquely long, sickle-shaped bill. Or maybe it is their razor-edged wariness of us as we attempt to approach them on an open beach or a grassy meadow. But one thing seems certain, at least to me— few natural sounds are more thrilling than this bird's clear, mellow whistle, a *cur-lee, cur-lee*. Indeed, I pity the man who has never in his lifetime stood alone at the edge of the sea, far from the usual discordant sounds of our civilization, and watched curlews probing their bills into the sand and giving out their wild cries at the slightest alarm.

As the name implies, the present species has the longest bill (six to eight inches in length) of all the curlew. It is also the largest. The head has no striping, lacking even a prominent line over the eye, and the underside of the wing is pinkish buff. The Long-billed Curlew breeds away from water in the dry, open prairies of the Great Plains region. But while it is in Louisiana it is a bird of the Gulf shores and adjacent meadows, where it is not uncommon from late July to late May and is especially numerous in fall and spring. A few nonbreeding individuals are found throughout the summer. It has been seen in the interior parishes of the state at only one place, Wallace Lake, near Shreveport, where a single individual, presumably the same bird, was noted on both October 18 and 24, 1953.

I have heard the name *corbigeau* applied to this species by the French-speaking inhabitants of Grand Isle and elsewhere along the coast, but I have never learned its meaning.

UPLAND SANDPIPER *Bartramia longicauda* Fig. 69

This species is well known in southern Louisiana under the French name of *papabotte*, which is one phonetic expression of the bird's call. There is an old French idea that those who eat the flesh of this bird are imbued with extraordinary amatory prowess. Possibly this belief, coupled with the alleged delicacy of its flesh, is the reason the *papabotte* was once killed in such great numbers. At one time it migrated throughout the length and breadth of the state in great flocks. Then, because of excessive hunting, it became extremely rare, so much so that doubts arose as to its ability to survive. The timely pas-

RET

Figure 69   Upland Sandpiper.

sage by Congress of the Migratory Bird Treaty Act, in 1918, which forbade the killing of a long list of migratory birds, was the salvation of this and many other shorebirds.

Under protection the Upland Sandpiper, or Upland Plover as it was for a long time incorrectly called, is once again becoming a regular and often quite common transient in our state, from mid-March to mid-May and from July to late September. It is never, to my knowledge, seen on beaches but is instead a bird of cultivated fields and pastures throughout the state. The body is somewhat larger and heavier than that of the Killdeer, but the neck is disproportionately slender and the head disproportionately small. The color above is brownish, mottled with black; the underparts are whitish or pale buffy. The bill is relatively short and thin, and the long legs are greenish yellow.

One of the best field characters of the Upland Sandpiper is its mellow, gurgling call, *quip, ip, ip, ip* or *kip, ip, ip, ip*. This is uttered either as it runs rapidly on the ground or as it flies high in the sky at night in its migrations up and down the Mississippi Valley on its way between the pampas of the Argentine and the fields of our own northern United States.

GREATER YELLOWLEGS   *Tringa melanoleuca*   Fig. 70

The Greater and Lesser Yellowlegs are almost identical except in size (Fig. 70) and in call notes. The call of the Greater has been described as a three- or four-syllable whistle *whew-whew-whew*, or *dear-dear-dear*. The corresponding call of the Lesser is a flatter cry of one or two notes, *cu* or *cu-cu*. The long, bright yellow legs serve to distinguish both species from other sandpipers, as does also the flight pattern of a white rump in combination with a back that is dark gray, heavily speckled with white instead of streaked.

In Louisiana, the Greater Yellowlegs is a nonbreeder that has been recorded in every month of the year, but only in periods of migration is it common over the state as a whole. Spring transients arrive in numbers toward the last of February or the first week of March and continue to pass through the state in force until mid-May. Fall migrants begin to return at the end of July and are unfailingly common from then until the middle of November. The main center of abundance is on the coast, where it remains fairly common even in winter, a season when it is hardly ever found elsewhere. The number seen in midwinter appears to depend mainly on whether hard

Figure 70 Lesser Yellowlegs (left) and Greater Yellowlegs (right).

freezes have occurred to cause the birds to desert their coastal haunts. One-day counts in Cameron Parish in winter normally produce from two dozen to as many as 75 or 80 individuals, but on December 30, 1956, the tally was 517, an all-time high for any of the 15 Sabine Christmas Bird Counts.

LESSER YELLOWLEGS *Tringa flavipes*   Fig. 70; p. 294

The critical differences between the two yellowlegs are noted in the account of the Greater Yellowlegs. The Lesser Yellowlegs might, however, be confused with several sandpipers in its own size class. Its bright yellow legs and the white basal portion of the tail will serve to separate it from the Solitary Sandpiper, which has the legs greenish and only the *outer* tail feathers whitish. In addition, the latter has a white eye-ring and a different call note. The Stilt Sandpiper, which in winter lacks the barring on the breast characteristic of the breeding plumage, has greenish legs. The winter-plumaged Wilson's Phalarope is plain, unmarked gray above, is immaculate white below, and has a bill that is exceedingly thin and needlelike.

The Lesser Yellowlegs occurs here throughout the year, but it does not nest. It is fairly common to abundant in migration all over the state, from March well into May and again from mid-July to late November. In some winters it is moderately common on the coast, but in other winters, especially following freezing weather, its numbers are greatly reduced. June records are doubtless based on belated migrants or else individuals that, for some reason, failed to go north with the remainder of their species.

SOLITARY SANDPIPER   *Tringa solitaria*   Fig. 71

The Solitary Sandpiper is very common throughout Louisiana in migration, and stragglers can sometimes be found in the southern part of the state in winter. It has been seen on several occasions in June and not infrequently in July; hence one cannot be sure whether a sighting, particularly one in late June, represents a bird belatedly headed northward or one on its way southward from its breeding grounds.

Lesser Yellowlegs

ALLAN D. CRUICKSHANK

Figure 71 Solitary Sandpiper.

The species is identified by the very dark coloration above, the white eye-ring, the dark greenish legs, and the white, conspicuously barred outer tail feathers, which show plainly when the bird takes flight. The call is a *peep-weep*, resembling the note of the Spotted Sandpiper but higher in pitch. The Solitary Sandpiper is well named, for usually it is seen alone instead of with flocks of its kind or with other shorebirds. It frequents lakeshores and the open edges of wooded swamps but is especially fond of drainage ditches. I have never seen it on the Gulf beach.

Despite the fact that this sandpiper has long been one of the best-known shorebirds in the United States, its nest was not discovered until 1903. The bird was found in summer in abundance around streams and lakes in northern Canada, but repeated search for its nest met with complete failure. Finally, one day when an ornithologist happened to be sitting on the edge of a small stream watching Solitary Sandpipers passing to and fro, he chanced to notice an individual that appeared to terminate its flight in one of the few trees that dotted the area. Casually strolling over to the tree, he looked up to see only a last year's robin's nest. What prompted this man to climb the tree to inspect the old dilapidated nest is not known, but when he did so he looked down upon the first eggs of the Solitary Sandpiper known to science. No wonder the eggs of the species had escaped detection, for sand-pipers are supposed to build their nests on the ground! Now it is well known that the Solitary Sandpiper is an exception, that it always uses abandoned nests of such birds as the robin, grackle, or waxwing, and that the site some-times may be as much as 40 feet from the ground.

WILLET   *Catoptrophorus semipalmatus*   Fig. 72; p. 296

The local names of this large shorebird, *vire-vire* and "pill-will-willet," are derived from two of its call notes. One can hardly set foot anywhere at any time on our Gulf Coast without seeing and hearing this striking bird. When at rest it appears to be an all-gray, nondescript wader, but the moment it takes to the air it erupts into a burst of bold black and white markings, as illustrated in Figure 72. Its loud cries frequently startle into flight all the shorebirds along a whole section of beach, just as the observer has ap-proached the aggregation close enough to permit identification of the smaller and more nondescript members. When one comes into the vicinity of a Willet nest, the adult birds raise a nerve-wracking commotion with their incessant *pill-will-willet* call and their terrifying power dives at the intruder.

Willets in Silhouette

ALLAN D. CRUICKSHANK

RET

Figure 72 Willet.

I always instinctively duck although I know full well that the attacker will swerve to one side a few feet from my head. But sometimes airplanes fail to pull out of their power dives, and this makes me wonder if the flight mechanism of a Willet is not subject, at least rarely, to some sort of failure.

The species nests in Louisiana only in the marshes along the Gulf Coast, where it is common to abundant the year around; elsewhere in the state it is a rare transient. The nest is a simple depression in the ground above the high-tide mark, sometimes with a few sticks or pieces of grass in the bottom or arranged around the periphery. The eggs are usually four in number and are various shades of buff, spotted with dark brown and gray.

In the molt after the nesting season the Willet loses the fine streaking on the breast and the dark mottling on the upperparts and hence becomes almost immaculate white below and ashy gray above. The wings, however, retain the sharply contrasting patches of black and white.

SPOTTED SANDPIPER   *Actitis macularia*   Fig. 73

The Spotted Sandpiper is a bird present in Louisiana the year around, common in the main periods of migration (mid-March to the end of May, late July to the end of October) but rare in midsummer and midwinter. As yet there is no satisfactory evidence that it nests here, despite the fact that it has been alleged to do so. Individuals seen in June may be late northbound migrants and those seen in July may be early southbound migrants. As noted previously, the mere presence of a species in the breeding season is by no means proof of nesting. An actual nest, a young individual just out of a nest, or one too poorly developed to undertake sustained flight is required to establish that a species is breeding in an area.

In spring the Spotted Sandpiper acquires the plumage that gives it its name, for the breast becomes heavily sprinkled with black spots. In the molt following the breeding season these spots are lost. The bird is still easily recognized at any season by its habit of bobbing the back end of its body up and down, by the fact that in flight it almost never lifts its wings much

Figure 73   Spotted Sandpiper (summer plumage).

above the horizontal and generally glides a few feet with its wings held at a downward tilt just before landing, and by its distinctive call note, a clear *pee-weet*. At Baton Rouge there are no records for the species between May 25 and July 20, but on the coast it has been seen in every week of the year.

RUDDY TURNSTONE *Arenaria interpres* Fig. 74; p. 300

The Ruddy Turnstone, or "calicoback" as it is sometimes called, is one of the easiest of all shorebirds to identify. Its unique harlequin pattern of black and reddish brown, interspersed with white patches, and its orange feet make it extremely attractive in appearance. It is principally a bird of the seashore and can nearly always be found at Grand Isle. Although numerous only in spring, late summer, and early fall, it has been observed in Louisiana in every month of the year. Midsummer records, however, are undoubtedly of nonbreeding individuals that have failed to migrate northward to the nesting grounds of the species on the tundra bordering the Arctic Ocean. No one knows whether the turnstones that come to the shores of the Gulf of

Figure 74 Purple Sandpiper (left) and Ruddy Turnstone (right).

Ruddy Turnstones Resting

Mexico migrate exclusively up and down the Mississippi Valley. Such a movement would not, however, seem to be the case, since the species is extremely rare at all inland localities in the state, having been observed only twice at Baton Rouge, only once at Shreveport, and nowhere else in the interior. Possibly a considerable part of the Gulf population works its way eastward in spring, makes a short overland flight across Florida, and then migrates up the Atlantic Coast.

WILSON'S PHALAROPE *Steganopus tricolor* Fig. 75

Phalaropes are peculiar shorebirds in several ways, and for this reason some experts accord them familial rank under the name Phalaropodidae. For one thing, the female, not the male, wears the bright colors—a contradiction to the general rule among birds that the male is the more handsome of the sexes. It should be noted, moreover, that the drab-plumaged male takes over the chores of incubation and is probably much less conspicuous in this role than the gaudy female would be. A feature of the Northern and

Red Phalaropes, not shared by the Wilson's, is their predilection for feeding, ducklike, out in the middle of large bodies of water, or even on the open sea. Indeed, the Red Phalarope winters entirely on the open Gulf or on the waters of the southern oceans, far from land. Phalaropes have marginally lobed toes, which they apparently hold in such a fashion as to make a cup-shaped paddle, for they swim with adeptness. They have the habit of whirling rapidly in a circle on the water, a behavior that must operate to some advantage in their quest for the tiny aquatic organisms on which they feed.

The Wilson's Phalarope is less inclined to swim in open water than either the Red or Northern Phalaropes; it is, in other words, more typically a *shorebird*. In spring the female has a rich chestnut streak on the side of the neck that blends into a black patch on the neck and face. The top of her head is pale gray, the back is gray with two longitudinal chestnut stripes, one of which is a continuation of this color from the sides of the neck, and the underparts are immaculate white. The less attractive male is similar but has only a tinge of reddish confined to the neck and has a gray rather than black facial patch. In fall both sexes are pale gray above and white below and resemble somewhat the Lesser Yellowlegs. They may be distinguished from the latter by their creamy yellow, instead of bright yellow, legs; by their thin, needlelike bill; and by the immaculate grayness of their backs.

The species winters mainly in faraway South America and is most likely to be encountered on the coast of Louisiana from late April to mid-May, a period in which it is sometimes moderately common. Fall records are mostly in July, August, and early September. Although most frequently observed on the coast, the species is also occasionally seen during periods of migration on edges of lakes, rivers, and ponds in the interior of the state. Exceptional, however, were the observations of one at the Natchitoches Fish Hatchery between November 12 and 20, 1958, and of two in a rice field nine miles west of Lafayette on December 24 and 26, 1969. The latter record is the only occurrence inland in the United States in winter known to me.

NORTHERN PHALAROPE *Lobipes lobatus*   Fig. 75

This species was added to the Louisiana list on May 8, 1966, when I collected an adult female at an impoundment adjacent to an oil installation 10 miles west of Johnsons Bayou, near Sabine Pass. On May 1, 1970, Robert J. Newman and I saw six phalaropes behind the Cameron courthouse that we are certain were this species. An effort to collect one of the birds unfortunately failed. On April 30, 1971, Newman and Gayle T. Strickland saw four phalaropes believed to be Northerns at a nearby pond, and on the following day several of us observed three in the same area. Finally, on September 12, 1971, a single individual at the impoundment near Sabine Pass, where the first record was obtained, furnished the only fall observation of this species in the state. It was studied by Newman and four other competent observers and was actually compared directly in the same binocular field with Wilson's Phalaropes that were also present. Its small size, short and slender bill, and dark top of the head were noted.

The distinguishing field marks of the Northern Phalarope are discussed in the account of the Red Phalarope. The species breeds principally north of the Arctic Circle, in both the Eastern and Western hemispheres, and winters at sea in the waters of the North and South Atlantic and the North and South Pacific.

RED PHALAROPE *Phalaropus fulicarius*   Fig. 75

Three Red Phalaropes have now been recorded in the state—a specimen obtained on the Baton Rouge campus of Louisiana State University on October 12, 1950, by Robert J. Newman; one collected a mile west of Holly Beach, in Cameron Parish, on September 16, 1961, by Laurence C. Binford and Delwyn G. Berrett, following Hurricane Carla; and an individual observed at the Natchitoches Fish Hatchery on November 29, 1970, by Robert B. Hamilton and Robert J. Newman. The last-mentioned bird remained at the fish hatchery until December 10 and during this interval was seen by Horace H. Jeter and was photographed.

The Red Phalarope should occur during the winter in Louisiana's offshore waters, since it is known to be common off Pensacola, Florida, where it has been recorded from October 13 to April 21, at distances of 5 to 65 miles out and in flocks sometimes numbering into hundreds of individuals.

This phalarope in breeding attire cannot be confused with any other species, for it is red breasted and has white cheek patches and a blackish crown. The winter plumages of the three phalaropes do, however, present identification problems. The Red Phalarope is simply gray above and white below and is, therefore, similar to other species of shorebirds, particularly the other species of phalaropes. In the Red Phalarope the bill is black, sometimes yellowish toward the base. Although the yellow at the base is diag-

Figure 75 Phalaropes: (1) Wilson's (female in breeding plumage on left, winter plumage on right); (2) Northern (female in breeding plumage on left, winter plumage on right); (3) Red (female in breeding plumage on left, winter plumage on right).

nostic when present, it should not be expected. The shortness and thickness of the bill, in comparison with the bills of the other two phalaropes, is more consistently dependable. The length of the bill in the Red Phalarope is about as long as, or slightly longer than, the head at the same level, and it is broad enough at the base to appear somewhat conical. In the Northern Phalarope the bill is at least as long as the head, usually longer, and is thin and needlelike. In the Wilson's Phalarope the bill is also thin and needlelike but at least half again as long as the head at the same level. The tail of the Wilson's is essentially white and pale gray (no black), and it lacks any white in the wings, but the other two species have some black or dark gray in the tail and a slash of white on the upper surfaces of the wings, marks that are visible when the birds are in flight.

AMERICAN WOODCOCK *Philohela minor*   Fig. 76

This prized game bird—*becasse* to the French—is abundant all over Louisiana, except the coastal marshes, from mid-October to early February and present but rare during the remainder of the year. Though anatomically

Figure 76   American Woodcock.

a shorebird, it inhabits woodlands by day and feeds in fields at night, special muscles enabling it to open the flexible tip of the long bill while probing deep into damp soil for earthworms and insects. The hugest winter woodcock concentrations known anywhere foregather after dark in pastures in the heavily wooded Atchafalaya Basin. There Professor Leslie Glasgow and his students, in a seven-year period, hand-netted and banded some sixteen thousand individuals and learned much about their migratory movements.

Uttering a comical nasal *beezp beezp*, local breeders begin aerial courtship antics in early January, and by February the four buffy eggs, spotted with brownish, are laid in a depression in the leaves on the ground. When flushed from a thicket or other hiding place, this chunkiest of shorebirds rises straightaway, with the stiff outer feathers of the rounded wings making a diagnostic whistling sound. The slimmer and much smaller-headed Common Snipe, the only other long-billed shorebird occurring near the haunts of woodcock, has pointed wings and a tendency to fly erratically. A good way to find woodcock is to station oneself at the border between woods and open fields and watch for them passing by during morning or evening twilight.

COMMON SNIPE *Capella gallinago*   Fig. 77

This species is the only shorebird, other than the American Woodcock, that is legal game. The Common Snipe, or "jacksnipe," is abundant in Louisiana in late fall, winter, and early spring, occurring in numbers from mid-October well into April, and has been recorded sporadically as early as August 14 and as late as June 18. It frequents marshes, grassy meadows, and lakeshores, blending so well with the ground that it often escapes detection. It is slimmer than the American Woodcock, and the outer tail feathers are orange-red. When flushed, it takes off on a rapid zigzag course, instead of flying straightaway. This peculiarity of flight and its harsh, rasping note are each diagnostic of the species.

Figure 77   Common Snipe.

The Common Snipe, or Wilson's Snipe as it is sometimes called, resembles the dowitchers in body form. In winter, however, the dowitchers are grayish with the rump and lower back white, while the Common Snipe is brownish below and very dark above except for a few longitudinal buffy streaks. In spring plumage the dowitchers are pinkish or reddish below; and, even though dark like the Common Snipe on most of the upperparts, they still have the extensive patch of white on the rump and lower back.

SHORT-BILLED DOWITCHER   *Limnodromus griseus*   Figs. 78, 79

Dowitchers are fairly large, snipelike shorebirds with a long, straight bill and a white patch that extends over the base of the tail, the rump, and most of the lower back. They are usually seen in groups on mud flats or wet grassy meadows, probing their bills into the earth in quest of food. Sometimes these flocks reach vast proportions. For instance, I once saw an aggregation estimated at two thousand individuals energetically feeding in a pasture in Cameron Parish in early April.

Not until the mid-1950s did authorities agree that dowitchers constitute two distinct species—one short billed, the other long billed. Nowhere do their breeding ranges come in contact, so whether they are capable of interbreeding cannot be tested. Each is further characterized by significant differences in behavior and call notes. Because of individual variation in bill length, the separation of *short-billed* Long-billed Dowitchers from *long-*

Figure 78 Sanderling (left); Short-billed Dowitcher (middle); and Buff-breasted Sandpiper (right).

Figure 79 Comparison of heads of Short-billed Dowitcher (lower left) and Long-billed Dowitcher (lower right). In shorebirds, females average larger than males in most of their measurements. The dowitcher in flight is shown to call attention to the white stripe extending from the base of the tail up the middle of the back, an excellent field mark for distinguishing dowitchers from other shorebirds.

billed Short-billed Dowitchers will always be difficult, but when the two species are viewed under favorable circumstances they can be distinguished with confidence. Criteria other than bill length that serve to separate them are given in the following account.

In my experience and in that of others with whom I have discussed the matter, any dowitcher seen in a strictly saltwater habitat, such as a mud flat along a Gulf shore, is almost certain to be the Short-billed. But both species occur in freshwater and brackish situations. In summer plumage, the underparts of both dowitchers are reddish with numerous dusky bars or spots, and the upper back is quite dark; but in winter, dowitchers are gray above and whitish below with only a faint indication of barring on the flanks. In any plumage, however, they differ from other shorebirds in having the extensive white patch on the lower back, rump, and basal portion of the tail. This patch is strikingly conspicuous when a bird takes flight but is otherwise hidden by the wings. The extreme lower rump, uppertail coverts, and tail feathers are heavily barred with black and white or black and reddish brown.

The Short-billed Dowitcher has been recorded in Louisiana in every month of the year, being moderately common in winter and abundant in spring and fall. Despite the frequent occurrence of both species of dowitchers along the coast and in the rice fields of the southwestern part of the state, comparatively few records are available from other interior localities.

LONG-BILLED DOWITCHER   *Limnodromus scolopaceus*   Fig. 79

This dowitcher breeds in Alaska and in extreme northwestern Canada, but it has been observed in Louisiana in every month of the year. It is numerous in freshwater and brackish situations near the coast in spring and fall and remains so throughout the winter, except when hard freezes create icy conditions in the marshes. Much remains, however, to be learned regarding the relative abundance of the two species of dowitchers at different seasons, a problem complicated by their close similarity.

The Long-billed Dowitcher in breeding plumage, as we sometimes see it in late April and May, is darker and more extensively reddish below, with the undertail coverts sometimes as reddish as the breast. The dusky markings on the flanks and sides of the breast tend to form bars instead of spots, and the upper back and scapulars are more extensively blackish (less brownish). Although extremes differ by as much as a full inch, bill length in the two species is subject to much overlapping. The call note of the Short-billed is a *tu-tu-tu*, while the Long-billed utters a *keek* that is only occasionally trebled.

RED KNOT   *Calidris canutus*   Fig. 80

In Louisiana this short-legged, heavy-bodied sandpiper is almost exclusively a bird of the sandy beaches of the Gulf shores. Only three Red Knots have ever been noted inland in the state: one seen on a rain-soaked parade field on the campus at Louisiana State University on September 18, 1943, fol-

Figure 80   Stilt Sandpiper (left) and Red Knot (right).

lowing a tropical disturbance in the Gulf of Mexico; an individual observed at Shreveport on September 1 and 8, 1951; and a third identified at the Natchitoches Fish Hatchery on March 15, 1956.

Even when it is in drab winter plumage its dumpy shape and short, thick bill form a combination that makes the Red Knot comparatively easy to separate from other sandpipers of its general size, such as the Common Snipe and the dowitchers. In spring one frequently sees this species with the prenuptial molt far enough advanced to give the birds the red breast characteristic of the breeding plumage, from which the vernacular name "robin snipe" stems.

The species breeds on the tundra bordering the Arctic Ocean and migrates in winter as far south as the shores of South America. Red Knots are encountered regularly in such coastal situations as at Grand Isle and on Cameron Parish beaches in periods of migration (March to mid-June, late July to early November), and records are available for all the winter months. Although the species is most often seen singly or in small groups, some exceptional counts include the following: 85 at Grand Isle on March 10,

1962; over 175 on Chandeleur Island on June 12, 1971; 60 on Grand Terre on August 1, 1971; 120 at Grand Isle on January 12, 1972; 261 on the Chandeleurs on June 19–21, 1973.

SANDERLING   *Calidris alba*   Fig. 78

Sanderlings are the little sandpipers that have aroused the curiosity of nearly everyone who has visited the seashore. On their short legs, which they move incredibly fast, they run down to the water's edge right behind a receding wave, probe their little bills into the wet sand, and then go scurrying back to higher ground as the succeeding wave comes rolling in. Oftentimes, with a heavy surf, it would seem certain that the sea must overtake them, but seldom do they get more than the pads of their toes wet.

In winter the Sanderling's plumage is nearly the color of dry sand, hence its name; but in spring, before it leaves us to go to its breeding grounds in the Arctic, it displays varying amounts of the summer dress, in which the head and breast, as well as the general tone of the dorsum, become rusty in color. In flight Sanderlings show a conspicuous white streak along the length of the wing, and they are by far the whitest of our sandpipers. Their preferred habitat is the front beach, where they are common from mid-August to the end of May and where a few can sometimes be found even in midsummer. Although they must migrate overland up and down the Mississippi Valley, the species has been seen less than a dozen times in the interior of our state.

SEMIPALMATED SANDPIPER   *Calidris pusilla*   Fig. 81

This species and the next, the first two of the "peeps," or sparrow-sized sandpipers, are not easy to distinguish in the field. Both resemble the Least Sandpiper, but that species has a thin, sharply attenuated bill, is browner on the upperparts and breast, and has yellowish, instead of black, legs. *Most* Semipalmated Sandpipers can be distinguished from *most* Western Sandpipers by bill length. If the bill is shorter than the length of the head at the same level, the bird in question is a Semipalmated; if the bill is definitely longer, it is a Western. But bill length in the two species is subject to much individual variation and sexual dimorphism; hence, we always find some birds with bills that are intermediate and therefore indeterminable as to

Figure 81 Heads of "peeps": Least Sandpiper (top); Semipalmated Sandpiper (middle); Western Sandpiper (bottom).

species in the field. The fact that the Western is conspicuously more rufous above than the Semipalmated in spring, however, is a help at that season.

The Semipalmated Sandpiper is an abundant migrant on the coast in April and May and again from early September to late November but is much less frequently observed inland, where it is decidedly less common than the Least Sandpiper and somewhat less common than the Western Sandpiper. It can almost always be found on the coast, even in midsummer. In midwinter its numbers are variable even on the coast; sometimes large flocks are present, and sometimes careful search is required to find a single individual.

WESTERN SANDPIPER *Calidris mauri* Fig. 81

The Western Sandpiper is abundant along the coast from August to late May, and it occurs in small numbers even in June and July, becoming more numerous toward the end of the latter month. Although less common inland, it is everywhere in the state one of the commonest members of the genus. The more reddish coloration of the upperparts in springtime and the generally longer bill that tends to droop near the tip serve to separate it from the Semipalmated Sandpiper, the species to which it bears the closest resemblance (see also the accounts for the Least and Semipalmated Sandpipers).

LEAST SANDPIPER   *Calidris minutilla*   Fig. 81

Of the five so-called peeps, the Least is the smallest, the commonest, and the most widespread. It is browner on the upperparts and on the breast than the Semipalmated and Western Sandpipers, the short bill is thinner, and the legs and feet are yellowish instead of blackish. Least Sandpipers are found inland, feeding in wet grassy meadows or along muddy lakeshores more frequently than Semipalmateds or Westerns, but they mingle freely with the other peeps on the seashore and on mud flats. Like all the others, they breed in the Far North, but there is no month of the year when at least a few may not be found within our borders. In the Baton Rouge area, which may be considered fairly typical of inland localities, the species has escaped detection only in the brief period between May 18 and July 15. It is fairly common there even in winter, notably on the shores of False River and at such places as the Natchitoches Fish Hatchery.

The peeps are comical little birds. They gang up in flocks and together methodically scour a beach or mud flat in search of food. I have often wondered what percentage of their pecking motions produces edible morsels, for their bills are probing continuously as they scamper about hurriedly from one spot to another. Another of their remarkable behavioral features is the compactness of their flocks in flight. Only a fraction of an inch seems to separate the fast-flying birds as they wheel and turn abruptly, first one way and then another. In order for the rear echelons not to crash into the leaders of the flock, as the latter begin to negotiate a turn, the whole maneuver would seemingly have to be simultaneous, with every member of the flock turning together. This supposition, however, must assume a system of communication that evokes instantaneous response.

WHITE-RUMPED SANDPIPER   *Calidris fuscicollis*   Fig. 82

This large-sized peep has been recorded in Louisiana as early as March 12 but does not ordinarily become common until late May or the first week of June, after the main movements of other transient shorebirds have ended.

RET

Figure 82 White-rumped Sandpiper.

It is a sandpiper that one does not need to go all the way to the coast to find, for it throngs the rice belt, appears regularly at the Natchitoches Fish Hatchery, and shows up at other places inland. The latest record for a northbound migrant is June 21.

The only notice of southbound migrants in the state is a report by Joseph C. Kennedy of five seen at New Orleans on August 13, 1968. This lone evidence compared with the abundance of sightings in spring encourages the idea that the White-rumped Sandpiper, like the American Golden Plover, ordinarily follows an elliptical migration route but with the lines of northward and southward flight not quite so far apart.

When this bird is feeding with a large aggregation of mixed sandpipers, it is easily confused with several other species, since it is intermediate in size between the smaller peeps on the one hand and the Pectoral Sandpiper on the other. Experts can generally pick out a White-rump in a flock by subtle characters, such as the combination of somewhat stocky build, black legs, and fine but crisply contrasted black streaking on the white chest; but even they prefer to delay identification until the bird has been made to fly and reveal the white patch at the base of its tail, a mark it shares with no other shorebird in its size range except the very rare Curlew Sandpiper, which has a conspicuously downcurved bill.

BAIRD'S SANDPIPER   *Calidris bairdii*   Fig. 83

The Baird's Sandpiper is a regular but uncommon spring and fall transient in Louisiana, recorded from mid-March to June 1 and from July 10 to November 17. Since the species migrates in numbers to the west of us, through Texas, its more frequent occurrence in our western parishes than elsewhere in the state is not surprising. Available records are preponderantly either from near Shreveport, the Natchitoches Fish Hatchery, or Cameron Parish, but the species has also been seen at Baton Rouge, Grand Isle, and New Orleans.

This rather nondescript peep is larger, with paler, browner upperparts, than either the Semipalmated or Western Sandpipers. The breast is a *pale buff* color and only lightly streaked, and the legs and feet are black. One of the best field marks is the long wings, which extend approximately a half inch beyond the tail when the bird is in standing posture. In the other peeps the wings never extend noticeably beyond the end of the tail. George M. Sutton, who studied the species on Southhampton Island, in Hudson Bay, where it breeds, syllabifies the call note as a distinctive *kreep, kreep*.

PECTORAL SANDPIPER   *Calidris melanotos*   Fig. 83

At certain seasons this is one of our commonest sandpipers and one that, unlike most species of the group, is almost as numerous inland as on the coast. It has a decided preference for grassy lakeshores and wet meadows but is not entirely averse to the muddy Gulf beaches. It resembles the peeps, as sparrow-sized sandpipers in general are sometimes called, but is considerably larger. The best field mark is the sharp line of demarcation between the heavy streaking on the neck, chest, and upper breast and the pure white of the lower breast and belly. A medium-sized brownish sandpiper with yellow legs and an abrupt termination to the pectoral streaking is almost certainly this bird.

Records for the species in our state are available for every month of

Figure 83 Dunlin (left); Baird's Sandpiper (middle); Pectoral Sandpiper (right).

the year, but in winter it is extremely scarce. Indeed, the three individuals seen on the muddy Gulf beach east of Cameron on December 23, 1950, were the only ones recorded on the nationwide Christmas Bird Count of that year. There are records of northbound migrants as late as June 7 and of southbound migrants as early as July 11. The main periods of occurrence are, however, March and April and August to the end of October.

PURPLE SANDPIPER *Calidris maritima*   Fig. 74

This sandpiper is a bird of rocky shores. For this reason, it is often found wintering on jetties along the coast of the North Atlantic, yet seldom farther south than Maryland. Since it had once been detected in winter on the jetties off Galveston Island, I had long expected its eventual appearance on the jetties projecting approximately a mile into the Gulf off the mouth of Calcasieu Pass in Cameron Parish. The end of these jetties was indeed the place where, on April 4, 1974, Robert B. Hamilton and Robert E. Noble found one and succeeded in obtaining the specimen, which now reposes in the LSU Museum of Zoology. In making this important discovery, Hamilton and Noble not only added the species to the state list, bringing the total to 411, but they provided one of the few records of the species anywhere on the shores of the Gulf of Mexico. The specimen was a female with considerable subcutaneous fat. The record was obtained after this edition was in press but not too late to be included here. The species could not, however, be added to the seasonal charts at the end of the book.

The Purple Sandpiper breeds in the Arctic Zone from Ellesmere Island, western and southern Greenland, Iceland, extreme northern Europe, and the coast and Arctic islands of northern Siberia south to islands on the east coast of Hudson Bay, the Faeroes, northern Norway, central Sweden, and the coast of Murmansk. In the western Atlantic it winters casually as far south as the coast of Georgia and Florida. The species is easily identified by its plump body, short legs, and rather stout bill. In winter the coloration is dark slaty gray to blackish above, gray on the throat and chest, and streaked with gray on the flanks, and it is white bellied. The central tail feathers are grayish black, the remainder are pale gray or white. The legs and feet and the base of the bill are golden yellow. A white line running lengthwise across the central portion of the wing is evident when the bird is in flight. The lores and a spot above and below the eye are indistinctly white. The species can hardly be confused with any other shorebird except the winter-plumaged Rock Sandpiper of the North Pacific, which, however, has never been recorded anywhere in eastern North America. In the latter species, the legs and feet are greenish in color, and the call notes are said to be a flickerlike, deep whistle repeated about a dozen times in quick succession. The call of the Purple Sandpiper is a *wit* or *weet-wit*.

DUNLIN *Calidris alpina*   Figs. 83, 84

The long, downcurved bill of the Dunlin is diagnostic among shorebirds of its size class unless a Curlew Sandpiper happens to be present. This is not a wholly unlikely possibility, since that species has been seen once at Cameron, once in the Galveston, Texas, area, twice in Alabama, and numerous times on the coast of the northeastern United States. In spring the Dunlin acquires a black belly and a red back, which make it unlike any other shorebird; but in fall both it and the Curlew Sandpiper are plain gray above and white below. At that season, the lack of white uppertail coverts eliminates the Curlew Sandpiper.

The species is common on the coast in winter but is not often seen inland, even in migration. It has, however, been noted at Baton Rouge twice in fall and at the Natchitoches Fish Hatchery on numerous occasions be-

Figure 84 Curlew Sandpiper (left) and Dunlin (right), both in winter plumage.

tween October 12 and December 8, with three individuals lingering to December 20 in 1968. One was also seen at Wallace Lake Dam, near Shreveport, on May 17, 1953. It differs from most of its allies in the greater amount of time it spends away from our shores; it is almost always gone by late May and has only once reappeared in southward migration as early as the first week of September.

CURLEW SANDPIPER *Calidris ferruginea*   Fig. 84

The Curlew Sandpiper is admitted here to the Louisiana list entirely on the basis of a single sight record, since the evidence in this particular case seems to be unequivocal. The bird in question was on the edge of a small pond 50 yards back of the front beach two miles east of Cameron, where John P. Gee and Marshall B. Eyster discovered it on September 13, 1953, and studied it at leisure for an hour, noting that the bill curved evenly downward without drooping at the tip, as does the bill of the Dunlin. They made the bird, which was in winter plumage, fly several times in order to observe the distinctive white lower rump and uppertail coverts. This feature ruled out the possibility of the bird's being the Dunlin, which, like the Curlew Sandpiper, has a decurved bill; and the decurved bill eliminated the White-rumped Sandpiper from consideration.

There can be little or no doubt that the bird observed by Gee and Eyster, two competent and painstaking ornithologists, was a Curlew Sandpiper, a species that breeds in Siberia, winters widely in the Old World, and occurs with fair regularity in Canada and the northern United States. In spring and summer plumage it is unmistakable because of its unique color, which is almost entirely brownish red. In winter, though, when it is pale grayish above and white below, it may escape detection among the hordes of similar-appearing Dunlins that throng our beaches.

STILT SANDPIPER   *Calidris himantopus*   Fig. 80

The heavy crossbarring of the underparts, reddish ear patches, and rather long greenish legs make this sandpiper easily identifiable in spring plumage. In fall and winter, however, its coloration is predominantly dark gray above and white below with a faint streaking on the chest, and therefore it is quite similar to several other species. It suggests a Lesser Yellowlegs, but the legs are greenish instead of bright yellow. It differs from the Solitary Sandpiper in having a white line over the eye instead of a white eye-ring and in having a white rump (the Solitary has only the outer tail feathers white, and the rump and central tail feathers are the same color as the back). From the Wilson's Phalarope in fall and winter plumage it differs in having a less needlelike bill, in being darker above, and in having greenish legs and a lightly streaked, instead of immaculate, lower throat and upper breast.

The Stilt Sandpiper has been recorded as a transient in suitable situations in many parts of the state. But it breeds, as do most of its kin, in the Far North in the vicinity of the Arctic Circle, and it migrates thousands of miles to winter in South America. Possibly because of the distance the species must cover in coming up from its wintering grounds, its spring passage through Louisiana does not commence in force until April. From then until mid-May it is common along our Gulf Coast. In midsummer, as soon as the young are able to fly, the family groups must immediately head southward again, for the second week of July finds some Stilt Sandpipers back on the Gulf Coast, and by late August fair numbers are again in evidence. Fall records in Louisiana extend through November, and a flock of three was observed in Cameron on January 1, 1973, by Robert J. Newman and Robert B. Hamilton.

BUFF-BREASTED SANDPIPER   *Tryngites subruficollis*   Fig. 78

The Buff-breasted Sandpiper once was considered a very rare transient in Louisiana. Now that its habitat preferences are better understood it is found regularly in both small and large flocks. The species is seldom observed in tidal situations but instead feeds almost exclusively in grassy situations, where the only other shorebirds are American Golden Plovers, Killdeers, and Upland Sandpipers. Once on September 1 we found these sandpipers abundant on the prairie a few miles west of Cameron, where they were feeding in the innumerable rain-filled cow tracks, and as many as 120 were counted on April 5 and 12, 1954, in a wet field near Duson. Other favorite haunts are golf courses, parade fields, new grainfields, pastures, and recently burned marshes.

The Buff-breasted Sandpiper is not easily confused with any other bird. It is scaly tan above and plain buffy below, sometimes with an admixture of white, often passing into solid buffy white on the abdomen and undertail coverts, more rarely doing so on the lower breast. The bill is short and slender and the legs are yellowish. Other important field marks are the general build and the white wing linings that show when the bird takes wing. Although not likely to be visible except in the case of a specimen in the hand, the greater primary underwing coverts and the terminal half of the flight feathers are uniquely barred or finely vermiculated with black. All other sandpipers in Louisiana show at least some indication of dark markings on the sides of the head, notably in the auricular area and on the underparts, but the cheeks and underparts of the Buff-breasted Sandpiper are immaculate except for a few tiny spots on the sides of the neck and occasionally on the edges of the upper chest. Baird's Sandpipers are buffy only on the upper breast (throat and belly are white), and the legs are blackish.

Dates extend from late March to mid-May and from mid-July until late October. The species breeds in the Arctic and winters near the delta of the Río de la Plata, in Argentina and Uruguay.

The Jaeger
Family
Stercorariidae

Jaegers (pronounced yā′gers) are the avian pirates of the sea. In fact, the name comes from the German *jäger*, meaning "huntsman." They pursue and plunder the gulls and terns, rob them of their food, and eat their eggs and young. Jaegers have longer and more pointed wings than their relatives the gulls, and the beak is strongly hooked. Although they come to land to nest on the Arctic tundra, they are truly birds of the open sea, roosting at night on the waves or on flotsam and coursing for hours on open wings during the day. Deep-sea fishermen, who go into offshore waters, are quite likely to encounter one or another of the three species.

The plumage varies appreciably since light, intermediate, and dark phases occur. A good field mark of all jaegers in all plumages is the white streak in the wings produced by the white basal color of the wing quills. Most adults can be relegated to their proper species by the shape of the central tail feathers, which, in mature jaegers, are longer than the lateral tail feathers. In the Long-tailed Jaeger, the projecting portion of the central tail feathers is long and pointed; in the Parasitic, relatively short and pointed; in the Pomarine, round ended and twisted into a vertical plane (Fig. 85).

At the time the second revised edition of this work was in preparation, in 1959, no satisfactory state record of any member of this family was available. Both the Pomarine and Parasitic Jaegers had been observed in our off-shore waters but too far out to satisfy the rules then followed. Now all three species are definitely known to occur in the state and are qualified members of our state's avifauna.

POMARINE JAEGER   *Stercorarius pomarinus*   Fig. 85

The Pomarine Jaeger was first recorded in Louisiana on April 20, 1962, when John P. Gee collected an immature female on the beach one mile west of the jetties at the mouth of Calcasieu Pass. The species has been seen in numbers in April along the continental shelf between points opposite Cameron and Morgan City by biologists on the U.S. Fish and Wildlife Service's exploratory and research vessel, the M/V *Oregon*. The following specimens were actually obtained in this section of the Gulf in the spring of 1952: one 82 miles due south of the Rockefeller Refuge on April 10, and two others 132 and 152 miles south of the same place on April 11. This and other species of jaegers should be looked for by fishermen who visit the waters off the mouths of the Mississippi River, where the continental shelf lies much closer to the mainland than it does off southwestern Louisiana. Indeed, when only approximately 20 miles off South Pass, Robert J. Newman sighted a Pomarine Jaeger on May 19, 1971.

The twisted central tail feathers are diagnostic of the species, but, unfortunately, immatures and birds in molt may lack this feature. The central tail feathers of adults are so twisted that they lie almost in a vertical plane and therefore show their full width when viewed from the side. Since in other jaegers these feathers under similar circumstances are viewed on edge, the difference is a striking one, visible at considerable distances. Figure 85 illustrates these differences in lateral aspect. The Pomarine Jaeger is the largest of the three species, being between the Ring-billed and Herring Gulls in body bulk. While the Parasitic sometimes approaches the Pomarine in body size, its bill is only half as large as that of the Pomarine. In the hand these features are extremely useful in determining the identity of an immature specimen, but they have only limited usefulness as field marks. Even the redoubtable master of field identification, Roger T. Peterson, considers many immature jaegers virtually indistinguishable under most field conditions. But any jaeger that flashes more than five white primary shafts in the wing is probably a Pomarine.

PARASITIC JAEGER   *Stercorarius parasiticus*   Fig. 85

This species is now entitled unequivocally to a place on the list of the state's avifauna. Although the Parasitic Jaeger has long been known to occur in our offshore waters, no completely satisfactory sighting within Louisiana's his-

Figure 85   Tails and silhouettes of adult jaegers: (1) Pomarine Jaeger; (2) Parasitic Jaeger; (3) Long-tailed Jaeger. Note shape and length of central tail feathers.

toric boundaries was made until the early 1960s. Now no less than seven records involving 13 identified birds make the Parasitic by far the most frequently observed jaeger close to Louisiana shores—recorded in all months except March, July, August, and December. On October 4, 1964, following Hurricane Hilda, Laurence C. Binford and Sidney A. Gauthreaux observed an adult over University Lake on the LSU campus at Baton Rouge.

The Parasitic Jaeger is no more parasitic than its relatives, for all jaegers get a great deal of their food by robbing other seabirds of their catches. As seen from Figure 85, pointed central tail feathers are characteristic of this species, provided, of course, that proper conditions of molt and age obtain. The bird is about the size of a Laughing Gull in body bulk. Usually four or five of the primaries show white at the base of the shafts, versus fewer in the Long-tailed and more in the Pomarine. For other comments on differences between the three species of jaegers, see the account of the Pomarine.

LONG-TAILED JAEGER *Stercorarius longicaudus* Fig. 85

The first unequivocal record for this species in the state is a light-phase subadult female collected at the west jetty of Calcasieu Pass on April 24, 1965, by A. W. Palmisano and Sidney A. Gauthreaux. The bird was first spotted sleeping on a sandbar, some 500 yards from shore. It was surrounded by a motley congregation of gulls and terns, and picking it out of the crowd at that distance was surely a real feat of sharp-sightedness. Having been shown its location through a spotting scope by Gauthreaux, Palmisano went out the jetty on the side away from the bird, jumping from rock to rock and bending low. Before he got into shotgun range, the gulls and terns became alarmed and departed. The jaeger stayed and permitted Palmisano to get closer, but before he was within easy range, it too flew. He fired—and missed. But his second shot brought the bird down. That was indeed fortunate, since neither of the observers had been able to identify the jaeger to species. Being a subadult, it had the tips of the two central tail feathers only barely extended beyond the others and therefore lacked the main diagnostic character of the species.

The Long-tailed Jaeger is apparently scarcer in the Gulf of Mexico than either of the other two species. In writing up the incident for publication, Palmisano and Gauthreaux cited eight previous Gulf records for the Long-tailed Jaeger.

Any jaeger with two pointed central tail feathers protruding more than four inches beyond the others is unquestionably this species. When the projecting portion is shorter—no matter how short it is—this character alone does not suffice to decide whether the bird is a Long-tailed or a Parasitic. Then supporting characters, although qualitatively not as clear-cut, assume increased importance. In body size (excluding the tail) the Long-tailed is the smallest of the three species—smaller than a Laughing Gull—and, as might be expected, it has the slimmest wings and the most buoyant ternlike flight. It has little white on the underside of the wing, and on the upper side only the first and second outermost primaries show white quills. Compared with their congeners, adults have the back a pearlier gray, the upper breast whiter (less tinged with gray), and the legs and feet grayish blue rather than black. Insofar as I know, the Long-tailed has no dark phase, although immatures have a great deal of dusky beneath that tends to form bars.

Figure 86 Great Skua.

[GREAT SKUA   *Catharacta skua*]   Fig. 86

Although, in the absence of a corroborating specimen, this species definitely does not merit inclusion on the state list, a single sight record by several competent observers of two birds in northern Chandeleur Sound on June 7, 1968, should be mentioned. The bracketing of the name in effect places the species on the list of birds of hypothetical occurrence. The party responsible for the sighting included Marshall B. Eyster and Jacob M. Valentine.

The species is fairly easily identified by its large size, which is close to that of a Herring Gull, its dark brown upperparts and rusty underparts, its short square-cut tail, and its *conspicuous* white patches at the base of the primaries. It resembles a dark-phase jaeger, and its flight is strong and swift, but the wings are wider and rounded at the tips, not long and pointed.

The Great Skua has two widely disjunct breeding populations, one in the North Atlantic, the other in the South Atlantic and South Pacific. While a northern Great Skua would not be likely to occur in the Gulf of Mexico in June, the possibility exists that the bird seen near the Chandeleurs was a wanderer from southern oceans, for June would be in the southern winter. Representatives of southern populations have occurred in the Pacific as far north as Washington, British Columbia, and Japan, and in the Atlantic to the Caribbean.

The Gull
Family
Laridae

This family in Louisiana includes 20 species of gulls and terns, water birds that frequent our rivers, lakes, or seashore. In south Louisiana, gulls and some of the larger terns are known to the French-speaking people by the name *goeland*. Elsewhere they go by the name "sea gull." All are long winged, and nearly all as adults have attractive patterns of black and white, usually with large areas of pearl gray. Gulls are generally more robust than terns; they do not plunge for their food as do terns but pick it off the water; and they fly with their *hooked bills* directed straight ahead, while a tern's *pointed bill* is held at a downward angle. Also, gulls have relatively much longer legs than do terns.

Of the eight kinds of gulls that are known to occur in Louisiana, only the Laughing Gull nests here. But of the 12 terns recorded here, 8 breed within our borders. Indeed, Louisiana's coastal islands are famous as nesting sites for these beautiful and graceful birds, which at one time were slaughtered unmercifully for the millinery trade or were robbed of their eggs for human consumption. Had it not been for the passage of the Lacey Act in 1909 and the Migratory Bird Treaty Act in 1918, it is quite probable that many of the terns would have joined the ranks of the two species of dodoes, Passenger Pigeon, Carolina Parakeet, and the other victims of man's once complete disregard of the potential exhaustibility of wildlife.

GLAUCOUS GULL *Larus hyperboreus*   Fig. 87

Although a specimen has not yet been taken in the state, the Glaucous Gull has been seen at least a dozen times by numerous competent observers and therefore definitely qualifies for inclusion on the state list. Observations

Figure 87 Glaucous Gull (upper) and Herring Gull (lower): adult, left; second winter, center; first winter, right.

of the species extend from December 4 to May 2, include every intervening month, and range from one side of the state to the other. Records on file are: a second-year bird at Holly Beach, December 4, 1938, Lowery and Thomas D. Burleigh; another second-year bird at Johnsons Bayou, December 4, 1960, Laurence C. Binford and Robert F. Andrle; one at Lake Pontchartrain, March 4, 1961, Sidney A. Gauthreaux, Mary Lewis, and others; one "immature" at Holly Beach, April 27, 1963, Gauthreaux, Stephen M. Russell, and A. W. Palmisano; one in "1st-year plumage" at west jetty of Calcasieu Pass, April 17, 1965, Gauthreaux, Binford, John P. Gee, and Burt L. Monroe, Jr.; second-year bird on Lake Pontchartrain at New Orleans, January 10, 1971, Robert J. Newman, R. D. Purrington, and H. Douglas Pratt; one at Mandeville, March 13, 1971, Pratt; one at Holly Beach, May 2, 1971, Pratt; one first-year bird on "Magnolia Road," Cameron Parish, April 11, 1971, Newman; second-year bird in Gulf short distance from mouth of Empire Canal, January 9, 1972, Newman and Pratt; second-year bird, three miles east of Gueydan, Vermilion Parish, February 12, 1972, Newman and others; second-year bird at Lake Pontchartrain, New Orleans, February 12–20, 1972, Purrington, Mac Myers, and Joseph C. Kennedy, photographed by Kennedy.

The Glaucous Gull is larger than a Herring Gull (26–32 inches in length instead of 23–26 inches). It is also paler *without* dark wing tips. First-winter birds are pale buffy, with the flight feathers edged with white. Second-year birds are *extremely white throughout*. Adults are pale gray above with *unmarked white primaries*.

HERRING GULL *Larus argentatus* Pl. XVIII; Fig. 87; p. 329

The Herring Gull is the second largest of the gulls that occur in Louisiana, being somewhat smaller than the Glaucous Gull, a species that is seen infrequently. In adults, which are rather uncommon in Louisiana in comparison with immatures, the upper surface of the wings and the back are pearl gray; the tips of the wings are black; the head, underparts, and tail are immaculate white; the bill is yellow; and the legs are flesh colored. Imma-

---

Plate XVIII Adult Gulls

1. Herring Gull (p. 328). 2. Ring-billed Gull (p. 329). 3. Laughing Gull (p. 330), breeding plumage in foreground, winter plumage behind. 4. Bonaparte's Gull (p. 334) in breeding plumage. 5. Franklin's Gull (p. 333) in breeding plumage. 6. Bonaparte's Gull (p. 334) in winter plumage.

1

2

3

4 .

5

6

AT
50

tures are a drab, dirty brown during their first year but somewhat lighter colored the second year. Four years or more are required for the Herring Gull to attain complete adult plumage. The immature Ring-billed Gull is also brownish, but its smaller size, its whitish tail with a prominent black subterminal band, and its yellowish, instead of flesh-colored, legs distinguish it.

The species breeds from the Arctic south to Long Island and on the larger lakes near the Canadian border of the United States; but immature birds and very old, senile adults sometimes do not migrate northward and instead summer on the Gulf Coast. The Herring Gull is fairly numerous in winter on our larger rivers, particularly the Mississippi, but only on the coast and in the vicinity of coastal waterways is it abundant. The main season is from mid-November to the end of April.

RING-BILLED GULL *Larus delawarensis* Pl. XVIII; pp. 330, 331

This abundant winter resident, which is especially numerous in southern Louisiana, may be distinguished by the black ring near the end of the bill, by its yellowish legs, and by the fact that it otherwise looks like a small

A Vociferous Adult Herring Gull

ALLAN D. CRUICKSHANK

edition of the Herring Gull. Immatures are much lighter colored than immatures of the other Louisiana gulls (except the very small Bonaparte's Gull), and the tail is crossed by a narrow, subterminal black band. The immature Laughing Gull also has a terminal tail band, but its breast is dirty gray in color, not white as in the Ring-bill.

A few Ring-billed Gulls are to be found on the coast of Louisiana every month of the year, but the species is uncommon to rare after the first of May. Fall migrants appear in numbers in October, and from then until spring the species is abundant, particularly along the larger rivers and on the coast. The Ring-billed Gull breeds in Canada and in the extreme northern part of the United States.

LAUGHING GULL   *Larus atricilla*   Pl. XVIII; Figs. 88, 89

The Laughing Gull is so strictly a coastal species that it occurs only casually even as short a distance inland as Baton Rouge. In its maritime habitat, however, it is an abundant permanent resident, somewhat more numerous in summer than in winter, but always present in considerable numbers. Its apparently reduced numbers in some areas in summer are probably attrib-

Subadult Ring-billed Gull

ALLAN D. CRUICKSHANK

Adult and Subadult Ring-billed Gulls

utable to its concentration near its main nesting grounds, many of which are located on coastal islands not readily accessible to ornithologists. It is the only gull that breeds in the state.

In late spring and early summer the adult Laughing Gull is separable from other gulls regularly present (see, however, the Franklin's and Bonaparte's Gulls) by its black head, red bill, dark slate-gray upper surfaces, and white underparts and tail. In winter the bill changes to black, and the head becomes white or grayish, yet the back and upper surface of the wings retain the distinctive slate-gray rather than pearl gray color. Immatures are brownish, with a white rump and a broad terminal black bar on the tail. The name of the species comes from its laughing call note, *ha, ha, ha, ha, haah, haah, haah, haah*—an excellent aid in identification.

The main nesting grounds for the species on the Gulf Coast are the islands in the Chandeleur chain and the mud lumps at the mouths of the Mississippi River. Four large greenish brown eggs with numerous dark blotches are laid in a poorly constructed nest located on or near the ground and made of trash, seaweed, and any other kind of litter that is available. Laughing Gulls work havoc in tern colonies, and even in colonies of their own species, by eating the eggs in unguarded nests. The first Gull-billed

PRATT

Figure 88   Three immature, winter-plumaged gulls: Laughing, left; Franklin's, center; Bonaparte's, right. Note particularly that the black subterminal band on the tail of the Franklin's does not extend onto the outer tail feathers and that the primaries of the Bonaparte's are extensively white. The last species is also the smallest, and it possesses the black spot behind the eye.

Tern nest ever found in Louisiana had its eggs destroyed, probably by a Laughing Gull, in the time it took me to walk several miles back to my boat at the other end of the island to obtain a camera. In studying the interesting tern eggs I had frightened away the adults, and on my departure a Laughing Gull evidently swooped down and ate the eggs before either of the rightful owners returned. When terns are not frightened from their nesting colonies by human intruders, there are probably enough birds on hand to protect the eggs and young from the marauding Laughing Gulls. For this reason the National Audubon Society and other conservation agencies, which protect the nests from illegal molestation by egg hunters, generally forbid visits to the colonies even by bird students.

FRANKLIN'S GULL *Larus pipixcan*   Pl. XVIII; Figs. 88, 89

This gull breeds in the northern prairies and migrates southward in numbers through Texas, apparently a bit too far to the west of our state for it to
visit us regularly. Over the years, several sightings have been made near
Shreveport, in the Baton Rouge area, and around New Orleans; but otherwise, notice has been confined to the coastal parishes, where it might be
found every year if the superabundance of closely similar Laughing Gulls
there did not make it so easy to overlook. Standing on the beach in a flock
of both species, adult Franklin's Gulls can usually be picked out by the
white tips of their primaries, but to make certain of their identity one must
put them into the air and note the white area that completely separates the
black of the wing tip from the gray of the remainder of the spread wing.
In first-winter plumage, Franklin's Gulls usually have a whiter breast and
forehead than Laughing Gulls of comparable age; and the relative proportions of the bills of the two species (Fig. 89) are a possible distinguishing
feature when direct comparison can be made. I would advise, however,
against attempting positive field identification of immature Franklin's Gulls
except on the infrequent occasions when a wheeling bird fans its tail and
reveals that the outermost tail feather at the level of the tail band is pure

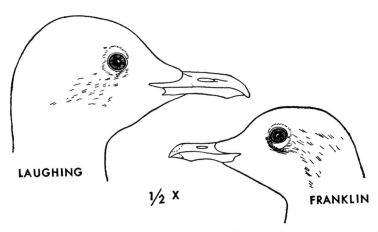

Figure 89 Heads of Laughing Gull and Franklin's Gull, showing particularly
the differences in the size and proportion of the bills.

white or has only a trace of gray or black on the inner web. The corresponding band of the Laughing Gull in first-winter plumage extends all the way across the tail.

Migrants flock through the vicinity of Rockport, Texas, by the "tens of thousands"; and the late Edward A. McIlhenny stated that just prior to 1880 they "passed over Avery Island each fall in unbelievably great numbers . . . in long, compact streams, requiring an hour or more to pass." The highest Louisiana count in the present century was 175 birds in two flocks seen over Lake Pontchartrain on October 25, 1959, by Sidney A. Gauthreaux and Mary Lewis. I cannot help surmising that McIlhenny's recollections may have been based not upon an annual spectacle but upon a few episodes when the weather happened to shift the great Texas flights abnormally far eastward. Dates of record extend from September 25 to May 17.

BONAPARTE'S GULL   *Larus philadelphia*   Pl. XVIII; Fig. 88; p. 334

This is our smallest gull of regular annual occurence, one that is considerably smaller even than several kinds of native terns. In winter plumage the adult, like the adult Laughing Gull, loses most of the black on the head. It retains

Immature Bonaparte's Gull in Winter

ALLAN D. CRUICKSHANK

Figure 90   Little Gull: adult in winter plumage, left; first winter plumage, right.

only a wash of gray on the nape and a distinctly defined dusky spot back of the eyes. The species is easily recognized by this spot and by a conspicuous elongated white area extending from the "wrist" almost to the tip of the wings. Immatures have a dusky spot back of the eye, a narrow black terminal tail band, a black rear border to the outspread wing, and white "wrist" marks.

The species is altogether a migrant and winter resident. It begins to arrive in late August or early September and remains until mid-May, only rarely later. In some years it is not uncommon in winter on our larger inland lakes; in other years it may be rare or even unrecorded in the interior. A few of these gulls are usually to be found any day in winter one spends by the seashore, especially if one watches the waters well beyond the breakers with binoculars or a telescope. The Bonaparte's Gull is definitely more pelagic than most of its relatives.

LITTLE GULL   *Larus minutus*   Fig. 90

The only record for this species in Louisiana and only the third evidence of its occurrence in any Gulf Coast state is an immature collected on the "Magnolia Road," three miles north of Holly Beach, in Cameron Parish, on March 31, 1973, by Dan Tallman and Robert J. Newman. The Little

Gull, as the name implies, is the smallest of the gulls, being even smaller than a Forster's Tern.

In Louisiana we are not likely ever to see the black-headed summer adult or the young immature, which has the back heavily barred with black. The white-headed winter adult is easily distinguished by the black undersurface of its wings and lack of any black on the dorsal wing tips. The advanced immature has a bold diagonal dark bar crossing the upper surface of the wing much as in a young kittiwake but lacks the dark collar across the back of the neck so prominent in the latter. However, its small size and slender bill are enough by themselves to separate it from the much larger kittiwake and, when direct comparison can be made, even from the less disparately large Bonaparte's Gull.

The Little Gull mainly breeds in the Old World and is only a rare nester in North America although it seems to be of regular annual occurrence in winter in favored places in New England and the Great Lakes region.

BLACK-LEGGED KITTIWAKE *Rissa tridactyla*   Fig. 91

The Black-legged Kittiwake is a medium-sized gull that has the hind toe absent or rudimentary. It breeds from the Arctic islands south, in eastern North America, to the St. Lawrence River. In winter it is mainly pelagic, spending most of its time well offshore and once thought only rarely to range farther south than the latitude of New Jersey. Consequently, the discovery of an immature individual on the front beach at Cameron on January 2, 1954, came as a great surprise to Louisiana ornithologists. This was the first definite record of a kittiwake for the Gulf of Mexico or for any of the lands immediately adjacent to that body of water. Fortunately, the bird lingered near the place where it was first seen and was collected on the following day. On April 18, 1954, a second kittiwake, also an immature, was shot at the west jetty at the mouth of the Calcasieu River, not more than two miles from the place where the first individual was found. The specimens now repose in the LSU Museum of Zoology, where they can always be inspected by anyone wishing to verify the correctness of the identifications.

Since 1954, three additional kittiwakes have been observed in the state on three occasions, all in Cameron Parish and all immatures: one seen on the beach a few miles west of Holly Beach by numerous observers attending the spring meeting of the LOS, on April 25 and 26, 1970 (excellent photo-

Figure 91   Black-legged Kittiwake: adult on left; immature on right.

graphs by both Joseph C. Kennedy and Larry P. O'Meallie); one observed
in the Calcasieu ship channel by Robert J. Newman and others, on December 4, 1971; and one tallied on the Sabine Christmas Bird Count by Newman and James C. Leak, on December 18, 1971. In spite of the pelagic
habits of the kittiwake, the only individual yet found in offshore waters adjacent to Louisiana was an immature that came close to the stern of a fishing
boat 20–30 miles from shore south of the Mississippi River delta on January
9, 1972, and was identified by Newman and H. Douglas Pratt.
    The immature, first-winter plumage of the kittiwake is a study in con-
trast, as shown by Figure 91. The general color is white or pearl gray, but the
back of the neck, the median upper surface of the wings, and the end of the
tail are all broadly banded with black, giving the bird a most striking appearance. In this plumage it resembles the winter-plumaged Bonaparte's Gull,

from which it differs by its much larger size (near that of the Laughing Gull) and in the distribution of the black areas when viewed from above. There is a broad black bar on the hindneck instead of a black spot back of the eye. The adult kittiwake is recognized by its black-tipped wings (with the black cut straight across as if the feathers had been dipped in black paint), by its black legs, and by its uniformly dull yellow bill.

GULL-BILLED TERN   *Gelochelidon nilotica*   Fig. 92

This is a medium-sized tern with an unusually heavy and unusually short, black bill, which is its main distinguishing feature. Relative size, however, means little as a guide to field identification until the student is familiar

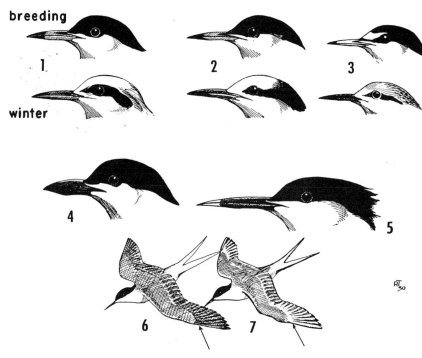

Figure 92 Heads of five terns: (1) Forster's Tern; (2) Common Tern; (3) Least Tern; (4) Gull-billed Tern; (5) Sandwich Tern; (6) Common Tern in flight; (7) Forster's Tern in flight.

enough with some of the common species in a group to be able to use them as standards of reference. For example, among the terns, if the student can acquaint himself with either the Caspian or the Royal Tern as a "large species" and the Least Tern as a "small species," rapid progress can be made in working out the identity of related species in the group. On this principle, a "medium-sized" tern would denote a bird not as large as the Royal Tern but also not as small as the Least Tern. The Gull-billed Tern loses the black cap after the breeding season and becomes, in winter plumage, the whitest of our terns.

The Gull-billed Tern is almost strictly coastal in its occurrence in the state, and within this general environment it has a strong preference for marshy areas, where it is frequently seen feeding in the water of canals and ponds. The only inland record is that of five individuals seen over the lakes on the LSU campus at Baton Rouge by Sidney A. Gauthreaux and Laurence C. Binford on September 10, 1965, during the passage of Hurricane Betsy.

The species is a permanent resident, fairly common during most of

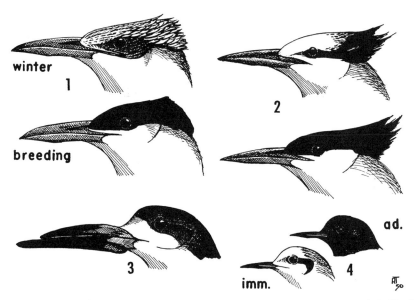

Figure 93   Heads of four terns: (1) Caspian Tern; (2) Royal Tern; (3) Black Skimmer; (4) Black Tern (adult above, immature below).

the year, least numerous in summer. It has been found nesting in small numbers on Isle au Pitre and on the Chandeleurs and adjacent islands, as well as on the mainland at the Rigolets. The three eggs are buffy white, indistinctly splotched with numerous chocolate markings, and are laid in a simple depression in the sand.

FORSTER'S TERN   *Sterna forsteri*   Fig. 92; p. 340

Accurate separation of Forster's and Common Terns in life is not easy but can be accomplished by attention to a combination of characters. In breeding condition the Forster's differs from the Common by the orange instead of red legs, feet, and base of bill and by having the primaries silvery and lighter than the remainder of the wing instead of dusky and darker than the adjoining feathers. In fall and early winter, the black patch through the eye extends only to the auriculars in the Forster's but passes completely around the nape in the Common. In the transition between plumages, however, in late summer and late winter, the black facial patches of the Forster's often connect around the back of the neck, much as in the Common. An excellent field mark is the dusky forepart of the wing in the imma-

Forster's Tern on Nest in the Marsh

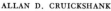
ALLAN D. CRUICKSHANK

ture Common Tern. In the hand—and sometimes when flying around at close range—the two species are distinguishable by the outer tail feathers, white on the outer web and gray or dusky on the inner web in Forster's Tern but reversed in color in the Common Tern.

A common permanent resident along our coasts, Forster's Tern breeds rather abundantly there, either in mainland marsh or on grassy islands in bays and lagoons, sometimes in groups of several hundred birds, sometimes as scattered, isolated pairs. It lays its three or four heavily spotted buffy or olivaceous eggs in a nest of grasses and stalks of marsh plants—well constructed compared with that of other terns, which is usually just a scooped-out depression in the sand. Inland, the species is a not so common migrant and winter resident, with extreme dates of July 15 and May 29.

COMMON TERN *Sterna hirundo* Fig. 92

On our inland lakes, this tern, which closely resembles the Forster's (see preceding account for distinguishing differences), is seen only in migration and during winter, and even then only infrequently. On our coast it is a rare breeder and a moderately common to locally common migrant and winter resident, although in statewide numbers it never approaches Forster's Tern. The first Louisiana breeding record resulted from the discovery by Robert J. Newman, R. D. Purrington, and Mac Myers of a bird incubating two eggs at the southern end of the main Chandeleur mass. Purrington's color photograph of this tern on the nest shows all diagnostic characters of this species except the dark outer webs of the outermost tail feathers, and these were carefully scrutinized through a spotting scope while the bird was hovering above the nest. On June 21, 1973, observers noted three adults with young nearby at the same place. Migrants from the North begin to arrive in late August, and some remain until late spring.

ROSEATE TERN *Sterna dougallii* Fig. 94

The standard guidebook prescription for recognizing this close counterpart of the Common and Forster's Terns is to note the all-black or nearly all-black bill (red only at the extreme base) and the all-white, deeply forked tail, which extends far beyond the wings when the bird is at rest. The formula works fairly well in areas where the only problem is to separate a Roseate from a Common Tern in breeding plumage. But in Louisiana,

Figure 94   Roseate Tern.

where great numbers of Forster's Terns and the wintering of other terns complicate matters, doubts arise; for Forster's Terns in some cases have longer streamer tails than Roseates, the dusky on their outermost tail feathers, being on the inner web, is largely concealed, and after the breeding season their orange bills sometimes turn dark.

In view of this situation, the evidence for the occurrence of the Roseate Tern in Louisiana is somewhat shaky. Stanley C. Arthur's 1918 annotated list of Louisiana birds mentions an alleged specimen taken at Grand Cheniere in February 1915; but this bird, which is apparently no longer extant, is not known ever to have been examined by a competent ornithologist. Arthur's own confidence in the record did not endure long enough for him to include the species in his expanded book on Louisiana birds 13 years later, and winter is not a favorable time for the presence of a Roseate Tern on the northern Gulf Coast. In reporting an individual of the species on the north end of the Chandeleur Islands on June 8, 1958, Ava R. Tabor, Mary Lewis, and Fannye Cook gave the nearly all-dark bill and long outer tail feathers as the identifying marks. Had they also noted seeing the bird at rest and ascertaining that the tail projected far beyond the folded wing, their record would rest on a much firmer foundation, for the Forster's Tern has longer wings than the Roseate, and hence its long tail does not project as far beyond the wing tips. In winter the Roseate Tern acquires an additional field character. Only the forehead and anterior portion of the crown become white, and hence at this season the bird is the most extensively dark-capped tern in its size range. On January 12, 1974, H. Douglas Pratt and Robert J. Newman spent 20 minutes studying a bird flying around the Cameron ferry slip that exhibited all the characters of a winter Roseate Tern—extensive dark cap, dark bill, and deeply forked all-white tail. The only difficulty is that in January it should not have been there. In the entire 74-year history of the Christmas Bird Count, only four Roseate Terns have ever been reported in the United States, all of them in peninsular Florida.

The Roseate Tern breeds at widely scattered sites from Nova Scotia to the Dry Tortugas and beyond, sometimes with only a pair or two attached to colonies of other terns. Ornithologists visiting Louisiana terneries should be on the lookout for it and should listen for its call notes—a unique, two-syllabled *chu-ick* and a less distinctive, rasping *aaak*.

SOOTY TERN *Sterna fuscata*   Figs. 95, 96

The Sooty Tern is now known to nest sparingly but regularly in the Chandeleur Islands. Although some evidence is available indicating that the species may have nested on islands off Vermilion Parish in the late 1890s, its breeding in the state was not actually established until June 5, 1933, when Harry C. Oberholser found a nest on Curlew Island in the Chandeleur chain. It was also found nesting there and on Stake Island in the 1960s, but these two islands were destroyed by Hurricane Camille in 1969. In the nesting season of 1971 the highest Louisiana count ever was obtained on the main Chandeleur Island: 34 adults and 19 nests. In 1973 only 19 adults, 1 chick, and no nests were found on a visit to the same island on June 21. I do not know whether this diminution in numbers from the 1971 high count forecasts eventual abandonment of this northernmost breeding colony of the species.

The species has been observed fairly often in our state's offshore waters. For example, Robert J. Newman saw four presumably separate individuals on June 18, 1970, approximately 38 miles off the mouth of South Pass of the Mississippi River delta. The following day he counted 28, of which at least 18 appeared to involve no possible duplication. On September 3, 1970, the same observer saw two individuals about 20 miles off South Pass, and on August 26, 1971, he counted 12 individuals between 20 and 30

Figure 95 Two pelagic terns that are infrequently seen in Louisiana: Brown Noddy on left; Sooty Tern on right.

miles southeast of South Pass. Several records of the species have been obtained on the mainland following the passage of hurricanes: singles one mile south of Leeville on the road to Grand Isle on September 16, 1961, and at Holly Beach on September 15, 1961, following Hurricane Carla; and two at Sabine National Wildlife Refuge and another west of Holly Beach, on September 6 and 8, 1973, during and following Hurricane Delia.

The Sooty Tern is mainly pelagic through most of the year but must necessarily come to land to lay its one egg, which is whitish or buffy and speckled or spotted with chocolate brown, in a depression in the sand amid clumps of sea purslane (*Sesuvium*). The desolate sandy islets known as the Dry Tortugas, 65 miles west of Key West, are one of the main nesting sites of the Sooty Tern in the Western Hemisphere. From still-unknown winter quarters over 100,000 individuals normally return each spring to engage in their family duties on the Dry Tortugas, and when these chores are done, they virtually disappear. Where they go, no one knows. Paradoxically, a set of carefully conducted experiments by two capable scientists showed that Sooty Terns cannot long remain afloat, because their feathers rapidly become soaking wet. That the birds rest or sleep on the open waters of the ocean during the period of their absence from the nesting islands seems therefore unlikely. But where they go is still a mystery. Consequently, the recovery of a banded bird off Atchafalaya Bay, approximately 25 miles south of Morgan City, on December 15, 1968, that had been banded as an adult more than six years earlier, on July 9, 1962, on the Dry Tortugas, is of great interest even though it provides no real clue as to where the tens of thousands of Sooty Terns from these islands actually go in winter.

Other birds banded on the Dry Tortugas and recovered in Louisiana include the following: one banded on June 12, 1940, and recovered near Ponchatoula, in Tangipahoa Parish, on August 10, 1940; one banded on June 5, 1941, and found near New Iberia, in Iberia Parish, on September 8, 1941; one banded on June 5, 1941, and recovered near Lena, in Rapides Parish, on September 9, 1941; and one banded on June 27, 1973, and recovered on the Sabine National Wildlife Refuge on September 8, 1973.

Only slightly larger than a Forster's Tern, the adult Sooty is the only tern that is black above and white below. Seen from an airplane, from too high overhead to discern size or bill shape, it can be picked out from the Black Skimmers with which it sometimes associates by its more buoyant flight and the lack of white trailing edges on the wings. Immatures are almost completely blackish though usually flecked on the back with whitish.

BRIDLED TERN *Sterna anaethetus*   Fig. 96

The first record of this species for Louisiana is that of a specimen found dead a few miles west of Holly Beach, in Cameron Parish, on September 16, 1961, by Keith A. Arnold and Edward T. Armstrong, following Hurricane Carla. A flying bird was seen over City Park Lake near the LSU campus at Baton Rouge on September 10, 1965, by Laurence C. Binford, Sidney A. Gauthreaux, and Robert J. Newman, during Hurricane Betsy.

The Bridled Tern occurs in tropical seas of the New and Old World and does not normally occur in waters off the United States except following hurricanes of West Indian or Caribbean origin. It resembles the Sooty Tern in being largely dark above and white below, but it differs from the Sooty

Figure 96   Adult Sooty Tern (left) and adult Bridled Tern (right).

not only by its somewhat smaller size but also by the wide *whitish* collar separating the black of its cap from the gray of its back, which is considerably lighter than that of the Sooty. The white of the forehead extends to a point *behind* the eye, while in the Sooty it extends only *to* the eye. In the Sooty only the base and the outer web of the outermost tail feathers are white and the remainder of the tail black, whereas in the Bridled the median tail feathers are light gray (not black) and the outermost feather on each side is essentially all-white except for some gray toward the tips.

LEAST TERN   *Sterna albifrons*   Fig. 92; p. 347

The Least Tern is the runt of our terns; indeed, it is one of the smallest in the world. The body, tail and all, is hardly more than eight inches in length. In summer the bird has a black cap, like most terns, but its nearly all-yellow bill (only the tip is black) is unique. Immatures and winter-plumaged adults have dark bills and a dusky patch from the eye around the back of the head.

    The Least Tern has been seen a few times in winter along our coast, but mainly it is a migrant and summer resident that arrives in late March or early April and remains until late October, only rarely any later. It is the commonest of our terns in summer, nesting in colonies on many of our coastal islands, on sandy patches along our coastal highways, and on sandbars inland along our rivers. The so-called nest is nothing more than a depression in the sand in which three or four creamy eggs with dark blotches are laid. In New Orleans it is even known to lay its eggs on the graveled top of a flat building. Some terns, such as the Royal and Caspian, prefer to nest in mixed colonies in which two or more species are associated. But Least Tern colonies more often than not are isolated from other species, although occasionally, in coastal situations, Black Skimmers may be nearby.

ROYAL TERN *Thalasseus maximus*   Fig. 93; p. 348

This large species and the even larger Caspian Tern are both common on our coast, where they are permanent residents. To distinguish between the two is not easy unless one knows just what to look for. The color of the bill is not an infallible character, but generally the Royal Tern has a more slender and more orange-colored bill, while the bill of the Caspian Tern is

Least Tern on "Nest"

ALLAN D. CRUICKSHANK

heavier and more intensely red in color. Except in seasons of molt the Royal Tern has a more deeply forked tail (outer feathers three inches longer than the ones in the middle); the tail of the Caspian is only shallowly indented. In winter the forehead of the Royal Tern becomes white, while that of the Caspian Tern retains a considerable amount of black and the black around the eye is much more extensive.

Colonies of Royal Terns, frequently numbering into hundreds of pairs, are found on our sandy coastal islands or on some isolated strand of Gulf beach. Generally this species nests in association with Caspian Terns, Laughing Gulls, Black Skimmers, and, at least from Grand Isle eastward, with the Sandwich Tern. The nest of the Royal Tern is a shallow depression in the sand in which only one egg is usually laid. The ground color of the egg is gray or slightly buffy and is profusely and evenly overlaid by small dark spots.

In winter the Royal Tern often travels short distances up the bayous and larger rivers in the southern part of the state, but the species has come as far inland as Baton Rouge only once—on September 10, 1965—when 39 were present on the lakes near the LSU campus during the passage of Hurricane Betsy.

Royal Tern in Winter

ALLAN D. CRUICKSHANK

SANDWICH TERN *Thalasseus sandvicensis* Fig. 92

The Sandwich Tern is an uncommon to locally abundant summer resident and breeder and a rare winter resident on the coast of Louisiana. It nests on sandy islands, usually in company with other terns and the Laughing Gull, placing its eggs in saucerlike depressions in the sand. The two (sometimes one or three) eggs are pinkish buff with brown, gray, and lavender markings. In 1941 there were approximately two dozen pairs and their young on Isle au Pitre and about the same number on North Island. But on June 10–12, 1971, Mac Myers, Robert J. Newman, R. D. Purrington, and Jacob M. Valentine made a census of tern colonies on North Island and on the southern end of the main Chandeleur Island. Their individual estimates varied rather widely, but Valentine's figures showed 23,400 Sandwich Terns and 2,600 Royal Terns. Of the Sandwich Terns, an estimated 3,000 were on North Island. The increase in the breeding population on the island from what it was in the early 1940s could be attributed to the virtual destruction of many of the islands in the Chandeleur chain, notably Stake and Curlew islands, by Hurricane Camille in 1969. Nesting colonies must also exist somewhere near Grand Isle and in Cameron Parish, for the species is seen in those places almost daily in June. The only inland record is the report of five over the lakes near the LSU campus at Baton Rouge on September 10, 1965, during Hurricane Betsy.

The Sandwich Tern is classed as a medium-sized tern, along with the Forster's Tern, although actually it is intermediate between the Forster's Tern on the one hand and the Royal Tern on the other. The Sandwich Tern is, however, the only tern with a yellow-tipped black bill, a character that immediately distinguishes it from all other species. The black on the top of the head is partially replaced with white in the molt that follows the breeding season—the forepart of the crown becomes white, streaked with black, and the back of the head and the nape become black, streaked with white.

CASPIAN TERN *Hydroprogne caspia* Fig. 93

The features that distinguish this species from the similar-appearing Royal Tern have already been discussed in connection with the latter and need not be repeated here. The Royal Tern is strictly coastal in its occurrence, but the Caspian Tern breeds in part on the Great Lakes and therefore passes up and down the Mississippi Valley in migration. From the third week of March to mid-May and from early August to mid-October it may be seen about our large inland, freshwater lakes and along our larger rivers, where it is also present casually in winter. Sizable breeding colonies are located on some of the islands along the coast of Louisiana such as, for example, Isle au Pitre and the Chandeleurs. Two to four creamy white eggs, scrawled and spotted with numerous chocolate-colored markings, are laid in a depression in the sand.

The Caspian Tern is definitely partial to the marshes instead of the front beaches, especially in winter. On the highways leading to or along the coast, through the great coastal marshes, Caspian Terns are often seen feeding up and down the canals along the roads or out over the marsh itself. The large terns observed along the Gulf beaches are predominantly Royal Terns.

BLACK TERN   *Chlidonias niger*   Fig. 93

The Black Tern in summer plumage is our only tern that is predominantly dark gray above and black below (only the undertail coverts are white). Thus it cannot be confused with any other species except possibly the blackish immature of the rare Sooty Tern, which is considerably larger and usually

Gulls and Terns Throng Our Beaches in Winter

ALLAN D. CRUICKSHANK

has some of the feathers of the brownish (not grayish) back edged with white. In the Black Tern the head, breast, and belly are black, and the upperparts are dark gray. The black crown and the black underparts become white in the postnuptial molt. Since the first migrants to return from the North are still in the process of their transformation, they are usually heavily blotched beneath. The immature of the year has a light breast and belly, dusky flanks, a white collar, and a black crown and nape. Such immatures may suggest the Sooty Tern; but the latter is larger, immaculate white below, black instead of gray above, and the tail is deeply instead of slightly forked.

The Black Tern breeds in the lake marshes of our northern states and in southern Canada. Spring migrants begin to pass through Louisiana in rather large numbers in late April and are seen regularly until about the end of the third week of June. Along the coast, however, the species occurs in numbers as a nonbreeder throughout the summer. Southward migration, as evidenced particularly by the appearance of juveniles, commences in early July and continues sometimes into October (single birds, or even more rarely several, have been recorded along the coast between November and the end of March). The great bulk of the population leaves the United States to spend the winter in southern South America.

BROWN NODDY *Anous stolidus*   Fig. 95

This pelagic tern has only twice been definitely recorded in Louisiana. The first occasion was on August 30, 1940, when Earl L. Atwood obtained a specimen on the Sabine National Wildlife Refuge, following a tropical storm attended by winds of gale intensity. The second record is based on a carcass found by Keith A. Arnold and Edward T. Armstrong on the beach two miles west of Holly Beach on September 16, 1961, in the wake of Hurricane Carla. The Brown Noddy is unique in coloration—uniform dark dusky brown except for the sharply contrasting white crown. Furthermore, unlike other terns, it has a rounded instead of a forked or emarginate tail.

Louisiana ornithologists should be on the watch for the Brown Noddy following any tropical disturbance that strikes the northern Gulf Coast. The species is abundant in the breeding season on the Dry Tortugas, and any hurricane passing close to these islands is likely to pick up some of these terns in its eye and carry them to our shores.

The species gets its name from the peculiar manner in which it nods its head in courtship antics in the vicinity of its nest, which, atypically for a tern, it builds in a bush or tree.

The
Skimmer
Family
Rynchopidae

BLACK SKIMMER   *Rynchops niger*   Fig. 93

The skimmers are large, long-winged, bizarre, ternlike birds in which the lower half of the greatly compressed bill is longer than the upper half. With the knifelike edge of its lower mandible cutting the surface of the water of coastal bays and lagoons, the skimmer scoops up the tiny fish that form its diet. The scissor shape of the bill is the basis of the name *bec à ciseaux*, by which it is known among our French-speaking inhabitants. The call note is a houndlike *yap, yap,* from which another local name, "sea dog," is derived.

The Black Skimmer is strikingly colored, with black upperparts, white underparts and bright red, black-tipped bill. It is a common permanent resident, exclusively coastal in its normal distribution, although on at least four occasions, mainly following hurricanes, the species has appeared as far inland as Baton Rouge. For example, on September 10, 1965, in association with Hurricane Betsy, 35 were present on the lakes near the LSU campus. The skimmer nests in large colonies on many of our coastal islands, notably in the Chandeleurs but elsewhere as well. In June 1970 approximately 25 pairs laid eggs at a mainland site along U.S. Highway 90 near the Rigolets, but all the nests were destroyed through some unknown cause. It lays four or five chalky white, heavily blotched eggs that blend perfectly with the mixture of pebbles, broken shells, and debris that litters a seabeach.

352

The Auk
Family
Alcidae

The auks and auklike birds of the family Alcidae are mainly denizens of northern oceans, over which they wander far and wide throughout most of the year. In the summer, however, they come to land, generally to form immense colonies and to raise their young either in burrows, in rocky crevices, or on narrow ledges alongside the sea. Their black and white patterns and their upright postures suggest penguins, which, however, occur entirely in the Southern Hemisphere and are flightless birds only remotely related to alcids. The Auk family includes the puffins, guillemots, murres, murrelets, auks, auklets, and the Dovekie.

Alcids are heavy-bodied, somewhat ducklike birds with short, rounded wings, which they beat in flight in a rapid whir and with much veering of their course. Even though the legs are extremely short, they are located far to the rear of the body and hence in flight extend beyond the tail, where they are held spraddle-fashion. Alcids dive and swim with great agility, pursuing underwater the various marine organisms that compose their diet. The Great Auk, the largest known member of the family, became so extremely adapted to a life in the sea that it lost its power of flight. This ultimately led to its extinction at the hands of unscrupulous men who slaughtered it for food and feathers when it waddled out of the ocean onto land to nest.

ANCIENT MURRELET *Synthliboramphus antiquum*   Fig. 97

The alcids are so restricted to cold ocean waters that on our Atlantic Coast only the little Dovekie ever occurs as far south as Florida and the entrance

Figure 97   Ancient Murrelet.

to the Gulf, and then only on the occasion of exceedingly rare southward
invasions involving a large segment of the population of the species. It was,
indeed, the Dovekie that until 1954 constituted the only representative of
the Auk family in Gulf waters—the species has been recorded a few times
in the vicinity of the Florida Keys and even once on the northern Gulf
Coast, at St. Andrews Bay, Florida. We might thus have expected the
Dovekie to be the first alcid to appear in Louisiana, but such was not the
case. On May 6, 1954, a small, plump bird, about the size of a "di-dipper,"
was seen by a fisherman on the waters of Lake Pontchartrain, just north of
Littlewoods, on the eastern outskirts of New Orleans. The little bird swam
up to the fisherman's skiff and was lifted aboard only to succumb shortly
thereafter. Fortunately the specimen was taken to the Louisiana Wild Life
and Fisheries Commission, which later transmitted it to the LSU Museum
of Zoology for permanent preservation. The bird proved to be an Ancient
Murrelet, a Pacific Coast species that breeds on the faraway Aleutian Islands
and other shores of the North Pacific. Although there are single records of
the occurrence of the Ancient Murrelet in Idaho, Ontario, Quebec, Wisconsin, and on Lake Erie, this is the first and only instance of any Pacific
Coast alcid reaching the Gulf of Mexico.

    This species is closely similar to the Dovekie but differs in being slightly
larger, in having the upperparts gray instead of black, and in possessing a
longer and thinner bill, instead of one that is stubby and conical. Both have
most of the head and throat black in the breeding season, but in the Ancient
Murrelet, streaked white lines, one on each side of the head, begin at a point

above the rear of the eye and converge on the nape. The resulting "silver threads among the black" effect is the basis of the bird's name. In winter both species lose the black throat, but the murrelet retains a small dusky patch on the chin, and the top of its head is dark gray instead of black.

PIGEONS
AND ALLIES
Order *Columbiformes*

The Pigeon
Family
Columbidae

THE PIGEON FAMILY is poorly represented in the United States, but it achieves great diversity in the tropical regions of the world, a fact well known to every GI who saw service in such places as the Philippines and the southwest Pacific. Pigeons are peculiar birds in many respects. Their bills are soft and fleshy, their heads are disproportionately small in comparison with their bodies, and they possess in their necks specialized glands that secrete the so-called pigeon's milk, which they feed to their young by regurgitation.

The famous and now extinct dodoes were species of flightless pigeons that lived on the islands of Mauritius and Réunion, not far from Madagascar. They were exterminated by early French explorers who beat the helpless birds down with clubs to provide themselves with food. Not a single specimen of a dodo is extant in the museums of the world, and our conception of their appearance is based mainly on several somewhat contradictory drawings made by the early seamen and travelers, who were responsible for the birds' extinction.

BAND-TAILED PIGEON *Columba fasciata*   Fig. 98

At least five of these large Rocky Mountain pigeons have now been recorded in the state: an adult female obtained by John Thibaut one mile south of Napoleonville on January 21, 1954; an adult male collected by Burt L. Monroe, Jr., at Baton Rouge on May 7, 1964; an unsexed specimen picked up several miles south of Lake Pontchartrain along U.S. Highway 11, on December 16, 1969; one shot by a hunter in the fall or early winter of 1969 in Lafayette Parish; and one observed by Robert Kimble of the Louisiana Wild Life and Fisheries Commission in the Loggy Bayou area near Minden, in Webster Parish, in January 1973. The species is ordinarily found in high mountain forests even during its migrations and in its winter range in western North America.

The Band-tailed Pigeon is about the same size as the Rock Pigeon, the common pigeon of our city streets. Its color is predominantly slate-gray, but the tail is crossed subterminally by a band of dusky gray, and there is a somewhat crescent-shaped spot of white on the lower nape. Like the Rock Pigeon, it has tail feathers of nearly equal length, which make the tail squarish terminally, quite unlike the pointed tail of the Mourning Dove.

Figure 98   Band-tailed Pigeon.

ROCK PIGEON   *Columba livia*   Fig. 99

The familiar Rock Pigeon, or "domestic pigeon" as it is more often called, is now highly variable in color as a result of selective breeding. But it was originally predominantly slate-gray with iridescent patches, a condition that still prevails in most of our present-day stock. No wild dove in Louisiana other than the rare Band-tailed Pigeon remotely resembles it. Since there is evidence that domestication of this species was accomplished as early as 3000 B.C., it is a bird with which man long has been intimately acquainted. Yet, despite its usual dependency on man in one way or another, it has established itself under semiferal conditions in many of the towns and cities of Louisiana and other parts of the nation. In fact, there are instances in the western United States of the domestic pigeon reverting to a completely wild state and building its nest on ledges and in crevices in isolated canyons, far from human dwellings.

The "carrier pigeon," as one breed of the domestic pigeon is called, is innately capable of remarkable homing feats. When carefully bred with this purpose in mind and given special training, it will fly unerringly and rapidly for great distances to return to its cote, and hence it can be used to transport messages. Despite improvements in nearly all phases of electronics and other

Figure 99   Rock Pigeon.

means of communication, the Signal Corps of the armed services long regarded the domestic pigeon as one of its most dependable message conveyers under certain circumstances.

WHITE-WINGED DOVE   *Zenaida asiatica*   Pl. XIX

This western species is an uncommon but fairly regular winter visitor in southern Louisiana, seen most often singly but sometimes in flocks of as many as 18. It is most frequently encountered in our coastal parishes, where it has been recorded in every month of the year and where it has been long suspected of occasionally nesting. For instance, cooing males have been heard on several occasions in the breeding season on the chenieres of Cameron Parish, but no nests have as yet been found there. Proof of actual breeding in the state was, however, established on the Delta National Wildlife Refuge, near the mouths of the Mississippi River, on June 19, 1971, when two adults and a newly fledged young bird that was barely able to fly were found by refuge personnel and a group of ornithologists from the LSU Museum of Zoology. Although an occasional White-winged Dove has been seen in the interior of the state, such as at Baton Rouge and even at Shreveport, the species is definitely only a casual visitor away from the coastal parishes.

The White-winged Dove resembles the Mourning Dove but has a conspicuous white patch in its wings, a somewhat greater body bulk, and a squarish, instead of pointed, tail.

MOURNING DOVE   *Zenaida macroura*   Pl. XIX

This species is one of Louisiana's commonest permanent residents and one of its most highly esteemed game birds. It is smaller than a domestic pigeon and has a long, pointed (instead of fan-shaped) tail with largely white outer feathers. The Mourning Dove gets its name from its mournful cooing note, which, in the breeding season, is uttered almost continuously throughout the day. The nest is a flimsy platform of sticks and grass stalks so open in construction that it barely suffices to hold the two pure white eggs. Rarely is this structure located on the ground and even more rarely near the top of a tall tree; most frequently it is placed at a height of 10 to 25 feet. The bird raises on the average two broods a year, the last sometimes being fledged as late as September or rarely as late as early October. Consequently, when the hunting season is set to begin in September, as is sometimes done, Louisiana hunters run the risk of killing a high proportion of local birds not long out of the nest.

A popular misconception is the idea that Louisiana gets an invasion of "large, western doves" late in the fall. No highly significant geographical size difference has been demonstrated in the dove populations of the United States—certainly none detectable in the field. Furthermore, banding returns clearly show that our migratory doves come mainly from Ohio, Indiana, Michigan, and adjoining states to the east and that we get only a sprinkling of doves from as far west as even Iowa or Kansas.

PASSENGER PIGEON   *Ectopistes migratorius*   Fig. 100

The story of the Passenger Pigeon has been told many times, but it should be repeated over and over again, if only to remind us continually that even the most abundant of our natural resources must never be regarded as inexhaustible—that wise use and management are essential if our generation is to pass on to the next the heritage it received from the generations that went before. There was a time, not so very long ago, when this fine North American bird was so abundant that in migration it passed in flocks that numbered into the millions—flocks that darkened the sky and that, by cutting off the sun's rays, cast huge shadows on the earth. In its nocturnal roosts large limbs of trees would break under the sheer weight of the birds perched on them. Indeed, it is difficult to imagine a bird as common as this becoming quite suddenly extinct, but that is what happened; and it will happen again with other species unless we are alert to the dangers that beset wild creatures under the impact of civilization.

The Passenger Pigeon resembled our Mourning Dove, but it was considerably larger in bulk, had a much longer tail, and was blue-gray instead of brown on the head and back. Because of their greater size, these "wild pigeons" were even more highly esteemed as food than Mourning Doves; and this is the primary factor that led to their destruction. At the height of their exploitation for the market, hundreds of *barrels* of their bodies were shipped daily into New York City alone. Men with torches and sticks invaded the roosts and even the nesting rookeries to lay low thousands of birds in a single night.

The Passenger Pigeon had a very low reproductive potential (see discussion under Bobwhite); it laid one or, rarely, two eggs. This low breeding

Plate XIX Doves

1. Mourning Dove (p. 359). 2. Common Ground Dove (p. 361). 3. White-winged Dove (p. 359).

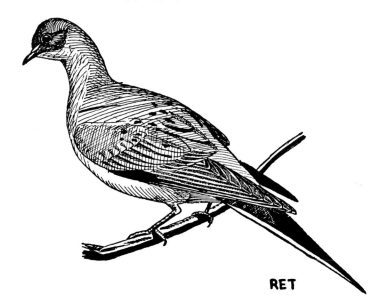

Figure 100 Passenger Pigeon.

rate was sufficient to maintain high populations only as long as some ex-
traneous decimating factor was not introduced. Man and the unbelievable
slaughter he engineered proved to be this critical factor. With its largest
breeding colonies disrupted, with its young often left to die in the nest, and,
at the same time, with many natural decimating forces still operating against
it—disease, predators, weather, and perils of migration—the Passenger
Pigeon suddenly became rare and then extinct. Apparently the last individuals to be seen in Louisiana were a few observed in the vicinity of Prairie
Mer Rouge, in Morehouse Parish, in the winter of 1902–1903. The species
passed completely from the face of the earth on September 1, 1914, when a
captive bird died in the Cincinnati Zoological Park.

COMMON GROUND DOVE *Columbina passerina* Pl. XIX

This small dove, which is not much larger than a House Sparrow, is an uncommon to locally common resident in Louisiana, seen least often in summer. Although nesting of the species in the southern parishes was long

RET

Figure 101   Inca Dove.

suspected, it was not verified until April 6, 1955, when John R. Walther and R. R. Rudolph made the eventful discovery of a nest containing two young in the wooded cheniere near Johnsons Bayou. Two years later, on July 22, 1957, Van T. Harris found a nest, also containing two young, six miles south of New Iberia. It was situated nine inches above the ground in a cane field. The structure is generally made of fine rootlets, twigs, and grass, is placed in a bush or small tree or amid leaves on the ground, and has scarcely any depression for the two white eggs.

The Common Ground Dove is grayish brown above and vinaceous below; its short, nearly square tail is black; and, in flight, the wings flash rufous red. It is seen frequently year around in some sections of southern Louisiana and is especially numerous in old cane fields and clearings near Carville and Reserve, although a few miles to the north at Baton Rouge it is decidedly uncommon. Records from somewhere in the state are available for every month of the year. The call is a two-syllable *woo, wooo*, with a slight rising inflection. The Common Ground Dove is a rather comical little bird as it walks along the ground nodding its head back and forth.

INCA DOVE   *Scardafella inca*   Fig. 101

The Inca Dove is a very rare visitor from western and southern Texas. It is somewhat larger than a Common Ground Dove but considerably smaller than a Mourning Dove. The color is light grayish with numerous horizontal black markings that produce a scaled effect. The tail is long and narrow, and the outer feathers are white tipped. The seven records for the state are of single birds found near Alexandria, on December 28, 1935 (collected); at Farmerville, on November 19, 1936; at Belcher, on April 25, 1943; northeast of Dixie, in Caddo Parish, on November 27, 1958 (collected); at Grand Cheniere, on January 29, 1959; at the Sabine National Wildlife Refuge, in Cameron Parish, from October 28 through November 1, 1969; and at Rockefeller Refuge headquarters from October 28, 1973, to at least the following April 21.

PARROTS
Order *Psittaciformes*

The Parrot Family
Psittacidae

CAROLINA PARAKEET   *Conuropis carolinensis*   Fig. 102

The Carolina Parakeet once roamed in flocks over most of Louisiana, but none have been recorded here with certainty since 1880, and it is unlikely that any remain elsewhere. The factors that led to its extermination are clear. Despite its resplendent beauty, adorned as it was with body feathers of vivid green, a head of yellow, and an area of orange surrounding the base of the bill, the bird was a rogue. It ate the farmer's corn and raided his orchards, destroying almost every kind of fruit indiscriminately. Consequently, it was slaughtered at every opportunity. Moreover, because its flesh was palatable, it was hunted as game. Professional bird catchers procured thousands of parakeets for sale as pets, and still more were obtained for the millinery trade.

The birds' fatal habit of not deserting a fallen comrade often led to the killing of every individual in a flock as the surviving members hovered over their stricken companions. So great was the parakeets' unpopularity that Audubon tells of seeing "several hundred destroyed in this manner in the course of a few hours." As early as Audubon's time the bird was rapidly decreasing in numbers, for in 1842 this famous naturalist lamented its scarcity in places where 25 years before it had been plentiful. In 1881, however, F. W. Langdon, in writing about the birds of West Baton Rouge Parish, told of flocks of two or three dozen individuals being seen in 1880 on the Cinclare Plantation, approximately opposite Baton Rouge; and Charles Wickliffe Beckham reports that a single bird was seen about that same year

364

Figure 102   Carolina Parakeet.

at Bayou Sara. The alleged occurrence of parakeets in the vicinity of Webster Parish, in north Louisiana, about 1900 is highly indefinite.

Parakeets formerly ranged from Florida north to Pennsylvania and New
York and west to Wisconsin, Colorado, and Texas. The populations occupy-
ing the western part of the birds' range differed slightly from those in the
east in being larger and less yellowish (more greenish) on the rump and
hindneck but in having the yellow of the wings more pronounced and extensive. These western representatives of the species have often been referred to as the Louisiana Parakeet, since the scientific name given to the
subspecies is *Conuropsis carolinensis ludovicianus,* a name bestowed by the
Swedish naturalist Gmelin in 1788 on the basis of Le Page du Pratz's description of the bird in his *Histoire de la Louisiane* (see p. 28).

[MONK PARAKEET *Myiopsitta monachus*]

The Monk Parakeet, a native of temperate regions of South America from Bolivia through Paraguay, southern Brazil, Uruguay, and the northern two-thirds of Argentina, is now well established in the eastern part of the United States as a result of accidental introductions. It appears to be multiplying at an alarming rate. Since in its native haunts it is highly destructive of crops, especially corn, rice, sorghum, and citrus fruit, its introduction is looked upon by biologists and agriculturists with grave concern. The species is now present in numbers in the New York City area and in adjacent parts of New Jersey and Connecticut, and it has been reported in no less than 25 states, including Louisiana. As of this writing, the Monk Parakeet has been seen in only two places in our state—in St. Mary Parish at Patterson, where a pair was captured in a garden in December 1973, and at Metairie, just outside of New Orleans, where a pair built a nest in March 1972 and were seen at frequent intervals through October 1973. As is evident from the brackets around the name in the heading of this account, I have not added the species to the official state list, although I am confident it is destined to become a permanent member of our avifauna whether we want it or not.

Several factors have doubtless contributed to the establishment of this exotic in the wild state. First of all, with the lifting in the 1960s of the ban on the importation of psittacine birds, thousands of Monk Parakeets were subsequently introduced for the pet trade. During 1968 alone nearly twelve thousand are said to have been imported into the United States. Free-living birds have come from a variety of sources, including broken crates at Kennedy International Airport and accidental escapes from pet shops and private aviaries across the country. Many are doubtless birds released when owners discover that these parrots cannot be taught to talk and tire of keeping them. Factors abetting their survival in the wild are their tolerance of cold winter temperatures and the readiness with which they come to bird feeders, where they find a year-round source of food. In such situations they compete with our native songbirds. I admit, though, that Monk Parakeets are not unattractive visitors to have in one's garden, provided they do not become obnoxious by eating the buds from our roses and camellias and by committing other nuisances.

The species is unique among the 332 living species of parrots in that it builds a nest of sticks in the open instead of in a tree cavity. It is also a communal nester, several pairs often sharing in the construction of the bulky structure in which each pair has its own nest compartment. The Monk Parakeet is highly gregarious, sometimes forming flocks of a dozen or more individuals. It is about the size of a Mourning Dove, being nearly 12 inches in length. The forehead, throat, and chest are gray; the feathers of the chest, edged terminally with grayish white, produce a scaly effect. The upperparts and lower belly, as well as the shoulders, wing coverts, and tail, are a pea soup green, but the flight feathers are bluish, only tinged with green. The gray hood is the basis of the name Monk Parakeet, as well as the names Quaker parakeet and gray-breasted parakeet, by which the species is sometimes known in the pet trade and among aviculturists.

As far as I know, only one state, Virginia, has so far officially outlawed the Monk Parakeet, and there wildlife experts are carrying out search-and-destroy missions. A 1972 ban on the importation of all exotic birds except under the most rigid regulations has stopped further introductions, but this measure carries no guarantee of permanence, for the ban could be lifted at any time. Most agricultural officials agree that the Monk Parakeet should be added to the list of noxious animals that are forbidden entry to the United States and that those existing in the wild should be destroyed at every opportunity. But eradication will now prove difficult if not impossible. Argentina has certainly met with no success in its program of shooting, netting, poisoning, and nest destruction. In one province alone between 1958 and 1960 bounties were paid on 427,206 pairs of feet. Yet none of these measures had any visible effect on the population as a whole.

CUCKOOS
AND ALLIES
Order *Cuculiformes*

The Cuckoo Family
Cuculidae

THE CUCKOOS and their allies are a large group of birds represented in the tropical or temperate regions of all the continents of the world except Antarctica. The members of this family in western Europe are notable for their parasitic nesting habits. Building no nests of their own, the females skulk here and there looking for nests with fresh eggs. When the rightful owners are away, they slip in, take out one of the eggs already there, and deposit their own egg. Then they quietly sneak away to let their victim assume all the responsibilities associated with the incubation and care of the young cuckoo. Although American cuckoos almost never parasitize other birds, they exhibit tendencies in that direction by sometimes parasitizing each other and by building extremely sloppy nests. Some of the anis, which are aberrant cuckoos, build communal nests in which two or more females lay their eggs together and share the chores of incubation. The roadrunners are giant cuckoos that have taken up a terrestrial existence.

YELLOW-BILLED CUCKOO *Coccyzus americanus* Fig. 103

The Yellow-billed Cuckoo, or "rain crow" as it is often called, is a common summer resident throughout most of Louisiana. It ordinarily arrives in late March and sometimes remains until after the middle of November or more rarely into December. One was seen at Peveto Beach, in Cameron Parish, on December 8, 1963, and another at Lafayette on December 26, 1969. An

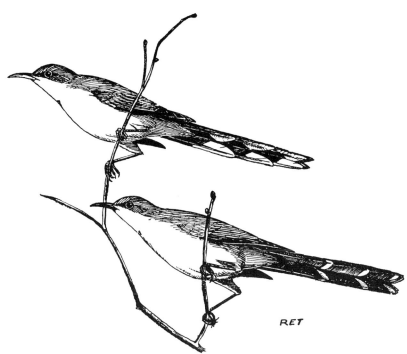

Figure 103   Yellow-billed Cuckoo (above) and Black-billed Cuckoo (below).

individual observed at Alligator Bayou, in Ascension Parish, on February 27, 1965, was either an extremely early migrant or a bird that had wintered in the area.

The nest is a fragile platform of sticks and bits of grass and bark, often so shallow and thin that the two to six unmarked bluish green eggs are visible to one standing beneath the structure. Generally it is placed not much more than 15 feet from the ground, in a tree on the edge of a clearing, in an open grove, or not infrequently adjacent to a human dwelling.

Cuckoos are slow and deliberate in their movements and sometimes alight on a limb and remain there almost motionless for several minutes. The yellow lower mandible, the rufous inner margins of the wing feathers, and the *extensive* white tips on the feathers of the long tail immediately distinguish this species from the Black-billed Cuckoo. The call is a unique,

guttural *ka ka ka ka ka ka ka ka ka ka ka ka ka kow kow kowp——kowp*
———*kowp*———*kowp*. Although the call is emitted continually, day
in and day out, there are many people who believe it is a sign of approaching
rain—hence the name "rain crow." Cuckoos are highly beneficial birds since
each one consumes thousands of caterpillars and other noxious insects in
the course of a summer.

BLACK-BILLED CUCKOO   *Coccyzus erythropthalmus*   Fig. 103

This species gets its name from the fact that its bill is uniformly black, while
the previous species has a yellow lower mandible. It can be further distinguished by the lack of rufous in its wings and by the more restricted whitish
tips of the tail feathers. The call note is a succession of three to five mellow
notes—*cow cow cow*. The Black-billed Cuckoo is strictly a transient throughout the state, uncommon in spring and moderately common in fall; dates
range from April 3 to May 26 and from August 11 to October 26.

GREATER ROADRUNNER   *Geococcyx californianus*   Fig. 104

This interesting, two-foot long, ground-dwelling cuckoo entered Louisiana
fairly recently, for when Oberholser wrote his *Bird Life of Louisiana*, published in 1938, he was unable to find a single satisfactory record of it in the
state. But immediately thereafter the LSU Museum of Zoology received
reports of its occurrence near Shreveport and obtained a specimen that was
shot in that vicinity and mounted by a taxidermist in Bossier City. Since
that time the bird has increased rapidly and is now seen regularly throughout the year in numerous localities in the western part of the state. It is
known to occur as far south as Calcasieu Parish and as far east as 12 miles
south-southeast of Alexandria, in Rapides Parish, and five miles south of
Lake Providence, in East Carroll Parish. Several nests have been found in
the state, some containing eggs, others unfledged young. The eggs number
three to five and are chalky white. The nest is a huge structure of sticks and
is placed in a bush or tree six to eight feet above the ground.

The Greater Roadrunner is well adapted by its long legs to a terrestrial
existence, and it usually seeks safety by running instead of by flight. In the
southwestern United States, where the species is common, it enjoys a good
reputation because of its propensity for killing rattlesnakes.

SMOOTH-BILLED ANI   *Crotophaga ani*   Fig. 105

Anis are solid black, slightly iridescent cuckoos with immense, parrotlike bills. Superficially they resemble grackles, but one glance at the bill is sufficient to make an ani stand out. This species lacks the grooves on the sides of the bill that characterize the next species.

The Smooth-billed Ani is normally restricted to peninsular Florida, the West Indies, and Central and South America. Evidence for its occurrence in Louisiana derives almost entirely from Dr. H. L. Ballowe, an old-time resident of Buras, in the delta of the Mississippi River. On July 18, 1893, Ballowe saw his first ani, a dead one brought to him by a man who had killed it at nearby Diamond. Ballowe sent the specimen to George E. Beyer, a distinguished Louisiana ornithologist of that day, who informed him that it was a Smooth-billed Ani. Years later, in the 1930s, the identification was presumably verified by Harry C. Oberholser, an avian taxonomist of formidable expertise; for while preparing to write on the birdlife of Louisiana, he had examined all the material in the Tulane University collection, where the ani reposed. And in the book that resulted he corrected the previously published date of the record, as he could hardly have felt entitled

Figure 104   Greater Roadrunner.

Figure 105 Heads of anis: Smooth-billed Ani, left; Groove-billed Ani, right.

to do without examining the specimen label and hence the specimen itself.

Meanwhile, in the years from 1893 to 1929, Ballowe continued to see birds he believed to be Smooth-billed Anis—some 20 altogether, all in the Mississippi delta and all except the first in the months of December to February. A reason for not accepting this observer's testimony at face value is that he never mentioned encountering the Groove-billed Ani, a closely similar species now known to be commonplace in the delta and even to nest in its orange groves. Indeed, the only serious claim that the Smooth-billed Ani has occurred in Louisiana since 1929 is a report of one found dead at the Delta National Wildlife Refuge headquarters by Claude Lard on January 30, 1952.

A complicating factor is that bills of immature Groove-bills sometimes have no detectable grooves, none visible even when held in the hand. Whether Beyer and Lard knew this is uncertain, so I base inclusion of the bird on the state list almost wholly on my confidence in Oberholser. Any doubt could be quickly resolved by inspection of a specimen in the light of current knowledge. Unfortunately none survives. The 1952 bird was not preserved, and the original specimen appears to be among many Tulane specimens that cannot now be located.

GROOVE-BILLED ANI *Crotophaga sulcirostris* Fig. 105

The Groove-billed Ani is an uncommon but regular winter resident in Louisiana that also presumably occurs in every month of the year somewhere in the state. It is most often seen in early winter and in southern Louisiana, particularly in Cameron and Plaquemines parishes, but it has also been observed at numerous other localities in the state, even in places far inland, such as at Cottonport, in Avoyelles Parish, and at Oak Ridge, in Morehouse Parish. Groove-bills are usually seen singly, in pairs, or in flocks of 3 to 15 birds. But the all-time high was the more than 40 counted in a span of four days in the Johnsons Bayou area of Cameron Parish in late November 1959.

Although actual breeding of the Groove-billed Ani in Plaquemines Parish had long been suspected, not until July 5, 1971, was strong evidence obtained of it doing so. On this date R. D. Purrington, Mary Lewis, and Wayne Blank found a closely knit family group, including two juveniles with grooveless bills, ruffled appearance, and lack of some facial feathering in an orange grove at Triumph. On July 10 a nest, presumed to be that of a Groove-billed Ani, was found in the same orchard, but, of course, no birds were in attendance and the identity of the former owner could not be definitely established.

Despite the fact that the Groove-billed Ani is now known to breed in the delta region below New Orleans, it is decidedly scarce there in summer and actual records for the month of June are still lacking. The only time that the species is even present anywhere in the state in appreciable numbers is in winter, and this increase must result from an infiltration from the lower Rio Grande Valley or Mexico, both places being within the main breeding range of the bird. But why this ani should move northeastward in fall, when other migratory birds are moving southward, is a mystery.

In the latter parts of severe winters, such as the one of 1972–1973, anis virtually vanish from all of Louisiana except their warmer southernmost sanctuary in the delta. Whether they retire to the tropics or simply perish is not known. But fears that the Louisiana-oriented part of the population may have been permanently wiped out always prove groundless. Unfailingly in the following fall a new influx of visitors takes place.

The Groove-billed Ani frequents orchards, mesquite, and weedy places and sometimes associates with cows in pastures. The extensive cultivation of citrus crops in the Mississippi River delta region below New Orleans may be one reason why anis show a preference for this area of the state. It is a noisy, querulous bird with a wide assortment of unmusical sounds. As the name implies, the bill of the adult is furrowed longitudinally, while the otherwise similar Smooth-billed Ani has a smooth bill.

OWLS
Order *Strigiformes*

ALTHOUGH THE ORDER Strigiformes is divided into two families, the barn owls and the typical owls, it is a remarkably homogeneous group, clearly differentiated from its closest relatives. Unlike other birds, owls are flat faced; the eyes are not located on the sides of the head with the bill interposed but are instead situated so that each peers straight ahead from a flat facial disc. This arrangement is probably of great value to the owl, contributing to the extraordinary sense of sight that enables it to see after dark. The lens of the eye is capable of considerable forward and backward adjustment, doubtless permitting rapid focusing, especially useful at night when the owl drops down swiftly and unerringly on its unsuspecting prey. The feathers, including even the large flight feathers, are extremely soft and flexible. Their loose texture permits owls to fly without making the usual "swooshing" sound normally associated with bird flight, and hence they are able to descend on a rat without disclosing their approach.

Owls are generally very early nesters, sometimes in the South having young as early as January. This adaptation is rather remarkable, for the birds gain a great advantage by bringing forth their young as close as possible to the annual peak of the small rodent population. Baby owls are voracious eaters. I once watched a pair of Barn Owls, which had a nest in a hollow tree on the campus of Louisiana Tech University at Ruston, bring in five field mice in as many trips and shove each mouse into the mouth of *one* nestling. When the sixth mouse was brought to the nest and given to the same favored offspring, this hapless individual could swallow no more. For more than an hour the tail of the last mouse hung from the corner of the little owl's mouth as if it were waiting to digest some of the initial mice and thereby make room for the others in its alimentary tract.

Our native woods mice, field mice, and rats provide an abundant source of winter food for our owl and hawk populations. Indeed, were it not for the service rendered to us by these birds of prey, the rat and mouse population of our state would doubtless increase to disastrous proportions. When a mouse is eaten by an owl, the hair and most of the bones are rolled into a pellet by the muscles of the owl's stomach and regurgitated onto the ground near the bird's roost or nest. Since the skull of each kind of mammal has striking individual peculiarities, a specialist can study the contents of an owl pellet and determine not only how many animals the owl has eaten but also exactly what species it has caught. For example, Dr. A. K. Fisher, who in his lifetime was one of the leading authorities on the food habits of North American birds, once studied the nesting site of a pair of Barn Owls in one of the towers of the Smithsonian Institution building in Washington and later wrote: "The floor was strewn with pellets, and the nest, which was in one corner, was composed of a mass of broken-down ones. An examination of 200 of these pellets gave a total of 454 skulls. Of these, 225 were meadow mice; 2, pine mice; 179, house mice; 20, rats; 6, jumping mice; 20, shrews; 1, a star-nosed mole; and 1, a vesper sparrow."

The Barn Owl Family
Tytonidae

Barn owls are structurally different enough from other owls to be placed in a family of their own. There are, however, only 10 species in the entire family, even though it is virtually worldwide in its distribution. The single species, *Tyto alba*, to which our Louisiana bird belongs, occurs also in such distant lands as Tierra del Fuego, the Fiji Islands, Australia, Madagascar, India, Palestine, Africa, Russia, Norway, England, and most of the countries and islands in between. I do not know of any other land bird with such a cosmopolitan distribution. Of course, the Barn Owl is by no means uniform in color or in size throughout its wide range, but most of the geographical variants are not different enough to be accorded recognition as species.

BARN OWL   *Tyto alba*   Pl. XX; p. 377

The Barn Owl, or "monkey-faced owl" as it is often called, occurs in two phases, a yellow- or buffy-breasted phase and one in which white predominates below. The latter color variation has often been the basis for erroneous local reports of the Snowy Owl, a giant-sized, white owl of the Arctic regions that sometimes spreads southward in winter over parts of the United States. The best distinguishing features of the Barn Owl are its heart-shaped facial disc, its extraordinarily long legs, and its hissing call note that sounds like escaping steam.

It is a common permanent resident that frequently nests in barns, attics, and church steeples, sometimes in hollow trees, and rarely in holes in the ground. The eggs are three to five in number and are white in color, like the eggs of most species that nest in the dark. The laying habits of the Barn Owl are unlike those of most birds, which generally do not commence incubation until all eggs in a clutch are laid and thereby insure that all eggs will hatch more or less simultaneously. If they did otherwise, birds such as the Bobwhite that lay large clutches would have young hatching and leaving the nest over a two-week period, and the problems of parental care would be terrifically compounded. Barn Owls, however, begin to incubate as soon as the first egg is laid, and for this reason their young sometimes vary immensely in size.

SAMUEL A. GRIMES

Barn Owl in Loft

The Typical
Owl Family
Strigidae

This family is represented on the Louisiana list by nine species, almost as many as all the species of Tytonidae in the entire world; but only three of these nine species are definitely known to nest within our borders.

COMMON SCREECH OWL *Otus asio* Pl. XX; facing p. 64

This little owl often comes to live in a hollow tree or in a dense thicket of shrubbery close to human habitations. Generally speaking, its presence is not looked upon with favor, for its tremulous, shivering note is superstitiously thought by many to be an omen of ill luck or even of an approaching death. Of course, it is very easy to forestall such misfortune, provided one is aware of the correct techniques. One method is to turn one's socks wrong side out; another, to turn one's hat around. As a matter of fact, however, the Common Screech Owl should be welcomed by man to his premises, for it is a far better mouser than any pussycat that ever lived. Moreover, many people, including myself, enjoy hearing the quavering notes that these little birds make as their contribution to the interesting chorus of voices that emanates from the darkness at night.

The Common Screech Owl has so-called "ear" tufts, which are charac-

---

Plate XX Heads of Owls
1. Barn Owl (p. 376). 2. Barred Owl (p. 381). 3. Great Horned Owl (p. 379). 4. Common Screech Owl (p. 378). 5. Short-eared Owl (p. 383). 6. Burrowing Owl (p. 381).

1

2

3

4

5

6

RT

teristic of many kinds of owls, and here it is the only common small owl possessing them. A red and a gray color phase may sometimes occur in the same brood (see photograph opposite p. 64), but Common Screech Owls in Louisiana are generally somewhat brownish and thus intermediate between these two color extremes. Four to six white eggs are laid in a hollow in a tree in March or early April. The species is common throughout the wooded sections of the state, including the chenieres along the coast.

FLAMMULATED OWL *Otus flammeolus* Pl. XXI

This little owl really has no business in Louisiana, for it is supposed to be a denizen of our western mountains from British Columbia southward through the United States to the highlands of Mexico. On January 2, 1949, however, one was captured in a willow thicket on the banks of the Mississippi River, a few miles below Baton Rouge, and is now preserved in the LSU Museum of Zoology. The unusual severity of the winter of 1948–1949 through the northwestern states may have been the factor responsible for the unexpected appearance of this individual far from its normal range.

The Flammulated Owl closely resembles the Common Screech Owl, but it is only slightly more than half as large, has brown instead of yellow eyes, and has more finely vermiculated feathers. Its call is a soft, single-syllabled *hoot* that is repeated at regular intervals.

GREAT HORNED OWL *Bubo virginianus* Pl. XX

The Great Horned Owl has often been referred to as the "tiger" of the bird world because of the ferocious manner in which it preys on many kinds of small mammals and birds. Its large size enables it to kill rabbits with ease and to subdue skunks, which it apparently relishes. Although it kills poultry, it also eats great quantities of rats and mice. The species is easily distinguished by its large size (over 20 inches in length), by its prominent widely spaced "ear" tufts, and by its deep, sonorous call note that is usually repeated three or four times, *whoo, whoo-whoo, whoo,* suggesting the barking of a deep-throated hound dog off in the distance. The call of the Barred Owl, or "hoot owl," is a laughing, higher-pitched call of six to eight notes with various inflections toward the end.

In December or January the Great Horned Owl lays its two or three eggs in an abandoned crow's or squirrel's nest, in hollows in trees, or even sometimes on the ledges of city buildings. It is a widespread permanent resident that is never as plentiful as the Barred Owl, except in the chenieres and in the small clumps of large trees planted as windbreaks in the prairies of southwestern Louisiana.

SNOWY OWL *Nyctea scandiaca*   Pl. XXI

This huge white diurnal owl, which averages larger than even the Great Horned Owl, is an Arctic species that about once every four winters invades the northern part of the United States in considerable numbers. Only rarely, however, have its wanderings extended into the South. The three reports for Louisiana prior to 1900, long the sole basis for occurrence in Louisiana, are less than satisfactory. In each case the bird was shot, but no evidence, not even in the form of supporting details, has survived to assure us that light-phase Barn Owls or albino Barred Owls were not mistaken for Snowy Owls. Most welcome, therefore, was a recent record that appears to be incontrovertible. On February 17, 1972, Charles Hollis, a biologist with the U.S. Soil Conservation Service, saw a Snowy Owl five miles north of Newellton, in Tensas Parish. It was perched on a fence post and allowed Hollis to approach to within 25 to 30 yards before it would take flight, and then it would fly only a short distance. Three times it was flushed, but it stayed within 100 yards of the place where it was first found. Hollis specifically noted the yellow eyes, which eliminated aberrant Barn or Barred Owls.

The Snowy Owl has a large, round head without "ear" tufts, and its predominantly white plumage is more or less barred with dusky. The legs and feet are heavily feathered, and the eyes are yellow. No other owl in normal plumage is as white as the Snowy Owl. In its white phase the Barn Owl is white only on the underparts and is, of course, also easily told by its smaller size, its heart-shaped face and black eyes, and its disproportionately long legs.

[HAWK OWL *Surnia ulula*]

Despite the fact that this species has been listed in old publications on the birds of Louisiana, there is, in my opinion, no satisfactory record of its occurrence in the state. A specimen is said to have been collected near St. Francisville in the winter of 1886, but since it was not preserved, there is no means now of verifying the identification. Actually the Hawk Owl is a bird of the

Far North that rarely gets into the United States at all even along the Canadian border. It feeds almost entirely in the daytime and perches on the topmost branch of a tree in a horizontal position (owls generally sit upright). Its medium size, grayish color, and the black "sideburn" patches on the head are diagnostic.

BURROWING OWL *Speotyto cunicularia* Pl. XX

The Burrowing Owl in the United States has a peculiar, discontinuous distribution. It is common in the western plains and again on faraway Kissimmee Prairie in peninsular Florida. In Louisiana it occurs as an uncommon winter resident from the first part of October until late May, and, although recorded in many parts of the state, it is most frequently observed in the southern parishes. The alleged discovery of the eggs of this species at Baton Rouge on April 10, 1935, is an erroneous record, but a pair did apparently spend the summer of 1972 on Delta Farms near Jonesville, in Catahoula Parish. No evidence of actual nesting was obtained, and a search for the pair in the late spring and summer of 1973 failed because of excessive flooding of the area.

This interesting little owl is easily distinguished by its light brown color, its small screech owl body size, and its extremely long legs. It sits on the ground, on a fence post, or atop piles of lumber and appears to be fond of perches around heaps of driftwood and debris on the Gulf beaches. It is often seen in daytime. This owl never seems to emit a sound while it is here in winter, but on its breeding grounds it has a hooting note with some of the quality of the song of the Mourning Dove.

BARRED OWL *Strix varia* Pl. XX

In Louisiana this species is by far the commonest and best-known member of the Owl family, for there is hardly any sizable wood in the state that does not support at least a pair of "hoot owls." Their comical calls can be expressed in southern lingo as "Who cooks for me? Who cooks for you? Who cooks for you-all-l-l-l?" Unlike the Horned Owl, which has a deep call of three or four syllables, the Barred Owl generally emits eight or more hoots. Occasionally the hoots are followed by a long drawn-out, weird scream that is enough to chill the bones of the uninitiated. I have heard this note frequently in the vicinity of Monroe but only rarely as far south as Baton

Rouge. The Barred Owl lays its two to four eggs in a hollow in a tree, usually not later than February, and sometimes much earlier.

The general color of this species is dark brown with numerous bars on the upper breast and vertical streaks on the belly. It has no "ear" tufts, and its eyes are so dark that they actually appear to be black. It and the Barn Owl are the only large owls in Louisiana that do not have yellow eyes.

The diet is made up largely of rats and mice and only in rare circumstances includes poultry. Under no conditions, however, should any owl be shot, for all are protected by federal and state law.

LONG-EARED OWL *Asio otus* Pl. XXI

In many northern states, bird enthusiasts search for this nocturnal owl in the isolated patches of evergreen trees that stand out in winter amid a generally leafless landscape. They scan the ground for the elongated pellets that betoken the presence of Long-eared Owls, sitting as immobile as if frozen, on the boughs above. In Louisiana, this method has not worked. We are surrounded by a winter sea of green—vast pine forests, augmented by live oaks, broad-leaved magnolias, and other trees that do not shed foliage in fall. In our surroundings, a searcher for Long-eared Owls does not know where to begin. One perceptive Baton Rougean, however, did not have to look far. On a short walk in downtown Baton Rouge, he spotted two of these owls perched in a live oak in a front yard, only a block from the State Capitol.

To Leslie Glasgow and his woodcock banders we are indebted for the information that Long-eared Owls hunt over the open fields at night. Along country roads squeaking will sometimes entice them to alight nearby on a fence. If a dashboard plug-in searchlight is then shined upon them, they will sit for a long time without flying, as though spellbound. Often, after the haunts of Long-ears have been located, a series of observations result. But if we count as separate records only definite occurrences in different winters or in different places, the all-time Louisiana score for the species is only 13 sets of observations, 3 of them supported by specimens. Sightings extend from October 20 to the last week of March and are confined to Caddo, Vermilion, Iberia, Iberville, Pointe Coupee, East Baton Rouge, Livingston, and St. Charles parishes.

In general appearance the Long-eared Owl suggests a Great Horned Owl but is not much more than half the size of the latter and is longitudinally streaked instead of horizontally barred below. Moreover, the excep-

Plate XXI   Heads of Owls

1. Snowy Owl (p. 380). 2. Northern Saw-whet Owl (p. 383). 3. Flammulated Owl (p. 379). 4. Long-eared Owl (p. 382).

tionally long "ear" tufts are situated closer together, near the center of the head. It is about the size of a Short-eared Owl, but that species is predominantly buffy in color, instead of dusky and gray with only a smattering of buffy. Flying at night in the beam of a spotlight, Long-ears exhibit dark "wrist" marks, much like those of the Short-eared Owl.

SHORT-EARED OWL *Asio flammeus* Pl. XX

The Short-eared Owl is another northern owl that comes to us only in winter. Among nonbreeding members of the family, it has vied with the Burrowing Owl for top ranking in numbers, despite the fact that it has gone unrecorded in some years. It often feeds in the daytime or at dusk and, therefore, in areas where it is present, it is frequently observed. For a long time, it seemed in its visitations to prefer expanses of open marsh, and hence it was more frequently observed in the southern parishes, which abound in such habitat, than elsewhere in Louisiana. So far in the 1970s, however, it has appeared more regularly in fields in the northwestern part of the state.

The Short-eared Owl is buffy with two prominent black spots near the bend of the wing on the underside, and its "ears" are so diminutive that they are scarcely ever visible. It is most often seen coursing erratically back and forth like a Marsh Hawk over open spaces in daylight, and, since our other owls virtually never appear in such circumstances, the Short-eared Owl can hardly be confused with them. Its food includes an occasional small marsh bird, but most of the time it eats only small rodents and insects. Fall migrants usually do not appear in Louisiana until after the middle of October, and departure in spring usually takes place in April, though records extend to as late as May 21.

NORTHERN SAW-WHET OWL *Aegolius acadicus* Pl. XXI

This little owl is smaller than a Common Screech Owl and has no "ear" tufts, a combination of characters that sets it apart from everything else except the Flammulated Owl, which has only inconspicuous "ears" and dark, instead of yellow, eyes. Only two definite records of its occurrence in Louisiana are available. A specimen was collected near Madisonville in the winter of 1889 and identified by Professor George E. Beyer, who, in his day, was one of Louisiana's most distinguished ornithologists. The second record is that of a bird found at Hackberry, in Cameron Parish, on December 29,

1962, by Sidney A. Gauthreaux, Robert B. Moore, and Gus Hannibal. The little owl was studied carefully by the observers at a distance of 20 feet and the following characters noted: bold rufous stripes on the front of the breast, fine dotted white lines on the forehead, yellow eyes, and lack of "ear" tufts.

The Northern Saw-whet Owl is probably a more frequent winter visitor to Louisiana than the two records would indicate, for it may simply escape detection because of its retiring habits in daytime. The call note is a monotonous whistle, *too, too, too, too, too, too,* that is repeated almost endlessly.

GOATSUCKERS
AND ALLIES
Order *Caprimulgiformes*

The Goatsucker Family
Caprimulgidae

THIS STRANGE GROUP of birds called goatsuckers acquired its equally strange name long ago in rural Europe. There, as elsewhere, these birds habitually feed on the wing, low over pastures, at dusk. Some of the simple and superstitious folk of olden times evidently believed that these deft fliers were pilfering milk when they swept in and out among the legs of the goats in quest of winged insects. At any rate, whatever may have been the basis for the name, it is now firmly implanted in our modern ornithological nomenclature.

The goatsuckers are a large group of birds of many bizarre species with equally bizarre names—Frogmouth, Potoo, Whip-poor-will, Chuck-will's-widow, Poor-will, nighthawk, and others. They all have long wings and long tails, but the most striking part of their anatomy is the immense mouth with its tiny, virtually useless bill. On each side of this huge mouth are bristles, often long and stiff, that fence in the edges of the gape and thus prevent their insect prey from escaping (Fig. 106). Since nearly all activity is on the wing, the minute and extremely weak feet are used only in perching. The exceptionally large eyes are an adaptation to twilight and night feeding. Indeed, nature could hardly have produced a bird more efficiently constructed for pursuit of its food on the wing at a time when nearly all other birds are at roost and fast asleep. During the day, most goatsuckers perch on a fence post, on the ground, or lengthwise on the limb of a tree.

Their colors so nearly match their surroundings that they almost always escape detection. The Mexican Potoo even goes so far as to assume awkward postures that conform with the curvature of the particular dead limb on which it is passing the daylight hours.

I think the most remarkable fact of all about goatsuckers is the discovery that at least one species hibernates. Zoologists long made issue of the fact that no bird was known to be able to go into a complete state of torpidity in order to survive the cold winter months. Most cold-blooded animals— such as frogs, toads, and various reptiles—as well as several mammals, have this remarkable physiological adaptation. Birds that cannot endure cold weather compensate by performing migrations to regions of warmer climate. But in December 1946, much to the surprise of zoologists, an ornithologist in California discovered a small goatsucker called a Poor-will hibernating in a rocky crevice in a canyon. He took this bird out of its retreat, handled it leisurely, and then replaced it in its nook, all without arousing it from its torpid slumber. The following winter, a Poor-will thought to be the same bird was in the same crypt and was again lethargic. The ornithologist banded this individual bird and commenced a series of weekly visits to its place of hiding, making recordings of the bird's internal temperature and the temperature of the surrounding air, as well as numerous other observations, including ones pertaining to heartbeat, respiration, and the effects of various stimuli. Its rectal temperature over a period of seven weeks in midwinter was not only far below normal and almost constant at 66°F (normal bird temperature is about 107°F), but was also below the temperature of the surrounding atmosphere near noonday. The bird stayed in a state of coma in its protecting nook throughout the second winter, at least until sometime between February 14 and 22; on the latter date it flew from the hand when picked up. As if all this were not enough to startle zoologists, the same bird, as its aluminum band proved, came back to the identical spot the following winter! The hibernating bird was further studied between November 24 and December 5, but on December 19, 1948, and on dates thereafter, the hiding niche was empty and the bird was not to be found.

CHUCK-WILL'S-WIDOW *Caprimulgus carolinensis* Figs. 106, 107

The Chuck-will's-widow is the common breeding goatsucker of the wooded upland regions of Louisiana, particularly numerous where there is a mixture

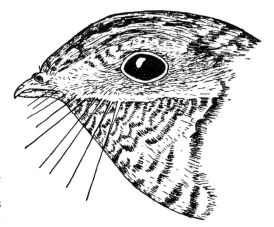

Figure 106 Head of Chuck-will's-widow, showing rictal bristles that fence the corners of the mouth when it is open.

of pines and oaks. It is the largest member of the family in the United States and is reddish brown, sprinkled with black. The other species in Louisiana have patches of white or pale buff either in the wings or at the corners of the tail; the female of the present species lacks both.

Throughout the state the Chuck-will's-widow is confused with the Whip-poor-will, which is presumably a transient species occurring only in spring and fall. The call of the latter is a *whip-poor-will'*, the major accent being on the last syllable. The call of the present species is a rapidly repeated *chuck-will's-wid'ow*, the emphasis being on the *will's* and first syllable of the *widow*. As a matter of fact, unless one is quite close to the singing bird, the *chuck* is inaudible, and all one hears is an often-repeated *-will's-wid'ow, -will's-wid'ow*.

Few sounds are to me more pleasant than the continued nocturnal calling, back and forth, of several of these ghosts of the night. In spring and early summer, especially on moonlit nights, the woods of their choice reverberate with their calls, and although often heard, the bird is seldom seen unless one happens, in walking through these woods, to flush one from the ground.

Migrant Chuck-will's-widows usually arrive in numbers in the first part of April, and from then to the end of summer they are common. After they cease to call, an estimate of their numbers is difficult, but we may safely presume that most of them are gone by the middle of October. In our coastal

Figure 107 The three common goatsuckers of Louisiana: (1) Common Night-hawk; (2) Whip-poor-will; (3) Chuck-will's-widow.

woods and chenieres an occasional Chuck-will's-widow remains throughout the cold months, but only by sheer luck do we ever find one of these silent, wintering individuals.

The food of the species consists almost entirely of insects, in spite of at least one instance of an individual engulfing a hummingbird in its two-inch gape and another of a Chuck-will's-widow swallowing a sparrow.

WHIP-POOR-WILL   *Caprimulgus vociferus*   Fig. 107

This species is an elusive but regular spring and fall transient and a rare winter resident in Louisiana. No less than a dozen and a half records are now available for localities in the southeastern part of the state during the winter months. It has been reported to nest in northern Louisiana, particularly in the vicinity of Shreveport and may have once done so in limited numbers. Why it should have discontinued nesting in this region is unexplainable, but repeated efforts have revealed no evidence that it is now even present there in summer.

2GOATSUCKERS

389

During its passage in spring, which takes place mainly in late March and the first three weeks of April, the Whip-poor-will is observed rather frequently on the coastal chenieres, where it is usually silent. In its passage through the interior of the state it is sometimes heard calling, although rarely is it seen, since, like the preceding species, it is active only in the twilight and at night. Indeed, during the period of its southward return when it is voiceless, comparatively few records of it are on file.

The Whip-poor-will is considerably smaller than the Chuck-will's-widow; the male has dirty white terminal spots on the outer tail feathers, and the call notes are different (see preceding account).

COMMON NIGHTHAWK   *Chordeiles minor*   Figs. 107, 108

The nighthawks are not hawks and are considerably less nocturnal than their relatives, the Whip-poor-will and the Chuck-will's-widow. Yet the local name "bull-bat," by which this species is generally known in Louisiana, is

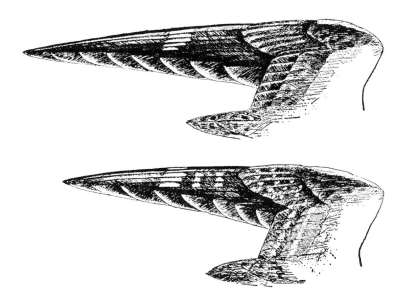

Figure 108   Wings of the Common Nighthawk (above) and the Lesser Nighthawk (below). In the latter, the white patch is closer to the end of the wing than it is in the Common Nighthawk.

no more appropriate than the name nighthawk, since nighthawks have no
proper association, real or fanciful, with either bulls or bats—unless the
booming sound made by their wings is considered suggestive of the bellow of
a bull. On Grand Isle I have heard the Common Nighthawk called the
"pee-ank zoom," a vivid name that combines its call with an allusion to one
of its interesting habits. The bird flies overhead emitting an eruptive *pee-ank*
sound and then suddenly dives earthward at considerable speed. Just before
crashing to the ground or on a rooftop, it swoops upward, and the rushing
of the air through its flight feathers causes the latter to vibrate and to produce the booming sound. The interesting performance is repeated over and
over again by the males and is doubtless done for the benefit of a female
perched nearby.

The species is migratory to faraway South America, generally leaving
Louisiana by late October and not returning until near the middle of April.
After this time it is abundant and widespread throughout the southern part
of the state. For some reason it is rather uncommon in the extreme northern
sections of Louisiana. The Lesser Nighthawk, a species very similar in appearance, has been recorded in southern Louisiana (see next account for its
distinguishing characteristics). In the winter of 1957–1958 two, possibly
three, Common Nighthawks wintered near Audubon Park in New Orleans.
They were seen and heard repeatedly by a host of competent observers between late November and the following February 3. The species was again
present in New Orleans in late December 1959 and in January 1960. On
December 30, 1965, three were seen at Baton Rouge, and again on January
22, 1973, one was noted at the same place. The midwinter occurrence in
Louisiana of a species that normally winters in South America is a matter
of great ornithological interest.

Nighthawks cannot be acclaimed as nest builders, for the two eggs are
merely placed in a slight depression in the ground in a clearing in the woods,
in the rough of a golf course, or in similar situations. Not infrequently
they lay their eggs on the flat graveled rooftops of downtown office buildings.

The chief field marks of the Common Nighthawk, besides its distinctive call notes, are its long, pointed wings, its erratic, zigzag flight, and the
presence of a white patch in the wing. Like its relatives, it feeds almost
entirely on flying insects, dragonflies being preferred.

LESSER NIGHTHAWK   *Chordeiles acutipennis*   Fig. 108

This western relative of the Common Nighthawk has been detected in our state on fairly numerous occasions. On April 10, 1942, a group of students and I collected two specimens from a small flock found feeding at dusk over the edge of a marsh six miles east of Cameron, in southwestern Louisiana. The following morning one was found roosting on the limb of a tree in a nearby cheniere. On April 7, 1957, one was found dead on the highway just north of Grand Isle by Buford Myers, and a wing was saved to corroborate the identification. Later in the same year, on May 2, Robert J. Newman collected an adult male on Grand Isle. On November 28, 1959, Mac Myers obtained a specimen of an adult male at Cameron. On December 18, 1959, Sidney A. Gauthreaux repeatedly observed and heard a male calling as it fed at dusk near the street lamps on the campus of Louisiana State University in New Orleans. The species has been observed over a dozen times at several places in Cameron Parish, as well as at LaBranche, in St. Charles Parish, on January 9, 1971, and at New Orleans, on October 2, 1965. Extreme dates are April 7 to May 23 and September 8 to January 9. Records are therefore lacking for June, July, August, February, and March.

The species, which has also been called the Texas Nighthawk, breeds in Texas and normally winters from central Mexico to South America. Its migrations in spring may quite often bring it into southwestern Louisiana, where it simply passes undetected because of its great similarity to the Common Nighthawk. In addition to being slightly smaller, a feature that would hardly be noticed in the field, the present species has the white patch in the wing relatively much closer to the tip. In the Lesser Nighthawk the white patch is centered on a point two-thirds the distance from the bend of the wing to the tip, while in the Common Nighthawk it is only a little more than halfway from the bend to the tip (Fig. 108). An adult Lesser Nighthawk in the hand can always be positively identified by the presence of buffy spots on the primaries and secondaries that are lacking in the Common Nighthawk. Moreover, in the Lesser Nighthawk the tip of the sixth primary (from the outside) does not extend beyond the white patch that crosses the first four, and sometimes the fifth, primaries, while in the Common Nighthawk the tip of the sixth primary extends well beyond the distal edge of the white patch. The seldom-heard call note of the Lesser Nighthawk is a hooting or grunting sound, totally unlike the *pee-ank* of the Common Nighthawk.

SWIFTS AND HUMMINGBIRDS
Order *Apodiformes*

TO ONE who is not an ornithologist, the fact that swifts and humming-birds are considered closely related will doubtless seem strange. Swifts, on the one hand, have bills that are minute and not often used, for they get their food by engulfing insects in the opened mouth as they fly through the air. Hummingbirds, on the other hand, have long bills and tongues highly modified for probing into the corollas of flowers and sucking up the nectar (Fig. 116). This seemingly important difference in bill and tongue structure is, however, merely an adaptation to certain specialized feeding habits, for in other anatomical characteristics swifts and hummingbirds have a great deal in common. Their feet, for instance, are small and weak—the ordinal name Apodiformes means literally, and of course incorrectly, "forms without feet." Other characteristics they have in common are: the wings are relatively long and narrow, hence knifelike; the legs are without the ambiens muscle, which, when present, is used in flexing the toes; the sternum, or breastbone, is wide, deeply keeled, and unnotched. The colon is without caeca, or pouches; the number of wing and tail feathers and the arrangement of the feather tracts are very similar; and the oil gland at the base of the tail is without a tuft of feathers, which is so often present in other groups. These and other internal features possessed by both hummingbirds and swifts point to a close relationship not readily apparent in the birds' external appearances.

The Swift Family

Apodidae

Swifts are small, long-winged birds that feed entirely on the wing. Since they are insectivorous, all but a comparatively few of the 78 species in the world are confined to tropical regions. Two of the four kinds that occur regularly in the United States also enter Louisiana, but only one breeds here. Both of our species are members of a group that is unique within the family in having the shafts of the tail feathers longer than the webs (Fig. 109), an adaptation for clinging vertically to the sides of caves, the interiors of hollow trees, and the insides of chimneys. Swifts are popularly confused with swallows, possibly because of a superficial similarity in feeding habits, but they are not closely related to swallows. Swifts use a secretion of their salivary glands to hold together their fragile nests, and one Asiatic and Philippine group, the Edible Nest Swiftlets, builds nests entirely of this substance, which is gathered by man and eaten as a delicacy.

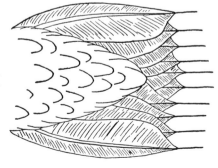

Figure 109   Tail of Chimney Swift. Note the extension of the rhachis beyond the tips of the webs, forming a stiff terminal spine on each tail feather. The tail is used by the swift as a prop as it clings to the interior of a hollow tree or chimney.

393

Figure 110   Chimney Swift (left) and Vaux's Swift (right).

CHIMNEY SWIFT   *Chaetura pelagica*   Figs. 109, 110

The Chimney Swift, or "chimney sweep" as it is sometimes called, is one of our commonest summer residents from the third week of March until near the end of October. It is indeed one of the best-known birds of the eastern United States. In the broad area extending eastward to the Atlantic Ocean from a line between Texas and Manitoba, there are probably very few towns uninhabited in summer by swifts. But, despite this widespread abundance, it was not until 1944 that this bird's winter home was discovered, and then

Figure 111   Photograph of Chimney Swift trap in position. Sections of seven-inch stove pipe connect the L-shaped box on top of the chimney with the receiving cage on ground level. The trap is placed on the chimney after the swifts go to roost. At daybreak on the following morning light begins to enter the trap through the screen wire top and through the plexiglass window on the front side of the box. As the birds fly toward the light in attempting to leave the chimney, they are deflected by the screen and the plexiglass window into the galvanized metal funnel and thence through the stove pipe tunnel to the receiving cage. Several thousand swifts can be banded in a single morning by the use of this apparatus.

it was discovered only in part. Aluminum bands that had been placed on 13 swifts in Tennessee, Alabama, Georgia, Illinois, Connecticut, and Ontario were obtained by a missionary from natives living along the Río Yanayaco, one of the headwaters of the Amazon in eastern Peru. How the natives came by the bands was never ascertained, but it can be presumed that they must have examined no less than 5,000 swifts in order to have found 13 wearing bands. This presumption is based on the experience of bird banders who have handled large numbers of swifts and have found that, on the average, for every 400 birds caught, 1 will be banded.

The dispersal of 21,414 swifts that were captured by a special trap (Fig. 111) and banded at Baton Rouge between 1937 and 1939, inclusive, and the recovery of "foreign" banded birds (that is, birds banded at other stations) at the same place is shown by the accompanying map (Fig. 112). One of the birds banded at Baton Rouge on September 24, 1938, presumably went to South America to spend the winter. It must have come back through the United States in 1939, for it was captured and released at Campbellton, New Brunswick, on June 11, 1939. It then presumably went back to South America in the fall, possibly passing through Baton Rouge as it did in 1938. Finally, on August 22, 1940, it was found dead at Upsalquitch, New Brunswick, 15 miles from the point of its capture and release in 1939. Case histories such as this serve to illustrate the great importance of bird banding as a means of learning about the movements of wild birds.

The Chimney Swift is very punctual in its migratory movements. In spring it arrives almost simultaneously throughout the state in the third week of March. In fall it congregates in vast flocks during October in the cities and larger towns in the southern part of the state. At Baton Rouge as many as seven thousand swifts have roosted in one night in a single large chimney. Such huge gatherings are noted in the late afternoon as the birds circle about a chimney chosen for a roost. Suddenly, on an evening when the temperature has dropped abruptly, the large flocks disappear en masse, and no Chimney Swifts are seen again until the following March.

The cigar-shaped body, long narrow wings, and brownish black coloration make this species easily identifiable. The color of the throat is actually white but is usually more or less obscured by chimney soot (the rare Vaux's Swift has nearly the entire underparts whitish). The song or call note is a loud twitter that is repeated almost continuously as the birds wheel about overhead. In feeding, swifts spend hours upon hours on the wing, and they

Figure 112 Map showing points of recovery (open circles) of 126 of 21,414 swifts banded at Baton Rouge and the sources (black dots) of 64 "foreign" birds recovered at Baton Rouge, 1937–1939. (Reprinted from Lowery, *Proceedings of the Louisiana Academy of Sciences*, 7, 1943:64.)

even get their nesting materials of sticks by flying through trees and snipping off small twigs. These they carry to a chimney (or, rarely, to a hollow tree, as in the days before the advent of man), where they make a fragile shelf of sticks, cemented together by their own saliva, to cradle the three or four white eggs.

VAUX'S SWIFT   *Chaetura vauxi*   Fig. 110

This species of the Pacific Coast states is a very rare winter visitor in south-eastern Louisiana. It has arrived as early as October 14 (when a single individual was found at Baton Rouge in a roosting flock of 3,300 Chimney Swifts that had been trapped for banding) and has remained as late as March 3.

The Vaux's Swift cannot always be distinguished in the field from the Chimney Swift, although it is slightly smaller and its twittering call note is decidedly weaker. Also, unlike the Chimney Swift, which has a white throat and a blackish brown breast and belly, this species is entirely light colored below (Fig. 110). The uniformly light underparts of the Vaux's Swift stand out rather prominently when the bird circles overhead, provided, of course, the individual in question is not soiled from roosting in a sooty chimney. Any swift seen in Louisiana after the first week of November and before the second week of March is almost certainly of this species, since there is no unequivocal evidence that the Chimney Swift is ever present anywhere in the United States in this period.

The Hummingbird Family
Trochilidae

Hummingbirds occur only in the Western Hemisphere, their main head-quarters being in the mountainous areas of the northwestern part of South America. No less than 115 species occur in diminutive Ecuador alone. Central America and southern Mexico likewise have a wide variety of species, but as one progresses northward into northern Mexico and into the United States, representation of the family rapidly diminishes. Including the forms that barely get across our southern border, there are in this country but 18 species. Of these, only the Ruby-throated Hummingbird breeds east of the Great Plains; the remaining species occur mainly in the southwestern states and in the Pacific Coast region.

One aid to correct species identification of male hummingbirds is the color of the glistening feathers of the throat, or gorget. These particular feathers are nearly always highly iridescent. Their remarkable sheen results from their peculiar physical structure and not from the presence or absence of pigments. The brilliant color appears only when light, striking the gorget at a certain angle, is broken up by the microscopic structures that go to make up the feathers. Since the minute details of structure of the feathers of the gorget in each species often vary somewhat, a wide variety of colors and shades of colors results. In some hummers the gorget is a flaming red, while in others it may be a rose red, or even blue, purple, or green, depending on the species.

RUBY-THROATED HUMMINGBIRD   *Archilochus colubris*

Figs. 113, 114; p. 401

The Ruby-throat arrives in Louisiana in early March and remains until late October. The few authenticated records of its occurrence here in winter include an individual that remained until late January 1952 in the garden of the late Mrs. W. W. Tennant at Baton Rouge. Hummers that otherwise have been found after the first week of December and that have been positively identified as to species have in nearly all cases proved to be either the Rufous or the Black-chinned Hummingbird, although the Broad-tailed Hummingbird has been noted once and the Buff-bellied at least three times. All these other species come to us from the west. The male Ruby-throat is easily distinguished from other hummers by its ruby-colored throat and its solid green back and tail. The female lacks the gorget, is uniformly grayish white below and emerald green above, and has the outer tail feathers tipped with white.

Ruby-throated Hummingbirds are found in numbers in the summer

RET

Figure 113   Male Ruby-throated Hummingbird.

Female Ruby-throat at Lichen-covered Nest

She Pauses in Midair Beneath a Bottlebrush Flower

throughout northern Louisiana, but they are not quite as common in the southern parishes. They build elaborate nests of finely woven hair and plant down, bedecked on the outside in the most delicate fashion with lichens and moss, held in place by cobwebs. These amazing structures are about the size of an eyewashing cup and are placed on a horizontal branch, where they can hardly be detected unless the bird is seen to come to the nest or to depart from it. The two eggs are white and no larger in diameter than a lead pencil.

BLACK-CHINNED HUMMINGBIRD *Archilochus alexandri* Pl. XLI

This species has been found in Louisiana only in winter, when it is rare but regular in its occurrence in the southern part of the state. The first record was that of a male that appeared in the garden of Mrs. W. W. Tennant, near downtown Baton Rouge, in late December 1955. It was seen there almost daily until December 27, when it was collected to verify its identification and to provide an indisputable record of the occurrence of the species in the state. On January 15, 1961, Mrs. H. A. J. Evans watched a male Black-chinned in her yard in New Orleans, observing it at a distance of a foot or two. In the winter of 1965–1966, Kenneth McGee had two Black-chins in his yard in New Orleans that he observed almost daily from shortly before Christmas until, in the case of one, April 12. The birds were observed by numerous individuals, including Buford Myers. Again in February and March 1969, two more Black-chins were in the same garden and at least one was there in the winters of 1969–1970 and 1970–1971, when two were photographed. Finally, on November 25, 1969, an adult male was captured in a butterfly net at Lafayette by Marshall B. Eyster and maintained alive for a week.

Females of this species are indistinguishable in the field from female Ruby-throated Hummingbirds. Male Black-chinned Hummingbirds, however, have the upper part of the gorget black and the lower part purple, a feature that immediately sets them apart from male Ruby-throats.

BROAD-TAILED HUMMINGBIRD *Selasphorus platycercus* Fig. 114

The occurrence of this far-western species in Louisiana is based on a single record. During December 1952 and until January 7, 1953, Mrs. W. W. Tennant of Baton Rouge had one under daily observation in her garden, where

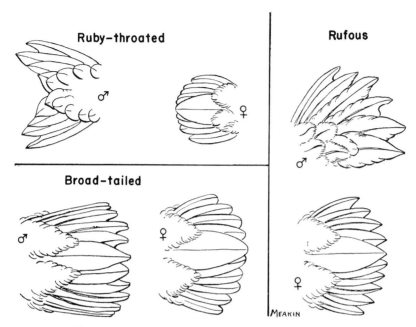

Figure 114 Tail feathers of three species of hummingbirds recorded from Louisiana. The symbol ♂ denotes male, ♀ female.

it was studied in the most minute detail by a half-dozen or more ornithologists. It fed mainly on the flowers of her salvia beds, but, in addition, also visited special hummingbird feeders that she kept filled with honey-sweetened water. Sometimes it would hover within three feet or less of the eyes of an observer standing by one of the feeders. The Broad-tail was often compared at close range with a male Rufous Hummingbird that was present in the same garden, as well as with a large series of museum skins carried to the garden in specimen trays. So ideal were the circumstances for studying the individual that I, for one, have no doubt at all regarding its identity. The little bird was studied as closely as it could have been in the hand in the museum, the only difficulty being that no measurements of its wing, tail, and bill could be made. But the shape of the tail feathers, which are diagnostic, was clearly noted.

The male of the Broad-tail is slightly larger than the common Ruby-throat, which it resembles somewhat in color, but its gorget is a purplish red instead of fiery, geranium red. Females and immature males have the flanks strongly washed with buffy and the basal half of the outer tail feathers reddish brown, followed by a broad band of black and finally a white tip. The Ruby-throat is never buffy on the flanks nor does it ever have brown on the basal portions of the outer tail feathers. The females and immatures of the Broad-tail, because of their green backs and green rectrices, resemble immature Rufous Hummingbirds, which also have a greenish back; but the latter have enough reddish brown in all but the two central tail feathers to give the spread tail a predominantly brownish appearance. In the Broad-tail, the brown on the lateral rectrices is very difficult, sometimes impossible, to see in the field. Any of these species in the hand are immediately distinguishable by the shapes of the primaries and rectrices (Fig. 114).

RUFOUS HUMMINGBIRD *Selasphorus rufus*   Fig. 114

This Rocky Mountain species is an uncommon but fairly regular winter visitor in southern Louisiana. Localities of record are Baton Rouge, Thibodaux, Lafayette, Sabine National Wildlife Refuge south of Hackberry, Grand Isle, Reserve, and New Orleans. In Baton Rouge and New Orleans the species is of almost regular annual occurrence. It has been known to appear in the state as early as the last week of August, but generally its arrival is not noted until the end of September or even later. Departure in the spring has been recorded as late as April 15, but when hard freezes occur in southern Louisiana in January and February the species often disappears at that time. Whether the birds succumb to the cold or instead move farther south to warmer climes is not known, but I suspect the former is more often the case. The flowers of hibiscus and late-blooming salvia are especially attractive to it; indeed, the bird's continued presence in any locality in winter may depend on the continued blooming of one or the other of these plants.

The adult male Rufous is reddish brown above and has a fiery red gorget. The female and immature, unlike the adult male, have the back and central tail feathers bronzy green (although never a distinctly emerald green as in the two preceding species) and, of course, lack the gorget. They differ further from the females and young of the Ruby-throat in having a wash of buff on the flanks. For a comparison with the Broad-tailed Hummingbird, which has been recorded only once, see the preceding account.

BUFF-BELLIED HUMMINGBIRD *Amazilia yucatanensis* Pl. XLI

Between November 23 and December 30, 1965, the late Mrs. Thelma von Gohren observed a hummingbird in her yard in New Orleans that seems unquestionably to have been this species. Color photographs that were made on several dates in December leave no doubt as to the bird's identity, and these pictures are on file in the LSU Museum of Zoology. More recently, on December 15, 1973, James C. Leak and Don Norman carefully studied a hummingbird that they found feeding in the town of Cameron on the flowers of the introduced hibiscus relative that is known locally as Turk's cap. The bird was positively identified as a Buff-bellied Hummingbird and full supporting details were furnished along with the record. Finally, also during the winter of 1973–1974, Mr. and Mrs. George De Soto of Franklin observed almost daily a hummingbird in their garden that they were certain was a member of the genus *Amazilia* and in all probability a Buff-bellied. On March 28 the bird was collected by Marshall B. Eyster and Garrie Landry and its identification was confirmed. Consequently, the species is now included on the state list on the basis of a preserved specimen, as well as two additional well-substantiated sight records.

The Buff-bellied Hummingbird breeds in the lower Rio Grande Valley in Texas and south through eastern Mexico to Guatemala and Belize. The back and head, including the throat, are green, the belly is buffy tan, the tail feathers are predominantly reddish brown, and the bill is orange-red except for the dusky tip.

KINGFISHERS AND ALLIES
Order *Coraciiformes*

The Kingfisher Family
Alcedinidae

BELTED KINGFISHER   *Megaceryle alcyon*   Fig. 115

The Belted Kingfisher is a familiar sight along the numerous waterways of
our state. It particularly likes to perch on telephone wires along bayous and
drainage canals, where it can look down into the water below and wait for a
minnow or some other small fish to come into view. It is one of the very
few birds adept at hovering in midair, a feat that certainly expedites its
capture of food, as well as one that provides an excellent aid in its identification. Kingfishers have bills that show a strong resemblance to those of terns,
which have the same general food habits but are only distantly related. Such
resemblances may be explained by the principle of adaptive convergence,
according to which diverse animals living in the same habitat and doing
the same things tend to become more and more similar by evolving similar
structures under selective pressure.

The best field marks of the kingfisher are its disproportionately large
head, its combination of bluish upperparts and white underparts, the broad
white collar that almost surrounds the neck, and the one or two wide bands
across the upper breast. In the males there is only one bluish gray band, but
in the female there is in addition a rufous band below the gray that not only
crosses the breast but also extends along the sides. This additional bright
color in the female makes the Belted Kingfisher one of the few species of
birds in which the male is less vividly marked than its mate.

Nests are usually built at the end of six-foot horizontal tunnels dug in

Figure 115   Female Belted Kingfisher.

the sides of banks of streams, and, like the eggs of nearly all other birds that
nest in dark cavities, the five to eight eggs are white. The call note is a loud
rattle that is often emitted just after a successful plunge for a fish, as the bird
rises shaking water from its feathers. With the advent of cold weather, the
arrival of northern Belted Kingfishers causes the species to increase in numbers throughout the state, and it becomes especially abundant in southern
Louisiana. Sometimes in January and other winter months scores of these
birds are seen perched on the telephone wires along the roadside canals
between Leeville and Grand Isle and in other similar situations.

WOODPECKERS
Order *Piciformes*

The Woodpecker Family
Picidae

WOODPECKERS SHOW remarkable structural adaptations that enable them to fill a special environmental niche—one in which they perform a great service to man. As even every child knows, woodpeckers spend their lives on the trunks and limbs of trees. There they eat millions of wood borers, bark lice, and other insects that, left uncontrolled, would do great damage to the trees of our forests. In order that they may successfully move about on vertical tree trunks or steep limbs, nature has provided them with a special foot structure and a special kind of tail. Instead of having the usual arrangement of three toes in front and one behind, as do most birds, woodpeckers generally have two toes in front and two behind, a condition termed zygodactyl, or yoke-toed (see Pl. XXII). The two toes that are directed backward, combined with the stiffened tail feathers, which are held against the tree trunks, provide the birds with props.

Other remarkable adaptations of woodpeckers are the evolutionary changes in their skulls and tongues that enable them to drill holes in trees and to extract insects from these excavations. The skull bones are exceedingly hard and rigidly ossified and therefore can withstand the terrific vibrations and shock that the birds impose on themselves when drumming and drilling. But the most amazing thing about the head is the modifications that have taken place in the tongue. This structure, which is part of what is known as the hyoid apparatus, is extremely elastic and is provided terminally with tiny hooks or barbs, like an arrow (Fig. 116). The woodpecker drills a hole only slightly larger in diameter than its bill, extrudes the elastic tongue, and literally spears or hooks out the insect that it seeks.

All woodpeckers use their chisellike bills to excavate their nest holes. They all lay pure white eggs, as is true of most cavity-nesting species.

COMMON FLICKER *Colaptes auratus*   Pl. XXIII; Fig. 117; p. 411

The "yellow-hammer," as this woodpecker is commonly called in the eastern United States, is easily identified by the yellow shafts of its tail and wing feathers, which from certain angles give the bird in flight an overall yellowish color; by its extensive white rump, which is also conspicuous in flight (we say that "its shirttail hangs out"); by the red crescent on the back of the head and the black crescent on the breast; and by the black "mustache" marks in the male. Its call is a rapidly repeated *wick, wick, wick, wick, wick*. When two birds come together they emit a loud *kee-you* and a *flick-a, flick-a* note that can be mistaken for the call of no other bird.

Flickers are less strictly arboreal than other woodpeckers and are often seen on the ground, where they search for ants, one of their favorite items of food. They are common and widespread permanent residents and are somewhat more numerous in winter than in summer because of the influx of birds from farther north.

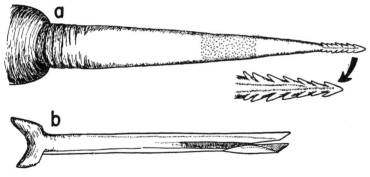

Figure 116 Tongues of a woodpecker (a) and a hummingbird (b), showing modifications to suit two different feeding habits. With the barbs on the end of its tongue, the woodpecker is able to rake insects out of the hole that it drills in a tree. The tubelike tongue of the hummingbird enables it to suck nectar from deep within the corolla of a flower. (After Lucas.)

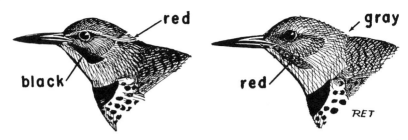

Figure 117   Heads of two subspecies of flickers: a "yellow-shafted" type, left; a "red-shafted" type, right.

In most parts of the western United States, flickers differ in having salmon red wing linings and shafts to the flight and tail feathers; in possessing red, instead of black, "mustache" patches; and in lacking a red nape. They were long considered a different species under the name Red-shafted Flicker, but are now treated as a subspecies of *Colaptes auratus*, as is the Gilded Flicker of the extreme southwestern United States and northwestern Mexico. Flickers of the "red-shafted" type interbreed freely with flickers of the "yellow-shafted" type wherever their respective ranges overlap, which happens in many places in our central Great Plains. Flickers in which the shafts of the feathers are red have been observed on infrequent occasions in winter in the western part of Louisiana, notably in the Shreveport area, as well as twice in the vicinity of New Orleans.

PILEATED WOODPECKER   *Dryocopus pileatus*   Pl. XXII; p. 417

This is the "log-god," "Indian hen," "woodchuck," or "cock-of-the-woods" that is so familiar to hunters, fishermen, and others who roam our woods and paddle our forest-lined streams. Except for the rare and almost extinct Ivory-billed Woodpecker, it is our largest woodpecker, for it is nearly the size of a crow. At rest on the side of a tree, the Pileated Woodpecker is predominantly black, but in flight it shows a great deal of white in the wings. In the male the top of the head and crest are bright red, while the female has the forehead dusky and only the posterior part of the crest is red. The call note resembles that of a flicker but is louder and more eruptive—*kuk—kuk—kukkuk—kuk-kuk*, sometimes with a rising pitch. Like that of all woodpeckers its flight is generally a bounding series of undulations and is punctuated by its resounding calls.

The species is a fairly common to common permanent resident in the wooded sections of the state, both in hardwoods and in pines, especially where forests of the latter are crossed by hardwood-bordered streams. The nest hole is made by the bird itself in the trunk of a tree or snag, sometimes at a considerable height above the ground. The cavity is often as much as three feet in depth, with an entrance hole that is three or four inches in diameter. The four or five pure white eggs are deposited simply on a layer of shavings in the bottom of the cavity.

RED-BELLIED WOODPECKER *Centurus carolinus* Pl. XXIII

Early naturalists were extremely clever in choosing names for birds, but not so in the case of this bird. Unless one has a specimen of the Red-bellied Woodpecker in the hand, there is little likelihood of seeing the color that gives the species its name, for generally the only red on the belly is a slight trace on the extreme lower underparts. It is otherwise white below, the back is barred transversely with black and white, and the top of the head is solid red in the male and partially red in the female. No other woodpecker in Louisiana has a color combination of this sort. This and the Downy Wood-

Male Common Flicker in Nest Hole

SAMUEL A. GRIMES

pecker are our commonest woodpeckers, for there is hardly a patch of woods in the state where there is not a pair or more of each residing.

The call of the Red-bellied Woodpecker is a rolling *chur-r-r-r-r-r-r*, and there is also a hoarse note that might be expressed as a *chaw, chaw*. Three to eight, usually four or five, eggs are laid in a cavity excavated jointly by the male and female in a dead snag or even sometimes in an old Red-cockaded Woodpecker nest site. Incubation is said to last about 14 days. Both sexes share in this chore and in the feeding and care of the young.

RED-HEADED WOODPECKER   *Melanerpes erythrocephalus*
Pl. XXII

This species was once one of our commonest and best-known birds throughout the state, but it is now rapidly diminishing in numbers. The causes of its decline are varied, but certainly the main factor operating against it is the competition afforded by the European Starling. Since the introduction of starlings in the vicinity of New York City in the last part of the nineteenth century, the species has spread south to Florida and Mexico and west to California. In a considerable part of this area it has become established as a common breeder. Since the starlings generally nest in tree cavities, their habits have brought them into conflict with the Red-headed Woodpecker. After a Red-head laboriously drills and excavates a nest hole, a starling usurps it through a technique of persistent, aggressive heckling. The Red-head abandons one cavity after another and finally fails to complete its own nesting routine and to rear its own young. At Baton Rouge, in the last 40 years, I have witnessed the arrival and the steady increase of the European Starling and the corresponding diminution in numbers of the Red-head. Nest holes in certain dead snags that once produced annually a brood of four to seven Red-heads are now devoid of these beautiful birds and instead are producing brood after brood of unwelcome starlings.

The Red-head can hardly be confused with any other bird; its whole head is bright red down to the shoulders. The back, tail, and flight feathers

---

Plate XXII   Four Woodpeckers
Upper left, Ivory-billed Woodpecker (p. 415), male above and female below. Upper right, male Red-cockaded Woodpecker (p. 415). Lower left, Red-headed Woodpecker (p. 412), adult above and juvenile below. Lower right, Pileated Woodpecker (p. 410), male above and female below.

are bluish black, while the remainder of its body appears immaculate white in the field. In the juvenal plumage the large areas of black and white are present, but the bird's head is dingy brown. The young bird of the year retains this plumage only until fall, when it undergoes a long postjuvenal molt. After this molt it cannot be distinguished from the adult. The call of the Red-head is a loud *queech*, as well as a variety of other notes, including a rolling sound that many kinds of woodpeckers make.

YELLOW-BELLIED SAPSUCKER *Sphyrapicus varius* Pl. XXIII

The sapsucker is a common winter resident in all wooded sections of Louisiana. It arrives in mid-September and is usually gone by the middle of April, although a few individuals may sometimes remain until early May. The species gets its name from its peculiar habit of drilling parallel rows of small holes in the bark of trees, which cause the sap to exude from the cambium layer. The bird then not only drinks the juice that fills the perforations, but it also eats the small insects that are attracted by the sap. That these holes ever cause the death of a tree, either directly or by allowing the intrusion of disease organisms, is doubtful, but scars may form on the cambium, depreciating the value of the wood for use as lumber. Fortunately, the sapsucker operates on only a small proportion of the trees destined for commercial use.

The best field mark that distinguishes this woodpecker is the conspicuous vertical white patch in the black wing, which, when folded, puts this mark on the *side* of the bird's body. In the Downy and Hairy Woodpeckers the somewhat similar appearing white patch is down the *middle of the back*. Moreover, no other woodpecker has head markings that resemble those of the sapsucker. The call note has been described as a nasal *cheer* that slurs downward.

HAIRY WOODPECKER *Dendrocopos villosus* Pl. XXIII

I have no idea how this woodpecker acquired its name, for it certainly does not possess a single hair on its body. It is almost an exact replica of the Downy Woodpecker but differs in its larger size (nine inches in total length, as opposed to six inches), its disproportionately larger bill (well over half as long as the head, instead of less than half), and the unbarred whiteness of its outer tail feathers. Both species have a broad white patch extending down the back. In the sapsucker there are two white patches, one extending down each wing; in other woodpeckers in Louisiana the back is either uniformly colored or conspicuously barred.

The calls of the Hairy Woodpecker are a sharp *pleek* and a rapid rattling sound. Like all woodpeckers it seems to delight in beating a rolling tattoo on a resonant limb, especially in late winter and early spring. These drummings of woodpeckers are somewhat different in each species, particularly in rhythm patterns, and probably serve the same primary function as the more musical songs and notes of other birds—the advertisement of its intention to defend a certain delineated territory.

The Hairy Woodpecker is a fairly common to common permanent resident that is more densely distributed in the northern parishes than elsewhere in the state. It does, however, occur in many of the coastal chenieres and islands, such as on Cheniere au Tigre, Pecan Island, and Grand Isle. The nest is placed in a tree cavity 12 to 40 feet from the ground, where three to six white eggs are laid.

DOWNY WOODPECKER   *Dendrocopos pubescens*   Pl. XXIII

The diminutive Downy Woodpecker is the commonest member of the family in Louisiana. It is numerous the year around in all parts of the state where there are trees, except on the coastal chenieres, where it is rather uncommon. As noted in the preceding account, the Downy is a miniature edition of the Hairy Woodpecker, being only six inches in total length. But it otherwise resembles its larger relative even in its call note, a nasal, but not quite so sharp, *peet*.

This little bird seems to spend nearly every wakeful moment of its life pecking at the bark of trees. In this pursuit it renders an inestimable service to man, as do all woodpeckers, by ridding our ornamental as well as our commercial trees of noxious insect pests.

The nest of the Downy Woodpecker is found in a variety of situations, but it is usually dug in a decaying limb of a tree and may be located anywhere from five to fifty feet above the ground. The white eggs vary in number, but ordinarily there are four or five.

Plate XXIII   Male Woodpeckers
1. Common Flicker (p. 409). 2. Red-bellied Woodpecker (p. 411). 3. Yellow-bellied Sapsucker (p. 413). 4. Hairy Woodpecker (p. 413). 5. Downy Woodpecker (p. 414).

RED-COCKADED WOODPECKER *Dendrocopos borealis*
Pl. XXII; p. 418

This ladder-backed woodpecker is primarily a denizen of the longleaf pine forests, although it does sometimes occur in forests of other kinds of pine (especially slash pine) and even more rarely in woods of mixed pine and hardwoods. It is a fairly common permanent resident in suitable forests in the state. Unlike most other woodpeckers, it excavates its nest hole in a *live* pine. The habit of using a live tree is tied in with its peculiar custom of puncturing a series of small holes around the entrance to the nest cavity. From these shallow perforations sticky pitch oozes to the surface (see photograph on p. 418). Three or four, rarely five, eggs are laid.

The call of this species is easily recognized, for it resembles the nasal *yank, yank* of a White-breasted Nuthatch, but it is louder, lower in pitch, and somewhat reedy. Two tiny patches of red feathers, which are seldom seen in the field, are located well back on the sides of the head; these are its "cockades," whence its name is derived. The only other ladder-backed woodpecker in Louisiana, the larger Red-bellied Woodpecker, has a conspicuous amount of red on the head.

IVORY-BILLED WOODPECKER *Campephilus principalis* Pl. XXII

One of the most exciting ornithological experiences of my life occurred on the rainy Christmas morning of 1933. On the previous evening my father and I, with two companions, had entered the Singer Preserve, near Tallulah. This area was at the time a great virgin hardwood bottomland forest. We were in quest of America's rarest bird, a species that few living ornithologists had ever seen except as a museum specimen. Indeed, until the year before, ornithologists had come to believe that this, the largest of all woodpeckers in the United States (total length 21 inches), had joined the vanished ranks of the two species of dodoes, the Labrador Duck, and the Passenger Pigeon. A comment to this effect in the offices of the Louisiana Wild Life and Fisheries Commission prompted a quick denial from Mason Spencer, a resident of Tallulah, who happened to be present. So incredulous was everyone of his assertion that Ivory-bills still lived near Tallulah that a permit was immediately issued to him to shoot one—this with the certainty that he would produce nothing more than a "log-god," or Pileated Woodpecker. Spencer, however, promptly vindicated himself, to everyone's amazement, by securing a male Ivory-bill. The specimen was mounted and is still on display in the Wild Life and Fisheries Commission Museum on Royal Street in New Orleans.

After several unsuccessful attempts to see this great woodpecker myself in the Singer Preserve in the summer of 1933, I was still trying on the Christmas Day mentioned above. My companions and I were out at daybreak, quietly stalking through that magnificent hardwood forest with our ears strained for only one sound—the high-pitched nasal *yamp, yamp,* or as some people interpret it, *kent, kent,* of an Ivory-bill. We saw flock after flock of Wild Turkeys, dozens of deer, and scores of log-gods, but no sign of the bird that we really sought. A slow drizzling rain that began to fall did not seem to better our prospects, but suddenly, far in the distance through the great wood, a telltale sound reached our ears. Approaching cautiously in the direction indicated by the calls, we soon beheld not one but *four* Ivory-bills feeding on a dead snag! There were two males and two females, which, with their powerful bills, were proceeding to demolish the bark on this dead tree, in search, no doubt, of flat-headed beetles, or "betsy-bugs."

I went back several times to this place, once when Drs. A. A. Allen and Paul Kellogg took motion pictures and sound recordings of an Ivory-bill at its nest. Once I even caught, before it hit the ground, a piece of wood that an Ivory-bill, in the tree above me, chipped off with a vigorous chisellike blow of its beak. But, at least in the Tallulah forest, all that is something of the past. The great forests where Ivory-bills were struggling to survive from 1933 to 1943 are now gone. The last virgin hardwood bottomland swamp on the North American continent fell to the ax because not enough sentiment could be raised to save it! The last authenticated report of the bird in that part of the state is of a lone female that lingered in this area in the spring of 1943 after the felling that same year of a tree that contained a nest and eggs. Possibly no future generation of Americans will be able to spend a Christmas morning, or any morning, watching four Ivory-billed Woodpeckers go about their daily routine amid huge redgums whose diameters are greater than the distance a man can stretch his arms. I wonder what natural beauties we shall have, aside from the mountains and the sky, a hundred years from now!

In May 1971, however, an exciting event occurred. A man whom I had been corresponding with for several years about alleged Ivory-bills in his area sent me two photographs that he had taken of one of two Ivory-bills that he had found. He saw the birds as they flew across a right-of-way

Female Pileated Woodpecker and Young

Red-cockaded Woodpecker at Nest in Live Pine

clearing in the forest, and, having a camera with him at the time, he pursued the birds and was able to get two photographs of one, a male. The photos are of poor quality, but the bird shown is absolutely, unequivocally an Ivory-bill! My wife and I have since made repeated trips to the area and have not, as yet, been rewarded with seeing or hearing the bird in question. But the swamp is extremely difficult to work, being largely under water and with vast tangles of undergrowth that are almost impossible to penetrate to any extent. I have not divulged, for obvious reasons, the location of the site, other than to say that it is south of U.S. Highway 90, thereby excluding possible speculation that it is in the vicinity of the old Singer tract, where Ivory-bills abounded in the 1930s. On the first visit to the area after receiving the photographs, my informant and I located a fresh excavation in a live baldcypress located within a hundred yards or so of where the photographs were made. Fresh chips on the ground at the base of the tree indicated recent activity. Perhaps the excavation was being made by a Pileated Woodpecker, but one thing is certain—it was either by a Pileated or an Ivory-bill, judging from its dimensions and the size of the chips. We picked up all the chips, and the next day my confidant found a few more, but on subsequent trips to the tree none were found, indicating that excavation of the cavity had ceased. Despite my failure to find the bird, I have no doubt at all, on the basis of the photographs, that a pair of Ivory-bills was present in the area in May 1971.

Ivory-bills are easily confused with the Pileated Woodpecker, and therefore many erroneous reports of them are received. Three characters should be looked for in a bird suspected of being an Ivory-bill (and all three should be noted before giving the slightest credence to thoughts that the bird in question is this rare species): (1) uniformly ivory-colored bill, instead of one that is black above and pale bluish below; (2) a tremendous amount of white on the back, covering the shoulders and a large portion of the wings, instead of a small amount of white in the wings that is usually seen only when the bird is in flight; (3) a high-pitched nasal call note that may be described as *yamp, yamp, yamp,* instead of a flickerlike, deep-voiced *chuck, chuck, chuck.*

PERCHING
BIRDS
Order *Passeriformes*

THE PASSERES, or perching birds, are but one of the 27 living orders of birds, yet approximately one-half of the eight-thousand-odd species of living birds in the world today belong to this single order. It is the pigeonhole, so to speak, that contains such birds as the crows, jays, wrens, warblers, blackbirds, orioles, tanagers, and sparrows. Despite the differences that set all these birds apart from one another, they all have in common many anatomical and behavioristic features not combined in other birds. Three toes are located in front and one behind, the latter being well developed and incumbent, that is, on the same level as the front toes and hence adapted for grasping limbs. The helpless, altricial young are hatched naked or nearly so, but soon acquire a fluffy natal down that is replaced by a juvenal plumage before the birds leave the nest. Nearly all Passeres have well-developed songs, and, in virtually all, the nest is an elaborately interwoven structure.

There are many adaptive modifications that enable different passerine groups to live under diverse ecological conditions, or to eat different foods, or in some way to escape severe competition with their close relatives; but these differences do not refute the fact that Passeres are otherwise a remarkably large and homogeneous array of species. Of the 411 species of birds known definitely to occur in Louisiana, the remaining 181 species in this book are Passeres.

The
Flycatcher
Family
Tyrannidae

This one family, which is confined to the Western Hemisphere, contains 358 species, but only 36 inhabit the United States and only 23 occur in Louisiana. The remainder are found mainly in the tropics, from Mexico through northern South America. There cannot be much doubt that the family originated in the tropics and that the comparatively few species that we possess are immigrants, or derivatives of immigrants, to the United States from a southern ancestral home.

Flycatchers are generally birds of the woods or orchards. They perch on dead trees or limbs, where they quietly survey their surroundings. Suddenly one will fly out, grab an insect out of the air, and then return to the same perch. The bill is generally flattened horizontally and equipped with hairlike structures at the base that fence the corners of the mouth when it is opened and thereby help prevent insects from escaping. Flycatchers as a group are among the poorest songsters of all perching birds, a fact that results from their less highly developed syrinx, the organ of voice. In all Louisiana species, with the exception of the Vermilion Flycatcher, the sexes are essentially alike.

EASTERN KINGBIRD *Tyrannus tyrannus* Pl. XXIV; Fig. 118

Whenever a small bird is seen chasing a large one, the chances are 10 to 1 that the diminutive aggressor is a member of this species. The Eastern Kingbird, or "bee martin" as it is often called, has a special grudge against crows and sometimes will chase one for a mile or more, all the while diving and pecking at the crow's back. Even hawks and vultures are not immune to attack, and heaven help any kind of bird that happens to intrude near a kingbird's nest.

The Eastern Kingbird commonly perches on fences and on telephone wires, where, in typical flycatcher fashion, it placidly awaits the passing of an insect, which, with superb deftness, it captures on the wing. Many kinds of birds have white *outer* tail feathers, but the Eastern Kingbird is almost unique among passerines in having a broad white band across the *end* of the tail. Otherwise it is blackish above and white below, with a concealed orange crown patch that is not seen except when the bird is in the hand.

The species normally arrives in mid-March and remains until late October, rarely into November, and throughout all but the first few days and the last few weeks of this time it is abundantly and widely distributed in the state. Huge daytime southward migrations have been observed in late August and the initial three weeks of September, after which time the bird becomes increasingly scarce. I observed one such spectacular passage of Eastern Kingbirds on August 30, 1944. At about 4:30 in the afternoon, while standing on the Mississippi River levee a few miles south of the LSU Baton Rouge campus, I began to see kingbirds passing from the north heading south in a continuous stream at a height of a hundred feet or so over the levee. In approximately one hour at least several thousand kingbirds of this species passed overhead. The species winters from southern Mexico, through Central America, to Bolivia.

GRAY KINGBIRD   *Tyrannus dominicensis*   Pl. XXIV; Fig. 118

This tropical species once occurred regularly in the United States only from South Carolina to Florida, where it is a fairly common summer resident along both coasts of the peninsula, nesting in moderate numbers on the northern Gulf Coast as far west as Pensacola. Now, breeding pairs have extended as far west as Dauphin Island, Alabama. Its inclusion on the list of Louisiana birds is based on four records. The first of these relates to an individual that I saw in migration just 32 miles off the mouth of the Mississippi River on May 11, 1948, as I was returning by boat from Yucatan. The bird passed several times within a few feet of the bridge on which I stood before it finally flew ahead of the boat in the direction of Southwest Pass. Since we were then almost in sight of land, toward which the bird was headed when it disappeared from view, it almost certainly made a landfall on the coast of Louisiana. The second record is of an individual that I observed with binoculars at close range on Grand Isle on May 3, 1954. Because it is desirable always to have at least one museum specimen of every

Figure 118 Heads and tails of three kingbirds: (1) Gray Kingbird; (2) Western Kingbird; (3) Eastern Kingbird.

species on the state list, I shot at the bird in an attempt to procure it but unfortunately failed to bring it down. Robert J. Newman, who was with me at the time but who did not see the bird until after it flew, clearly noted its large bill and pale coloration as it passed close to him before disappearing from the view of each of us. Newman asked if the bird were not a Gray Kingbird before I had a chance to convey to him my own conclusions regarding it. Almost 16 years later to the day, on May 1, 1970, Newman and I found another Gray Kingbird, in Peveto Beach wood, in Cameron Parish, and the specimen was obtained, the first for Louisiana. The only other record is that of one seen a mile south of Creole, also in Cameron Parish, on April 25, 1964, by Robert LaVal and others.

The Gray Kingbird resembles the Eastern Kingbird but is slightly larger, is gray above instead of black, and lacks the white tips to the tail feathers. The head is prominently marked by a dusky gray auricular patch.

TROPICAL KINGBIRD *Tyrannus melancholicus* Pl. XLI

The only record of the occurrence of this species in the state is that of an adult male collected 4.3 miles east of Johnsons Bayou, in Cameron Parish, on October 9, 1965, by Laurence C. Binford and Sidney A. Gauthreaux.

The species breeds from southeastern Arizona and southern Texas to Argentina but is known to have straggled as far east as Galveston, Texas. It resembles the Cassin's and Western Kingbirds but differs from the former in having the upper breast yellow instead of gray and from both in having the tail slightly forked, not square, and without any white on the sides or on the tips of the rectrices.

WESTERN KINGBIRD   *Tyrannus verticalis*   Pl. XXIV; Fig. 118

The Western Kingbird, a species of the Great Plains and the West, is an uncommon spring transient, a rare breeder, a moderately common fall migrant, and a casual winter resident. The one known instance of breeding in the state is that of a nest attended by two adults found by A. W. Palmisano on the Rockefeller Refuge on June 11, 1966. One of the adults was still incubating on June 23, but the ultimate fate of the nesting attempt is not known. A bird that R. D. Purrington found three miles north of Lebeau, in St. Landry Parish, on June 20, 1970, may have been nesting. Of the numerous sightings of the species in May some could have also represented breeding birds. An individual seen by Robert B. Hamilton at the Natchitoches Fish Hatchery on May 10–12, 1971, was actually performing territorial displays, but no other evidence of nesting was later obtained.

The 95 records on file in the LSU Museum of Zoology are distributed as follows: 15, involving 18 birds, in December through March; 17, involving 27 birds, in April and May; 2, involving 3 birds, in June; none in July; 3, involving 8 birds, in August; 23, involving 51 birds, in September; 20, involving 41 birds, in October; and 15, involving 29 birds, in November. Obviously, the best chance of seeing this species in Louisiana is to scrutinize closely all kingbirds seen on telephone and fence wires from late August to December. As many as five have been seen on a drive between Golden Meadow and Grand Isle, and an equal number have been observed in going from Cameron to Little Cheniere.

This kingbird is approximately the same size as its close relative the Eastern Kingbird but is easily distinguished from it by its yellowish, instead of white, underparts; by its gray head and greenish-colored back, instead of all-blackish upperparts; and by its white-bordered, instead of white-tipped, tail. Thus in color it resembles a Great Crested Flycatcher somewhat more than it does the Eastern Kingbird, but it differs in having a shorter tail that is predominantly black instead of reddish brown and in having the top of the head and shoulders pale gray, contrasting with the color of the back, instead of as dark as the middle of the back. The Western Kingbird resembles even more closely the Tropical and Cassin's Kingbirds, but it differs from them in a number of important details, the most important of which is that the outer web of the outermost tail feathers is white. In Cassin's Kingbird the upper breast is gray, not yellow, and in the Tropical Kingbird the tail is deeply emarginate, not square.

CASSIN'S KINGBIRD *Tyrannus vociferans* Pl. XLI

This species has been observed only one time in the state—Ralph Andrews found one on a fence 4.6 miles east of Holly Beach, in Cameron Parish, on November 7, 1964. He was able to collect the specimen, which now reposes in the LSU Museum of Zoology, in order to verify the identification and to provide an incontrovertible record of the occurrence of the species in Louisiana. Cassin's Kingbird so closely resembles some of its congeners that a mere sight record would have hardly sufficed as a basis for adding the species to the state list. It is quite similar to both the Western and Tropical Kingbirds but differs in having a whiter chin that stands out in sharp contrast with the dark gray breast, which is pale gray in the Western and yellow in the Tropical. It differs further from the Western in lacking the whitish outer web to the outer tail feathers. The tips of the dusky tail feathers are narrowly tipped with white in fresh plumage but never to the extent of remotely suggesting the broad white tipping of the tail feathers in the Eastern Kingbird, a species that is pure white below and grayish black above. The Tropical Kingbird differs from the present species in having the breast yellow, not dark gray, and in possessing a deeply notched, instead of square, tail.

Cassin's Kingbird breeds in the Rocky Mountains from Montana to southern Mexico. It winters in Mexico and Guatemala.

SCISSOR-TAILED FLYCATCHER *Muscivora forficata* Pl. XXIV

This superbly colored and agile-winged flycatcher is unquestionably one of our most attractive birds. It is observed regularly in migration in the southern and western portions of the state. Although its nesting within our borders was once confined to the Shreveport area, the species has in recent years expanded its breeding range eastward to Ruston, in Lincoln Parish, and to Colfax, in Grant Parish. It has also extended southward and now breeds sparingly in Calcasieu and Cameron parishes (Holmwood, Gum

Cove, and possibly Grand Cheniere). Records are available for every month of the year, but the species is most numerous during periods of migration. It is, however, seen with surprising regularity in winter in the delta area south of New Orleans, as well as elsewhere in southern Louisiana. For example, an aggregation of 25 individuals spent the winter of 1959–1960 between Buras and Venice. The only winter record in the northern half of the state is that of an individual seen at Powhatan, in Natchitoches Parish, on December 31, 1971, by James Boswell.

The color of the Scissor-tailed Flycatcher is predominantly pearl gray, but the underwing linings and sides of the breast vary from a brilliant salmon pink to a saturn red. Its exceedingly long, nine-inch, "scissor" tail on a body that is no larger than that of an Eastern Bluebird lends it unusual gracefulness. When it perches, the "scissors" are often closed, but, when the bird becomes excited near its mate or its nest or when it is in pursuit of an insect, the deeply forked tail opens and closes.

Pecan orchards are a preferred breeding habitat in Louisiana, as are also scattered tall trees in open fields and pastures. The nest, a rather bulky structure often lined with a heavy layer of cotton, is generally placed toward the end of a limb 20 to 30 feet from the ground. The eggs are usually five in number and are clear white or pinkish white, blotched with shades of dark brown.

Herbert Brandt, in his *Texas Bird Adventures*, describes the interesting courtship behavior of the male Scissor-tailed Flycatcher in the following well-chosen words: "During his courting days and even until the eggs are hatched, the male engages in one of the most fantastic of feathered skydances. Mounting the air to a height of perhaps a hundred feet, he starts his routine by plunging downward for about a fourth of the distance, then turns sharply upward to nearly the previous height; and he repeats this up and down zigzag course several times, emitting meanwhile a rolling, cackling sound like rapid, high-pitched hand-clapping. This he seems to produce by

---

Plate XXIV   Flycatchers

1. Eastern Kingbird (p. 421). 2. male Scissor-tailed Flycatcher (p. 425). 3. Great Crested Flycatcher (p. 428). 4. Western Kingbird (p. 424). 5. Gray Kingbird (p. 422). 6. Ash-throated Flycatcher (p. 430). 7. Olive-sided Flycatcher (p. 436). 8. Eastern Phoebe (p. 430). 9. Eastern Wood Pewee (p. 435). 10. Vermilion Flycatcher (p. 437), male on right, female on left. 11. Yellow-bellied Flycatcher (p. 431). 12. Acadian Flycatcher (p. 432). 13. "Traill's" Flycatcher (p. 433). 14. Least Flycatcher (p. 434).

Robert E. Tucker

loud snapping of the mandibles, or it may be a vocal effort, or both, though I observed it to be the former. The last upward flight may take him still higher, and his path then becomes a vertical line. When the flycatcher reaches the zenith of this flight, so vivacious is his ardor that over he topples backward, making two or three consecutive reverse somersaults, descending like a Tumbler Pigeon, all the while displaying to his mate the soft, effective, under-wing colors."

GREAT KISKADEE *Pitangus sulphuratus* Fig. 119

A single individual shot at Cheniere au Tigre, in Vermilion Parish, on May 23, 1930, furnished the first positive record for this species in Louisiana. It has since been found nesting at Gum Cove by Mrs. Babette Odom, and it has been observed repeatedly by numerous observers in Vincents Wood at Hackberry, where a nest was found in 1968 but never with more than one bird in attendance. It has been recorded in Vincents Wood as early as February 14 and as late as December 8.

The Great Kiskadee's chunky shape, rufous wings and tail, brilliant

Figure 119 Great Kiskadee. The underparts and crown patch are yellow; the line over the eye is white.

yellow underparts, and the heavy black lines on the crown and from the bill through the eye and ear regions are the combination of characters that serves to set this species apart. Its note is a clearly enunciated *kisk-ka-dee*, from which the bird derives its name, although for a long time it was called the Derby Flycatcher. The species normally occurs in the United States only in the lower Rio Grande Valley, but from there it extends southward to central Argentina. The nest is a football-shaped structure of moss, grass, and small twigs with the opening on the side. The three or four eggs are creamy white with the large end sprinkled with small reddish brown spots.

SULPHUR-BELLIED FLYCATCHER   *Myiodynastes luteiventris*
Fig. 120

On September 30, 1956, two experienced observers, Robert J. Newman and Edwin O. Willis, found what was unquestionably this species in the oaks on Grand Isle. The bird, studied through binoculars at distances of as little as 20 feet, had a massive bill, a whitish superciliary line, bold black malar patches, a streaked yellow breast, and a reddish brown tail. The only other species bearing a resemblance to the Sulphur-bellied Flycatcher is the Streaked Flycatcher (*Myiodynastes maculatus*), whose range overlaps with the former in Mexico and Central America, as well as parts of South America. Since both species occur in Yucatan and since the Grand Isle bird was seen within a week of the passage of Hurricane Flossy, one might suspect it of being a Yucatan waif, in which case it could have been either species. The observers—one intimately familiar with the Sulphur-bellied in life, the other acquainted with both species—are convinced, though, that the bird was a Sulphur-bellied, for they were able to note all the diagnostic features of that species. Attempts to collect the bird were futile.

The Sulphur-bellied Flycatcher nests in southern Arizona and Middle America south to Costa Rica, and it winters normally south to Panama and northwestern South America.

GREAT CRESTED FLYCATCHER   *Myiarchus crinitus*   Pl. XXIV

Nearly every kind of bird has some special behavior pattern or peculiarity that the ornithologist finds interesting, and this species is certainly no exception. What does it do but place a discarded snakeskin in its nest! I have known of only one nest of a Great Crested Flycatcher without this accessory, and strangely enough, it contained a twentieth-century substitute—a piece

Figure 120 Sulphur-bellied Flycatcher.

of cellophane! Why a bit of old snakeskin is placed in the nest, only the Great Crested Flycatcher knows. One common explanation is that it scares away the bird's enemies, but another explanation is simply that snakeskins are readily available material and that their presence in the nests of Great Crested Flycatchers is no more peculiar than the presence in other birds' nests of special materials, such as horsehair, mud, thistle, or some particular fiber or kind of grass, depending on the species of bird and its special desideratum.

The Great Crested Flycatcher has the upperparts brown, tail reddish, throat gray, and belly yellow. The feathers of the crown are capable of being raised as a sort of crest, particularly when the bird gives its characteristic *pwet, pwet* or *wheeep* call notes. The Great Crested Flycatcher cannot be readily confused with any other species in the state except the rare Ash-throated and Wied's Crested Flycatchers, which are browner above, much paler gray on the throat, and paler yellow on the belly.

The nest is placed in a tree cavity or old woodpecker hole, and contrary to the general rule that eggs laid in such darkened places are white, the Great Crested Flycatcher lays creamy-colored eggs that are heavily streaked longitudinally with purplish brown. The species is strictly a summer resident that is statewide in its occurrence in the wooded portions of Louisiana. To me it is one of the real harbingers of spring. It arrives in the last two weeks of March to remain here until late October, rarely to the end of November.

WIED'S CRESTED FLYCATCHER   *Myiarchus tyrannulus*   Pl. XLI

This western species, which is sometimes called the Brown-crested Flycatcher, is a rare winter visitor in extreme southeastern Louisiana. It has been recorded seven times in the Venice area (two collected), once at New Orleans, and twice at Reserve, in St. John the Baptist Parish. Extreme dates are November 24 and January 27. The species resembles the Great Crested Flycatcher, but the overall size is greater, the top of the head is browner, the lower underparts are paler yellow, and the bill is larger and wholly black (not horn colored). It differs from the Ash-throated Flycatcher by its much larger body size and its more massive and all-black bill.

ASH-THROATED FLYCATCHER   *Myiarchus cinerascens*   Pl. XXIV

This species is an even paler edition of the Great Crested Flycatcher. The throat is pale gray or grayish white, and the belly, instead of being a rich lemon yellow, is only slightly yellow in color. The species is rare but of fairly regular annual occurrence in winter in southern Louisiana, particularly in the New Orleans area and in the delta region south of that city. It has also been seen on Grand Terre Island, at False River, and on at least five occasions in Cameron Parish. The only record in the northern half of the state is one seen 18 miles south of Ferriday, in Concordia Parish, on January 7, 1966. Extreme dates are October 4 and April 1, except for two May records submitted without supporting details. The normal range of the species is in the western part of the United States and in Mexico.

EASTERN PHOEBE   *Sayornis phoebe*   Pl. XXIV

The Eastern Phoebe is primarily a common winter resident that occurs in all parts of the state. It sometimes arrives by the middle of September, rarely earlier, and it remains until April or early May. Although its diet, like that of all flycatchers, is composed principally of insects, it will, on occasion, eat berries. The latter fact doubtless accounts for its ability to survive periods of cold, inclement weather, when insect life is dormant.

The species breeds uncommonly in northwestern Louisiana, where, in a manner typical of the species, it builds its bulky nest on beams under bridges. Horace H. Jeter discovered the first nest located in the state in such a situation on June 10, 1956, near Four Forks in extreme southwestern Caddo Parish, and in 1958 he and James R. Stewart found several breeding pairs, some of which were known to have successfully reared young, near Bethany, in Caddo Parish, and near Benton and Bellevue, in Bossier Parish. The easternmost breeding record for the state is that of a nest, containing five nestlings, observed 3.5 miles west of Calhoun, in Lincoln Parish, by John W. Goertz and William Roloph, on May 13 and 17, 1971.

The Eastern Phoebe may be recognized by its dark, olive color above and its pale yellowish underparts and by its lack of wing bars or contrasting markings. It is, indeed, a quite nondescript bird. The best field mark of all is its behavior of constantly wagging its tail. The somewhat similar Eastern Wood Pewee does not wag its tail and has two prominent wing bars.

SAY'S PHOEBE *Sayornis saya*   Pl. XLI

Credit for the discovery here of this western flycatcher goes to David Weber, who obtained a specimen at Reserve on September 29, 1957. On November 23 of the same year another individual appeared at Howze Beach, near New Orleans, and was seen regularly by a host of observers until the following February 16. The third record is that of a bird seen at Johnsons Bayou, in Cameron Parish, on October 5, 1958, by Sidney A. Gauthreaux and John P. Gee. Finally, a female was taken at Baton Rouge on October 10, 1964, by Gauthreaux and Allan Hayse.

The Say's Phoebe resembles the common Eastern Phoebe in size but is grayish brown above with a black tail. The throat and upper breast are also grayish brown, but the lower breast and abdomen, including the flanks, are pale rusty. The species breeds from central Alaska south through western Canada and the western United States into Mexico.

YELLOW-BELLIED FLYCATCHER *Empidonax flaviventris*
Pl. XXIV

The genus *Empidonax* comprises one of the most difficult groups of species to identify in the field, and for this reason the inexperienced observer should be extremely cautious in making positive specific determinations. This and the following five species are all small, rather nondescript birds, greenish or olive above and gray, whitish, or slightly yellowish below. A great deal of individual and seasonal variation in color is evident. For instance, some fall examples of the Acadian Flycatcher are just as extensively yellow below as most Yellow-bellied Flycatchers.

With the exception of the locally very common Acadian Flycatcher, the species of *Empidonax* are birds of passage in Louisiana, numerous only in fall when they are generally silent. This is unfortunate, for the call notes are universally regarded as the best means of field identification of birds in this genus. Despite the great similarity of the various species, they are unquestionably perfectly good biological entities in nature, for they do not interbreed insofar as is known, and they all have remarkably different behavior patterns. One species will nest in a northern coniferous forest, another in a southern bottomland swamp. One will build its nest of moss, lined with grasses, on the ground beside a root, while another will construct its nest of plant fibers, rootlets, and fine strips of bark in a tree crotch 5 to 15 feet up. In one species the eggs may be immaculate white, in another cream colored with cinnamon-brown spots on the larger end. So, despite the great difficulties that the field ornithologist may have in distinguishing these little flycatchers, the birds themselves apparently can always recognize their own kind.

On the basis principally of specimens in the LSU Museum of Zoology, the Yellow-bellied Flycatcher appears to be an uncommon spring and only a moderately common fall migrant throughout the state, recorded from March 29 to May 28 and from August 9 to October 23. Its apparent rarity in spring may be due in part to the fact that it is a late migrant, possibly passing through mainly in May, when we seldom have adverse weather conditions to pile up migrants; hence these little birds may go through without being detected.

ACADIAN FLYCATCHER *Empidonax virescens* Pl. XXIV

This is one of the commonest small birds in the wooded sections of Louisiana in summer, the only member of the genus *Empidonax* that breeds here. It swings its cup-shaped nest hammockwise between horizontal twigs, usually 10 to 15 feet from the ground and usually in a swamp or at its edge. It lays two to four whitish eggs that are finely spotted, particularly near the large end. Its call is a *peet* or a rather explosive *pee-e-yuk*.

A world-famous ornithologist once wrote: "This species has the upperparts fully as olive green as the Yellow-bellied Flycatcher, but the underparts are never entirely yellow, and the throat is always white." Apparently, however, this distinguished scientist had never seen a representative collection of fall specimens, for the series at Louisiana State University contains numerous examples in which the entire ventral surface, including the throat, is a clear, pale yellow, save for the slight duskiness of the chest. The color of the underparts of the Yellow-bellied Flycatcher is, if anything, duller by contrast, but the color of the underparts is not a reliable field character in autumn.

The Acadian Flycatcher arrives in early April and stays with us until mid-October or, rarely, the beginning of November. It winters in Colombia and Ecuador.

WILLOW FLYCATCHER *Empidonax traillii* Pl. XXIV

The species formerly called the Traill's Flycatcher has now been shown to consist of *two* perfectly valid species that are separable more readily on the basis of behavioral and song differences than on structural characters. One is *Empidonax traillii*, the generally more southern and western bird, whose vocalizations have been described as a *fitz-bew*, and the other is *Empidonax alnorum*, the generally more northern bird, of the forest of the Boreal Region, whose vocalizations have been interpreted as a *fee-beé-o*. For the first, as here restricted, the English name is Willow Flycatcher. For the second, the English name is Alder Flycatcher. Where circumstances do not permit specific identification of a particular individual as either the Willow or the Alder Flycatcher, but the bird in question is definitely one or the other, the vernacular name "Traill's flycatcher" can be used.

The Yellow-bellied and Acadian Flycatchers are olive-green above and yellowish below, while the "Traill's" and Least Flycatchers tend to be olive-brown above and whitish below. As noted in the account of the Yellow-bellied Flycatcher, all four may be confused with each other, and, consequently, museum specimens are often the only reliable basis for determining the exact seasonal status of the different species. But in the case of "Traill's flycatchers" even specimens usually cannot be identified with certainty unless accompanied by a description of the call notes uttered by the bird before it was collected. As noted above, the call of the Willow Flycatcher is a *fitz-bew*, that of the Alder, a sneezy *fee-beé-o*. The call of the Least Flycatcher is a sharp *che-bec'*, that of the Yellow-bellied a simple, lackadaisical *chu-wie*. The Acadian Flycatcher says *peet* or *pee-e-yuk*.

On May 5 and 12, 1973, five miles south of St. Francisville, Robert B. Hamilton heard the *fitz-bew* notes of the Willow Flycatcher and the *fee-beé-o* of the Alder Flycatcher. On May 12 at the same place he identified the call of the latter. Also in the spring of 1973, Horace H. Jeter found what may have been a mated pair of Willow Flycatchers in the Shreveport area. The two birds appeared to be territorial, and one of the individuals was emitting the *fitz-bew* call notes. Unfortunately, although the birds were present on June 16, they could not be found on June 18 or thereafter.

Exclusive of the Shreveport area, extreme dates of occurrence for the Willow Flycatcher, positively identified on the basis of call notes heard or on specimens in the LSU Museum of Zoology, are April 28 through May 21 and from August 14 through October 1.

ALDER FLYCATCHER *Empidonax alnorum* Pl. XXIV

The Alder Flycatcher, as noted in the account of the Willow Flycatcher, can be identified with complete certainty only when it is heard to emit its *fee-beé-o* call notes. The vocalizations of the morphologically similar, if not almost identical, Willow Flycatcher are a distinctive *fitz-bew*. In fall, though, both species are usually silent. Consequently, their relative abundance at that season is uncertain to say the least. In cases where an observer is confident than an *Empidonax* under observation is either a Willow or an Alder Flycatcher, but cannot be sure which because the bird is silent, I recommend the use of the noncommittal vernacular name "Traill's flycatcher."

On the basis of positive field records or specimens in the LSU Museum of Zoology, the occurrence of the Alder Flycatcher in spring is limited to the period from May 12 through May 21. Fall records, based almost wholly on museum specimens, range from August 17 through September 24.

LEAST FLYCATCHER *Empidonax minimus* Pl. XXIV

This species has a whiter and more distinct eye-ring than the other species of the genus *Empidonax* in Louisiana. This character combines with its smaller size and its tendency to sit low in a bush or tree and to jerk its tail to provide fairly reliable field marks. The call note is a distinctive *che-bec'*. On the basis of the available evidence, the Least Flycatcher seems to be moderately common in spring in northern Louisiana but rare elsewhere. It is fairly plentiful throughout the state in fall. Recorded normal dates of occurrence are from March 30 through May 16 and from July 17 through December 1. Several winter records are available from the southern part of the state, including two collected, one of them on December 31, 1954, at Johnsons Bayou, in Cameron Parish, and the other on January 1, 1957, near New Orleans.

HAMMOND'S FLYCATCHER   *Empidonax hammondii*   Pl. XLI

The only record of the occurrence of this small, nondescript, western flycatcher in the state is that of a specimen collected at Woodworth, in Rapides Parish, on January 17, 1957, by Brooke Meanley and now deposited in the LSU Museum of Zoology. The species is hardly distinguishable in the field from the Willow, Alder, and Least Flycatchers, not to mention other representatives of the genus that could accidentally stray as far east as Louisiana. In general aspect Hammond's Flycatcher is more olive above and has the yellow of the belly standing out in sharp contrast to its gray chest. The white eye-ring is prominent, and the throat is gray, not white. The species possesses a tiny bill in comparison with most of its relatives. It breeds in mountainous areas from southern Alaska south to eastern California and New Mexico and normally winters from the southwestern United States south to Nicaragua.

EASTERN WOOD PEWEE   *Contopus virens*   Pl. XXIV

The Eastern Wood Pewee rivals the Acadian Flycatcher for the honor of being the commonest woodland representative of this family in Louisiana in summer. But, whereas the Acadian Flycatcher is mainly a bird of shaded bottomlands, the pewee more often frequents dry wooded uplands and pine forests. It is a nondescript bird with very dark upperparts ranging between olive and olive-gray, colors that separate it, the Eastern Phoebe, and the Olive-sided Flycatcher from the more greenish species of the genus *Empidonax* but not from each other. The underparts are grayish, washed with olive-gray on the sides. The wing coverts are narrowly tipped with whitish, forming two indistinct wing bars. The somewhat similar Eastern Phoebe is larger and darker than the Eastern Wood Pewee, is generally more yellowish beneath, and continually wags its tail. The large, chunky Olive-sided Flycatcher has white tufts near the base of the tail on each side. Neither the Eastern Phoebe nor the Olive-sided Flycatcher has wing bars.

Fortunately, this pewee is one of the most vociferous of all small birds, calling its name with a plaintive *pee-a-wee, pe-wee* from dawn to dusk, even in the hottest part of the day. It remains for a long time with us, arriving in late March and staying until late October, or rarely into November, before its return to Central and South America. An unusually early record is that of February 26, 1967, at Buras by Joseph C. Kennedy. Winter records are limited to one seen and heard calling at Baton Rouge on January 3, 1959, and for a week thereafter, by Mrs. Barbara M. Bodman, and one observed by Kennedy and others at New Orleans, on December 21, 1968.

The nest is made of grasses, rootlets, and mosses, is densely covered with lichens, and is saddled on a horizontal limb 20 to 40 feet up. The three or four eggs are white except for a wreath of dark markings around the large end.

WESTERN WOOD PEWEE *Contopus sordidulus* Pl. XLI

The only record of the Western Wood Pewee in Louisiana is that of a male specimen collected two miles west of Grand Cheniere, in Cameron Parish, on October 10, 1965, by Laurence C. Binford. The specimen is now in the LSU Museum of Zoology. It was identified by Allan R. Phillips as the race *saturatus* that breeds in southeastern Alaska south through western British Columbia to western Washington and Oregon. The species is extremely similar to the Eastern Wood Pewee but is strongly olive-gray (not pale gray) on the breast and sides, and it often shows no trace of yellowish on the belly. Its song has a much more nasal quality than that of its eastern counterpart and has been described as a *peeyee* or *peeeer*.

OLIVE-SIDED FLYCATCHER *Nuttallornis borealis* Pl. XXIV

This species was once regarded as a very rare transient in the state, but it is now recorded with considerable regularity, particularly in late summer and early fall. In spring it is still looked upon as a rare and late migrant, having been recorded less than a dozen times, once on April 22 and all other times between May 2 and 23. Fall records, now numbering over 30, range from July 31 through October 20, with all but four of the observations being in August and September.

The species breeds in the coniferous forest, across the entire breadth of

Canada and the United States and even southward along the Alleghenies. It winters in northern South America from Colombia and Venezuela to Peru.

The Olive-sided Flycatcher is a rather large-headed, chunky flycatcher, about the size of an Eastern Bluebird. Above it is dark greenish fuscous, and the breast has a dark grayish patch on either side, separated by a white streak passing from the throat to the lower belly. A tuft of white feathers usually protrudes on each side from beneath the wings near the base of the tail. Although the Olive-sided Flycatcher might conceivably be confused with the Eastern Wood Pewee, the latter is not so heavy breasted and chunky, nor does it have the white tuft on each side of the base of the tail. The note of the Olive-sided Flycatcher is an emphatic three-syllabled "Come right *here*," or "Hip, three *beers.*"

VERMILION FLYCATCHER   *Pyrocephalus rubinus*   Pl. XXIV

The regular presence in winter of Vermilion Flycatchers in Louisiana and elsewhere on the northern Gulf Coast is not easy to explain, since the species is a bird of the southwestern United States and Mexico. To reach Louisiana in fall these little flycatchers must, as a minimum, move more than a thousand miles eastward (if our birds come from Nevada or Utah) or hundreds of miles to the *northeast* (if they come from the lower Rio Grande Valley). In either case, they come at a time when migratory birds ordinarily are moving southward. The species arrives in mid-September and departs usually by early March, but it has been known to remain as late as April 17 at the Natchitoches Fish Hatchery. City Park in New Orleans used to be the one place where individuals could be found almost every winter, although an adult male wintered on the Louisiana State University campus in Baton Rouge for several years in succession, and one or two individuals are found nearly every winter on the headquarters grounds of the Sabine National Wildlife Refuge in Cameron Parish. Actually it can be expected almost anywhere in the state, even in the northern sections, for it is fairly regular in winter in the Shreveport area.

The favorite habitat of the Vermilion Flycatcher when it is in Louisiana is the periphery of a small pond that has at least a few willows on its edge. The male is resplendent in color and is so distinctively marked that it could hardly be mistaken for any other bird.

The top of the head and entire underparts are a brilliant vermilion, and the back, wings, tail, and a line through the eye are black or slaty black. The immature males and the females have the throat and upper breast whitish and the lower underparts dull reddish or saffron yellow, streaked with dusky.

The Lark Family
Alaudidae

HORNED LARK   *Eremophila alpestris*   Fig. 127

This species is a true lark and hence is in no way related to the meadowlarks, which are members of the Oriole family. The Horned Lark is very common in the northern and western parts of the United States and it is migratory but once was rather seldom seen in Louisiana. Up to 1960 fewer than a half-dozen records were available from the state—that is, excluding those from Cameron Parish, where the small Texas coastal plains subspecies probably once nested and may still do so in small numbers. Now the species appears to be far more regular and somewhat more widespread in its occurrence in Louisiana in winter. I believe the greater frequency of records is, however, attributable to a more thorough coverage of the state by an increasing number of ornithologists rather than to an actual change in the winter movements of the species.

Records in the last decade include the following: 56 seen five miles southwest of Lafayette on December 17, 1972, by Marshall B. Eyster; 21 at the same place on February 3, 1973, by the same observer; 2 at Mansfield on November 29, 1970; 20 at Lecompte on December 16, 1972; and 2 at Baton Rouge on January 11, 1973 (only the third record for this well-worked locality in the last 30 years), by Robert J. Newman and Robert B. Hamilton.

The species has been seen quite frequently in recent years in winter in the Shreveport area and at other places in the northern part of the state. Horace H. Jeter located a flock of 20 near Missionary on November 28, 1969, and he saw 12 near Ida on February 7, 1970. On November 27, 1970, several flocks, the largest containing 16 birds, were located three miles east of Ida, and 12 were counted at nearby Missionary on January 16, 1972. But on May 23, 1971, Jeter found a fledgling still unable to fly, and he photographed it on May 25. The birds were present and presumably breeding there in 1972, but none could be found in 1973, probably because the area was unsuitable at the time the birds came into breeding condition. At about the same time D. T. Kee located over 50 birds in a cotton field 2 miles south of Collinston, in Morehouse Parish, on December 27, 1970, and 28 in a similar situation 2.6 miles north of Start, in Richland Parish. In both places he found scattered Horned Larks in summer and at both places he observed newly fledged young. He also noted sizable flocks, totaling at least 200 individuals, on several occasions near Quimby, in Madison Parish, in the winter of 1973–1974.

Ernest Thompson Seton has described the Horned Lark as follows: "It is strictly a ground-bird, never perching in trees, although it commonly alights on the top of a fence post, or other low level surface. When encountered on a pathway it often runs before the pedestrian after the manner of a Vesper Sparrow, from which bird, however, it may be distinguished by the black feathers in its tail, by its brown back, and by the black marks on its face; also by the fact that it *runs*, but does not *hop*, and when it flies it usually utters a whistle."

Periods of cold weather, especially those producing a blanket of sleet or snow in the regions north of Louisiana, are probably the best times to look for visitations of Horned Larks in south Louisiana. The grassy fields of airports are a favorite habitat of this lark and, if watched regularly in winter, might also produce other interesting species of birds that prefer this kind of situation to all others, such as the Sprague's Pipit and the various longspurs. The nest of the Horned Lark is built in a saucer-shaped hole scratched out by the birds and lined with prairie grasses and a variety of soft materials, on which three or four grayish, densely speckled eggs are laid.

The Swallow
Family
Hirundinidae

Swallows are birds of small size with long pointed wings and great powers of flight. Indeed, they are among the most graceful of all birds on the wing, wheeling and turning with ease, first one way and then another, or skimming low over the ground or the waters of a lake, in quest of their diet of insects.

In late summer and fall, resident and migrant populations of swallows congregate in immense flocks, lining telephone wires along our roads and over our marshes (see photograph on p. 441). Although these aggregations, sometimes of thousands of individuals, may remain fairly constant in size from August to November, the species composition of the flocks definitely changes. First the assemblages are made up of Rough-winged Swallows, which are later joined by migrant Barn and Bank Swallows and still later by Cliff and Tree Swallows. The last large aggregations of swallows are almost wholly comprised of Tree Swallows, for the other species, except for a few Rough-wings, have moved on to warmer regions south of the Gulf of Mexico.

TREE SWALLOW *Iridoprocne bicolor* Pl. XXV; p. 441

The Tree Swallow is an abundant migrant throughout Louisiana (from early March to early May and from September to late November) and usually a common winter resident in the southern half of the state, being particularly numerous in fall and early winter. When the latter season is not too severe, the bird remains in south Louisiana in sizable numbers, but always in the vicinity of a lake or a large expanse of coastal marsh. If, however, the weather in January is marked by several days of continuous cold, the Tree Swallow may become greatly diminished in numbers and remain so until migrants begin to reappear in early spring.

The only known instance of the species nesting in the state is that of a small colony that resided in some hollows in dead snags near the middle of Eagle Lake, on the boundary of Louisiana and Mississippi, northeast of Tallulah. The species has been observed on a few dates in June and July at

Migrating Tree Swallows Pause to Rest

Baton Rouge, Reserve, Cameron, and Venice, in southern Louisiana, but without evidence that the birds in question were breeding anywhere near these places. The Eagle Lake nesting was in a situation typical of that used by the Tree Swallow, except that in the North it sometimes comes in close to human habitations and occupies nesting boxes. The nest is usually composed of straw, weed stalks, and a copious supply of feathers. The four to six eggs are immaculate white.

The Tree Swallow is easily distinguished from other swallows by its color, which is bluish green above and immaculate white below. The outer tail feathers are slightly longer than the middle ones. Immatures are dull brownish gray above with only a slight greenish tinge, but their all-white underparts still make them easily separable from the other species.

BANK SWALLOW   *Riparia riparia*   Pl. XXV

The statements by some early writers on Louisiana birds that this species nested in the state probably resulted from confusion of the Bank Swallow with the Rough-winged Swallow, since both are brown in color and both build their nests in tunnels in clay banks. There is no satisfactory evidence that this species has ever bred within our borders, although it does occur here numerously in migration. It can be separated from the Rough-winged Swallow by its slightly smaller size and by the distinct grayish brown band across its otherwise white breast.

The Bank Swallow generally arrives at the end of March or in the first week of April and remains until mid-May, rarely to the end of the month and even into June. In fall it reappears sometimes as early as the first week of July and continues to pass through until the first week of November. It has twice been seen in the first week of December in Cameron Parish.

ROUGH-WINGED SWALLOW   *Stelgidopteryx ruficollis*
Pl. XXV; Fig. 121

This swallow was first discovered by John James Audubon on the banks of Bayou Sara. Late one afternoon, standing on the edge of the bayou, he shot a swallow as it circled about him, and his dog retrieved it. Taking the specimen from the dog's mouth, he stood idly examining it, thinking at first that it was a Bank Swallow. Then to his surprise he noted a peculiar roughness to the fore edge of the outer primary, which, on close inspection, he found to be due to a tiny, recurved hooklet on each barb of the outer web. Later, at Charleston, South Carolina, he obtained another specimen and was then convinced that he had found a species new to science. Indeed, the Rough-winged and Bank Swallows are rather easily confused unless one knows what to look for. Both are brown backed, but their underparts are very dissimilar. In the Bank Swallow, the throat and belly are pure white separated by a brown band across the breast. In the Rough-wing, the throat and

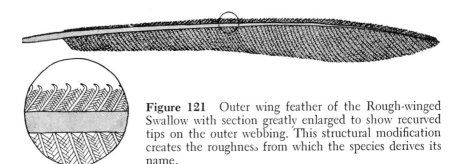

Figure 121   Outer wing feather of the Rough-winged Swallow with section greatly enlarged to show recurved tips on the outer webbing. This structural modification creates the roughness from which the species derives its name.

upper breast are dingy brown, and only the lower belly is white; there is no indication of a breast band.

The Rough-wing winters in small numbers in most of southern Louisiana, notably at False River, in Pointe Coupee Parish, but the species is mainly a summer resident, arriving here in early March and sometimes remaining in large numbers until mid-November. Nests are built at the end of a tunnel in a riverbank or a highway cut. The four or five eggs are pure white.

BARN SWALLOW   *Hirundo rustica*   Pl. XXV

This is the only swallow in Louisiana with a reddish breast, bluish back, and deeply forked tail. Young birds of the year are paler beneath and somewhat resemble Cliff Swallows but lack the pale rufous rump patch of the latter and have a forked tail.

Barn Swallows migrate thousands of miles in passing from their main summer range in the northern United States and Canada to their winter home in South America. In doing so a considerable part of the population crosses the broad expanse of the Gulf of Mexico, winging its way across this trackless 600 miles of water as easily as if guided by a map, chronometer, and sextant. When Barn Swallows reach the lower Mississippi Valley in spring, we see them singly and in flocks feeding over our fields and levees as they move northward to their breeding grounds.

Nests are built of mud, grasses, and feathers and are placed under eaves of barns and other buildings or on rafters and sleepers under bridges along highways. The Barn Swallow has only recently been found breeding in the state in other areas besides certain coastal islands and other coastal situations, such as under bridges on the Sabine National Wildlife Refuge in Cameron Parish. Now it is also known to nest, mostly under highway bridges, in northwestern Louisiana in Caddo, De Soto, and Natchitoches parishes. The males of coastal-breeding populations are for the most part pale breasted and appear to belong to the insular race known otherwise only from the islands off the coast of Texas, Mississippi, Alabama, and western Florida. The presence, however, in our coastal populations of red-breasted, rather than white-breasted, males requires much additional study. The birds build their nests on the walls of old forts, as well as under the eaves of the few man-made structures that are occasionally present. Where they nested before these structures were built is a mystery.

By early August migrants from the north of us begin to arrive in Louisiana, and the species is present until the end of October and early November, occasionally later. In spring Barn Swallows return in mid-March and are abundant transients until the middle of May. An occasional individual is seen in extreme southern Louisiana in December and January.

CLIFF SWALLOW *Petrochelidon pyrrhonota* Pl. XXV

The Cliff Swallow breeds extensively across the breadth of North America but is absent from Louisiana and other parts of the Gulf coastal plain of southeastern United States except as a migrant. It winters in South America. Being essentially a blue-backed swallow, it is hardly to be confused with any other species except possibly the Barn Swallow. Instead of having the upperparts uniformly blue and the underparts reddish, as does the latter species, it displays a variety of colors and markings; the forehead is white, the back streaked lightly with white, the rump pale rufous, the tail blackish, the sides of the head chestnut, the breast gray with only the belly white, and the lower throat black. Unlike its relatives, which have the tail forked (Barn Swallow) or notched (Rough-winged, Bank, and Tree Swallows), the Cliff Swallow has tail feathers of almost equal length.

The species is a fairly common but late migrant in spring, passing through Louisiana in its greatest numbers in May and early June, but occasionally appearing as early as the first week of April. In southward migration it may be seen regularly and in moderate numbers from late July until late October. One was seen at Triumph, in Plaquemines Parish, on November 24, 1961, and another was recorded at Natchitoches on January 23, 1973. Two individuals observed by Horace H. Jeter near Mira, in northern Caddo Parish, on June 28, 1959, suggested the possibility that the species might breed sparingly in the northwestern part of the state, but so far no evidence of its doing so has materialized.

PURPLE MARTIN *Progne subis* Pl. XXV; p. 445

This species is my favorite of all swallows, and possibly of all land birds. Almost as far back as I can remember I have had martin boxes in my yard and each year have looked forward to the return of the occupants. The cheery, gurgling note that these birds make is generally the first harbinger of spring, for the Purple Martin is the earliest bird to return to Louisiana after a

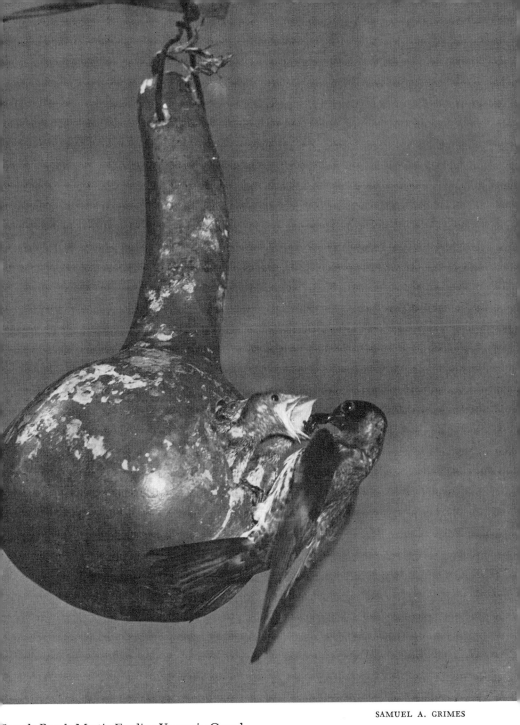

Female Purple Martin Feeding Young in Gourd

winter sojourn in the lands south of the Gulf of Mexico. Almost always, in the southern part of the state, the species is back with us by the first week of February, and sometimes the advance guard arrives in late January.

My high regard for the martin has come about in part through having handled more than 500 of them alive in the course of banding the inhabitants of my nesting boxes. There can be few greater thrills to the naturalist than that of banding an adult bird or nestling and witnessing its return to the exact spot of its banding after it has traveled a thousand miles or more to spend the winter in some distant land. What an excitement it is to hear again the familiar twitter of the first Purple Martin in spring and to see one perched on the nesting box with an aluminum band on one of its legs and a series of color bands on the other, labeling it as a "return"! In the 1940s and 1950s nearly all the martins in my boxes were marked with band combinations of one to three of the following colors: white, red, green, blue, black, yellow, and orange. Each bird had its own special arrangement of colors and hence did not need to be recaptured for the purpose of reading the actual number on the aluminum band. For example, a male bird with red, yellow, and blue bands (reading from top to bottom) on the left leg and the aluminum band on the right leg was U.S. Fish and Wildlife Service band number 47-157223. The same arrangement on a female was number 46-111760. The various colors can be utilized in hundreds of different combinations and thus provide an almost unlimited means of individually identifying each bird in a colony over a period of many years. This permits detailed studies of interrelationships and social behavior within the framework of the colony. It is a way of ascertaining if mating between two individuals extends over from one season to the next, if any brother-sister matings or other forms of inbreeding occur, if any form of polygamy exists, if more than one brood is raised, and numerous other details in the lives of the birds, including facts relating to longevity, migration routes, and winter homes.

The Purple Martin, which is our largest swallow and the only one that is black bellied, cannot easily be mistaken for any other bird. The male is such a dark blue that it appears in many circumstances to be jet black. Even a bird

---

Plate XXV   Adult Swallows

1. male Barn Swallow (p. 443). 2. Cliff Swallow (p. 444). 3. Bank Swallow (p. 441). 4. Purple Martin (p. 444), male in foreground, female behind. 5. Rough-winged Swallow (p. 442). 6. male Tree Swallow (p. 440).

in the hand is best described as *blue-black*. The female is grayish white on the throat and breast and white on the belly and undertail coverts. An indistinct light collar extends around the neck, and the forehead is pale, grayish brown; the top of the head, back, wings, and tail are predominantly grayish black, usually with only a trace of blue, hence much duller than in the adult male. Young males cannot be distinguished with certainty from females. I used to think I could tell them apart by the amount of gray on the forehead until several birds that I banded and recorded as "immature females" returned in a later year in full male regalia. The molt transforming young males into their adult plumage generally takes place after the end of the first breeding season, although sometimes it occurs during the first-year breeding activities.

Martins arrive early, as already noted, and selection of compartments in a nesting box begins promptly. Actual nesting, however, is delayed until April, with subadults sometimes commencing as late as the end of May or early June. The three to five (rarely eight) dead-white eggs are laid in a nest made of leaves and sticks on a thin foundation of mud, which is banked up in front to prevent the eggs from rolling out. Often during the period of incubation a few fresh green leaves are found on top of the eggs during the day. The suggestion has been made that the evaporation of moisture from the leaves may serve a useful function in raising the humidity within the nesting compartment.

Incubation takes an average of 13 days, but one set of eggs that I checked required 19 days to hatch. Such variation could be the result of discontinuous brooding, which causes arrested development of the embryo, for there is some evidence that both the male and female martins sometimes leave the eggs unattended at night, presumably to go to huge communal roosts. This departure at night from the nest boxes is definitely true of the males after the end of April. Very few of them can then be trapped by closing the boxes after dark, for they simply do not regularly spend the nights there. I often wondered what became of them until I discovered that an estimated ten thousand or more birds roost nightly on the superstructure of a hydrogen tank in the center of the huge Exxon refinery north of Baton Rouge.

The young remain in the nest for about four or five weeks, and, although some writers have said that they return to the nest box for a week or ten days after first leaving it, this claim is not substantiated by my own banding studies. Never have I known either the young or the parents to return, even momentarily, after the last of the brood has departed. Martins frequently alight on the boxes after all young are out of the nests, and these visitors would be regarded as the original occupants were it not for the absence of telltale leg bands. Some authors have claimed that the martin raises two, or sometimes even three, broods; but again no support to this assertion has come forth from banding studies—the only reliable means whereby the matter can be analyzed. I have found fresh eggs in my boxes as late as June 4, but they belonged in most instances to new and not yet banded subadult males and presumably subadult females.

When the chores of nesting are over, martins from a large area congregate in huge flocks. The Baton Rouge roost mentioned above has been estimated to contain as many as fourteen thousand birds in early August. After this time the number gradually diminishes until by mid-September nearly all the birds are gone. The observation of a Purple Martin any time in October is exceptional. However, 11 martins, 2 adult males and 9 female-plumaged individuals, were carefully studied by Father J. L. Dorn in a large winter aggregation of Tree Swallows near New Orleans on December 26 and 27, 1956. There are to my knowledge no other records for the United States in this month. The species winters for the most part in Brazil.

Martins are sociable birds that like each other's company and hence usually occupy any sort of multicompartmented house, whether it be made of mahogany or of a soapbox and whether it be painted or unpainted. Martins are great aerial acrobats that require open spaces to perform their maneuvers. Many times they may be seen to come in at a height of a hundred feet or more, and, when nearly over the nesting box, fold their wings back close to the body and literally plummet earthward. It would seem for a moment that they would surely crash, but, just as the birds reach the level of the box, the wings are thrown out, the tail is spread, and the birds abruptly halt in midair as they gently alight on the porch of the box. Because of antics and performances such as these, martins seem to prefer boxes more or less in the open and situated 10 to 15 feet above the ground. Instructions and specifications for the building of martin boxes are given on page 91.

Indians were very fond of martins, and long before the arrival of the white man they put up hollowed-out gourds on poles for them to nest in, like the one shown on page 445. This practice was taken up by plantation Negroes and persists until this day. Despite the martin's popularity and the great number of houses erected for it, there is still apparently a "housing shortage." Consequently, many of the birds nest in holes under the eaves of buildings, in open horizontal pipes, and in a variety of other situations. The most unorthodox nesting site with which I am familiar was in a rural-type mail box, four feet above the ground, on the edge of the Louisiana State University campus at Baton Rouge.

The Crow Family
Corvidae

BLUE JAY *Cyanocitta cristata*   Fig. 122; p. 451

John James Audubon's magnificent portrait of the Blue Jay depicts three of these birds devouring eggs stolen from the nest of another species. In referring to the drawing, the famous naturalist has this to say about his subjects: "Reader, look at the plate in which are represented three individuals of this beautiful species—rogues though they may be, and thieves, as I would call them, were it fit for me to pass judgment on their actions. See how each is enjoying the fruits of his knavery, sucking on the egg which he has pilfered from the nest of some innocent Dove or harmless Partridge! Who could imagine that a form so graceful, arrayed by Nature in a garb so resplendent, should harbour so much mischief;—that selfishness, duplicity, and malice should form the moral accompaniments of so much physical perfection!" In so writing, Audubon sums up what most of us feel with regard to the Blue Jay. We disapprove of its habit of eating the eggs and young of other birds, but we would not wish our surroundings to be without its beauty, its querulous but pleasing calls, and its garrulous, raucous screams. And, after all, these depredations are not very serious. Even in places where I have seen it taking a heavy toll of the eggs and young of the melodious Wood Thrush, there never seemed to be any shortage of the latter species.

The Blue Jay is an abundant permanent resident in Louisiana, and its

Figure 122   Blue Jay.

numbers are augmented in winter by the arrival of migrant populations from farther north, possibly from as far away as Canada. The calls of the species are varied. One has been alluded to as the "pump handle" note, so closely does it resemble the sound made by that device. A roving band moving through a wood often shouts "jay, jay." Commonly jays imitate the Red-shouldered Hawk by emitting a loud scream that can hardly be distinguished from the call of the hawk. Rarely one will be heard singing a low, gurgling, ventriloqual song as it perches quietly in a tree, probably near its mate and nest. The latter is a bulky but compact structure of sticks and rootlets, usually located 10 to 20 feet up in a tree crotch and containing four to six olive-green eggs variously blotched with brown.

COMMON CROW   *Corvus brachyrhynchos*   Figs. 123; 124

Aside from students of ornithology, probably few people in Louisiana realize that we have in our state two species of crows, the Common Crow and the Fish Crow. Like most crows the world over, both of ours are solid black, and were it not for their dissimilar calls, we could hardly distinguish them except in the case of a specimen in the hand. The Common Crow is slightly the

Young Blue Jay Among Weigela Blossoms

RET

Figure 123   Common Crow.

larger of the two, but this size difference is not readily apparent in the field. Its call, however, is a deep-voiced *caw-caw*, while that of its relative is a nasal, rather tin horn *car-car*.

The Common Crow occurs abundantly over most of the state lying north of the coastal marches, while the Fish Crow ranges along the coast and extends northward only along the major rivers. The two species build bulky, virtually indistinguishable nests of sticks, twigs, and rootlets, lined with grasses and moss, thirty to fifty feet up in trees. The variably colored eggs, which are generally bluish green and heavily blotched with various shades of brown, are likewise so similar in the two species that only an expert oologist can tell them apart with a high degree of accuracy.

Crows are thoroughly disliked by nearly everyone because of the damage they do to crops, especially corn, and because of the toll they take of the eggs and young of other species. But despite their bad reputation, crows are highly respected for their seeming intelligence by those who know them. Indeed, the facetious statement has been made that "if human beings were birds, very few of them would be crows." So wary has the species become of man that only by partially concealing oneself and employing a vocal or mechanical imitation of its call can one bring a crow into gun range.

I am in favor of "crow shoots" because I am convinced that the species is highly destructive of crops and other birds and because I believe its numbers are now far beyond the normal limits set by nature. The excessive number of crows is probably the result of changes in our landscape coincident with the great expansion of agriculture in this country in the last hundred years. Therefore, the crow may need control methods applied against it.

I am further convinced that a segment of the American public, which no longer has access to an abundance of game, must have something to shoot at. Unlike most other peoples in the world, we are, in the twentieth century, still a nation of "shotguns over every mantelpiece." With this ample supply of guns at hand and with ammunition obtainable in the corner grocery, the legions of would-be hunters in this country are unfortunately encountering greater and greater difficulty in finding an outlet for their hunting instincts. This dilemma becomes acute when the short hunting seasons are over, and thus many are turning to shooting nongame birds. I would prefer to see this enthusiasm vented on the noxious crow rather than, as is often the case, on our beneficial hawks. This indiscriminate killing of hawks and virtually everything that flies is deplorable and reprehensible, as well as illegal, and is, of course, an offense committed by no true sportsman. However, if gunners must shoot nongame birds, let it be Common and Fish Crows, European Starlings, and House Sparrows, *not hawks* or any of our other birds for which there are permanently closed seasons.

FISH CROW   *Corvus ossifragus*   Fig. 124

Fish Crows are fairly abundant permanent residents in the southern part of the state, where they frequent the edges of our marshes and the farmlands of the bayou country. The species was once thought to be restricted to such

Figure 124   Heads of two species of Louisiana crows.

areas, both here in Louisiana and elsewhere in its range, which extends from the coast of Massachusetts south to Florida and west along the Gulf Coast to Texas. Now, however, it is known to range far inland along many of the larger rivers that empty into the Atlantic Ocean and into the Gulf of Mexico. In our section it is present at least as far north as Shreveport on the Red River and Memphis on the Mississippi River.

Despite the great similarity of the Fish Crow to the Common Crow, no instance of hybridization has been found. As noted in connection with the Common Crow, the call notes are the only means by which the two species are distinguishable with certainty in the field.

The Tit Family
Paridae

CAROLINA CHICKADEE　*Parus carolinensis*　　　Pl. XXVI

The field identification of birds would be simple indeed if all species in uttering their calls or songs pronounced their names. But, unfortunately, all too few are so obliging. The Dickcissel shouts *dick-ciss-ciss-ciss*, the Eastern Phoebe says *phee-be*, and the Carolina Chickadee moves through the woods uttering repetitiously a cheery, high-pitched, whistled *chick-a-dee-dee-dee*, or sometimes a simple *dee-dee-dee*. This diminutive "ball of feathers" is a member of a rather large family that occurs mainly in the Temperate Zone forests of the New and Old Worlds. In England these birds are called tits, and the Britishers have their Coal Tit, Blue Tit, Great Tit, Bearded Tit, and even their Penduline Tit.

Though resembling many species of tits in other parts of the world, our own Carolina Chickadee is distinctively marked, insofar as Louisiana birds are concerned, by its black cap and black throat on a coat that is otherwise dull gray. It occurs in virtually every patch of woods in the state except for some of the chenieres along the coast that are isolated by wide expanses of marshland. It is so sedentary in habit that no individual probably ever wanders very far from its place of birth. But in winter in the confines of its home district the Carolina Chickadee joins with the Tufted Titmouse, the kinglets, and other small birds to form roving bands. A squeaking noise made with the fingers pressed against the lips elicits great excitement on the part of these flocks and will generally bring the birds to within a few feet of the observer. They nervously search for the source of the sound, which apparently they interpret as a distress call on the part of another bird.

Chickadees build their nests in tree cavities and sometimes in bird boxes. They lay five to eight eggs that are white speckled with reddish brown. The sexes are alike and the young, even in juvenal plumage, closely resemble the adults. This is a general rule among species in which the female is like the male. In those species where the sexes are dissimilar, the young males are usually colored like the females.

TUFTED TITMOUSE *Parus bicolor* Pl. XXVI

This species is a close relative of the Carolina Chickadee but differs from it principally in having a plain throat and a topknot or crest. The Tufted Titmouse is a nondescript bird in color, wholly mouse gray, except for a wash of rufous along the sides and flanks. The song is a distinct *peter-peter;* the call, a *dee-dee* note that resembles one of the utterances of the Carolina Chickadee but is coarser and lower pitched.

The species is a widespread and common permanent resident in Louisiana, wandering through the woods in winter with bands of other small denizens of the forest but apparently never crossing the coastal marshes to the wooded chenieres. It nests in old Downy Woodpecker holes, tree cavities, and even bird boxes when available. The eggs are three to five in number, white or creamy white, and coarsely and evenly marked with rufous brown.

The Nuthatch
Family
Sittidae

Nuthatches are small, arboreal birds that spend their lives creeping about on the trunks and limbs of trees in search of bark beetles and other insects. They do not hold their tails against the tree for support, in the fashion of woodpeckers. The little birds nevertheless exhibit great agility in working even upside down on the underparts of branches. Although nuthatches are northern birds in a worldwide sense, Louisiana has two resident species and one that is an erratic, although sometimes abundant, winter visitor. The call notes of all three are nasal in quality and not easily confused with those made by any other bird.

WHITE-BREASTED NUTHATCH *Sitta carolinensis*

Pl. XXVI; p. 457

This species has a black cap; bluish gray upperparts, with black and white edges to the secondaries; and immaculate white underparts, except for a mixture of rufous on the lower belly and undertail coverts. The other nuthatches are either red breasted or brown headed.

White-breasted Nuthatches inhabit the oak and oak-pine forests of the northern half of our state in considerable numbers, and a few are to be found scattered through the extreme northern part of the Florida Parishes. Their call is a nasal *yank-yank-yank*, but when spring comes the males utter a rather high-pitched *hah-hah-hah-hah-hah* that sounds more like a kind of laughter than a song. The nest is made of feathers and leaves and is placed in a cavity

---

Plate XXVI   Tits, Nuthatches, and the Brown Creeper

1. Carolina Chickadee (p. 454). 2. Tufted Titmouse (p. 455). 3. White-breasted Nuthatch (p. 456). 4. Red-breasted Nuthatch (p. 457). 5. Brown Creeper (p. 458). 6. Brown-headed Nuthatch (p. 458).

1

2

3

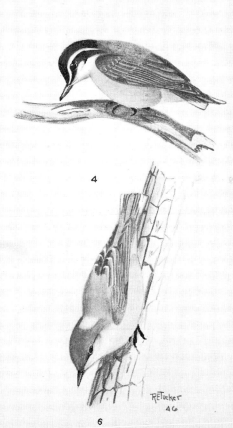

4

5

6

R.E.Tucker
46

of a tree or stump. The five to eight eggs are white or creamy white, heavily speckled with rufous or lavender.

RED-BREASTED NUTHATCH *Sitta canadensis* Pl. XXVI

This nuthatch is intermediate in size between the other two species that occur in Louisiana. It somewhat resembles the White-breasted Nuthatch in color but has a white line over the eye and a dark line through the eye (shiny black in the male, bluish gray in the female) extending from the bill to the nape. The underparts, exclusive of the white throat, are reddish buff in color. The last character alone makes the species easily recognizable.

The Red-breasted Nuthatch breeds mainly in the extreme northern part of the United States and in Canada. It is an irregular visitor to Louisiana in winter that has been recorded from September 21 to May 7, and it is often rare except in certain years when it literally inundates the state by mass invasions. In the 46 years that I have closely observed the birds of Louisiana, this phenomenon has occurred only five times. The greatest invasion of all was in the winter of 1940–1941, but lesser invasions have taken place in the winters of 1954–1955, 1961–1962, 1965–1966, and 1969–1970. In the winter

White-breasted Nuthatch and Young

SAMUEL A. GRIMES

of the record invasion of 1940–1941, Red-breasted Nuthatches were virtually everywhere, and they were abundant as far south in the state as the narrow wooded ridges along our coast, on the south side of the great coastal marshes. Strange indeed was it to see these small birds feeding within a stone's throw of the Gulf beach.

BROWN-HEADED NUTHATCH *Sitta pusilla* Pl. XXVI

The Brown-headed Nuthatch is a common permanent resident in many of the pine forests of Louisiana. Indeed, this little nuthatch, the Red-cockaded Woodpecker, Pine Warbler, and Bachman's Sparrow are the most characteristic birds of the pinelands of the South.

The Brown-headed Nuthatch has gray upperparts and a grayish white breast, but the *dull brownish cap* immediately identifies it. Its call note is uttered continually as it scurries about among the boughs of the tall pines in which it lives most of its life. Although definitely nasal in tone, the sound is somewhat more of a twitter than the calls of the other nuthatches. One writer has described it as a thin, metallic *dee-dee-dee* or *tnee-tnee-tnee*. The nest is usually located in a cavity or old woodpecker hole in a pine snag, generally only a few feet from the ground. The five or six white or creamy white eggs are heavily marked with cinnamon-brown or olive-brown.

The Creeper Family
Certhiidae

BROWN CREEPER *Certhia familiaris* Pl. XXVI

The creepers are a small Old World family of only 12 species, one of which, the Brown Creeper, has reached North America. Here it breeds in the northern forests and in the Allegheny and Rocky mountains, as well as at high elevations all the way down to the southern edge of the Mexican table-land. In Louisiana it occurs solely as a winter resident.

Creepers parallel woodpeckers in certain specializations adapting them to tree climbing. The tail feathers are stiff and attenuated on the tips and are held firmly against the tree trunk as the little birds inch their way upward. After reaching the upper limits of the tree trunk or of one of its main upper forks, the creepers glide down to the base of a nearby tree and begin their ascent all over again. The upperparts are brownish with streaks of dusky and tawny, the rump is pale rufous, and the underparts are grayish white. The thin, rather elongated bill is slightly downcurved.

The Brown Creeper arrives in Louisiana in the first half of October and remains sometimes through early April. The species is regular and generally fairly numerous in northern Louisiana, but in the southern part of the state it is quite uncommon in some winters. The call is a high-pitched *see* that often provides the first clue to the bird's presence in a wood. Indeed, the little birds blend so well with the bark of tree trunks, to which they cling closely, that they would hardly ever be detected if we were not attracted to them by their almost continuous movements and by their sounds.

The Wren Family
Troglodytidae

Wrens are small, elusive birds that usually inhabit thickets or heavily wooded areas, where they are more often heard than seen. The family occurs both in the Old and the New Worlds, but the headquarters of the group is in the American tropics. Of the 10 kinds that occur in the United States, 6 are known from Louisiana, but of these only 2 remain the year around.

Wrens, and some of their close relatives such as the members of the Mimic Thrush family, have only one molt a year, the postnuptial molt following the breeding season. Hence they are in their finest plumage in the early fall, immediately after the postnuptial molt is completed. Inhabiting, as they do, brushy situations or, in some cases, marshy places with coarse grasses, wrens soon have their feathers abraded. By the time spring comes they are faded and worn, but this poor dress must suffice during courtship, nest building, and family raising. Most other birds, however, have at least a partial prenuptial molt that puts them in fine feather during the period when they are seeking, or being sought after by, the opposite sex.

NORTHERN HOUSE WREN *Troglodytes aedon* Pl. XXVII

As its name implies, the Northern House Wren, over a large part of its breeding range, is especially common near human habitations. During its sojourn with us it lacks the sociable nature that it exhibits in summer and instead skulks about in the woods and brushy fields. In Louisiana it is strictly a migrant and winter resident, arriving here in early September and remaining in numbers until April, sparingly until early May. As a winter resident it is uncommon and irregular in north Louisiana but fairly numerous in the southern part of the state.

The Northern House Wren is one of the most nondescript of our wrens, being neither the largest nor the smallest and being simply dark brown above and grayish brown below. It has no obvious facial markings, such as a white line over the eye. But the absence of such marks readily distinguishes it from its relatives, all of which have some special pattern on the head.

WINTER WREN *Troglodytes troglodytes* Pl. XXVII

From our point of view in Louisiana, this wren is particularly well named, for it occurs here only in winter. It resembles the Northern House Wren but is much darker in color, the underparts are barred instead of almost immaculate, there is an indistinct line over the eye, and the tail is much stubbier. The tail is actually only slightly more than an inch in length and is usually held perpendicular or at an acute angle to the back. This species, the smallest of the wrens, lives in the densest tangles and brush heaps and is thus extremely difficult to see. Sometimes a squeaking sound made by placing the fingers against the lips will entice one of the elusive little birds to hop momentarily into view. But these fleeting glimpses are usually barely sufficient to verify one's identification.

Plate XXVII Wrens

1. Winter Wren (p. 460). 2. Northern House Wren (p. 460). 3. Marsh Wren (p. 463). 4. Sedge Wren (p. 465). 5. Carolina Wren (p. 461). 6. Bewick's Wren (p. 461).

1

2

3

4

R.E.Tucker
46

5

6

The Winter Wren is generally less common than the Northern House Wren, except in north Louisiana, where it is sometimes much the commoner of the two species from late November to early March. The Winter Wren is also quite numerous in the brushy, willow thickets in the battures along the Mississippi River at St. Francisville, at Baton Rouge, and presumably from there southward. It does not arrive in our state until the first part of October, nearly a month later than the Northern House Wren; departure is in late March or April. The call note of the Winter Wren is quite distinctive once it is learned. I cannot describe actually how it differs in quality from the *chip* of the Song Sparrow, which one often finds in the same habitat, but the Winter Wren more often sputters out two or more of these notes in rapid succession.

BEWICK'S WREN *Thryomanes bewickii*   Pl. XXVII

The Bewick's (pronounced "Buicks") Wren is similar to the Northern House Wren and to some extent to the Carolina Wren. It is distinguished from either by its black-barred and white-tipped outer tail feathers. The dull, reddish brown color of its back is markedly different from the plain grayish brown of the Northern House Wren and the rich, rusty brown of the Carolina. The distinct white line over the eye quickly distinguishes the Bewick's from the Northern House Wren, which has no eyeline at all or at best only a very faint indication of one. In the Carolina Wren the line over the eye is buffy except in faded and worn plumage, when it becomes whitish. One of the most diagnostic field characters of the Bewick's Wren is, however, the manner in which the tail is continually wobbled from side to side as if it were loosely joined to the body.

The species arrives in late September (an August 9 record is possibly erroneous) and is usually gone by the middle of March. It is earlier in its departure than either the Northern House Wren or the Winter Wren. It is never common in the state and in some years is decidedly uncommon.

The bird was first described scientifically by John James Audubon on the basis of a specimen obtained by him on October 2, 1821, at the Oakley Plantation near St. Francisville. He named the bird for his friend Thomas Bewick.

CAROLINA WREN *Thryothorus ludovicianus*   Pl. XXVII; p. 462

This species was first made known to science in 1790 by the famous English

Carolina Wren at Entrance to Nest

ornithologist, John Latham, who based his description on a specimen received by him from "Louisiana" (most likely from near New Orleans), hence the specific name *ludovicianus*. It is one of the commonest resident birds of Louisiana and one of the better known. Its vociferous outbursts, which are unbelievably loud for such a small bird, can be heard in our gardens, as well as throughout the forests of the state. The song suggests the words *tea-kettle, tea-kettle* or *wheedle, wheedle*. Often one of a pair will emit the *tea-kettle* note and be answered nearby by its mate with a monosyllabic rattling sound.

Carolina Wrens build their bulky nests of leaves and sticks in all sorts of places near our houses. Not infrequently they select the most inconvenient kind of situation. This may be an old work hat, which we left in the garage and must now abandon temporarily until the little birds are raised and leave the nest. As I write this account, I have a pair nesting in my outdoor workshop on a small ledge where I keep various instruction booklets on the use and care of the lawnmower and other power tools. I can only hope that none of these booklets has to be consulted in the next few weeks!

The Carolina Wren is the largest of the six species of wrens in Louisiana, among which it is unique in being rich rusty brown above and very buffy below, except for its white throat. There is a light buffy line over the eye that gradually becomes whitish through fading. The five creamy white eggs have numerous rufous brown, cinnamon brown, and lavender markings, which sometimes form a wreath about the larger end.

MARSH WREN *Telmatodytes palustris* Pl. XXVII; p. 464

The Marsh Wren, formerly referred to as the Long-billed Marsh Wren, inhabits marshy places almost throughout the country, but for some reason in Louisiana it nests only in our coastal marshes, where, however, it is abundant the year around. Elsewhere in the state it occurs only as an uncommon transient or, in suitable situations, as a fairly common winter visitor. In northern Louisiana, however, it is quite scarce during the cold months. Not surprising is the fact that a large breeding population exists in our southern marshes, for this area provides an ideal habitat for the species. Probably as a result of the isolation of these coastal birds, they have become markedly different in color from populations in the interior of the United States; for this reason they are recognized as a distinct subspecies or geographical race.

Any wren in tall marsh vegetation is often suspected of being a Marsh Wren simply on the basis of its presence in such a habitat, but the light brown color, white eyeline, black cap, and black back marked with longitudinal white stripes serve as the real basis for separation of this species from its relatives. The Sedge Wren prefers low, densely matted grassy situations in salt grass marsh or broom sedge (*Andropogon*) fields. Moreover, the Sedge Wren's crown is streaked and not solid black like that of the Marsh Wren.

Migrants of the present species arrive in late September and do not complete departure for their northern nesting areas until late April. The resident birds in our southern marshes build their globular nests of coarse grasses and reed stalks and line them with fine grasses, attaching them to reeds or bushes. The entrance hole is on the side, generally near the top. The five to nine eggs are uniform chocolate or else pale brown speckled with olive- or cinnamon-brown. The male is the nest builder and sometimes he is overzealous to the extent that he will construct as many as five (rarely 10) nests, from which the female possibly makes a choice. But the real purpose of the extra or dummy nests is not known; they are not complete structures with lining and all, and they are not used as night roosts by the males.

The singing of the male Marsh Wren is no less energetic than his nest-building propensities. He gives voice continually throughout the day

Marsh Wren Entering Nest

to a most pleasing medley of bubbling and gurgling notes that ripple across the marsh.

SEDGE WREN   *Cistothorus platensis*   Pl. XXVII

This small elusive marsh wren is not particularly a *marsh* bird during its winter sojourn in Louisiana, although it was formerly called the Short-billed Marsh Wren. In the upland areas, at least, it is found in dry, grassy fields, especially those with strands of broom sedge, which the Le Conte's, Henslow's, and Grasshopper Sparrows also frequent. In coastal areas it occurs in grassy marshes. It is not, in other words, a denizen of deep marshes where there are cattails, rushes, and roseau cane.

The Sedge Wren is a seldom-recorded transient and winter visitor in northern Louisiana, but in the southern part of the state it is known as a common winter resident. The first arrivals appear early in October, and the last individuals to depart do so in late April or early May. The bird's main distinguishing features are its pale buffy color and its small size (only the exceedingly dark Winter Wren is smaller), along with its *finely streaked* crown and back. All other wrens in Louisiana have the top of the head unstreaked and, while the Marsh Wren is streaked on the back, the crown is unstreaked. The call of the Sedge Wren is a *chick* note that, once learned, serves readily to identify the species in the grass whether it is seen or not.

The
Mimic Thrush
Family
Mimidae

The mockingbirds and their allies, which include the Gray Catbird and numerous species of thrashers, are confined to the Western Hemisphere. They rank among the world's most accomplished avian songsters, and, since their musical renditions are generally given from some exposed perch, they are familiar to most people. Mockingbirds are closely akin to thrushes, but they possess relatively longer tails, and their bills are usually longer and more curved than those of thrushes. The adults of some species in the family have plain breasts, others streaked or spotted breasts, but the juvenal plumage of nearly all species shows some degree of spottedness.

GRAY CATBIRD   *Dumetella carolinensis*   Pl. XXVIII

The Gray Catbird, which gets its name from its mewing, catlike call note, is a common summer resident in the northern half of the state but rare at that season in the southern half. I have known of fewer than a dozen breeding pairs at Baton Rouge in the 40 years or more that I have lived here. In the seasons of migration, however, notably in April and early May and again in September and October, the Gray Catbird is often abundant throughout the state. In winter it is found only occasionally, hiding away in a dense thicket somewhere in the southern parishes or, still more rarely, lingering in similar situations in north Louisiana.

The song is a jumbled potpourri of notes, remotely resembling those of the Northern Mockingbird. In the breeding season Gray Catbirds come in close to human habitations, with the males singing from exposed perches, but at other seasons the species is shy and retiring. The plumage is a dark slate color above and below, except for the tail and the top of the head, which are black, and the undertail feathers, which are brick red. The eye is black, not yellowish as in the Northern Mockingbird and the Brown Thrasher. The Gray Catbird builds its bulky nest of sticks, grasses, and leaves, lined with rootlets, in dense thickets or tangles of vines. The three to five eggs are a rich, waxy greenish blue, unblemished by spots, and thus are more like those of the American Robin than like the eggs of most of the other members of the Gray Catbird's own family.

The modifier Gray in the vernacular name of our catbird is required because another species, the Black Catbird, occurs in Yucatan and parts of Central America.

NORTHERN MOCKINGBIRD   *Mimus polyglottos*
Pl. XXVIII; p. 467

Few birds anywhere provide more human enjoyment than does the mockingbird to the people of the South. The bird's delightful habit of singing day and night, especially when the landscape is bathed in moonlight and fragrant with the odors of summer flowers, makes its song appealing even to the man least sensitive to the sounds of nature. Mockingbirds have a song of their own, but their reputation stems mainly from their ability to imitate many other birds. The scientific name *Mimus polyglottos* means literally "mimic of many tongues." Some individual mockers are more adept than others. The Massachusetts Audubon Society has issued a phonograph record reproducing the vocal efforts of a single mockingbird that had over 50 songs in its repertoire, and there is a published report of another mockingbird that so successfully imitated a dinner bell that it frequently caused the farmhands to come out of the field expecting their noon meal.

A few zoologists contend that mockingbirds do not mock—that they simply have a diverse assortment of sounds that by sheer chance sometimes duplicate the notes made by other birds. If this were so, we would hear them rendering calls of exotic, extralimital species, but such is not the case. I have never heard a mockingbird in Louisiana that seemed to imitate any of the purely Mexican birds whose songs I know, nor as a matter of fact any other kind of bird not occurring in the specific mocker's own home range.

The Northern Mockingbird is an abundant permanent resident in Lou-

orthern Mockingbird at Nest

ALLAN D. CRUICKSHANK

isiana. Indeed, the adult mockingbirds that I have ringed and color-banded in my own yard never seem to leave their individual sections of the neighborhood. A male that sings from a perch near the living room windows and regularly visits the feeding table nearby has never been seen on the other side of the house in the territory of the male that resides there. For either male to enter the territory of the other would invite combat. These territories, surprisingly enough, seem to be maintained throughout the year.

Though the Northern Mockingbird really needs no description I may briefly state that it is robin sized but slimmer and has long legs and a long black tail, the outer feathers of which are white. The bird is gray above and white below, and the wings have a white "window" patch. When the wings are raised, they flash a great deal of black and white. The bird's habit of running across a lawn flitting its wings is a behavior that is not fully understood. Some people claim that it is done to scare up winged insects. Others contend that it is done by an incubating or brooding parent, exercising its cramped wings. And still others would have us believe that it is without any significance whatever. None of these explanations appear to me to be wholly correct. I have often seen such performances in the nonbreeding season, and I have witnessed the action on the part of juvenile birds not long out of the nest. Moreover, I have failed to note that the wing flittering achieves any marked success in scaring up insects. Finally, with regard to the claim that it has no significance, I can only say that I doubt if any behavior pattern ever persists without a function, however slight. Thus, here is one of our commonest birds whose behavior is obviously in need of much more careful study—a study that could be made to advantage just outside one's front door.

Mockingbirds raise several broods, beginning nesting activities sometimes as early as February. The nest of sticks and small rootlets, lined with finer materials, contains from three to five greenish blue eggs, spotted or splotched with cinnamon or rufous. It is usually placed in a dense shrub or hedge and is seldom located far from a human dwelling.

The addition of the modifier Northern to the name of our mockingbird

---

Plate XXVIII Mimic Thrushes and True Thrushes

1. Northern Mockingbird (p. 466). 2. Gray Catbird (p. 466). 3. Brown Thrasher (p. 469). 4. American Robin (p. 472). 5. male Eastern Bluebird (p. 476). 6. Wood Thrush (p. 473). 7. Hermit Thrush (p. 474). 8. Veery (p. 475). 9. Gray-cheeked Thrush (p. 475). 10. Swainson's Thrush (p. 474).

1

2

3

4

5

6

7

8

9

10

R. E. Tucker

is required because other kinds of mockingbirds, such as the Tropical, Long-tailed, and Patagonian, occur in Middle and South America.

BROWN THRASHER   *Toxostoma rufum*   Pl. XXVIII; p. 469

No sound in the forest or in the dense shrubbery around our homes is more indicative of fall than the *wheeu* note that the Brown Thrasher begins to make again after its comparative silence in late summer. Although commonly but erroneously called the "brown thrush," this species is actually a "first cousin" of the mockingbirds, which it closely resembles except in color. The songs of the two seem almost identical except to those who know that the thrasher sings in spurts of two or three notes disrupted by slight pauses, whereas the mocker's song is delivered without pause. Neither does the thrasher imitate other birds to any noticeable extent. The color of the upperparts of the Brown Thrasher is a rich brown, that of the underparts buffy, heavily streaked with dusky—not spotted as in the case of our true thrushes.

Brown Thrashers are abundant permanent residents throughout the state, and in winter Louisiana is the home for many northern members of the species that come south to escape the cold weather and to find adequate

Brown Thrasher Surveys Four Hungry Mouths

ALLAN D. CRUICKSHANK

food. The rather bulky nest of the thrasher is made of sticks and rootlets, lined with finer materials. The three to six eggs are bluish or grayish white, sprinkled with brown or rufous.

CURVE-BILLED THRASHER *Toxostoma curvirostre*   Pl. XLI

The first record of this western species for Louisiana was that of a bird seen by John P. Gee at Hackberry on August 26, 1958. Gee reported that when he first located the bird it was in plain view at close range but later, when he attempted to collect it, the bird proved to be exceedingly elusive even though he saw it repeatedly throughout a three-hour chase. Although I have never had the slightest doubt concerning the authenticity of Gee's identification, I nevertheless in earlier editions of this book placed the species on the list of hypothetical occurrences, pending the collecting of at least one specimen within our borders. Such is now available. On December 7, 1963, John J. Morony obtained a female on the east end of Willow Island, several miles east of Cameron. Also, on December 31, 1972, one was observed by a host of ornithologists along the road leading to the west jetties at the mouth of Calcasieu Pass.

The Curve-billed Thrasher is easily recognized by its robin size, grayish coloration, faintly spotted breast, narrow wing bars, strongly curved bill, and orange eyes. It occurs normally from southern Texas to eastern and south-central Mexico.

SAGE THRASHER *Oreoscoptes montanus*   Fig. 125

Five individuals of this western, desert species were discovered and one was collected on January 2, 1926, near the Gulf beach in Cameron Parish. There were no other records for the state until December 1, 1957, when John P. Gee and Sidney A. Gauthreaux saw one near Venice. Then, on December 29 and 30, 1962, Ava R. Tabor, Electa Levi, Gauthreaux, and others saw the species in a dooryard in the town of Hackberry, and on June 26, 1963, Lovett E. Williams and Mac Myers found it on North Island in the Chandeleurs. Finally, on November 8, 1964, and again in Cameron Parish, near the town of Cameron, Joel Cracraft, in company with Gauthreaux and A. W. Palmisano, collected a specimen.

The fact that as many as five Sage Thrashers once appeared simultaneously at the same place on the Louisiana coast in midwinter suggests that

Figure 125   Sage Thrasher.

a small flock of these birds was moving southward from the species' Great Plains breeding grounds in the migratory period of the previous fall and·was displaced eastward from a regular route that normally would have carried them into southern Texas or even into Mexico. Moreover, since the birds were found close to the shores of the Gulf of Mexico, this large body of water had apparently once again, as it seems so often to have done in the past, imposed a barrier to further southward movement. In Cameron Parish, where the chenieres are studded with acacia, cacti, and other examples of a more western flora, the habitat is not unattractive to western birds that fortuitously find their way into the region, and hardly a winter goes by that several distinctly western species are not found there.

The Sage Thrasher resembles a short-tailed Northern Mockingbird with a heavily streaked breast and without prominent white patches in the wings. The white in its tail is confined to spots on the tips of the feathers, while in the Northern Mockingbird the entire outer tail feathers are white.

The
True Thrush
Family
Turdidae

When we say the word *thrush*, we generally think of a spotted-breasted, brown-backed denizen of dark, shaded woods, and, indeed, most of the thrushes in Louisiana do conform to this pattern. Over the world as a whole, however, a high proportion of the members of the family are without spots as adults and are, like our own Eastern Bluebird and American Robin, inhabitants of open country. But even the plain-breasted thrushes disclose their relationships by having the breast heavily spotted in the juvenal plumage.

AMERICAN ROBIN   *Turdus migratorius*   Pl. XXVIII

Our robin got its name from the early settlers who were reminded by it of the European Robin or "robin redbreast." Our bird, however, is much larger, and the breast is a rusty red, rather than a pale orange-red as in the European bird. Because of the great mass migrations that our bird performs, it would have been better if another of its old names, the "migratory thrush," had been retained instead of American Robin.

The species breeds commonly in parts of northern Louisiana, notably in the larger towns from Alexandria northward. At Baton Rouge and New Orleans it is also present in summer in small to moderate numbers, the breeding pairs there being restricted to cemeteries or to better residential sections where there are spacious lawns and numerous shade trees. In winter, migrants from the North inundate the state, and the species is abundant almost everywhere. It arrives in numbers in mid-October and does not begin to depart until early March. In the first half of the winter robins are most numerous in the wooded swamps, but by the time January arrives they begin to enter the cities and towns to feed on lawns and golf courses.

The song, which is given mainly on the breeding grounds, is a loud carol made up of short phrases of two or three notes. The call is a *chuck, chuck.*

The robin builds its nest in a variety of situations but most often places it in a tree crotch or on a horizontal limb. The structure is made up of sticks and grasses plastered together with mud and lined with fine, soft materials. The three to five eggs, as one would naturally guess, are robin's-egg blue in color. An exceptionally early breeding record for anywhere in the United States was a nest found by Earl R. Smith on Jefferson Avenue in New Orleans on February 10, 1953, that contained nearly fully fledged young.

WOOD THRUSH *Hylocichla mustelina* Pl. XXVIII

The Wood Thrush is a common summer resident in all parts of the state, except some of the coastal areas. It is found in secluded woods and in residential sections of our cities and towns. The song is a beautiful flutelike carol that is surely one of the most restful sounds to which one can listen, especially when heard in the quiet of the evening between sundown and the passing of twilight. Like most thrushes, the Wood Thrush prefers dense shade, and, although we may hear its song or its sharp call note, *quirk*, we usually have to search for the performer. The bird feeds on insects or on berries and small fruits. The planting of red mulberry trees is a sure means of attracting not only this species but numerous other delightful songbirds.

The Wood Thrush is easily distinguished from other thrushes by its reddish brown head, which contrasts with its olive-brown back, and by the large size of the black spots on its breast. It usually arrives in Louisiana by the last week of March and remains until November. An occasional individual is found in the southern part of the state in winter, but I know of no place where it is of regular annual occurrence at that season.

The nest of the Wood Thrush is made of sticks plastered together with mud and almost invariably interspersed with pieces of old newspaper or rags. The three to five eggs are greenish blue and are almost indistinguishable from those of the American Robin.

HERMIT THRUSH *Catharus guttatus* Pl. XXVIII

The Hermit Thrush breeds in the great woods of the North and the high mountain forests of the West and comes to us only after the leaves have begun to fall. It is the only member of its genus that winters regularly and abundantly in the United States; the others go to the tropics, some of them to northern South America or even as far as Argentina and Peru. None of this group of thrushes is well marked, except the Wood Thrush, which has large black spots on its underparts. If, however, the observer can manage to get a clear view of the Hermit Thrush in fairly good light, it can be separated from its relatives by its reddish brown tail, which contrasts with an olive-gray or brownish olive back. All thrushes of this group have the habit of sometimes nervously flitting the wings and of jerking the tail upward above the horizontal and then slowly lowering it. The Hermit Thrush, however, moves the tail up and down so continually that the behavior is a good field mark.

One of the most delightful experiences I have ever had was that of camping on the top of the Guadalupe Mountains in western Texas, at over eight thousand feet elevation, and hearing the ethereal song of the Hermit Thrush at dawn and again at twilight. Frank M. Chapman says that its notes are not remarkable "for variety or volume, but in purity and sweetness of tone and exquisite modulation they are unequaled."

The species is a common winter resident throughout the state. It arrives in numbers in late October and does not depart until April, while occasionally individuals linger well into May.

SWAINSON'S THRUSH *Catharus ustulatus* Pl. XXVIII

This species is a fairly common spring and fall transient through Louisiana. Although occasionally it has appeared in late March, normally it does not arrive in numbers until the third week of April. The spring passage is usually completed by mid-May but infrequently it stays until the last days of the month. In fall, en route southward, it returns to Louisiana by the middle of September and sometimes lingers until well after the middle of November. It has been observed twice in late December. One was seen near Oak Ridge, in Morehouse Parish, on December 31, 1972, by D. T. Kee and others, and another was noted at Triumph, in Plaquemines Parish, on December 30, 1971, by R. D. Purrington.

The Swainson's Thrush is not easily separated from either the Hermit Thrush or the Gray-cheeked Thrush. From the former it differs in lacking a reddish tail, and from the latter it may be separated by its buffy eye-ring and its buffy cheeks.

A. A. Saunders, who was a specialist on bird songs, masterfully described the complicated notes and song pattern of the Swainson's Thrush as follows: "The song consists of phrases of eight to fourteen or fifteen notes each, all more or less connected and with liquid-consonant sounds between them. The quality is sweet and melodious, but not quite so clear as the Hermit Thrush's, and sometimes somewhat windy. Each phrase begins with a low note, and though all the notes are connected and about equal in time, the ones following this first note seem grouped in pairs. The second note of each pair is lower-pitched than the first, but each succeeding pair begins on a higher pitch than the last, so that the whole phrase rises regularly in pitch." In the Gray-cheeked Thrush the pitch is more even and the notes seem to be slurred. Both of these species and the Veery as well are not infrequently heard to sing as they pass through the state in spring although sometimes the song is a *sotto voce* performance rather than a full-voiced rendition.

GRAY-CHEEKED THRUSH *Catharus minimus* Pl. XXVIII

This species has almost the same habits in Louisiana as the Swainson's Thrush, but it appears to be slightly less numerous here. It has never been recorded in fall beyond October 29, whereas the Swainson's sometimes remains nearly a month longer. This is not particularly surprising, for even though the winter range of the Swainson's extends much farther south, all the way to Argentina, it also extends farther north, to southern Mexico, much nearer to Louisiana. The Gray-cheeked Thrush spends the winter in Colombia, Ecuador, Peru, Venezuela, and Guyana. The pale gray cheeks and the *lack of an eye-ring* are the best field marks of this species.

VEERY *Catharus fuscescens* Pl. XXVIII

The Veery is somewhat less difficult to identify than any of the three preceding species, which are all very similar, particularly in the grayish olive or brownish olive color of their backs. The Veery, in contrast, is a tawny-brown or light cinnamon-brown above. The throat is *faintly* spotted with the same color as the back, and the belly and *sides* are conspicuously whitish. The Wood Thrush has the sides heavily spotted, and the other thrushes have these parts more strongly washed with gray or brown.

The Veery, like the Swainson's and Gray-cheeked Thrushes, is a fairly common transient through Louisiana (March 31 to June 4, August 31 to October 29). It breeds much nearer to us than does either of these species. In the higher mountains of western North Carolina and northern Georgia it is common in summer, and there one can hear its pleasant melody of *whee'-o* or *whee'-you* notes that rate it among the most gifted of avian songsters. This vocal performance has a peculiar echoing double quality that makes the bird sound as if it were singing from the bottom of a well.

EASTERN BLUEBIRD *Sialia sialis* Pl. XXVIII

Bluebirds do not much remind us of thrushes; their color is not thrushlike; they are birds of the open spaces instead of dark secluded woods; and, unlike our other thrushes, they build a nest in a cavity in a tree or fence post or sometimes in a birdhouse. But the proof that they are members of the True Thrush family lies in their anatomical characteristics and the fact that the young are spotted like a typical thrush.

The Eastern Bluebird is a fairly abundant permanent resident, particularly numerous in winter, when northern populations come south to escape the cold and to find their staple food of insects. Despite the statewide abundance of the species in winter, I have a friend who never seems to see one except in spring, whereupon he comes up each year with the exclamation, "Spring must be here; the bluebirds are back!" The truth is that they have never left!

The call of the Eastern Bluebird is a soft, cheery *chur-wee*. The eggs are a pale bluish color, although sometimes they may be nearly white.

As startling as the statement may seem, our bluebird is *not* really blue, but brown! Blue pigment does not exist in feathers. Birds have pigments that are actually red, yellow, and a variety of other colors, but not blue. Hence, technically there is no such thing as an Eastern *Blue*bird, a *Blue* Jay, or a Great *Blue* Heron. We perceive blue color in these birds simply because the minute physical structures in the feathers break up white light striking them at an angle and refract certain components that yield blue color. This fact can be convincingly verified by viewing a blue feather through a microscope admitting only transmitted light from the stage mirror. We then see only a dense brown color. Another way is to observe an Eastern Bluebird or Blue Jay while looking as nearly toward the sun as possible. Neither bird is then blue but is instead black. A Northern Cardinal in the same position is red, and a Yellow Warbler is yellow, since red and yellow pigments are actually present. To perceive them we do not have to depend on a particular angle of reflected light.

MOUNTAIN BLUEBIRD   *Sialia currucoides*   Pl. XLI

This western bluebird has been observed only twice in Louisiana. On January 28, 1968, Kenneth P. Able obtained a female three miles southwest of Alford, in West Baton Rouge Parish, and on February 14, 1970, Robert J. Newman and others observed one five miles north of New Roads on the river road. The latter record was of an adult male perched on a fence post and studied at leisure in good light at a distance of 30 feet through binoculars. The sky blue plumage of the male that lacks any rusty brown, such as that of the throat and breast of both the male and female Eastern Bluebird, is diagnostic. The female possesses a gray breast and does not exhibit the hunched posture characteristic of the Eastern Bluebird. The species breeds in Alaska south to California and New Mexico, and it normally winters in northern Mexico.

NORTHERN WHEATEAR   *Oenanthe oenanthe*   Fig. 126

A single Northern Wheatear captured near New Orleans on September 12, 1888, supplies the only record for this species in Louisiana and, as a matter of fact, one of the few records for the bird anywhere south of Canada. The specimen, taken by Professor George E. Beyer, proved to be identical with examples of the population of the species that breeds in Iceland and Greenland, west to Ellesmere Land, in our North American Arctic Zone.

Figure 126   Northern Wheatear.

Wheatears of this general region normally migrate through England and France to winter in West Africa, and, in order for one to appear in Louisiana, an occasional bird must go astray.

The Northern Wheatear is about the size of an Eastern Bluebird, and it possesses a striking color pattern—upperparts light gray; cheeks and wings black; the rump and basal two-thirds of the tail white with the end black, tipped with buffy; underparts buffy. As it flits over open ground it bobs and jerks its tail and utters a sharp *chack*.

The Old World Warbler Family
Sylviidae

This diverse family comprises over 300 species, but of these only 15 occur in the Western Hemisphere—2 kinglets, 2 willow warblers, the Grasshopper Warbler (in Alaska only), and 10 gnatcatchers (which perhaps are not properly classified in this family at all). The hundreds of remaining species are confined to the Eastern Hemisphere. Sylviids are in many ways the counterpart of our own large family of warblers, the Parulidae, which in turn fails entirely to reach the Old World except for one minor intrusion into extreme eastern Siberia. The virtually complete mutual exclusion of each of these families from the range of the other provides good argument for zoogeographers who wish to consider the Palearctic Realm (including Europe, North Africa, and that part of Asia west of the Indus River and north of the Himalayas) separate from the Nearctic Realm (North America south to the edge of the Mexican Plateau). The continental faunas of these two realms are, to be sure, in many ways similar—so much so that they all might be considered as parts of a single circumpolar zoogeographical realm, the Holoarctic. But the peculiarities of the several families characteristic of each are striking, as in the case of the families Sylviidae and Parulidae, not to mention the contrast of the Old World Flycatchers (Muscicapidae) versus the Tyrant Flycatchers (Tyrannidae), or the Old World Orioles (Oriolidae) versus our own peculiar family of orioles and blackbirds (Icteridae).

As noted above, the gnatcatchers are of uncertain systematic position. Until recently most ornithologists regarded them as aberrant members of the family Sylviidae, but now they are considered by certain authorities to be members of the Muscicapidae, the Old World Flycatchers. As such, they would become the only New World representative of that large and diverse group of birds, which ranges throughout Europe, Asia, and Africa but which has been eminently unsuccessful in reaching the Western Hemisphere. But a decision as to the true familial affinities of the gnatcatchers must await the outcome of much additional study.

BLUE-GRAY GNATCATCHER *Polioptila caerulea* Pl. XXIX; p. 479

This diminutive bird, whose body is not much larger than a thimble, is bluish gray in color, as the name states. Its long tail, though, is black except for the outer feathers, which are white. Adult males have a thin black line over each eye, the lines joining at the base of the bill. The Blue-gray Gnatcatcher has been described as a miniature replica of our mockingbird. This characterization is, however, not precisely correct, for the mockingbird is not nearly so bluish gray in color, lacks the black lines on the head, and, of course, differs

Blue-gray Gnatcatcher at Nest

SAMUEL A. GRIMES

in various other respects. Nevertheless, one cannot look at a Blue-gray Gnat-catcher without being reminded of this striking superficial resemblance.

The species is a common summer resident from early March to late October throughout Louisiana, particularly where there are oak trees. It generally, but not always, deserts north Louisiana in late fall, but in the southern part of the state a few can be found in winter on nearly any day one spends in the field.

The nest is a beautifully fabricated structure that is covered with lichens and placed astride a horizontal limb, with which it blends so perfectly that it is almost impossible to locate unless one follows the bird to it (see photograph on p. 479). The four or five bluish white eggs are thickly spotted with cinnamon-brown or umber.

GOLDEN-CROWNED KINGLET   *Regulus satrapa*   Pl. XXIX

This and the following species are among the smallest birds in North America. Both breed in the far-northern woods, visiting us only in winter. The Golden-crowned Kinglet is greenish above and grayish white below and can be distinguished easily from the following species by the white line over the eye, bordered above by black. The males have the center of the crown golden orange, surrounded by yellow; the females possess only yellow in the crown. Two very closely related species occur in Europe, where they are called the Firecrest and the Goldcrest.

The note of the Golden-crowned Kinglet is a high-pitched, almost supersonic, *ti-ti*. Indeed, there are many people who cannot hear it at all. Unless I consciously listen for it, I likewise do not always hear it.

The species is rather consistently common in winter in north Louisiana, but in some years it is rare in the lower half of the state. The first arrivals reach us in mid-October, rarely somewhat earlier, and by the middle of April the species is usually gone. Kinglets travel through the forest in small bands, generally in close proximity to a group of chickadees, titmice, or other small denizens of our winter woodlands.

RUBY-CROWNED KINGLET   *Regulus calendula*   Pl. XXIX

The Ruby-crowned Kinglet is almost ubiquitous in Louisiana in winter. In our 49,000 square miles of land there must be, on the average, at least one to every 25 acres. This is surely a conservative estimate and indicates a winter population in Louisiana of over one million Ruby-crowned Kinglets. And since each of these tiny sprites spends nearly its entire time catching and eating minute insects one after another, just think of the millions that all of them consume each day!

The Ruby-crowned Kinglet differs from the Golden-crowned mainly in the color of the crest. In the male the crest is a brilliant red (lacking in the female), but, unfortunately, except when the bird is alarmed, or in spring just before it heads northward, the crest is kept concealed. The conspicuous white *eye-ring* is diagnostic, since the Golden-crowned Kinglet has a *white line* over the eye, bordered above with black. The Ruby-crowned Kinglet arrives as early as late September and sometimes lingers until early May. The song is a jumbled, repetitious series of soft, pleasing sounds that are seldom heard this far south except in spring just before the birds start northward. The call note, however, is a chatter or grating sound that is an excellent aid to field identification.

The Wagtail Family

Motacillidae

The Wagtail family, like the two preceding families, is predominantly Old World in distribution. Six species, four pipits and two wagtails, occur in the continental U.S., and the Water Pipit is but a geographical variant of a species that is found across northern Europe and Asia. The pipits are birds of open shortgrass fields and lakeshores. Instead of hopping over the ground, like most small birds, they walk, and in doing so they constantly bob the tail up and down. The outer tail feathers are white and are conspicuously flashed when the flocks arise to take flight. In the latter regard, as well as in several other features of their superficial appearance, they somewhat resemble the Vesper Sparrow and the longspurs, but their habits of walking and of wagging their tails are diagnostic.

WATER PIPIT *Anthus spinoletta*   Fig. 127

The Water Pipit is one of our commonest winter birds. It arrives in the state in early October, and from the first of November until late March, sometimes much later, it is abundant in almost every place where there is open ground. Favorite haunts are golf courses, plowed fields, levees, airstrips, or any other open expanse, such as a lakeshore, the Gulf beach, a spoil bank through the coastal marsh, or even the edges of our heavily traveled highways. All these habitats are in sharp contrast to its preferences in summer, when it retreats to the Arctic Zone and to alpine situations above tree line on the high peaks of the Rockies.

In winter the species goes in flocks numbering from a few individuals up to 50 or more, and when alarmed into flight the whole group ascends, usually circling widely in a series of bounding undulations, only to come back near to its point of departure. The Water Pipit has a weak but distinctive note, a simple *wit-wit* or *wit-wit-wit-wit*, which, once learned, serves to identify it as it flies overhead, whether or not the bird is actually seen. It is a plain-colored, brownish species, with streaked, buffy underparts, that is quite nondescript and is thus similar to some of the sparrows and longspurs. But the combination of its white outer tail feathers, thin bill, slender form, bobbing tail, peculiar call notes, and habit of walking instead of hopping, separates it from everything else with which it can be confused—except the Sprague's Pipit, which is discussed in the following account.

RET

Figure 127   (1) Horned Lark; (2) Sprague's Pipit; (3) Water Pipit.

SPRAGUE'S PIPIT *Anthus spragueii* Fig. 127

This species of pipit is rather rare in Louisiana, except in certain localities in the western part of the state. On the prairies in Cameron Parish it is noted with fair regularity, and it is not infrequently observed near Shreveport. It differs from the Water Pipit in its slightly smaller size, its yellow instead of dusky legs, its paler but streaked instead of plain upperparts, and its white or only slightly buffy underparts, which are faintly streaked on the upper breast but not elsewhere. Unlike the preceding species, it seldom wags its tail. The call is a hard, sharply enunciated *cleep*, frequently doubled, occasionally tripled, and totally unlike the note given by the Water Pipit.

The present species sometimes arrives in Louisiana in September but ordinarily is not seen until October. Occasionally one will linger until the last week of April. Grassy areas, such as pastures and airfields, are its preferred habitat. It seldom occurs in flocks like the Water Pipit, being more frequently encountered singly or in pairs.

The Waxwing Family
Bombycillidae

[BOHEMIAN WAXWING *Bombycilla garrulus*]

This boreal species seldom reaches as far south as the latitude of Louisiana. A single individual, however, was observed by Eugene W. Wilhelm, Jr., near the Louisiana State University campus on January 6 and 7, 1960. It was found in a large flock of Cedar Waxwings, with which it was compared at close range. Although the brown instead of yellow under tail feathers, the distinctive white wing patches, and the much larger size were clearly noted by the competent observer, the species probably should not be formally added to the state list without at least one record supported by a preserved specimen.

CEDAR WAXWING   *Bombycilla cedrorum*   Pl. XXIX

In no part of the world is there what we might term a "slicker, trimmer" bird than the "cedarbird." It is about the size of an Eastern Bluebird, and its general color is a rich cinnamon-brown. The belly and a band across the end of the tail are yellow. The forehead, the chin, and a line through the eye are a velvety black. The secondaries have tiny, seedlike structures on their tips that look exactly like solidified drops of bright red sealing wax. The function of these peculiar structures, if they have any function, is unknown. But, the thing that really lends distinction to the waxwing is its long crest or topknot.

These elegant birds have been seen in Louisiana as early in the fall as late September, but not until late November do they appear in numbers and frequently not until mid-January are they overly abundant. By the end of March they virtually inundate the entire state, but nowhere are they more numerous than in our cities, where they come to eat the ripe pyracantha, camphor, and ligustrum berries. The flocks fly in compact groups from one food tree to another, wheeling and turning in unison and all the while uttering a high-pitched, lisping note. When a flock alights to rest in the top of a tree, the crests are held erect and all the birds generally face the same way. Flocks often remain in the state until well into May, and 25 were once observed in Shreveport on the extremely late date of June 18.

Sometimes Cedar Waxwings eat so many berries at a time that digestion must be accomplished rapidly in order to make room for the continuous intake into the esophagus and stomach. Occasionally a bird is found prostrate on the ground, seemingly "drunk" from having consumed too much berry juice. But I am inclined to think that another explanation is more plausible. These stupefied birds always have their throats packed beyond capacity with berries or fruit, which surely must exert undue pressure on the adjacent blood vessels. The possibility exists that the pressure against the internal

---

Plate XXIX   Vireos and Some of Their Allies

1. Solitary Vireo (p. 492). 2. Yellow-throated Vireo (p. 492). 3. White-eyed Vireo (p. 490). 4. Red-eyed Vireo (p. 494). 5. Warbling Vireo (p. 496). 6. Philadelphia Vireo (p. 495). 7. Bell's Vireo (p. 490). 8. Cedar Waxwing (p. 484). 9. Loggerhead Shrike (p. 485). 10. Blue-gray Gnatcatcher (p. 479). 11. Golden-crowned Kinglet (p. 480), male in foreground, female behind.   12. male Ruby-crowned Kinglet (p. 480).

Robert E Tucker

carotid artery, which carries blood to the brain, causes a temporary blackout until digestive action allows some of the food in the esophagus to move down into the stomach and thereby relieve the congestion.

The Shrike Family
Laniidae

LOGGERHEAD SHRIKE   *Lanius ludovicianus*   Pl. XXIX; p. 485

The terms "butcher bird," "French mockingbird," or "catbird" instead of Loggerhead Shrike would probably be more often recognized in Louisiana as the name for this species. It is an abundant and conspicuous bird that is no-

The Loggerhead Shrike Sometimes Lays Six Eggs

SAMUEL A. GRIMES

where more likely to be seen than on a telephone wire. The bill is sharply hooked and possesses a supplementary "tooth," rendering it especially useful for tearing apart the insects, small mammals, and sometimes sparrow-sized birds that the shrike is able to catch. The feet, on the other hand, are weak and nonraptorial. Consequently a most peculiar behavior on the part of the species has evolved. It impales its prey on a thorn and proceeds to dismember it without the need for talons. A modern innovation is for the shrike to hook its prey on a barbed-wire fence.

The breeding shrike population in Louisiana is probably entirely sedentary, but elsewhere the bird must be at least partially migratory, for we get an occasional large, pale, white-rumped individual here in winter that is typical of the breeding populations of the Great Plains region. Shrikes are modestly attired, gray above and white below, with a broad black line through the eye and with the wings and tail largely black. The outer tail feathers are broadly tipped with white, and the wing has a small white patch in the secondaries. Beginners sometimes confuse the shrike with a mockingbird, but the massive head of the shrike, its black facial markings, and its largely black wings are excellent points of difference. Also, the shrike has a shorter tail than does a mockingbird. When it flies from the top of one tree to the top of another, it nearly always swoops low to the ground—a performance which the French call the *révérence*, or the "curtsy." The flight of a mockingbird is straight-away on the level.

Shrikes have a variety of querulous, rather nonmusical notes, one of which has a mewing quality that accounts for the name "catbird." The nest is a bulky structure made up of moderately large sticks on the outside and fine grasses on the inside. It is placed in a thorny hedge or low tree, usually seven to ten feet above the ground. The three to six eggs are dull creamy white, heavily blotched with brown or lavender. The young are essentially like the adults in color except for a series of fine vermiculations on the breast.

Shrikes are members of a family that is abundantly represented by species in the Old World. Only two species, however, the Loggerhead and the Northern Shrikes, inhabit the Western Hemisphere.

The Starling Family
Sturnidae

EUROPEAN STARLING   *Sturnus vulgaris*   Fig. 128

A sad day in the history of this country occurred back in 1890, when a group of 60 European Starlings was introduced into New York City from Europe. From this shipment, and another of 40 liberated a year later, the millions of starlings now inhabiting the United States and Canada apparently have descended. The food habits of the European Starling are beneficial, for it feeds almost entirely on insects that it gets from the ground, but, unfortunately, it roosts and nests on the cornices of our buildings, which it literally "whitewashes" with its droppings. In Washington, D.C., alone it causes hundreds of thousands of dollars' damage each year in this regard, not to mention that it ruins the paint on cars parked under trees where it roosts.

The European Starling lays its four or five pale bluish or greenish white eggs in tree cavities and nesting boxes. This leads to one of the worst indictments against it—the fact that it drives away native songbirds and usurps the nesting cavities of such birds as the Red-headed Woodpecker. This beautiful woodpecker is now near extirpation in some sections of the eastern United States, and right here in Louisiana it is becoming alarmingly scarce in certain areas. For instance, at Baton Rouge, several dead snags in City Park and University lakes, which for years produced brood after brood of Red-headed Woodpeckers, are now completely taken over by European Starlings, and the woodpecker has disappeared from the neighborhood. Ironically, the latter species, amply equipped by nature to drill and excavate its own nest cavity, does so only to be harassed and heckled into abandoning it to the overbearing European Starling, which itself is incapable of making the hole. Naturally, if any bird fails to breed and to produce a complement of young each year, it cannot offset the inroads of its natural enemies and the other decimating factors operating against it. Consequently, a species such

Figure 128 European Starling: unworn fall plumage on left; worn spring plumage on right.

as the Red-headed Woodpecker can in a very few years disappear from a wide area of its range. Unfortunately there is nothing much that man can do about the ever-increasing starling. It is here to stay, and our only hope is that some disease or parasite peculiar to the species will intervene in our behalf.

The European Starling was rare in Louisiana until the winters of 1930–1931 and 1931–1932, when several small flocks were seen. Then, in the winter of 1932–1933, great hordes of them arrived. Thousands of individuals covered the parade ground on the Louisiana State University campus and similar situations elsewhere. Each winter thereafter larger and larger flocks appeared, but at first they would disappear in early spring. As late as 1937 there were but very few records of nesting and then only of isolated pairs. Finally, in the summer of 1938, a sizable number bred in downtown Baton Rouge and in the vicinity of LSU. Since then the summer population has increased steadily until now starlings are seen in numbers throughout the year in nearly every town in the state.

The European Starling is not an unattractive bird. In breeding plumage the males and females alike are glossy black with metallic purple and green reflecting from their bodies in good light. In the nesting season, the bill turns bright yellow, and the legs are a dull red. In fresh fall plumage the bird appears grayish at a distance because each feather is tipped with grayish white or buffy, and it is only by the wearing off of these light tips that the bird assumes its black, iridescent appearance. The juvenal plumage, in which the young leave the nest, is dull brownish, totally unlike that of the parents. But this dress is lost by a postjuvenal molt in September that puts the young birds in their first winter plumage, which is indistinguishable from that of the older birds. The European Starling walks instead of hops, and, unlike the blackbirds, which it resembles, it has a bill that is not robust or conical but long and rather flat. The tail is relatively short, giving the bird the shape of an Eastern Meadowlark. When in flight, it frequently glides on out-stretched wings. Starlings have a series of musical whistles and still other notes that are coarse and rattling. A frequently uttered sound is something suggesting the syllables *p-e-e-u-u*. They are accomplished mimics, frequently imitating the call of the Bobwhite.

The family is fairly well distributed through Europe, Asia, and Africa. Although absent from Australia and New Guinea, it is represented in the Philippines and on many of the islands of the Southwest Pacific.

The Vireo Family
Vireonidae

Vireos are endemic to the New World; that is, they are found nowhere else. They reside mainly in wooded regions, although a few species prefer low, brushy areas. They resemble the wood-warblers (Parulidae), but are more deliberate in their movements and their songs are generally less musical and less complicated. Structurally the vireos are in some respects intermediate between the shrikes and the wood-warblers, having, as they do, slightly hooked instead of pointed bills and heads that are rather large like those of the shrikes. Their plumages are for the most part drab and unspectacular, whereas those of the wood-warblers are usually well marked and in many instances resplendent.

WHITE-EYED VIREO   *Vireo griseus*   Pl. XXIX; p. 491

This is one of our most abundant birds in summer, when it is present in nearly every thicket in the state, from the coastal ridges to the border of Arkansas. It is yellowish green above and white below, except for the flanks, which are yellow, and it possesses two very distinct creamy white wing bars. A prominent yellow ring around the eye and a yellow line from the eye to the bill are two points that clearly separate it from the somewhat similar Bell's Vireo (see next account). The iris in the adult is white, as the name implies, but in young birds it is brown. The song is a complicated jumble of notes that in some renditions suggests the words "chip-fell-off-the-white-oak."

White-eyed Vireos build their pensile nests in bushes, usually in some dense growth. The three to five eggs are white with tiny specks of black or brown. A few of these birds are nearly always to be found in southern Louisiana in winter, but they are never common until the spring migrants begin to arrive in numbers in mid-March. From that time until late October the species is encountered frequently.

BELL'S VIREO   *Vireo bellii*   Pl. XXIX

The Bell's Vireo is extremely rare in Louisiana, except in the northwestern part of the state, where painstaking search by Horace H. Jeter of Shreveport has resulted in the discovery of quite a few breeding pairs. Jeter found the species in a habitat of willow and shrubs in the bottomlands of the Red River. Nowhere else in Louisiana is it known with certainty to breed, and there are few records of it in migration. It has been seen as early as March 18 and as late as September 11, with isolated records in November, December, and January. A single Bell's Vireo that I collected in the salt cedars (*Tamarix*) near the Gulf beach in southwestern Louisiana on December 29, 1952, one seen on the Sabine Christmas Bird Count on December 30, 1972, by Ronald J. Stein, and another collected by Ralph Cambre at Reserve on January 17, 1959, are, I believe, the only wintering individuals ever found in the United States.

The Bell's Vireo is a nondescript little bird, resembling the White-eyed Vireo but having dark-colored eyes. Instead of possessing a yellow eye-ring and yellow lores, it has only a faint, white line, which extends around the top of the eye and thence to the bill. The flanks, although not nearly as yellow as those of the White-eyed Vireo, are nevertheless lightly washed

White-eyed Vireo Inspects Its Pensile Nest

with that color. Its white wing bars separate it from the Warbling Vireo, which it also resembles. Roger T. Peterson describes the song as a *cheedle, cheedle, chee? cheedle, cheedle, chew!*

Although Jeter found the Bell's Vireo spending the better part of its time in willow trees, its hanging, cup-shaped nest was in his experience always suspended between two horizontal limbs of another plant. Six out of the seven nests he found were between three and five feet above the ground, three being in the marsh-elder (*Baccharis*) and one each in the blackhaw (*Viburnum*), sumac (*Rhus*), and persimmon (*Diospyros*). The seventh nest was at a height of 12 feet or so in a cottonwood (*Populus*). The contents of five of the seven nests were examined. Three contained complete clutches of four vireo eggs, two contained clutches of three vireo eggs plus one Brown-headed Cowbird egg, and both of these nests were abandoned. The eggs are practically indistinguishable from those of the White-eyed Vireo.

YELLOW-THROATED VIREO   *Vireo flavifrons*   Pl. XXIX

This vireo is a common summer resident throughout the part of Louisiana lying north of the coastal marshes. It normally arrives in the first or second week of March, but at least five records in December, January, and February are available from the southern part of the state. It usually remains until late October, but, as just noted, it has been seen in winter. The song is a simple but pleasant-sounding phrase, "sweetie, come here!" It is repeated over and over, but not nearly so frequently as the notes of the Red-eyed Vireo, which are similar. The greenish yellow head and back and *bright yellow throat and breast*, which contrast with the white belly, distinguish this species from other vireos at a glance. In addition it has a conspicuous yellow eye-ring and yellow lores, along with the prominent white wing bars. The Philadelphia Vireo, which lacks wing bars, is yellow below, but the shade of yellow is radically different, being not nearly so intense, and the top of the head is gray, bordered with a white eyeline.

SOLITARY VIREO   *Vireo solitarius*   Pl. XXIX

The Solitary Vireo is a northern species that occurs in Louisiana only as a winter resident. Aside from two anomalous August records and a few scattered records in September, its appearance in fall is in early October, and the latest date in spring is May 5. Although this vireo can be encountered almost anywhere in the wooded sections of the state in winter, it is particularly common at that season in the southern part of the state. In the northern parishes its is decidedly uncommon even though a few can usually be found during the cold months. When alarmed, it gives a scolding *churrr* that helps one locate it as it moves deliberately through the treetops or occasionally through a low myrtle thicket.

The species is easily identified by the contrast between its bluish gray head and its green back, by its conspicuous white eye-ring and white lores, and by its immaculate white throat, breast, and belly. There is a wash of yellow or yellowish green on the sides and flanks. It has two white wing bars, but these are of little need as field marks, since the other plumage characteristics are more diagnostic.

BLACK-WHISKERED VIREO   *Vireo altiloquus*   Fig. 129

Although this species was until fairly recently considered only accidental in Louisiana, it now appears to be of regular annual occurrence in the extreme southern part of the state and may actually nest casually in certain coastal situations. It has been observed on at least a dozen dates in Cameron Parish in spring, as well as on Grand Isle and Grand Terre Island. The dates range from March 18 to May 4. Particularly exciting, though, was the discovery by a host of observers on June 19 and July 4, 1971, of two presumptively mated pairs singing on the Delta National Wildlife Refuge, near the mouth of the Mississippi River. The four Black-whiskered Vireos observed on these occasions appeared to be birds on their nesting territories. Although one of the birds repeatedly returned to the same tree, search for a nest was futile. On July 1 and 2, 1973, the same area was combed, but no Black-whiskered Vireos were found. Admittedly, though, the opposite bank of the Mississippi River contains much suitable habitat that has not as yet been carefully investigated.

The frequency with which the species is now known to occur along the Louisiana coast in spring, and the fact that it is also known from Galveston Island to the west and on Dauphin Island and at Pensacola to the east, may be attributable in many cases to strong easterly winds displacing migrants over the Gulf of Mexico that are actually bound for southern Florida, where the species is a regular summer resident. A few degrees shift in course would cause migrants to miss the tip of Florida and the Keys and

LOUISIANA BIRDS

Figure 129   Black-whiskered Vireo (left) and Red-eyed Vireo (right).

thereby commit these migrants to a trans-Gulf crossing with a landfall taking place anywhere on the northern Gulf Coast.

The only records for the species in the state outside the extreme dates mentioned above are of one observed by Sidney A. Gauthreaux and Mary Lewis in City Park in New Orleans on August 29, 1959, and of one collected on the eastern outskirts of New Orleans on August 17, 1963, by A. W. Palmisano. Its presence in these localities on these two dates is puzzling, since New Orleans is so far removed from the kinds of habitat with which we associate the species.

The Black-whiskered Vireo is very similar to the Red-eyed Vireo except that it possesses a noticeably larger bill and has the two thin, black streaks or "mustache" marks on either side of the chin.

RED-EYED VIREO   *Vireo olivaceus*   Pl. XXIX; Fig. 129

This abundant summer resident is to be found virtually everywhere in the hardwood section of the state, arriving in the last half of March and staying until the last of October. Only casually does one remain into November, and but one winter record is available, a bird seen and carefully studied at Venice on January 3, 1965, by Buford Myers and others. On some days during the main periods of migration, in April and again in September and early October, the woods seem literally filled with Red-eyed Vireos. No less than a hundred can often be counted in the confines of a few acres. In spring and early summer the song of the Red-eye is heard from dawn to late afternoon, being repeated over and over again, sometimes with hardly any pause. To me the bird sounds as if it is saying, "Here I am. Where are you?"

In addition to having a distinctive song, the species is also recognized by the bluish gray on top of the head, bordered on each side by a black line beneath which a broad white line extends *over the eye* down to the bill. There are *no wing bars* and the underparts are almost pure white. The red eye cannot be seen in the field and is therefore of no value as an aid in field identification.

The small pensile nest is suspended in a fork anywhere from 5 to 40 feet up, usually in an oak or sweetgum tree. The three or four eggs are white except for a few tiny blackish spots around the larger end.

PHILADELPHIA VIREO *Vireo philadelphicus* Pl. XXIX

Some ornithologists have expressed concern because the Philadelphia Vireo is quite rare in Philadelphia and for this reason think the name should be changed, but all this seems to me to be a matter of small moment. After all, a name is just a name, and this one commemorates an interesting bit of history, for this bird remained unknown to science until as late as 1851, when the famous naturalist John Cassin secured the first specimen in one of the most populous sections of the country, at Philadelphia.

With us the Philadelphia Vireo is a rare spring but very common fall transient. It appears infrequently in late March and during April and May, along with the waves of warblers that arrive in Louisiana at that time, but by the last week of August it returns in numbers and can be seen almost daily through the third week of October, sometimes to the second week of November, at least in the southern sections of the state. I have found it nowhere more numerous than in the willows along the Mississippi River near Baton Rouge in autumn. Only twice has it been seen in winter, once at Johnsons Bayou, in Cameron Parish, on December 3, 1960, and the other time at Buras, in Plaquemines Parish, on February 5, 1961 (specimen collected).

The Philadelphia Vireo has a faint white eye stripe but no wing bars, and it is grayish green above except for the top of the head, which is gray. Below it is mostly very pale yellow. Both the Philadelphia Vireo and some fall examples of the Warbling Vireo are yellow and white below, but in the Philadelphia the yellow is overwhelmingly predominant, being particularly evident on the chest, whereas in the Warbling Vireo the white predominates and the chest is never yellow. The Yellow-throated Vireo has the throat and breast intensely yellow, and, in addition, possesses a prominent yellow eyering and white wing bars.

WARBLING VIREO *Vireo gilvus* Pl. XXIX

The Warbling Vireo is the plainest member of the genus in Louisiana. Most examples are simply greenish gray above and white below with no other markings except a white line over the eye; there are no wing bars. Most Warbling Vireos show a wash of yellow on the flanks but never approach the Philadelphia Vireo in the yellowness of the underparts. The Red-eyed Vireo is descriptively similar to the Warbling Vireo, but in life the two are quite distinct, since the Red-eye is somewhat larger and has the white eye stripe bordered above by black.

The favorite haunts of the Warbling Vireo are large trees along the banks of a river or a lake. It is particularly fond of cottonwood trees, although oaks and pecans are also frequented. The nest is pensile, like those of other vireos, and is located from 10 to 40 feet above the ground. The eggs are similar to those of the Red-eyed Vireo but smaller.

The song bears little or no resemblance to the songs of the other vireos. It consists of a jumble of warbling notes with a slight rising inflection toward the end. Although the refrain is not wholly displeasing to hear, I find it sometimes annoying, possibly because it lacks a smooth pattern and also because it is repeated so persistently and without pause or variation throughout the day.

The species usually arrives in Louisiana in early March but is not common until the first days of April. It departs rather soon after its nesting season, though an occasional bird may be seen as late as November 24.

The Wood-Warbler Family
Parulidae

This family is primarily North American, being virtually absent from the Old World, where it is replaced by the vast array of species making up the family Sylviidae. The Parulidae have been described as the "butterflies of the bird kingdom," in tribute to their diverse and spectacular color patterns. All except one of the 40 species that occur regularly in the eastern half of the United States also occur in Louisiana at one season or another. Fourteen species are definitely known to nest here, and two others almost certainly do so, although their nests have not yet been found. Many of the warblers are merely birds of passage, stopping here only en route to and from their breeding grounds in the North and their winter homes in the tropics. But in the brief period of their migration, warblers of both categories may be unbelievably numerous, particularly in spring on our coastal islands and chenieres, where they have just made a landfall after crossing the Gulf of Mexico. I have seen every tree and every bush in such places filled with warblers of dozens of species, and what a spectacle that is! The uninitiated would suppose that a storm had blown a host of *tropical* birds to our shores, not realizing that many of these gems of color nest in the trees of their yards or in some nearby wood.

The ability to find and identify the members of this family of birds poses a challenge to the ornithological neophyte. This would not be an easy task if we were confronted only with the spring plumages of the males, but there is the compounded difficulty of having to learn to recognize the females and the less well-marked fall plumages of the adults, both male and female, as well as the different-appearing young of the year, where again the sexes may be dissimilar. Careful study and observation are essential if one is to learn them all, both as to sex and age, as well as to season. Yet this is precisely what makes ornithology the intriguing subject that it is. It is laden with unlimited potentialities for providing one with an unending source of pleasure and fascination, as well as wholesome outdoor exercise and recreation.

The wood-warblers are extremely active little birds that seem continuously on the move in search of their food, which consists almost wholly of insects. They must find a tremendous number of tiny leafhoppers, plant lice, and other minute animals in order to fill their dietary requirements and thereby produce the energy to carry on their high rate of metabolism. In this quest they employ the technique of "rapid peering," as Joseph Grinnell once termed their habit of moving quickly one way and then another in order to see better as much surface area as possible from many angles. The system is much the same as the one we employ when we search the ground for a lost object, such as a golf ball. We rapidly zigzag back and forth, quickly looking one way then another. The lost object may then suddenly appear in plain sight before us when viewed from one particular angle. The warblers similarly, it would seem, detect their quarry, which might otherwise escape notice amid the leaves or in the cracks and crevices of a tree trunk. But whatever the device used by the energetic little birds they seem continually to be picking up objects in their small, pointed bills.

BLACK-AND-WHITE WARBLER *Mniotilta varia* Pl. XXX

The Black-and-white Warbler is just what its name suggests, a small bird that is streaked all over with black and white. The great early naturalists, John James Audubon and Alexander Wilson, called it the "black and white creeper," thereby alluding to its habit of snooping around all sides of a limb in its search for insects. Sometimes it works upside down on the underside of a bough, creeping one way and then another. Its distinctive black and white pattern renders it easily identifiable. The somewhat similar-appearing Blackpoll Warbler has a solid black cap (no white center stripe) and white cheek patches. The Black-throated Gray Warbler, a rare western visitor, likewise has a solid black cap and has an almost solid gray back. A small streaked black and white bird that creeps all over the limbs of a tree, poking its head around the underside of branches, is almost certain to be the Black-and-white Warbler. The song is an extremely high pitched *we-see* rapidly repeated four or five times.

The species is a common transient everywhere in the state and a fairly common summer resident in the oak forests in the northern two-thirds of the state. It arrives very early from its winter home, appearing sometimes in late February, and is largely gone by November, although a few sometimes remain throughout the winter in southern Louisiana. The four or five speckled eggs are laid in a nest that is usually placed on the ground at the base of a tree and is well concealed above by an arch of leaves or pine needles. Occasionally the nest is placed in a broken-off stump.

BACHMAN'S WARBLER *Vermivora bachmanii* Pl. XXX

The Bachman's Warbler is a species that is shrouded in considerable mystery. It first became known to science in July 1833, when Dr. John Bachman shot two individuals and observed several more, all within a short distance of Charleston, South Carolina. He turned the specimens over to Audubon, who described them as representatives of a new species, which he named in honor of his friend and collaborator. Over 50 years passed before another individual of the species was seen, this time in Louisiana. Charles G. Galbraith, a professional plume collector, who was procuring feathers for the millinery trade, shot 38 of them in the springs of 1886, 1887, and 1888, and still others in 1891, all on dates between February 27 and March 20, and all in the vicinity of Mandeville on Lake Pontchartrain. His interest was primarily that of getting any kind of small, bright-colored bird that would be suitable for skinning and drying with wings spread and with the head turned back, ready for pinning on fashionable ladies' hats. The species must then have been exceedingly abundant for him to have obtained so many specimens of it. At about the same time, it was plentiful, at least in migration, in southern Florida (where on March 3, 1889, alone, 21 birds struck the lighthouse on Sombrero Key) and in other localities in the southeastern United States.

Since the time of Galbraith there have been fewer than a dozen records of the Bachman's Warbler in Louisiana, despite an intensive search for it, even in the vicinity of Mandeville. It is now not regular in its occurrence anywhere; some years pass without any being seen. It is indeed today the most rarely observed North American warbler.

The species inhabits heavily wooded swampy areas, and hence breeding pairs probably occur here and there through many parts of Louisiana, despite the fact that only two or three records of it are known in the breeding season. No nest has yet been found in the state.

The male Bachman's Warbler is readily recognizable by its black throat and yellow breast, in combination with the fact that the forehead is yellow, bordered posteriorly by black. The remotely similar male Hooded Warbler is decidedly larger and has the black of the head and throat broadly connected in the form of a hood. The back of the Bachman's is olive-green, and all except the middle tail feathers are marked with white on the inner web. The female lacks the black cravat and the black on the crown and hence somewhat resembles the female Hooded Warbler and the first-year female Wilson's Warbler, which are also yellow below and greenish yellow above. The female Bachman's, however, has the top of the head and cheeks pale gray, punctuated by a yellow eye-ring. The female Hooded is much larger and shows a great deal of white in the tail.

The song of the Bachman's Warbler is described as a buzz, similar to the song of the Northern Parula Warbler but without the rise at the end. It must also, therefore, resemble the songs of the Worm-eating Warbler and Chipping Sparrow. For over 40 years I have listened and looked for this bird.

In early March I have searched the woods near Mandeville, where Galbraith found them plentiful over 80 years ago, and I have walked for miles along the banks of the Suwannee River where William Brewster and Frank M. Chapman reported them common in 1890. Despite these efforts the Bachman's Warbler remains the only breeding bird of the southeastern United States that has eluded me. My failure to find it is not the source of regret that it might seem to be. The out-of-doors would lose some of its appeal if there were nothing new left to look for. At this moment I am planning where I shall search for the Bachman's Warbler next spring, or, if that fails, where I shall search the spring thereafter!

GOLDEN-WINGED WARBLER *Vermivora chrysoptera*
Pls. XXX, XXXI

The Golden-winged Warbler is a fairly common spring and a common fall transient. It gets its name from the yellow patch in the wing, which is only one of its several distinctive features. Others are the yellow forehead, black eye patch, black bib on otherwise immaculate white underparts, and bluish gray upperparts. The female has the black replaced by blackish gray. In spring the species is most likely to be found in the heavily wooded uplands, but in fall it is numerous in such places as the cottonwood-studded battures along the Mississippi River and other large streams.

Spring arrivals usually appear with the first wave of migrants after the

---

Plate XXX Wood-Warblers

(Spring plumage unless otherwise specified; when only one bird of a species is shown, the sexes are quite similar) 1. male Black-and-white Warbler (p. 498); 1a. female. 2. male Blackpoll Warbler (p. 517); 2a. female. 3. male Black-throated Gray Warbler (p. 510); 3a. female. 4. male Golden-winged Warbler (p. 500). 5. male Myrtle Warbler of the white-throated type (p. 514) in late spring and summer plumage; 5a. male in winter plumage. 6. male Myrtle Warbler of the yellow-throated type (p. 515) in winter plumage. 7. male Black-throated Blue Warbler (p. 508); 7a. female. 8. Yellow-throated Warbler (p. 509). 9. male Canada Warbler (p. 531); 9a. female. 10. male Mourning Warbler (p. 529); 10a. female. 11. male Connecticut Warbler (p. 528); 11a. female. 12. Nashville Warbler (p. 503). 13. male Hooded Warbler (p. 530); 13a. female. 14. male Bachman's Warbler (p. 498); 14a. female. 15. male Kentucky Warbler (p. 527). 16. male Wilson's Warbler (p. 530); 16a. female. 17. male Pine Warbler (p. 509); 17a. female. 18. male Prairie Warbler (p. 512); 18a. female. 19. male Cape May Warbler (p. 513); 19a. female. 20. male Magnolia Warbler (p. 514); 20a. immature in fall. 21. Louisiana Waterthrush (p. 521). 22. Northern Waterthrush (p. 520). 23. Ovenbird (p. 520). 24. Swainson's Warbler (p. 522). 25. Worm-eating Warbler (p. 524).

Robert E. Tucker

beginning of April, and the bird is seen irregularly until the middle of May or slightly later. Fall migration is early, for the species regularly appears as far south as New Orleans by the first week of August, after which time it may be seen frequently until the last part of October. The only winter record is that of a male seen at Monroe on January 5, 1971, by D. T. Kee. The song is a simple buzz that W. M. Tyler describes as *zee, zer, zer, zer*. The Golden-wing breeds mainly in the upper Mississippi Valley and in central-southern Canada; it winters in northwestern South America.

BLUE-WINGED WARBLER *Vermivora pinus* Pl. XXXI

The Blue-winged Warbler is a somewhat irregular and uncommon spring transient but fairly common fall transient (extreme dates: March 22 to May 20, July 27 to October 18). What might have been a potential wintering individual was one seen at Boothville, in Plaquemines Parish, on November 29, 1963, by Sidney A. Gauthreaux and Laurence C. Binford. The alleged nest building of the species in Bienville Parish in 1934 has not been supported by any additional evidence of breeding there or elsewhere in the state.

This bird has the top of the head yellow and the underparts yellow, a narrow black line extends through the eye, and the bluish wings possess two prominent but narrow white wing bars. It therefore bears no color resemblance to the Golden-winged Warbler, yet in places where the breeding ranges of the two species overlap in the northeastern United States, hybridization is frequent and two general types of intermediates result. One is called the Brewster's Warbler, the other the Lawrence's Warbler, since at one time, before their true nature was understood, they were each regarded as a distinct species (see Pl. XXXI). The first-generation offspring of a cross between a typical Blue-wing and a typical Golden-wing results in birds all of the Brewster type, which is similar to the Blue-wing except that the throat and belly are white (or with only a tinge of yellow) and the wing patch is broadly yellow. This may be explained on the basis of current genetic theory, by postulating (1) that plain throat is dominant over black throat, (2) that white underparts are partially dominant over yellow underparts, and (3) that the single broad yellow wing bar is partially dominant over the two narrow white wing bars. A cross between two of the first-generation hybrids would result in what is known as segregation, a genetic phenomenon wherein the expected 9-3-3-1 ratio in the offspring of such a cross would be nine Brewster's to three apparent (phenotypic) Golden-wings to three apparent Blue-wings to one pure recessive, the Lawrence's Warbler, which is like a Golden-wing but has yellow replacing the white. These interhybrid crosses are believed, however, to be extremely rare in nature (only two cases known) and not sufficient to account for the numerous examples of the Lawrence's Warbler that have been recorded by field observers. The combination of recessive characters needed to produce the Lawrence type can result, however, from a number of possible crosses between first-generation Brewster's and genetically impure (heterozygous) Golden-wing and Blue-wing parental stocks. Both the Brewster and the Lawrence type of warblers have been recorded in Louisiana.

TENNESSEE WARBLER   *Vermivora peregrina*   Pl. XXXI

The Tennessee Warbler breeds in Canada and the extreme northern part of the United States and winters in southern Mexico, Central America, and northern South America. In Louisiana it is a common spring and fall transient, as it is elsewhere in the Mississippi Valley. Although occasionally the Tennessee Warbler is seen in March, it does not appear in numbers until the first week of April, whereupon it remains quite common until well after the first of May. Fall migrants appear in the second week of September and are seen regularly until the end of October, occasionally into November. The latest record in fall is that of an exceedingly fat individual collected at Johnsons Bayou, in Cameron Parish, on December 1, 1962, by Laurence C. Binford.

The adult male in spring is bright olive-green on the back, pale gray on top of the head, and white below (sometimes with a faint tinge of yellow); there is a faint light grayish line over the eye and a thin dusky line through it. In fall the adult male resembles the adult female, which is yellowish green above and faintly yellowish below, with white undertail coverts. Immatures of both sexes in the fall also resemble the adult female but are even more yellowish. The white under tail coverts serve to separate females and immatures from the somewhat similar Orange-crowned Warbler. The lack of wing bars or any pronounced facial pattern renders the Tennessee Warbler quite nondescript and may sometimes cause confusion with some of the small vireos, but its thin, pointed bill should classify it at a glance as a warbler.

The species is quite common in spring in the large trees of our cities, where it can be heard uttering its twittering song, which one author describes thus: *wi-chip-wi-chip-wi-chip-wi-chip-wi-chip-wi-chip-chip-chip-chip-*

chip-chip, the last syllables louder and more emphatic than those at the beginning. In fall the bird seems to prefer the wooded borders of streams and is especially numerous in the willows and cottonwoods along the battures of the Mississippi River.

ORANGE-CROWNED WARBLER *Vermivora celata* Pl. XXXI

When in winter a small olive-green or grayish green almost completely nondescript warbler is seen in a woodland thicket or in the shrubbery of one's yard, it is probably this species. Its name is a fortunate one, since it calls attention to a feature of the bird that bird students might otherwise not even realize exists. The orange can hardly ever be seen except in a bird in the hand, and then only by parting the feathers on top of the head. The species lacks all the marks that warblers usually possess in one form or another—wing bars, eye stripes and other facial patterns, and differently colored flank or rump feathers. It is so dark below that at a distance it appears greenish gray all over, and this uniformity itself serves as an excellent field mark. It frequently utters a sharp *chip*, which has a distinctive quality once it is learned and properly associated.

The Orange-crowned Warbler is a common winter resident, particularly in the southern part of Louisiana. No less than 281 were counted in the Buras-Venice area on December 30, 1959, on a Christmas Bird Count, and this was the highest number seen anywhere in the nation that year. Fall arrivals do not usually appear in the state until past the middle of October, but within a month the species is common and remains so until the first part of April. Most have gone by the end of the month, but the latest record is of one seen at New Orleans on May 2, 1961.

NASHVILLE WARBLER *Vermivora ruficapilla* Pl. XXX

Alexander Wilson, the contemporary of Audubon and author of the great work *American Ornithology*, was the first to describe this warbler. He obtained two specimens near Nashville, Tennessee, and hence gave the species the name Nashville Warbler. The gray head, white eye-ring, yellowish green back, yellow underparts, and the absence of wing bars or any white in the tail are, in combination, distinguishing marks of the species. In the fall it is duller, being more brownish on the sides of the head, back, and flanks.

The Nashville Warbler is a fairly regular and moderately common spring and fall transient that has been recorded from March 29 to May 10 and from August 31 to November 20. On April 11, 1942, the bird was unusually common on Willow Island, a cheniere near Cameron, and it has been found to be one of the regular and more numerous migrants in spring near Shreveport. It is, however, seldom observed in spring anywhere in the eastern half of the state. Fall occurrences are spread throughout Louisiana and are quite regularly recorded. A specimen that was taken in a dense patch of weeds along the shore of University Lake at Baton Rouge on December 19, 1938, and one seen at Grand Isle by Sidney A. Gauthreaux and Brian Donlan on December 28, 1957, are the only definite winter records for the species in the state.

LUCY'S WARBLER   *Vermivora luciae*   Pl. XLI

The only record in the state for the Lucy's Warbler is that of an adult individual collected near Triumph, in Plaquemines Parish, on December 30, 1959, by Sidney A. Gauthreaux. It is one of the smallest of the warblers and is distinguished by its gray dorsum except for a dark red crown patch and rump. The species breeds from southwestern Colorado, southern Nevada, and Utah south into northwestern Mexico. It winters normally in southwestern Mexico and has been previously recorded casually only as far east as El Paso, Texas.

NORTHERN PARULA WARBLER   *Parula americana*

Pl. XXXI; p. 505

The Northern Parula Warbler is an extremely abundant summer resident throughout the hardwood forests of the state, except in the northwest corner, where it is only fairly common. It nests even on the narrow oak-lined chenieres adjacent to the Gulf. Its weak, lisping trill that "kicks up" on the end can be heard wherever there are large trees, from early March until late summer, when the song period of nearly all birds terminates. The Northern Parula is not only one of the first migrants to arrive, reaching southern Louisiana in late February or the first days of March, but it is also one of the last to complete its exodus in fall. Although an occasional individual winters in the southern part of the state, this is the exception rather than the rule, for most Northern Parulas are gone by the first part of November.

One would think that the Spanish moss that profusely drapes the trees

A Northern Parula Warbler Entering Its Nest in a Clump of Spanish Moss

SAMUEL A. GRIMES

of our state would harbor the nests of many small birds, but the Northern Parula Warbler is one of the very few birds that actually makes its home inside it (see photograph on p. 505). It lays four or five white eggs with rufous markings in a wreath around the large end.

Both Audubon and Wilson called this bird the Blue Yellow-backed Warbler, but to the generation that followed them this name did not seem an appropriate one; so the bird became the Parula Warbler. The addition of the modifier Northern is required to distinguish this species from its close relative, the Tropical Parula Warbler (*Parula pitiayumi*) of southern Texas and Middle and South America. The word *Parula* is the diminutive of *Parus*, the generic name for titmice and chickadees, and was applied to this warbler because of its habit of searching under foliage for insects in the manner of a chickadee. Now the fashion is again for literally descriptive names, such as Blue Yellow-backed Warbler. But I hope that authors will not go back to Audubon's and Wilson's name even though it is a perfectly fitting one. Either name is appropriate in its own way, but the policy of always trying to find a *more* appropriate one than the one currently in vogue leads to nothing but confusion and instability in our nomenclature. As the older name suggests, the bird is light bluish gray above, except for the middle of the back, which is greenish yellow.

In the male, a narrow band of dark chestnut or rufous separates the yellow of the throat from the yellow breast. Females lack this breast band but may be distinguished by their bluish upperparts and yellow breast, and by the prominent white wing bars, white-tipped outer tail feathers, and white eyelids. Immature birds are strongly tinged above with yellowish green but otherwise closely resemble adult females.

YELLOW WARBLER *Dendroica petechia*   Pl. XXXI

Although nearly all warblers possess some yellow, none has more than this species. Even the normally white patches that most warblers have in their outer tail feathers are replaced in the Yellow Warbler by yellow. The upperparts may tend toward greenish yellow and the breast may be minutely streaked, but basically the bird is entirely yellow. Adult males in spring have the forehead more intensely yellow than the remainder of the upperparts, and the breast is finely marked with reddish streaks. Females and immatures are duller in color, particularly in fall, when some are greenish yellow above and below. But in all cases the yellow on the inner webs of the tail feathers is diagnostic of the species.

In Louisiana the Yellow Warbler is quite common in spring and abundant in fall, as it passes to and from its breeding grounds in the northern part of the United States and its winter quarters south of the Gulf of Mexico. There are records for Louisiana in every month of the year, but this is only because stray individuals will sometimes spend the winter here and because the last migrants to go north in spring virtually meet the first to come back, leaving only a short period of a few weeks in midsummer when none are present. Although the Yellow Warbler has been reported several times to breed in the state, there is no indisputable record of its actually having done so. Somewhat surprising, though, is the fact that no nesting populations are present on any of the mangrove-covered islands along our Gulf Coast, for the species breeds abundantly in this habitat in the West Indies, Yucatan, and eastern Mexico.

Francis H. Allen describes the song of the Yellow Warbler as *wee see wee see wiss wiss'-u*. Although this interpretation may not be perfect, it certainly comes closer than that of the lady who claimed that the bird says, "I want to see all the world." I have a thousand times since listened to the song of the Yellow Warbler, and for the life of me I cannot find in it any resemblance to her verbal rendition.

CHESTNUT-SIDED WARBLER   *Dendroica pensylvanica*   Pl. XXXI

If a variegated color pattern is of real survival value to an animal, then the Chestnut-sided Warbler should be eminently protected. To be sure, its bright, multicolored plumage does blend remarkably with the leaves of a tree, particularly where beads of sunlight are interspersed with various shades of green foliage. The top of the bird's head and the two wing bars are yellow, the back is yellow streaked with black, the underparts and a patch on the side of the face are immaculate white, and the flanks are rich chestnut. No other warbler has chestnut on the flanks, except the Bay-breasted, which has a black mask and dark chestnut-colored crown. In autumn the adults are not as distinctly marked, although there is always some trace of chestnut on the flanks. The immatures, however, are very plain, simply grayish white below and light greenish above, with two yellowish wing bars. The *sharp line* of demarcation between the green of the upperparts, including the head, and the gray of the underparts is a good field mark.

The Chestnut-sided Warbler is quite common in northern Louisiana in spring, but in the southern parishes it is ordinarily less common and less regular, except for its occasional abundance on the coastal ridges, where as many as 100 can be observed in a small area in periods of bad weather. In spring it appears usually with the first concentration of transient migrants arriving after the first of April and may be seen as late as the third week of May. Its return in the fall commences in late August and extends through October. During most of this time it is regular and fairly frequent in its occurrence throughout the state.

The song can be verbalized as an emphatic "I wish to see Miss Beecher," a rather ridiculous description but one that is nevertheless remarkably suggestive of the bird's song. The species breeds across Canada and the northern half of the eastern United States and winters in Central America.

CERULEAN WARBLER   *Dendroica cerulea*   Pl. XXXI

Although the Cerulean Warbler is a widespread and fairly common, occasionally abundant, migrant in spring, it is much more regular in occurrence in fall. There are several published statements asserting that the species breeds widely in the state, and indeed it has been observed on several occasions in June, but apparently no nest or fledglings have yet been found. Spring transients appear in late March or early April and are seen until early May. Fall migrants reappear in southern Louisiana as early as July 22, as evidenced by the presence of the bird in willow thickets along the lower reaches of the Mississippi River. The bulk of the southward movement takes place in August and early September, but an occasional individual may be seen past the middle of October.

The color of the upperparts of the male Cerulean Warbler is sky blue; below it is immaculate white, except for a very narrow blue or bluish black band across the upper breast and a few black streaks along the flanks. The female and the immatures are bluish green or greenish blue above, with two white wing bars and a yellowish line over the eye; the plain underparts are strongly tinged with yellow, especially in the immatures. Female and immature Tennessee Warblers are similar but lack the white wing bars. The song of the Cerulean is very much like that of the Northern Parula Warbler and has been described as *wee wee wee wee bzzz*. In the Northern Parula the *bzzz* comes first, followed by a trill of monosyllables, whereas in the Cerulean there is a trill then the *bzzz*.

BLACK-THROATED BLUE WARBLER   *Dendroica caerulescens*
Pl. XXX

This locally rare species, like the Cape May Warbler, seems to migrate mainly to the east of us. Its occurrence in spring often appears to follow several days of strong prevailing easterly winds that may have been responsible for having displaced migrants much farther west than they would normally have passed. The comparatively few spring records, numbering less than two dozen, are on dates between February 25 and May 20, at the following localities: Monroe, Pelican, Grand Isle, Lafayette, St. Francisville, New Orleans, Pilottown, Chandeleur Island, and various places in Cameron Parish. Southbound migrants appear in early September and are seen casually from then to late October and early November. There are, however, at least six records in extreme southeastern Louisiana (New Orleans and Venice) between November 24 and January 3 and a single sighting at Lafayette on December 19.

The male is blue above and black below, except for the white lower belly and white patch in the wing at the base of the main flight feathers. The female and immatures are buffy below and dark olive-green above, sometimes with a faint bluish tinge. This unstreaked dark coloration and the very dark cheeks, along with the white patch in the wing, make them easily separable from their relatives.

The Black-throated Blue Warbler breeds mainly in the north-central and northeastern part of the United States. It is also abundant in summer on the higher ridges of the Alleghenies as far south as northern Georgia.

PINE WARBLER *Dendroica pinus* Pl. XXX

The Pine Warbler is an abundant permanent resident throughout the pinelands of Louisiana; in late fall and winter it also appears in other situations. The resident population is augmented in fall by the arrival of migrants from the North, and these are possibly the birds that we see outside of the species' normal pine habitat. Pine Warblers sometimes appear in hardwood forests and even on our coastal islands and chenieres, where they certainly seem strange and out of place.

The male of the species is identified by its white wing bars, its greenish yellow upperparts, and its bright yellow throat and breast. The female is not as yellow as the male, and immature birds have only a tinge of yellow, being mainly greenish above and light-colored below. The song is a prolonged, liquid trill that is heard through our pine forests throughout the year, except possibly for the brief period of the bird's annual molt in late summer. The somewhat similar trill of the Chipping Sparrow, which often occurs in the same habitat, is much drier and more staccato.

The cup-shaped nest of the Pine Warbler is often saddled between two cones, near the top of a tall pine. Four or five eggs are laid that are white or grayish white, usually with a wreath of cinnamon-brown to blackish markings around the larger end.

YELLOW-THROATED WARBLER *Dendroica dominica* Pl. XXX

The Yellow-throated Warbler is a common summer resident throughout Louisiana. It occupies two distinct habitats, the dry pine-oak forests on the one hand and the wet, wooded bottomland swamps on the other, and it seems equally at home in either place. The species is one of the first migrants to appear in spring; sometimes a few individuals are present on the coastal ridges before the end of February. At Baton Rouge the bird can always be heard singing in the tupelogum swamps before March 10. Throughout the day from that time until late in summer it continues to render its song, two or three clear notes followed by a short trill. Like the Northern Parula Warbler it often builds its nest in clusters of Spanish moss, where it lays four or five whitish eggs with numerous distinct or obscure cinnamon- or olive-brown markings, sometimes evenly distributed, sometimes in a wreath around the larger end.

The species is easily recognized by its yellow bib, bluish gray upperparts, and the prominent black facial marks consisting of a black forehead, black ear patches, and black malar streaks. In birds from central and western Louisiana, the line over the eye is white all the way to the bill, but birds from southeastern Louisiana have the white superciliary line ending in a tiny yellow spot on the lores.

The winter home of the Yellow-throated Warbler extends from South Carolina, Georgia, and Florida to the West Indies and from central-eastern Mexico to Central America. In Louisiana the species is rare but of fairly regular annual occurrence in winter in the extreme southeastern corner of the state, and it has also been observed on one occasion in northwestern Louisiana in that season, on January 2, 1966, at Natchitoches.

BLACK-THROATED GRAY WARBLER *Dendroica nigrescens*
Pl. XXX

More than two dozen records for this western species in Louisiana are now available. It has been observed at 18 localities, all in the southern part of the state, on dates extending from October 3 to March 21. The species is easily recognized by its black throat, black ear patch, and black crown. Otherwise it is blue-gray above and white below, except for the black streaks on the flanks and its two white wing bars. In contrast, the Black-and-white Warbler has a white streak down the center of the crown and the back is streaked with white. The male Blackpoll Warbler has the entire top of the head black down to the level of the eye; the remainder of the cheeks is white (no black ear patch); and the black bib is lacking.

HERMIT WARBLER *Dendroica occidentalis*
Pl. XLI

This far-western species has only twice been recorded in the state. R. D. Purrington observed one on Grand Isle on January 12, 1972, and another was seen and collected at Johnsons Bayou, in Cameron Parish, on April 20, 1973, by Mac Myers and H. Douglas Pratt.

The Hermit Warbler resembles the Black-throated Green Warbler, but the yellow of the face and top of the head is more extensive, the nape and hindneck possess a small patch of black, the black bib is more restricted (not extending across the chest and sides), and the back is grayish (not greenish). The species breeds from southwestern Washington south through the Coast Ranges and the Sierra Nevada to California. It normally winters in the area of central-southern Mexico south to Costa Rica.

BLACK-THROATED GREEN WARBLER *Dendroica virens*
Pl. XXXI

In northern Louisiana this attractive warbler is a fairly common transient in spring. In southern Louisiana, at the latitude of Baton Rouge, records at this season are few because of the effect of the so-called coastal hiatus, but along the coast itself, in such places as Grand Isle and Cameron, the bird is often abundantly represented in concentrations of grounded migrants following the passage of cold-front storms. In the fall it is an abundant transient throughout the state. Its periods of migration extend from March 14 to May 24 and from early September (rarely mid-August) to sometimes as late as mid-November or even later. The species is of virtual regular annual occurrence in winter from New Orleans south through the delta region near the mouth of the Mississippi River, and it has been seen in winter at Grand Isle and in Cameron Parish. Although seldom during the winter season is more than a single individual seen in the course of a day, no less than three were present at Fort Jackson, in Plaquemines Parish, on January 8, 1972.

In the male Black-throated Green Warbler the back and top of the head are yellowish green, the cheeks are yellow, the throat and sides of the neck black, and the breast and belly white, except for black streaks along the flanks. Females are similar, but the black of the throat is more or less mixed with yellow. Adults in fall are not as well marked as they are in spring, and the immatures lack the black throat. All fall birds are, however, easily recognized by the prominent yellow cheeks and greenish color of the back.

One of the best descriptions of the song is the graphic representation of straight lines, which John Burroughs proposed many years ago: ———, ——— V ———. There are, to phrase it differently, two monosyllabic notes, then a short one on a different pitch, and, finally, a single repetition of the first note. Although migrants are found in wooded areas, one of their favorite haunts in the fall is the swamp privet, which grows abundantly in the battures along our rivers and in other low places.

PRAIRIE WARBLER *Dendroica discolor*   Pl. XXX

In Louisiana, as elsewhere, the Prairie Warbler is not an inhabitant of prairies. Here it is a locally common summer resident in dry woods, usually ones containing a mixture of pine and scrub oak. In the last days of March it arrives almost simultaneously on its nesting grounds in the northern part of the Florida Parishes and in extreme northern Louisiana. Strangely enough, it is seldom seen elsewhere in the state, except in fall, when northern populations are drifting southward toward the Gulf Coast.

The Prairie Warbler is yellowish green above with fine red marks on the back. The underparts are yellow except for heavy black streaks that begin on the side of the head and continue down the sides of the neck and the flanks. There are two yellowish wing bars and considerable white in the outer tail feathers, but since both of these characters are possessed by a number of warblers, they are of little diagnostic value. Neither are the red streaks on the back, for they are too difficult to see in the field. But the bird's habit of wagging its tail, in combination with the two bold black stripes on its yellow face and the fact that the entire underparts are yellow, serves as an excellent field mark. Fortunately, adults of both sexes are nearly alike at all seasons and therefore pose fewer problems than we usually encounter in learning to recognize warblers whose appearance varies drastically with sex, age, and season. But the Prairie Warbler, too, is not without some of these handicaps, for the immatures in their first fall plumage possess only faint dusky indications of the facial and side stripes and lack the wing bars almost altogether. Again the tail-wagging habit and the combination of the bright yellow underparts and a distinctive dusky mark on the side of the neck are features that identify the bird.

The song of the Prairie Warbler is a simple *tzee tzee tzee tzee tzee* on a rising scale. Three to five whitish eggs that are spotted or speckled with various shades of reddish brown are laid in a cup-shaped nest that is placed in a low bush or sapling several feet from the ground. Breeding birds and their young desert the nesting grounds by the end of August, but migrants are seen in other habitats as late as the middle of October and sometimes into November. At least eight winter records are now available from the extreme southern part of the state that include sightings at Peveto Beach, Cameron, Johnsons Bayou, Grand Cheniere, New Orleans, Gretna, and Venice.

CAPE MAY WARBLER   *Dendroica tigrina*   Pl. XXX

This species winters in the West Indies and migrates northward mainly through Florida; hence it is not frequently seen as far west as Louisiana. Although not long ago considered quite rare in the state, it has now been recorded on well over two dozen dates between April 5 and May 15. Its occurrence in Louisiana in spring, the only season in which it is known, appears most often to be associated with several days of strong easterly winds over the Gulf of Mexico that may serve to displace Florida-bound migrants from the Caribbean area to the west, committing them to a trans-Gulf crossing and resulting in their making a landfall on the northern Gulf Coast.

The spring male of the Cape May Warbler is quite yellow, particularly on the breast and face. It has a black cap, reddish cheek patch, broad white bar on the wing, and dense streaking of black on the breast and flanks. Both sexes have a yellowish rump and a yellow patch on the side of the neck, which is especially useful in distinguishing the female, since she lacks most of the other features that identify her mate. The yellow area on the *side of the neck* in combination with yellowish wing bars and yellowish underparts, which are heavily streaked with black on the flanks, might serve to identify the fall adults and immatures. But this should be attempted only with great caution, even by experienced observers. Indeed, the only wholly reliable fall record would be one involving a specimen.

BLACKBURNIAN WARBLER   *Dendroica fusca*   Pl. XXXI

This beautiful warbler is a fairly regular transient in Louisiana, somewhat uncommon in spring but moderately common in fall. The spring passage begins the second week of March and extends into May, rarely to the end of that month. On the bird's return southward it occurs here from the end of August to the first part of November, rarely later. The only winter record is of one seen on the Venice Christmas Bird Count of January 3, 1965, and carefully studied by four persons.

The male Blackburnian Warbler in nuptial plumage is black and white with flaming orange on the head and throat. The female is not so brilliant but is still easily recognized. In fall the adults and immatures alike lack the orange on the head and throat, but the basic pattern is there—yellow throat, dark ear patch, black and white stripes on the back, and white wing bars. The song has been described as a *chiddle chiddle chiddle chick-a chick-a cheet.*

The species breeds in the evergreen forests of eastern Canada and the northern fringe of the United States, as well as in the Alleghenies as far south as northern Georgia. It winters in Central America and northern South America.

MAGNOLIA WARBLER *Dendroica magnolia* Pl. XXX

The Magnolia Warbler is a regular and common transient in the northern part of the state in spring, but it is less frequently seen at that season in the southern part except on the coast, where it is irregularly common to abundant. Although there are March records for the species, it generally does not appear until mid-April or later, and the bulk of migration passes through in the last days of April and in early May. In fall it is abundant almost everywhere from the second week of September until the last week of October, occasionally remaining into November or even later. On at least eight occasions it has been seen on dates ranging from December 3 to January 12 in the extreme southern part of the state.

The Magnolia Warbler in spring is so conspicuously marked that it can hardly be confused with any other bird. The top of the head is gray, the cheeks and back are black, the rump is yellow, and the underparts are yellow, heavily streaked with black across the breast and on the flanks. The wings have a broad white patch, as does each side of the tail, midway between the base and the tip. In fall the Magnolia is more soberly dressed, but the *white rectangular patch* on the outer tail feathers is always distinctive.

In 1877 the distinguished New England ornithologist William Brewster gave his interpretation of the song as "She knows she was right; yes, she knows she was right." As ridiculous as such verbal expressions may seem, they are of tremendous aid in helping one to remember and to recognize bird songs.

MYRTLE WARBLER *Dendroica coronata* Pl. XXX

Until recently the Myrtle Warbler was treated as a separate species from the so-called Audubon's Warbler. Each was considered polytypic, that is, comprised of two or more subspecies. But because the two entities have now been found to interbreed in their zone of contact in the mountains of the Pacific Northwest, they are considered part of a complex array of geographical variants of a single species. When the two entities were combined, the scientific name *Dendroica coronata* took precedence over *D. auduboni* because of nomenclatural priority. But I still consider the vernacular name Myrtle Warbler entirely appropriate for the species as a whole, even though the AOU Committee on Classification and Nomenclature proposed that Yellow-rumped Warbler, one of the old names for the complex, be resurrected for the species. Indeed, this was the name used by Audubon over a century ago. I prefer, however, to retain the name Myrtle Warbler for the species.

When the field ornithologist wishes to specify in the vernacular to which group of races he is referring, he can use the terms Myrtle Warbler (white-throated type) or Myrtle Warbler (yellow-throated type). A more professional alternative would be the terms *"coronata* complex" and *"auduboni* complex."

One of the most difficult tasks of the field zoologist is that of estimating animal populations and relative abundance with some degree of accuracy. Species of retiring habits that seem uncommon may in reality be far more numerous than other so-called common species that live in the open, where they are easily seen. But even with due allowance for the fact that the Myrtle Warbler is conspicuous, there can be little doubt that it is one of the commonest winter birds in Louisiana. Almost from the time it arrives, which is usually toward the end of September, until it leaves in late April or early May, it seems to be virtually everywhere. It occupies nearly every type of habitat from one end of the state to the other and is incredibly abundant in the myrtle thickets of our southeastern parishes.

The Myrtle is one of the largest members of the Wood-Warbler family. In late spring it molts into a nuptial plumage that is striking in appearance, mainly black and white, but with patches of yellow on the crown, on the sides, and at the base of the tail. In fall, however, we see it as a grayish brown bird, dingy white, streaked with dingy brownish, below; white on the throat; with less prominent patches of yellow on each side of the breast; and with a conspicuous yellow patch at the base of the tail. The Palm Warbler is only faintly washed with greenish yellow on the rump; furthermore, the undertail feathers are yellow instead of white, and the bird wags its tail continuously. A grayish brown warbler in a bush, on the ground, or in a tree-top that has a conspicuous yellow patch on the rump is almost certainly a Myrtle Warbler. Its distinct liquid *chip* is also a good aid in field identification and should be learned at once by the beginning student.

The Myrtle Warbler breeds in the coniferous forests across the breadth of North America, from Alaska to Labrador, south to the northern part of

the United States. It winters from Kansas to New England, southward to
Panama and the Greater Antilles. The more southern wintering birds probably cross the Gulf of Mexico from Yucatan, arriving in Louisiana in late
March and in April. These transients evidently molt before leaving their
winter quarters, for they appear here in full breeding plumage and are quite
distinct from the remnants of the local wintering population that have not
yet finished their prenuptial molt.

The yellow-throated "Audubon's" type of Myrtle Warbler has been
seen in at least a dozen places in the state, mostly in southern Louisiana but
also at Shreveport and Alexandria, on dates ranging from October 25 to
May 7.

PALM WARBLER   *Dendroica palmarum*   Pl. XXXI

The Palm Warbler is an uncommon spring and fall transient and a rare
winter visitor in northern Louisiana. In southern Louisiana, however, it is at
least moderately common as a winter resident, particularly in the eastern
Florida Parishes. It sometimes appears as early as the end of August and
remains until the end of April or slightly later. Nowhere in the state is it ever
seen in numbers and, unless certain specific habitats are visited, it can be
overlooked altogether. For example, on the census of birds that is made
each year on one day around Christmastime, a project that has been going
on for many years at various localities in the state, the Palm Warbler is
always regarded as a species likely to be missed. In the St. Francisville–Port
Hudson area a few individuals may sometimes be found in the dense stands
of willows in the bottomlands along the Mississippi River. In the pine flats
of the southeastern part of the state the species shows a preference for
burned-over ground and may be seen feeding in such situations along with
Pine Warblers and various sparrows.

The adult male Palm Warbler is predominantly brown above, with a
reddish crown and a yellowish rump patch. Some individuals are all-yellow
below except for brownish streaks on the sides and flanks. Others may have
the yellow of the underparts restricted to the throat, lower belly, and undertail feathers, with the remainder of the breast and belly a dingy white. Immatures, particularly those of the pale western population of the species (see
p. 39 and Pl. XXXI), may lack any vestige of yellow above or below. Consequently, one of the best field characters of all is the manner in which the

Palm Warbler continually wags its tail. The Prairie Warbler also wags the tail, but it can be eliminated either by its prominent black facial and side stripes, by its wing bars, by the absence of a reddish brown cap, by its citrine-yellow underparts, or, in the immature, by the dusky spot on the side of the neck.

BLACKPOLL WARBLER *Dendroica striata*   Pl. XXX

The Blackpoll Warbler is a fairly common spring transient between April 9 and May 26. Although the species has been reported to occur in Louisiana regularly in fall, only one record at that season seems acceptable, a specimen taken by Laurence C. Binford on September 17, 1965, at Baton Rouge. The fall plumages of the Blackpoll and the Bay-breasted Warblers are almost identical in being simply olive-greenish above and whitish or faintly yellow, more or less washed with buff, below. Both have white wing bars, and, whereas the adult males of the Bay-breasted in fall sometimes have a trace of chestnut on the flanks, the females and immatures of the two species are very similar at this season. The color of the legs is the best means of telling them apart. The Blackpoll has flesh-colored legs, the Bay-breasted Warbler, black. In spring the male Blackpoll is identified by its general black and white plumage. The top of the head is black, there is a black malar streak, and the sides and back are heavily streaked with black. The prominent white cheek patch is also distinctive. The female is more olive-drab with less black streaking. For comparison with other warblers that are predominantly black and white, see the account of the Black-throated Gray Warbler.

The song of the Blackpoll is a ticking note that rises in volume and then descends. It is suggestive of the clicking sounds heard in department stores that have an overhead conveyor system for carrying money to the cashier and bringing back change in small metal containers. If one happens to be standing in the middle of the store, the metallic sounds made by one of the containers running on its track increases in loudness until it is opposite the listener and then diminishes as it gets farther away.

Among the favorite haunts of the Blackpoll Warbler, as it passes through Louisiana, are pecan orchards. Its rarity in fall is due to the fact that, although it migrates northward through the Mississippi Valley after a trans-Gulf crossing, it returns southward by a more eastern route through the Atlantic Coast states, Florida, and the West Indies.

BAY-BREASTED WARBLER   *Dendroica castanea*   Pl. XXXI

This warbler is another in a long list of small woodland birds that merely pass through our state in spring and again in late summer and fall. Like most other spring transients, it is irregular in occurrence in the southern part of the state, but on occasions, particularly in the face of adverse weather, it may be abundant for a day or two at a time. In the northern part of Louisiana it appears more regularly from day to day. In fall it hardly ever occurs in large concentrations, but a few can be seen almost daily, particularly in October, as the species drifts southward to the shores of the Gulf, whence it takes off on a great overwater flight to its winter home in Central America. The spring passage is brief, taking place between April 16 and May 28, while the fall records cover the period from September 21 to December 3. The species has twice appeared on Christmas Bird Counts: one seen at New Orleans on December 30, 1967, by Sidney A. Gauthreaux and James J. Hebrard, and one observed at Lafayette on December 19, 1971, by William Gardner, Jr.

In spring the Bay-breasted Warbler cannot be confused with any other species. The top of the head is dark chestnut as are also the throat and flanks; there is a black mask through the eye and a cream-colored patch on the side of the head and neck. The female is similar but has less chestnut on the throat and flanks and the eye mask is dusky instead of black. Fall birds, however, are radically different. Their backs are greenish with black streaks, and the underparts are pale buffy and white; there are also two wing bars. The fall-plumaged male may have a trace of chestnut on the flanks, but this color is always absent in the female and the immatures. In this plumage the Bay-breasted Warbler and the Blackpoll Warbler can be distinguished only with great difficulty. In the former the undertail feathers are buff; in the latter, white. The best diagnostic character, however, is the color of the legs, which are blackish in the Bay-breasted, flesh colored in the Blackpoll. The identification of Bay-breasted and Blackpoll Warblers in fall should not be undertaken by the beginner until he is familiar with the also nondescript immature Pine Warbler, for the three are easily confused. The immature Pine Warbler lacks any streaks on the back, which is generally darker and browner (less greenish). The song of the Bay-breasted Warbler is a high-pitched *teesi, teesi, teesi,* much like that of the Black-and-white Warbler.

AMERICAN REDSTART *Setophaga ruticilla* Pl. XXXI

This beautifully attired bird is another aberrant member of the Wood-Warbler family. It differs from the other representatives of the family in several striking features, including its disproportionately long tail that is fanned out broadly at the end, its flat, flycatcherlike bill, and its behaviorisms. The male is unusually attractive, being jet black, except for the white belly, the reddish orange on the base of the outer tail feathers, and the reddish orange patches in the wings and on the shoulders. The female and the immatures are gray or greenish gray everywhere that the male is black, yellow where the male is reddish orange. Immature males sometimes have the yellow replaced by salmon color. The American Redstart is continually flitting from limb to limb, and habitually it holds the wings down alongside the body with the tips below the tail. The tail is narrow at the base but fans out broadly at the end. The males can be mistaken for nothing else; neither can the females and immatures, since the rectangular yellow patch at the base of the outer tail feathers, easily seen from below as well as from above, is unique.

The species is a common, sometimes locally abundant, migrant in spring, and it is abundant in fall. It breeds locally in various parts of Louisiana, such as in the Pearl River swamp opposite Bogalusa, in deep beech-magnolia ravines near St. Francisville, and in the wooded areas near Minden. The southernmost breeding record is that of a nest found by J. Stan Landry and William Dupre, Jr., on May 26, 1973, on the edge of a swamp seven miles southwest of Donaldsonville, in Assumption Parish. Spring arrivals appear in the last few days of March. Fall migration, as evidenced by the appearance of the bird in areas where the species does not breed, begins in late July and continues in volume until after the last days of October. The American Redstart is of fairly regular annual occurrence in winter somewhere in southern Louisiana. It has been recorded in December and January on numerous occasions in the New Orleans and the Venice-Buras areas of the delta region, as well as in Cameron Parish. One was also found near New Roads, in Pointe Coupee Parish, on December 19, 1954.

The four or five grayish white or bluish white eggs, which are spotted and blotched with cinnamon- or olive-brown, chiefly at the larger end, are laid in a nest of finely interwoven tendrils and rootlets 5 to 20 feet from the ground in the crotch of a sapling. The song is high pitched and rather monotonous, a sort of *tsee, tsee, tsee, tset.*

OVENBIRD   *Seiurus aurocapillus*   Pl. XXX

The Ovenbird is a familiar species in the northern part of the United States, mainly because of its loud, ringing song and its interesting habits. It is sometimes called the "teacher-bird," since it seems to say "teacher, teacher, teacher, teacher." The name Ovenbird is in reference to its domed, Dutch-oven-shaped nest. It is a common breeding bird in deciduous woodlands from northwestern Canada to Newfoundland south to northern Arkansas and northern Mississippi, but in Louisiana it is merely a bird of passage. One possible instance of breeding in the state is that of an Ovenbird at what was described as a typical nest of the species found by W. D. Reese along a stream about 13 miles west of Bogalusa, in Washington Parish, on April 21, 1963. Professor Reese was collecting bryophytes at the time and was extremely confident of his identification of both the bird and the nest.

The species usually arrives in late March and is more regularly seen than some transient warblers, though never in large numbers even on the coastal ridges. Usually none are encountered after the middle of May, but it has occasionally been seen as late as May 30. Southbound migrants return in August and are moderately common until the first part of November. An occasional individual has been found in southern Louisiana in winter, particularly in the delta area south of New Orleans. It has also been seen in winter at Reserve, in St. John the Baptist Parish, and at Henderson, in St. Martin Parish. At the latter place as many as five were counted and one was collected on February 14, 1970, by Michael J. Musumeche. The bulk of the population, however, spends the cold months in the West Indies, Mexico, and Central America.

The bird is dark olive-green or greenish olive above and white below, with numerous blackish streaks on the sides and flanks. It has a white eyering and an orange stripe down the center of the crown, bordered on each side by black. These markings, in conjunction with the fact that it walks instead of hops and continually bobs its tail, combine to make it readily identifiable. It inhabits the forest floor and is usually seen in some shaded, secluded place.

NORTHERN WATERTHRUSH   *Seiurus noveboracensis*   Pl. XXX

The two species of waterthrushes and the Ovenbird are closely related, as evidenced by their general similarity in appearance and by the many behavioral characteristics that they have in common. All three walk instead of hop and all of them bob their tails in the most ludicrous manner. This species is dark olive-drab above, and its underparts are yellowish, heavily streaked with dusky, even on the throat. The prominent line over the eye is usually yellowish. The Louisiana Waterthrush is darker above and whiter below, has the line over the eye white, and lacks the streaks on the throat.

Unevenly distributed like most transient migrants, the Northern Waterthrush is never more than fairly common anywhere in Louisiana in spring but is exceedingly numerous over a wide area in fall. It usually appears in the first part of April, but it has been recorded in mid-March. February records, of which several are on file, probably represent birds that have overwintered. In spring the species is usually gone by the middle of May. On its return southward it is often present in the last half of July, but the main period of abundance is from the end of August to the first week of October, after which it declines rapidly. The species has been seen frequently in New Orleans and in the delta area below that city during the winter months, from early December through February and early March.

Deep, shaded woods are among its favorite haunts, but in fall it is nowhere more numerous than in the willow thickets bordering our larger streams.

Francis H. Allen describes the song as *wheet wheet chip chip chip wheedleyou*. The notes are loud and musical and accelerate toward the end.

LOUISIANA WATERTHRUSH *Seiurus motacilla*   Pl. XXX; p. 522

The Louisiana Waterthrush is an uncommon transient in the southern part of the state and a locally common summer resident in northern Louisiana, occurring regularly but less commonly in the St. Francisville–Jackson area and other parts of the Florida Parishes. A nest with three young was found at Goodbee, in St. Tammany Parish, on June 15, 1962, by Mac Myers. It builds its bulky nest of dead leaves, sticks, fine grasses, and rootlets, all plastered together with mud, near the banks of woodland streams, often where the structure is concealed under an overhanging bank and amid ferns and other foliage. Breeding birds arrive in mid-March, but the four to six finely speckled white eggs are not laid until late April. Southward migration, as evidenced by the appearance of the bird in areas where it does not breed (such as in the willow thickets along the battures of the Mississippi River at Baton Rouge), begins as early as July 1 and continues until late in October. Casual winter records during the last week of December have been obtained at New Orleans and in the delta area below that city, and twice it has been

Louisiana Waterthrush at Its Nest Under a Root in a Stream Bank

seen in winter at Thibodaux, once on January 27 and again on February 16, both sightings probably representing birds that had overwintered.

The Louisiana Waterthrush is darker above than the Northern Waterthrush, the line over the eye is white instead of yellowish, and the throat is immaculate instead of streaked. Its song is a wild, ringing, musical rendition that begins with three slurred whistles and ends in a profusion of twittering sounds.

SWAINSON'S WARBLER *Limnothlypis swainsonii* Pl. XXX; p. 523

The Swainson's Warbler is, for some reason, often overlooked even by good ornithologists. There are periods, comprising many decades, in the bird's history when it has been virtually a lost species. Following its discovery in 1832 by the Reverend John Bachman, the good friend and collaborator of Audubon, it was practically unknown until 1884. From then until 1910 it received considerable notice, but after 1910 and until 1930 it was again seldom mentioned in ornithological writings. In the last 35 years much has been learned of its habits, one of the most notable facts being that it is not confined in its nesting to swampy places, but that it also nests in dense, dark rhododendron thickets at an altitude of several thousand feet in the Allegheny Mountains. Strangely, though, the bird can be present in an area and still escape detection. Indeed, I know one excellent ornithologist who had never succeeded in finding a Swainson's Warbler and was astounded when we stood on the edge of a woodland no more than a few miles from his home and I casually commented, "There I hear a Swainson."

I suspect the species is overlooked for several reasons, one being that it is a drab-colored bird and another that it is reluctant to expose itself to view. The back is olive-brown, the top of the head is dark russet, the underparts are soiled white or faintly yellowish, and a white line extends over the eye that is accentuated by a faint dusky streak through and posterior to the eye. No white is present in the wings or tail. None of these characteristics add up to anything very distinctive. The Swainson's is, however, the only brown-backed warbler with a solid brown cap and unstreaked underparts.

Another factor possibly accounting for the fact that the species is overlooked is the similarity of its song to that of the Hooded Warbler on one hand and to that of the Louisiana Waterthrush on the other. The best trans-

Adult Swainson's Warbler Feeding Its Young

SAMUEL A. GRIMES

literation of it to come to my attention is that given by Maurice Brooks and William Legg. These two highly trained ornithologists describe the song as a *whee, whee, whip-poor-will*, the first two notes being uttered slowly, the last more rapidly and on a descending scale, and with no pause between the two sections. The accents in the last part of the song are on the *whip* and on the *wi-* part of *will*.

The nest of the Swainson's Warbler is built in dense tangles of "switch cane," briers, or thick bushes. The ones I have seen have been rather bulky structures attached to the upright stalks three to five feet from the ground and always in or near a swampy area. The usual complement of three eggs is variable in color, being plain whitish with either a bluish, greenish, or pinkish tinge. Rarely the eggs are faintly speckled with reddish brown.

The Swainson's Warbler usually arrives in Louisiana in the last few days of March or in the first week in April. It departs, as a rule, by late September or early October. The earliest record ever is March 21 and the latest is October 27, both in wooded chenieres in Cameron Parish.

WORM-EATING WARBLER   *Helmitheros vermivorus*   Pl. XXX

This warbler is a rather uncommon transient and extremely local summer resident in Louisiana. Although the species has been observed on fairly numerous occasions in the vicinity of Jonesboro in summer, actual evidence of breeding has been found in only one locality, near St. Francisville, and even there the actual nest (a well-hidden structure of rootlets, strips of bark, and leaves, placed on the ground) is yet to be discovered. Jas. Hy. Bruns found Worm-eating Warblers present in summer in the deep-gullied and well-shaded beech-magnolia woods and although he has not succeeded so far in locating an actual nest, he has more than once seen young birds just out of a nest and still partially covered with natal down. Strangely enough, John James Audubon, who lived for a considerable time near St. Francisville, never saw the bird there.

The Worm-eating Warbler is greenish olive above and olive-buff below and has four prominent black lines on the head, two enclosing a buffy stripe in the middle and one passing through each eye from the bill to the nape. No other North American warbler is olive-buff below; nor is there any other with a buffy stripe on the crown bordered by black. The Worm-eating Warbler further lacks wing bars or any white in the tail, and the sexes are alike. The song, a simple buzzing *che-e-e-e-e*, is difficult to distinguish from the notes of the Chipping Sparrow. Fortunately, the two never occur in the same habitat, for the Chipping Sparrow is typically a bird of the pine woods or pastures.

Worm-eating Warblers appear on their nesting grounds at St. Francisville sometimes as early as March 14, which is well in advance of the main migratory flights. Fall migrants continue to pass through the state until near the end of October. The only winter record is that of one seen at Fort Jackson, in Plaquemines Parish, on December 30, 1971, by R. D. Purrington, who furnished corroborating details.

PROTHONOTARY WARBLER *Protonotaria citrea* Pl. XXXI

Beginners in bird study often look with disfavor on the name of this bird; they find it difficult to spell, to pronounce, and to understand. Actually, however, the title Prothonotary (pronounced pro-thon'-o-ta-ry) possesses the same high degree of distinction and appropriateness that we recognize in the name of the Northern Cardinal. For centuries of ecclesiastical history, the prothonotary, who is legal advisor to the pope, has worn yellow vestments, as the cardinals have worn red. When the Creoles of Louisiana found in the swamps of our state a bird that wore a similarly resplendent golden surplice, they had the inspiration to call it the "prothonotary"—or, at least, so the story goes. At any rate, the Prothonotary Warbler has ever since occupied its fitting position in the world of southern swamp birds as a properly sanctified associate of the Northern Cardinal. How colorless and unimaginative in comparison is the name Golden Swamp Warbler, which some people would like to use in place of Prothonotary! It tells us nothing we do not already know the moment we see the bird, and, while it is perhaps desirable that many names should be of this purely descriptive sort, it is certainly refreshing to find an occasional one that widens our horizons by providing a challenge to our intellectual curiosity.

The species is everywhere in Louisiana an abundant denizen of swampy places and is, therefore, a bird with which nearly every fisherman of our swamp lakes and bayous is familiar. Although it sometimes comes up into our gardens to nest in bird boxes or gourds, it never strays far from water and normally builds its nest in a hole in a stump standing in water. The male of the species is unquestionably one of our most attractive birds. Its golden yellow head and yellow underparts contrast with its yellowish green back and bluish wings and tail. The outer tail feathers have a considerable amount of white that is often flashed when the bird is excited. The female, though somewhat duller in plumage, closely resembles the male. The Blue-winged Warbler is descriptively similar, but its much smaller bill, narrow black line through the eye, and white wing bars are all points that it does not share with the Prothonotary Warbler.

The song of the Prothonotary is a loud, ringing *peet, tweet, tweet, tweet* that reverberates through the swamps from the time of its arrival in mid-March until late summer. Southward migration begins in September, but the bird's departure from the state is not normally completed until the end of October. An occasional individual sometimes remains until well into November, but the only winter record is that of one seen by Marshall and Grace Eyster at Lafayette on December 25, 1950. The three to eight beautiful rose-tinted eggs are liberally blotched with chestnut-brown, intermingled with blotches of gray or lavender.

COMMON YELLOWTHROAT *Geothlypis trichas* Pl. XXXI

The Common Yellowthroat (whose name is not to be confused with that of the Yellow-throated Warbler) is one of our commonest birds, and it is the only species of warbler that breeds in all 49 continental states. In southern Louisiana the Common Yellowthroat is present the year around and is always at least fairly common, even in winter. In the northern part of the state, at least from Alexandria northward, it is almost entirely a summer resident. An occasional yellowthroat is seen in the Shreveport area in midwinter, but I was never able to find it at that season near Monroe. After making its appearance in late March or early April, it is common until near the middle of September. In spring, when migration is in progress, it is often incredibly abundant everywhere, particularly on some of our coastal ridges during adverse weather that "dams up" the flow of transients. Once in the spring of 1953, in a 10-acre tract of woodland near the Gulf beach of Cameron Parish, the yellowthroat population jumped from one lone individual on April 17 to a number in excess of 250 on April 20.

The favorite haunt of the Common Yellowthroat in the breeding season is a marshy place, particularly where there are cattails and other aquatic plants. It is also fond of dense thickets and rank stands of grass where there is exposure to sunlight. The male yellowthroat is recognized at a glance by its greenish olive back, yellow underparts, and the *rectangular* black mask through the eye and across the face and along the upperpart of the neck. The upper edge of the black mask is usually bordered with white. The female lacks the mask and is "just another little yellowish bird" until one learns to recognize her by her few intangible characteristics (among which the lack of bars or tail patches is notable) and by the distinctive yellowthroat call note, a sharp *tchep*. Most students begin by learning the appearance of the female through her association with the male. She is the brownest of the plain yellowish warblers and usually the whitest on the belly.

The song of the yellowthroat is a distinct *witchity-witchity-witchity-witchity-witchity-witch* or a *witchity-ta-witchity-ta-witchity-ta-witch*. Although the species is retiring in habits and lives in situations where it cannot be easily approached by stealth, a squeaking noise made by placing one's fingertips against the lips is a sure means of bringing one of these little birds into plain view.

KENTUCKY WARBLER   *Geothlypis formosa*   Pl. XXX; p. 527

The Kentucky Warbler is a common breeding bird throughout most of the dense hardwood regions of Louisiana. It arrives in mid-March and is present until late October. The only winter record is of one seen at New Orleans on January 2, 1967, by Ronald J. Stein and Joseph Cambre.

The nest is ordinarily built on the ground or very close thereto. This

Female Kentucky Warbler Brings One Worm to Satisfy Four Offspring

SAMUEL A. GRIMES

location is not surprising, for the bird itself is habitually a denizen of the forest floor, usually where there are dark, damp, shaded areas and a profusion of ferns. The male will often mount to an elevated perch in a tree to pour forth its song that simulates the words *tur-dle tur-dle tur-dle*, in a manner strongly suggestive of the song of the Carolina Wren. The song should be learned at once, for it frequently leads the observer to Kentucky Warblers that otherwise would never be seen because of the denseness of the habitat they frequent.

The Kentucky Warbler is quickly identified by its dark greenish upperparts, its bright yellow underparts, and the prominent black streak that runs from the bill and the lower side of the eye down along the side of the neck. It also has a black forehead, and this, with the other black of the face, causes the yellow eye-ring and yellow lores to stand out conspicuously. The Common Yellowthroat likewise possesses a black patch, but the black area is broader and more rectangular and forms a solid mask across the entire face and forehead of the bird, uninterrupted by light-colored eye-rings, superciliary lines, or lores. The legs of the Kentucky Warbler are flesh colored, and it possesses no wing bars or white in the tail.

CONNECTICUT WARBLER   *Geothlypis agilis*   Pl. XXX

The Connecticut Warbler is a very rare spring and fall transient in Louisiana that has been recorded in the state on only five occasions, all involving single birds, as follows: at Monroe on October 9, 1931; another at the same place on April 27, 1936; at Pelican, in De Soto Parish, on May 19, 1957; on Shreve Island, near Shreveport, on April 27, 1964; and on the edge of University Lake at Baton Rouge on October 6, 1965. Everywhere it is a notably late migrant in spring, sometimes not even reaching Florida, which is on its main northward route, until after the first of May. The best time to look for it, then, would be in periods of bad weather (which nearly always cause a precipitation of migrants) in late April and in May.

The species in spring is recognized by its olive-green upperparts, yellow breast and belly, and gray hood punctuated by a *complete* white eye-ring. The Mourning Warbler also has a gray hood, but it lacks the eye-ring, and in the male the throat is black. Immatures of both species in the fall are greenish brown or brownish green above and yellowish below, with only the Connecticut showing a suggestion of a hood. They are, however, so similar to each other and to female and immature Common Yellowthroats that field identification is often impossible. I have never heard the song, but it is said to resemble the words *three three three three,* uttered without inflections or other variations.

MOURNING WARBLER   *Geothlypis philadelphia*   Pl. XXX

The Mourning Warbler is a rare spring and rather uncommon fall transient in Louisiana. In spring the only place where it has been observed with any consistency is in the Shreveport area. There, as well as elsewhere, it appears in northward migration only in April and May. A bird seen at Shreveport between May 24 and June 3 had what seemed to be a slightly injured wing, which might have been responsible for it lingering so late. In fall the species is recorded with some regularity between the first part of August and mid-October, especially by those who know its haunts and habits. In the latter season it seems most often to frequent brier thickets and dense stands of grass and coffeeweed and is thus very difficult to locate and to study satisfactorily.

In spring the species closely resembles the Connecticut Warbler to the extent that it is olive-green above and yellow below and has a gray hood. The male Mourning Warbler, however, has a conspicuous black throat and no white eye-ring. The female and immature lack the black on the throat, but the absence in spring of the eye-ring is diagnostic, since the Connecticut Warbler always has it. The difficulty of identifying immatures in fall is rendered insurmountable in many cases by the fact that many immature Mourning Warblers also exhibit an eye-ring.

MACGILLIVRAY'S WARBLER   *Geothlypis tolmiei*   Pl. XLI

The only record of this western species in the state is that of an adult male collected by Sidney A. Gauthreaux near Triumph on November 15, 1959. The MacGillivray's Warbler is almost identical with the Mourning Warbler except that adult males possess a small white spot on both the upper and lower eyelids, whereas the male Mourning has no eye-ring at all. The Connecticut Warbler possesses a complete eye-ring in all plumages. Females and immatures of the MacGillivray's and Mourning Warblers can hardly be identified even with specimens in the hand.

MacGillivray's Warbler breeds from southern Alaska south through western Canada and the western United States to central Arizona and central New Mexico. It normally winters in southern Mexico or Guatemala.

HOODED WARBLER   *Wilsonia citrina*   Pl. XXX

The Hooded Warbler is a common summer bird in Louisiana, for it breeds in nearly every hardwood bottomland from one end of the state to the other, except possibly in the northwestern corner, where it seems to be only moderately common. The male is one of the most readily identified of all warblers. The yellow face is completely surrounded by the black of the head, neck, and throat. The remainder of the body is greenish yellow above and bright yellow below. Although no wing bars are present, both sexes possess considerable white in the tail, which is conspicuously flashed as the bird flicks its tail. Females and immature birds are otherwise very nondescript, simply greenish yellow above and bright yellow below; therefore, they are similar to the first-year female and young of the Wilson's Warbler, which, however, are smaller and lack any white in the tail.

The Hooded Warbler arrives in Louisiana early in March and remains until the end of October, rarely later. The only truly winter records are: an adult male seen by Kenneth P. Able at New Orleans on January 18, 1969, and another male observed regularly and on numerous occasions by Robert S. Kennedy in the Atchafalaya Floodway near Palmetto until January 14, 1974. Four or five white or creamy white eggs with tiny reddish brown spots, usually forming a wreath around the larger end, are laid in a nest located in a crotch of a sapling or bush, four to five feet above the ground. In spring and early summer the woods fairly ring with the Hooded's song, a loud *whee, whee, whee-a-whee*. It also has a sharp *chirp* that can hardly be expressed phonetically but which is highly diagnostic when it is once learned by the field observer.

WILSON'S WARBLER   *Wilsonia pusilla*   Pl. XXX

In Louisiana in spring this species is everywhere a rare transient, but it is fairly common in fall migration. Normally the species is seen in late April or May and from the second week of September through the third week of October. Every year an appreciable number remain in southern Louisiana through the cold months, but in some winters it is far more numerous than in others. Indeed, in the winter of 1952–1953 the bird seemed to be virtually everywhere. This was the year when no less than nine species of birds never before recorded from Louisiana were found within our borders. Along with these novelties were numerous other species that, although not being seen for the first time, were nevertheless birds of highly unexpected occurrence in Louisiana at that season. One such species was the little Wilson's Warbler, which seemed literally to inundate the southern part of the state. The species was noted in counts of one to five on twenty-four separate dates between December 6 and March 28, at twenty-three widely separated stations, by more than a score of different observers. For so many of these little birds to have been recorded in the dense thickets that they frequent, there must have been immense numbers of them distributed through the vast expanse of suitable habitat available in southern Louisiana.

The male has a square black patch on top of the head and is otherwise simply yellowish green above and bright yellow below, with no wing bars or white in the tail. The immatures and many females lack the black cap and thus resemble the female and young of the Hooded Warbler. The latter, however, is larger and shows white in the outer tail feathers. Also the immature Wilson's Warbler has the bright yellow of the throat extending up on the face around the black eye, thereby forming a sort of light superciliary line. This aids in its separation from other plain yellowish warblers with which it might be confused. The female Common Yellowthroat has no such light line over the eye, is much browner above, and generally has brownish flanks and a whitish belly. The female Hooded Warbler is darker green above (less yellowish) and shows white when it flicks the tail. Immature Yellow Warblers have bright yellow patches on the inner margins of the tail feathers and are more uniformly pale yellowish all over.

CANADA WARBLER *Wilsonia canadensis* Pl. XXX

Other names for this bird might have alluded in some way to the diagnostic black "necklace" markings across the chest, or to its bluish gray back and yellow underparts, or even to its yellow "spectacle" marks. The female and immatures in fall have only an indication of the black necklace, but the combination of plain bluish gray upperparts and yellow underparts, along with the absence of white in the wings or tail, provides conclusive points in its identification.

In Louisiana, the Canada Warbler is strictly a bird of passage that is rather uncommon in spring, although occasionally as many as a dozen can be seen in a day. The highest count ever was the 28 seen by James R. Stewart at Shreveport on May 7, 1960. It is fairly common in fall, being often quite numerous in the cottonwood-willow thickets on the banks and in the battures of our larger streams. Extreme periods of occurrence are March 31 through May 22 and from August 9 through November 4.

PAINTED REDSTART   *Myioborus pictus*   Pl. XXXI

The normal occurrence of the Painted Redstart in the United States is limited to Arizona, New Mexico, and the Chisos Mountains of western Texas, where it breeds in high montane forests, and whence almost the entire population migrates southward into Mexico in winter. The inexplicable appearance of an adult individual in City Park in New Orleans on November 17, 1952, and its subsequent observation in the same place almost daily until December 7 provide one of the very few known instances of the presence of the species anywhere in the United States in winter except for the mountains west and northwest of Nogales, Arizona. The bird was first detected by Mrs. Thelma von Gohren and then two weeks later by Henry B. Chase, Jr., each without the other's knowledge.

The Painted Redstart is easily recognized by its striking combination of colors. It has predominantly lustrous black upperparts and hood, carmine red breast and belly, and conspicuous white wing patches, white outer tail

---

Plate XXXI Wood-Warblers

(Spring plumage unless otherwise specified; when only one bird of a species is shown, the sexes are quite similar) 1. male Palm Warbler (pp. 39 and 516), western subspecies; 1a. female of same; 1b. male of eastern subspecies. 2. male Blackburnian Warbler (p. 513); 2a. female; 2b. male in fall; 2c. immature. 3. male Black-throated Green Warbler (p. 511); 3a. female. 4. male Chestnut-sided Warbler (p. 507); 4a. female; 4b. immature in fall. 5. male Bay-breasted Warbler (p. 518); 5a. female; 5b. immature male in fall. 6. male Orange-crowned Warbler (p. 503) in winter; 6a. immature in winter. 7. male Tennessee Warbler (p. 502); 7a. immature in fall. 8. male Blue-winged Warbler (p. 501). 9. male Prothonotary Warbler (p. 525); 9a. female or immature. 10. male Yellow Warbler (p. 506); 10a. immature in fall. 11. adult male American Redstart (p. 519); 11a. female; 11b. immature male. 12. male Painted Redstart (p. 532). 13. male Common Yellowthroat (p. 526); 13a. female. 14. Yellow-breasted Chat (p. 533). 15. male Cerulean Warbler (p. 507); 15a. female. 16. male Northern Parula Warbler (p. 504); 16a. female; 16b. male in fall. 17. male Blue-winged Warbler (p. 501); 17a. male "Brewster's" Warbler (p. 501); 17b. male "Lawrence's" Warbler (p. 501). 18. male Golden-winged Warbler (p. 500).

feathers, and white undertail coverts. The species was until recently considered a member of the genus *Setophaga*, to which our summer resident American Redstart belongs. Now the Painted Redstart is considered unequivocally a member of the genus *Myioborus*, in a different segment of the family Parulidae.

YELLOW-BREASTED CHAT *Icteria virens* Pl. XXXI; p. 533

The chat has been labeled the "buffoon of the brier patch" because of its ludicrous antics and the medley of whistling, chuckling, barking, scolding, mewing sounds that pass as its song. The fact that it is classified as a wood-warbler always comes as a surprise to students of ornithology, possibly because of its larger size, which approaches that of the Eastern Bluebird, and because of its large bill. Despite its peculiarities, however, various anatomical characteristics indicate familial relationship to the warblers. Both sexes are olive-green above and yellow below, except for the white abdomen and the white undertail coverts. There is a white line above and below the eye, the former extending to the base of the bill, but there is no white in the tail and no white bars are present on the wing.

ellow-breasted Chat—The Buffoon of the Brier Patch

SAMUEL A. GRIMES

Although the chat is generally retiring in habits, hiding away in a dense thicket to give voice to its repertoire of comical sounds, it does often mount to the top of a tall tree to perform its "flight song." Sometimes it flings itself straight upward to a considerable height with its legs dangling, its head up, and its wings beating spasmodically. When it reaches the apex of its flight it bursts forth in an ecstasy of gurgles and whistles and then, as if physically spent, it drops back to its perch, only soon to repeat the performance. An even more remarkable exhibition is performed when the "flight song" is rendered as the bird flies straightaway, from the top of one tall tree to another 50 feet or more away. Its incredibly slow transit in doing this is accomplished by a laborious flapping of the wings, barely sufficient to sustain flight, and with the legs dangling and the tail held down at a right angle to the body. All the while there is a flood of assorted sounds that the great New England ornithologist Edward H. Forbush recorded as follows: *c-r-r-r-r-r, whrr, that's it, chee, quack, cluck, yit-yit-yit, now hit it, t-r-r-r-r, wher, caw, caw, cut, cut, tea-boy, who, who, mew, mew,* repeated over and over in almost identical sequence. With notes like that, can there be any wonder that the chat is regarded as comical?

The one thing that above all makes the chat one of my favorite birds is its habit of singing at night, in the manner of a mockingbird. Hence I am always delighted when, in mid-April, the species returns to Louisiana after its winter sojourn in the tropics. It regularly remains with us until the end of October, and a few can almost always be found somewhere in southern Louisiana in the middle of the winter.

The chat lays three to five speckled white eggs. Its bulky nest of coarse grasses and leaves, lined with finer grasses, is placed in a crotch in a dense thicket.

The Weaver Finch Family
Ploceidae

HOUSE SPARROW   *Passer domesticus*   Fig. 130

The House Sparrow, or English Sparrow, certainly requires no introduction. It is common in and about cities, as well as near farmhouses, and is everywhere a general nuisance and a source of economic loss to man. Its presence discourages beneficial native songbirds from entering our yards and gardens in greater numbers; it usurps nesting boxes that we build for martins, bluebirds, and woodpeckers; it denudes our bird-feeding tables of the food we place there for Blue Jays, Northern Cardinals, and other more attractive species; its large, massive nests clutter the drains and gutters of our houses; it consumes great quantities of our chicken feed; and its droppings defile our sidewalks and stain our automobiles. In brief, it is the *persona non grata* of America's avian population—an alien that unfortunately cannot now be deported.

The species was first introduced in Brooklyn, in 1850 and 1852, and by 1870 it had begun its phenomenal spread throughout nearly all of North America where there were settlements. The bird's period of greatest productivity and abundance seems to have been during the horse-and-buggy days. Now that automobiles have replaced the horse, its population has declined somewhat. Even so, the bird is still tremendously abundant. One year in August alone I trapped and destroyed 360 House Sparrows in my yard. When on the last day of the month I caught 17 individuals, more than I had caught the first day, I decided that the project of trying to eradicate the House Sparrow in that particular neighborhood was virtually hopeless. As birds were eliminated, others were simply moving in to fill the gaps.

The House Sparrow is a member of the Weaver Finch family of the Old World. Unlike our native sparrows of the family Fringillidae, which build cup-shaped nests, the Weaver Finches build nests that are large, domed structures into which the bird enters through a hole on the side; a

535

Figure 130   House Sparrow: male in front; female behind.

tunnel leads upward and then downward toward the rear. There, in a mass of chicken feathers and other soft materials, four to seven whitish eggs, densely but finely speckled with black, are laid.

The male House Sparrow, with its predominantly chestnut back and wings, is not unattractive. In fall, following the postnuptial molt, the characteristic black throat is obscured by the grayish tips of the feathers. As the winter season progresses, however, these light tips wear off, revealing the black beneath. The female is grayish brown above, except for a few black streaks on the back, and dirty white or pale buffy below. Although superficially she resembles some of the plain-colored native sparrows, the bird student quickly learns to know her, first by her association with the male and then by certain indefinable but distinctive qualities that go with her position as a member of the Weaver Finch family. Juvenile males resemble the female until after the postjuvenal molt that takes place in late summer.

The Blackbird, Oriole, and Meadowlark Family

Icteridae

This large family includes blackbirds, orioles, meadowlarks, and their allies. The group is confined to the Western Hemisphere, where there are nearly 100 species, most of which are tropical or subtropical in distribution. Some, like the orioles, build deep, pendulous nests, are brilliantly colored, and are capable of rendering superb songs. Others build cup-shaped nests, are drab in appearance, and emit squeaky, unmusical sounds. And one, the Brown-headed Cowbird, even builds no nest at all but instead lays its eggs in other birds' nests.

BOBOLINK   *Dolichonyx oryzivorus*   Pl. XXXII

The Bobolink is a common spring transient throughout Louisiana but extremely rare this far west in fall on its return journey southward. It seldom appears before the last of April, but from then until late May or early June, casually to June 16, it can be seen in small flocks, mainly in uncut hay fields. The rarity of the Bobolink in Louisiana in fall is demonstrated by the fact that at Baton Rouge it has been recorded only three times in that season, despite more than 40 years of intensive fieldwork there. Two of the three records were TV tower kills.

The male Bobolink is strikingly and diagnostically attired in black, punctuated by white patches on the wings, yellow on the nape, and an extensive white area on the rump and lower back. The female is simply buffy yellow, streaked above with black. The remotely similar female Red-winged Blackbird is dull brownish or brownish black above and dingy white, heavily streaked with blackish, below.

537

The song has been described as a rollicking melody that seems to suggest to some people the phrase *bob-o-link, spink, spank, spink*. It may be heard in our fields as the males move northward toward their breeding grounds in the northern United States and southern Canada. The species winters in South America, south of the Amazon River.

EASTERN MEADOWLARK   *Sturnella magna*   Pl. XXXII; Fig. 131

The Eastern Meadowlark, or "field lark" as it is often called, is in no sense related to the true larks (which are uncommon here). It is instead more closely kin to the blackbirds. The bright yellow breast with the V-shaped band across the chest and its habit of singing loudly from fence posts, telephone wires, and haystacks in the vicinity of fields that are its home make it both conspicuous and attractive. It is common the year around, going about in loose flocks in winter and breaking up into pairs in early spring.

The song to me seems to say, "Laziness will kill you," the last two notes being slurred downward. The nest is built on the ground and is roofed over, making it very difficult to locate. The four to six eggs are white, spotted with brownish. For the distinctions between the Eastern and Western Meadowlarks, see the following account.

WESTERN MEADOWLARK   *Sturnella neglecta*   Fig. 131

Despite the fact that seven states have either officially or unofficially adopted the meadowlark as their state bird, there are probably very few people, aside from ornithologists, who know that there are two kinds of meadowlarks. This is not surprising, since the two species are barely distinguishable and then only under the most favorable circumstances. The significant color differences between them are that the Western Meadowlark is noticeably lighter above, being olive-brown or grayish brown instead of reddish brown, and the bars on its inner wing feathers, rump, and tail are not connected along the shaft (Fig. 131). The chief distinction between the two species,

---

Plate XXXII   Three Members of the Blackbird Family
1. male Bobolink (p. 537) in spring. 2. female Bobolink (p. 537) in spring. 3. male Red-winged Blackbird (p. 541) in spring. 4. female Red-winged Blackbird (p. 541) in spring. 5. Eastern Meadowlark (p. 538).

Figure 131 The two species of meadowlarks: Eastern Meadowlark, left; Western Meadowlark, right. Also shown is one of the innermost secondaries of each species. The fact that the black crossbars are connected along the shaft of the feather in the Eastern Meadowlark but not connected in the Western is a useful field mark under favorable circumstances.

however, is in their songs, which are totally dissimilar. The Eastern Meadowlark has generally a four-noted, slurred song, while the Western Meadowlark's song consists of nine or ten notes, some double, that are both flutelike and gurgling. Where the summer ranges of the two species overlap, there has been little indication of interbreeding. Consequently, regardless of the difficulties we have in telling them apart, the birds themselves evidently experience no uncertainty in this regard.

In Louisiana the Western Meadowlark is a winter resident that occurs mainly from November to March. In northwestern Louisiana, however, it remains much later. Singing males, apparently with well-defined territories, were seen near Gilliam in Caddo Parish in April and May 1952. One of the dome-shaped nests of this species containing five eggs, indistinguishable from those of the Eastern Meadowlark, was discovered in the same area on May 11. Also, in April 1960, one member of a pair was watched almost daily as it built a nest on the Mississippi River levee opposite the Louisiana

State University campus at Baton Rouge. The birds were last observed on April 20, but a day or so later the levee was mowed, the nest destroyed, and the birds could not be found. The main breeding grounds of the Western Meadowlark are in the Great Plains region, westward to British Columbia and southward into Mexico.

YELLOW-HEADED BLACKBIRD   *Xanthocephalus xanthocephalus*

Fig. 132

The Yellow-headed Blackbird is a rare winter visitor and a rare spring and fall transient for which only some three dozen definite records in Louisiana are on file. The male is as large as an American Robin or Common Grackle and is easily distinguished by its bright yellow head and white wing patches contrasting with an otherwise black body. Young males and the females are browner and have most of the yellow confined to the throat and chest.

This strikingly attired inhabitant of the marshes of the Great Plains region of the United States and Canada migrates in fall mainly into the

Figure 132   Male Yellow-headed Blackbird.

southern part of its breeding range, in Mexico. In Louisiana it has been seen most frequently in the southern part of the state, particularly in Cameron Parish, but it has also appeared occasionally in the northern section, in De Soto, Caddo, and Morehouse parishes. Horace H. Jeter and James R. Stewart regard it as a rare and irregular spring transient in the Shreveport area. Extreme dates of occurrence, considering all available records, are from August 13 through May 16, but as yet no sightings have been made in the month of February. Approximately half of the records are in April.

RED-WINGED BLACKBIRD   *Agelaius phoeniceus*   Pl. XXXII

Few birds are more attractive than the jet black Red-winged Blackbird, particularly in spring when it pours forth its gurgling *konk-ker-ree* song from a fence post and flaunts its brilliant red "epaulets," or patches on the bend of its wings. The female, in sharp contrast, is dull brownish above and dingy white below, heavily streaked above and below with brownish black.

The species is a common summer resident throughout the state, and in winter its numbers are augmented manyfold by the hordes of Red-wings that come down from the North and West to take advantage of our mild weather and the abundance of food that is here available to them. The sexes segregate into separate flocks at the end of the breeding season, males in one place and females and young elsewhere. Sometimes in the rice fields of southwestern Louisiana, a single compact flock may number thousands of individuals, which wheel and turn in the sky in unison, oftentimes appearing at a distance like a huge cloud of smoke. When spring comes, many of these birds head back northward to lend their beauty and charm to the lakeshores and little patches of marsh. But before they are gone, our own breeding population has set about the task of establishing territories, building nests, and raising one or two broods of young. The three to five bluish eggs, spotted or splotched with purple or black, are laid in a cup-shaped nest of grasses suspended between stalks of reeds or limbs of bushes and small trees, sometimes 20 to 30 feet up but usually only a few feet from the ground. The call note is a sharp *chuck* or a slurred *teeer*.

ORCHARD ORIOLE   *Icterus spurius*   Pl. XXXIV

This abundant summer resident occurs in all parts of Louisiana, including even such places as the spoil banks in the coastal marshes and the mangrove-covered islands along the edge of the Gulf. The fully adult male has the head, back, tail, and part of the wings black. The remainder of the wing is chestnut, as are also the rump and the underparts. Hence it is not nearly so resplendent as its close relative, the Baltimore Oriole, which is black and orange. The female and young of the year are greenish yellow above and bright yellow below, hence resemble immature Yellow Warblers, but are, of course, more than twice as large. The female Baltimore Oriole is slightly larger than the Orchard Oriole, more orange colored below, and darker above. First-year male Orchard Orioles acquire a black bib; otherwise they, too, resemble the female. Finally, in the second year, the male acquires the full-dress coat of black and chestnut.

The Orchard Oriole builds its partially pendulous nest of closely inter-woven grasses in a bush or tree, usually 8 to 15 feet above the ground. In it are placed three to five bluish white eggs, blotched and scrawled with black markings. The song is a highly pleasing but jumbled outburst of clear whistles that can be heard almost continuously from the time the bird arrives in mid-March until it departs in late summer and early fall. Although an occasional individual is seen up to late October, and even casually to the end of November, the bulk of the breeding population leaves in late sum-mer. In the New Orleans area, and especially in the delta region below that city, the Orchard Oriole is fairly regular in occurrence in winter. At least a dozen sightings have been made of the species there in December, January, and early February. One December 5, 1965, record from Grand Cheniere, in Cameron Parish, is also on file, but as yet none have been seen on any of the Sabine Christmas Bird Counts.

SCOTT'S ORIOLE   *Icterus parisorum*   Pl. XLI

This western species of oriole is known from Louisiana on the basis of only six records. The first was that of an immature male collected by Sidney A. Gauthreaux at Cameron on December 27, 1958, and the specimen is now in the LSU Museum of Zoology. Ava R. Tabor observed a male in full plumage on a bird feeder at Thibodaux on May 6, 1962, and Mr. and Mrs. Kenneth McGee and Buford Myers saw one at New Orleans on January 29, 1967. On November 9, 1969, Robert J. Newman and Kenneth P. Able observed a female near Holly Beach, in Cameron Parish, and, finally, Mrs. Claudia Morton reported the appearance of a male Scott's Oriole at one of the feeders in her yard at Eunice in two successive winters. It arrived on January 26, 1973, and remained until March 15. In 1974 it appeared on January 29 and was present daily until March 8.

The adult male Scott's Oriole is mainly black, with the shoulders, rump, basal half of the outer tail feathers, and posterior underparts bright yellow. Females and immature males are rather nondescript but differ from our other orioles in being decidedly more greenish above and below.

BALTIMORE ORIOLE *Icterus galbula* Pl. XXXIV; Fig. 133

In Louisiana the Baltimore Oriole is represented by orioles of two types, each of which was until recently treated as a distinct species. In one the male is brilliant orange with a solid black hood. It is primarily a summer resident throughout the eastern United States and Canada and is the bird long known as the Baltimore Oriole (*Icterus galbula*). The other type lacks the solid black hood, having only the top of the head, lores, and the throat black with the remainder of the head orange-yellow, and possesses a prominent patch of white on the shoulders and bend of the wing. It is present here only as an uncommon migrant and winter visitor, and it breeds in the Great Plains and other parts of the western United States and southwestern Canada; it has long gone under the name of Bullock's Oriole (*I. bullockii*). The two forms are now known to hybridize freely where their ranges meet in the Great Plains of the central part of the United States. Since the name *Icterus galbula* has nomenclatural priority over *I. bullockii*, the former became the scientific name of the enlarged species. Some ornithologists would prefer to coin a new vernacular, such as Northern Oriole, for the species, because, according to their arguments, the use of the name Baltimore Oriole might imply that only the population of the eastern United States was being re-

Figure 133 Male Bullock's type of the Baltimore Oriole (left) and male black-hooded type (right).

ferred to, just as the use of the name Bullock's Oriole might imply that the western population was intended. Unfortunately, though, the name Baltimore Oriole is deeply engrained in ornithological literature, and I believe it should be retained as the name of the species. When an ornithologist wishes to specify one or the other of the two forms now treated as a single species, without resorting to a trinomial scientific name, the designation for the eastern bird can be Baltimore Oriole (black-hooded type). And for the western bird it can be Baltimore Oriole (Bullock's type).

Of all the vividly plumaged orioles that inhabit the tropics, none is more brilliant than our own Baltimore Oriole. It is larger than the Orchard Oriole and is a fiery reddish orange on the belly, shoulders, and rump, instead of drab chestnut. The female and immatures are more soberly dressed, being dusky gray above and only slightly orange below. The song is a clear, flutelike whistle that is heard from the first week of April until late summer.

The species is particularly numerous as a breeding bird in the large shade trees of our cities, from at least the latitude of Baton Rouge northward, but it also inhabits stands of cottonwoods along our rivers and is quite fond of pecan orchards. The nest is a rather long, pendent structure of closely knitted grasses, firmly anchored to each side of a fork of a horizontal limb. Although the nest sways widely in a strong wind, the four to six bluish eggs, which are scrawled with blackish marks, are perfectly safe; only by turning the nest upside down could they be made to roll out.

The black-hooded type of Baltimore Oriole arrives in early April and remains with us until October, but it is also fairly regularly present in winter. Although most of the records of it in the cold months are in the southern part of the state, it has likewise been seen at that time in our northern parishes at such places as Alexandria, Natchitoches, Shreveport, Monroe, and a few miles northeast of Ferriday on Durango Island. Many, but by no means all, winter records are of birds seen on feeding tables in residential situations, especially where suet is used as an attractant.

The Bullock's type of the Baltimore Oriole is widespread in its occurrence in the state in winter, having been noted on over 150 occasions at well over 25 different localities from Cross Lake and Coushatta in the northwestern section to Venice in the Mississippi River delta below New Orleans on dates ranging from September 11 through May 24. The Bullock's type closely resembles the black-hooded type, but instead of the male possessing a black hood, as does the male of the latter, it has the black largely confined to a bib on the throat and to the top of the head. It has a great deal of orange-yellow on the face and sides of the neck. The male also shows a conspicuous white patch in the wings, whereas the male black-hooded type has the shoulders orange and the white is limited to the tips of the greater wing coverts and to white emarginations on the primaries and secondaries. The female Bullock's type is decidedly paler above and is much whiter (less yellowish) below than the female of the black-hooded type.

RUSTY BLACKBIRD *Euphagus carolinus*   Fig. 134

The Rusty Blackbird is a fairly common to abundant winter visitor throughout nearly all of Louisiana from late October until the second week of April, rarely occurring later. It is seen in large flocks feeding in fields, orchards, and open, wet woods. The male is all-black except for the brownish tips to the feathers. The brown emarginations that are the basis for the bird's vernacular name, gradually wear off as winter progresses, so that by the time spring arrives the males are usually a solid shiny black, punctuated by yellow eyes. Females and immatures in fall are slate-gray, with a great deal more rusty tipping to the feathers than in adult males, but they too undergo great plumage change through wear. As the brown tips to the feathers disappear, the female assumes a uniform dark gray color, very similar to the color of the female Brewer's Blackbird. The yellow eye is, however, diagnostic, since the eye color in the female of the latter species is dark. The call of the bird, according to A. A. Saunders, is a loud *chack*, and the song, though musical, suggests "a slowly rotating wheel which has one or two different squeaks at regular intervals in its rotation."

BREWER'S BLACKBIRD *Euphagus cyanocephalus*   Fig. 134

This and the preceding species are sometimes seen together. Under these circumstances they are not too difficult to separate, particularly in the fall. The male Brewer's Blackbird is always blacker in the fall since it does not usually possess the brownish tips to the feathers that render the Rusty Blackbird almost as much rusty brown as black. Another fairly good feature of the Brewer's Blackbird is its whiter (less yellowish) eye. The plumage of the female in fall is decidedly more grayish (less brownish) than that of the female Rusty Blackbird, but by spring the female Rusty actually becomes the grayer of the two. Fortunately, the eye color is always diagnostic —dark in the female Brewer's, yellow in the female Rusty.

The Brewer's Blackbird is here only in winter, arriving in early October and remaining until late April. It breeds mainly from the eastern edge of the

Figure 134   Males of two similar species of blackbirds that visit Louisiana in winter: Rusty Blackbird, left; Brewer's Blackbird, right.

Great Plains westward to the Pacific Coast and southward into Mexico and was until rather recently believed to be only a rare winter visitor in the southeastern United States. Fieldwork in this area in the last three decades has, however, shown it to be common or even sometimes abundant. It shows a predilection for open situations, such as pastures, burned fields, pine woods, and orchards, where it feeds entirely on the ground.

The beginning student usually confuses the Rusty and Brewer's Blackbirds with the Common Grackle. The latter, however, is decidedly larger, with a bigger bill, has a wedged-shaped and much more graduated tail, and, though subject to variation in southeastern Louisiana, has the head usually iridescent bottle green and the back metallic bronze colored or rich purplish. The Brewer's Blackbird, on the other hand, shows only faint purplish reflections on the head and a dull greenish sheen on the back.

GREAT-TAILED GRACKLE   *Cassidix mexicanus*

Pl. XXXIII; Figs. 4, 135

The Great-tailed and Boat-tailed Grackles were originally regarded as separate species, but then for a considerable period of time they were considered conspecific, that is, members of a single species but of two distinct subspecies. Now, the consensus of experts is that the two should again be treated as distinct species. The Great-tailed Grackle is larger than the Boat-tailed, slightly different in color, and distinguishable by marked behavioral peculiarities. Where their ranges overlap in extreme southwestern Louisiana, occasional breakdowns occur in the reproductive isolating mechanisms that normally serve to keep the two apart, and, as a result, hybridization sometimes takes place. But this interbreeding of the two has never occurred with sufficient frequency to produce a hybrid population.

The adult male Great-tailed Grackle possesses a more purplish (less greenish) iridescence than does the adult male Boat-tail, and the female is more olive (less brownish) in color. The eye of the adult male and female Great-tail is yellow, while that of the Boat-tail in Louisiana is usually brown. Eye color is the best visual way to distinguish the two species in the field, but call notes are also useful. H. Douglas Pratt, one of the artists to whom I am indebted for the new illustrations in this edition of *Louisiana Birds*, has made a detailed study of the relationships of the two species of grackles in their zone of contact in southwestern Louisiana. This experienced student of the problem considers the varied repertoire of calls of the Great-tail to contain more musical notes, as well as more mechanical-sounding ones than the vocalizations of the Boat-tail. He describes one of the main calls of the Great-tail as a series of loud *clacks* or *clocks* that resemble the sound produced by a child's toy machine gun. The species also emits a clear, ascending whistle. The notes of the Boat-tail are harsher but never as mechanical sounding as some of those of the Great-tail. Pratt verbalizes the Great-tail's most frequent performance as a series of *shrib* or *jeeb* notes. He describes a commonly heard call of the Boat-tail as a sound resembling that produced by a coot pattering its feet on the water at takeoff.

In the courtship behavior of the two species, Boat-tails fluff the feathers of the head and neck (Fig. 135). This display gives them a rather thick-headed appearance. Great-tails, on the other hand, slick down the feathers of the head and take on a thin-headed, even pointed, appearance. Males of the two species, when proclaiming their territories or attempting to attract mates, indulge in the most bizarre antics. Stretching the neck upward, with the bill pointed to the sky and with wings and tail fanned, the birds emit series of weird, discordant squeaks and whistles that only technically can be classed as "song."

The species, unlike the Boat-tail, often occurs far removed from coastal situations. Indeed, in Mexico the Great-tailed Grackle extends across

Great—tailed Grackle   Boat—tailed Grackle

Figure 135   Posturing position in the Great-tailed Grackle and the Boat-tailed Grackle.

the breadth of the republic, occurring both in the tropical lowlands and on the high central plateau. The only large grackle of the genus *Cassidix* ever recorded in northern Louisiana was a yellow-eyed female Great-tail found by Horace H. Jeter and James R. Stewart on April 6, 1957, at Wallace Lake Dam, near Shreveport. Since Great-tails have extended their range in Texas northward and now breed in numbers in the Dallas area, they may also eventually expand farther inland in Louisiana. Actual nesting within our borders is presently limited to Cameron and Calcasieu parishes, but the species may be in the process of expanding its range eastward. Pratt has found that, although Great-tails are sometimes found in southern Louisiana in winter, most of them desert the state at that time and do not return until early spring.

BOAT-TAILED GRACKLE   *Cassidix major*   Figs. 4, 135

No one can visit the coastal marshes of Louisiana without seeing this large, long-tailed blackbird, which is sometimes called the "chock" or "crow black-bird." Although it is much smaller in body size than the Fish Crow, its exceedingly long tail makes it equal in total length to some examples of that species. The male Boat-tail appears to be all-black when viewed at a distance, but at close range, in good light, it turns out to be highly iridescent with intermingled blue, purple, and even dark green. The female is a nondescript tawny brown, except for the wings and tail, which are blackish brown. Young males just out of the nest resemble females in color. Within two months or so, however, they undergo a postjuvenal molt that puts them in their first winter plumage, which is dull uniform black. The following summer, at the time of the annual molt, the drab plumage gives way to the shiny, iridescent coat of steel blue and metallic greens and purple.

The Boat-tailed Grackle in Louisiana has brown eyes, a feature that readily sets it apart from the Great-tailed Grackle, in which the eye color is bright golden yellow. The eye of the male Boat-tail sometimes shows a narrow rim of yellow around the perimeter of the iris, and occasionally it may even appear to be a dull yellowish brown. The flashing of the white nictitating membrane across the eye also lends to it a light appearance under certain circumstances, but as H. Douglas Pratt has so adeptly expressed the matter, if there is ever any doubt as to whether a grackle has the eye a bright enough yellow to belong to a Great-tail, then the bird in question is *not* a Great-tail. This statement applies, however, only to Louisiana and other northern Gulf Coast populations, for Boat-tails on the Atlantic Coast do, indeed, have yellow eyes.

The species gets its common name from the huge keel-shaped or wedge-shaped tail, which is particularly evident, both when the bird is in flight and when it is perched. The extremely long legs are utilized to the fullest, for the bird holds its body high. It also keeps the long tail elevated at an angle as it walks or hops over the ground, usually in wet marsh areas but also in plowed fields near the coast.

In Louisiana the Boat-tail is primarily a resident of the coastal marshes, although it occurs commonly in the city parks of New Orleans and occasionally in fall and winter wanders a short distance inland along the numerous waterways in the southern part of our state. Only three times, however, has the bird been known to range as far up the Mississippi River as Baton Rouge.

Boat-tailed Grackles build their massive nests of grasses in colonies between upright stalks of marsh vegetation, in bushes such as mangrove, or in the top branches of trees that grow on the chenieres. The large bluish green eggs are beautifully blotched and scrawled with irregular purplish, vinaceous, and black markings.

COMMON GRACKLE *Quiscalus quiscula* Pl. XXXIII

The Common Grackle is a familiar bird everywhere in the state, except in the coastal marshes, where it is replaced by its much larger relative, the Boat-tailed Grackle. Like the latter bird, it has a long, plicate, graduated tail, which it often folds keellike into the form of a V. Its size, however, is only slightly larger. than that of an American Robin, and although it somewhat resembles the Boat-tail, its colors are different in hue and are distributed in well-defined areas or plumage tracts.

Two general types of Common Grackles inhabit the state. One is the bronze-backed type, with a bottle green head, that breeds north of a line roughly from Lake Charles to Bunkie. The other type, with its metallic green back and purplish head, breeds in the extreme southeastern corner of the state, mainly in the area south of Lake Pontchartrain. Where the ranges of the two meet, a zone of overlap occurs in which the hybrids are variously intermediate in color. Since the hybrid population tends to show a preponderance of purple, both on the head and the back, the name Purple Grackle has been used for it by some authors. Contact between the two types takes place along a line extending from south Louisiana to New Jersey and always with the same results. Consequently, there seems to be no basis for considering the two as separate species.

Common Grackles associate in small colonies, building their bulky nests of mud and grasses in the upper part of trees. In late summer, when the task of rearing a family is completed, the birds undergo a complete molt and then gather into large flocks, which forage over the countryside, cover our lawns and parks, and are in every way conspicuous. In late afternoon these bands assemble from far and wide at one huge nighttime roost, which is usually in a large swampy wood. Aggregations running into the tens of thousands are common.

Although on occasion grackles may do some damage to crops, their food habits are for the most part beneficial, since they eat great quantities of insects. The usual call note is a coarse *chock*, and the song is a squeaky sound that is almost identical with that produced by a rusty hinge on a door or gate.

BROWN-HEADED COWBIRD *Molothrus ater* Fig. 136

Cowbirds are renowned for one thing—the female lays her eggs in the nests of other birds. When the time comes for her to deposit her clutch, she skulks about through the trees and underbrush until she locates her victim, usually a small bird such as a warbler, vireo, or sparrow. Stealthily, when the rightful owner is away, she sneaks in, drops an egg, and then disappears, never to have any share in the task of incubation or rearing of the young. The foster parents

Plate XXXIII Adult Grackles

1. male Great-tailed Grackle (p. 546). 2. female Great-tailed Grackle (p. 546). 3. male Common Grackle (p. 549).

RET

Figure 136   Male Brown-headed Cowbird.

occasionally abandon their nest in these circumstances, but generally they work tirelessly to give the cowbird egg proper incubation and to feed the young bird all the food it needs. Because of their much smaller size, usually the legitimate young suffer both from the crowded conditions of the nest and the fact that they cannot raise their heads high enough to get food from their parents as regularly as does the baby cowbird.

Various theories purport to explain the parasitic egg-laying habits of the cowbird. One holds that the cowbird has lost some of its territoriality, causing it also to lose the urge to build a nest. Another theory contends that there is a "lack of attunement" in the normal sequence of territory establishment, territory defense, courtship, mating, nest building, and egg laying. In other words, the female cowbird gets the urge to lay and has eggs ready for laying before getting the urge to build a nest.

The cowbird receives its name from its habit of feeding around cows; for a similar reason it was once called the "buffalo bird." The male is solid black except for a brown head. The female is gray without any distinctive markings except a dirty whitish throat. The absence of streaks visible in the field serves to distinguish her from the female Red-winged Blackbird. In the juvenal plumage, which lasts only until late summer, the underparts are prominently streaked, but the conical bill alone is usually sufficient to distinguish young birds from the female Red-wing. This same character also differentiates the female cowbird from the larger female Rusty and female Brewer's Blackbirds. The song of the Brown-headed Cowbird is a gurgling, bubbling rendition given by the male from some high, treetop perch. Like all blackbirds, it also has a chuckling call note.

The Brown-headed Cowbird is a common and widespread permanent resident in Louisiana. In both summer and winter the species is more numerous in the southern part of the state than it is in northern Louisiana.

BRONZED COWBIRD   *Tangavius aeneus*   Pl. XLI

This predominantly Middle American species, which normally occurs from southern Texas to Panama, has been recorded only five times within our borders. The first observation of it was on December 31, 1961, on Little Cheniere, in Cameron Parish, where Robert B. and Mary Ann Moore and others saw a male at a distance close enough to note the greenish bronze sheen to the plumage and the red eyes. Perhaps this record alone would not have provided an adequate basis for adding the species to the state list, but fortunately this decision is not required, for on March 14, 1964, Murrell Butler collected a specimen from one of his banding traps, three miles west of Port Allen, in West Baton Rouge Parish. The specimen is now in the LSU Museum of Zoology. Again, on April 12, 1971, and subsequently until at least June 5, C. J. Cuculu, and later numerous other observers, studied a male that made regular visits to a bird feeder in Metairie, near New Orleans. One was also noted, again on Little Cheniere, the scene of the initial discovery, on April 12, 1972, by H. Douglas Pratt, and at Gum Cove, in extreme Cameron Parish, on May 27, 1972, by Stephen M. Russell, Pratt, and Mr. and Mrs. Robert J. Newman. In all instances, the observers carefully supplied supporting details, including the color of the eye, the presence of the neck ruff, and the bronzy sheen to the contour feathers.

The Bronzed Cowbird is easily distinguished from the Brown-headed Cowbird because it lacks the brown head in contrast to an otherwise black plumage that is characteristic of the latter. The eye is red (not brown), the general coloration is slightly greenish bronze (not glossy black), and the feathers of the neck form a pronounced ruff. The female is similar, but the ruff of the neck is less conspicuous. In the female Brown-headed Cowbird the general body color is grayish and the throat is whitish.

The Tanager Family

Thraupidae

The tanagers are members of another strictly New World family. Some of them are so similar to certain finches that authorities do not always agree as to their proper allocation. Indeed, some experts now treat the tanagers as a subfamily of the family Emberizidae, which contains in addition only the buntings and American sparrows, the cardinal-grosbeaks, the Plush-capped Finch, and the Swallow-Tanager, as well as a portion of the species that are otherwise assigned to the family Coerebidae. The present taxon, whether it be a family or a subfamily, embraces 240 species, and of these only four reach the United States. The remainder are mainly tropical or subtropical in their distribution. The group includes some of the most vividly colored of all birds.

WESTERN TANAGER *Piranga ludoviciana* Fig. 137

This Rocky Mountain species is an uncommon transient in spring and fall and a casual winter resident that has been observed nowhere in the state except in our southern parishes. It has been definitely recorded on no less than 39 occasions at some 18 different localities in Cameron, Lafayette, Pointe Coupee, West Feliciana, East Baton Rouge, Tangipahoa, Lafourche, St. John the Baptist, Jefferson, Orleans, and Plaquemines parishes. Twenty-three of the records are in spring, eight in late summer and fall, and seven in winter. One is an anomalous sighting by Ralph Cambre, Ronald J. Stein, and Melvin Weber of two males and a female at Reserve on June 15, 1963. Extreme dates of occurrence are otherwise from August 30 through May 23.

The male of the Western Tanager has a red face; yellow neck, rump, and underparts; and black tail, wings, and back. It is easily recognized not

Figure 137   Male Western Tanager.

only by this combination of characters but also by its two prominent yellow
wing bars; no other tanager in the United States possesses wing bars of any
sort. Females are simply dull greenish above and yellowish below but, like
the male, can be quickly identified by the yellowish wing bars.

SCARLET TANAGER   *Piranga olivacea*   Pl. XXXIV

I think that of all the brilliant birds I have ever seen, including those of the
tropics, none excels the male Scarlet Tanager in splendor. The jet black
wings and black tail add to its trim appearance and accentuate the scarlet
color of its body. The female is a sober olive-green, which is fortunate, since
she does all the incubating of the eggs. It would certainly be disastrous to the
species if the conspicuous male should attempt to share these duties, for he
would surely attract predators.

The sequence of molt in the Scarlet Tanager is particularly noteworthy.

Plate XXXIV   Tanagers, Orioles, Rufous-sided Towhee, and Red Crossbill
1. adult male Summer Tanager (p. 555); 1a. spring male changing into adult plumage;
1b. female. 2. adult male Scarlet Tanager (p. 554) in spring; 2a. adult female; 2b. adult
male in second or adult winter plumage; 2c. male in first winter plumage. 3. male
Rufous-sided Towhee (p. 569); 3a. female. 4. male Red Crossbill (p. 567). 5. adult male
Orchard Oriole (p. 541) two years old or more in spring; 5a. female (juvenile male is
very similar); 5b. male in first spring plumage. 6. adult male Baltimore Oriole of the
black-hooded type (p. 543) in spring; 6a. adult female in spring.

Robert E Tucker

Juvenal-plumaged males and females, just out of the nest, are solid greenish, much like the adult female. Before beginning their first fall migration, however, they undergo a postjuvenal molt in which they acquire black feathers on the forepart of the wing on what are called the wing coverts. In early spring a prenuptial molt gives males their first scarlet and black plumage. Following the nesting season, the postnuptial molt returns them to the sober green, second winter plumage, but this time the entire wing remains black. Thenceforth the males alternate between a scarlet and black summer dress and a green and black winter dress. The interesting point is that males that are less than a year old and in their first winter plumage have only the coverts black, while birds that are over a year old have the entire wing black, both the coverts and the flight feathers.

The Scarlet Tanager is a fairly common, sometimes fairly abundant, spring transient from March 27 to May 31. It is seen with the greatest regularity and in the largest numbers in northern Louisiana and on the coastal ridges but somehow manages to traverse the intervening area without often being reported. Of special interest in the latter connection is the fact that during a hailstorm between 8:30 and 9:00 P.M. on the night of April 20, 1933, hundreds of Scarlet Tanagers must have been flying over the Louisiana State University campus at Baton Rouge, for on the following day no less than 27 were there found dead or injured.

On the bird's return to its winter home in northern South America it passes again through the state, being fairly common from the last of August until the end of October. But the sober dress of both the male as well as the female makes the species rather inconspicuous at this season. Two anomalous records are the observation of a male in breeding plumage in Johnsons Bayou wood, in Cameron Parish, on July 26, 1971, by Robert J. Newman and H. Douglas Pratt and one seen at Venice, in Plaquemines Parish,.on December 28, 1965, by John P. Gee and others.

SUMMER TANAGER *Piranga rubra*   Pl. XXXIV

The Summer Tanager, or "summer redbird," is a common nesting bird throughout the state wherever there are trees. It arrives the last week of March and remains at least in fair numbers until late in October. Eighteen observations of the species in December and January are on file. Three of these are from Baton Rouge, seven from New Orleans, three from Shreveport, and the remainder are of single birds seen on one occasion each at

Lafayette, Bonnet Carré Spillway, Venice, Triumph, and Smiths Island (Cameron Parish).

The male Summer Tanager is solid rose red and differs from the Northern Cardinal, with which it is sometimes confused by careless observers, in that it lacks the black facial mark; its bill is horn colored, not red; and, of course, it lacks the crest. The female is yellowish green above and dull yellowish below. She differs from the female Scarlet Tanager in being more yellowish (less greenish) and from the female Orchard and Baltimore Orioles in lacking any vestige of wing bars and in having a heavy, conical bill.

The Summer Tanager is one of the most persistent songsters of our woodlands. Its caroling, robinlike song, consisting of two or three phrases, is repeated over and over again, almost to the point that it becomes monotonous. The call and alarm note is a loud series of *clucks*, which it pours forth when a person or other intruder is in the vicinity of its nest. The latter is generally placed on a horizontal limb, near its extremity, 20 to 30 feet up. The three to five bluish white or greenish blue eggs are heavily spotted with cinnamon-brown and olive-brown markings.

The Finch Family
Fringillidae

This huge family of birds contains many more species than any other and is worldwide in its distribution, except for Australia, New Zealand, and, of course, Antarctica. It is mainly an aggregation of small to medium-sized ground-dwelling birds, in which the bill is generally conical in shape and thereby adapted for crushing seeds. Some species, however, are frugivorous and exclusively arboreal, and nearly all eat an appreciable number of insects.

Although I am here maintaining the family Fringillidae as presently constituted by Wetmore and others, including the AOU *Check-list of North American Birds*, I am nevertheless aware that rather drastic revisions of this arrangement are imminent. Almost certain to be adopted soon is a new classification that will include in the family Fringillidae the genus *Fringilla* and, as far as Louisiana birds are concerned, only the present genera *Carpodacus*, *Loxia*, *Spinus*, and *Hesperiphona*. The last-named genera cover, respectively, the Purple Finch, Red Crossbill, goldfinches, Pine Siskin, and the Evening Grosbeak. All other sparrows and sparrowlike birds in Louisiana will then be assigned to the subfamily Emberizinae of the family Emberizidae, which, in addition to the buntings and American sparrows, will include as subfamilial categories the Plush-capped Finch, the cardinal-grosbeaks, the true tanagers, and the Swallow-Tanager (see also p. 553).

NORTHERN CARDINAL   *Cardinalis cardinalis*   Pl. XXXV

The well-known Northern Cardinal is a widely and abundantly distributed permanent resident everywhere in Louisiana, except in the coastal marshes and some of the deepest inland swamps. It is often called the "redbird," but this name is to be avoided, since the male Summer Tanager is likewise red in color and is sometimes called the "summer redbird." The male cardinal has a narrow area of black on the throat and around the base of its blood red bill. Otherwise it is entirely red, darker above and brighter below. A prominent topknot gives it a debonair appearance. The male Summer Tanager, on the other hand, lacks the topknot and the black on the face, and its bill is horn colored instead of red. The female cardinal differs from her mate in being more soberly attired in grayish brown, although her bill and crest are red, and she has a touch of red on the wings and tail. Juvenal-plumaged males and females are similar to the adult female except that they lack any red and the bill is black. By late summer, however, the young males have undergone a postjuvenal molt that puts them in the full coat of the adult.

The nest of the cardinal is built of grasses of various textures and is generally placed in a bush or shrub only five to eight feet above the ground. The three or four eggs are bluish white, heavily spotted with brown or umber. The song is a loud, clear whistle, "boys, boys, get up." In most species of birds only the male is a gifted songster, but this is not so in the case of the cardinal. The female is, according to some listeners, more accomplished in this regard than her mate, possibly because her notes are softer in tone. The species has a distinctive call or alarm note that is best described as a *tsip*.

ROSE-BREASTED GROSBEAK   *Pheucticus ludovicianus*   Pl. XXXV

The male "rosebird," as it is often called, is black and white except for a prominent patch of rose red in the center of its breast that extends beneath the wings and is therefore partly concealed except when the bird flies or flutters to another perch. The large conical bill is white, unless it happens to be stained by the juices of berries or wild fruits that form the chief items in this bird's diet. The female is grayish brown above and has a buffy line through the center of the crown, a brownish ear patch, and a whitish line over the eye; the wing coverts are tipped with white, forming indistinct wing bars; the underwing coverts are saffron yellow (not lemon yellow as in the female Black-headed Grosbeak); the underparts are buffy, streaked with grayish brown. Immatures are similar to the adult female but are even more buffy and more profusely streaked below.

The Rose-breasted Grosbeak is a fairly common and regular spring transient in northern Louisiana that is also occasionally numerous on the coastal ridges but only rarely observed in the intervening area. Its passage takes place mainly from the middle of April to the middle of May. In fall it is moderately common throughout the state, from the last of September until the beginning of November. An occasional individual sometimes remains throughout the winter, when the species has been recorded from 11 localities, as follows: Shreveport, Monroe, Lafayette, Baton Rouge, Thibodaux, Reserve, New Orleans, Gretna, Hackberry, Cameron, and Grand Isle.

The species seldom sings while in migration through the state, but should it be heard to do so, its song would remind the listener of an American Robin. Heard more often is the sharp metallic *kick* that serves as its call note.

The famous Swedish zoologist, Linnaeus, who devised the system of nomenclature that we use today, is accredited with making the Rose-breasted Grosbeak known to science. Linnaeus, however, based his technical diagnosis on an earlier drawing and description by the French ornithologist, Brisson, who called it *Le Grosbec de la Louisiane*.

BLACK-HEADED GROSBEAK *Pheucticus melanocephalus*

Pl. XXXV; Fig. 138

This Rocky Mountain species is a casual winter visitor. Of the 66 individual Black-headed Grosbeaks that have now been reported from the state, approximately half were observed on bird feeders in urban residential areas. Localities where it has been recorded are distributed almost statewide, and recorded dates of occurrence extend from October 10 to April 28, with every intervening month represented. Sixty-two percent of the observations were in the months of December, January, and February.

In the adult male Black-headed Grosbeak the head, upperparts, and tail are black, except for a brownish collar, brownish streaks on the back, and prominent white wing bars; below it is rich cinnamon-brown, except for the center of the abdomen and lower belly, which is yellow. Adult females resemble the female Rose-breasted Grosbeak in the streaking on the head,

RET

Figure 138 Black-headed Grosbeak: male on left; female on right.

but the underparts are rich, rusty brown, not pale buffy. Juvenile males and females in the first winter plumage have a prominent brown ear patch and a white line over the eye and are dingy brown above and buffy on the chest, with scant streaking below. They are, therefore, similar to the immature Rose-breasted Grosbeak and can be distinguished from it only with difficulty. However, a bird at close range that raises its wings and allows the observer to see the color of the underwing feathers can be identified with certainty. In the Black-headed Grosbeak the color of these parts is lemon yellow, whereas in the Rose-breasted Grosbeak the color is saffron yellow.

BLUE GROSBEAK *Guiraca caerulea* Pl. XXXV

The Blue Grosbeak is a common summer bird in northern Louisiana and in the northern part of the Florida Parishes. Elsewhere in the state it is a fairly common to common transient, mainly from the first part of April to the middle of May and from early August to late October. Casual records of its presence in the southern part of the state in winter are available from Lafayette, Baton Rouge, Reserve, Grand Isle, and Venice. In summer the species shows a proclivity for mixed woods of oak and pine, particularly where there are stands of scrub oak. In fall, however, it is met with most often in dense stands of grass, in old cornfields, and in places where there are a great many brush and brier thickets.

The male is easily recognized in spring by its two wide, brownish wing bars and its otherwise all-blue plumage. The female is dark brown above and light brown below, with two buffy wing bars. Juvenal-plumaged males closely resemble the adult female. The adult male in winter is extensively washed with brown but still shows a considerable amount of blue. The song is similar to that of the Orchard Oriole, but decidedly less forceful and without the clear whistles. The call is a sharp *pink* that is often heard overhead at night in fall when birds are migrating relatively close to ground level.

Plate XXXV Grosbeaks and Other Fringillids

(Spring plumage unless otherwise specified) 1. male Northern Cardinal (p. 557); 1a. female. 2. male Rose-breasted Grosbeak (p. 558); 2a. female. 3. female Black-headed Grosbeak (p. 559). 4. male Blue Grosbeak (p. 560); 4a. female. 5. male Purple Finch (p. 564); 5a. female. 6. Pine Siskin (p. 565). 7. male American Goldfinch (p. 565) in summer; 7a. male in winter. 8. male Indigo Bunting (p. 561); 8a. female. 9. male Dickcissel (p. 562). 10. male Painted Bunting (p. 562); 10a. female.

Robert E. Tucker

The Blue Grosbeak builds its nest of grasses and rootlets, lined with hair and other very fine materials, in a low bush or thicket, seldom more than a few feet from the ground. But a nest with three eggs was found by Horace H. Jeter, three miles south of Longwood, in Caddo Parish, that was in a ten-foot sweetgum sapling, some eight feet above the ground. Three young were still being fed by the female on August 4. The three to five eggs are pale blue and unmarked.

INDIGO BUNTING   *Passerina cyanea*   Pl. XXXV

This beautiful little bunting is seen literally in swarms during its north-ward migration in spring. These flocks attract much attention, since the color of the male in good light is a brilliant shade of blue (except for the color of the head, which is usually a dark blue or even black at the base of the bill). It is the only bird in the United States that is so uniformly blue and, therefore, should not be confused with any other species. The Indigo Bunting, unlike the Blue Grosbeak, has no wing bars. Also it possesses a smaller bill and its color is a much lighter blue. The females and juveniles, however, are brownish above and dingy white, tinged with brownish and sometimes indistinctly streaked below. Consequently, they resemble certain sparrows and would be difficult to recognize in the field were it not for the fact that the back appears uniformly brown and for the fact that the wings and tail generally show a trace of bluish.

The Indigo Bunting is a common breeding bird throughout the state, except in the coastal marshes and along the coastal ridges. It is especially numerous in brushy clearings along the edges of heavy woods and along high-ways and railroad rights-of-way. The song is a rather weak jumble of musical sounds, somewhat squeaky in quality, but pleasing nevertheless. The call is a sharp, thin *pseet* and, like the call of the Blue Grosbeak, it is often heard at night in fall, particularly on cloudy nights when a heavy volume of migrants is passing low overhead.

The main periods of migration are from late March to the first part of May and from early September through October. In winter the species is of fairly regular annual occurrence in the southern part of the state. Observations at this season most often involve only one or two individuals, but on December 1 and 8, 1957, no less than nine were tallied at Venice.

This species is known locally as the "blue pop," or the *pape bleu* to our French-speaking inhabitants. The following species is called the "red pop," or *pape rouge*.

PAINTED BUNTING   *Passerina ciris*   Pl. XXXV

To one who has never seen a male Painted Bunting, the description of this bird must sound fantastically unreal—head and sides of the neck, indigo blue; upper back, yellow to golden green; rump, underparts, and eye-ring, red. Strange as it may seem, these *are* the colors of this gaudy finch, which, moreover, is a common summer bird through most of Louisiana. The upper-parts of the female are plain green, shading into dull yellow on the under-parts. The immature male resembles the adult female.

The species arrives in the first half of April and is locally abundant during the period of migration, when sometimes it occurs in great flocks alongside our rural roads. Most of the birds of these large aggregations disperse or pass on, but the species remains as one of the more common summer residents of the state. This bunting is mainly a bird of the edges of wood-lands, particularly where there is an abundance of dense cover in the form of low thickets and brush. The three or four bluish white eggs, which have numerous brownish or chestnut markings, are laid in a cup-shaped nest in a bush or low tree. The song is a rather weak warble that lacks conciseness.

Fall migration begins in August and continues well into October. In the middle of this period the species is exceptionally common, particularly in the southern part of the state. Occasionally one or two individuals at a time are seen somewhere in southern Louisiana in winter. The 17 records that are on file cover the months of December, January, and February and include observations at Baton Rouge, Lottie, Thibodaux, Grand Isle, New Orleans, Gretna, and Venice. One was also seen on the Saline Wildlife Management Area, in La Salle Parish, on November 26, 1971, by Kermit Cummings.

DICKCISSEL   *Spiza americana*   Pl. XXXV

The Dickcissel is a common, locally abundant, summer resident in most of Louisiana, which usually arrives in the middle of April from its winter home in South America. It is a conspicuous bird, for it seems to like nothing better than to perch on telephone wires or on roadside fences when it pours forth its emphatic song, a loud *dick, ciss ciss ciss*. In size it is about the equivalent of the House Sparrow. The male has a white chin, black throat, and yellow belly; the cheeks and top of the head are ash gray; the line over the eye is yellow; and the back is brown, heavily streaked with black. The female is browner on the head, lacks the black throat, and is much whiter (less yellowish) below. She resembles a female House Sparrow somewhat, but differs in having at least a faint wash of yellow on the breast, rufous patches on the shoulders, and a prominent line over the eye.

Despite the abundance of Dickcissels in June and early July, the bulk of them suddenly disappear in late July, and the species is uncommon from August to mid-November. Thereafter the species is quite rare, although not infrequently a few spend the winter in the state, even as far north as Springhill, in Webster Parish, and at Shreveport. In the winter season the Dickcissels that are present are often found in company with flocks of House Sparrows at feeding stations in urban areas.

The rather bulky nest of coarse grasses and leaves, lined with finer materials, is placed on the ground or in bushes, usually at the edges of fields, where doubtless many are destroyed each summer by mowing operations. The four or five eggs are plain bluish.

EVENING GROSBEAK *Hesperiphona vespertina* Pl. XLI

The Evening Grosbeak did not first appear in Louisiana until January 1962, and for this reason the species was not included in earlier editions of this work. The initial record was that of four males and a female that visited a feeder at the home of James B. Avant in West Monroe on January 9, 1962. Later, on January 25, Virginia Cazedessus found a flock of approximately 50 feeding at a seam in a highway a few miles northeast of Amite, apparently in quest of sand and salt that had been sprinkled on the road during an earlier hard freeze. Others were seen near Pride, Bogalusa, Gramercy, and Natchitoches.

The species did not appear again in Louisiana until the winter of 1968–1969, when they literally inundated the state, being recorded in no less than 32 towns and cities, from one end of the state to the other. At Weiss, in Livingston Parish, Dale Newsom estimated that he saw over one thousand individuals on January 1, and flocks numbering a hundred or more were noted at many places.

As is so often the case following a massive invasion of a species into an area, what is known as an "echo" invasion occurs at the same place the following year. Such indeed was what took place in Louisiana in the winter of 1969–1970, for the Evening Grosbeak reappeared at Shreveport and Natchitoches in limited numbers. None were reported in the winters of

1970–1971 or 1971–1972, but in 1972–1973 the species was again abundantly present in many widespread localities in the state.

The Evening Grosbeak breeds in the boreal forest across Canada south to the northeastern edge of the United States and in the western mountains to southern Mexico. It is a hardy bird that in the eastern United States seldom moves in winter as far south as the Gulf Coast states. This large yellow-billed, yellow-and-black-plumaged grosbeak cannot be confused with any bird. In the male the breast, belly, lower back, line over the eye, and forehead are dull yellow; the top of the head, wings, and tail are black except for the secondaries and their coverts, which are white; the remainder of the head and upper breast are dingy brown. The female is gray with a yellow wash on the neck and sides of the breast, and it possesses black malar stripes on each side of the white throat. The white patch in the wing that is so prominent in the male is limited in the female to the secondary coverts and a spot near the base of the inner primaries, and the tail feathers and their upper coverts possess large terminal white spots.

PURPLE FINCH   *Carpodacus purpureus*   Pl. XXXV

One of the redeeming features of the severe cold waves that occasionally push into Louisiana in winter, sometimes bringing sleet and snow and sub-freezing temperatures, is the fact that with such weather Purple Finches often come in great numbers. In warm winters these beautiful birds may be quite scarce, particularly as visitors to our towns and cities. When cold weather brings a real invasion of Purple Finches, large numbers generally swarm into our berry trees or cover the ground of our lawns in search of seeds and possibly grit. The species has never been recorded in the state, even in extreme northern Louisiana, earlier than November 7, and, although there are isolated records as late as April, it is usually gone by the end of February.

The Purple Finch is about the size of a House Sparrow, but the color of the fully adult male is rose or raspberry red, which is especially bright on the head and rump. The females and the young males are heavily streaked above and below and thus resemble some of the striped sparrows. The thick bill that is almost round at the base, the rather deeply notched tail, and the fact that females and immatures go in flocks that nearly always contain the easily identifiable males, all serve to aid in their recognition. I have never heard the warbling song of the Purple Finch anywhere in Louisiana, and my ear is not particularly sensitive to the often-uttered metallic *tick* that the bird makes.

PINE SISKIN *Spinus pinus* Pl. XXXV

A few Pine Siskins visit Louisiana each winter, but in some years the species is scarce and may even go undetected in one part of the state or another. In other years it is fairly numerous and rather widespread. Siskins habitually go in flocks, often in association with American Goldfinches, and more often than not are found feeding on seeds of the sweetgum. Extreme dates of occurrence are October 20 and May 14.

Pine Siskins are mainly birds of the evergreen forests of Canada and of the mountains of the West, but in winter they gather in flocks and wander over the greater part of the United States in search of favorable food conditions. The bird's diminutive size, its streaked plumage, and the yellow patches on the base of the outer tail feathers and in the wing are excellent field marks. The flocks feed energetically but are quick to take wing and wheel away to another part of a wood. While feeding, as well as when in flight, the siskins utter a wheezy note that Peterson describes as a loud *clee-ip*. The most distinctive call, though, is its rather drawn-out buzzing *screeee*, a note that bears no close resemblance to any other bird sound.

AMERICAN GOLDFINCH *Spinus tristis* Pl. XXXV; Fig. 139

The American Goldfinch is a common, sometimes abundant, winter resident from November to April in most of Louisiana and a rare summer resident in the north-central part of the state. In summer plumage the male is resplendent in its coat of bright canary yellow, which is broken only by a small black cap and the predominantly black wings and tail. The wings have prominent white bars, the inner webs of the tail feathers are also white, and the unusually long uppertail coverts are grayish white. The female is a dull olive-yellow with blackish wings and conspicuous white wing bars. But we do not see many goldfinches in their bright summer dress, since the bird is very scarce in the season in which this plumage is worn. In winter the male is grayish brown on the back, and the head has only a moderate tinge of yellow; the throat and chest are dull yellowish, and the belly is whitish; and the

RET

Figure 139 (1) Lesser Goldfinch (male in front; female behind) and (2) American Goldfinch (male in winter plumage).

wings and tail are as they are in summer, except that the white bars and edgings to the secondaries are broader. The female is similar but has even less yellow on the head and less black in the wings.

One of the best aids in the identification of the American Goldfinch is its bounding flight and the peculiar call note that is often uttered when a flock is on the wing. Frank M. Chapman adequately describes the latter as *per chic-o-ree*, uttered as a hum. It has a pronounced whiney quality. The species has a great preference for the seeds of sweetgums and is more often seen hanging from sweetgum balls than in any other situation.

Proof of the nesting of the American Goldfinch in Louisiana rests on the discovery of a single nest a few miles west of Monroe. There are, however, quite a few summer records in the northern part of the state. Since the species is noted for being a late nester, its mere presence in a locality in full nuptial plumage as late as June provides no certainty that it is nesting there. The nest, constructed of fine grasses and lined with thistledown, is placed in trees or bushes 5 to 30 feet above the ground. The three to six eggs are pale bluish white.

LESSER GOLDFINCH   *Spinus psaltria*   Fig. 139

The sole record in Louisiana and the easternmost occurrence anywhere for this western species is that of a female collected by John P. Gee in the village of Cameron on April 17, 1954. The Lesser or Dark-backed Goldfinch, as it is sometimes called, is noticeably smaller than the American Goldfinch, and in summer plumages the males of the two are radically different in color. The eastern bird in breeding plumage is bright yellow except for its black tail, black frontal patch, black and white wings, and white rump. In contrast, the male Lesser Goldfinch, in both winter and summer plumages, has only the underparts yellow, the upperparts being all-black except for white markings on the wings and tail. Winter-plumaged American Goldfinches are brownish above with only a tinge of yellow on the breast, while the female Lesser Goldfinch in both winter and summer is greenish above and entirely yellow below. Moreover, in the American Goldfinch, the white on the central tail feathers extends to the tips and the undertail coverts are white, but in the western species the central tail feathers are black terminally and the undertail coverts are yellow.

RED CROSSBILL *Loxia curvirostra* Pl. XXXIV

As the name signifies, the upper and lower mandibles of this bird do not meet but instead cross each other. One would think that the crossbill would be hopelessly handicapped, but this is apparently not the case. I have stood under a pine tree in which a flock of these birds was feeding and have been amazed at the great number of sheaths of pine seeds that were literally raining down—the birds were opening pinecones that I do not believe could have been opened better with a chisel and a hammer. Apparently their success depends on a rapid prying motion in which they somehow get a high degree of leverage.

Until recently the Red Crossbill was known from Louisiana solely on the basis of two birds collected on March 27, 1888, near Mandeville. In the winter of 1972–1973, however, crossbills again came into the state. Several flocks, totaling 80 birds, were first found on January 27 by James R. Stewart and Robert J. Newman, a few miles north of Cross Lake, in Caddo Parish. They were seen in the same general area on several occasions during the following week. On March 20, D. T. Kee and others found three crossbills four miles north of Monroe, and on March 22 Kee located two more four miles north of Swartz, both places in Ouachita Parish.

Red Crossbills are notorious vagrants. Indeed, the specimens collected in Louisiana in 1888 are representative of the subspecies that breeds from the Sitkan district of Alaska southward to the northwestern coast region of

Figure 140   Green-tailed Towhee.

the United States. The movements of the species seem largely to be determined by the success of pine seed crops in the United States and Canada. The failure of pines to produce an abundance of seeds in the bird's normal, northern range and the simultaneous success of the crop in the pine forests of the southeastern United States are probably the proper conditions under which we may anticipate the appearance of the Red Crossbill this far south.

GREEN-TAILED TOWHEE   *Chlorura chlorura*   Fig. 140

This western finch has now been recorded on four occasions in Louisiana. I collected one in a thicket on a cheniere near Johnsons Bayou in Cameron Parish, less than a mile from the Gulf shore on December 28, 1952, another was seen at Lecompte by Brooke Meanley on November 4, 1956, one was taken at Cameron by John P. Gee and Robert J. Newman on April 13, 1957, and another was seen at the same place by a large group of observers on December 28, 1958. The species breeds from central Oregon and southern Montana to southern California, southern New Mexico, and central-western Texas. Normally it winters from the southern part of its breeding range south to central-southern Mexico.

The Green-tailed Towhee is somewhat smaller than a Northern Cardinal and is predominantly greenish or greenish gray above, except for its rufous cap, the throat and belly are white, and the remainder of the underparts are gray. No other bird in the United States is colored in this distinctive manner.

RUFOUS-SIDED TOWHEE *Pipilo erythrophthalmus*
Pl. XXXIV; Fig. 141

The Rufous-sided Towhee is certainly one of the more attractive members of our avifauna. The names "towhee," "joree," or "chewink" are all allusions to some of its calls; the name "ground robin" is in reference to its remote resemblance to the American Robin and the fact that the bird spends a considerable part of its time on the ground. In spring, however, the male will be seen to mount to the top of a tall tree, where it sings loudly. The phrase "drink your teeeeeeeee," the latter part wavering and drawn out, is an excellent phonetic representation of the song.

The male Rufous-sided Towhee is largely black, for its entire head, back, and tail are of that color. The sides and flanks are rufous, and the breast and abdomen are white. The outer secondaries are white basally, producing a

Figure 141 Male of western population (left) and male of eastern population (right) of Rufous-sided Towhee.

largely concealed white wing patch, and the tips of the outer tail feathers are also white, showing conspicuously when the bird flies. The female is identical in pattern, but where the male is black, she is reddish brown. The eye is red in both sexes of towhees in the eastern and northern United States, cream colored or white in the Southeast and Florida.

The Rufous-sided Towhee is a common winter resident throughout nearly all of Louisiana. It is a common summer resident in the southeastern part of the state, west to the Tunica Hills, Baton Rouge, and Napoleonville. Aside from a few breeding pairs in the vicinity of Oak Grove, in West Carroll Parish, in extreme northeastern Louisiana, the species is apparently entirely absent in summer from the northern half of the state. The towhee would seem to have occupied the southeastern corner of the state as a breeding bird quite recently, at least in the last hundred years, for John James Audubon failed to find it nesting in the vicinity of either St. Francisville or New Orleans—places where he spent a great deal of time and where the towhee is now one of our common summer birds.

The nest of the Rufous-sided Towhee, which is usually placed in a low bush, is made of dead leaves and is lined with fine grasses. The four or five white eggs are evenly speckled with rufous, sometimes blotched on the larger end.

In winter we often receive an influx of towhees from the western United States that were once regarded as members of a distinct species under the name Spotted Towhee but which are now considered only subspecies of eastern populations of the Rufous-sided Towhee.

Despite the similarity of the two populations, they can often be distinguished in the field (see Fig. 141). The western birds are heavily marked on the back and scapulars with white streaks, which the eastern towhees lack almost completely. The female "spotted" towhees are a dark chocolate brown and, for this reason, show much less color contrast with the male than do the females of eastern towhees with their mates. The eye color is orange in the western population, and the call note is a distinct, twangy zreee, a sound seldom made by our native towhees. Northern populations of the Rufous-sided Towhee, which visit Louisiana in numbers in winter, have a few white or buffy emarginations to the inner secondaries and hence might suggest a "spotted" towhee to one not familiar with the conspicuous white streaking on the wings and back of the latter. Examples of the western population have been seen or collected in the state between October 23 and April 13.

LARK BUNTING *Calamospiza melanocorys*   Fig. 142

The Lark Bunting has been recorded only twice in Louisiana. I obtained a
specimen along the highway through the marsh a few miles from Grand
Isle, on September 4, 1952, and Robert J. Newman and Sidney A. Gauthreaux secured another below New Orleans, between Triumph and Fort
Jackson, on December 23, 1973. The species breeds in the Great Plains
region of the western United States and normally winters from southern
Texas and Arizona southward over most of the Mexican plateau. It is slightly
longer and a good deal chunkier than the House Sparrow. In spring and
summer the male is all-black except for the large patch of white in the
wings and the white inner margins to the tail feathers. The females, immatures, and winter males are grayish, heavily streaked with dusky, and
possess white or buffy wing patches. This drab, streaked plumage is the one
most likely to be worn by birds occurring in Louisiana, and indeed both
specimens mentioned above were so attired. The profuse streaking and the
conspicuous patches of white in the wings should serve in most instances to
distinguish the Lark Bunting from all other ground-dwelling finches.

Figure 142   Lark Bunting: male on left; female on right.

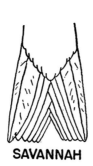

SAVANNAH   **SONG**

Figure 143 Tails of two similar sparrows. That of the Savannah Sparrow is short, square cornered, and slightly notched in the middle. In the Song Sparrow the tail is longer and wider and prominently rounded.

SAVANNAH SPARROW *Passerculus sandwichensis*

Pl. XXXVI; Fig. 143

This species is unquestionably the commonest sparrow of fields and open situations in Louisiana in the winter months. It arrives in numbers in the last week of September and sometimes stays until mid-May or even into June. It is a rather small, streaked sparrow that is white below, marked on the throat and breast with fine streaks, which sometimes tend to be concentrated in the center, forming a large spot. In the latter respect it resembles a Song Sparrow, but, unlike that species, the Savannah Sparrow has a pale streak down the center of the crown, a touch of yellow on the bend of the wing, and usually a yellow spot in front of the eye. It is one of the first winter sparrows that the beginning student of ornithology encounters in the field and should be learned at once so that it is not confused with other similar-appearing species, such as the Song Sparrow.

GRASSHOPPER SPARROW *Ammodramus savannarum*

Pl. XXXVI; Fig. 144

The Grasshopper Sparrow is a rather uncommon or at least a seldom-observed winter resident in Louisiana. Although recorded in every month of the year, it is generally not seen until late September or after the end of

April. To Horace H. Jeter goes the credit for having discovered, on July 7, 1968, the first and only nest of the species in the state, in an alfalfa field near Gilliam, in Caddo Parish. The nest contained five eggs and was subsequently photographed by G. Dale Hamilton.

The species is a small, short-tailed sparrow with a dark, striped back and a buffy, unmarked breast. It also has a buffy line over the eye and a median stripe of pale buff down the center of the crown. It is the only one of the "grass sparrows" (that is, sparrows that are habitual denizens of dense stands of grass) with a plain breast. Other distinctive features are its flatheadedness, its pale face, and its squarish tail. Its favorite haunts are broom sedge fields in which there are a few small trees or brush piles. It is, however, the easiest of the grass sparrows to chase to a perch in a hedgerow or a thicket on a woods border. The majority of the few birds seen in summer were in fields of alfalfa or vetch.

HENSLOW'S SPARROW   *Ammodramus henslowii* Pl. XXXVI; p. 573

This sparrow is often found in the same broom sedge situations as the following species, but it appears to be less numerous there. It is most common in the grass of "pine flats," particularly in the Florida Parishes. It resembles

Henslow's Sparrow, a Skulker in the Grass, Obligingly Poses in the Open

SAMUEL A. GRIMES

closely the Le Conte's Sparrow but is darker. The nape is olive-green instead of rufous brown, and the wings are quite reddish. The Henslow's Sparrow is also like the Le Conte's in that it is seldom seen except when suddenly flushed at one's feet. When it flies away it zigzags slightly just over the top of the grass. After traveling 20 yards or so, it abruptly pitches into the grass and disappears. A good technique that often yields a perched view of both this species and the Le Conte's is to run as rapidly as possible to the spot where the bird disappeared, flush it again, and repeat this process over and over. Sooner or later the little bird apparently becomes curious as to the identity of its pursuer and alights briefly in a bush or on a tall weed stalk. If the binoculars are immediately brought to play, the observer obtains a good look at the bird.

Henslow's Sparrows arrive in Louisiana in mid-October. They are usually gone by the end of March, but occasionally a few remain longer.

LE CONTE'S SPARROW   *Ammospiza leconteii*   Pl. XXXVI; Fig. 144

Le Conte's and Henslow's Sparrows are both commonly called "stink birds" by quail hunters because sometimes even well-trained bird dogs point them or are distracted by them. Both species occur mainly in broom sedge (*Andropogon*) fields where, even though they are often common, they are seldom seen except for the few moments when a bird jumps out of the grass at one's feet, flies 20 yards or so, and then pitches back into the grass.

The Le Conte's and Henslow's Sparrows, along with the Sharp-tailed and Seaside Sparrows, are distinguished by their narrow, sharp-pointed tail feathers, which are so steeply graduated that the whole tail has a pointed effect (Fig. 144). Adults of all four possess some streaking on the breast and sides, a broad buff, yellow, or gray line over the eye, and a median stripe on the crown. In the field the Le Conte's Sparrow appears to be the palest of the four and has a somewhat purplish or rufous brown nape. As a rule its habitat in Louisiana in winter is somewhat drier than that of the Henslow's Sparrow, and it is nowhere more numerous than in slightly rolling terrain where there is a dense stand of broom sedge. On the coast of southwestern

---

Plate XXXVI   Six Sparrows, All Adults

1. Savannah Sparrow (p. 572). 2. Sharp-tailed Sparrow (p. 575). 3. Henslow's Sparrow (p. 573). 4. Le Conte's Sparrow (p. 574). 5. Grasshopper Sparrow (p. 572). 6. Seaside Sparrow (p. 576).

1

2

3

4

5

6

RÉTucker
46

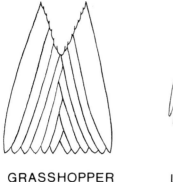

GRASSHOPPER   LE CONTE'S

Figure 144 Tails of two similar, grass-inhabiting sparrows. Note the narrowness and the distinct attenuation of the feathers in the tail of the Le Conte's Sparrow.

Louisiana, however, it is also plentiful in the shortgrass prairies paralleling the Gulf beach, as, for example, along the highway between Cameron and Johnsons Bayou.

The Le Conte's Sparrow arrives in Louisiana in the latter part of October and remains sometimes until after the first of May. The bird is somewhat more numerous in southern Louisiana in midwinter than it is in northern Louisiana.

SHARP-TAILED SPARROW *Ammospiza caudacuta*   Pl. XXXVI

Although the Sharp-tailed Sparrow breeds across the better part of southern Canada and in the northern part of the United States and is common in the marshes of southern Louisiana in winter, it has been recorded at inland localities in the state on only a few occasions. Four specimens have been picked up on four dates in October at a TV tower in Baton Rouge, but the species has otherwise been found only rarely at this well-worked locality. Other interior localities where it has been seen are at Shreveport on October 19, 1963, at Natchitoches on December 17, 1972, and at St. Francisville on December 22, 1962. Inland lakes with cattails and other aquatic plants around their peripheries should be watched for individuals of this species in migration.

Sharp-tailed Sparrows arrive in the coastal marshes in late October and have been known to stay as late as June 7, although generally most of them are gone by the first of May. They are the most buffy of the "sharp-tailed" sparrows. The cheeks, the line over the eye, and often the chest are rich ochraceous-buff, and the ear patch and median stripe in the crown are gray. Immatures, before the postjuvenal molt, are faintly streaked on the upper breast and are generally darker and duller.

SEASIDE SPARROW *Ammospiza maritima* Pl. XXXVI

No species of bird is more appropriately named than the Seaside Sparrow. Except where our coastal marshes are very broad and deeply indented with wide saltwater bays, around which these little birds occur, the Seaside Sparrow is synonymous with the pounding of the surf. It occurs as an abundant permanent resident mainly in densely matted and usually sharp-pointed grass and sedges that line our shores in places where the ground just back of the beach is flooded at high tide. Here they run about on the ground, or on masses of debris washed up by the waves, and would escape detection if we did not know that by making a squeaking noise we can cause them to mount the taller stalks of grass and even fly toward us from every direction. It is then that we see the Seaside Sparrow and are able to note its sober gray and dark olivaceous coloration, its massive bill, and, possibly, the yellow spot in front of its eye and the yellow on the bend of the wing. Young birds in juvenal plumage are dark brown above and dingy buff below, with numerous fine streaks of dusky on the breast. Individuals that have passed through the postjuvenal molt resemble full adults but have a stronger wash of buff on the breast and about the face.

In spring the weak, buzzing song of the Seaside Sparrow pours forth from all quarters of the marsh, and occasionally the observer will see one of them jump into the air a few feet above the top of the grass to sing in mid-air. The notes have been perfectly described by Peterson as *cutcut, zhe'-eeeeeeee.* The nest is made of coarse grasses, lined with fine material, and is placed close to the ground, often a foot or so high in a mangrove bush. The three or four whitish eggs are spotted finely with brown.

Plate XXXVII Five Sparrows and the Slate-colored Junco, All Adults

1. Vesper Sparrow (p. 577). 2. Lark Sparrow (p. 577). 3. Bachman's Sparrow (p. 578). 4. Slate-colored Junco (p. 578). 5. Chipping Sparrow (p. 582). 6. Field Sparrow (p. 584).

VESPER SPARROW   *Pooecetes gramineus*   Pl. XXXVII

When one is driving along a rural road or walking across an open field, a rather pale, streaked sparrow will sometimes take flight from the ground ahead of the observer. If the bird has conspicuous white outer tail feathers, it may or may not be a Vesper Sparrow, since quite a few sparrows and sparrowlike birds have the outer tail feathers white. If the bird in question, however, is also seen to have a narrow white eye-ring, indistinctly streaked buffy underparts, and rufous wing coverts, it is certainly this species. The Vesper Sparrow is a fairly common to common winter resident in Louisiana from early October, casually as early as the first part of August, until late in April. In addition to open pastures and roadsides, favorite haunts are burnt ground and old cornfields.

LARK SPARROW   *Chondestes grammacus*   Pl. XXXVII

This species inhabits approximately the same situations as does the Vesper Sparrow but at somewhat different seasons. The Lark Sparrow is a common summer resident in north-central Louisiana, where it arrives in early April and is seen in numbers until mid-September. In the southern part of the state the species is mainly a transient during April and again in late summer, but it is also rare and irregular in winter. Two individuals seen two miles south of Greenwood, in Caddo Parish, by Horace H. Jeter on February 14, 1954, form the only winter record for the northern part of the state.

The Lark Sparrow is a highly attractive bird, especially for a sparrow. The head is prominently marked with a patch of chestnut below and behind the eye and with a stripe of chestnut along the side of the crown; a line down the center of the crown and over the eye is whitish. There is a black streak on each side of the chin and throat; the upperparts are brownish and the underparts white, except for a small black spot in the center of the breast. The slightly graduated tail is blackish, and the outer tail feathers are tipped with white. The head pattern, the black spot on the otherwise immaculate breast, and the white-tipped outer tail feathers are diagnostic.

Like many of its close relatives, this sparrow nests in hedgerows, in old grown-up pastures, and in the vicinity of small clearings in woods of oak and pine. The nest is made of rather coarse grasses and rootlets, lined with fine grasses, and is located either on the ground or in a low bush. The three to five eggs are white or pinkish, scrawled and blotched with black, mainly on the larger end. The song is a difficult-to-describe series of trills and buzzing notes.

BACHMAN'S SPARROW   *Aimophila aestivalis*   Pl. XXXVII

One of the most melodious sounds to be heard anywhere is the clear, ethereal medley that resounds through our pine forests when the Bachman's or Pine-woods Sparrow pours forth its song. It is most frequently rendered early in the morning and late in the afternoon, when the woods are quiet save for the gentle murmur of a slight breeze through the pine boughs. One author interprets it as *che-e-e-de, de, de; che-e–chee-o, chee-o, chee-o.* Although doubtless recognizable as a reasonable transliteration of the bird's song by anyone already familiar with it, the words do not suffice to describe its quality to the uninitiated.

Bachman's Sparrows are chestnut above, and the underparts are chiefly pale grayish brown. There is a barely discernible grayish line over the eye, and the bend of the wing is yellow. The other plain-breasted sparrows likely to be encountered in the habitat of the Bachman's Sparrow all have either distinctive facial patterns, pink bills, white outer tail feathers, or profuse black streaks on the back. The present species has none of these markings, its sole unique feature being the extensiveness of the chestnut above that is virtually unbroken by noticeable streaks or other marks. The species is highly secretive and when approached usually slinks away among the boughs or along the trunk of a fallen tree, where its colors are a perfect blend with its background of pine needles and grass.

Bachman's Sparrows from the upper Mississippi Valley sometimes come southward to Louisiana in winter, but our own birds are almost certainly resident the year around. The species is not often found in this state outside of pine woods or woods of mixed scrub oak and pine. It is always seen singly or in pairs, never in flocks as are most other kinds of sparrows. The cup-shaped nest is a compact structure of grasses built on the ground in an open pine wood. The three to five eggs are pure white.

SLATE-COLORED JUNCO   *Junco hyemalis*   Pls. XXXVII, XXXVIII

I am using the name Slate-colored Junco to cover what were until recently called two species, the Slate-colored and Oregon Juncos. The two are now considered to be members of a single species since they hybridize freely in

Plate XXXVIII Males of Two Subspecies of the Slate-colored Junco

Oregon type, *Junco hyemalis oreganus*, on left (p. 578). Slate-colored type, *J. h. hyemalis*, on right (p. 578).

their zones of contact in our western mountains. The name *Junco hyemalis* has priority over *J. oreganus* and hence becomes the scientific name of the enlarged species, although some ornithologists would prefer to change the name of the resulting complexes of subspecies, including the one originally given specific rank under the name Oregon Junco, to Dark-eyed Junco. The eyes of these juncos are indeed dark, whereas the eyes of other juncos are yellow. But changing a vernacular name of such long standing as Slate-colored Junco seems to me to be entirely unnecessary. When the field ornithologist wishes to designate whether a given junco is of the "slate-colored type" or the "Oregon type," he can feel free to do so simply by using those terms. I would say that we should definitely continue to record juncos as one or the other types when conditions permit positive identification. Valuable information would be lost by referring to all juncos observed under the name Slate-colored. In the field the females and immatures of the Oregon type cannot always be distinguished with certainty from the females and immatures of the slate-colored type, although individuals of the former that possess extreme amounts of pink on the sides and flanks are recognizable. Adult males of the two types are, however, easily told apart, since the Oregon type has a black head and a *brown* back, while the slate-colored type is slate-black over the entire upperparts and lacks the distinct wash of pink on the sides and flanks. The Oregon type of the Slate-colored Junco has been recorded in the state on more than two dozen occasions, mainly in northern Louisiana but in the extreme southern parishes as well, between October 15 and March 26.

In southern Louisiana, Slate-colored Juncos are mainly "weather migrants." That is to say, they come into the southern half of the state in their greatest numbers when severe cold and particularly snow and sleet blanket their more northern winter range, inducing them to move farther and farther southward. The little birds feed entirely on the ground and are hence greatly handicapped when the ground is covered. They are often called "snowbirds" because they are most often seen in bad weather. I shall never forget the severe cold spell of January 1940 in which the entire state was covered with snow. Countless thousands of ground-dwelling birds perished, and some species were virtually wiped out over large areas of their winter range (for example, the American Woodcock, Common Snipe, Eastern Phoebe, and Northern House Wren). As soon as U.S. Highway 190 was opened, I was in one of the first cars to pass through en route to southwestern Louisiana, for I wanted to observe the effects of the cold on the birdlife of that area. One of my more vivid recollections of what I saw was that of great numbers of Slate-colored Juncos feeding at the *edge of the surf* on the Cameron Parish beach, this being the only place where the ground was not buried under a blanket of snow.

The Slate-colored Junco is easily identified by its distinctive slaty black and white pattern (see illustrations). In flight the large amount of white at the sides of the tail is particularly conspicuous. Immatures are brownish slate on the head and back and hence do not show as much sharp contrast with the white of the breast and belly. Sometimes they show a tinge of pinkish on the sides and flanks but not as prominently as do most pink-sided Oregon-type juncos.

Records of this species in Louisiana are mainly from the middle of October until late in March, extending rarely into April. It is far more plentiful in northern Louisiana than in the southern part of the state. In the latter area it is found principally in pine woods. The bird is generally clustered in small flocks, and it frequently utters a sort of twittering note and also a sharp smacking *tsip* that is highly diagnostic.

GRAY-HEADED JUNCO *Junco caniceps*   Pl. XLI

Our first Louisiana record of this junco was a bird collected by Horace H. Jeter at Shreveport, on February 3, 1957. Like the Oregon type of the Slate-colored Junco, this species comes to us from the western United States. It was found in a flock of Slate-colored Juncos that contained both the slate-colored and Oregon types. Interestingly enough, other Gray-headed Juncos that were seen near Tyler and Houston, Texas, in January of the same year provided the first records for the species in eastern Texas. On December 19, 1966, another Gray-headed Junco was seen in Louisiana, between Johnsons Bayou and Holly Beach, by J. P. Prevett and C. D. MacIness. The species is recognized quite easily by the presence of a prominent reddish patch on the upper back that serves to separate it from the females and immatures of the other species.

AMERICAN TREE SPARROW *Spizella arborea*   Fig. 145

There are only six records of the occurrence of the American Tree Sparrow in Louisiana. First were individuals seen from February 11 to 16, 1904, at Mer Rouge in Morehouse Parish, where it was said to have been common on

Figure 145 American Tree Sparrow.

the dates cited. A single bird was noted at Shreveport, on October 31, 1954, by James R. Stewart and Horace H. Jeter. Also I am certain that I saw an American Tree Sparrow on January 27, 1940, feeding with a horde of other sparrows on the side of the highway near Lottie during the severe cold spell of that memorable winter. After I had studied the bird for a few moments through binoculars, a large truck roared past, causing all the birds in the flock to take flight, and I was never able again to locate the individual believed to have been an American Tree Sparrow. Finally, in 1958, one was seen by James R. Stewart and Horace H. Jeter near Hackberry on December 6; two were seen on December 7 by Mr. and Mrs. H. A. J. Evans and Mac Myers at Cameron; and four were noted at the same place on December 27 by Rose Feingold.

The species breeds across northern Canada and appears to be very hardy, for its main winter range is no farther south than the central part of the United States. Hence the bird should be expected here only in periods of severe winter weather. In the center of the gray breast is a large black spot that is its main badge of identification. Otherwise, it resembles the Chipping Sparrow but is larger, has a gray (instead of white) line over the eye, and a rufous brown line behind the eye, not a black line through it. The bird also has two white wing bars, and the bill is dark above, light below.

Chipping Sparrows—Two Looked the Wrong Way

CHIPPING SPARROW *Spizella passerina* Pl. XXXVII; p. 582

The diminutive Chipping Sparrow is a common permanent resident throughout the pine regions of the state, where it inhabits the edges of pastures and orchards, as well as open deciduous woods and stands of pine. In winter it occurs not infrequently in pastures and open situations in the alluvial bottomlands, sometimes even on the coastal ridges. The adult has a black forehead, a rufous cap, a white line over the eye, and a black line through it. The lower back and rump are grayish and the underparts are grayish white, while the upper back is brownish streaked with black. The bill is jet black in the breeding season. Immatures have a streaked crown with little or no rufous, and the underparts, cheeks, and line over the eye are buffy instead of white.

The song of the Chipping Sparrow is a dry, rattling trill, all on one pitch. The four or five greenish blue eggs with brown or black markings on the larger end are laid in a nest of grasses and fine twigs, heavily lined with hairs, 5 to 20 feet above the ground in a bush or tree.

CLAY-COLORED SPARROW *Spizella pallida* Fig. 146

The Clay-colored Sparrow, a predominantly western species, is a decidedly uncommon winter visitor to Louisiana. Seventeen records of it on file are from False River, Baton Rouge, New Orleans, Pilottown, Thibodaux, Lake Charles, and seven localities in southern Cameron Parish. Extreme dates of occurrence are September 29 and May 8.

So closely do some individuals of the Clay-colored Sparrow resemble some immature Chipping Sparrows that field identifications in many instances are extremely hazardous, unless one is able to study the birds minutely and to see clearly the color of the rump. In Chipping Sparrows of all ages this part is gray in contrast to the brown of the back, but in Clay-colored

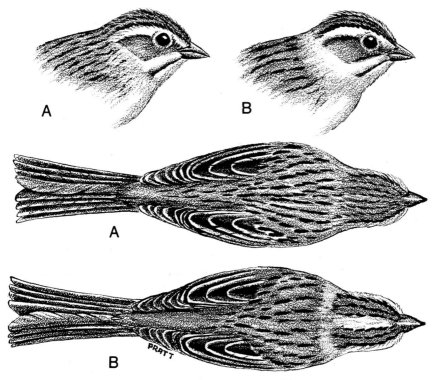

Figure 146   (A) Brewer's Sparrow; (B) Clay-colored Sparrow.

Sparrows, as well as in Brewer's Sparrows, the rump is brown like the back. In the Clay-colored Sparrow the ocular patch is a light tan with the upper edge, which forms the postocular streak, only a dark shade of brown—not black or blackish as it is in the Chipping Sparrow. Neither immature Chipping nor any Brewer's Sparrows ever have a prominent light stripe down the center of the crown, as do most Clay-colored Sparrows. The Brewer's Sparrow is further distinguished by the numerous fine, black streaks on its crown and by its overall grayer (less brownish) coloration. In the Clay-colored the brown of the head is noticeably separated from the brown of the back by a grayish collar.

BREWER'S SPARROW *Spizella breweri*   Fig. 146

There are only two records in the state for this western species. One was seen on a ridge near the Gulf beach at Cameron on December 6, 1952, and was collected the following day to verify positively its identification. The specimen is now on display in the mounted bird collection in the LSU Museum of Zoology. Another was reported from Thibodaux on November 19, 1955, by Ava R. Tabor.

The Brewer's Sparrow resembles an immature Chipping Sparrow except that it is slenderer, is more pale grayish buff (less reddish brown), and has many more tiny streaks on the crown. The color of the rump is the same as the ground color of the back, while in the immature Chipping Sparrow the rump is gray, in sharp contrast to the brownish ground color of the back. The distinctions between the Brewer's and the Clay-colored Sparrows are given in the account of the latter species.

FIELD SPARROW *Spizella pusilla*   Pl. XXXVII

The Field Sparrow is a moderately common to common permanent resident throughout nearly all of Louisiana. It inhabits, as its name indicates, fields, pastures, and other open places. It resembles the Chipping Sparrow but lacks the distinct facial marks of that species. The crown is reddish, as is also the ear patch, and, instead of a black line through the eye and a black bill, it has a rather prominent white eye-ring and a pink bill. The upperparts are decidedly more reddish than those of the Chipping Sparrow.

The song of the Field Sparrow is a highly pleasing but somewhat plaintive whistle of two or three notes ending in a trill. The song of a single individual is remarkably constant, but the songs of individual birds differ noticeably from each other. An expertly compiled collection of bird songs reproduced on phonograph records amply illustrates this individual variability by giving successively five slightly different songs of the Field Sparrow as rendered by five different birds. The eggs of this species vary from buffy white to very pale bluish green and are profusely streaked with brown.

HARRIS' SPARROW *Zonotrichia querula* Pl. XXXIX

This large sparrow breeds in extreme northern Canada from the western shores of Hudson Bay, possibly as far west as Great Bear Lake. In fall it migrates to Kansas, Oklahoma, and Texas, and only occasionally at our latitude does it wander as far east as the lower Mississippi Valley. Aside from the Shreveport area and the general situation that prevailed in the winter of 1952–1953, when the species was found in numerous places and on numerous dates, there are comparatively few records for the state. Extreme dates are November 7 and April 29. In extreme northwestern Louisiana the Harris' Sparrow appears to be a regular but uncommon winter visitor, occurring here and there, singly or in small flocks, and usually in the company of other winter sparrows. Although the species has been observed on a few occasions in other parts of the state, such as at Lake Charles, Indian Bayou, Baton Rouge, and New Orleans, only at localities in Cameron Parish has it been seen as many as a dozen times in the last 20 years.

The Harris' Sparrow is easily recognized by its large size and by the presence in the adults of a black crown, black face, and black throat patch, Immatures have the feathers of the crown edged with brownish and those of the breast and sometimes the throat streaked or blotched with black but never a solid black mask and throat; the cheeks and flanks are washed with buffy. Its habitat is similar to that of the White-crowned or White-throated Sparrows, species with which it often associates.

WHITE-CROWNED SPARROW *Zonotrichia leucophrys* Pl. XXXIX

Few birds possess the debonair appearance of the adult White-crowned Sparrow. The manner in which it holds itself erect, with the feathers on the back of its head slightly raised, gives it a peculiar distinction that is further heightened by the black and white stripes of its head and by its pinkish bill. Immatures have the black of the head replaced by rufous brown and the white replaced by light buffy brown.

The White-crowned Sparrow breeds across northern North America and at high elevation in the Rockies, and it winters in the southern United States and Mexico. Fall migrants appear in Louisiana generally in October, and a few may linger as late as mid-May. The bird frequents hedgerows, overgrown pastures, and other similar situations where there are brush heaps, blackberry tangles, or any sort of thickets in the open. Immatures are seen much more frequently in Louisiana than are adults, at least until after the prenuptial molt is completed that puts the first-year birds into their first breeding plumage.

The White-crowned Sparrow is at no time very common in Louisiana, but sometimes a small flock will take up its winter residence in a corner of a certain pasture or along one short section of a railroad right-of-way. There the flock will remain until late the following spring, when evidently the entire group departs together for some distant coniferous clearing in a far-away Canadian wilderness.

GOLDEN-CROWNED SPARROW *Zonotrichia atricapilla*
Pl. XXXIX

This species has been recorded only twice in Louisiana. A specimen was taken at Grand Isle by P. A. Daigre on April 20, 1936, and Ava R. Tabor reported seeing one at the same place on October 26, 1957. The Golden-crowned Sparrow breeds in Alaska and British Columbia and migrates southward in winter to Oregon, California, and Baja California. There are very few instances of its occurrence east of the Rocky Mountains, even as far as eastern Colorado; thus its presence in Louisiana is anomalous. It resembles the White-crowned Sparrow, but it lacks the white line over the eye; and the center of the head, instead of being white, is golden yellow. The general color of the body is of a much darker tone, tending toward olive rather than either grayish or reddish brown.

Plate XXXIX Five Sparrows, All Adults
1. White-throated Sparrow (p. 587). 2. White-crowned Sparrow (p. 585). 3. Golden-crowned Sparrow (p. 586). 4. Fox Sparrow (p. 588). 5. male Harris' Sparrow (p. 585).

46

WHITE-THROATED SPARROW   *Zonotrichia albicollis*

Pl. XXXIX; p. 587

White-throated Sparrows are unquestionably among the commonest winter birds in Louisiana. They occur in all places where there is shrubbery or other woody vegetation but do not like to venture far into the open. Where there is one of them, there are usually a dozen or more. The flocks arrive in late September or early October and are ubiquitous until the latter part of April, when they begin to thin out, finally to disappear completely by mid-May. A White-throat shot at Madisonville on May 30, 1886, and one observed at Lafayette between July 30 and August 8, 1969, probably were individuals that for one reason or another had failed to migrate.

The underparts of the species are grayish, which causes the white throat to stand out prominently. Adults have a broad white line over the eye, a yellow spot at the base of the bill, and a prominent buffy stripe down the center of the crown. Immatures have the head markings and throat patch more obscure and a few indistinct streaks on the breast.

The most frequently heard call note is a *tseet*. Its song is often rendered even in midwinter and is one of the most pleasing sounds to be heard in our

Adult White-throated Sparrow

ALLAN D. CRUICKSHANK

woods. It consists of five or six high-pitched, clear whistles, the first being very high, the others on a uniformly lower pitch. Then sometimes this pattern is reversed, with the first note an octave lower than the last series. The song has been likened to the refrain, "Old Sam Peabody, Peabody, Peabody."

FOX SPARROW   *Passerella iliaca*   Pl. XXXIX

Those finches that we call sparrows constitute a highly interesting group but not a colorful one. The Fox Sparrow, however, comes close to being an exception. Its bright rusty tail and general reddish tone throughout, which includes a heavy streaking and spotting of rufous and black on the underparts, give it an exceedingly attractive appearance and differentiate it from all its allies. Furthermore, on clear winter mornings when the rays of the sun are beginning to add warmth to the air, the Fox Sparrow often bursts forth into its full-toned medley of whistles that rise in cadence and then taper off in a series of soft utterances of the most pleasing sort.

The species is fairly numerous in winter in northern Louisiana, but it is not common in the southern part of the state. The first arrivals appear somewhat later than do most winter residents, for Fox Sparrows are not usually seen until after the first of November. The sojourn of these handsome birds is also briefer; their departure is generally in March and only twice has one been noted after the beginning of April.

LINCOLN'S SPARROW   *Melospiza lincolnii*   Pl. XL

The Lincoln's Sparrow is seldom a common bird in Louisiana except in April when northbound migrants from south of the Gulf of Mexico sometimes accumulate on the coastal ridges along our shores. A few can be found in winter in the thickets throughout most of the state, but the bird is never so plentiful that it is recorded on every field trip or even on the majority of them.

The Lincoln's Sparrow is a rather difficult bird to diagnose. It is essentially a streaked sparrow that is olive-brown and grayish above and grayish

Plate XL   Three Sparrows, the Lapland Longspur, and the Snow Bunting
1. Song Sparrow (p. 589). 2. Swamp Sparrow (p. 589). 3. Lincoln's Sparrow (p. 588).
4. Lapland Longspur (p. 590). 5. Snow Bunting (p. 593).

below, with a strong buffy wash on the breast. It can be confused with the immature Swamp Sparrow and with the Song Sparrow. However, its olive-brown color, finely streaked crown, and faint eye-ring and the fact that the streaks on the breast and flanks are fine and do not form a spot in the middle of the breast are all distinctive characteristics that eliminate in one way or another the other two species when the observer is in doubt. The combination of the olive-green color of the upperparts and the buffy breast band with its coextensive fine streakings is by itself diagnostic.

The species appears in Louisiana in late September or in early October and remains until the first part of May, rarely to the end of the month. It is most numerous during the period of spring migration, which takes place mainly in April. The largest numbers ever recorded in one day were the 40 seen by John P. Gee near Cameron on May 3, 1957, the 45 recorded on the Sabine Christmas Bird Count on December 29, 1962, and the 47 tallied on the Sabine count of December 27, 1964.

SWAMP SPARROW *Melospiza georgiana* Pl. XL

The Swamp Sparrow is an exceedingly common winter resident throughout most of Louisiana from the last days of September until late April, and a few remain into early May. As the name implies, its habitat preference is for swampy situations or damp fields. Adults are easily recognized by the reddish wings, the plain grayish underparts and cheeks, the rufous cap, and the heavy black streaks on the back. A fine dusky line extends from the ear through the eye to the base of the black bill. Immatures lack the rufous crown and gray cheeks, and the breast is lightly streaked instead of immaculate.

SONG SPARROW *Melospiza melodia* Pl. XL; Fig. 143

Many migrant birds exhibit an entirely different personality in their winter haunts from that which they display in their breeding range. In the northern part of the eastern United States the Song Sparrow in summer is an abundant inhabitant of farmyards, towns, and the residential sections and suburbs of cities. A single city block may have two or three or even more breeding pairs with their well-defined territories, each ruled over by a vociferous singing male. Hence, it is a conspicuous and familiar bird, liked by everyone who seeks its acquaintance. In the winter, though, large numbers of the birds leave their summer home to spend the cold months in the Southland. In doing so they take on new attitudes and new behavior patterns. Instead of being sociable and often urban dwelling, they become shy and rural. Sometimes their presence is detected only by the observer who is able to recognize the low, nasal *tchip* in the depth of a thicket or in a rank growth of broom sedge. A squeak on the part of the observer will usually bring one of the little birds into view, but not for long, for it always seems reluctant to show itself and reveal its markings.

The Song Sparrow is approximately the size of a House Sparrow and is reddish brown in color, with the heavy streakings on the underparts concentrated in a prominent black spot in the center of the breast (an excellent field mark). The Savannah Sparrow also often has a spot on its streaked underparts. Ways of distinguishing the two are discussed in the account of the Savannah Sparrow. Another field mark particularly useful when the bird is flying away is the shape of the tail, which is rounded in the Song Sparrow, indented in the Savannah (Fig. 143).

The Song Sparrow arrives in early October and is common from then until the first part of April. An occasional individual may sometimes remain until the end of the month. A male that was observed and heard singing at Port Hudson, in the northwestern corner of East Baton Rouge Parish, on July 5, 1948, by Mr. and Mrs. Robert B. Moore, is anomalous because the species is not known to breed in the lower Mississippi Valley south of northern Arkansas and southwestern Tennessee.

LAPLAND LONGSPUR   *Calcarius lapponicus*   Pl. XL; Fig. 147

When a bird that has not been previously recorded in the state is seen for the first time, it is usually a lone straggler that has for some reason wandered outside its normal range. Only rarely does a "first record" involve several

---

Plate XLI   Some of the Species Added to the State List Since the First Edition

1. male Mountain Bluebird (p. 477); 1a. female. 2. Western Wood Pewee (p. 436). 3. male Scott's Oriole (p. 542); 3a. female. 4. Tropical Kingbird (p. 423). 5. adult Buff-bellied Hummingbird (p. 405). 6. male Evening Grosbeak (p. 563); 6a. female. 7. male Hermit Warbler (p. 510); 7a. female. 8. male Black-chinned Hummingbird (p. 402). 9. Cassin's Kingbird (p. 425). 10. Hammond's Flycatcher (p. 435). 11. male Gray-headed Junco (p. 580). 12. male MacGillivray's Warbler (p. 529); 12a. female. 13. Say's Phoebe (p. 431). 14. Curve-billed Thrasher (p. 470). 15. male Lucy's Warbler (p. 504); 15a. female. 16. Wied's Crested Flycatcher (p. 430). 17. male Bronzed Cowbird (p. 552); 17a. female.

1 1a

2

3a

3

5 6a

7

7a

4

6

9 8

10 11 12

12a

13 14 15 16

17 17a

O'Neill

Figure 147   Longspurs in winter plumage and their respective tail patterns: (1) Chestnut-collared Longspur; (2) McCown's Longspur; (3) Lapland Longspur; (4) Smith's Longspur.

individuals or a flock. Technically, the initial appearance of the Lapland Longspur in Louisiana was no exception, for when I first discovered it, at Monroe, on December 19, 1932, I encountered only a single bird, feeding in the shortgrass along the shore of a small lake. Two days later two more individuals were seen at a different place several miles away. On the next day, however, I made an extraordinary and wholly unexpected find—a flock of no less than two thousand longspurs in an old cotton field a few miles south of Monroe. The species thus came close to being added to the state list on the basis of an unprecedented number of individuals. As far as most of the state is concerned, it has since proven to be an irregular winter visitor that is sometimes abundant when the state is blanketed in snow. At other times, its occurrence is rather erratic, except possibly in the vicinity of Shreveport, where it seems to occur almost every year whether there is snow or not.

Finding longspurs is largely a matter of visiting exactly the right place. Airport landing fields are one of their favorite haunts, as is almost any shortgrass area. Judging from my experience in 1932, I would expect old cotton fields to be likewise a good place in which to look for longspurs.

Three species of longspurs have been recorded in the state—Lapland, Smith's, and Chestnut-collared. A fourth species, the McCown's Longspur, is almost certain eventually to be discovered here and, therefore, cognizance is given to it in the following analysis of field marks. Adults of the four species in spring plumage differ radically, but that we shall ever encounter one of these birds in Louisiana late enough in spring for it to have acquired its full summer dress is unlikely. In winter plumage the four species are distressingly similar and can best be distinguished by the amount of white in the tail and the pattern that it forms with the black. These differences are shown by the accompanying diagrams (Fig. 147), which should be studied carefully by the student of Louisiana birds. In addition, the following key characters may be of help: Lapland—black smudge on the upper breast, rusty nape, and two prominent white wing bars; McCown's—rusty shoulders; Smith's—buffy underparts; Chestnut-collared—no ear patch.

Figure 127 shows the Horned Lark, Sprague's Pipit, and Water Pipit, three species occurring in habitat similar to that of the longspurs and also having white in the tail. Note in Figure 147 that among the longspurs, the Lapland has the least amount of white and that in both it and the Smith's, the white is entirely lateral. In the McCown's and Chestnut-collared the black forms a terminal bar, Y-shaped in the latter species and definitely T-shaped in the former.

The winter call notes of longspurs provide another means of field identification. The Lapland, Smith's, and McCown's Longspurs all have a dry, rattling note. It is so distinct and characteristic of a longspur that I at once recognized it the instant I heard it after an interim of nine years. The Lapland Longspur has a *tew* note, which is usually tacked onto the end of a rattle but is sometimes given alone, particularly on the bird's takeoff from the ground. The Smith's Longspur does not make the *tew* note but instead has a weak and not too often uttered *whit* (one of the calls of the Eastern Meadowlark is a similar, but a much stronger, *whit*). The Chestnut-collared Longspur does not give a rattling note, but instead has a finchlike call that as a rule consists of two or four syllables. Horace H. Jeter, of Shreveport, informs me that the note can be expressed as *ji-jiv* or *ji-jiv, ji-jiv*.

SMITH'S LONGSPUR *Calcarius pictus*   Fig. 147

This species has been recorded at only two localities in Louisiana. Horace H. Jeter, of Shreveport, found it at the old Municipal Airport of that city on several occasions in the winter of 1952–1953 and once in the winter of 1953–1954. He detected a single individual on December 13, 1952, but there were no less than 35 present on the airport grounds on December 21; 45 on January 25, 1953; 33 on February 22; and 10 on March 1. In the fall of 1953 the bird returned for the second year, appearing at the airport on November 26, but shortly thereafter the field was burned over and the longspurs disappeared. Five individuals were observed near Shreveport by Jeter and James R. Stewart on January 16, 1955, and three were seen on November 22, 1956, four on December 21, 1963, and one on December 27, 1971. The only record outside the Shreveport area is that of a single individual observed at the Natchitoches airport on January 17, 1956, by D. S. Payne. The diagnostic characteristics of the species are discussed in the preceding account.

CHESTNUT-COLLARED LONGSPUR   *Calcarius ornatus*   Fig. 147

The Chestnut-collared Longspur has been recorded in the state almost exclusively in the Shreveport area, where Horace H. Jeter first discovered it on March 23, 1952, and where he, James R. Stewart, and others have since seen it on several occasions in subsequent winters. On November 22, 1956, Jeter and Stewart found a flock of 34 individuals at the Caddo Parish Penal Farm. To my knowledge the only locality in the state outside of Caddo Parish where the species has been noted is 4 miles west of Cameron, where I obtained a specimen on November 20, 1966. Extreme dates of occurrence are October 18 and March 30. The distinctions between this species and the other longspurs of the United States are discussed in the account of the Lapland Longspur.

SNOW BUNTING   *Plectrophenax nivalis*   Pl. XL

The Snow Bunting breeds in the Arctic Zone north to within 7° of the North Pole. It winters in southern Canada and the northern part of the United States, rarely farther south. It is predominantly white in color, at least in winter, and its wings are almost entirely white. No other sparrow or sparrow-like bird possesses nearly as much white.

The sole basis for the inclusion of this species on the list of the birds of Louisiana hinges on a mounted specimen that reposed in the Louisiana State Museum in New Orleans until its transfer to the LSU Museum of Zoology in Baton Rouge. The printed label has a penciled notation in what appears to be the handwriting of Robert Glenk, longtime curator of the New Orleans museum. This notation states that the bird was collected by George E. Beyer at Covington. I have been advised, however, by H. H. Kopman, who collaborated with Beyer and Andrew Allison in writing one of the first annotated lists of the birds of the state, that Beyer informed him before his death that it was not he (Beyer) who had collected the Snow Bunting, but a taxidermist by the name of Schmidt. These facts are important, for until they were learned, the circumstances had always seemed paradoxical. If Professor Beyer had actually collected a bird as unusual in Louisiana as the Snow Bunting, he surely would have placed it in his own collection at Tulane University, rather than in the Louisiana State Museum.

SUMMARY
OF SEASONAL
OCCURRENCES

IN PREPARING the following charts (Table 3), I have attempted to show in condensed form the seasons or periods of occurrence and the approximate relative abundance of the 411 species of birds that are known to have occurred in Louisiana. Although this graphic presentation provides a quick reference to many useful data, it cannot portray all the facts that may be desired. I have made no attempt to indicate the fine degrees of abundance among the various species. The top category, "common to abundant, at least locally," includes many shades of commonness. It includes not only the Red-winged Blackbird, which sometimes blackens the rice fields, but also the Belted Kingfisher, which is widespread and conspicuous along our bayous and streams but which is seldom seen by a single observer in numbers of more than a dozen in the course of a day. Variations in the relative abundance of a bird in its different habitats and variations in a bird's abundance in different parts of the state are often very great. Although the Seaside Sparrow, for example, is entirely absent in all the inland parishes of the state, it is abundant in its one habitat, the salt marshes of the coast. I have, therefore, designated it as "common." Neither can the charts tell much about the year-to-year fluctuations in the numbers of a given species. The Red-breasted Nuthatch inundated the state in 1940, and to a lesser extent in 1941, in numbers that would have placed it high in the top category. Yet it has been all but absent in some years since the big invasion. Consequently, I have felt obliged to class it with the "very rare or irregular" species.

In a further attempt to overcome some of these difficulties, I have shown the status of each bird in the state as a whole (top line by each species), as well as its status in the Baton Rouge area (second line), which is interpreted here to include East and West Baton Rouge, East and West Feliciana, Pointe Coupee, Iberville, and Ascension parishes. The Baton Rouge area may not be regarded as truly indicative of the situation with respect to all inland localities, but at least it is noncoastal. Moreover, the Baton Rouge area happens to be one of the few areas in the interior of the state where there has been fairly complete coverage over a long number of years. An ideal arrangement, of course, would have been to have had four lines for each species: one for a strictly coastal locality, one for an area in the central-southern part of the state, one for an area in northern Louisiana, and, finally, a line summarizing the data for the state as a whole.

The numbers on the charts are the extreme dates of arrival and departure based on carefully sifted records in the literature or on file in the LSU Museum of Zoology. They cover the period from the time of Audubon to March 1, 1974. Birds definitely known to breed in the state are indicated by a star after the name. Proof of breeding in the state is based on the discovery of an actual nest with eggs or with young, but the detection of juveniles barely capable of flight is also considered sufficient. In the case of several species such unimpeachable evidence of breeding in Louisiana is still lacking, although the birds in question almost surely do so.

Observations that extend any of the migration dates or the seasons of occurrence, as well as any new information relating to the birds of Louisiana, should be transmitted along with full particulars to the LSU Museum of Zoology in order that the new facts may be put on file for future use by anyone who is interested. This does not mean to imply that every sight record of a bird that comes into the museum is automatically accepted and used. Sight records of birds are particularly subject to error, even when made by the most competent ornithologist. Consequently, to be of value they should invariably be accompanied by full supporting details. Scientific data of any sort must always be subject to the closest scrutiny and to the most rigid tests of their validity. Science is truth. When we seek the truth, we must always demand unimpeachable evidence.

Table 3   Charts Showing the Seasonal Occurrence of Louisiana Birds

■ (solid black) — Common to abundant, at least locally.

▨ (dark stipple) — Uncommon or only moderately common, but found regularly in smaller numbers.

▒ (light stipple) — Rare; found infrequently, not every day, but to be expected, particularly at certain times of the year.

•••• — Very rare or irregular; not found every week or even every month during its season, sometimes skipping a year or more, but when present possibly locally common for a short period.

★ — Breeding known.

Note: The first line by each species shows the status of the bird in the state as a whole; the second line shows the status in the Baton Rouge area as geographically defined on page 596. One species, the Purple Sandpiper, was recorded for the first time in Louisiana too late to be included in the charts (see page 315).

SPECIES	JAN	FEB	MAR	APR	MAY	JUN	JUL	AUG	SEP	OCT	NOV	DEC
COMMON LOON	▨	▨	▒	▲	••••	••••	••• 23		8 ▨	▨	▨	▨
	▒	▒	▒	20					22 ▒			
RED-THROATED LOON	••••	••••	•• 14								4• •30	
											23•30	
RED-NECKED GREBE											•2	
HORNED GREBE	▨	▨	▨	▒ 16					14 ▒	▨	▨	▨
	▒	▒	20							8 ▒		
EARED GREBE	▨	▨	▨	▒	• ••13				18 ▒	▨	▨	▨
	••••	•• 17									24•	
LEAST GREBE											•14	
											•14	
WESTERN GREBE	••••	••••	••• 26								3••••	
PIED-BILLED GREBE ★	■	■	■	▨	▨	▨	▨	▨	▨	■	■	■
	■	■	■	▨	▒	▒	▒	▒	▨	■	■	■
YELLOW-NOSED ALBATROSS					•9							
GREATER SHEARWATER					•3		•16	• 11	4•5			
AUDUBON'S SHEARWATER		29•		4 ••••	••••	••••	••••	••••	••15			
LEACH'S STORM-PETREL									•23			• 5
WILSON'S STORM-PETREL				8 ••••	••••	▒	▒	▒	9			
WHITE-TAILED TROPICBIRD								•15				
AMERICAN WHITE PELICAN	■	■	■	▨	■					▨	■	■
	▨	▨	▨	▨	••	••••	••••	••••	•• ▒	▒	▨	▨
BROWN PELICAN ★	▨	▨	▨	▨	▨	▨	▨	▨	▨	▨	▨	▨
	•11							•30				
MASKED BOOBY				1 ••••	••••	••••	••••	••••	••13			
									• 13			
BROWN BOOBY	•			•			•		•		•	
RED-FOOTED BOOBY										1•		
NORTHERN GANNET	••••	••••	••••	••••	• 5						29 •	••••

597

SPECIES	JAN	FEB	MAR	APR	MAY	JUN	JUL	AUG	SEP	OCT	NOV	DEC
DOUBLE-CRESTED CORMORANT ★												
OLIVACEOUS CORMORANT ★	• 20											
AMERICAN ANHINGA ★		4										
MAGNIFICENT FRIGATEBIRD						• 26	6 • 11	• 18				
GREAT BLUE HERON ★												
GREEN HERON ★		25								17		
LITTLE BLUE HERON ★	• • • •	9								26		• • • •
CATTLE EGRET ★												
REDDISH EGRET ★												
GREAT EGRET ★												
SNOWY EGRET ★			17									30
LOUISIANA HERON ★					29 • • • • •				• • • • • •	• 13		
BLACK-CROWNED NIGHT HERON ★												
YELLOW-CROWNED NIGHT HERON ★			27					8				
LEAST BITTERN ★	• • • •	23 •	• • •					8		• • • •	• • • •	
AMERICAN BITTERN ★						• • • •	• • • •	• • • •				
WOOD STORK	•	• • •	24 • • • 15			21		28				•
GLOSSY IBIS ★												
WHITE-FACED IBIS ★												
WHITE IBIS ★			24							• • • • • •	• 6	
ROSEATE SPOONBILL ★								• 16				
GREATER FLAMINGO	• 11										• 6	
WHISTLING SWAN	• • • •	• • •								15 • •	• • • •	
TRUMPETER SWAN	• 7									•		
CANADA GOOSE	• 4	29 • • • 11		• •	• • • •	• • • •	• • • •	• •	7 • • •	• • • •	• • • •	
COMMON BRANT	15 • 17									• 30		

598

SPECIES	JAN	FEB	MAR	APR	MAY	JUN	JUL	AUG	SEP	OCT	NOV	DEC
BLACK BRANT									21•			
WHITE-FRONTED GOOSE					27				29•			
				•27					29•			
SNOW GOOSE	•	•	•	•	•	•	•	•	•		•	•
ROSS GOOSE	••••	•••23									24•	••••
BLACK-BELLIED TREE-DUCK											26•	20•
FULVOUS TREE-DUCK ★												
MALLARD ★					••••	••••	••••		26• •••			
			14									
BLACK DUCK					16				7			
				23					30			
MOTTLED DUCK ★					•23		•26	•18				
GADWALL					13		8					
			23						5			
NORTHERN PINTAIL ★					••••	••••	••					
			23						5			
GREEN-WINGED TEAL				••3	23•	••••	•••					
			13						24			
BLUE-WINGED TEAL ★												
	3				27		20			24		
CINNAMON TEAL	••••	••••	••••	••21					20•	••••	••••	
NORTHERN SHOVELER					•• ••••	••••	•••					
			16					25				
AMERICAN WIGEON					30	•	11					
			3						16			
WOOD DUCK ★												
REDHEAD					22		27					
			17						3			
RING-NECKED DUCK					•• ••••	••••	•••					
			27						3			
CANVASBACK				• ••••	••••	••••	••••					
			27						28			
GREATER SCAUP			6			•24			2			
		3							4			
LESSER SCAUP					• ••••	••••	••••	••				
				••••	••••	••••	••					
COMMON GOLDENEYE			22						8			
		8							16			
BUFFLEHEAD			23					13				
		20							4			
OLDSQUAW				3					15			
		8							15			
HARLEQUIN DUCK			•1									

SPECIES	JAN	FEB	MAR	APR	MAY	JUN	JUL	AUG	SEP	OCT	NOV	DEC
WHITE-WINGED SCOTER	• • •13	•	• •	•	• •1				17•	•	•	• • • •
SURF SCOTER	•		•	•	• •13					8• • • •24	• •	•
BLACK SCOTER	•		•	• • • •	• •25					25•	• • •24	
RUDDY DUCK ★	▓	▓	▓	▓	• • • • • •12	• • • •	• • • •	•		4▓ 4▓	▓	▓
MASKED DUCK	•7			•3	• 5							23 •
HOODED MERGANSER ★	▓	▓	▓	▓	▓	▓				▓	▓	▓
COMMON MERGANSER	▓	▓	▓	19	•3				24▓	20• • • •21		
RED-BREASTED MERGANSER	▓	▓	▓	▓	• • •20	• •22			25▓	9▓	▓	▓
TURKEY VULTURE ★	██	██	██	██	██	██	██	██	██	██	██	██
BLACK VULTURE ★	██	██	██	██	██	██	██	██	██	██	██	██
WHITE-TAILED KITE									•11			
SWALLOW-TAILED KITE ★	15 • •8	• ▓	▓	▓	▓	▓	▓	• • •3	• • • • •24		30 •
MISSISSIPPI KITE ★	1 • • • •4	• • ▓	▓	██	██	██	██	• • •	• • • • •30	• • • •2	
GOSHAWK										• •30 •30		
SHARP-SHINNED HAWK ★	▓	▓	▓	▓	• • • • • • • •	• • • •	• • • • • •• •	•	▓	▓	▓	▓
COOPER'S HAWK ★	▓	▓	▓	▓	▓	▓	▓	▓	▓	▓	▓	▓
RED-TAILED HAWK ★	██	██	██	██	██	██	██	██	██	██	██	██
RED-SHOULDERED HAWK ★	██	██	██	██	██	██	██	██	██	██	██	██
BROAD-WINGED HAWK ★	▓ 7• • •	•	▓	██	██	██	██	██	▓14	▓	▓	▓
SWAINSON'S HAWK	• 5		7• •16					8 •9	•7 •26	28•6•28•	
WHITE-TAILED HAWK	•19									•18		
ROUGH-LEGGED HAWK	▓	▓	• • • •• •18	• •12					30• • • • •	12▓	
FERRUGINOUS HAWK	• • • •14	• • • •	• 8						1• • • •	• • • •		
HARRIS' HAWK									•			
GOLDEN EAGLE	▓ •	▓	▓12						8▓ •15	▓ •24	▓	▓
BALD EAGLE ★	▓ • • • •	▓ • • • •	▓ • • • •	• • • •	• • • •	• • • •	• • • •	▓	▓ • • • •	▓ • • • •	▓ • • • •	• • • •

600

SPECIES		JAN	FEB	MAR	APR	MAY	JUN	JUL	AUG	SEP	OCT	NOV	DEC
MARSH HAWK				23		25		28 •••	2				
OSPREY	★	••••	•4		21•	••17	••••	••••	•16 •9	••14 5•• ••12			
AUDUBON'S CARACARA	★	••••	••••	••••	••••	••••	••••	••••	••••	••••	••••	••••	••••
PEREGRINE FALCON	★				19	13			9 / 9				
MERLIN	★	•••• ••••	••••	••• 23		•••	••15		7	14 •• ••••	••••	••••	
AMERICAN KESTREL	★												
GREATER PRAIRIE CHICKEN	★	FORMERLY A PERMANENT RESIDENT: NOW EXTIRPATED IN LOUISIANA											
BOBWHITE	★												
BLACK FRANCOLIN	★												
WILD TURKEY	★												
WHOOPING CRANE	★	FORMERLY A MODERATELY COMMON RESIDENT AND WINTER VISITOR BUT NOW EXTIRPATED											
SANDHILL CRANE	★	••••	••••	••••	••••	••••		••••		••••	••••	••••	
KING RAIL	★												
CLAPPER RAIL	★												
VIRGINIA RAIL	★	2			•	••• 25				•••• 9			
SORA				27		24	20•		3				
YELLOW RAIL					1					6 / 6			21
BLACK RAIL		•17	••••	•14 ••••	••13					2•••	••••	••••	••••
PURPLE GALLINULE	★	••••	•16 ••••	••						••••	••••		
COMMON GALLINULE	★	••••	••••	17						••	••••	••••	
AMERICAN COOT	★												
AMERICAN OYSTERCATCHER	★			26					1		•6		
BLACK-NECKED STILT	★												
AMERICAN AVOCET						•7				•10	5	19	
SEMIPALMATED PLOVER		•4			22	17		7			30		
WILSON'S PLOVER	★	••••	•••									•	••••

601

SPECIES	JAN	FEB	MAR	APR	MAY	JUN	JUL	AUG	SEP	OCT	NOV	DEC
KILLDEER ★												
PIPING PLOVER							8	12				
SNOWY PLOVER				29		18						
AMERICAN GOLDEN PLOVER	23 / 3			25 / 22			10			•22		17
BLACK-BELLIED PLOVER				•26			22		22			
HUDSONIAN GODWIT			17	5		6•••	••••	••••30				
MARBLED GODWIT			•13	•	••••	••••	••	•10				
ESKIMO CURLEW	FORMERLY AN ABUNDANT SPRING MIGRANT; NOW VIRTUALLY EXTINCT											
WHIMBREL	••••	••••	•••		••••	••••	••••	••••	••••	••••	••••	••••
LONG-BILLED CURLEW												
UPLAND SANDPIPER	3 / 3			26 22• / 9	•••	7	25	••16				
GREATER YELLOWLEGS	8			••19 / 16	20		24			••••	••20	
LESSER YELLOWLEGS	9			9	21			24				
SOLITARY SANDPIPER	•••• / 2•••	••••		•• / 11	•••• / •	•• / 4••			4	••	•••• / ••	
WILLET ★						•7	•10					
SPOTTED SANDPIPER				••25	20							
RUDDY TURNSTONE				••	••	7 •••	•••19					
WILSON'S PHALAROPE	21•		27	21	12 / 10•12		•••	•				
NORTHERN PHALAROPE		30••8			•							
RED PHALAROPE					•16 •12 / •12	29	•••10					
AMERICAN WOODCOCK ★												
COMMON SNIPE			•••18 / 22	14••		10						
SHORT-BILLED DOWITCHER			••••	••••	10•15							
LONG-BILLED DOWITCHER			••••	•••								
RED KNOT					•18							
SANDERLING			•28	10•••	•••29							

602

SPECIES	JAN	FEB	MAR	APR	MAY	JUN	JUL	AUG	SEP	OCT	NOV	DEC
SEMIPALMATED SANDPIPER					•12		••••					
WESTERN SANDPIPER					15	16						
LEAST SANDPIPER					18	15						
WHITE-RUMPED SANDPIPER			12••• ••			21	•13					
		16••	•••• ••17									
BAIRD'S SANDPIPER		14				1	10				•	••17
					•16				14••	••••	• 9	
PECTORAL SANDPIPER	• ••••• •					7	11					•• 23
	• •		11	18			21				12	
DUNLIN						••• •10	4					
										25 •	•11	
CURLEW SANDPIPER									•13			
STILT SANDPIPER	• 1		7		29	12						28
						24			19			
BUFF-BREASTED SANDPIPER			28		15	11			25			
				•7			1	24				
POMARINE JAEGER				10•••	•••19							
PARASITIC JAEGER	6••21• 6			•11	•3	•4 •21			•12	•4	•14	
										•4		
LONG-TAILED JAEGER				•24								
GLAUCOUS GULL					2						4	
HERRING GULL						•• ••••	•••• ••••			14		
					••••• 2							
RING-BILLED GULL						•• ••••		11				
				8								
LAUGHING GULL ★		•29					6•11	•10	•4			
FRANKLIN'S GULL					••17			25				
		•29							3 ••• 27			
BONAPARTE'S GULL					•• ••14		29••					
			20						8			
LITTLE GULL				•31								
BLACK-LEGGED KITTIWAKE	•2			18•• 26							4 •• 18	
GULL-BILLED TERN ★									•10			
FORSTER'S TERN ★				25			23					
COMMON TERN ★		•11	•11						5•• 16			
ROSEATE TERN		•				•8						
SOOTY TERN ★				•6								•15

603

SPECIES		JAN	FEB	MAR	APR	MAY	JUN	JUL	AUG	SEP	OCT	NOV	DEC
BRIDLED TERN									10 •16 / 10•				
LEAST TERN	★	••••	••••	••••								••••	••••
						4				24			
ROYAL TERN	★												
SANDWICH TERN	★								•10				
									•10				
CASPIAN TERN	★	•3 •22		19			21		7	16			
BLACK TERN		••••	••••	••••						•••	••••	••••	••••
					20		7	2		9			
BROWN NODDY									•30 •16				
BLACK SKIMMER	★							•9	10• •	•2			
ANCIENT MURRELET						•6							
BAND-TAILED PIGEON		•21				•7							•16
						•7							
ROCK PIGEON	★												
WHITE-WINGED DOVE	★									•25	21•	•1	
MOURNING DOVE	★												
PASSENGER PIGEON		FORMERLY AN ABUNDANT WINTER RESIDENT; NOW EXTINCT											
COMMON GROUND DOVE	★	•6 •18		15			•••• 1			4		1	
INCA DOVE		••••	••••	••••	••• 25					28•	••••	••••	
CAROLINA PARAKEET	★	FORMERLY A COMMON PERMANENT RESIDENT; NOW EXTINCT											
YELLOW-BILLED CUCKOO	★		27•	•••								••	••••
			27•	•••						16			
BLACK-BILLED CUCKOO				3		26		11		26			
				21	8			24		18			
GREATER ROADRUNNER	★												
SMOOTH-BILLED ANI		14••	•8				•18						
GROOVE-BILLED ANI	★												
		3•8								•8	•7 3•••	••••	
BARN OWL	★												
COMMON SCREECH OWL	★												
FLAMMULATED OWL		•2											
		•2											
GREAT HORNED OWL	★												

SPECIES	JAN	FEB	MAR	APR	MAY	JUN	JUL	AUG	SEP	OCT	NOV	DEC
SNOWY OWL		•17		•								
BURROWING OWL			22	1	•	•	•	•	7 / 10			
BARRED OWL ★	████	████	████	████	████	████	████	████	████	████	████	████
LONG-EARED OWL	•••• / 21•	•••• / ••••	••• 25 / ••• 25							•20		22•
SHORT-EARED OWL				3	21				15 / 30			
NORTHERN SAW-WHET OWL												29•
CHUCK-WILL'S-WIDOW ★	••••	••••	• / 28						25	•••	••••	••••
WHIP-POOR-WILL	••••	••••	•• / •• 7					12	11 •••	•••	••••	••••
COMMON NIGHTHAWK ★	••••	•••• / •22	••••	•••• / 10	••					••••	••••	•••• / 30•
LESSER NIGHTHAWK		•9		7	23			8	13		28•	•4•18
CHIMNEY SWIFT ★			6 / 10							••10 / •8		
VAUX'S SWIFT			3 / 3						14 / 14			
RUBY-THROATED HUMMINGBIRD ★	••••	••••	• / •							••	••••	••••
BLACK-CHINNED HUMMINGBIRD	••••	••••	••••	•• 12						25•		27•
BROAD-TAILED HUMMINGBIRD		•7 / •7										•••• / ••••
RUFOUS HUMMINGBIRD				15 / 7				26• / 26•	25			
BUFF-BELLIED HUMMINGBIRD	••••	••••	••• 28							23••	••••	
BELTED KINGFISHER ★	████	████	████	████	████	████	████	████	████	████	████	████
COMMON FLICKER ★	████	████	████	████	████	████	████	████	████	████	████	████
PILEATED WOODPECKER ★	████	████	████	████	████	████	████	████	████	████	████	████
RED-BELLIED WOODPECKER ★	████	████	████	████	████	████	████	████	████	████	████	████
RED-HEADED WOODPECKER ★	████	████	████	████	████	████	████	████	████	████	████	████
YELLOW-BELLIED SAPSUCKER			/ 29		7 / 29				10 / 10			
HAIRY WOODPECKER ★	████	████	████	████	████	████	████	████	████	████	████	████
DOWNY WOODPECKER ★	████	████	████	████	████	████	████	████	████	████	████	████
RED-COCKADED WOODPECKER ★	████	████	████	████	████	████	████	████	████	████	████	████

605

SPECIES	JAN	FEB	MAR	APR	MAY	JUN	JUL	AUG	SEP	OCT	NOV	DEC

IVORY-BILLED WOODPECKER ★ — FORMERLY A COMMON PERMANENT RESIDENT: NOW EXTREMELY RARE OR EXTIRPATED

EASTERN KINGBIRD ★ 6•• ••• 26 / 6•• 28

GRAY KINGBIRD 25• ••11

TROPICAL KINGBIRD •9

WESTERN KINGBIRD ★ •••• •••• •• •••• •• • ••••• / •24 5 28

CASSIN'S KINGBIRD •7

SCISSOR-TAILED FLYCATCHER ★ 28 21 1 21

GREAT KISKADEE ★ •14 • •• • • • •8

SULPHUR-BELLIED FLYCATCHER •30

GREAT CRESTED FLYCATCHER ★ 12• •••• 26 / 25 19

WIED'S CRESTED FLYCATCHER •3 •27 24• ••••

ASH-THROATED FLYCATCHER •••• •••• ••••1 1•9 4•••• •••• •••• / 20•24 23•

EASTERN PHOEBE ★ ••• •7 1

SAY'S PHOEBE •••• ••16 29 •••10 23• ••••

YELLOW-BELLIED FLYCATCHER 29• ••• 28 9 23 / 29• •••26 2 22

ACADIAN FLYCATCHER ★ 8 •••1 / 11 ••19

WILLOW FLYCATCHER 28 •••16 14 1 / 5••12 30 1

ALDER FLYCATCHER 12 22 17 24 / •12 17 24

LEAST FLYCATCHER •1 30 16 17•• ••• •••• / 15 5

HAMMOND'S FLYCATCHER •17

EASTERN WOOD PEWEE ★ 3•10 •26 27 • ••11 21• / 3•10 1 •• •9

WESTERN WOOD PEWEE •10

OLIVE-SIDED FLYCATCHER 22• •••23 31 •••20 / 7••22

VERMILION FLYCATCHER 17 16 / 3 2

HORNED LARK ★ 28 27 / •••• 28 26•

TREE SWALLOW ★ •• •••• •••• • / •• •••• •••• •

SPECIES		JAN	FEB	MAR	APR	MAY	JUN	JUL	AUG	SEP	OCT	NOV	DEC
BANK SWALLOW				23•		•9	4•						••3
				12	18		18				12		
ROUGH-WINGED SWALLOW	★												
BARN SWALLOW	★			20		•• ••• 25	3					•••28	
CLIFF SWALLOW		•23		2		••28	18•			•	•••24		
					9	5			5	•••24			
PURPLE MARTIN	★	23•••								•••11		26•	
		23•••								••••10			
BLUE JAY	★												
COMMON CROW	★												
FISH CROW	★												
CAROLINA CHICKADEE	★												
TUFTED TITMOUSE	★												
WHITE-BREASTED NUTHATCH	★												
RED-BREASTED NUTHATCH		••••	••••	••••	••••	•7				21•	••••	••••	••••
		••••	••••	••••	•••20					27•	••••	••••	••••
BROWN-HEADED NUTHATCH	★												
BROWN CREEPER					12					10			
					12					11			
NORTHERN HOUSE WREN						9				7			
					27					7			
WINTER WREN						23				8			
					4					17			
BEWICK'S WREN					•••20				•9	26			
					•9					26			
CAROLINA WREN	★												
MARSH WREN	★				27					19			
SEDGE WREN						•• ••• 12				2			
					•19					2			
NORTHERN MOCKINGBIRD	★												
GRAY CATBIRD	★												
BROWN THRASHER	★												
CURVE-BILLED THRASHER									•26			7•31•	
SAGE THRASHER		•2					•26					•8 1•	31•
AMERICAN ROBIN	★					•• •••	••••	••••	••••	••			

SPECIES		JAN	FEB	MAR	APR	MAY	JUN	JUL	AUG	SEP	OCT	NOV	DEC
WOOD THRUSH	★	•3	5••• •									••	••••
		•3		18								•18	
HERMIT THRUSH						•••15				26			
						21					21		
SWAINSON'S THRUSH				31		30			12				2 •
				20	19				12	15			
GRAY-CHEEKED THRUSH				7	26			31		29			
				22	25				26	14			
VEERY				31	4			31		29			
				20	19				11	27			
EASTERN BLUEBIRD	★												
MOUNTAIN BLUEBIRD		28•	•14										
		28•	•14										
NORTHERN WHEATEAR										•12			
BLUE-GRAY GNATCATCHER	★												
GOLDEN-CROWNED KINGLET					••24					7•			
				•••	•10					15			
RUBY-CROWNED KINGLET					11				17				
					5				29				
WATER PIPIT					•• ••14					3			
				12						18			
SPRAGUE'S PIPIT					26				20•				
		18• 24								30•• 3			
CEDAR WAXWING						18			27				
					21					7			
LOGGERHEAD SHRIKE	★												
EUROPEAN STARLING	★												
WHITE-EYED VIREO	★												
BELL'S VIREO	★	•••17		18•						11	11•• 21	29•	
YELLOW-THROATED VIREO	★	••••	••••								25		23•
			3•••								25		
SOLITARY VIREO					5			•?	12				
				19						5			
BLACK-WHISKERED VIREO				18 •	••	•• ••••• 4		•29					
RED-EYED VIREO	★	•3		15							8		
				20						26			
PHILADELPHIA VIREO			•5	25•	•	30		2			12	•3	
					•13			24		26			
WARBLING VIREO	★			4							•••24		
				26						3			
BLACK-AND-WHITE WARBLER	★	••••	••••								••••	••••	
			6•••	•						•	•••29	25•	
BACHMAN'S WARBLER			27 •	••••	••••	•••• •3							
					•9								

608

SPECIES	JAN	FEB	MAR	APR	MAY	JUN	JUL	AUG	SEP	OCT	NOV	DEC
GOLDEN-WINGED WARBLER	•5		2		16	5			21			
				13 2			15		21			
BLUE-WINGED WARBLER			22		20	27				18	•29	
			30		20			4		14		
TENNESSEE WARBLER			12		22				9		••21•1	
				6	16				9	31		
ORANGE-CROWNED WARBLER					2				9			
				30					9			
NASHVILLE WARBLER			29		10			31		•	•••20	••
									1	25	19•	
LUCY'S WARBLER												30 •
NORTHERN PARULA WARBLER ★	••••	•••								••••	••••	
		28								•7		••
YELLOW WARBLER	••••	••••	••••		••	•16•				••••	••••	
			11••		14	•16•				20	•• •3	
CHESTNUT-SIDED WARBLER			21		22			27		1		
				6	17			27		27		
CERULEAN WARBLER			23		••••••	••			18			
			31		•16	22			20			
BLACK-THROATED BLUE WARBLER	•3	25•	••••		20			8		••••	••••	
									19	20		
PINE WARBLER ★												
YELLOW-THROATED WARBLER ★	••••	••							•	••••	••••	
		1	••••	•						••••	••••	
BLACK-THROATED GRAY WARBLER	••••	••••	•••21						3•••	••••	••••	
			• 21						•5			
HERMIT WARBLER	•12			•20								
BLACK-THROATED GREEN WARBLER	•5	••	•	14	24			12		23	•18	
				18	11			11		17		
PRAIRIE WARBLER ★	••••	••••	•••						•	••••	••••	
			25						30			
CAPE MAY WARBLER				5	15							
BLACKBURNIAN WARBLER	•3	10			29			22		••	•8	
			2	16				2		27		
MAGNOLIA WARBLER	••12		21		28			30		8	3•••	
			16	18				8		7		
MYRTLE WARBLER					15	•16	•5	15				
				5		•16	•5	16				
PALM WARBLER					5			29••••				
				8					9			
BLACKPOLL WARBLER				9	26			•17				
				22	13			•17				
BAY-BREASTED WARBLER				16	28			21		•• •30•		
				17	17			8		15		
AMERICAN REDSTART ★	••••		28							••	••••	
			7							7	•19	
OVENBIRD	•	•	••	•	30			9		••	••••	
				15	16			25		25		

609

SPECIES	JAN	FEB	MAR	APR	MAY	JUN	JUL	AUG	SEP	OCT	NOV	DEC
NORTHERN WATERTHRUSH	• •	•••• ••			18	13			•••	••••
			16	16			15	24		
LOUISIANA WATERTHRUSH ★		10							25	
		14							25	
SWAINSON'S WARBLER ★		21							27	
		30						5		
WORM-EATING WARBLER ★		14							26		30•
		14						12		
PROTHONOTARY WARBLER ★		3							18	•29 25
		5						15		
COMMON YELLOWTHROAT ★										
KENTUCKY WARBLER ★	•2	14							25	
		19						16		
CONNECTICUT WARBLER			27•	•19				6•9		
								6•		
MOURNING WARBLER			2	24		8		18		
							15	18		
MACGILLIVRAY'S WARBLER									•15	
HOODED WARBLER ★	14•18	7						•••	•7
		15						26		
WILSON'S WARBLER	••••	••••	••••	••		•4		25••	•	••••	••••
		•19			•4		7	24	•••	••••
CANADA WARBLER		31	22		9		4		
		29	17		13		4		
PAINTED REDSTART								17••	•7
YELLOW-BREASTED CHAT ★	••••	••••	••••					•	••••	••••
		• •	15••	•				27	• •
HOUSE SPARROW ★										
BOBOLINK		1••	••16	•13	4•••	••••	•5	
		19	23			30•	•3		
EASTERN MEADOWLARK ★										
WESTERN MEADOWLARK ★				17	•18		7		
			20				22		
YELLOW-HEADED BLACKBIRD	•22	••••	••16		•13	•16 ••	•	•17
		27•				• 8	•11	
RED-WINGED BLACKBIRD ★										
ORCHARD ORIOLE ★	••••	••••	•					•	••••	••••
		14						25		
SCOTT'S ORIOLE	26•	••••	••15	•6				•9	28•
BALTIMORE ORIOLE ★	••••	••••	•••					•	••••	••••
		••••	••••	•••				3		•••
RUSTY BLACKBIRD			••	•10			21		
			1					22	
BREWER'S BLACKBIRD			26				5		
			14					12	

610

SPECIES	JAN	FEB	MAR	APR	MAY	JUN	JUL	AUG	SEP	OCT	NOV	DEC
GREAT-TAILED GRACKLE ★	•	••	••••							••••	••••	••••
BOAT-TAILED GRACKLE ★	•7											22••
COMMON GRACKLE ★												
BROWN-HEADED COWBIRD ★												
BRONZED COWBIRD			•14 / •14	12••	•••• •5							31•
WESTERN TANAGER	••	• •	••••		•23 •15		30•	••		••••	••••	
	•	•		•••• •••23							26•	
SCARLET TANAGER			27	16	31 / 13		•26 30		14		•7	28•
								30				
SUMMER TANAGER ★	••••	••••	•••							••••	••••	
	••••	••••	•••							••••	••••	
NORTHERN CARDINAL ★												
ROSE-BREASTED GROSBEAK	••••	••••	••••	21	16 / 16	•8			22 / 24	25	••••	••••
												28•
BLACK-HEADED GROSBEAK					28				10			
	••••	••••	•••• •3								2	••••
BLUE GROSBEAK ★	••••	••••	•							••	••••	
	••	8			••	•••						
INDIGO BUNTING ★	••••	••••	•							••	••••	
											••	••••
PAINTED BUNTING ★	••••	••••	••••	•						••••	••••	
	••	••••	••••	•					23			
DICKCISSEL ★	••••	••••	••••	•							••	••••
	••••	••••	••••	•							••	••••
EVENING GROSBEAK	••••	••••	••••	••••	•••21					26•	••••	
	••••	••••	••••	•••• •4						26•	••••	
PURPLE FINCH				•	•••25					7		
				•	•8					23		
PINE SISKIN					••••14					20		
				3								18
AMERICAN GOLDFINCH ★					18					13		
LESSER GOLDFINCH				•17								
RED CROSSBILL	•27		20••27									
GREEN-TAILED TOWHEE				•13							•4	28•
RUFOUS-SIDED TOWHEE ★												
LARK BUNTING									•4			23•
SAVANNAH SPARROW					•• ••17				18			
					14				28			
GRASSHOPPER SPARROW ★					•••	••••	•••	•1	18			
					•••	••18			3			

611

SPECIES	JAN	FEB	MAR	APR	MAY	JUN	JUL	AUG	SEP	OCT	NOV	DEC
HENSLOW'S SPARROW					••15				18			
		4								24		
LE CONTE'S SPARROW					6				6			
				10						31		
SHARP-TAILED SPARROW					••••	•7			23•	•••		
									23•	•• •		22•
SEASIDE SPARROW ★												
VESPER SPARROW					30		2••••	•••				
			26							18		
LARK SPARROW ★	••••	••••	•••• •							••	••••	••••
	••••	••		•13		•21		24		14	26•	••••
BACHMAN'S SPARROW ★												
SLATE-COLORED JUNCO			•	•••25					5			
				•••	••14					12		
GRAY-HEADED JUNCO		•3										•19
AMERICAN TREE SPARROW	27•	•••16								•31	6•27•	
	27•											
CHIPPING SPARROW ★												
CLAY-COLORED SPARROW	•	•30		••••	•8				29•	••••	•• •	•
		•30									•13	
BREWER'S SPARROW											19•	•7
FIELD SPARROW ★												
HARRIS' SPARROW			••	••••29						7		
										13•	•	•14
WHITE-CROWNED SPARROW					17				8			
				27					28			
GOLDEN-CROWNED SPARROW				•20						•26		
WHITE-THROATED SPARROW					••• 30		••		12			
					6				12			
FOX SPARROW				•10					21•			
		19								14		
LINCOLN'S SPARROW					30				25			
			14						11			
SWAMP SPARROW					13				25			
				5					10			
SONG SPARROW					30		•5		4			
				8			•5		23			
LAPLAND LONGSPUR			20							12		
	3•••	••14										
SMITH'S LONGSPUR	••••	••••	•1							22••	••••	
CHESTNUT-COLLARED LONGSPUR	••••	••••	•••30							18••	••••	••••
SNOW BUNTING	SPECIMEN TAKEN AT COVINGTON ON AN UNSPECIFIED DATE											

612

BIBLIOGRAPHY

ONE OF THE MANY notable features of Oberholser's *Bird Life of Louisiana* is its superb bibliography. Every publication up to 1938 that contains an important reference to Louisiana birds is listed therein, beginning with Le Page du Pratz's *Histoire de la Louisiane,* which appeared in 1758. To list again all the 477 titles cited by Oberholser, even though I have consulted virtually every one of the original works at one time or another, would be superfluous. Consequently, except for a few works to which direct reference has been made in the text, I have included here only the publications incorporating significant references to the birds of the state that have appeared since the termination of Oberholser's compilation. But I have done one thing more. I have included in the present bibliography a number of general ornithological works, such as guides, manuals, and textbooks, as well as a selection of technical treatises on specialized aspects of the science. If the more serious student consults even a small assortment of this last category of listings, he cannot fail to be apprised of the great scope of the science and hence may be led from the delightful but hobbyist pathway of mere "bird listing" to the no less delightful but more fruitful pursuit of real ornithology—the scientific study of birds and avian biology.

ABLE, KENNETH P. [see GAUTHREAUX, SIDNEY A., JR., and KENNETH P. ABLE]

ALDRICH, JOHN W.
   1944. Geographic variation of Bewick Wrens in the eastern United States. Occas. Papers Mus. Zool., Louisiana State Univ., 18:305–309.
      Contains numerous references to specimens from Louisiana.

ALLEN, A. A.
1930. The book of bird life. D. Van Nostrand Co., New York.
> A general introduction to bird study.

ALLEN, GLOVER M.
1937. Birds and their attributes. Marshall Jones Co., Francestown, N.H.
> One of the best of all introductions to avian biology; often used as a text-book in college courses in ornithology.

ALLEN, ROBERT PORTER
1942. The Roseate Spoonbill. National Audubon Society Research Report No. 2.
> Mentions former and current nesting rookeries of the Roseate Spoonbill in the state; an excellent life history account.

1952. The Whooping Crane. National Audubon Society Research Report No. 3.
> An excellent life history study containing numerous references to the occurrence of the Whooping Crane in Louisiana.

ALLISON, ANDREW
1904. The birds of West Baton Rouge Parish, Louisiana. Auk, 21:472–484.
> An annotated list of 130 species.

ALLISON, ANDREW [see BEYER, GEORGE E., ANDREW ALLISON, and H. H. KOPMAN]

AMERICAN ORNITHOLOGISTS' UNION COMMITTEE ON NOMENCLATURE
1957. Check-list of North American birds. 5th ed. Amer. Ornith. Union.
> An annotated list giving the classification, the approved vernacular and scientific names, and the distribution of all species of birds occurring in the continental United States, Canada, and Baja California.

1973. Thirty-second supplement to the American Ornithologists' Union check-list of North American birds. Auk, 90:411–419.
> An extremely important publication affecting the nomenclature of North American birds with respect to both vernacular and scientific names.

ARMSTRONG, EDWARD A.
1947. Bird display and behavior. Oxford University Press, New York.

ARTHUR, STANLEY CLISBY
1918. The birds of Louisiana. Bull. Louisiana Dept. Conserv., 5:1–80.
> A list of the species and subspecies then accredited to Louisiana.

1931. The birds of Louisiana. Bull. Louisiana Dept. Conserv., 20:1–598.
> This work is a popular account of the birds then known to occur in Louisiana.

1937. Audubon: an intimate life of The American Woodsman. Harmanson, New Orleans.
> One of the best of the many biographies of Audubon; contains numerous references to birds in the state.

ATWOOD, EARL L.
1943. Recent interesting Louisiana records. Auk, 60:453–455.
> Contains records of the Vermilion Flycatcher, Blue-winged Teal (nesting), Audubon's Caracara, Prairie Chicken, and Brown Noddy. The last-named species was here recorded from Louisiana for the first time.

AUDUBON, JOHN JAMES [LA FOREST]
1827–1838. Birds of America. Vols. 1–4, folio. 435 plates. London.
> Figures of several birds obtained in Louisiana are included in this double elephant folio.

1831–1839. Ornithological biography, or an account of the habits of the birds of the United States of America. Vols. 1–5. Edinburgh.
> This work is the letterpress text that supplemented the double elephant folio of colored plates.

1840–1844. The birds of America, from drawings made in the United States and their territories. Vols. 1–7. Philadelphia and New York.
> Includes many references to Louisiana birds, mostly the same as those in the above-mentioned Ornithological Biography.

BAILEY, ALFRED M.
1945. Birds of the Louisiana Gulf Coast. Aud. Mag., 47:166–172.
> A nontechnical account of some of the author's experiences with birds along the Louisiana coast.

BAILEY, ALFRED M., and EARL GROVER WRIGHT
1931. Birds of southern Louisiana. Wilson Bull., 43:114–142.
> An annotated list of 215 species and subspecies of birds observed by the authors in the southern part of the state, including the coastal islands.

BATEMAN, HUGH A., JR.
1965. Clapper Rail (*Rallus longirostris*) studies on Grand Terre Island, Jefferson Parish, Louisiana. La. Wild Life and Fisheries Comm., Baton Rouge. 144 p.

BATULIS, JOHN C., and SALVATORE E. BONGIORNO
1951. Effect of water depth on diving times in the American Coot (*Fulica americana*).
> Based on observations made in Orleans Parish, La.

BECKHAM, CHARLES WICKLIFFE
1882. Short notes on birds of Bayou Sara, Louisiana. Bull. Nuttall Ornith. Club, 7:159–165.
> An annotated list of 86 species.

1887. Additions to the avifauna of Bayou Sara, Louisiana. Auk, 4:299–306.
> An annotated list of 27 species.

BENT, ARTHUR CLEVELAND, and collaborators
   1919–1968. Life histories [of North American birds]. Bull. U.S. Natl. Mus.:
      Diving Birds, Bull. 107, 1919; Gulls and Terns, Bull. 113, 1921; Petrels
      and Pelicans and Their Allies, Bull. 121, 1922; Wild Fowl (part),
      Bull. 126, 1923; Wild Fowl (part), Bull. 130, 1925; Marsh Birds, Bull.
      135, 1927; Shore Birds (pt. 1), Bull. 142, 1927; Shore Birds (pt. 2),
      Bull. 146, 1929; Gallinaceous Birds, Bull. 162, 1932; Birds of Prey (pt.
      1), Bull. 167, 1937; Birds of Prey (pt. 2), Bull. 170, 1938; Wood-
      peckers, Bull. 174, 1939; Cuckoos, Goatsuckers, Hummingbirds, and
      Their Allies, Bull. 176, 1940; Flycatchers, Larks, Swallows, and Their
      Allies, Bull. 179, 1947; Jays, Crows, and Titmice, Bull. 191, 1947; Nut-
      hatches, Wrens, Thrashers, and Their Allies, Bull. 195, 1948; Thrushes,
      Kinglets, and Their Allies, Bull. 196, 1949; Wagtails, Shrikes, Vireos,
      and Their Allies, Bull. 197, 1950; Wood Warblers, Bull. 203, 1953;
      Blackbirds, Orioles, Tanagers, and Allies, Bull. 211, 1958; North
      American Cardinals, Grosbeaks, Buntings, Towhees, Finches, Sparrows,
      and Allies (pts. 1, 2, and 3), Bull. 237, 1968.

      Contains detailed life history accounts of all Louisiana birds in the orders
      and families treated. Mr. Bent's death on December 30, 1954, prevented
      him from finishing his great work. Fortunately, however, volumes treating
      the remaining species were compiled and edited by Oliver L. Austin, Jr.,
      and appeared in three parts as Bulletin 237 of the U.S. National Museum.
      All volumes in the series, including the early numbers that have long been
      out of print, are now available in paperback editions by Dover Publica-
      tions, Inc., New York.

BERGER, ANDREW J. [see VAN TYNE, JOSSELYN, and ANDREW J. BERGER]

BEYER, GEORGE E.
   1900. The avifauna of Louisiana, with an annotated list of the birds of the
      state. Proc. Louisiana Soc. Nat. for 1897–1899:75–120.
      An annotated list of the birds then known to occur in the state.

BEYER, GEORGE E., ANDREW ALLISON, and H. H. KOPMAN
   1906–1908. List of birds of Louisiana. Auk, 1906, 23:1–15, 275–282; 1907,
      24:314–321; 1908, 25:173–180, 439–448.

BICK, GEORGE H.
   1942. Ivory-billed Woodpecker and Wild Turkeys in Louisiana. Auk, 59:
      431–432.
   1947. The Wild Turkey in Louisiana. Jour. Wildlife Management, 11:126–
      139.
   1954. A bibliography of the zoology of Louisiana. Proc. Louisiana Acad. Sci.,
      17:1–48.
      Contains many titles of publications relating to Louisiana birds.

BIGGS, JOSEPH D.
   1949. Scissor-tailed Flycatcher in southern Louisiana in winter. Auk, 66:286–
      287.

BISSONNETTE, THOMAS H.
1937. Photoperiodicity in birds. Wilson Bull., 49:241–270.
A pioneer study in that field of avian biology concerned with the physiological aspects of migration.

BODMAN, BARBARA M.
1973. Check list of the birds of the United States and Canada (excluding Hawaii). Privately printed by the compiler, 9555 Jefferson Hwy., Baton Rouge. 7 p.
This list is one of the few of its kind (and perhaps the best). It includes all the species presently known from North America north of Mexico.

BOLEN, ERIC G. [see RYLANDER, M. KENT, and ERIC G. BOLEN]

BONGIORNO, SALVATORE E. [see BATULIS, JOHN C., and SALVATORE E. BONGIORNO]

BROLEY, C. L.
1947. Migration and nesting of Florida Bald Eagles. Wilson Bull., 59:3–20.
An important study of the life history and seasonal movements of the Bald Eagle as revealed mainly by banding.

BULLIS, HARVEY R., JR.
1954. Trans-Gulf migration, spring 1952. Auk, 71:298–305.
Describes the observation of certain pelagic species and of numerous land birds in migration over the open Gulf, some of which were seen in Louisiana's offshore waters.

BULLIS, HARVEY R., JR., and FREDERICK C. LINCOLN
1952. A trans-Gulf migration. Auk, 69:34–39.
One of the most important papers on the subject of trans-Gulf migration.

BURLEIGH, THOMAS D.
1942. A new Barn Swallow from the Gulf Coast of the United States. Occas. Papers Mus. Zool., Louisiana State Univ., 11:179–183.
Includes reference to a nesting colony of the insular race of the Barn Swallow on Isle au Pitre.
1944. The bird life of the Gulf Coast region of Mississippi. Occas. Papers Mus. Zool., Louisiana State Univ., 20:324–490.
An eminent contribution to the ornithology of the central-northern Gulf Coast region.

BURLEIGH, THOMAS D. [see McATEE, W. L., THOMAS D. BURLEIGH, GEORGE H. LOWERY, JR., and HERBERT L. STODDARD]

BURLEIGH, THOMAS D., and ALLEN J. DUVALL
1952. A new Ovenbird from the southeastern United States. Wilson Bull., 64:39–42.
Mentions a specimen of *Seiurus aurocapillus furvior* from New Orleans.

BURLEIGH, THOMAS D., and GEORGE H. LOWERY, JR.
   1942. An inland race of *Sterna albifrons*. Occas. Papers Mus. Zool., Louisiana State Univ., 10:173–177.
      Contains numerous references to Louisiana populations of the Least Tern.
   1944. Geographic variation in the Red-bellied Woodpecker in the southeastern United States. Occas. Papers Mus. Zool., Louisiana State Univ., 17:293–301.
      Contains critical comments on the geographic variability of Louisiana populations of the species.
   1945. Races of *Vireo griseus* in eastern United States. Amer. Midl. Nat., 34: 526–530.
      Contains numerous references to specimens of the White-eyed Vireo from Louisiana.

BURLEIGH, THOMAS D., and MERRIAM L. MILES
   1942. Tree Swallow breeding in northeastern Louisiana. Auk, 59:312.

CADBURY, JOSEPH M. [see KURY, CHANNING R., and JOSEPH M. CADBURY]

CAMPBELL, JOHN S., GEORGE H. PENN, JR., H. EUGENE WALLACE, and M. GEORGE GREIG, JR.
   1943. Quail investigations in Louisiana. I. Analyses of reported returns from artificially-raised Bobwhites in 1941. Proc. Louisiana Acad. Sci., 7:38–43.

CHABRECK, ROBERT H.
   1963. Breeding habits of the Pied-billed Grebe in an impounded coastal marsh in Louisiana. Auk, 80:447–452.
      An important contribution to the breeding biology of the species in the state.
   1966. Molting Gadwall (*Anas strepera*) in Louisiana. Auk, 83:664.

CHAPIN, JAMES P.
   1946. The preparation of birds for study. Science Guide No. 58. Amer. Mus. Nat. Hist., New York.
      An excellent, well-illustrated description of the proper technique for preparing study skins.

CHAPMAN, FRANK M.
   1939. *Quiscalus* in Mississippi. Auk, 56:28–31.
      Contains references to specimens of the Common Grackle taken in Louisiana.
   1940. Handbook of birds of eastern North America. 2nd rev. ed. D. Appleton-Century Co., New York.
      A superbly written handbook that was for many years one of the most popular single-volume works dealing primarily with the birds of eastern North America. Contains descriptions of 532 species, notes on their nests and eggs, migration dates, and much other useful information.

CHAPMAN, H. H.
1947. Some observations on the Carolina Wren in La Salle Parish, Louisiana. Auk, 64:199–201.
>Describes the local abundance of the Carolina Wren in La Salle Parish.

CHILDS, V. L. [see GRIFFITH, R. E., V. L. CHILDS, and FAXON W. COOK]

CLEMENT, ROLAND C.
1946. Some Louisiana observations. Auk, 63:97–99.
>Contains notes on the White-faced Ibis, Gull-billed Tern, Burrowing Owl, Brown-headed Nuthatch, and Loggerhead Shrike—all in the Lake Charles area.

COOK, FAXON W. [see GRIFFITH, R. E., V. L. CHILDS, and FAXON W. COOK]

COUES, ELLIOTT
1926. Key to North American birds. 2 vols., 6th ed. Page Co., Boston.
>The first volume of this work includes superb discussions of avian anatomy and keys to the orders and families of North American birds, as well as chapters on collecting and preparing specimens, the history of ornithology, and other miscellaneous topics.

CRAFT, BILLY RONALD
1966. An ecological study of the Black Francolin in the Gum Cove area of southwestern Louisiana. La. Wild Life and Fisheries Comm., Baton Rouge. 79 p.

CURTLER, MARTIN
1941. A British bird-lover's wanderings in North America. Bird Notes and News, 19:137–141.
>Describes a trip to the old Singer Preserve in Madison Parish; also notes occurrence of Blue-winged and Cerulean Warblers.

DORST, JEAN
1962. The migration of birds. Houghton Mifflin Co., Boston.

DUFRESNE, FRANK
1947. Bobolink on the Gulf of Mexico. Auk, 64:138.
>Describes an observation of a Bobolink over the open Gulf 20 miles west of Trinity Shoals.

DUVALL, ALLEN J. [see BURLEIGH, THOMAS D., and ALLEN J. DUVALL]

EISENMANN, EUGENE
1952. Olivaceous Cormorant. Wilson Bull., 64:195.
>Mentions the nesting of the species in Louisiana.

EMFINGER, JAMES W.
1966. Survival, dispersal and reproductive success of the Black Francolin (*Francolinus francolinus*) in Morehouse Parish, Louisiana. La. Wild Life and Fisheries Comm., Baton Rouge. x + 82 p.

FARNER, DONALD S.

    1949. Age groups and longevity in the American Robin: comments, further discussion, and certain revisions. Wilson Bull., 61:68–81.

        A paper that should be consulted in connection with any study pertaining to longevity in birds.

    1950. The annual stimulus for migration. Condor, 52:104–122.

        An excellent résumé of the problems related to the physiology of bird migration.

FRIEDMANN, HERBERT

    1941. The birds of North and Middle America. Bull. U.S. Natl. Mus., 50, pt. 9. "By Robert Ridgway, continued by Herbert Friedmann."

        Contains technical descriptions, ranges, and bibliographies of the cranes, rails, and their allies that occur in Louisiana.

    1946. The birds of North and Middle America. Bull. U.S. Natl. Mus., 50, pt. 10. "Commenced by the late Robert Ridgway, continued by Herbert Friedmann."

        Contains technical descriptions, ranges, and bibliographies of the fowl-like birds that occur in Louisiana.

    1950. The birds of North and Middle America. Bull. U.S. Natl. Mus., 50, pt. 11.

        Contains technical descriptions, ranges, and bibliographies of the hawks and hawklike birds that occur in Louisiana.

GAUTHREAUX, SIDNEY A., JR.

    1962. Winter specimen of the Philadelphia Vireo. Auk, 79:120.

        Reports the first winter specimen taken in the United States.

    1970. Weather radar quantification of bird migration. Bio-Science, 20(1): 17–20.

        A major contribution to the quantification of radar displays of birds migrating at night, based on studies conducted at Lake Charles and New Orleans.

    1971. A radar and direct visual study of passerine spring migration in southern Louisiana. Auk, 88:343–365.

        An extremely important contribution to the study of bird migration as a whole and to the phenomenon in Louisiana in particular.

GAUTHREAUX, SIDNEY A., JR. [see PALMISANO, ANGELO W., and SIDNEY A. GAUTHREAUX, JR.]

GAUTHREAUX, SIDNEY A., JR., and KENNETH P. ABLE

    1970. Wind and the direction of nocturnal songbird migration. Nature, 228: 476–477.

        This study was done in part at Lake Charles, La., and is an important contribution to the subject of the mechanics of nocturnal bird migration.

GLASGOW, LESLIE L., CLAUDE H. GRESHAM, and STEPHEN HALL
  1950. The Flammulated Screech Owl, *Otus f. flammeolus,* in Louisiana. Auk,
     67:386.

GODFREY, W. EARL
  1946. A new Carolina Wren. Auk, 63:564–568.
       Contains references to Louisiana specimens of the Carolina wren.

GOWANLOCH, JAMES NELSON
  1951. Rare bird captured. Louisiana Conserv., 3:4, 24.
       Describes the capture on April 7, 1951, of a Roseate Spoonbill on the open
       Gulf at a point approximately 40 miles south of Grand Isle.

GRASSÉ, PIERRE-P. (Editor)
  1950. Traité de Zoologie. Tome XV (Oiseaux). Masson et Cie, Paris.
       Possibly the best and most comprehensive one-volume treatise on the anat-
       omy, systematics, and biology of birds.

GREIG, M. GEORGE, JR. [see CAMPBELL, JOHN S., GEORGE H. PENN, JR.,
H. EUGENE WALLACE, and M. GEORGE GREIG, JR.]

GRESHAM, CLAUDE H. [see GLASGOW, LESLIE L., CLAUDE H. GRESHAM,
and STEPHEN HALL]

GRIFFITH, R. E., V. L. CHILDS, and FAXON W. COOK
  1946. Roseate Spoonbill nesting on the Sabine Refuge, Louisiana. Auk, 63:
     259–260.

GRIFFITH, RICHARD E. [see STEVENSON, JAMES O., and RICHARD E.
GRIFFITH]

GRISCOM, LUDLOW
  1944. A second revision of the Seaside Sparrows. Occas. Papers Mus. Zool.,
     Louisiana State Univ., 19:313–328.
       Contains numerous critical references to Louisiana specimens and popu-
       lations of the species in the state.

  1945. Modern bird study. Harvard University Press, Cambridge.
       An excellent book, delightfully written, and covering many aspects of orni-
       thology; highly recommended reading for the beginner in bird study.

  1948. Notes on Texas Seaside Sparrows. Wilson Bull., 60:103–108.
       Contains references to Louisiana specimens.

HALL, STEPHEN [see GLASGOW, LESLIE L., CLAUDE H. GRESHAM, and
STEPHEN HALL]

HAMERSTROM, FREDERICK N., JR.
  1947. Status of the Whooping Crane. Wilson Bull., 59:127–128.
       Mentions the occurrence and nesting of the Whooping Crane in the
       White Lake district of Vermilion Parish in 1939 and the disastrous losses
       to this colony that took place after the storm and floods of early August
       1940.

Hann, Harry W.
    1953. The biology of birds. Edwards Brothers, Inc., Ann Arbor, Mich.
        A good supplementary text on avian biology, especially recommended for
        beginners in bird study.

Hasbrouck, Edwin M.
    1944. Apparent status of the European Widgeon in North America. Auk,
        61:93–104.
        Mentions the occurrence of the species in southwestern Louisiana in the
        winter of 1915.

    1944. Fulvous Tree-ducks in the Louisiana rice fields. Auk, 61:305–306.

Hebrard, James J.
    1971. The nightly initiation of passerine migration in spring: a direct visual
        study. Ibis, 113:8–18.
        An important study dealing with the mechanics of nocturnal migration
        that was done at Grand Isle.

    1972. Fall nocturnal migration during two successive overcast days. Condor,
        74:106–107.
        Illuminating observations of nocturnal migrations at Grand Isle.

Herbert, Richard, Roger T. Peterson, and Walter R. Spofford
    1943. Duck Hawk eyries in southern states. Auk, 60:274.
        Describes discovery of a nest in a broken-topped baldcypress [in Madison
        Parish, fide Peterson] on May 11, 1942.

Hewes, S. Elizabeth
    1941. Common birds of Louisiana. La. Dept. Conserv., New Orleans.
        A brief, popular account of some common Louisiana birds.

Hickey, Joseph J.
    1951. Mortality records as indices of migration in the Mallard. Condor, 53:
        284–297.
        Mentions recovery of banded birds in Louisiana.

    1953. A guide to bird watching. Garden City Books, Garden City, N.Y.
        A "must" reading for beginners in bird study.

Howard, Julian A.
    1943. Status of the White-winged Scoter in Louisiana. Auk, 60:453.

Howell, Arthur H.
    1908. Notes on the winter birds of northern Louisiana. Proc. Biol. Soc. Wash-
        ington, 21:119–124.
        A list of birds observed by Howell in the northern part of Louisiana during
        January and February 1908.

HOWELL, THOMAS R.
1953. Racial and sexual differences in migration in *Sphyrapicus varius*. Auk, 70:118–126.

> Louisiana specimens of the Yellow-bellied Sapsucker included in analysis of the sex ratios of winter populations.

JETER, HORACE H.
1952. Nesting of Bell's Vireo, *Vireo bellii*, in Louisiana. Auk, 69:89–90.

1953. Chestnut-collared Longspur: an addition to the Louisiana list. Wilson Bull., 65:48–49.

1953. Smith's Longspur: an addition to the Louisiana list. Wilson Bull., 65:212.

1957. Eastern Phoebe nesting in Louisiana. Wilson Bull., 69:360–361.

KENDEIGH, S. CHARLES
1952. Parental care and its evolution in birds. Illinois Biol. Monographs, 22:1–356.

KESSEL, BRINA
1953. Distribution and migration of the European Starling in North America. Condor, 55:49–67.

> Discusses the recovery in Louisiana in winter of starlings banded in the northern part of the United States.

KIDD, J. B. [see NEWSOM, J. D., J. B. KIDD, and ROBERT E. MURRY]

KOPMAN, H. H.
1915. List of the birds of Louisiana. Pt. 6. Auk, 32:15–29. Pt. 7. Auk, 32:183–194.

> These two papers are the continuation and completion of the list of Louisiana birds by Beyer, Allison, and Kopman started in The Auk in 1906.

KOPMAN, H. H. [see BEYER, GEORGE E., ANDREW ALLISON, and H. H. KOPMAN]

KORTWRIGHT, FRANCIS H.
1942. The ducks, geese and swans of North America. Amer. Wildlife Inst., Washington, D.C.

> An excellent account of the birds belonging to the duck family; especially recommended to sportsmen.

KURY, CHANNING R., and JOSEPH M. CADBURY
1970. The winter distribution of Maine's Double-crested Cormorants. Auk, 87:815.

> Notes the recovery in Louisiana of individuals of the species banded in Maine.

LABORATORY OF ORNITHOLOGY
[CORNELL UNIVERSITY]
   American bird songs. Comstock Publishing Co., Inc., Ithaca, N.Y.
      Two albums of 11 records; recordings by P. P. Kellogg and A. A. Allen.
   Florida bird songs. Comstock Publishing Associates, Ithaca, N.Y.
      One record with songs or calls of 10 species, all but 1 of which occur in
      Louisiana; hence of interest and value to ornithologists of this state. Re-
      cordings by P. P. Kellogg and A. A. Allen.

LACK, DAVID
   1946. The life of the robin. H. F. & G. Witherby, Ltd., London.
      A model life history study of a single species. The "robin" referred to is,
      of course, the European bird (*Erithacus rubecula*), not our American
      Robin (*Turdus migratorius*).

LE PAGE DU PRATZ, ANTOINE SIMON
   1758. Histoire de la Louisiane. Vol. 2 (Oiseaux). Paris.

LIGDA, G. H.
   1958. Radar observations of blackbird flights. Texas Jour. Sci., 10:255–265.
      Reports the occurrence daily between July 20 and August 9, 1957, of ring
      echoes thought to be flocks of Red-winged Blackbirds entering and leaving
      a communal roost at Black Bayou Wildlife Reservation in Caddo Parish.

LINCOLN, FREDERICK C.
   1939. The migration of birds. Doubleday, Doran & Co., Inc., New York.
      One of the best books available dealing exclusively with the subject of bird
      migration.
   1950. Migration of birds. U.S. Fish and Wildlife Serv. Circ. 16:1–102.
      A brief but well-prepared brochure on some of the main features of bird
      migration.

LINCOLN, FREDERICK C. [see BULLIS, HARVEY R., JR., and FREDERICK C.
LINCOLN]

LORENZ, KONRAD Z.
   1935. Der Kumpan in der Umvelt des Vogels. Jour. für Ornith., 83:137–213,
      289–413.
      A classic contribution to the literature on bird behavior and its interpre-
      tation. (For English summary, see Auk, 1937, 54:245–273).

LOWERY, GEORGE H., JR.
   1931. Birds of north Louisiana. Bull. Louisiana Polytechnic Inst., 29:1–52.
      An annotated list of 252 species of birds recorded from northern Louisiana.
   1938. A new grackle of the *Cassidix mexicanus* group. Occas. Papers Mus.
      Zool., Louisiana State Univ., 1:1–11.
      Contains numerous references to Louisiana specimens of the Boat-tailed
      Grackle.

1938. Hummingbird in a Pigeon Hawk's stomach. Auk, 55:280.

1939. Vaux Swift in Louisiana. Wilson Bull., 51:199–201.

1940. Geographical variation in the Carolina Wren. Auk, 57:95–104.
   Contains numerous references to Louisiana specimens of the Carolina Wren.

1943. The dispersal of 21,414 Chimney Swifts banded at Baton Rouge, Louisiana, with notes on probable migration routes. Proc. Louisiana Acad. Sci., 7:56–74.

1945. Trans-Gulf spring migration of birds and the coastal hiatus. Wilson Bull., 57:92–121.
   A discussion of the visible evidences of the effects of weather on spring migration of birds on the central-northern Gulf Coast and in the lower Mississippi Valley. Contains many references to Louisiana birds and to the migration of birds in this state.

1946. Evidence of trans-Gulf migration. Auk, 63:175–211.
   The retort to George Williams' first paper (1945), which contended that "there is no direct evidence to show that birds migrating from regions south . . . [of the United States] in spring actually cross the Gulf of Mexico in any appreciable numbers. . . ."

1947. Extreme arrival and departure dates for migratory birds in the Baton Rouge region of Louisiana. Proc. Louisiana Acad. Sci., 10:42–48.

1947. Additions to the list of the birds of Louisiana. Univ. Kansas Publ. Mus. Nat. Hist., 1:177–192.
   Contains records of 45 species of birds involving 6 species and many subspecies not previously reported to occur in the state.

1951. A quantitative study of the nocturnal migration of birds. Univ. Kansas Publ. Mus. Nat. Hist., 3:361–472.
   A comprehensive report on the results of the 1948 nationwide cooperative study of nocturnal migration. Statistical data were obtained on the hourly and nightly variations in the volume and directional flow of migration at 30 stations by counting the birds passing before the moon as seen through small telescopes. The paper contains many references to the migration of birds in Louisiana and in the Gulf Coast area.

1964. The woodpeckers, family Picidae. Pp. 78–97, in Song and garden birds of North America. National Geographic Soc., Washington, D.C.

LOWERY, GEORGE H., JR., and ROBERT J. NEWMAN
   1950. The Mexican Grebe, Colymbus d. brachypterus, at Baton Rouge, Louisiana. Auk, 67:505–506.

   1954. The birds of the Gulf of Mexico. Fishery Bull. 89, Fishery Bull. U.S. Fish and Wildlife Serv., 55:519–540.
      Includes an annotated list of Louisiana's coastal and offshore birds.

   1965. The mysteries of migration. Pp. 352–371, in Water, prey, and game birds of North America. National Geographic Soc., Washington, D.C.

1966. A continentwide view of bird migration on four nights in October. Auk, 83:547–586.
> Contains numerous references to migrants in Louisiana.

LOWERY, GEORGE H., JR. [see BURLEIGH, THOMAS D., and GEORGE H. LOWERY, JR.]

LOWERY, GEORGE H., JR. [see McATEE, W. L., THOMAS D. BURLEIGH, GEORGE H. LOWERY, JR., and HERBERT L. STODDARD]

LUDWIG, FREDERICK E.
1943. Ring-billed Gulls of the Great Lakes. Wilson Bull., 55:234–244.
> Records the recovery in Louisiana of Ring-billed Gulls banded in the Great Lakes region.

LUNK, WILLIAM A.
1952. Notes on variation in the Carolina Chickadee. Wilson Bull., 64:7–21.
> Contains critical comments on Louisiana populations of the Carolina Chickadee.

LYNCH, JOHN J.
1943. Fulvous Tree-Duck in Louisiana. Auk, 60:100–102.
> Describes the nesting of the species in the rice fields of southwestern Louisiana.

McATEE, W. L., THOMAS D. BURLEIGH, GEORGE H. LOWERY, JR., and HERBERT L. STODDARD
1944. Eastward migration through the Gulf states. Wilson Bull., 56:152–160.
> A geographical analysis of the frequency of occurrence of western birds in the Gulf Coast states.

McCARTNEY, ROBERT BRUCE
1963. The Fulvous Tree Duck in Louisiana. La. Wild Life and Fisheries Comm., New Orleans. 156 p.

McDANIEL, JAMES W.
1973. Vagrant albatrosses in the western North Atlantic and Gulf of Mexico. Amer. Birds, 27:563–565.

McILHENNY, E. A.
1938. Whooping Crane in Louisiana. Auk, 55:670.
1939. An unusual migration of Broad-winged Hawks. Auk, 56:182–183.
> Describes the passage of a large aggregation of Broad-winged Hawks at Avery Island on September 22, 1938. From 500 to 1,000 individuals were involved.
1939. Feeding habits of Black Vulture. Auk, 56:472–474.
> Describes the killing and immediate consumption by Black Vultures of skunks and opossums at Avery Island; also records the eating by Black Vultures of fresh cattle excrement in early morning.

1940. Effect of excessive cold on birds in southern Louisiana. Auk, 57:408–410.

> An interesting account of bird mortality during the severe cold wave that struck Louisiana in January 1940.

1941. The passing of the Ivory-billed Woodpecker. Auk, 58:582–584.

> A historically important account of the author's experiences in witnessing the extirpation of the Ivory-billed Woodpecker at Avery Island.

1943. Major changes in the bird life of southern Louisiana during sixty years. Auk, 60:541–549.

> The author describes the changes, as witnessed by him over a period of more than five decades, in the status of 29 species of Louisiana birds. Of particular interest are his notes on the Passenger Pigeon, Carolina Parakeet, and Ivory-billed Woodpecker. His notes on certain other species are somewhat paradoxical.

1945. An unusual feeding habit of the Black Vulture. Auk, 62:136–137.

> Describes the eating by the Black Vulture of chopped sweet potatoes intended for captive deer and nutria.

McIlhenny, E. A., and Rosemary McI. Osborn
1938. Black Vultures following aeroplanes. Auk, 55:521.

> Describes two observations in the vicinity of Avery Island of Black Vultures presumably following an airplane.

Meanley, Brooke
1959. Notes on Bachman's Sparrow in central Louisiana. Auk, 76:232–234.

1969. Natural history of the King Rail. N. Amer. Fauna, 67:xiii–108.

> Contains numerous references to the species based on observations in Louisiana.

Meanley, Brooke, and Anna Gilkeson Meanley
1959. Observations on the Fulvous Tree Duck in Louisiana. Wilson Bull., 71:33–45.

Meanley, Brooke [see Wetherbee, David Kenneth, and Brooke Meanley]

Miles, Merriam L.
1943. Nevada Savannah Sparrow and Northern Pine Siskin in Louisiana and Mississippi. Auk, 60:606–607.

> Records the taking of the first example of *Passerculus sandwichensis nevadensis* in the state and the first specimens of the Pine Siskin (*Spinus pinus pinus*) since 1879.

1950. Three unusual records from Louisiana and Mississippi. Auk, 67:247–248.

> Records the taking of a Rose-breasted Grosbeak specimen in winter at Slaughter and the inland occurrence of the Boat-tailed Grackle at Anchor.

Miles, Merriam L. [see Burleigh, Thomas D., and Merriam L. Miles]

MORSE, DOUGLASS H.

1967. Competitive relationships between Parula Warblers and other species during the breeding season. Auk, 84:490–502.

> Since the study was done in Louisiana it contains many references to Louisiana birds.

1972. Habitat utilization of the Red-cockaded Woodpecker during the winter. Auk, 89:429–435.

> A valuable contribution to the life history and habits of this species based on a study made in Louisiana.

MURRY, ROBERT E. [see NEWSOM, J. D., J. B. KIDD, and ROBERT E. MURRY]

NATIONAL AUDUBON SOCIETY

1947–. Central Southern Region. American Birds (incorporating Audubon Field Notes, including the annual Christmas Bird Counts and Breeding Bird Censuses. Vols. 1–.

> Six issues of this publication appear each year. No. 1, February, Fall Migration, August 16 to November 30. No. 2, April, Christmas Bird Count. No. 3, June, Winter Season, December 1 to March 31. No. 4, August, Spring Migration, April 1 to May 31. No. 5, October, Nesting Season, June 1 to August 15. No. 6, December, Breeding Bird Census.
>
> Observations on the birdlife in the United States and Canada are summarized in 19 regional accounts among which is the Central Southern Region, embracing Louisiana, Arkansas, Mississippi, western Tennessee, western Florida, and all of Alabama except the extreme northeastern corner. Many important distributional and seasonal records of Louisiana birds are to be found in these accounts and in the Christmas Bird Counts that have been published over the years. At the end of each period, records of unusual birds, effects of weather on birdlife, apparent changes in status or in relative abundance, or other seasonal information pertaining to birds in the Central Southern Region should be sent to the LSU Museum of Zoology, where the material will be added to the permanent files maintained there and then forwarded to the person who is preparing the current seasonal account, for incorporation into his or her summary.

NEWMAN, ROBERT J. [see LOWERY, GEORGE H., JR., and ROBERT J. NEWMAN]

NEWSOM, J. D., J. B. KIDD, and ROBERT E. MURRY

1953. Mourning Dove management in Louisiana. Louisiana Conserv., 5 (8): 16–18.

> An analysis of the dispersal of doves banded in Louisiana and the source of "foreign" banded birds recovered in the state. Recommendations with regard to season and bag limits are made.

NORRIS, RUSSELL T.

1942. Cooper's Hawk takes crippled coot. Wilson Bull., 54:250.

OBERHOLSER, HARRY C.
  1938. The bird life of Louisiana. Louisiana Dept. Conserv. Bull. 28:1–834.
    A comprehensive and authoritative treatment of the 348 species of birds
    then known to occur in Louisiana; contains life history notes and a de-
    tailed listing of specimens and other records up to 1938.

OSBORN, ROSEMARY McI. [see McILHENNY, E. A., and ROSEMARY McI.
OSBORN]

PALMISANO, ANGELO W., and SIDNEY A. GAUTHREAUX, JR.
  1966. First specimen of the Long-tailed Jaeger from the northern Gulf Coast.
    Auk, 83:673.
  1971. Ibises in Louisiana. Wildlife Technical Report 71–1. La. Wild Life and
    Fisheries Comm., Baton Rouge. 22 p.

PAYNTER, RAYMOND A., JR.
  1951. Autumnal trans-Gulf migrants and a new record for the Yucatan Pe-
    ninsula. Auk, 68:113–114.
  1953. Autumnal migrants on the Campeche bank. Auk, 70:338–349.
    Two important papers dealing with the subject of trans-Gulf migration.

PENN, GEORGE H., JR.
  1943. Quail investigations in Louisiana. III. A study of the grit requirements
    of Bobwhites by gizzard analyses. Proc. Louisiana Acad. Sci., 7:49–56.

PENN, GEORGE H., JR., and H. EUGENE WALLACE
  1943. Quail investigations in Louisiana. II. Inventory of Bobwhite in northern
    Louisiana. Proc. Louisiana Acad. Sci., 7:43–48.

PENN, GEORGE H., JR. [see CAMPBELL, JOHN S., GEORGE H. PENN, JR.,
H. EUGENE WALLACE, and M. GEORGE GREIG, JR.]

PETERS, JAMES LEE
  1931–1951. Check-list of birds of the world. Vols. 1–7. Harvard University
    Press, Cambridge.
    A complete list, with a delineation of the ranges, of all species of recent
    birds in the orders and families covered in the seven volumes completed
    before the author's death. The remaining species are in the process of
    being treated in eight additional volumes, each by different authors who
    are specialists on their respective groups. In the continuation of Peters'
    Check-list, six volumes (9, 10, 12, 13, 14, and 15) have now been pub-
    lished by Harvard University Press under the editorship of Ernst Mayr,
    James C. Greenway, Jr., or Raymond A. Paynter, Jr. Volumes 8 and 11,
    treating the Old World Warblers and certain suboscine families, including
    the Tyrannidae, await completion of the manuscripts.

PETERSON, ROGER T.
  1947. A field guide to the birds. 2nd ed. Houghton Mifflin Co., Boston.
    Contains a brief description, diagnostic characteristics and field marks,

statement of range, one or more illustrations, etc., of each species of bird in the eastern United States.

1948. Birds over America. Dodd, Mead & Co., New York.

An account of some of the author's experiences in his pursuit of birds. Contains references to Louisiana birds, including mention of the tree nesting of the Peregrine Falcon in the northeastern part of the state. Both highly entertaining and informative reading.

1960. A field guide to the birds of Texas. Published for Texas Game and Fish Commission by Houghton Mifflin Co., Boston.

Contains a brief description, diagnostic characteristics and field marks, statement of range, and an illustration of each of the 542 species of birds known from Texas and is therefore especially useful to ornithologists in Louisiana.

PETERSON, ROGER T. [See HERBERT, RICHARD, ROGER T. PETERSON, and WALTER R. SPOFFORD]

PETTINGILL, OLIN SEWALL, JR.

1946. A laboratory and field manual of ornithology. Burgess Publishing Co., Minneapolis.

1951. A guide to bird finding east of the Mississippi. Oxford University Press, New York.

1953. A guide to bird finding west of the Mississippi. Oxford University Press, New York.

Two volumes that are of great value to ornithologists who contemplate traveling. Gives names and directions for reaching places where certain birds may be found, the names and addresses of local ornithologists, and much other information of great use to a bird student visiting an area for the first time.

1970. Ornithology in laboratory and field. 4th ed. Burgess Publishing Co., Minneapolis.

An excellent manual covering most aspects of ornithology and providing an introduction to field and laboratory techniques and procedures; highly recommended for all beginners in the study of birds.

POUGH, RICHARD H.

1946. Audubon bird guide: small land birds. Doubleday & Co., Inc., Garden City, N.Y.

1951. Audubon water bird guide. Doubleday & Co., Inc., Garden City, N.Y.

Two highly useful guides that together treat all the birds of the United States; profusely illustrated in color.

PURRINGTON, ROBERT D.

1970. Nesting of the Sooty Tern in Louisiana. Auk, 87:159–160.

Describes the nesting and other occurrences of the species in the Chandeleurs between September 1961 and August 1968.

REICHERT, ROBERT J. and ELSA

1951. The inside story of binoculars. Amer. Rifleman.

> An excellent analysis of specifications desired in binoculars intended for use in bird study. Reprints are obtainable by writing to the Mirakel Repair Co., Mt. Vernon, N.Y.

ROBBINS, CHANDLER S., BERTREL BRUUN, and HERBERT S. ZIM

1966. Birds of North America: a guide to field identification. Illustrated by Arthur Singer. Golden Press, New York.

ROWAN, WILLIAM

1929. Experiments in bird migration. Proc. Boston Soc. Nat. Hist., 39:151–208.

> A classic study in the physiology of bird migration.

1931. The riddle of migration. Williams & Wilkins Co., Baltimore.

> Recommended reading for anyone particularly interested in the subject of bird migration.

RYLANDER, MICHAEL KENT

1969. Pathological changes associated with birdshot embedded in sandpiper muscle tissue. Auk, 86:132–133.

> Describes a condition found in a Dunlin collected at Cameron, La.

RYLANDER, M. KENT, and ERIC G. BOLEN

1970. Ecological and anatomical adaptations of North American Tree Ducks. Auk, 87:72–90.

> Study based in part on Fulvous Tree-Duck material obtained in Louisiana.

SAUNDERS, ARETAS

1951. A guide to bird songs. Doubleday & Co., Inc., Garden City, N.Y.

> An unexcelled treatise on the subject.

SIEBENALER, J. B.

1954. Notes on autumnal trans-Gulf migration of birds. Condor, 56:43–48.

> An important contribution to the subject of trans-Gulf migration.

SPEIRS, J. MURRAY

1953. Winter distribution of robins east of the Rocky Mountains. Wilson Bull., 65:175–183.

> Mentions the recovery in Louisiana of robins banded farther north.

SPOFFORD, WALTER R. [see HERBERT, RICHARD, ROGER T. PETERSON, and WALTER R. SPOFFORD]

STANLEY, ALLAN J.

1941. Sexual dimorphism in the cowbird, *Molothrus ater*. Wilson Bull., 53:33–36.

> The author concludes that sexual dimorphism in the Brown-headed Cowbird is not under hormonal control but is determined genetically. The study was based on specimens taken in winter at Baton Rouge.

STEVENSON, HENRY M., JR.
  1944. Southeastern limits of the Spotted Sandpiper's breeding range. Auk, 61: 247–251.
      Includes reference to the alleged breeding of the Spotted Sandpiper in Louisiana.
  1957. The relative magnitude of the trans-Gulf and circum-Gulf spring migrations. Wilson Bull., 69:39–77.
      Incorporates many Louisiana migration data.

STEVENSON, JAMES O., and RICHARD E. GRIFFITH
  1946. Winter life of the Whooping Crane. Condor, 48:160–178.
      An important contribution to the life history of this bird. Reference is made to the occurrence of the species in Louisiana, especially in the period between 1939 and 1944.

STEWART, PAUL A.
  1952. Dispersal, breeding behavior, and longevity of banded Barn Owls in North America. Auk, 69:227–245.
      Records the capture in Louisiana of Barn Owls banded in Ohio and Oklahoma.

STILLWELL, JERRY and NORMA
  1952–1954. Bird songs of dooryard, field and forest. 2 vols. (33-1/3 rpm records). Ficker Recording Service, Old Greenwich, Conn.
      Superb recordings of the songs and calls of many wild birds. Volume 1 includes 49 species; Volume 2 treats 58 species.

STODDARD, HERBERT L.
  1931. The Bobwhite Quail, its habits, preservation, and increase. Charles Scribner's Sons, New York.
      A classic among life history studies. Now out of print but occasionally offered by second-hand bookdealers.

STODDARD, HERBERT L. [see MCATEE, W. L., THOMAS D. BURLEIGH, GEORGE H. LOWERY, JR., and HERBERT L. STODDARD]

STRECKER, JOHN KERN
  1928. Notes on summer birds of the northwestern parishes of Louisiana. Contrib. Baylor Univ. Mus., 14:1–13.
      Includes a list of 82 species of birds observed in Caddo, Bossier, and De Soto parishes in April, August, and September 1925, April and September 1926, April and May 1927, and June 1928.

STREET, PHILLIPS B.
  1948. The Edward Harris collection of birds. Wilson Bull., 60:167–184.
      Contains reference to Harris' travels in Louisiana and the birds encountered by him.

SUTTON, GEORGE MIKSCH
1941. A new race of *Chaetura vauxi* from Tamaulipas. Wilson Bull., 53: 231–233.
Mentions specimens of the Vaux's Swift taken in Louisiana.

1951. A new race of Yellow-throated Warbler from northwestern Florida. Auk, 68:27–29.
Contains reference to characteristics of populations of the Yellow-throated Warbler in Louisiana.

TABOR, AVA R.
1940. Bullock's Oriole in Thibodaux, Louisiana. Auk, 57:257.

TANNER, JAMES T.
1939. Observations in Madison Parish, Louisiana. Auk, 56:90.
Describes the observation in Madison Parish of the Swallow-tailed Kite on April 2, 1937; of the Golden Eagle from March 6 to 12, 1938; and of the Bachman's Warbler between May 25 and June 3, 1937.

1941. Three years with the Ivory-billed Woodpecker, America's rarest bird. Aud. Mag., 43:5–14.
An interesting account of the author's study of the Ivory-billed Woodpecker, mainly in Madison Parish.

1942. Present status of the Ivory-billed Woodpecker. Wilson Bull., 54:57–58.
A plea is made to set aside the Singer Tract in Madison Parish as a sanctuary for the Ivory-billed Woodpecker. This area is noted as one of three places where the species still had a chance of survival.

1942. The Ivory-billed Woodpecker. National Audubon Society Research Report No. 1.
A superb life history account based in large part on the author's field studies in Louisiana.

TAYLOR, WALTER KINGSLEY
1965. Nesting heights of some Louisiana birds. Wilson Bull., 77:146–150.
The study was made in and near Ruston, in Lincoln Parish. An analysis of the height of 522 nests, representing 28 species, is made.

THOMSON, A. L.
1949. Bird migration. H. F. & G. Witherby, Ltd., London.
A classic treatise on the subject.

TINBERGEN, N.
1948. Social releasers and the experimental method required for their study. Wilson Bull., 60:6–51.
Highly recommended reading for the student of bird behavior.

VAN TYNE, JOSSELYN, and ANDREW J. BERGER
1959. Fundamentals of ornithology. John Wiley & Sons, Inc., New York.
A superb textbook that no serious student of ornithology can be without.

WALLACE, GEORGE J.
1955. An introduction to ornithology. Macmillan Co., New York.

A general introduction to ornithology especially designed for use as a textbook; highly recommended for the beginning and intermediate student.

WALLACE, H. EUGENE [see CAMPBELL, JOHN S., GEORGE H. PENN, JR., H. EUGENE WALLACE, and M. GEORGE GREIG, JR.]

WALLACE, H. EUGENE [see PENN, GEORGE H., JR., and H. EUGENE WALLACE]

WELLER, MILTON W.
1965. Chronology of pair formation in some Nearctic *Aythya* (Anatidae). Auk, 82:227–235.

WETHERBEE, DAVID KENNETH, and BROOKE MEANLEY
1965. Natal plumage characters in rails. Auk, 82:500–501.

Contains reference to the presence of white neossoptiles in the plumage of the downy young of the Clapper Rail in Louisiana.

WETMORE, ALEXANDER
1930. The migration of birds. Harvard University Press, Cambridge.

A well-written general treatise on the subject.

1951. A revised classification for the birds of the world. Smithsonian Misc. Coll., 117(4):1–22.

A revised classification and arrangement of the orders and families of birds. Nearly all current ornithological works adhere to this author's arrangement.

WILLIAMS, GEORGE G.
1945. Do birds cross the Gulf of Mexico in spring? Auk, 62:98–111.

The highly controversial paper in which Williams first contended that "there is no direct evidence to show that birds migrating from regions south of us in spring actually cross the Gulf of Mexico in any appreciable numbers; but there is abundant evidence to show that vast numbers of these birds, both individuals and species, take the coastwise routes *around* the eastern and western edges of the Gulf."

1947. Lowery on trans-Gulf migration. Auk, 64:217–238.

Williams' reply to Lowery's 1946 paper.

1950. Weather and spring migration. Auk, 67:52–65.

An attempt on theoretical grounds to account for the appearance of migrants in abnormal, off-course areas by assuming that displacements have come about as a result of the influence of meteorological forces on migratory flights. These forces cause birds "to alter their course at some time, retreat in the face of bad weather, suffer dissemination indiscriminately over the continent, seek refuge in unfamiliar areas, and return to their regular course along abnormal routes."

1950. The nature and causes of the 'coastal hiatus.' Wilson Bull., 62:175–182.

The paper in which the author contends that the so-called coastal hiatus appears to be no more than "a lacuna south of and between two great spring migration triangles, one extending north and northeast from southern Texas, the other extending northwest, north, and northeast from Florida."

1951. Birds against the moon. Nature Notes from the Gulf States (winter, 1951), 1:5–7, 22.
A nontechnical account of the lunar method of studying nocturnal migration but particularly important as the place where the author first clearly expounds, contrary to his earlier claims that he did not deny trans-Gulf migrations in fall, that autumnal migrations are, like those in spring, largely coastwise.

1952. Birds on the Gulf of Mexico. Auk, 69:428–431.
An attempt at rebuttal of the evidence of trans-Gulf migation presented by Bullis and Lincoln (1952).

WILLIAMS, LOVETT E.
1962. Parasitic Jaeger in Louisiana. Auk, 79:483.
This record is the first for the species in the state.

1965. Jaegers in the Gulf of Mexico. Auk, 82:19–25.
Records of the Long-tailed, Parasitic, and Pomarine Jaegers off Louisiana.

WING, LEONARD
1943. Relative distribution of Mallard and Black Duck in winter. Auk, 60:438–439.
Gives the Mallard–Black Duck winter ratio of abundance (1900–1939) for the eastern half of the United States. In Louisiana the ratio is 12.22 Mallards to 1 Black Duck. The ratio decreases to the east of Louisiana and increases to the west.

WOLFSON, ALBERT
1942. Regulation of spring migration in juncos. Condor, 44:237–263.

1945. The role of the pituitary, fat deposition, and body weight in bird migration. Condor, 47:95–127.

1952. Day length, migration, and breeding cycles in birds. Scient. Monthly, 74:191–200.
Three papers of great fundamental importance in connection with the physiology of bird migration.

1953. The seventieth stated meeting of the American Ornithologists' Union [at Baton Rouge, La.]. Auk, 70:183–195.
A résumé of the first and only American Ornithologists' Union convention held in Louisiana.

WOOLFENDEN, GLEN E.
1965. A specimen of the Red-footed Booby from Florida. Auk, 82:102–103.
Contains reference to the specimen of Red-footed Booby taken in Louisiana near the mouth of the Mississippi River.

WRIGHT, EARL GROVER [see BAILEY, ALFRED M., and EARL GROVER WRIGHT]

YANCEY, RICHARD K.
    1953. The Louisiana waterfowl kill. Louisiana Conserv., 5(7):7–9.

> A geographical analysis of hunter bag checks with special reference to (1) the ratio of the number of ducks killed to the number of hunters and (2) the species composition of bags in different parts of the state. The author laments the scarcity in southern Louisiana of public shooting grounds.

INDEX

WHERE MORE THAN one reference to the official English name is given, the page on which the account of the species begins is listed first. The page or pages on which a species is illustrated are shown in italics. In the case of scientific and colloquial names, only the main page reference is given.